HOCKEY GUIDE

1986-87 EDITION

Editor/Hockey Guide
LARRY WIGGE

Compiled by
FRANK POLNASZEK

Contributing Editors/Hockey Guide
JOHN HADLEY
BARRY SIEGEL
DAVE SLOAN

President-Chief Executive Officer
RICHARD WATERS

Editor
TOM BARNIDGE

Director of Books and Periodicals
RON SMITH

Published by

The Sporting News
1212 North Lindbergh Boulevard
P.O. Box 56 — St. Louis, MO 63166

Copyright © 1986
The Sporting News Publishing Company

A Times Mirror
Company

IMPORTANT NOTICE

The Hockey Guide is protected by copyright. All information, in the form presented here, except playing statistics, was compiled by the publishers and proof is available.
Information from the Hockey Guide must not be used elsewhere without special written permission, and then only with full credit to the Hockey Guide, published by THE SPORTING NEWS, St. Louis, Missouri.

ISBN 0-89204-231-1   ISSN 0278-4955

TABLE OF CONTENTS

1985-86 NHL Season in Review 3-11
NHL Office Directory 12
NHL Divisional Alignment 13
NHL Team Directories and Rosters 14-55
THE SPORTING NEWS 1985-86 NHL All-Star Team 56
National Hockey League Summary and Statistics, 1985-86 59-88
NHL Miscellaneous Achievements in 1985-86 89-99
NHL Departmental Leaders 100-102
Stanley Cup Playoffs, 1986 103-110
Year-by-Year NHL Standings 111-121
Stanley Cup Winners 122
Stanley Cup Records 123
NHL Awards and Leaders 124-129
NHL Entry Draft 130-134
All-Time Individual Records (National Hockey League, World Hockey
    Association, Central Hockey League, American Hockey League,
    International Hockey League) 135-137
American Hockey League 138
International Hockey League 155
Atlantic Coast Hockey League 167
Memorial Cup Winners 172
Ontario Hockey League 173
Western Hockey League 187
Quebec Hockey League 200
American College Hockey 209
National Hockey League Schedule for 1986-87 233

ON THE COVER: Claude Lemieux, one of the key figures in Montreal's surprising stretch run, hoists the Stanley Cup, symbolic of the Canadiens' 23rd NHL title, after the team's final victory over Calgary.
—Photo by Paul Bereswill

Canadiens Beat Odds, Capture 23rd Cup Title

By JIM MATHESON

In a season spliced with agony and ecstacy, the National Hockey League's cup ranneth over with tears of joy and tears of grief, punctuated by the rebirth of the Montreal Canadiens' legendary mystique and the tragic death of Philadelphia Flyers goaltender Pelle Lindbergh.

The Canadiens, longshots when the 1985-86 season opened, rediscovered their old winning formula after a seven-year itch and captured their 23rd Stanley Cup title while the supposedly invincible Edmonton Oilers waved goodby to their two-year reign as hockey's best team.

The Flyers' loss went deeper than that. They lost a friend and one of the best goalies in the game. There wasn't a dry eye in Philadelphia's Spectrum on a rainy November night as both fans and players hung their heads and mourned Lindbergh. "He carries such a wonderful report card to the Almighty God," said the Flyers' chaplain, Father John Casey, in a moving eulogy prior to an Edmonton-Philadelphia game.

The Swedish netminder had lost control of his Porsche 930 and crashed into a wall on November 10. Tests showed later that he was intoxicated.

"When he went through the last intersection he was going so fast it looked like his back wheels weren't on the ground. It looked like the back of the car came up like a rocket or something," said a 19-year-old girl who witnessed the accident.

"Pelle was a victim of one poor judgment," said former Flyers coach Bob McCammon. "He was a good kid, I don't care what the blood alcohol level was. Day in and day out, there wasn't a better kid in hockey."

The 26-year-old Lindbergh was pronounced brain dead, but remained on a life-support system for several days before his organs were donated. "In the end, he made one last save," said Flyers Coach Mike Keenan.

It was a sad start to an unusual season. Among the highs: Edmonton's Paul Coffey passed Bobby Orr as the highest-scoring defenseman in a single season (48 goals), Los Angeles Kings center Marcel Dionne passed Phil Esposito and moved into second place on the all-time scoring list, and the incomparable Wayne Gretzky passed the 200-point plateau for a fourth

Jari Kurri and the Edmonton Oilers scored goals in bunches, but fell short on their attempt to defend their Stanley Cup title.

time with an NHL-record 215 points. Unfortunately for Gretzky and his Oilers teammates, their season ended ahead of schedule when the insolent Calgary Flames knocked the crowns from their heads in a shocking seven-game Clarence Campbell Conference final series.

Among the lows: There was a series of serious eye injuries in what one observer dubbed "The Year of the Stick-Up." It got so bad that such stars as Dionne and Edmonton's Jari Kurri donned face shields after getting nicked by sticks or pucks. It was hockey under glass.

All eyes focused on the high-scoring

Oilers as the regular season began. Nobody was disappointed. Edmonton, the only NHL team ever to score 400 or more goals in one season, reached that plateau for the fifth straight time. The Oilers remained the NHL's most entertaining team, if not its most artistic. That point can be driven home by the 21-goal salute the Oilers and Chicago Black Hawks fired one December night in Chicago. Edmonton won the game, 12-9, as the teams combined to tie a 45-year-old record for most goals in a single game. The Canadiens beat the Toronto St. Pats, 14-7, in 1941.

"There's never been another game like this," said Gretzky. "We led 6-0, then 8-6, then 11-7, then 12-9. After two periods, when we scored six goals and so did they, I'm sure the coaches in both dressing rooms didn't know what to say."

Later in the year, the Oilers came out on the wrong end of an embarrassing 11-9 loss to the Toronto Maple Leafs. "I don't know whether to drink this stuff or put it on my face," said McCammon, an Oilers assistant coach, while debating whether to slap aftershave on his cheeks or down his throat.

The Leafs, who finished with the 19th best record (62 points behind the Oilers), were one of 15 teams to score 300 or more goals as the netminders around the NHL took another beating. Only one goalie who played 25 games or more (Bob Froese of the Flyers) had a goals-against average under 3.00. One of the league's best, Greg Stefan of Detroit, finished with an embarrassing 4.50 average. "No place for a nervous person," laughed one shooter.

Six players scaled the 50-goal plateau and 23 had 40 or more. Kurri became the first European to lead the league in goals (68) and enjoyed a streak in which he scored in 10 straight games. New York Islanders winger Mike Bossy was next at 61, extending his run of 50-or-more goal seasons to a record nine. The other 50-goal men were Philadelphia's Tim Kerr (58), Edmonton's Glenn Anderson (54), Quebec's Michel Goulet (53) and Gretzky (52).

Gretzky won his sixth straight scoring title, thanks to a record 163 assists. No other NHL player has ever scored more than 152 points (goals and assists combined) in a single season. "I wish the kid would give me a break," joked Phil Esposito, who once held the single-season point record.

"Wayne should get a point and a half for some of the assists he gets, the way he sets up some of his teammates," said Chicago co-Coach Roger Neilson. "He doesn't get any cheap ones." Gretzky's 163 assists beat his mark of 135, set in the 1984-85 season.

Gretzky, who had a 39-game point streak, outdistanced young Pittsburgh sensation Mario Lemieux, considered the heir-apparent to his scoring crown, by 74 points. He had a point in all but three of the 80 games he played (only Buffalo, Chicago and Minnesota held No. 99 off the scoresheet).

"It seems like only yesterday they said I couldn't play in this league. I had the pressure to prove I belonged. They said I was too young, too small, too slow....now they're saying I'm over the hill," joked the 25-year-old Gretzky at the midseason All-Star Game. "Now they're wondering who will take my place. It makes you feel old, believe me."

Record-breaking performances have become old hat for Gretzky, but Oilers teammate Coffey savored his moment in the sun.

"It's an honor to be mentioned in the same sentence with Orr," said the defenseman who broke the former Boston star's record with a great solo rush against Vancouver goalie Wendell Young late in the season.

"The record wasn't tainted in any sense. He went end-to-end, split the defense, went one-on-one with the goalie and put it away. It was a classic, a typical Bobby Orr goal," said Vancouver Coach Tom Watt.

Coffey missed Orr's record 139 points (for a defenseman) by one en route to earning his second straight Norris Trophy as the NHL's best defenseman. In mid-March against Detroit, Coffey scored eight points (two goals, six assists), tying Philadelphia's Tom Bladon for the best single-game mark by a defenseman.

"I keep pinching myself," said Coffey. He also had a 28-game point streak, tying Gretzky, Guy Lafleur and Lemieux for the fourth longest in history. Ironically, Gretzky's 39-game run and Coffey's 28-gamer both ended the same January night in Chicago.

Kurri (131) and Bossy (123) rounded out the top five in the scoring race. In all, 13 players managed more than 100 points. And Minnesota's Neal Broten (105) became the highest-scoring American-born player in history, surpassing his own record of 98 points in 1981-82.

Dionne didn't make it to 100 (94), but he now has 1,599 points, nine more than Esposito. He's 251 behind all-time leader Gordie Howe.

"I don't know if it makes a difference. Gretzky will probably beat us both," shrugged Dionne, who turned 35 in Au-

The Philadelphia Flyers and the rest of the hockey world were stunned in November when goaltender Pelle Lindbergh (left) died after crashing his Porsche (above).

Los Angeles Kings veteran Marcel Dionne moved into second place on the all-time scoring list.

gust. Kerr broke Bossy and Esposito's record of 28 power-play goals, clicking for an amazing 34. Goulet tied Bossy and Esposito's mark. Coffey had nine shorthanded goals, the fourth-highest figure ever. Buffalo's Dave Andreychuk had the season's best single-game scoring outburst, scoring five times against Boston in an 8-6 February win.

The Oilers collected $200,000 as the team with the most points (119). The Flyers, who were No. 1 in 1984-85 and enjoyed the longest 1985-86 winning streak (13), were nine points back. The pivotal point in the Great Race came March 2 when Kurri scored in overtime to give Edmonton a 2-1 victory over the Flyers. The Oilers pulled away after that and Philadelphia had to settle into a fight with Patrick Division rival Washington (107 points) for second place.

The Quebec Nordiques won the Adams Division with 92 points and the Black Hawks prevailed in the Norris with 86.

One of the biggest stories was the demise of Buffalo in the Adams Division. The Sabres, under hockey's winningest-ever coach, Scotty Bowman, missed the playoffs after a torrid race with the Hartford Whalers. It was the Whalers' first playoff berth since 1979 when proud father Gordie Howe was playing with his two boys, Mark and Marty. And it was the first time since 1973-74 that the Sabres had missed the playoffs.

The season's biggest flop occurred in Detroit, where the Red Wings, who used up $6.7 million of Owner Michael Ilitch's money to sign free agents in the summer of '85, struggled to a 17-57-6 season. They finished 21st in the league and went through two coaches—Harry Neale and Brad Park. During the off-season, Ilitch replaced Park with former St. Louis Coach Jacques Demers.

"We were like oil and water, which don't mix," said Wings' General Manager Jim Devellano after firing Park.

Bowman was involved in one of several other coaching changes as the NHL kept its revolving-door policy intact. He stepped down from his general manager's job to replace Buffalo Coach Jim Schoenfeld midway through the season. In Winnipeg, Barry Long was fired after finishing near the top in the 1984-85 coach-of-the-year race.

After watching his team finish with a 39-29-12 season and a first-round playoff elimination by the Washington Capitals, Islanders Coach Al Arbour surprised the hockey world when he informed his boss, Bill Torrey, that he was quitting after 13 excellent seasons. Arbour, the dean of NHL coaches, had directed the Islanders to four Stanley Cups. But he said that his desire had waned after the New Yorkers lost their crown to Edmonton in 1984. He was replaced by Prince Albert (Western Hockey League) Coach Terry Simpson.

The other new faces heading into the 1986-87 season will be Dan Maloney (Winnipeg), Jacques Martin (St. Louis) and John Brophy (Toronto). Maloney refused to sign a one-year contract with the Maple Leafs after the season and walked into a three-year deal with the Jets. Martin guided Guelph (Ontario Hockey League) to the Canadian junior title last spring. Brophy coached St. Catharines of the American Hockey League.

On the executive level, Esposito took over for Craig Patrick as general manager of the New York Rangers. Patrick's contract wasn't renewed after six years.

Nine players and one coach (Park) were suspended during the 1985-86 season. Glenn Anderson and Montreal's Chris

Al Arbour, who guided the New York Islanders to four straight Stanley Cup titles in the early 1980s, stunned the hockey world when he retired after the 1985-86 season.

Nilan were rapped hardest for stick-swinging incidents (Anderson at Detroit's Dave Silk; Nilan at Boston's Rick Middleton). They both got eight-game sentences. Park got a six-game holiday for admitting to sending his team onto the ice in a bench-clearing brawl with the Maple Leafs.

There was a flurry of trading, particularly at the March 11 deadline. The biggest names to change teams were Islanders' left wing John Tonelli, New Jersey goalie Chico Resch and Detroit's Ron Duguay. Tonelli, a hero for New York in its four Cup victories, went to Calgary for winger Richard Kromm and defenseman Steve Konroyd. Resch, the league's oldest player at age 38, was traded to Philadelphia for a third-round draft pick. Duguay went to Pittsburgh for winger Doug Shedden.

Earlier major deals involved Jets defenseman Dave Babych and Blues sniper Joey Mullen. Babych, Winnipeg's No. 1 draft pick in 1980, was peddled to Hartford for winger Ray Neufeld. Mullen, who has scored 125 goals in the last three seasons, went to the Flames in a six-player swap just before the All-Star Game.

One of the most disturbing stories of the year involved the number of players hit with eye injuries. Former Islanders winger Hector Marini lost his left eye in a freak mishap in an International League game. He was standing in front of the net when a puck smacked him in the eye.

"It was such an innocent thing," Marini said. "I was minding my own business. The puck hit me right on the eyeball....unbelievably, there wasn't a drop of blood on the ice. I got off the ice on my own steam, but I knew something was terribly wrong."

Islanders winger Bob Nystrom was clipped in the eye during a playful practice game by defenseman Gerald Diduck in December and eventually was forced to retire after an operation to repair the damage. Boston's Charlie Simmer suffered bleeding around his eyeball when felled by an errant stick, but returned with a visor.

Kurri, the Islanders' Denis Potvin, Calgary's Paul Reinhart, Montreal's Ryan

Walter and many other players also donned visors after scary incidents. Dionne was cut and immediately went to a shield when his 10-year-old daughter came home from school with a classmate and said, "That's my dad, look at his scars." By season's end, more than 50 players were regularly wearing face protection and countless others were experimenting with glass visors.

"Medical science can mend a shoulder or leg, but it can't mend a head smashed into a gate or an eye that's had a stick in it," said Demers.

There was much discussion during the off-season about whether the NHL should make the wearing of visors mandatory, as it did helmets several years ago. Nothing's been passed yet, however, probably because there's a nagging worry that visors might increase more stickwork by players who aren't worried about hitting somebody in a protected face.

"The game is faster and the players are bigger now," said Bowman. "Many players have grown up wearing helmets and visors as kids. Their reflexes aren't as attuned to the dangers of carrying their sticks high."

The words of former Rangers winger Anders Hedberg, who had his career shortened by a high stick, echo loudly. He strongly advocates facial protection.

"What would happen to this game if Wayne Gretzky lost an eye? These things just don't happen to the Hector Marinis," he said.

Gretzky, who has not suffered a serious injury in his seven-year NHL career, had to stomach the Oilers' shocking loss to the Flames. Oilers rookie defenseman Steve Smith delivered the crowning blow when he inadvertently shot the puck off his own goalie, Grant Fuhr, with 15 minutes left in the seventh game. That proved to be a winner for Calgary.

"It was a human error. I guess I've just got to live with it," said Smith.

The Flames won the game, 3-2, and the series, 4-3, to end the Oilers' hopes of a third straight Stanley Cup.

"Calgary won fair and square. We had an unfortunate goal in the last game but we shouldn't have been in the position of having to play a seventh game anyway," said Gretzky, refusing to stickhandle around the harsh facts.

Among those facts are that the Oilers lost three games at home to the Flames, allowed Calgary to score the first goal and dictate the style of play in six of the seven games and scored just six goals in the four losses.

Two of the Oilers' big guns—Kurri and Coffey—never got untracked. Kurri managed just one goal in the series; Coffey was shut out.

"Every time I carried the puck and got to center, five guys were on me. I felt like I was in Boston Garden," said Coffey.

"I have no excuses," said Kurri. "When you score 68 goals in the regular season and only two in the entire playoffs, you have to expect criticism. I was fighting the puck."

Oilers Coach Glen Sather resisted the urge to set up a conference call with Keenan in Philadelphia, Bryan Murray in Washington and Michel Bergeron in Quebec City. With the Oilers' ouster, the top four 1985-86 teams were eliminated from Cup contention.

It was a wacky postseason script. The Flyers, who met the Oilers in the 1985 Cup final, surprisingly fell to the New York Rangers in the first round of the Patrick Division playoff. Washington then lost to the Rangers in the Patrick Division final. Quebec was clobbered in three straight games by Hartford in the Adams Division preliminary round. And the Oilers—well, they simply didn't give the Flames enough respect.

"I've always worried about Calgary. And when they made the trades for Mullen and Tonelli it really finished off their team," said Sather, who went into the Flames dressing room to shake hands after the Uncivil War. "They had the balance they needed to do this. Guys like Doug Risebrough, Tonelli and Lanny McDonald—this may be the last hurrah for them and I knew they wouldn't go down easily."

Sather admitted the obvious. "We still have some growing to do," he said. "This is a great hockey team but there are still some people who don't believe what the coaches tell them. I don't think it was intentional, but what works in regular season doesn't always work in the playoffs when teams devise strategies to overcome strengths. We had to play well enough to overcome the fluke goal in the last game, but really we didn't."

Sports Illustrated suggested that the Oilers might have been done in by alleged drug problems involving several players. But Sather scoffed at the inference.

"If they'd said in the article, 'here are the names,' then we'd have to accept that," he said. "But it's a shame that any organization should have to defend its integrity from such obvious innuendo. I have to think this is one of the lowest points I've had in hockey."

While the Oilers were being criticized for their failure to win, the Canadiens

Lanny McDonald and other members of the Calgary Flames had problems getting the puck past Montreal goalie Patrick Roy.

were being praised for their resiliency. They finished with the seventh-best record (87 points) and entered the playoffs with a young lineup that included eight rookie players and a rookie coach (Jean Perron), yet breezed to the title. They whipped Boston three straight, got past the Rangers in five and and dispatched Calgary in a five-game finale. Only Hartford, which took the Canadiens to a seventh game in the Adams Division final, proved a problem.

The Flames, who were extended to a seventh game by the surprising St. Louis Blues in the Campbell Conference semifinal round, jumped to a quick 1-0 lead in the finals, but then hit a brick wall. The Canadiens proceeded to sweep four straight with a suffocating defense, excellent goaltending from rookie Patrick Roy (1.92 average in the playoffs) and a few heroics from Claude Lemieux, who had four game-winners in the postseason march to the crown.

One of the most interesting aspects to the Montreal-Calgary matchup was that each team was backstopped by a rookie goaltender, Roy for the Canadiens and Mike Vernon for the Flames. It was the first time two rookies had appeared between the pipes in the finals since 1945, when Frank McCool of Toronto got the better of Harry Lumley of Detroit in a seven-game series. Prior to Vernon and Roy, only 18 rookie goalies had worked a Stanley Cup final game, the last one being Minnesota's Don Beaupre in 1981.

Controversy was an uninvited guest in the opener in Calgary as the Flames capitalized on a disputed goal. Roy was bruised by an apparent high-stick goal by Jim Peplinski 19 minutes into a 5-2 Calgary victory. Where was Peplinski's stick? "Right on the puck. I would say it was within the rules by 6 inches to a foot," said Peplinski.

Roy, whose playoff story was embellished by his humorous accounts of having talked to the goalposts, spent the next few minutes arguing with and bumping into the linesmen and referee Kerry Fraser— but to no avail. The arguing got him nowhere; the bumping got him a misconduct penalty. Roy was beaten four more times (Risebrough scored into an empty net), the most goals he allowed in any of the Canadiens' 20 playoff games.

Game 2 was more intense. It ended when Montreal's Brian Skrudland scored nine seconds into overtime. Skrudland banged Mike McPhee's pass past Vernon for the fastest overtime goal in history (J.P. Parise of the Islanders scored in 11 seconds 11 years earlier) to give the Habs a 3-2 win. It took Skrudland, a rookie, longer to describe the goal than to score it.

Claude Lemieux produced four game-winning goals in Montreal's run to the Stanley Cup title.

"I just hope my folks, who'd driven in for the game from Saskatoon, weren't out buying hot dogs and cokes and saw it," he said. "I couldn't have predicted this in 1,000 years. I might have scored an overtime goal before but it was in peewee." Skrudland's goal capped a Montreal comeback that wiped out an early 2-0 deficit.

The script for Game 3 was written by Swedish winger Mats Naslund, who had two goals and an assist in a 5-3 Canadiens victory. Naslund, who'd been writing a column in a Swedish paper for months, may have had to use the first person in his playoff report.

"I am not shy when I think I deserve to have my name mentioned," the winger said with a laugh. "My stories are mainly surrounding the games though. Maybe you guys with the cameras and pens will be in my corner of the paper."

Naslund set up Bobby Smith's tip-in to tie the game 2-2 late in the first period, then scored on a wild scramble 52 seconds later. Bob Gainey's 30-footer capped a three-goal blitz in 68 seconds.

"Mats is a winner. He wants to win as much as Gainey and Larry Robinson. He motivates the team and does what he has to do," said Perron.

Lemieux did what he does best in Game 4. He ripped a shot through Vernon's pads with nine minutes left for the game-winner in a 1-0 victory. Lemieux connected after pouncing on a miscue by the usually-alert Risebrough. After the game, Lemieux pounced on Peplinski as both benches joined in a brawl.

"He (Lemieux) grabbed my hand and pushed it into my mouth," said Peplinski. "I didn't know I'd have to worry about cannibalism."

The postgame altercation provided a sad ending to a fine game. Eight players were handed game misconducts and NHL President John Ziegler slapped the teams with a record $42,000 in fines the next day.

"There was absolutely no excuse for what happened. The conduct of the players served only to degrade the otherwise outstanding game," Ziegler said.

Both coaches agreed with Ziegler. "This was crazy. Hockey really has a problem when players can't control themselves. We're trying to be an influence on kids," said Perron. "Very expensive...these playoffs."

Tempers were kept in check in Game 5 as the Canadiens won, 4-3. They used two goals in 19 seconds by Smith and Rick Green in the final period, then held on to win their first Cup since 1979.

"I don't know why, but this one is much sweeter," said Robinson, who has six Stanley Cup rings. "It's been seven years since this club has been here. When you wait that long you begin to wonder."

Gainey, who has participated in five Cup victories, chuckled softly as he described the feeling of winning against long odds.

"We weren't written as one of the all-time favorites to win," he said. "But we've played well against good teams in this league the past two years. In the past you could look at the caliber of some teams and say they'd win the Stanley Cup two or three times in a row. Now I really think there's no reason a team can't come from sixth or eighth and be a contender for the Cup."

Lemieux, who finished second to Roy in balloting for the playoff MVP, put the victory in perspective.

"I know some people are going to say some teams like Edmonton and Philadelphia weren't here," he said, "but we deserved to win. We're the champions because we won the games we had to win. We deserve this."

The Incomparable Wayne Gretzky (left) and teammate Paul Coffey posted record-setting numbers for the high-flying Edmonton Oilers.

National Hockey League

Organized November 22, 1917

NHL Offices

John A. Ziegler, Jr.

Sun Life Building
1155 Metcalfe Street, Suite 960
Montreal, Que., Canada H3B 2W2
Phone—(514) 871-9220
TWX—(610) 421-3260

Central Scouting & Officiating
Suite 200, 1 Greensboro Drive
Rexdale, Ont. M9W 1C8
Phone—(416) 245-2926
TWX—(610) 492-2703

34th Floor
500 Fifth Avenue
New York, NY 10110
Phone—(212) 398-1100
TWX—(710) 581-2736

Chairman of the Board	WILLIAM W. WIRTZ
President	JOHN A. ZIEGLER, JR.
Vice-Chairman	FRANK A. GRIFFITHS
Secretary	ROBERT O. SWADOS
Executive Vice-President	BRIAN F. O'NEILL
Vice-President and General Counsel	GILBERT STEIN
Vice-President, Finance	KENNETH G. SAWYER
Vice-President, Project Development	IAN "SCOTTY" MORRISON
Vice-President, Broadcasting	JOEL NIXON
Vice-President, Marketing-Public Relations	STEVE RYAN
Director of Communications	John Halligan
Director of Central Registry	Garry Lovegrove
Executive Director of Hockey Operations	Jim Gregory
Director of Officiating	John McCauley
Director of Information (Prince of Wales Conference)	Dan Leary (New York)
Director of Information (Clarence Campbell Conference)	Gary Meagher (Montreal)
Supervisors of Officials	Bryan Lewis, John Ashley, Matt Pavelich
Director of Administration	Phil Scheuer
Director of Security	Frank Torpey
Assistant Director of Security	Al Wiseman

National Hockey League

1986-87

Campbell Conference
Smythe Division

Calgary Flames
Edmonton Oilers
Los Angeles Kings
Vancouver Canucks
Winnipeg Jets

Norris Division

Chicago Black Hawks
Detroit Red Wings
Minnesota North Stars
St. Louis Blues
Toronto Maple Leafs

Prince Of Wales Conference
Patrick Division

New Jersey Devils
New York Islanders
New York Rangers
Philadelphia Flyers
Pittsburgh Penguins
Washington Capitals

Adams Division

Boston Bruins
Buffalo Sabres
Hartford Whalers
Montreal Canadiens
Quebec Nordiques

Board of Governors

Paul A. Mooney .... Boston	John O. Pickett, Jr. .... N. Y. Islanders
Seymour H. Knox, III .... Buffalo	John H. Krumpe .... N. Y. Rangers
Cliff Fletcher .... Calgary	Jay T. Snider .... Philadelphia
William W. Wirtz .... Chicago	J. Paul Martha .... Pittsburgh
Michael Ilitch .... Detroit	Marcel Aubut .... Quebec
Peter Pocklington .... Edmonton	Harry Ornest .... St. Louis
Howard Baldwin .... Hartford	Harold E. Ballard .... Toronto
Dr. Jerry Buss .... Los Angeles	Frank A. Griffiths .... Vancouver
Gordon Gund .... Minnesota	Abe Pollin .... Washington
Ronald Corey .... Montreal	Barry Shenkarow .... Winnipeg
John J. McMullen .... New Jersey	

Boston Bruins
Adams Division

President and Governor	Paul A. Mooney
General Manager and Alternate Governor	Harry Sinden
Assistant General Manager	Tom Johnson
Coach	Butch Goring
Assistant Coach	Mike Milbury
Director of Public Relations	Nate Greenberg
Coordinator of Minor League Player Personnel/Scouting	Bob Tindall
Director of Player Evaluation	Bart Bradley
Special Assignment Scout	Jean Ratelle
Scouting Staff	Jim Morrison, Andre Lachapelle, Joe Lyons, Don Saatzer, Lars Waldner
Controller	John J. Dionne
Trainers	Jim Narrigan, Larry Ness
Public Relations Assistant	Heidi Holland
Sales and Marketing	Steve Nazro
Home Ice	Boston Garden
Address	150 Causeway Street, Boston, Mass. 02114
Seating Capacity	14,451
Club colors	Gold, Black and White
Phone	(617) 227-3206

Paul Mooney

Harry Sinden

Tom Johnson

Butch Goring

Boston Bruins 1986-87 Roster

FORWARDS	Hgt.	Wgt.	Place of Birth	Date	1985-86 Club	G.	A.	Pts.
Buettgen, Jim	6:04	215	Chicago, Ill.	3-8-60	Milwaukee-Moncton	6	6	12
Burridge, Randy	5:09	180	Fort Erie, Ont.	1-7-66	Peterborough-Boston	32	36	68
Byers, Lyndon	6:01	190	Nipawin, Sask.	2-29-64	Milwaukee-Moncton-Boston	2	8	10
Carter, John	5:10	175	Winchester, Mass.	5-3-63	RPI-Boston	23	18	41
Courtnall, Geoff	6:00	185	Victoria, B.C.	8-18-62	Moncton-Boston	29	24	53
Crowder, Keith	6:00	195	Windsor, Ont.	1-6-59	Boston	38	46	84
Foster, Dwight	5:11	190	Toronto, Ont.	4-2-57	Detroit-Boston	6	12	18
Gradin, Thomas	5:11	170	Solleftea, Sweden	2-18-56	Vancouver	14	27	41
Johnston, Greg	6:01	190	Barrie, Ont.	1-14-65	Moncton-Boston	19	28	47
Kasper, Steve	5:08	170	Montreal, Que.	9-28-61	Boston	17	23	40
Kostynski, Doug	6:01	170	Castlegar, B.C.	2-23-63	Moncton	18	36	54
Lehman, Tommy	6:01	185	Solna, Sweden	2-3-64	AIK Sweden	6	9	15
Linseman, Ken	5:11	175	Kingston, Ont.	8-11-58	Boston	23	58	81
Markwart, Nevin	5:10	185	Toronto, Ont.	12-9-64	Boston	7	15	22
McCarthy, Tom	6:02	200	Toronto, Ont.	7-31-60	Minnesota	12	12	24
Middleton, Rick	5:11	175	Toronto, Ont.	12-4-53	Boston	14	30	44
Miller, Jay	6:02	205	Wellesley, Mass.	7-16-60	Moncton-Boston	7	6	13
Neely, Cam	6:01	205	Comox, B.C.	6-6-65	Vancouver	14	20	34
Nienhuis, Kraig	6:02	205	Sarnia, Ont.	5-9-61	Boston	16	14	30
Pasin, Dave	6:01	205	Edmonton, Alta.	7-8-66	Boston	18	19	37
Podloski, Ray	6:02	210	Edmonton, Alta.	1-5-66	Portland	59	75	134
Reid, Dave	6:00	215	Toronto, Ont.	5-15-64	Moncton-Boston	24	28	52
Simmer, Charlie	6:03	205	Terrace Bay, Ont.	3-20-54	Boston	36	24	60
Sleigher, Louis	5:11	200	Nouvelle, Que.	10-23-58	Boston	4	2	6
Sweeney, Bob	6:03	190	Boxborough, Mass.	1-25-64	Boston College	15	24	39

DEFENSEMEN	Hgt.	Wgt.	Place of Birth	Date	1985-86 Club	G.	A.	Pts.
Blum, John	6:03	205	Detroit, Mich.	10-8-59	Moncton-Boston	2	12	14
Bourque, Ray	5:11	210	Montreal, Que.	12-28-60	Boston	19	58	77
Campbell, Wade	6:04	220	Peace River, Alta.	1-2-61	Sherbrooke-Winn.-Boston-Monc.	2	5	7
Cote, Alain	6:00	200	Montmagny, Que.	4-4-67	Granby-Boston-Moncton	4	18	22
Hynes, Gord	6:01	165	Montreal, Que.	7-22-66	Medicine Hat	22	39	61
Kluzak, Gord	6:04	210	Climax, Sask.	3-4-64	Boston	8	31	39
Larson, Reed	6:00	195	Minneapolis, Minn.	7-30-56	Detroit-Boston	22	45	67
Pedersen, Allen	6:03	180	Edmonton, Alta.	1-13-65	Moncton	1	8	9
Simonetti, Frank	6:01	185	Melrose, Mass.	9-11-62	Moncton-Boston	1	0	1
Thelin, Mats	5:10	185	Stockholm, Sweden	3-30-61	Moncton-Boston	2	4	6
Thelven, Michael	5:11	180	Stockholm, Sweden	1-7-61	Boston	6	20	26

GOALTENDERS	Hgt.	Wgt.	Place of Birth	Date	1985-86 Club	Mins.	GA.	SO.
Daskalakis, Cleon	5:09	175	Boston, Mass.	9-29-62	Moncton-Boston	2463	151	0
Keans, Doug	5:07	190	Pembroke, Ont.	1-7-58	Boston	1757	107	0
Ranford, Bill	5:10	170	Brandon, Man.	12-12-66	New Westminster-Boston	3031	235	1
Riggin, Pat	5:09	175	Kincardine, Ont.	5-26-59	Washington-Boston	2641	150	1

Buffalo Sabres
Adams Division

Chairman of the Board	Seymour H. Knox III
President	Northrup R. Knox
Vice-Chairmen of the Board	David G. Forman, Robert E. Rich, Jr.
Vice-President and Counsel	Robert O. Swados
Administrative Vice-President	Mitchell Owen
Vice-President, Finance	Robert W. Pickel
Secretary and Assistant General Manager	Gerry Meehan
Treasurer	Joseph T. J. Stewart
Director of Hockey Operations, General Manager and Coach	Scotty Bowman
Assistant Coaches	Don Luce, Craig Ramsay, Barry Smith
Director of Communications	Paul Wieland
Head Trainer	Jim Pizzutelli
Assistant Trainer	Bob Simonick
Home Ice	Memorial Auditorium
Address	Memorial Auditorium, Buffalo, N.Y. 14202
Seating Capacity	16,433 (including standees)
Club Colors	Blue, White and Gold
Phone	(716) 856-7300

Seymour Knox III

Northrup Knox

Scotty Bowman

Gerry Meehan

Buffalo Sabres 1986-87 Roster

FORWARDS

Name	Hgt.	Wgt.	Place of Birth	Date	1985-86 Club	G.	A.	Pts.
Andersson, Mikael	5:11	187	Malmo, Sweden	5-10-66	Buffalo-Rochester	5	17	22
Andreychuk, Dave	6:03	200	Hamilton, Ont.	9-29-63	Buffalo	36	51	87
Arneil, Scott	6:01	170	Cornwall, Ont.	9-17-62	Winnipeg	18	25	43
Brydges, Paul	5:11	180	Guelph, Ont.	6-21-65	Guelph	17	40	57
Corkum, Bob	6:02	195	Salisbury, Mass.	12-18-67	Windsor	7	26	33
Creighton, Adam	6:05	205	Burlington, Ont.	6-2-65	Buffalo-Rochester	18	22	40
Cyr, Paul	5:10	185	Port Alberni, B.C.	10-31-63	Buffalo	20	31	51
Foligno, Mike	6:02	195	Sudbury, Ont.	1-29-59	Buffalo	41	39	80
Fraser, Jay	6:01	200	Ottawa, Ont.	10-26-61	Carolina-Rochester	4	5	9
Gage, Jody	6:00	185	Toronto, Ont.	11-29-59	Buffalo-Rochester	45	59	104
Gardner, Paul	6:00	195	Fort Erie, Ont.	3-5-56	Buffalo-Rochester	61	51	112
Gretzky, Keith	5:09	157	Brantford, Ont.	2-16-67	Windsor	31	62	93
Guay, Francois	6:00	183	Gatineau, Que.	6-8-68	Laval	19	55	74
Hajdu, Richard	6:00	170	Victoria, B.C.	4-10-65	Buffalo-Rochester	10	27	37
Hamilton, Jeff	6:00	180	Montreal, Que.	2-23-64	Rochester	19	10	29
Harper, Warren	6:00	175	Prince Albert, Sask.	5-10-63	Rochester	18	30	48
Hartman, Mike	6:00	189	Detroit, Mich.	2-7-67	North Bay	23	17	40
Hogue, Benoit	5:10	180	Repentigny, Que.	10-28-66	St. Jean	54	54	108
Hughes, Pat	6:00	180	Calgary, Alta.	3-25-55	Buffalo-Rochester	7	12	19
Jackson, Jim	5:08	181	Oshawa, Ont.	2-1-60	Rochester	16	32	48
Kaese, Trent	5:11	205	Nanaimo, B.C.	9-9-67	Lethbridge	24	41	65
Kerr, Kevin	5:10	172	North Bay, Ont.	9-18-67	Windsor	21	51	72
Lacombe, Normand	5:11	205	Pierrefonds, Que.	10-18-64	Buffalo-Rochester	16	20	36
Langevin, Chris	6:00	190	Montreal, Que.	11-27-59	Buffalo	2	1	3
Larose, Guy	5:09	172	Hull, Que.	7-31-67	Guelph-Ottawa	31	61	92
Lever, Don	5:11	185	South Porcupine, Ont.	11-14-52	Buffalo-Rochester	13	12	25
Logan, Bob	6:00	190	Montreal, Que.	2-22-64	Yale University	21	23	44
McKinnon, Brian	5:11	185	Toronto, Ont.	10-4-64	Rochester	4	7	11
Orlando, Gates	5:08	175	Montreal, Que.	11-16-62	Buffalo-Rochester	13	12	25
Parker, Jeff	6:03	198	St. Paul, Minn.	9-7-64	Michigan State	15	20	35
Priestlay, Ken	5:10	172	Vancouver, B.C.	8-24-67	Rochester	0	2	2
Ristau, Andrew	6:05	230	Winnipeg, Man.	1-28-61	Carolina-Rochester	1	2	3
Rooney, Larry	5:11	165	Boston, Mass.	1-30-68	Thayer	20	35	55
Ruff, Lindy	6:02	190	Warburg, Alta.	2-17-60	Buffalo	20	12	32
Seiling, Ric	6:01	180	Elmira, Ont.	12-15-57	Buffalo	12	13	25
Sheppard, Ray	6:01	196	Pembroke, Ont.	5-27-66	Cornwall	81	61	142
Smith, Doug	5:11	180	Ottawa, Ont.	5-17-63	Buffalo-Los Angeles	18	20	38
Trapp, Doug	6:00	182	Balcarres, Sask.	11-28-65	Rochester	21	42	63
Tucker, John	6:00	185	Windsor, Ont.	9-29-64	Buffalo	31	34	65
Verret, Claude	5:09	165	Lachine, Que.	4-20-63	Rochester	19	32	51

DEFENSEMEN

Name	Hgt.	Wgt.	Place of Birth	Date	1985-86 Club	G.	A.	Pts.
Anderson, Shawn	6:01	191	Montreal, Que.	2-7-68	Team Canada	2	6	8
Arndt, Troy	6:00	195	Regina, Sask.	4-30-68	Portland	3	20	23
Baldris, Miguel	6:00	192	Montreal, Que.	1-30-68	Shawinigan	2	31	33
Brown, Greg	5:11	182	Hartford, Conn.	3-7-68	St. Marks High	22	28	50
Burton, James	6:01	187	Brantford, Ont.	11-13-61	Fort Wayne	30	64	94
Dunn, Richie	6:00	195	Boston, Mass.	5-12-57	Buffalo-Rochester	11	22	33
Dykstra, Steve	6:02	190	Edmonton, Alta.	2-3-62	Rochester-Flint	4	21	25
Engblom, Brian	6:02	190	Winnipeg, Man.	1-27-55	Buffalo-Los Angeles	4	17	21
Fenyves, Dave	5:11	190	Dunnville, Ont.	4-29-60	Buffalo	0	7	7
Ferner, Mark	6:00	180	Regina, Sask.	9-5-65	Rochester	3	13	16
Gasseau, James	6:02	205	Carleton, Que.	5-4-66	Drummondville	20	31	51
Hajt, Bill	6:03	205	Radisson, Sask.	11-18-51	Buffalo	1	16	17
Halkidis, Bob	5:11	196	Toronto, Ont.	3-5-66	Buffalo	1	9	10
Hofford, James	6:00	188	Sudbury, Ont.	10-4-64	Buffalo-Rochester	2	7	9
Hoover, Tim	5:10	175	North Bay, Ont.	1-9-65	Rochester	2	5	7
Housley, Phil	5:10	180	St. Paul, Minn.	3-9-64	Buffalo	15	47	62
Matikainen, Petri	6:00	185	Savonlinna, Finland	1-7-67	Oshawa	14	42	56
Meyer, Jason	5:10	185	Regina, Sask.	2-21-65	Rochester	7	28	35
Moylan, Dave	6:02	194	Tillsonburg, Ont.	8-13-67	Sudbury	17	20	37
Ramsey, Mike	6:03	190	Minneapolis, Minn.	12-3-60	Buffalo	7	21	28
Reekie, Joe	6:03	195	Petawawa, Ont.	2-22-65	Buffalo-Rochester	3	25	28
Russell, Phil	6:02	200	Edmonton, Alta.	7-21-52	Buffalo-New Jersey	4	6	10
Virta, Hannu	6:00	180	Turku, Finland	3-22-63	Buffalo	5	23	28

GOALTENDERS

Name	Hgt.	Wgt.	Place of Birth	Date	1985-86 Club	Mins.	GA.	SO.
Barrasso, Tom	6:03	195	Boston, Mass.	3-31-65	Buffalo	3248	144	5
Cloutier, Jacques	5:07	155	Noranda, Que.	1-3-60	Buffalo-Rochester	868	40	0
Craig, Mike	6:00	165	Calgary, Alta.	11-1-62	Rochester	2573	183	0
Puppa, Daren	6:03	195	Kirkland Lake, Ont.	3-23-65	Buffalo-Rochester	1830	78	0
Rein, Kenton	5:11	198	Saskatoon, Sask.	9-12-67	Prince Albert	1302	71	0
Wakaluk, Darcy	5:11	181	Pincher Creek, Alta.	3-14-66	Spokane	2562	224	1

Calgary Flames
Smythe Division

Owners	Norman Green, Harley Hotchkiss, Mrs. Ralph Scurfield, B. J. Seaman, D. K. Seaman, Norman Kwong
President, General Manager and Governor	Cliff Fletcher
V.P., Business and Finance	Clare Rhyasen
Assistant to the President and Director of Marketing	Al Coates
Assistant General Manager	Al MacNeil
General Counsel	Howard Mackie & Assoc.
Coach	Bob Johnson
Assistant Coaches	Bob Murdoch, Pierre Page
V.P., Sales and Broadcasting	Leo Ornest
Director of Public Relations	Rick Skaggs
Assistant Public Relations Director	Mike Burke
Chief Scout	Gerry Blair
Coordinator of Scouting	Ian McKenzie
U.S. and College Scout	Jack Ferreira
Scouting Staff	Bill White, Larry Popein, Lars Normann, Ben Hayes, Al Godfrey
Controller	Lynne Tosh
Trainer	Jim Murray
Equipment Manager	Bobby Stewart
Home Ice	The Olympic Saddledome
Address	P.O. Box 1540, Station M, Calgary, Alta. T2P 3B9
Seating Capacity	16,762
Club colors	White, Red and Gold
Phone	(403) 261-0475

Cliff Fletcher

Al MacNeil

Bob Johnson

Bob Murdoch

Calgary Flames 1986-87 Roster

FORWARDS

Name	Hgt.	Wgt.	Place of Birth	Date	1985-86 Club	G.	A.	Pts.
Bakovic, Peter	6:01	190	Thunder Bay, Ont.	1-31-65	Moncton	18	36	54
Berezan, Perry	6:02	192	Edmonton, Alta.	12- 5-64	Calgary	12	21	33
Bodak, Bob	6:02	190	Thunder Bay, Ont.	5-28-61	Moncton	27	15	42
Bozek, Steve	5:11	175	Kelowna, B.C.	11-26-60	Calgary	21	22	43
Bradley, Brian	5:10	170	Kitchener, Ont.	1-21-65	Moncton-Calgary	23	43	66
Courteau, Yves	6:00	194	Montreal, Que.	4-25-64	Moncton-Calgary	27	23	50
Doucet, Benoit	5:10	180	Montreal, Que.	4-23-63	Moncton	26	34	60
Fotiu, Nick	6:02	210	Staten Island, N.Y.	5-25-52	Calgary	0	1	1
Hull, Brett	5:11	195	Belleville, Ont.	8- 9-64	U. of Minn.-Duluth	52	32	84
Hunter, Tim	6:02	202	Calgary, Alta.	9-10-59	Calgary	8	7	15
Loob, Hakan	5:09	175	Karlstad, Sweden	7- 3-60	Calgary	31	36	67
McDonald, Lanny	6:00	190	Hanna, Alta.	2-16-53	Calgary	28	43	71
Mullen, Joe	5:09	180	New York, N.Y.	2-26-57	St. Louis-Calgary	44	46	90
Otto, Joel	6:04	220	St. Cloud, Minn.	10-29-61	Calgary	25	34	59
Patterson, Colin	6:02	195	Rexdale, Ont.	5-11-60	Calgary	14	13	27
Peplinski, Jim	6:03	209	Renfrew, Ont.	10-24-60	Calgary	24	35	59
Pickell, Doug	6:01	185	London, Ont.	5- 7-68	Kamloops	27	20	47
Quinn, Dan	5:11	175	Ottawa, Ont.	6- 1-65	Calgary	30	42	72
Risebrough, Doug	5:11	183	Kitchener, Ont.	1-29-54	Calgary	15	28	43
Roberts, Gary	6:01	190	North York, Ont.	5-23-66	Ottawa-Guelph	44	40	84
Tonelli, John	6:01	200	Milton, Ont.	3-23-57	N.Y. Islanders-Calgary	23	45	68
Wenaas, Jeff	6:00	185	Eastend, Sask.	9- 1-67	Medicine Hat	20	26	46
Wilson, Carey	6:02	198	Winnipeg, Man.	5-19-62	Calgary	29	29	58

DEFENSEMEN

Name	Hgt.	Wgt.	Place of Birth	Date	1985-86 Club	G.	A.	Pts.
Baxter, Paul	5:11	189	Winnipeg, Man.	10-25-55	Calgary	4	3	7
Degray, Dale	6:00	201	Oshawa, Ont.	9- 3-63	Moncton	9	31	40
Glynn, Brian	6:04	224	Iserlohn, W. Ger.	11-23-67	Saskatoon	7	25	32
Gregoire, Bill	6:00	175	Victoria, B.C.	4- 9-67	Victoria	13	19	32
Guy, Kevan	6:03	202	Edmonton, Alta.	7-16-65	Moncton	4	20	24
Johnson, Terry	6:03	210	Calgary, Alta.	11-28-58	St. Louis-Calgary	1	8	9
Kivell, Rob	6:02	200	North Bay, Ont.	1-14-65	Moncton	7	3	10
Lessard, Rick	6:02	198	Timmins, Ont.	1- 9-68	Ottawa	1	20	21
MacDonald, Chris	6:01	175	Barrie, Ont.	7- 9-63	U. of Western Michigan	12	38	50
MacInnis, Al	6:02	193	Inverness, N.S.	7-11-63	Calgary	11	57	68
Macoun, Jamie	6:02	197	Newmarket, Ont.	8-17-61	Calgary	11	21	32
McCutcheon, Darwin	6:05	210	Listowel, Ont.	4-19-62	Moncton	0	2	2
Melrose, Kevan	5:10	180	Calgary, Atla.	3-28-66	Penticton	18	15	33
Mercier, Don	6:04	210	Grimshaw, Alta.	1-21-63	U. of Denver	3	10	13
Mersch, Mike	6:02	210	Skokie, Ill.	9-29-64	U. of Illinois-Chicago	4	19	23
Reierson, Dave	6:00	185	Bashaw, Alta.	8-30-64	Michigan Tech	7	16	23
Reinhart, Paul	5:11	205	Kitchener, Ont.	1- 8-60	Calgary	8	25	33
Rivington, Dale	6:01	193	Ottawa, Ont.	3- 7-64	Rochester Tech	16	23	39
Sabourin, Ken	6:04	204	Scarborough, Ont.	4-28-66	Cornwall	3	12	15
Sheehy, Neil	6:02	215	Fort Francis, Ont.	2- 9-60	Calgary-Moncton	3	17	20
Suter, Gary	6:00	199	Madison, Wis.	6-24-64	Calgary	18	50	68

GOALTENDERS

Name	Hgt.	Wgt.	Place of Birth	Date	1985-86 Club	Mins.	GA.	SO.
Blair, Grant	6:00	160	Ancaster, Ont.	8-15-64	Harvard	1812	82	0
Dadswell, Doug	5:10	175	Scarborough, Ont.	2- 7-64	Cornell	1815	92	1
D'Amour, Marc	5:10	165	Sudbury, Ont.	4-29-61	Calgary-Moncton	1689	104	0
Kosti, Rick	5:10	185	Kincaid, Sask.	9-13-63	Moncton-Salt Lake City	2035	143	1
Lemelin, Rejean	5:11	170	Quebec City, Que.	11-19-54	Calgary	3369	229	1
Vernon, Mike	5:09	155	Calgary, Alta.	2-24-63	Moncton-SLC-Calgary	1895	107	2

Chicago Black Hawks
Norris Division

President	William W. Wirtz
Vice-President	Arthur M. Wirtz, Jr.
Vice-President and Assistant to the President	Thomas N. Ivan
General Manager and Coach	Bob Pulford
Assistant G.M. and Director of Player Personnel	Jack Davison
Assistant Coaches	Cliff Koroll, Roger Neilson
Scouts	Jimmy Walker, Don Smith, Dave Lucas, Michel Dumas, Jim Pappin, Jan Spieczny
Public Relations	Jim DeMaria
Trainers	Charles "Skip" Thayer, Lou Varga, Randy Lacey
Home Ice	Chicago Stadium
Address	1800 W. Madison Street, Chicago, Illinois 60612
Seating Capacity	17,317
Club colors	Red, Black and White
Phone	(312) 733-5300

William W. Wirtz

Bob Pulford

Jack Davison

Arthur M. Wirtz

Chicago Black Hawks 1986-87 Roster

FORWARDS

Name	Hgt.	Wgt.	Place of Birth	Date	1985-86 Club	G.	A.	Pts.
Belland, Brad	6:00	180	Windsor, Ont.	1- 4-67	Sudbury-Hamilton	20	26	46
Benic, Geoff	6:02	198	Toronto, Ont.	9- 1-68	Windsor	3	7	10
Boudreau, Bruce	5:10	170	Toronto, Ont.	1- 9-55	Nova Scotia-Chicago	31	36	67
Braccia, Rick	6:00	195	Revere, Mass.	9- 5-67	Boston College	0	3	3
Brown, Bill	6:01	170	Dayton, O.	10- 9-66	Ohio State	4	4	8
Camazzola, Jim	5:11	190	Vancouver, B.C.	1- 5-64	Saginaw-Nova Scotia	16	22	38
Eriksson, Tom	5:11	183	Umea, Sweden	5- 3-66	Modo Div. 1	..	..	..
Fraser, Curt	6:00	200	Cincinnati, O.	1-12-58	Chicago	29	39	68
Greenough, Glenn	5:11	198	Sudbury, Ont.	7-20-66	Sudbury	30	41	71
Hudson, Mike	6:01	185	Guelph, Ont.	2- 6-67	Sudbury	38	44	82
LaPlante, Richard	5:11	175	Boucherville, Que.	3-15-67	U. of Vermont	1	17	18
Larmer, Steve	5:10	189	Peterborough, Ont.	6-16-61	Chicago	31	45	76
LaVarre, Mark	5:11	170	Evanston, Ill.	2-21-65	Nova Scotia-Chicago	15	19	34
Loach, Lonnie	5:10	181	New Liskeard, Ont.	4-14-68	Guelph	41	42	83
Lowes, Glenn	6:00	184	Burlington, Ont.	1-17-68	Toronto Jrs.	8	14	22
Ludzik, Steve	5:11	186	Toronto, Ont.	4- 3-62	Chicago	6	5	11
Lysiak, Tom	6:01	204	High Prairie, Alta	4-22-53	Chicago	2	19	21
Mackey, David	6:03	190	N. Westminster, B.C.	7-24-66	Medicine Hat	28	36	64
Murray, Troy	6:01	195	Calgary, Alta.	7-31-62	Chicago	45	54	99
Nanne, Marty	6:00	180	Edina, Minnesota	7-21-67	U. of Minnesota	5	5	10
Noonan, Brian	6:01	180	Boston, Mass.	5-29-65	Saginaw	39	39	78
Olczyk, Ed	6:01	195	Chicago, Ill.	8-16-66	Chicago	29	50	79
Paterson, Rick	5:09	187	Kingston, Ont.	2-10-58	Chicago	9	3	12
Persson, Joakim	5:08	163	Gavle, Sweden	5-15-66	Gavle Div. 1	..	..	..
Posa, Victor	6:00	193	Bari, Italy	11- 5-66	Toronto Jrs.-Chicago	28	34	62
Presley, Wayne	5:11	172	Detroit, Mich.	3-23-65	Nova Scotia-Chicago	13	17	30
Sanipass, Everett	6:01	192	Big Cove, N.B.	2-13-68	Verdun	23	66	89
Savard, Denis	5:10	167	Pt. Gatineau, Que.	2- 4-61	Chicago	47	69	116
Sceviour, Darin	5:10	185	Lacombe, Alta.	11-30-65	Nova Scotia-Saginaw	13	14	27
Secord, Al	6:01	212	Sudbury, Ont.	3- 3-58	Chicago	40	36	76
Stapleton, Mike	5:10	163	Sarnia, Ont.	5- 5-66	Cornwall	39	65	104
Sutter, Darryl	5:11	176	Viking, Alta.	8-19-58	Chicago	17	10	27
Thayer, Chris	6:02	190	Exeter, N.H.	11-9-67	Kent H.S.	7	10	17
Torkki, Jari	6:00	163	Finland	8-11-65	Lukko (Finland)	..	..	..
Vincellette, Dan	6:01	202	Verdun, Que.	8- 1-67	Drummondville	37	47	84
Watson, Bill	6:01	190	Pine Falls, Man.	3-30-64	Chicago	8	16	24
Williams, Sean	6:00	182	Oshawa, Ont.	1-28-68	Oshawa	15	23	38
Yaremchuk, Ken	5:11	187	Edmonton, Alta.	1- 1-64	Chicago	14	20	34

DEFENSEMEN

Name	Hgt.	Wgt.	Place of Birth	Date	1985-86 Club	G.	A.	Pts.
Beck, Brad	5:11	185	Vancouver, B.C.	2-10-64	Michigan State	3	15	18
Bergevin, Marc	5:11	178	Montreal, Que.	8-11-65	Chicago	7	7	14
Brown, Keith	6:01	191	Cornerbrook, Nfld.	5- 6-60	Chicago	11	29	40
Cassidy, Bruce	5:11	176	Ottawa, Ont.	5-20-65	Nova Scotia-Chicago	0	0	0
DiFiore, Ralph	6:01	181	Montreal, Que.	4-20-66	Trois-Rivieres	0	21	21
Doyon, Mario	6:00	174	Quebec City, Que.	8-27-68	Drummondville	5	14	19
Dupont, Jerome	6:03	201	Ottawa, Ont.	2-21-62	Chicago	2	13	15
Hamilton, Brad	6:00	175	Calgary, Alta.	3-30-67	Michigan State	3	10	13
Heed, Jonas	6:00	174	Sodertalje, Sweden	1- 3-67	Sodertalje (Sweden)	..	..	..
Herbert, Rick	6:01	180	Toronto, Ont.	7-10-67	Portland-Spokane	4	37	41
Howard, Tarek	6:01	185	Tucson, Arizona	2- 6-65	Univ. of North Dakota	2	11	13
Kucera, Frantisek	6:01	180	Stibrova, Czech.	2- 3-68	Sparta Praha	1	2	3
Kurzawski, Mark	6:03	199	Chicago, Ill.	2-25-68	Windsor	11	25	36
Manson, Dave	6:02	190	Prince Albert, Sask.	1-27-67	Prince Albert	14	34	48
Murray, Bob	5:10	186	Kingston, Ont.	11-26-54	Chicago	9	29	38
O'Callahan, Jack	6:01	189	Charleston, Mass.	7-24-57	Chicago	4	19	23
Paynter, Kent	6:00	186	Summerside, P.E.I.	4-27-65	Nova Scotia	1	2	3
Pound, Ian	6:01	183	Brockville, Ont.	1-22-67	Kitchener	2	12	14
Williams, Dan	6:02	180	Oak Park, Ill.	4-15-66	Elmira	4	16	20
Wilson, Behn	6:03	210	Toronto, Ont.	12-19-58	Chicago	13	38	51
Wilson, Doug	6:01	187	Ottawa, Ont.	7- 5-57	Chicago	17	47	64
Yawney, Trent	6:03	183	Hudson Bay, Sask.	9-29-65	Team Canada	6	15	21

GOALTENDERS

Name	Hgt.	Wgt.	Place of Birth	Date	1985-86 Club	Mins.	GA.	SO.
Bannerman, Murray	5:11	185	Ft. Francis, Ont.	4-27-57	Chicago	2689	201	1
Clifford, Chris	5:09	139	Kingston, Ont.	5-26-66	Kingston	2988	178	1
Helmuth, Andy	5:10	172	Detroit, Mich.	3-18-67	Ottawa-Guelph	1795	136	0
Lehkonen, Timo	5:11	165	Helsinki, Finland	1- 8-66	Finland	..	..	..
Pang, Darren	5:05	155	Medford, Ont.	2-17-64	Saginaw	2638	148	2
Ralph, Jim	5:11	167	Sault Ste. Marie, Ont.	5-13-62	Nova Scotia-Saginaw	1368	104	1
Reid, John	5:11	202	Windsor, Ont.	2-18-67	Belleville-North Bay	2627	164	1
Sauve, Bob	5:08	165	St. Genevieve, Que.	6-17-55	Chicago	2099	138	0
Skorodenski, Warren	5:08	165	Winnipeg, Man.	3-22-60	Nova Scotia-Chicago	1776	115	0

Detroit Red Wings
Norris Division

President and Owner	Michael Ilitch
Executive Vice-President	James Lites
Secretary/Treasurer	Marian Ilitch
General Counsel	Denise Ilitch-Lites
Vice-President, General Manager	Jim Devellano
Asst. General Manager/Director of Player Development	Nick Polano
Coach	Jacques Demers
Assistant Coaches	Danny Belisle, Colin Campbell, Dave Dryden, Don MacAdam
Director of Public Relations	Bill Jamieson
Director of Scouting/Player Procurement	Neil Smith
Director Scouting/United States	Billy Dea
Eastern USA Scout	Jerry Moschella
Director Scouting/Eastern Canada	Alex Davidson
Director Scouting/Western Canada	Ken Holland
Scouts	Chris Coury, Frank Michalek, Dave Polano, Christer Rockstrom, Carl Wetzel, Mike Daski
Director of Marketing	Rosanne Kozerski-Brown
Director of Advertising Sales/Promotions	Terry Murphy
Physical Therapist	Jim Pengelly
Home Ice	Joe Louis Sports Arena
Address	600 Civic Center Drive, Detroit, Mich. 48226
Seating Capacity	19,275
Club colors	Red and White
Phone	(313) 567-7333

Mike Ilitch

Jim Devellano

Nick Polano

Jacques Demers

Detroit Red Wings 1986-87 Roster

FORWARDS

Name	Hgt.	Wgt.	Place of Birth	Date	1985-86 Club	G.	A.	Pts.
Bissett, Tom	6:00	180		3-13-66	Michigan Tech	19	19	38
Bjur, Thomas	6:01	207	Stockholm, Sweden	8-28-66	AIK (Sweden)	0	1	1
Burr, Shawn	6:00	180	Sarnia, Ont.	7- 1-66	Kitchener-Detroit-Adirondack	63	69	132
Carroll, Bill	5:10	190	Toronto, Ont.	1-19-59	Edmonton-Nova Scotia-Detroit	9	24	33
Chiatto, Chuck	5:08	160	Pittsburgh, Pa.	9-24-64	Western Michigan Univ.	4	10	14
Cichocki, Chris	5:10	185	Detroit, Mich.	9-17-63	Detroit-Adirondack	14	15	29
Donnelly, Dave	5:11	185	Edmonton, Alta.	2- 2-62	Boston	0	0	0
Fedyk, Brent	6:00	180	Yorkton, Sask.	3- 8-67	Regina	43	34	77
Gallant, Gerard	5:10	168	Summerside, P.E.I.	9- 2-63	Detroit	20	19	39
Garpenlov, Johan	5:11	178	Stockholm, Sweden	3-21-68	NACKA (Sweden)	8	12	20
Graves, Adam	5:11	185	Toronto, Ont.	4-12-68	Windsor	27	37	64
Higgins, Tim	6:01	185	Ottawa, Ont.	2- 7-58	New Jersey	9	17	26
Karsson, Lars	6:03	176	Karlstad, Sweden	6-14-65	Bjorkloven-Farjestad	7	13	20
Klima, Petr	6:00	190	Chaomutov, Czech.	12-23-64	Detroit	32	24	56
Kocur, Joe	6:01	204	Calgary, Alta.	12-21-64	Detroit-Adirondack	15	8	23
Krentz, Dale	5:11	187	Steinbach, Man.	12-19-61	Adirondack	19	27	46
Lundstrom, Mats	5:10	178	Skelleftea, Sweden	4-23-66	Skelleftea (Sweden)	..	..	..
McKay, Randy	6:01	185	Montreal, Que.	1-25-67	Michigan Tech	12	22	34
McRae, Basil	6:02	205	Beaverton, Ont.	1- 5-61	Detroit-Adirondack	22	30	52
Merkosky, Glenn	5:10	176	Edmonton, Alta.	4- 8-60	Detroit-Adirondack	24	35	59
Murphy, Joe	6:01	190	London, Ont.	10-16-67	Michigan State Univ.	24	37	61
Nordin, Urban	6:01	181	Ornskioldsvik, Sweden	4-11-66	MoDo (Sweden)	0	0	0
Oates, Adam	5:11	190	Weston, Ont.	8-27-62	Detroit-Adirondack	27	39	66
Ogrodnick, John	6:00	189	Ottawa, Ont.	6-20-59	Detroit	38	32	70
Potvin, Marc	6:01	185	Ottawa, Ont.	1-28-67	Stratford	22	43	65
Probert, Bob	6:03	208	Windsor, Ont.	6- 5-65	Detroit-Adirondack	20	28	48
Robertson, Geordie	6:00	165	Victoria, B.C.	8- 1-59	Adirondack	36	56	92
Shedden, Doug	6:00	185	Wallaceburg, Ont.	4-29-61	Pittsburgh-Detroit	34	37	71
Shibicky, Bill	5:11	180	Burnaby, B.C.	1-25-64	Michigan State Univ.	17	39	56
Speers, Ted	5:11	190	Ann Arbor, Mich.	1-21-61	Detroit-Adirondack	33	36	69
Staszak, Ray	6:00	200	Philadelphia, Pa.	12- 1-62	Detroit-Adirondack	13	9	22
Svanberg, Bo	5:11	165	Farjestad, Sweden	1- 5-67	Farjestad	4	2	6
Yaremchuk, Gary	6:00	185	Edmonton, Alta.	8-15-61	Adirondack	12	32	44
Young, Warren	6:03	195	Toronto, Ont.	1-11-56	Detroit	22	24	46
Yzerman, Steve	5:11	175	Cranbrook, B.C.	5- 9-65	Detroit	14	28	42

DEFENSEMEN

Name	Hgt.	Wgt.	Place of Birth	Date	1985-86 Club	G.	A.	Pts.
Chiasson, Steve	6:00	210	Barrie, Ont.	4-14-67	Guelph	12	30	42
DeGaetan, Phil	6:01	203	Roslyn, N.Y.	8- 9-63	Indianapolis	9	39	48
Djoos, Per Olav	5:11	176	Mora, Sweden	5-11-68	Mora (Sweden)	9	5	14
Ekroth, Peter	6:03	211	Sodertalje, Sweden	4- 2-60	Sodertalje	13	19	32
Friday, Tim	6:00	190	Burbank, Calif.	3- 5-61	Detroit-Adirondack	2	34	36
Hamalainen, Eerik	6:01	187	Rauma, Finland	4-20-65		..	..	..
Houda, Doug	6:02	190	Blairmore, Alta.	6- 3-66	Medicine Hat-Detroit	13	33	46
Korol, David	6:02	175	Winnipeg Man.	3- 1-65	Adirondack	3	9	12
Ladouceur, Randy	6:02	200	Brockville, Ont.	6-10-60	Detroit	5	13	18
Larsson, Stefan	5:11	160	Goteborg, Sweden	6-14-65	Vasta Frolunda (Sweden)	..	..	..
Lindman, Mikael	5:11	174	Stockholm, Sweden	5-15-67	Skelleftea (Sweden)	..	..	..
Luckraft, Mike	6:01	186	Jackson, Mich.	11-28-66	University of Minnesota-Duluth	..	..	..
Luongo, Chris	6:00	180	Detroit, Mich.	3-17-67	Michigan State Univ.	1	5	6
Mayer, Derek	6:00	185	Rossland, B.C.	5-21-67	University of Denver	2	7	9
Melrose, Barry	6:00	205	Kelvington, Sask.	7-15-56	Detroit-Adirondack	4	4	8
Morton, Dean	6:00	196	Peterborough, Ont.	2-27-68	Oshawa-Ottawa	5	7	12
O'Connell, Mike	5:09	185	Chicago, Ill.	11-25-55	Boston-Detroit	9	28	37
Richmond, Steve	6:01	205	Chicago, Ill.	12-11-59	N.Y. Rang.-N. Haven-Det.-Adir.	4	17	21
Rose, Jay	6:00	181	Newton, Mass.	7- 6-66	Clarkston Univ.	0	7	7
Schenna, Rob	6:01	190	Saugus, Mass.	2- 5-67	Rensselaer Poly. Institute	0	6	6
Sharples, Jeff	6:01	185	Terrace B.C.	7-28-67	Portland	2	6	8
Smith, Jim	6:01	215	Castlegar, B.C.	1-18-64	Univ. of Denver	10	40	50
Snepsts, Harold	6:03	215	Edmonton, Alta.	10-24-54	Detroit	0	6	6
Stark, Jay	6:00	190	Vernon, B.C.	2-29-68	Portland	2	13	15
Trader, Larry	6:01	178	Barry's Bay, Ont.	7- 7-63	Adirondack	10	46	56
Veitch, Darren	6:00	195	Saskatoon, Sask.	4-24-60	Washington-Detroit	3	14	17
Zombo, Rick	6:01	195	Des Plaines, Ill.	5- 8-63	Detroit-Adirondack	7	35	42

GOALTENDERS

Name	Hgt.	Wgt.	Place of Birth	Date	1985-86 Club	Mins.	GA.	SO.
Cheveldae, Tim	5:10	176	Melville, Sask.	2-15-68	Saskatoon	2030	165	0
Gowans, Mark	5:11	160	Bay City, Mich.	3-26-67	Oshawa	1187	84	0
Hanlon, Glen	6:00	175	Brandon, Man.	2-20-57	N.Y. Rangers-Adirondack	1775	98	0
Hansch, Randy	5:11	170	Edmonton, Alta.	2- 8-66	Kamloops	1821	172	0
King, Scott	6:01	170	Thunder Bay, Ont.	6-25-67	Vernon	1718	133	..
Laforest, Mark	5:10	178	Welland, Ont.	7-10-62	Detroit-Adirondack	2525	171	1
Micalef, Corrado	5:08	172	Montreal, Que.	4-20-61	Detroit-Adirondack-Kalamazoo	2400	172	0
Pusey, Chris	6:00	180	Brantford, Ont.	6-20-65	Detroit-Adirondack	1211	79	1
Stefan, Greg	5:11	178	Brantford, Ont.	2-11-61	Detroit	2068	155	1

Edmonton Oilers
Smythe Division

Owner/Governor	Peter Pocklington
Alternate Governor	Glen Sather
General Counsels	Bob Lloyd, Gary Frohlich
President, General Manager and Co-Coach	Glen Sather
Co-Coach	John Muckler
Assistant General Manager	Bruce MacGregor
Assistant Coach	Bob McCammon
Director of Player Personnel/Chief Scout	Barry Fraser
Scouting Staff	Lorne Davis, Ace Bailey, Bob Freeman, Ed Chadwick, Bucky Kane, Matti Vaisanen
Controller	Werner Baum
Executive Secretary	Diana Hrynchuk
Director of Public Relations	Bill Tuele
Assistant Public Relations Director	Trish Wilson
Director of Marketing	Mark Hall
Trainer	Barrie Stafford
Assistant Trainer	Lyle Kulchisky
Athletic Therapist	Peter Millar
Team Physician	Dr. Gordon Cameron
Home Ice	Northlands Coliseum
Address	Edmonton, Alta. T5B 4M9
Seating Capacity	17,308 (Standing 190)
Club colors	Blue, Orange and White
Phone	(403) 474-8561

Peter Pocklington

Glen Sather

John Muckler

Bob McCammon

Edmonton Oilers 1986-87 Roster

FORWARDS	Hgt.	Wgt.	Place of Birth	Date	1985-86 Club	G.	A.	Pts.
Anderson, Glenn	5:11	185	Vancouver, B.C.	10- 2-60	Edmonton	54	48	102
Biggs, Don	5:08	175	Mississauga, Ont.	4- 7-65	Springfield-Nova Scotia	21	39	60
Brubaker, Jeff	6:02	210	Frederick, Md.	2-24-58	Toronto-Edmonton-N.S.	5	3	8
Crawford, Louis	6:00	185	Belleville, Ont.	11- 5-62	Nova Scotia	8	11	19
Eaves, Murray	5:10	185	Calgary, Alta.	5-10-60	Sherbrooke-Winnipeg	22	51	73
Graves, Steve	5:10	190	Kingston, Ont.	4- 7-64	Nova Scotia	19	18	37
Gretzky, Wayne	6:00	170	Brantford, Ont.	1-26-61	Edmonton	52	163	215
Hopkins, Dean	6:01	210	Cobourg, Ont.	6- 6-59	Nova Scotia	23	32	55
Hunter, Dave	5:11	200	Petrolia, Ont.	1- 1-58	Edmonton	15	22	37
Jalo, Risto	5:11	185	Humppila, Finland	7-18-62	Edmonton	0	3	3
Krushelnyski, Mike	6:02	200	Montreal, Que.	4-27-60	Edmonton	16	24	40
Kurri, Jari	6:00	190	Helsinki, Finland	5-18-60	Edmonton	68	63	131
MacTavish, Craig	6:00	190	London, Ont.	8-15-58	Edmonton	23	24	47
McClelland, Kevin	6:00	200	Oshawa, Ont.	7- 4-62	Edmonton	11	25	36
McSorley, Marty	6:01	210	Hamilton, Ont.	5-18-63	Edmonton-Nova Scotia	13	16	29
Messier, Mark	6:01	205	Edmonton, Alta.	1-18-61	Edmonton	35	49	84
Moller, Mike	6:00	190	Calgary, Alta.	6-16-62	Nova Scotia	16	15	31
Napier, Mark	5:10	185	Toronto, Ont.	1-28-57	Edmonton	24	32	56
Semenko, Dave	6:03	215	Winnipeg, Man.	7-12-57	Edmonton	6	12	18
Sherven, Gord	6:00	185	Mankota, Sask.	8-21-63	Minn.-Edmon.-Springfield-N.S.	18	27	45
Summanen, Raimo	5:11	185	Jyvaskyla, Finland	3- 2-62	Edmonton	19	18	37
Tikkanen, Esa	5:11	185	Helsinki, Finland	1-25-65	Edmonton-Nova Scotia	11	14	25
Turcotte, Alfie	5:09	170	Gary, Ind.	6- 5-65	Sherbrooke-Montreal	29	36	65
DEFENSEMEN								
Beukeboom, Jeff	6:04	210	Ajax, Ont.	3-28-65	Nova Scotia	9	20	29
Coffey, Paul	6:00	200	Weston, Ont.	6- 1-61	Edmonton	48	90	138
Fogolin, Lee	6:00	200	Chicago, Ill.	2- 7-55	Edmonton	4	22	26
Gregg, Randy	6:04	205	Edmonton, Alta.	2-19-56	Edmonton	2	26	28
Huddy, Charlie	6:00	200	Oshawa, Ont.	6- 2-59	Edmonton	6	35	41
Jackson, Don	6:03	210	Minneapolis, Minn.	9- 2-56	Edmonton	2	8	10
Lowe, Kevin	6:02	195	Lachute, Que.	4-15-59	Edmonton	2	16	18
Miner, John	5:10	190	Moose Jaw, Sask.	7-28-65	Nova Scotia	10	33	43
Playfair, Jim	6:03	205	Vanderhoof, B.C.	5-22-64	Nova Scotia	2	12	14
Smith, Steve	6:02	210	Glasgow, Scotland	4-30-63	Edmonton-Nova Scotia	4	22	26
GOALTENDERS						Mins.	GA.	SO.
Fuhr, Grant	5:10	185	Spruce Grove, Alta.	9-28-62	Edmonton	2184	143	0
Moog, Andy	5:09	170	Penticton, B.C.	2-18-60	Edmonton	2664	164	1
Reaugh, Daryl	6:04	200	Prince George, B.C.	2-13-65	Nova Scotia	2205	156	0

Hartford Whalers
Adams Division

Managing General Partner, Chairman and Governor	Howard L. Baldwin
President, G.M. and Alternate Govenor	Emile Francis
Alternate Governor	Donald G. Conrad
Coach	Jack Evans
Assistant General Manager	Bob Crocker
Special Assistant to Managing General Partner	Gordie Howe
Assistant Coach	Claude Larose
Director of Player Personnel	Steve Brklacich
Scouts	John Cunniff, David McNab, Leo Boivin
Trainer	Tommy Woodcock
Equipment Manager	Skip Cunningham
V.P., Marketing and Public Relations	William E. Barnes
V.P., Finance and Development	W. David Andrews III
Assistant to Managing General Partner	Camille Beck
Treasurer	Robert L. Kelly
Controller	Michael J. Amendola
Director of Public Relations	Phil Langan
Assistant Director of Public Relations	Dennis Buden
Chief Statistician	Frank Polnaszek
Home Ice	Hartford Civic Center
Address	One Civic Center Plaza, Hartford, Conn. 06103
Seating Capacity	15,126
Club colors	Blue, Green and White
Phone	(203) 728-3366

Howard Baldwin

Emile Francis

Bob Crocker

Jack Evans

Hartford Whalers 1986-87 Roster

FORWARDS

Name	Hgt.	Wgt.	Place of Birth	Date	1985-86 Club	G.	A.	Pts.
Anderson, John	5:11	180	Toronto, Ont.	3-28-57	Quebec-Hartford	29	45	74
Babych, Wayne	5:11	195	Edmonton, Alta.	6-6-58	Pitt-Que-Hartford	17	22	39
Brant, Chris	6:01	190	Belleville, Ont.	8-26-65	Binghamton	7	6	13
Callaghan, Gary	5:11	175	Oshawa, Ont.	8-12-67	Belleville	29	16	45
Channell, Todd	5:10	185	Chicago, Ill.		Miami (O.) Univ.	27	27	54
Churla, Shane	6:01	200	Fernie, B.C.	6-24-65	Binghamton	4	10	14
Dineen, Kevin	5:10	180	Quebec City, Que.	10-28-63	Hartford	33	35	68
Evason, Dean	5:10	180	Flin Flon, Man.	8-22-64	Binghamton-Hartford	29	45	74
Fenton, Paul	6:00	180	Springfield, Mass.	12-22-59	Binghamton-Hartford	53	35	88
Ferraro, Ray	5:11	185	Trail, B.C.	8-23-64	Hartford	30	47	77
Francis, Ron	6:02	200	Sault Ste. Marie, Ont.	3-1-63	Hartford	24	53	77
Gardner, Bill	5:10	170	Toronto, Ont.	3-19-60	Chicago-Hartford	4	18	22
Gaume, Dallas	5:10	180	Innisfal, Alta.		University of Denver	32	67	99
Gavin, Stewart	5:11	185	Ottawa, Ont.	3-15-60	Hartford	26	29	55
Glasgow, Robert	6:00	205	Edmonton, Alta.	4-22-68	Sherwood Park	23	18	41
Hoffman, Mike	5:11	190	Cambridge, Ont.	2-26-63	Binghamton	14	14	28
Hoover, Ron	6:01	185	Oakville, Ont.	10-28-66	Western Michigan Univ.	10	23	33
Jarvis, Doug	5:09	175	Brantford, Ont.	3-24-55	Washington-Hartford	9	18	27
Lawless, Paul	5:11	185	Scarborough, Ont.	7-2-64	Hartford	17	21	38
MacDermid, Paul	6:01	200	Chesley, Ont.	4-14-63	Hartford	13	10	23
MacLean, Dave	6:00	195	Newmarket, Ont.	1-12-65	Binghamton-Salt Lake City	9	14	23
Newberry, John	6:01	180	Port Alberni, B.C.	4-8-62	Binghamton-Moncton	16	35	51
Robertson, Torrie	5:11	200	Victoria, B.C.	8-2-61	Hartford	13	24	37
Quinn, Joe	5:11	185	Calgary, Alta.	2-10-67	Calgary Jrs.	17	24	41
Tippett, Dave	5:10	180	Moosomin, Sask.	8-25-61	Hartford	14	20	34
Torrel, Steve	6:03	195	Hibbing, Minn.	5-27-67	Hibbing H.S.	7	30	37
Turgeon, Sylvain	6:00	195	Noranda, Que.	1-17-65	Hartford	45	34	79
Verbeek, Brian	5:09	195	Wyoming, Ont.	10-22-66	Kingston	50	40	90
Young, Scott	6:00	185	Clinton, Mass.	10-1-67	Boston University	16	13	29

DEFENSEMEN

Name	Hgt.	Wgt.	Place of Birth	Date	1985-86 Club	G.	A.	Pts.
Babych, Dave	6:02	215	Edmonton, Alta.	5-23-61	Winnipeg-Hartford	14	55	69
Bothwell, Tim	6:03	190	Vancouver, B.C.	5-6-55	Hartford	2	8	10
Brown, Cal	6:00	195	Calgary, Alta.	1-13-67	Penticton	..	..	..
Brownschidle, Jack	6:02	195	Buffalo, N.Y.	10-2-55	Hartford-Binghamton	5	26	31
Chapman, Brian	6:00	185	Brockville, Ont.	2-10-68	Belleville	6	31	37
Cote, Sylvain	5:11	175	Quebec City, Que.	1-19-66	Hartford-Hull	8	23	31
Cronin, Shawn	6:01	205	Melrose, Mass.	9-9-60	Univ. Ill. at Chicago	3	8	11
Kleinendorst, Scot	6:03	215	Grand Rapids, Minn.	1-16-60	Hartford	2	7	9
Laforge, Mike	6:02	201	Sudbury, Ont.	1-3-68	Kingston	1	13	14
McEwen, Mike	6:01	185	Hornepayne, Ont.	8-10-56	Det-NYR-N. Haven-Hart.	5	20	25
Mokosak, John	5:11	200	Edmonton, Alta.	9-7-63	Binghamton	0	9	9
Murzyn, Dana	6:02	200	Regina, Sask.	12-9-66	Hartford	3	23	26
Paterson, Mark	5:11	180	Ottawa, Ont.	2-22-64	Hartford-Binghamton	2	16	18
Quenneville, Joel	6:01	200	Windsor, Ont.	9-15-58	Hartford	5	20	25
Samuelsson, Ulf	6:01	195	Fagursta, Sweden	3-26-64	Hartford	5	19	24
Shaw, Brad	5:11	180	Cambridge, Ont.	4-28-64	Binghamton	10	44	54
Vellucci, Mike	6:01	180	Farmington, Mich.	8-11-66	Belleville	11	32	43

GOALTENDERS

Name	Hgt.	Wgt.	Place of Birth	Date	1985-86 Club	Mins.	GA.	SO.
Evoy, Sean	6:00	190	Sudbury, Ont.	2-11-66	Cornwall	1391	122	1
Horn, Bill	5:08	150	Regina, Sask.	4-16-67	Western Michigan Univ.	1797	114	0
Liut, Mike	6:02	195	Weston, Ont.	1-7-56	Hartford	3262	197	2
Sidorkiewicz, Peter	5:09	180	Dabr. Bialo., Poland	6-29-63	Binghamton	2819	150	2
Weeks, Steve	5:11	165	Scarborough, Ont.	6-30-58	Hartford	1544	99	1
Whitmore, Kay	5:11	165	Sudbury, Ont.	4-10-67	Peterborough	2467	114	3

Los Angeles Kings

Smythe Division

Owner	Dr. Jerry Buss
Alternate Governors	Ken Doi, Rogie Vachon
General Manager	Rogie Vachon
Coach	Pat Quinn
Assistant Coaches	Mike Murphy, Phil Myre
Administrative Assistant	John Wolf
Head Scout	Ted O'Connor
Scouting Staff	Ross Tyrell, Alex Smart, Skip Schamehorn, Jim Anderson, Don Perry, Bob Owen, Serge Blanchard, Gary Sargent
Director of Public Relations	David Courtney
Public Relations Assistant	Diane Reesman
Trainer	Pete Demers
Assistant Trainer	Mark O'Neill
Home Ice	The Forum
Address	3900 West Manchester Blvd., P. O. Box 10, The Forum, Inglewood, Calif. 90306
Seating Capacity	16,005
Club Colors	Purple and Gold
Phone	(213) 674-6000

Dr. Jerry Buss

Rogie Vachon

Pat Quinn

Los Angeles Kings 1986-87 Roster

FORWARDS

Name	Hgt.	Wgt.	Place of Birth	Date	1985-86 Club	G.	A.	Pts.
Benoit, Guy	5:10	187	St. Hyacinthe, Que.	3- 8-59	New Haven-Toledo-Muskegon	48	57	105
Carson, Jimmy	6:00	185	Southfield, Mich.	7-20-68	Verdun	70	83	153
Ciprick, Trenton	6:01	176	Russell, Man.	7-21-67	Brandon	13	19	32
Crossman, Jeff	6:00	200	Toronto, Ont.	12- 3-64	Western Michigan U.	13	19	32
Currie, Glen	6:02	180	Montreal, Que.	7-18-58	New Haven-Los Angeles	1	6	7
Deegan, Shannon	6:02	190	Montreal, Que.	3-19-66	Univ. of Vermont	9	9	18
Dionne, Marcel	5:08	185	Drummondville, Que.	8- 3-51	Los Angeles	36	58	94
Duncanson, Craig	6:00	190	Naughton, Ont.	3-17-67	Cornwall-Sudbury	43	67	110
Edlund, Par	5:11	180	Nynashamn, Sweden	4- 9-67	Bjorkloven	1	0	1
Erickson, Bryan	5:09	170	Roseau, Minn.	3- 7-60	Binghamton-N. Haven-Los Ang.	32	29	61
Fishback, Jeff	6:01	185	White Bear Lake, Minn.	1-19-65	Univ. of Minn.-Duluth	2	3	5
Flanagan, Tim	6:00	185	Red Deer, Alta.	3- 6-67	Penticton-Michigan Tech	6	11	17
Fox, Jim	5:08	175	Coniston, Ont.	5-18-60	Los Angeles	14	17	31
Gans, Dave	5:11	185	Brantford, Ont.	12- 7-66	Los Angeles-N. Haven-Hershey	35	44	79
Grannis, David	6:00	190	St. Paul, Minn.	3-25-66	Univ. of Minnesota	5	7	12
Gratton, Dan	6:00	185	Brantford, Ont.	12- 7-66	Oshawa-Ottawa-Belleville	33	37	70
Guay, Paul	6:00	193	No. Smithfield, R.I.	9- 2-63	Los Angeles-N. Haven-Hershey	18	41	59
Hanley, Tim	6:00	200	Greenfield, Mass.	10-10-64	U. of New Hampshire	9	13	22
Horner, Steve	6:01	195	Cowansville, Que.	6- 4-66	U. of New Hampshire	3	5	8
Horwath, Marion	5:11	176	Bratislava, Czech.	11-28-65	Bratislava	5	7	12
Kelly, John Paul	6:01	215	Edmonton, Alta.	11-15-59	Los Angeles	6	9	15
Lofthouse, Mark	6:01	185	New Westminster, B.C.	4-21-57	New Haven	32	35	67
Lukowich, Morris	5:09	170	Speers, Sask.	6- 1-56	Boston-Los Angeles	12	13	25
Martin, Brian	6:00	195	St. Catharines, Ont.	3-27-66	Windsor	42	41	83
McKenna, Sean	6:00	190	Asbestos, Que.	3- 7-62	Buffalo-Los Angeles	10	12	22
McSorley, Chris	5:11	185	Hamilton, Ont.	3-22-62	Toledo	27	28	55
Nicholls, Bernie	6:00	185	Haliburton, Ont.	6-24-61	Los Angeles	36	61	97
Paterson, Joe	6:02	205	Toronto, Ont.	6-25-60	Phila.-Hershey-Los Angeles	14	32	46
Phair, Lyle	6:01	195	Pilot Mound, Man.	3- 8-61	Los Angeles-New Haven	9	10	19
Robitaille, Luc	6:01	190	Montreal, Que.	2-17-66	Hull	68	123	191
Sykes, Phil	5:10	175	Dawson Creek, B.C.	3-18-59	Los Angeles	20	24	44
Taylor, Dave	6:00	195	Levack, Ont.	12- 4-55	Los Angeles	33	38	71
Wilks, Brian	5:11	175	No York, Ont.	2-27-66	Los Angeles	4	8	12
Williams, Tiger	5:11	190	Weyburn, Sask.	2- 3-54	Los Angeles	20	29	49

DEFENSEMEN

Name	Hgt.	Wgt.	Place of Birth	Date	1985-86 Club	G.	A.	Pts.
Baumgartner, Ken	6:01	200	Flin Flon, Man.	3-11-65	Prince Albert	4	23	27
Duchesne, Steve	6:00	190	Sept-Iles, Que.	6-30-65	New Haven	14	35	49
English, John	6:02	190	Toronto, Ont.	5-13-66	Hamilton-Ottawa	10	37	47
Florio, Perry	6:00	190	Glen Cove, N.Y.	7-15-67	Providence College	4	5	9
Galley, Garry	5:11	190	Ottawa, Ont.	4-16-63	Los Angeles-New Haven	11	19	30
Hammond, Ken	6:01	190	Pt. Credit, Ont.	8-22-63	Los Angeles-New Haven	4	13	17
Hardy, Mark	5:11	187	Semaden, Switzerland	2- 1-59	Los Angeles	6	21	27
Kennedy, Dean	6:02	200	Redvers, Sask.	1-18-63	Los Angeles	2	10	12
Larocque, Denis	6:01	197	Hawkesbury, Ont.	10- 5-67	Guelph	2	17	19
Ledyard, Grant	6:02	190	Winnipeg, Man.	11-19-61	N.Y. Rangers-Los Angeles	9	27	36
Playfair, Larry	6:04	220	Fort St. James, B.C.	6-23-58	Buffalo-Los Angeles	1	3	4
Prajzler, Petr	6:00	180	Pardubice, Czech.	9-21-65	Pardubice	4	4	8
Redmond, Craig	5:10	187	Dawson Creek, B.C.	9-22-65	Los Angeles	6	18	24
Sawkins, Peter	6:03	190	Skagen, Denmark	8-29-63	New Haven-Toledo	5	11	16
Tuite, Steve	6:01	195	Brockton, Mass.	1-14-62	New Haven-Toledo	6	33	39
Wells, Jay	6:01	205	Paris, Ont.	5-18-59	Los Angeles	11	31	42

GOALTENDERS

Name	Hgt.	Wgt.	Place of Birth	Date	1985-86 Club	Mins.	GA.	SO.
Eliot, Darren	6:01	175	Milton, Ont.	11-26-61	Los Angeles-New Haven	1661	140	0
Franzosa, John	5:07	175	Reading, Mass.	3- 3-63	Toledo-New Haven	2200	182	0
Healy, Glenn	5:09	183	Pickering, Ont.	8-23-62	Los Angeles-N. Haven-Toledo	2860	194	0
Hyduke, John	5:10	160	Hibbing, Minn.	6-23-67	U. of Minn.-Duluth	1401	84	0
Janecyk, Bob	6:01	180	Chicago, Ill.	5-18-57	Los Angeles	2083	162	0
Melanson, Roland	5:10	178	Moncton, N.B.	6-28-60	Minn.-Los Angeles-New Haven	1750	124	0
Strome, Greg	5:09	160	Muenster, Sask.	7-18-65	U. of North Dakota	1189	78	0

Minnesota North Stars

Norris Division

Co-Chairmen of the Board	George Gund III and Gordon Gund
President	John Karr
Vice-President, General Manager	Lou Nanne
Assistant General Manager	John Mariucci
Director of Player Development	Glen Sonmor
Administrative Assistant	Murray Oliver
Coach	Lorne Henning
Assistant Coaches	J.P. Parise, Les Jackson
Chief Scout	Harry Howell
Special Assignment Scout	Dick Bouchard
Director of Media Relations	Dick Dillman
Publications Manager	Joe Janasz
Community Relations Director	Patty Connolly
Scouts	George Agar, Gump Worsley, Smokey Cerrone
Trainer	Dick Rose
Assistant Trainer	Dave Smith
Equipment Manager	Mark Baribeau
Home Ice	Metropolitan Sports Center
Address	7901 Cedar Avenue S., Bloomington, Minn. 55420
Seating Capacity	15,449
Club colors	Green, White, Gold and Black
Phone	(612) 853-9333

George Gund III

Gordon Gund

Lou Nanne

Lorne Henning

Minnesota North Stars 1986-87 Roster

FORWARDS

Name	Hgt.	Wgt.	Place of Birth	Date	1985-86 Club	G.	A.	Pts.
Acton, Keith	5:09	172	Stouffville, Ont.	4-15-58	Minnesota	26	32	58
Archibald, Jim	5:11	180	Craik, Sask.	6-6-61	Springfield-Minnesota	1	7	8
Babe, Warren	6:02	188	Medicine Hat, Alta.	9-7-68	Lethbridge	33	24	57
Bellows, Brian	5:11	195	St. Catharines, Ont.	9-1-64	Minnesota	31	48	79
Bergen, Todd	6:03	185	Prince Albert, Sask.	7-11-63	Minnesota	Did not play		
Bjugstad, Scott	6:01	175	St. Paul, Minn.	6-2-61	Minnesota	43	33	76
Broten, Neal	5:09	169	Roseau, Minn.	11-29-59	Minnesota	29	76	105
Ciccarelli, Dino	5:10	180	Sarnia, Ont.	2-8-60	Minnesota	44	45	89
Coulis, Tim	6:00	200	Kenora, Ont.	2-24-58	Springfield-Minnesota	7	9	16
DePalma, Larry	6:00	180	Trenton, Mich.	10-27-65	Saskatoon-Minnesota	61	51	112
Graham, Dirk	5:11	190	Regina, Sask.	7-29-59	Minnesota	22	33	55
Habscheid, Marc	6:00	180	Swift Current, Sask.	3-1-63	Minnesota	20	35	55
Hallin, Mats	6:02	202	Eskilstuna, Sweden	3-19-58	Minnesota-Springfield	3	2	5
Helmer, Tim	6:00	185	Woodstock, Ont.	11-6-66	Ottawa	13	12	25
Houck, Paul	5:11	185	N. Vancouver, B.C.	8-12-63	Springfield-Minnesota	16	17	33
Lawton, Brian	6:00	173	New Brunswick, N.J.	6-29-65	Minnesota	18	17	35
Lomow, Byron	5:11	180	Sherwood Park, Alta.	4-27-65	Brandon	52	67	119
Maruk, Dennis	5:08	174	Toronto, Ont.	11-17-55	Minnesota	21	37	58
McColgan, Gary	6:00	192	Scarborough, Ont.	3-27-66	Oshawa	49	54	103
McKegney, Tony	6:01	200	Montreal, Que.	2-15-58	Minnesota	15	25	40
Micheletti, Pat	5:10	175	Hibbing, Minn.	12-11-63	Univ. of Minn.-Springfield	33	48	81
Nilsson, Kent	6:01	195	Nynashamn, Sweden	8-31-56	Minnesota	16	44	60
Payne, Steve	6:02	215	Toronto, Ont.	8-16-58	Minnesota	8	4	12
Plett, Willi	6:03	220	Paraguay, S. America	6-7-55	Minnesota	10	7	17
Poner, Jiri	6:02	175	Pardubice, Czech.	2-9-64	Indianapolis-Muskegon	17	43	60
Roy, Stephane	5:11	181	Ste. Foy, Que.	6-29-67	Granby	33	52	85
Servinis, George	5:11	175	Willowdale, Ont.	4-29-62	Springfield	2	14	16
Smith, Randy	6:03	180	Saskatoon, Sask.	7-15-65	Saskatoon-Minnesota	60	86	146

DEFENSEMEN

Name	Hgt.	Wgt.	Place of Birth	Date	1985-86 Club	G.	A.	Pts.
Giles, Curt	5:08	179	The Pas, Man.	11-30-58	Minnesota	6	21	27
Hartsburg, Craig	6:01	195	Stratford, Ont.	6-29-59	Minnesota	10	47	57
Hirsch, Tom	6:04	211	Minneapolis, Minn.	1-27-63	Minnesota	Did not play		
Jensen, David	6:01	190	Minneapolis, Minn.	5-3-61	Springfield-Minnesota	4	18	22
Kolstad, Dean	6:06	200	Edmonton, Alta.	6-16-68	Prince Albert	2	20	22
Langevin, Dave	6:02	215	St. Paul, Minn.	5-15-54	Minnesota	0	8	8
Lucyk, Carey	6:01	195	Winnipeg, Man.	3-8-62	University of Manitoba	..	..	..
Musil, Frantisek	6:03	215	Czechoslovakia			..	..	..
Pryor, Chris	6:00	200	St. Paul, Minn.	1-23-61	Springfield-Minnesota	4	17	21
Roberts, Gordie	6:00	193	Detroit, Mich.	10-2-57	Minnesota	2	21	23
Rouse, Bob	6:02	215	Surrey, B.C.	6-18-64	Minnesota	1	14	15
Viveiros, Emanuel	5:11	160	St. Albert, Alta.	1-8-66	Prince Albert-Minnesota	22	71	93
Wilkinson, Neil	6:03	190	Selkirk, Man.	8-15-67	Selkirk	14	35	49
Wilson, Ron	5:10	170	Windsor, Ont.	5-28-55	Davos-Minnesota	36	46	82

GOALTENDERS

Name	Hgt.	Wgt.	Place of Birth	Date	1985-86 Club	Mins.	GA.	SO.
Beaupre, Don	5:08	162	Kitchener, Ont.	9-19-61	Minnesota	3073	182	1
Casey, Jon	5:10	155	Grand Rapids, Minn.	3-29-62	Springfield-Minnesota	1867	121	0
Sands, Mike	5:09	146	Sudbury, Ont.	4-6-63	Springfield	1490	94	0
Takko, Kari	6:02	182	Kaupunki, Finland	6-23-63	Springfield-Minnesota	2453	164	1

Montreal Canadiens
Adams Division

President	Ronald Corey
Managing Director	Serge Savard
Senior Vice-President, Corporate Affairs	Jean Beliveau
Special Ambassador	Maurice Richard
Senior Vice-President, Operations and Special Events	Aldo Giampaolo
Vice-President, Finance and Administration	Fred Steer
Vice-President, Marketing	Francois-Xavier Seigneur
Director of Hockey Personnel	Jacques Lemaire
Coach	Jean Perron
Assistant Coach	Jacques Laperriere
Director of Player Development	Claude Ruel
Director of Scouting	Andre Boudrias
Chief Scout	Doug Robinson
Director of Special Events	Camil DesRoches
Director of Advertising Sales	Floyd Curry
Director of Public Relations	Claude Mouton
Director of Press Relations	Michel Lapointe
Director of Publicity	Yvon Robert
Club Physician	Dr. D.G. Kinnear
Physiotherapist	Gene Gaudette
Trainer	Eddy Palchak
Assistant Trainers	Gaetan Lefevre, Sylvain Toupin
Home Ice	Montreal Forum
Address	2313 St. Catherine Street West, Montreal, Que. H3H 1N2
Seating Capacity	16,074
Club colors	Red, White and Blue
Phone	(514) 932-2582

Ronald Corey

Serge Savard

Jacques Lemaire

Jean Perron

Montreal Canadiens 1986-87 Roster

FORWARDS

Name	Hgt.	Wgt.	Place of Birth	Date	1985-86 Club	G.	A.	Pts.
Anastos, Tom	6:00	185	Dearborn, Mich.	7- 5-63	Sherbrooke	9	18	27
Boisvert, Serge	5:09	170	Drummondville, Ont.	6- 1-59	Sherbrooke-Montreal	42	50	92
Bonar, Graeme	6:03	208	Toronto, Ont.	1-21-66	Peterborough	53	40	93
Bucyk, Randy	6:00	183	Edmonton, Alta.	11- 9-62	Sherbrooke-Montreal	22	35	57
Carbonneau, Guy	5:11	180	Sept-Iles, Que.	3-18-60	Montreal	20	36	56
Charbonneau, Jose	6:00	190	Ferme-Neuve, Que.	11- 2-66	Drummondville	44	45	89
Corson, Shayne	6:00	175	Barrie, Ont.	8-13-66	Hamilton	41	57	98
Dahlin, Kjell	6:00	175	Timra, Sweden	2- 2-63	Montreal	32	39	71
DeBlois, Lucien	5:11	200	St. Tho.-de-Jol., Que.	6-21-57	Montreal	14	17	31
Demers, Eric	6:03	192	Montreal, Que.	3- 1-66	Drummondville	13	10	23
Desjardins, Martin	5:11	165	Ste. Rose, Que.	1-28-67	Trois-Rivieres	49	69	118
Dufresne, Donald	6:01	190	Rimouski, Que.	4-10-67	Trois-Rivieres	8	32	40
Dundas, Rocky	6:00	200	Edmonton, Alta.	1-30-67	Spokane	31	70	101
Gainey, Bob	6:02	200	Peterborough, Ont.	12-13-53	Montreal	20	23	43
Ganchar, Perry	5:09	175	Saskatoon, Sask.	10-28-63	Sherbrooke	25	29	54
Gilchrist, Brent	5:11	175	Moose Jaw, Sask.	4- 3-67	Spokane	45	45	90
Harlow, Scott	6:00	190	E. Br'dg'w't'r, Mass.	10-11-63	Boston College	38	41	79
Keane, Mike	5:10	175	Winnipeg, Man.	5-28-67	Moose Jaw	34	49	83
Kolioupoulos, Tom	6:01	185	Detroit, Mich.	2-10-64	Did not play	..	..	..
Lemieux, Claude	6:01	206	Buckingham, Que.	7-16-65	Sherbrooke-Montreal	22	34	56
Maley, David	6:02	205	Beaver Dam, Wisc.	4-24-63	Univ. of Wisconsin	20	40	60
McPhee, Mike	6:01	200	Riviere Bourgeois, N.S.	7-14-60	Montreal	19	21	40
Momesso, Sergio	6:03	203	Montreal, Que.	9- 4-65	Montreal	8	7	15
Moore, Charlie	6:02	219	Ottawa, Ont.	3-27-66	Belleville	4	4	8
Naslund, Mats	5:07	160	Timra, Sweden	10-31-59	Montreal	43	67	110
Nesich, Jim	5:11	170	Dearborn, Mich.	2-22-66	Verdun-Sherbrooke	19	34	53
Nilan, Chris	6:00	200	Boston, Mass.	2- 9-58	Montreal	19	15	34
Richer, Stephane	6:02	200	Ripon, Que.	6- 7-66	Montreal	21	16	37
Rooney, Steve	6:02	200	Canton, Mass.	6-28-62	Montreal	2	3	5
Rouleau, Guy	5:09	174	Beloeil, Que.	2-16-65	Hull	92	99	191
Skrudland, Brian	6:00	188	Peace River, Alta.	7-31-63	Montreal	9	13	22
Smith, Bobby	6:04	210	North Sydney, N.S.	2-12-58	Montreal	31	55	86
Svoboda, Karel	6:01	192	Most, Czech.	12- 2-60	Did not play	..	..	..
Tremblay, Mario	6:00	190	Alma, Que.	9- 2-56	Montreal	19	20	39
Vargas, Ernie	6:02	195	St. Paul, Minn.	3- 1-64	Univ. of Wisconsin	20	23	43
Walter, Ryan	6:00	195	New Westminster, B.C.	4-23-58	Montreal	15	34	49
Williams, Brian	5:09	172	Fargo, N.D.	6-27-63	Univ. of North Dakota	22	40	62

DEFENSEMEN

Name	Hgt.	Wgt.	Place of Birth	Date	1985-86 Club	G.	A.	Pts.
Bergeron, Jean-Guy	6:01	204	Montreal, Que.	4-14-65	Drummondville	12	52	64
Campbell, Billy	6:00	175	Montreal, Que.	3-20-64	Sherbrooke-Hershey	1	12	13
Campedelli, Dominic	6:01	205	Cohasset, Mass.	4- 3-64	Sherbrooke	4	10	14
Chelios, Chris	6:01	186	Chicago, Ill.	1-25-62	Montreal	8	26	34
Gingras, Gaston	6:00	185	T'camingue, Que.	2-13-59	Sherbrooke-Montreal	19	38	57
Green, Rick	6:03	210	Belleville, Ont.	2-20-56	Montreal	3	2	5
Hayward, Rick	6:00	173	Toledo, Ohio	2-25-66	Hull	3	40	43
Herring, Graham	6:01	170	Montreal, Que.	10-27-65	Sherbrooke	0	9	9
Kordic, John	6:01	200	Edmonton, Alta.	3-22-65	Sherbrooke-Montreal	3	15	18
Kurvers, Tom	6:00	190	Minneapolis, Minn.	9-14-62	Montreal	7	23	30
Lalor, Mike	6:03	200	Buffalo, N.Y.	3- 8-63	Montreal	3	5	8
Ludwig, Craig	6:03	217	Rhinelander, Wisc.	3-15-61	Montreal	2	4	6
MacTavish, Scott	6:03	204	Fredericton, N.B.	1-25-66	Verdun	7	14	21
Robinson, Larry	6:03	217	Winchester, Ont.	6- 2-51	Montreal	19	63	82
Sandelin, Scott	6:00	191	Hibbing, Minn.	8- 8-64	U of N. Dakota-Sherbrooke	7	33	40
Svoboda, Petr	6:01	170	Most, Czech.	2-14-66	Montreal	1	18	19

GOALTENDERS

Name	Hgt.	Wgt.	Place of Birth	Date	1985-86 Club	Mins.	GA.	SO.
Knickle, Rick	5:10	170	Chatham, N.B.	2-26-60	Saginaw	2336	135	2
Penney, Steve	6:01	190	Ste. Foy, Que.	2- 2-61	Montreal	990	72	0
Riendeau, Vincent	5:09	173	St. Hyacinthe, Que.	4-20-66	Drummondville	3336	215	2
Roy, Patrick	6:00	174	Quebec City, Que.	10- 5-65	Montreal	2651	148	1

New Jersey Devils
Patrick Division

Chairman	John J. McMullen
President	Robert J. Butera
Vice President, Hockey Operations and G.M.	Max McNab
Coach	Doug Carpenter
Assistant Coach	Ron Smith
Director of Player Personnel	Marshall Johnston
Scouts	David Conte, Frankie Jay, Russ LeClair, Ed Thomlinson
Athletic Trainer	Chris Ipson
Director of Public Relations	Larry Brooks
Assistant Director of Media Relations	David Freed
Executive Offices	Byrne Meadowlands Arena
Home Ice	Byrne Meadowlands Arena
Address	Meadowlands Arena, P.O. Box 504, East Rutherford, N.J. 07073
Seating Capacity	19,040
Club Colors	Red, Green and White
Phone	(201) 935-6050

John McMullen

Robert Butera

Max McNab

Doug Carpenter

New Jersey Devils 1986-87 Roster

FORWARDS

Name	Hgt.	Wgt.	Place of Birth	Date	1985-86 Club	G.	A.	Pts.
Adams, Greg	6:02	185	Nelson, B.C.	8- 1-63	New Jersey	35	42	77
Anderson, John	6:00	175	Toronto, Ont.	1-18-68	Oshawa	13	11	24
Anderson, Perry	6:00	195	Barrie, Ont.	10-14-61	New Jersey	7	12	19
Brady, Neil	6:02	180	Montreal, Que.	4-12-68	Medicine Hat	21	60	81
Brickley, Andy	6:00	195	Melrose, Mass.	8- 9-61	Maine	26	34	60
Bridgman, Mel	6:00	190	Trenton, Ont.	4-28-55	New Jersey	23	40	63
Broten, Aaron	5:10	175	Roseau, Minn.	11-14-60	New Jersey	18	25	43
Carlsson, Anders	5:11	185	Galve, Sweden	11-25-60	Sodertolje	12	26	38
Chernomaz, Rich	5:09	175	Selkirk, Man.	9- 1-63	Maine	21	28	49
Conacher, Pat	5:08	185	Edmonton, Alta.	5- 1-59	New Jersey-Maine	15	32	47
Crowder, Troy	6:04	200	Sudbury, Ont.	5- 3-68	Hamilton	4	4	8
Dorian, Dan	5:09	180	New York, N.Y.	3- 2-63	Western Mich-N. Jersey	43	63	106
Evtushevski, Greg	5:08	180	St. Paul, Alta.	5- 4-65	Maine-Kamloops	32	51	83
Floyd, Larry	5:08	180	Peterborough, Ont.	5- 1-61	Maine	29	58	87
Gagne, Paul	5:10	180	Iroquois Falls, Ont.	2- 6-62	New Jersey	19	19	38
Henderson, Archie	6:06	220	Calgary, Alta.	2-17-57	Maine	4	6	10
Johnson, Mark	5:09	160	Madison, Wis.	9-22-57	New Jersey	21	41	62
Kirton, Doug	6:02	180	Penetanguishene, Ont.	3-21-66	Orillia	34	45	79
Loiselle, Claude	5:11	190	Ottawa, Ont.	5-29-63	Detroit-Adirondack	22	26	48
Ludvig, Jan	5:10	190	Liberec, Czech.	9-17-61	New Jersey	5	9	14
MacLean, John	6:00	195	Oshawa, Ont.	11-20-64	New Jersey	21	36	57
McKinley, Jamie	6:01	165	Moncton, N.B.	5- 1-67	Guelph	23	30	53
McMillan, Bill	6:02	185	North Bay, Ont.	4- 3-67	Peterborough	16	31	47
McNab, Peter	6:03	205	Vancouver, B.C.	5- 8-52	New Jersey	19	24	43
Muller, Kirk	6:00	195	Kingston, Ont.	2- 8-66	New Jersey	25	41	66
Ojanen, Janne	6:02	185	Tampere, Finland	4- 9-68	Tampere	5	17	22
Pardoski, Ryan	6:02	175	Calgary, Alta.	8-19-64	Calgary Jrs.	16	27	43
Stewart, Al	5:11	175	Fort St. John, B.C.	1-31-64	New Jersey-Maine	7	12	19
Sulliman, Doug	5:09	185	Glace Bay, N.S.	8-29-59	New Jersey	21	22	43
Todd, Kevin	5:11	180	Winnipeg, Man.	5- 4-68	Prince Albert	14	25	39
Trottier, Rocky	5:11	185	Climax, Sask.	4-11-64	Maine	12	19	31
Tsujiura, Steve	5:05	155	Coaldale, Alta.	2-28-62	Maine	31	55	86
Verbeek, Pat	5:09	190	Sarnia, Ont.	5-24-64	New Jersey	25	28	53
Wilson, Mitch	5:09	190	Calgary, Alta.	2-15-62	Maine	4	3	7

DEFENSEMEN

Name	Hgt.	Wgt.	Place of Birth	Date	1985-86 Club	G.	A.	Pts.
Blomqvist, Timo	6:00	200	Helsinki, Finland	1-23-61	Binghamton	6	18	24
Bolduc, Michel	6:02	210	Angeardion, Que.	3-13-61	Maine	1	6	7
Cirella, Joe	6:03	210	Hamilton, Ont.	5- 9-63	New Jersey	6	23	29
Copeland, Todd	6:02	200	Ridgewood, N.J.	5-18-68	Belmont Hill H.S.	4	19	23
Daneyko, Ken	6:00	195	Windsor, Ont.	4-16-64	New Jersey-Maine	3	12	15
Davey, Neil	6:02	205	Edmonton, Alta.	12-29-65	Maine-Toledo	5	8	13
Driver, Bruce	6:00	185	Toronto, Ont.	4-29-62	New Jersey-Maine	7	22	29
Ferguson, Ian	6:02	175	Winnipeg, Man.	6-24-66	Oshawa	6	10	16
Hepple, Alan	5:09	200	Blaydon-en-Tyne, Eng.	8-16-63	New Jersey-Maine	4	21	25
Hiemer, Uli	6:01	190	Fussen, W. Germany	9-21-62	New Jersey-Maine	13	18	31
Huscroft, Jamie	6:02	200	Creston, B.C.	1- 9-67	Seattle	6	21	27
Laniel, Marc	6:02	185	Oshawa, Ont.	1-16-68	Oshawa	9	25	34
Lorimer, Bob	6:00	200	Toronto, Ont.	8-25-53	New Jersey	2	2	4
Mark, Gord	6:03	205	Edmonton, Alta.	9-10-64	Maine	9	13	22
McCormack, Scott	6:01	185	Minneapolis, Minn.	9-25-67	St. Pauls Prep	3	17	20
Palmer, Rob	5:11	190	Sarnia, Ont.	9-10-56	Maine	2	10	12
Pichette, Dave	6:03	200	Grand Falls, Nfld.	2- 4-60	New Jersey-Maine	11	27	38
Velischek, Randy	6:01	206	Montreal, Que.	2-10-62	New Jersey-Maine	2	11	13
Wolanin, Craig	6:03	205	Grosse Pt., Mich.	7-27-67	New Jersey	2	16	18

GOALTENDERS

Name	Hgt.	Wgt.	Place of Birth	Date	1985-86 Club	Mins.	GA.	SO.
Billington, Craig	5:10	150	London, Ont.	9-11-66	New Jersey-Belleville	1082	88	0
Burke, Sean	6:03	180	Windsor, Ont.	1-29-67	Toronto Jrs.	2840	233	0
Chabot, Frederic	5:10	160		2-12-68	St. Foy Midgets	..	..	..
Chevrier, Alain	5:08	170	Cornwall, Ont.	4-23-61	New Jersey	1362	143	0
Friesen, Karl	6:00	165	Winnipeg, Man.	6-30-58	Maine	1983	115	2
McLean, Kirk	6:00	175	Willowdale, Ont.	6-26-66	Oshawa-New Jersey	2941	180	1
St. Laurent, Sam	5:10	190	Arvida, Que.	2-16-59	Maine-New Jersey	2350	174	2
Terreri, Chris	5:09	155	Warwick, R.I.	11-15-64	Providence College	1539	96	0

New York Islanders
Patrick Division

Chairman of the Board/Governor	John O. Pickett, Jr.
President and General Manager	William A. Torrey
Vice-President, Finance	Joseph H. Dreyer
Alternate Governor	William M. Skehan
Vice-President/Player Development	Al Arbour
Coach	Terry Simpson
Assistant General Manager/Director of Scouting	Gerry Ehman
Director of Hockey Administration	Darcy Regier
Scouting Staff	Harry Boyd, Richard Green, Hal Laycoe, Mario Saraceno, Jack Vivian, Earl Ingarfield
Publicity Director	Les Wagner
Assistant Publicity Director	Greg Bouris
Publicity Assistant	Kathy Schutte
Communications Consultant	Barney Kremenko
Director of Finance	Arthur McCarthy
Controller	Ralph Sellitti
Trainer	Craig Smith
Assistant Trainer	Jim Pickard
Home Ice	Nassau Veterans Memorial Coliseum
Address	Uniondale, N. Y. 11553
Seating Capacity	16,265
Club colors	Blue, White and Orange
Phone	(516) 794-4100

John Pickett

Bill Torrey

Al Arbour

Terry Simpson

New York Islanders 1986-87 Roster

FORWARDS	Hgt.	Wgt.	Place of Birth	Date	1985-86 Club	G.	A.	Pts.
Bassen, Bob	5:10	180	Calgary, Alta.	5- 6-65	N.Y. Islanders-Springfield	14	22	36
Bossy, Mike	6:00	185	Montreal, Que.	1-22-57	N.Y. Islanders	61	62	123
Bourne, Bob	6:03	197	Netherhill, Sask.	6-21-54	N.Y. Islanders	17	15	32
Breton, Rene	5:11	190	Princeville, Que.	10- 1-64	Flint	8	24	32
Coulter, Neal	6:02	190	Toronto, Ont.	1- 2-63	N.Y. Islanders-Springfield	20	13	33
Dalgarno, Brad	6:03	205	Vancouver, B.C.	8-11-67	Hamilton-N.Y. Islanders	23	43	66
Flatley, Patrick	6:02	197	Toronto, Ont.	10- 3-63	N.Y. Islanders	18	34	52
Gilbert, Greg	6:01	192	Mississauga, Ont.	1-22-62	N.Y. Islanders-Springfield	9	19	28
Gillies, Clark	6:03	214	Moose Jaw, Sask.	4- 7-54	N.Y. Islanders	4	10	14
Haanpaa, Ari	6:01	185	Nokis, Finland	11-28-65	N.Y. Islanders-Springfield	3	8	11
Hamway, Mark	6:00	190	Detroit, Mich.	8- 9-61	N.Y. Islanders-Springfield	10	20	30
Henry, Dale	6:00	205	Prince Albert, Sask.	9-24-64	N.Y. Islanders-Springfield	15	29	44
Herom, Kevin	5:11	195	Regina, Sask.	7- 6-67	Moose Jaw	22	18	40
Kerr, Alan	5:11	195	Hazelton, B.C.	3-28-64	N.Y. Islanders-Springfield	35	37	72
King, Derek	6:01	205	Hamilton, Ont.	2-11-67	Oshawa	20	30	50
Kortko, Roger	5:11	175	Hafford, Sask.	2- 1-63	N.Y. Islanders-Springfield	7	18	25
Kromm, Rich	5:11	180	Trail, B.C.	3-29-64	Calgary-N.Y. Islanders	19	24	43
Lacey, Garry	5:11	178	Sudbury, Ont.	5-24-64	Springfield	12	11	23
Lackten, Kurt	6:00	177	Kamsack, Sask.	5-20-67	Calgary Jrs.	5	20	25
LaFontaine, Pat	5:10	177	St. Louis, Mo.	2-22-65	N.Y. Islanders	30	23	53
Lauer, Brad	6:00	195	Humboldt, Sask.	10-27-66	Regina	36	38	74
Makela, Mikko	6:00	185	Tampere, Finland	2-28-65	N.Y. Islanders-Springfield	17	21	38
McKechney, Garnet	6:01	170	Swift Current, Sask.	4-28-63	London	16	14	30
Sutter, Brent	5:11	176	Viking, Alta.	6-11-62	N.Y. Islanders	24	31	55
Sutter, Duane	6:01	195	Viking, Alta.	3-16-60	N.Y. Islanders	20	33	53
Trottier, Bryan	5:11	195	Val Marie, Sask.	7-17-56	N.Y. Islanders	37	59	96
Wiest, Rich	5:11	170	Lethbridge, Alta.	6-22-67	Calgary Jrs.	13	16	29
DEFENSEMEN								
Boutilier, Paul	6:00	200	Sydney, N.S.	5- 3-63	N.Y. Islanders	4	30	34
Boyd, Randy	5:11	192	Coniston, Ont.	1-23-62	N.Y. Islanders	2	12	14
Diduck, Gerald	6:02	195	Edmonton, Alta	4- 6-65	N.Y. Islanders	7	16	23
Dineen, Gord	5:11	195	Toronto, Ont.	9-21-62	N.Y. Islanders-Springfield	3	11	14
Finley, Jeff	6:02	185	Edmonton, Alta	4-14-67	Portland	11	59	70
Johannesen, Glenn	6:02	220	Lac La Ronge, Sask.	2-15-62	N.Y. Islanders-Springfield	8	21	29
Jonsson, Tomas	5:10	185	Falun, Sweden	4-12-60	N.Y. Islanders	14	30	44
Konroyd, Steve	6:01	195	Scarborough, Ont.	2-10-61	Calgary-N.Y. Islanders	7	25	32
Leiter, Ken	6:01	195	Detroit, Mich.	4-19-61	N.Y. Islanders-Springfield	8	29	37
MacPherson, Duncan	6:01	195	Saskatoon, Sask.	2- 3-66	Saskatoon	10	54	64
Morrow, Ken	6:04	205	Flint, Mich.	10-17-56	N.Y. Islanders	0	12	12
Paddock, Gord	6:00	180	Hamiota, Man.	2-15-64	Springfield-Indianapolis	2	2	4
Potvin, Denis	6:00	205	Ottawa, Ont.	10-29-53	N.Y. Islanders	21	38	59
Smith, Vern	6:01	190	Winnipeg, Man.	5-30-64	Springfield	3	11	14

GOALTENDERS	Hgt.	Wgt.	Place of Birth	Date	1985-86 Club	Mins.	GA.	SO.
Hrudey, Kelly	5:10	180	Edmonton, Alta	1-13-61	N.Y. Islanders	2557	137	1
Johnson, Gary	5:10	165	Winnipeg, Man.	2-16-65	Brandon	553	44	0
Lumbard, Todd	6:00	185	Brandon, Man.	8-31-63	Erie	1446	102	0
Smith, Bill	5:10	185	Perth, Ont.	12-12-50	N.Y. Islanders	2303	143	1
Volpe, Mike	5:11	165	Vancouver, B.C.	1- 2-67	Kitchener	1927	138	0

New York Rangers
Patrick Division

President	John H. Krumpe
Vice-President, Finance and Administration	Mel Lowell
Treasurer	Stephen Schwartz
Vice-President and General Manager	Phil Esposito
Coach	Ted Sator
Assistant Coaches	Jack Birch, Reg Higgs
Goaltending Coach and Special Assignment Scout	Ed Giacomin
Assistant to General Manager	Joe Bucchino
Vice-President-Communications	John Halligan
Public Relations Assistants	Matthew Loughran, Barry Watkins
Statistician	Arthur Friedman
Scouting Staff	Chuck Grillo, Lou Jankowski, Richard Rose, Lars-Erik Sjoberg, Wayne Cashman
Trainers	Jerry Maloney, Joe Murphy, Dave Smith
Home Ice	Madison Square Garden
Address	4 Pennsylvania Plaza, New York, N. Y. 10001
Seating Capacity	17,500
Club colors	Blue, Red and White
Phone	(212) 563-8000

Ted Sator

Phil Esposito

New York Rangers 1986-87 Roster

FORWARDS

Name	Hgt.	Wgt.	Place of Birth	Date	1985-86 Club	G.	A.	Pts.
Allison, Mike	6:00	200	Ft. Francis, Ont.	3-28-61	N.Y. Rangers	2	13	15
Bernard, Larry	6:02	195	Prince George, B.C.	4-16-67	Seattle	17	25	42
Brooke, Bob	6:02	205	Melrose, Mass.	12-18-60	N.Y. Rangers	24	20	44
Brown, Newell	5:09	178	Cornwall, Ont.	2-14-62	Team Canada	15	21	36
Caufield, Jay	6:04	240	Philadelphia, Pa.	7-17-60	New Haven-Toledo	7	7	14
Crawford, Bob	5:11	175	Belleville, Ont.	4- 6-59	Hartford-N.Y. Rangers	15	22	37
Elik, Todd	6:00	191	Brampton, Ont.	4-15-66	North Bay	12	34	46
Erixon, Jan	6:00	190	Skellaftea, Sweden	7- 8-62	N.Y. Rangers	2	17	19
Filbey, Ken	5:08	181	Prince Rupert, B.C.	1- 5-63	Colorado College	5	7	12
Gagner, Dave	5:10	180	Chatham, Ont.	12-11-64	N.Y. Rangers	4	6	10
Gropp, Brent	5:11	195	Edmonton, Alta.	11-16-63	Colorado College	19	23	42
Helminen, Raimo	6:00	185	Tampere, Finland	3-11-64	N.Y. Rangers	10	30	40
Jensen, Chris	5:11	169	Salmon Arm, B.C.	10-28-63	U. of N. Dakota-N.Y. Rangers	26	43	69
Kisio, Kelly	5:09	170	Wetaskwin, Alta.	9-18-59	Detroit	21	48	69
Koebel, Gerald	6:00	190	Edson, Alta	12- 7-64	University of Alberta	..	..	..
Kontos, Chris	6:01	195	Toronto, Ont.	12-10-63	Ilves (Finland)-New Haven	24	30	54
Lambert, Lane	5:11	178	Melfort, Sask.	11-18-64	Adirondack-Detroit	18	28	46
Larouche, Pierre	5:11	175	Taschereau, Que.	11-16-55	Hershey-N.Y. Rangers	42	24	66
MacLellan, Brian	6:03	212	Guelph, Ont.	10-17-58	Los Angeles-N.Y. Rangers	16	29	45
Maloney, Don	6:01	190	Lindsay, Ont.	9- 5-58	N.Y. Rangers	11	17	28
McPhee, George	5:09	170	Guelph, Ont.	7-2-58	N.Y. Rangers	4	4	8
Miller, Kelly	5:11	185	Detroit, Mich.	3- 3-63	N.Y. Rangers	13	20	33
Moeser, Duanne	5:10	170	Waterloo, Ont.	4- 3-63	Cornell University	13	20	33
Mongeau, Michel	5:10	175	Montreal, Que.	2- 9-65	Laval	71	109	180
Moria, Steve	6:00	175	Vancouver, B.C.	2- 3-61	New Haven	19	37	56
Nasheim, Rick	5:11	185	Regina, Sask.	1-15-63	University of Regina	22	28	50
Natyshak, Peter	5:10	185	Oakville, Ont.	2-14-64	Cornell University	12	21	33
Nemeth, Steve	5:08	162	Calgary, Alta.	2-11-67	Lethbridge	42	69	111
O'Dwyer, Bill	6:00	190	S. Boston, Mass.	6-25-60	New Haven	10	15	25
Osborne, Mark	6:02	200	Toronto, Ont.	8-13-61	N.Y. Rangers	16	24	40
Paiement, Wilf	6:01	210	Earlton, Ont.	10-16-55	Quebec-N.Y.Rangers	8	18	26
Poeschek, Rudy	6:01	208	Kamloops, B.C.	9-29-66	Kamloops	3	13	16
Raedeke, Mark	5:11	190	Regina, Sask.	1- 7-63	Univ. of Regina	15	19	34
Reifenberger, Paul	5:11	191	St. Paul, Minn.	5-27-63	College of St. Thomas (Minn.)	29	31	60
Ridley, Mike	6:01	200	Winnipeg, Man.	7- 8-63	N.Y. Rangers	22	43	65
Sandstrom, Tomas	6:02	200	Fagersta, Sweden	9- 4-64	N.Y. Rangers	25	29	54
Sanko, Ron	6:01	195	Windsor, Ont.	6-30-65	Kitchener	43	89	132
Shea, Neil	5:11	194	Boston, Mass.	7-15-63	Boston College	12	18	30
Stepan, Brad	5:11	185	Hastings, Minn.	8-27-67		..	..	..
Strueby, Todd	6:01	190	Lannigan, Sask.	6-15-63	Muskegon	25	40	65
Sundstrom, Peter	6:00	180	Skelleftea, Sweden	12-14-61	N.Y. Rangers	8	15	23
Tait, Terry	6:02	190	Thunder Bay, Ont.	9-10-63	Springfield	11	19	30
Talakoski, Ron	6:02	215	Thunder Bay, Ont.	6- 1-62		..	..	..
Vinge, Ken	5:10	175	Edmonton, Alta.	1-21-63	University of Calgary	30	50	80
Walker, Gordon	6:00	175	Castlegar, B.C.	8-12-65	New Haven	11	28	39

DEFENSEMEN

Name	Hgt.	Wgt.	Place of Birth	Date	1985-86 Club	G.	A.	Pts.
Andonoff, Jim	6:02	200	Grosse Pointe, Mich.	8- 7-65	Salt Lake-Flint-New Haven	15	21	36
Beck, Barry	6:03	215	Vancouver, B.C.	6- 3-57	N.Y. Rangers	4	8	12
Bumbacco, Nick	6:02	200	Sault Ste. Marie, Ont.	4-19-64	Sault Ste. Marie Sr. A	35	43	78
Carkner, Terry	6:03	200	Smith Falls, Ont.	3- 7-66	Peterborough	12	32	44
Duggan, Ken	6:03	210	Toronto, Ont.	2-21-63	University of Toronto	13	41	54
Feltrin, Tony	6:01	185	Ladysmith, B.C.	12- 6-61	New Haven-N.Y. Rangers	0	2	2
Greschner, Ron	6:02	205	Goodsoil, Sask.	12-22-54	N.Y. Rangers	20	28	48
Huber, Willie	6:05	225	Strasskirchen, W. Ger.	1-15-68	N.Y. Rangers	7	8	15
Laidlaw, Tom	6:02	215	Brampton, Ont.	4-15-58	N.Y. Rangers	6	12	18
Leavins, Jim	5:11	185	Dinsmore, Sask.		Adirondack-Detroit	6	32	36
Meckling, Brent	6:02	205	Kelowna, B.C.	9-14-64	University of Calgary	..	..	..
Melnyk, Larry	6:00	180	Saskatoon, Sask.	2-21-60	Edmonton-N.Y. Rangers	3	11	14
Patrick, James	6:02	185	Winnipeg, Man.	6-14-63	N.Y. Rangers	14	29	43
Pilon, Neil	6:04	182	Merritt, B.C.	4-26-67	Moose Jaw	2	18	20
Saint Cyr, Chris	5:10	190	Winnipeg, Man.	9-14-63	University of Manitoba	9	29	38
Salo, Vesa	6:02	194	Rauma, Finland	4-17-65	Lukko (Finland)	1	8	9
Samuelson, Kjell	6:06	227	Tyringe, Sweden	10-18-56	New Haven-N.Y. Rangers	6	21	27
Smith, Scott	6:01	185		10-16-62	Univ. of Maine-New Haven	6	15	21
Whistle, Rob	6:02	195	Thunder Bay, Ont.	4-30-61	New Haven-N.Y. Rangers	5	6	11
Wiemer, Jim	6:04	200	Sudbury, Ont.	1- 9-61	New Haven-N.Y. Rangers	27	49	76

GOALTENDERS

Name	Hgt.	Wgt.	Place of Birth	Date	1985-86 Club	Mins.	GA.	SO.
Crouse, Peter	6:01	190	Trenton, Ont.	11-13-63		..	..	..
Kleisinger, Terry	6:00	190	Nanaimo, B.C.	10-22-60	Flint-New Hav.-N.Y. Rngs.-Tol.	1674	149	0
Labillois, Judes	5:09	163	Nuvelle-Gaspesie, Que.	6-15-65		..	..	..
Scott, Ron	5:08	155	Guelph, Ont.	7-21-60	New Haven-N.Y. Rangers	1225	77	1
Soetaert, Doug	6:00	180	Edmonton, Alta.	4-21-55	Montreal	1215	54	3
Trakalo, Derril	5:09	165	Winnipeg, Man.	1- 3-63		..	..	..
Vanbiesbrouck, John	5:10	180	Detroit, Mich.	9- 4-63	N.Y. Rangers	3326	184	3

Philadelphia Flyers
Patrick Division

Chairman of the Executive Committee	Edward M. Snider
Chairman of the Board Emeritus	Joseph C. Scott
President	Jay T. Snider
Executive Vice-President	Keith Allen
Vice-President, Finance and Administration	Donn Patton
General Manager	Bob Clarke
Coach	Mike Keenan
Assistant General Manager	Gary Darling
Assistant Coaches	E.J. McGuire, Paul Holmgren, Bill Barber
Goaltending Instructor	Bernie Parent
Physical Conditioning and Rehabilitation Coach	Pat Croce
Scouts	Jerry Melnyk, Walt Atanas, Dennis Patterson, Red Sullivan
Assistant to the President	John Brogan
Public Relations Director	Rodger Gottlieb
Assistant Public Relations Director	Mark Piazza
Ticket Manager	Ceil Baker
Vice-President, Sales	Jack Betson
Director of Team Services	Joe Kadlec
Director of Broadcast Sales	Pete Huver
Trainer	Dave Settlemyre
Assistant Trainer	Kurt Mundt
Controller	Bob Baer
Team Physician	Edward Viner, M.D.
Home Ice	The Spectrum
Address	Pattison Place, Philadelphia, Pa. 19148
Seating Capacity	17,211
Club colors	Orange, White and Black
Phone	(215) 465-4500

Ed Snider

Bob Clarke

Mike Keenan

Jay Snider

Philadelphia Flyers 1986-87 Roster

FORWARDS	Hgt.	Wgt.	Place of Birth	Date	1985-86 Club	G.	A.	Pts.
Allison, Ray	5:10	195	Cranbrook, B.C.	3- 4-59	Hershey	32	46	78
Berube, Craig	6:02	195	Calihoo, Alta.	12-17-65	Medicine Hat	27	25	52
Brown, Dave	6:05	205	Saskatoon, Sask.	10-12-62	Philadelphia	10	7	17
Carson, Lindsay	6:02	195	N. Battleford, Sask.	11-21-60	Philadelphia	9	12	21
Craven, Murray	6:02	175	Medicine Hat, Alta.	7-20-64	Philadelphia	21	33	54
Dobbin, Brian	5:11	195	Petrolia, Ont.	8-18-66	London-Hershey	39	55	94
Dzikowski, John	6:03	190	Point LaPrarie, Man.	1-28-66	Seattle	53	35	88
Eklund, Per-Erik	5:10	170	Stockholm, Sweden	3-22-63	Philadelphia	15	51	66
Fitzpatrick, Ross	6:01	195	Penticton, B.C.	10- 7-60	Hershey-Philadelphia	50	47	97
Hawley, Kent	6:03	213	Kingston, Ont.	2-20-68	Ottawa	21	30	51
Hill, Al	6:01	175	Nanaimo, B.C.	4-22-55	Hershey	17	40	57
Holmes, Daril	6:06	200	Cornwall, Ont.	2-15-67	Kingston	25	37	62
Horacek, Tony	6:03	200	Vancouver, B.C.	3- 3-67	Spokane	19	28	47
Kerr, Tim	6:03	225	Windsor, Ont.	1- 5-60	Philadelphia	58	26	84
Kypreos, Nick	6:00	190	Toronto, Ont.	6- 4-66	North Bay	62	35	97
Lamoureaux, Mitch	5:06	175	Ottawa, Ont.	8-22-62	Baltimore	22	31	53
Martinson, Steve	6:01	205	Minnetonka, Minn.	6-21-57	Hershey	3	6	9
Maxwell, Kevin	5:09	170	Edmonton, Alta.	3-30-60	Maine	14	17	31
McLay, Dave	5:11	175	Chilliwack, B.C.	5-13-66	Portland	37	49	86
Mellanby, Scott	6:01	195	Montreal, Que.	6-11-66	U. of Wisconsin-Phila.	21	23	44
Murray, Mike	6:00	185	Kingston, Ont.	8-29-66	Guelph	27	38	65
Nachbaur, Don	6:02	200	Kitimat, B.C.	1-30-59	Hershey-Philadelphia	24	25	49
Poulin, Dave	5:11	180	Timmons, Ont.	12-17-58	Philadelphia	27	42	69
Propp, Brian	5:10	190	Lanigan, Sask.	2-15-59	Philadelphia	40	57	97
Seabrooke, Glen	6:01	175	Peterborough, Ont.	9-11-67	Peterborough	8	12	20
Seguin, Steve	6:01	191	Cornwall, Ont.	4-10-64	Hershey	25	29	54
Sinisalo, Ilkka	6:01	190	Valeakoski, Finland	7-10-58	Philadelphia	39	37	76
Smith, Derrick	6:01	185	Scarborough, Ont.	1-22-65	Philadelphia	6	6	12
Sutter, Ron	5:11	175	Viking, Alta.	12- 2-63	Philadelphia	18	42	60
Tocchet, Rick	6:00	195	Scarborough, Ont.	4- 9-64	Philadelphia	14	21	35
Tookey, Tim	5:11	185	Edmonton, Alta.	8-29-60	Hershey	35	62	97
Zezel, Peter	5:09	200	Toronto, Ont.	4-22-65	Philadelphia	17	37	54

DEFENSEMEN	Hgt.	Wgt.	Place of Birth	Date	1985-86 Club	G.	A.	Pts.
Armstrong, Ian	6:04	200	Peterborough, Ont.	1-25-65	Hershey	0	8	8
Chychrun, Jeff	6:04	183	LaSalle, Que.	5- 3-66	Kingston	4	21	25
Crossman, Doug	6:02	190	Peterborough, Ont.	6-30-60	Philadelphia	6	37	43
Daigneault, J.J.	5:11	180	Montreal, Que.	10-12-65	Vancouver	5	23	28
Hospodar, Ed	6:02	210	Bowling Green, O.	2- 9-59	Philadelphia-Minnesota	3	3	6
Howe, Mark	5:11	190	Detroit, Mich.	5-28-55	Philadelphia	24	58	82
Huffman, Kerry	6:02	180	Peterborough, Ont.	1- 3-68	Peterborough	3	24	27
Marsh, Brad	6:03	220	London, Ont.	3-31-58	Philadelphia	0	13	13
Maurice, Paul	6:02	180	Sault Ste. Marie, Ont.	1-30-67	Windsor	3	10	13
McCarthy, Kevin	5:11	195	Winnipeg, Man.	7-14-57	Hershey-Philadelphia	15	40	55
McCrimmon, Brad	5:11	197	Dodsland, Sask.	3-29-59	Philadelphia	13	42	55
Murphy, Gordon	6:01	180	Willowdale, Man.	2-23-67	Oshawa	7	15	22
Smith, Steve	5:09	200	Trenton, Ont.	4- 4-63	Hershey-Philadelphia	1	11	12
Smyth, Greg	6:03	194	Oakville, Ont.	4-23-66	London-Hershey	12	43	55
Stanley, Daryl	6:02	200	Winnipeg, Man.	12- 2-62	Philadelphia-Hershey	0	6	6
Stevens, John	6:01	185	Completon, N.B.	5- 4-66	Oshawa	1	7	8
Stothers, Mike	6:04	210	Toronto, Ont.	2-22-62	Hershey-Philadelphia	4	10	14
Villeneuve, Andre	6:00	190	Alma, Que.	1-19-63	Hershey	2	7	9

GOALTENDERS	Hgt.	Wgt.	Place of Birth	Date	1985-86 Club	Mins.	GA.	SO.
Froese, Bob	5:11	180	St. Catharines, Ont.	6-30-58	Philadelphia	2728	116	5
Gilmour, Darryl	5:11	160	Winnipeg, Man.	2-13-67	Moose Jaw	3482	276	1
Hextall, Ron	6:03	180	Brandon, Man.	5- 3-64	Hershey	3061	174	5
Jensen, Darren	5:09	165	Creston, B.C.	5-27-60	Philadelphia-Hershey	2231	126	3
Kemp, John	6:00	185	Burlington, Ont.	7-31-63	Hershey-Team Canada	..	..	..
Resch, Glenn	5:09	165	Moose Jaw, Sask.	7-10-48	New Jersey-Philadelphia	1976	136	0

Pittsburgh Penguins
Patrick Division

Chairman of the Board and President	Edward J. DeBartolo, Sr.
Vice-President	Marie Denise DeBartolo York
Vice-President and General Counsel	J. Paul Martha
Vice-President and Treasurer	Thomas F. Rosetti
General Manager	Eddie Johnston
Director of Player Personnel and Assistant G.M.	Ken Schinkel
Coach	Bob Berry
Assistant Coach	Jim Roberts
Ontario Scout	Paul Goulet
Western Scout	Bruce Haralson
Quebec Scout	Albert Mandanici
Mid-Western Scout	John Gill
Director of Marketing	Paul Steigerwald
Director of Media Relations	Cindy Himes
Director of Team Services	Terry Schiffhauer
Trainer	Steve Thomas
Equipment Manager	John Doolan
Strength Coach	Doug McKenney
Home Ice	Civic Arena
Address	Civic Arena, Gate No. 7, Pittsburgh, Pa. 15219
Seating Capacity	16,033
Club colors	Black, Gold and White
Phone	(412) 642-1800

Edward DeBartolo

Eddie Johnston

Bob Berry

Pittsburgh Penguins 1986-87 Roster

FORWARDS

Name	Hgt.	Wgt.	Place of Birth	Date	1985-86 Club	G.	A.	Pts.
Aitken, Brad	6:03	202	Scarborough, Ont.	10-30-67	Sault Ste. Marie	17	47	64
Belanger, Roger	6:00	192	St. Catharines, Ont.	12- 1-65	Baltimore	17	21	38
Blaisdell, Mike	6:01	195	Moose Jaw, Sask.	1-18-60	Pittsburgh	15	14	29
Bourque, Phil	6:01	190	Chelmsford, Mass.	6-18-66	Baltimore-Pittsburgh	8	18	26
Brown, Rob	5:11	170	Kingston, Ont.	4-10-68	Kamloops	58	115	173
Bullard, Mike	5:10	185	Ottawa, Ont.	3-10-61	Pittsburgh	41	42	83
Cain, Kelly	5:06	180	Toronto, Ont.	4-19-68	London	46	51	97
Capuano, Dave	6:02	188	Cranston, R.I.	7-27-68	Mt. St. Charles H.S.	43	42	85
Chabot, John	6:03	190	Summerside, PEI	5-18-62	Pittsburgh	14	31	45
Choules, Greg	5:09	170	Montreal, Que.	5- 1-66	Chicoutimi	20	32	52
Clemens, Kevin	5:11	187	McLennan, Alta.	2- 2-67	Regina	26	32	58
Cunneyworth, Randy	6:00	180	Etobicoke, Ont.	5-10-61	Pittsburgh	15	30	45
Daniels, Jeff	6:01	187	Oshawa, Ont.	6-24-68	Oshawa	13	19	32
Del Col, John	5:10	190	St. Catharines, Ont.	5-11-65	Baltimore-Toledo	7	9	16
Drulia, Stan	5:10	188	Elmira, N.Y.	1- 5-68	Belleville	43	36	79
Duguay, Ron	6:02	210	Sudbury, Ont.	7- 6-57	Detroit-Pittsburgh	25	36	61
Errey, Bob	5:10	185	Montreal, Que.	9-21-64	Pittsburgh-Baltimore	19	13	32
Frawley, Dan	6:00	170	Sturgeon Falls, Ont.	6- 2-62	Pittsburgh	10	11	21
Giffin, Lee	5:11	177	Chatham, Ont.	4- 1-67	Oshawa	29	37	66
Gotaas, Steve	5:10	175	Camrose, Alta.	5-10-67	Prince Albert	40	61	101
Hannan, Dave	5:10	175	Sudbury, Ont.	11-26-61	Pittsburgh	17	18	35
Johnson, Scott	5:11	185	New Hope, Minn.	10-12-63	Lake Superior State	21	24	45
Lemieux, Mario	6:04	200	Montreal, Que.	10- 5-65	Pittsburgh	48	93	141
Lindstrom, Willy	6:00	180	Grunns, Sweden	5- 5-51	Pittsburgh	14	17	31
Loney, Troy	6:03	215	Bow Island, Alta.	9-21-63	Pittsburgh-Baltimore	15	20	35
Mathiasen, Dwight	6:01	190	Brandon, Man.	5-12-65	Denver U.-Pittsburgh	41	49	90
McGeough, Jim	5:08	170	Regina, Sask.	4-13-63	Pittsburgh-Baltimore	17	15	32
McIlwain, Dave	6:00	189	Seaforth, Ont.	1- 9-67	North Bay	37	35	72
Mokosak, Carl	6:01	180	Ft. Saskatchewan, Alta.	9-22-62	Hershey	30	42	72
Ruskowski, Terry	5:09	180	Prince Albert, Sask.	12-31-54	Pittsburgh	26	37	63
Shaw, Brian	6:00	190	Edmonton, Alta.	5-20-62	Adirondack-Peoria	44	24	68
Simpson, Craig	6:02	185	London, Ont.	2-15-67	Pittsburgh	11	17	28
Stevens, Kevin	6:03	207	Brockton, Mass.	4-15-65	Boston College	17	27	44
Wilson, Mitch	5:08	190	Kelowna, B.C.	7- 5-57	Maine	4	3	7

DEFENSEMEN

Name	Hgt.	Wgt.	Place of Birth	Date	1985-86 Club	G.	A.	Pts.
Bodger, Doug	6:02	200	Chemainus, B.C.	6-18-66	Pittsburgh	4	33	37
Buskas, Rod	6:01	197	Wetaskiwin, Alta.	1- 7-61	Pittsburgh	2	7	9
Charlesworth, Todd	6:01	190	Calgary, Alta.	3-22-65	Muskegon-Balt-Pittsburgh	10	31	41
Dahlquist, Chris	6:01	190	Fridley, Minn.	12-14-62	Baltimore-Pittsburgh	5	23	28
Goertz, Dave	5:11	210	Edmonton, Alta.	3-28-65	Baltimore	1	15	16
Hillier, Randy	6:00	180	Toronto, Ont.	3-30-60	Pittsburgh-Baltimore	0	8	8
Hobson, Doug	5:11	186	Prince Albert, Sask.	4- 9-68	Prince Albert	2	17	19
Johnson, Jim	6:00	190	New Hope, Minn.	8- 9-62	Pittsburgh	3	26	29
Mantha, Moe	6:02	195	Lakewood, O.	1-21-61	Pittsburgh	15	52	67
Marston, Stuart	6:02	183	Montreal, Que.	5- 9-67	Laval	7	18	25
McDonnell, Joe	6:02	200	Kitchener, Ont.	5-11-61	Baltimore-Pittsburgh	1	14	15
Paek, Jim	6:00	188	Seoul, Korea	4- 7-67	Oshawa	5	21	26
Schmidt, Norm	5:11	185	Sault Ste. Marie, Ont.	1-24-63	Pittsburgh	15	14	29
Siren, Ville	6:01	185	Tempre, Finland	2-11-64	Pittsburgh	4	8	12
Wilson, Rob	6:03	187	Toronto, Ont.	7-18-68	Sudbury	1	5	6
Zalapski, Zarley	6:01	196	Edmonton, Alta.	4-22-68	Ft. Sask'wan-Team Canada	22	37	59

GOALTENDERS

Name	Hgt.	Wgt.	Place of Birth	Date	1985-86 Club	Mins.	GA.	SO.
Cooper, Jeff	5:10	170	Ottawa, Ont.	6-12-62	Baltimore	1099	77	2
Ford, Brian	5:10	170	Edmonton, Alta.	9-22-61	Baltimore-Muskegon	2743	169	1
Guenette, Steve	5:09	170	Montreal, Que.	11-13-65	Guelph	2910	165	3
Meloche, Gilles	5:09	185	Montreal, Que.	7-12-50	Pittsburgh	1989	119	0
Romano, Roberto	5:06	170	Montreal, Que.	10-10-62	Pittsburgh	2684	159	2
Titus, Steve	5:10	151	St. John, N.B.	2- 2-67	Cornwall	1846	163	0

Quebec Nordiques
Adams Division

President and Governor	Marcel Aubut
General Manager	Maurice Filion
Director of Personnel Development	Gilles Leger
Director of Recruiting and Chief Scout	Martin Madden
Coach	Michel Bergeron
Associate Coach	Simon Nolet
Special Counsellor to Hockey Department	Charles Thiffault
Scouts	George Armstrong, Serge Aubry, Red Fleming, Pierre Gauthier, Darwin Bennett
General Counsel	Jean Pelletier
Director of Finance	Jean Laflamme
Director of Marketing	Jean Methot
Director of Communications and Press Relations	Bernard Brisset
Supervisor of Public Relations	Marius Fortier
Physician	Dr. Pierre Beauchemin
Trainers	Rene Lacasse, Rene Lavigueur, Jacques Lavergne
Home Ice	Quebec Coliseum
Address	2205 Ave. du Colisee, Quebec, Que. G1L 4W7
Seating Capacity	15,434
Club colors	Blue, White and Red
Phone	(418) 529-8441

Marcel Aubut

Maurice Filion

Gilles Leger

Michel Bergeron

Quebec Nordiques 1986-87 Roster

FORWARDS	Hgt.	Wgt.	Place of Birth	Date	1985-86 Club	G.	A.	Pts.
Ashton, Brent	6:01	210	Saskatoon, Sask.	5-18-60	Quebec	26	32	58
Cota, Darren	5:11	193	McLellan, Atla.	4- 7-66	Medicine Hat	34	37	71
Cote, Alain	5:10	203	Matane, Que.	5- 3-57	Quebec	13	21	34
Eagles, Mike	5:10	180	Sussex, N.B.	3- 7-63	Quebec	11	12	23
Gaulin, Jean-Marc	5:10	182	Balve, Germany	3- 3-62	Quebec-Fredericton	17	26	43
Gerlitz, Paul	5:11	205	Calgary, Alta.	3-23-63	Boston University	6	7	13
Gillis, Paul	5:11	190	Toronto, Ont.	12-31-63	Quebec	19	24	43
Goulet, Michel	6:01	185	Peribonka, Que.	4-21-60	Quebec	53	51	104
Groulx, Wayne	5:09	176	Welland, Ont.	2- 2-65	Fredericton-Muskegon	24	33	57
Heroux, Yves	5:11	185	Terrebonne, Que.	4-27-65	Fredericton-Muskegon	26	18	44
Hough, Mike	6:01	190	Montreal, Que.	2- 6-63	Fredericton	21	33	54
Hunter, Dale	5:09	190	Petrolia, Ont.	7-31-60	Quebec	28	42	70
Kumpel, Mark	6:00	190	Wakefield, Mass.	3- 7-61	Quebec-Fredericton	14	14	28
Lafreniere, Jason	5:11	185	St. Catharines, Ont.	12- 6-66	Belleville	49	82	131
Latta, Dave	6:00	185	Thunder Bay, Ont.	1- 3-67	Kitchener-Quebec	36	34	70
Malone, Greg	6:00	185	Fredericton, N.B.	3- 8-56	Hartford-Quebec	9	12	21
McRae, Ken	6:01	196	Winchester, Ont.	4-23-68	Sudbury	25	49	74
Middendorf, Max	6:04	194	Syracuse, N.Y.	8-18-67	Sudbury	40	42	82
Patrick, Steve	6:04	205	Winnipeg, Man.	2- 4-61	N.Y. Rangers-Quebec	8	16	24
Peer, Brit	6:00	189	Toronto, Ont.	6-14-66	Windsor	22	33	55
Perkins, Terry	6:01	190	Campbell River, B.C.	7-21-66	Spokane	71	46	117
Quinney, Ken	5:10	190	New Westminster, B.C.	5-23-65	Fredericton	11	26	37
Routhier, Jean-Marc	6:01	177	Quebec City, Que.	2- 2-68	Hull	18	16	34
Stastny, Anton	6:00	185	Bratislava, Czech.	8- 5-59	Quebec	31	43	74
Stastny, Peter	6:01	195	Bratislava, Czech.	9-18-56	Quebec	41	81	122
Stienburg, Trevor	6:01	185	Kingston, Ont.	5-13-66	London-Quebec	13	18	31
Zemlak, Richard	6:02	190	Wynard, Sask.	3- 3-63	Muskegon-Fredericton	6	7	13
DEFENSEMEN								
Andersson, Peter	6:02	200	Ferdertalve, Sweden	3- 2-62	Washington-Quebec	6	16	22
Brown, Jeff	6:01	185	Ottawa, Ont.	4-30-66	Sudbury-Quebec	25	30	55
Delorme, Gilbert	6:01	205	Boucherville, Que.	11-25-62	Quebec	2	18	20
Donnelly, Gord	6:02	195	Montreal, Que.	4- 5-62	Fredericton-Quebec	5	9	14
Finn, Steven	6:00	192	Laval, Que.	8-20-66	Laval-Quebec	4	16	20
Guerard, Stephane	6:02	182	St. Elisabeth, Que.	4-12-68	Shawinigan	4	16	20
Karalis, Tom	6:01	205	Montreal, Que.	5-24-64	Fredericton-Muskegon	9	16	25
Moller, Randy	6:02	205	Red Deer, Alta.	8-23-63	Quebec	5	18	23
Picard, Robert	6:02	205	Montreal, Que.	5-25-57	Winnipeg-Quebec	9	32	41
Poudrier, Daniel	6:02	185	Thetford Mines, Que.	2-15-64	Fredericton-Quebec	6	31	37
Price, Pat	6:02	195	Nelson, B.C.	3-24-55	Quebec	3	13	16
Rochefort, Normand	6:01	200	Trois-Rivieres, Que.	1-28-61	Quebec	5	4	9
Shaw, David	6:02	187	St. Thomas, Ont.	5-25-64	Quebec	7	19	26
Siltanen, Risto	5:09	180	Tampere, Finland	10-31-58	Hartford-Quebec	10	27	37

GOALTENDERS	Hgt.	Wgt.	Place of Birth	Date	1985-86 Club	Mins.	GA.	SO.
Brunetta, Mario	6:03	180	Quebec City, Que.	1-25-67	Laval	3383	279	0
Gosselin, Mario	5:08	160	Thetford Mines, Que.	6-15-63	Quebec-Fredericton	2030	126	2
Guenette, Luc	5:09	162	St. Jerome, Que.	7-22-64	Fredericton	1021	76	0
Malarchuk, Clint	5:10	172	Grand Prairie, Alta.	5- 1-61	Quebec	2657	142	4
Sevigny, Richard	5:08	178	Montreal, Que.	11- 4-57	Quebec-Fredericton	830	54	1

St. Louis Blues
Norris Division

Board of Directors	Harry Ornest, Ruth Ornest, Michael Ornest, Cindy Ornest, Maury Ornest, Laura Ornest, Jack Quinn
Chairman of the Board, President and Governor	Harry Ornest
Vice-Chairwoman and Treasurer	Ruth Ornest
Executive Vice-President	Jack Quinn
Vice-President and Secretary	Michael Ornest
Vice-President, Administration	Cindy Ornest
Vice-President	Maury Ornest
Vice-President/General Manager	Ron Caron
Director of Scouting	Ted Hampson
Assistant Director of Scouting	Jack Evans
Coach	Jacques Martin
Assistant Coach	Barclay Plager
Special Assignment Scout	Bob Plager
Public Relations Director	Susie Mathieu
Assistant Public Relations Director	Charlie Hodges, Mark Niebling
Trainer	Norm Mackie
Home Ice	The Arena
Address	5700 Oakland Avenue, St. Louis, Missouri 63110
Seating Capacity	17,666
Club colors	Blue, Gold, Red and White
Phone	(314) 781-5300

Harry Ornest

Jack Quinn

Ron Caron

Jacques Martin

St. Louis Blues 1986-87 Roster

FORWARDS	Hgt.	Wgt.	Place of Birth	Date	1985-86 Club	G.	A.	Pts.
Barr, Dave	6:01	195	Toronto, Ont.	11-30-60	St. Louis	13	38	51
Beers, Eddy	6:02	195	Zwaag, Netherlands	10-12-59	Calgary-St. Louis	18	21	39
Bozon, Phillipe	5:11	180	Chamoix, France	11-30-66	St. Jean	59	52	111
Carlson, Kent	6:03	200	Concord, N.H.	1-11-62	Montreal-St. Louis	2	3	5
Cavallini, Gino	6:01	215	Toronto, Ont.	11-24-62	Calgary-St. Louis	13	12	25
Dumont, Marc	6:01	185	Quebec City, Que.	1-28-67	Laval	14	12	26
Evans, Doug	5:09	178	Peterborough, Ont.	6- 2-63	Peoria-St. Louis	47	51	98
Federko, Bernie	6:00	195	Foam Lake, Sask.	5-12-56	St. Louis	34	68	102
Flockhart, Ron	5:11	185	Smithers, B.C.	10-10-60	St. Louis	22	45	67
Gilmour, Doug	5:11	160	Kingston, Ont.	6-25-63	St. Louis	25	28	53
Hunter, Mark	6:00	205	Petrolia, Ont.	11-12-62	St. Louis	44	30	74
Lemieux, Jocelyn	5:11	207	Mont Laurier, Que.	11-18-67	Laval	57	68	125
Meagher, Rick	5:08	175	Belleville, Ont.	11- 4-53	St. Louis	11	19	30
Paslawski, Greg	5:11	189	Kindersley, Sask.	8-25-61	St. Louis	22	11	33
Raglan, Herb	6:00	204	Peterborough, Ont.	8- 5-67	Kingston-St. Louis	10	9	19
Reeds, Mark	5:10	190	Toronto, Ont.	1-24-60	St. Louis	10	28	38
Ronning, Cliff	5:08	157	Vancouver, B.C.	10- 1-65	Team Canada	51	57	108
Sutter, Brian	5:11	180	Viking, Alta.	10- 7-58	St. Louis	19	23	42
Wickenheiser, Doug	6:01	196	Regina, Sask.	3-30-61	St. Louis	8	11	19
DEFENSEMEN								
Bell, Bruce	6:00	190	Toronto, Ont.	2-15-65	St. Louis	2	18	20
Benning, Brian	6:00	175	Edmonton, Alta.	6-10-66	Team Canada	4	12	16
Bourgeois, Charlie	6:04	220	Moncton, N.B.	11-19-59	Calgary-St. Louis	7	12	19
Dark, Michael	6:03	225	Sarnia, Ont.	9-17-63	Rensselaer Poly. Inst.	7	29	36
Dirk, Robert	6:04	207	Regina, Sask.	8-20-66	Regina	19	60	79
Evans, Shawn	6:02	195	Kingston, Ont.	9- 7-65	Peoria-St. Louis	8	26	34
Nattress, Ric	6:02	210	Hamilton, Ont.	5-25-62	St. Louis	4	20	24
Norwood, Lee	6:00	195	Oakland, Calif.	2- 2-60	St. Louis	5	24	29
Pavese, Jim	6:02	205	New York, N.Y.	5- 8-62	St. Louis	4	7	11
Posavad, Mike	5:11	196	Brantford, Ont.	1- 3-64	Peoria-St. Louis	1	17	18
Ramage, Rob	6:02	210	Byron, Ont.	1-11-59	St. Louis	10	56	66
Ruff, Marty	6:01	195	Warburg, Alta.	5-19-53	Peoria	3	6	9

GOALTENDERS						Mins.	GA.	SO.
Jablonski, Pat	6:00	170	Toledo, O.	6-20-67	Windsor	1600	119	1
May, Darrell	6:00	175	Edmonton, Alta.	3- 6-62	Peoria-St. Louis	3491	192	1
Millen, Greg	5:09	175	Toronto, Ont.	6-25-57	St. Louis	2168	129	1
Perry, Alan	5:08	155	Providence, R.I.	8-30-66	Windsor	2424	131	3
Wamsley, Rick	5:11	185	Simcoe, Ont.	5-25-59	St. Louis	2517	144	1

Toronto Maple Leafs
Norris Division

President, Governor and Managing Director	Harold E. Ballard
Chairman of the Board	Paul McNamara
Vice-President	Frank "King" Clancy
General Manager	Gerry McNamara
Coach	John Brophy
Assistant Coach	Garry Lariviere
Assistant to General Manager	Gord Stellick
Scouts	Johnny Bower, Frank Currie, Jacques Toupin, Dick Duff, Floyd Smith, Jack Faulkner, Jim Easdell, Anders Bengston
Publicity Director	Bob Stellick
Treasurer	Donald Crump
Box Office Manager	Gordon Finn
Trainers	Guy Kinnear, Dan Lemelin
Home Ice	Maple Leaf Gardens
Address	60 Carlton Street, Toronto, Ont. M5B 1L1
Seating Capacity	16,382 (including standees)
Club Colors	Blue and White
Phone	(416) 977-1641

Harold Ballard

King Clancy

Gerry McNamara

John Brophy

Toronto Maple Leafs 1986-87 Roster

FORWARDS

Name	Hgt.	Wgt.	Place of Birth	Date	1985-86 Club	G.	A.	Pts.
Armstrong, Tim	5:10	160	Toronto, Ont.	5-12-67	Toronto Jrs.	35	69	104
Bean, Tim	6:00	194	Sault Ste. Marie, Ont.	3-9-67	North Bay	32	34	66
Bellefeuille, Brian	6:02	185	Natick, Mass.	3-21-67	Canterbury H.S.	57	58	115
Brennan, Stephen	6:01	190	Winchester, Mass.	3-22-67	New Prep	..	..	..
Clark, Wendel	5:11	197	Kelvington, Sask.	10-25-66	Toronto	34	11	45
Costello, Rich	6:00	175	Framingham, Mass.	6-27-63	St. Catharines-Toronto	18	23	41
Courtnall, Russ	5:11	180	Duncan, B.C.	6-2-65	Toronto	22	38	60
Damphousse, Vincent	6:01	190	Montreal, Que.	12-17-67	Laval	45	119	164
Daoust, Dan	5:11	160	Montreal, Que.	2-29-60	Toronto	7	13	20
Davidson, Sean	5:11	177	Toronto, Ont.	4-13-68	Toronto Jrs.	18	34	52
Donahue, Andy	6:01	180	Boston, Mass.	1-17-67	Dartmouth University	11	7	18
Fergus, Tom	6:01	200	Chicago, Ill.	6-16-62	Toronto	31	42	73
Frycer, Miroslav	6:00	180	Opava, Czech.	9-27-59	Toronto	32	43	75
Giguere, Stephane	6:00	182	Montreal, Que.	2-21-68	St. Jean	13	20	33
Hie, Danny	6:00	178	Mississauga, Ont.	6-21-68	Ottawa	7	18	25
Hodgson, Dan	5:10	175	Ft. Vermillion, Alta.	8-29-65	Toronto-St. Catharines	26	28	54
Holick, Mark	6:02	185	Saskatoon, Sask.	8-6-68	Saskatoon	6	11	17
Hulst, Kent	6:00	180	St. Thomas, Ont.	4-8-68	Windsor	12	27	39
Ihnacak, Miroslav	6:00	185	Poprad, Czech.	2-19-62	Toronto-St. Catharines	6	8	14
Ihnacak, Peter	6:01	195	Poprad, Czech.	5-3-57	Toronto	18	27	45
Jackson, Jeff	6:01	193	Chatham, Ont.	4-24-65	Toronto-St. Catharines	18	30	48
James, Val	6:02	205	Ocala, Fla.	2-14-57	St. Catharines	0	3	3
Jarvis, Wes	5:11	156	Toronto, Ont.	5-30-58	St. Catharines-Toronto	37	60	97
Korn, Jim	6:03	210	Hopkins, Minn.	7-28-57	Toronto	0	0	0
Laxdal, Derek	6:01	176	St. Boniface, Man.	2-21-66	Brandon-St. Catharines	43	42	85
Leeman, Gary	5:11	168	Toronto, Ont.	2-19-64	Toronto-St. Catharines	24	36	60
MacInnis, Joseph	6:00	165	Cambridge, Mass.	5-25-66	Northeastern University	4	3	7
Maguire, Kevin	6:02	200	Toronto, Ont.	1-5-63	St. Catharines	6	9	15
McRae, Chris	6:00	178	Beaverton, Ont.	8-25-65	St. Catharines	1	1	2
Poddubny, Walt	6:01	200	Thunder Bay, Ont.	2-14-60	Toronto-St. Catharines	40	49	89
Reynolds, Bobby	5:11	175	Flint, Mich.	7-14-67	Michigan State	9	10	19
Ruzicka, Vladimir	6:01	175	Czechoslovakia	6-6-63	Czechoslovakia	..	..	..
Smith, Brad	5:11	180	Quebec City, Que.	7-31-54	Toronto-St. Catharines	18	46	64
Terrion, Greg	5:11	175	Marmora, Ont.	5-2-60	Toronto	10	22	32
Thomas, Steve	5:10	185	Stockport, England	7-15-63	Toronto-St. Catharines	38	51	89
Thomlinson, Dave	6:01	184	Edmonton, Alta.	10-22-66	Brandon	25	20	45
Vaive, Rick	6:01	190	Ottawa, Ont.	5-14-59	Toronto	33	31	64
Verstraete, Leigh	5:11	183	Pincher Creek, Alta.	1-6-62	St. Catharines	8	12	20
Vey, Greg	6:00	190	Toronto, Ont.	6-20-67	Peterborough	14	20	34
Waslen, Gerrard	6:00	187	Humbolot, Sask.	10-5-62	Colgate University	28	36	64
Whittemore, Todd	6:01	175	Taunton, Mass.	6-20-67	Kent School	..	..	..
Wurst, Mike	6:04	210	Edina, Minn.	10-5-64	Ohio State	1	3	4

DEFENSEMEN

Name	Hgt.	Wgt.	Place of Birth	Date	1985-86 Club	G.	A.	Pts.
Abrecht, Cliff	6:00	200	Bramalea, Ont.	5-24-63	Princeton Univ.-St. Catharines	15	27	42
Benning, Jim	6:00	183	Edmonton, Alta.	4-29-63	Toronto	4	21	25
Boland, Sean	6:03	180	Toronto, Ont.	2-18-68	Toronto Jrs.	2	10	12
Buckley, David	6:04	195	Newton, Mass.	1-27-66	Boston College	0	2	2
Capuano, Jack	6:02	210	Cranston, R.I.	7-7-66	Univ. of Maine	9	18	27
Clements, Scott	6:01	205	Sudbury, Ont.		St. Catharines	1	10	11
Gill, Todd	6:01	180	Brockville, Ont.	11-9-65	Toronto-St. Catharines	9	27	36
Iafrate, Al	6:03	215	Dearborn, Mich.	3-21-66	Toronto	8	25	33
Kitchen, Bill	6:02	198	Schomberg, Ont.	10-2-60	St. Catharines	7	32	39
Kotsopoulos, Chris	6:03	215	Scarborough, Ont.	11-27-58	Toronto	6	11	17
Latal, Jiri				2-2-67	Sparta, Czech.	..	..	..
Loven, Tim	6:00	189	Red River, N.D.	10-14-63	Univ. of North Dakota	0	1	1
Maxwell, Brad	6:02	195	Brandon, Man.	7-8-57	Toronto	8	18	26
McGill, Bob	6:01	190	Edmonton, Alta.	4-27-62	Toronto	1	4	5
Nylund, Gary	6:03	210	North Delta, B.C.	10-28-63	Toronto	2	16	18
Plante, Cam	6:00	195	Brandon, Man.	3-12-64	St. Catharines	6	15	21
Root, Bill	6:00	210	Toronto, Ont.	9-6-59	Toronto-St. Catharines	7	5	12
Salming, Borje	6:01	195	Kiruna, Sweden	4-17-51	Toronto	7	15	22
Serowik, Jeff	6:00	190	Manchester, N.H.	10-1-67	Lawrence Academy	..	..	..
Shannon, Darryl	6:02	190	Barrie, Ont.	6-21-68	Windsor	6	21	27
Slanina, Peter	6:02	185	Czechoslovakia			..	..	..
Spangler, Ken	5:11	196	Edmonton, Alta.	5-2-67	Calgary Jrs.-St. Catharines	19	36	55
Taylor, Scott	6:00	182	Toronto, Ont.	3-23-68	Kitchener	4	13	17
Uvira, Edourd			Czechoslovakia			..	..	..
Wesley, Blake	6:01	200	Red Deer, Alta.	7-10-59	Toronto-St. Catharines	3	5	8

GOALTENDERS

Name	Hgt.	Wgt.	Place of Birth	Date	1985-86 Club	Mins.	GA.	SO.
Bernhardt, Tim	5:09	164	Sarnia, Ont.	1-17-68	Toronto-St. Catharines	2042	145	1
Bester, Allan	5:07	155	Hamilton, Ont.	3-26-64	Toronto-St. Catharines	2875	175	1
Edwards, Don	5:09	160	Hamilton, Ont.	9-28-55	Toronto	2009	160	0
Reese, Jeff	5:09	150	Brantford, Ont.	3-24-66	London	3281	215	0
Wregget, Ken	6:01	195	Brandon, Man.	3-25-64	Toronto-St. Catharines	2624	191	1

Vancouver Canucks
Smythe Division

Chairman of the Board	Frank A. Griffiths
Assistant to the Chairman	Arthur R. Griffiths
Director of Hockey Operations/General Manager	Jack Gordon
Vice-President, Finance	John Chesman
Vice President, Marketing	John Whitman
Vice-President, Communications	Glen Ringdal
Assistant to the General Manager/Coach	Tom Watt
Assistant Coach	Jack McIlhargey
Director of Player Development	Darcy Rota
Director of Scouting	Mike Penny
Scouts	Jack McCartan, Ken Slater, Ron Delorme
Director of Team Services	Norm Jewison
Assistant/Hockey Information	Frank Bohmer
Public Relations Assistant	Babe Pratt
Trainers	Ken Fleger, Larry Ashley
Home Ice	Pacific Coliseum
Address	100 North Renfrew St., Vancouver, B.C. V5K 3N7
Seating Capacity	16,553
Club Colors	Black, Red and Gold
Phone	(604) 254-5141

Frank A. Griffiths

Arthur R. Griffiths

Jack Gordon

Tom Watt

Vancouver Canucks 1986-87 Roster

FORWARDS

Name	Hgt.	Wgt.	Place of Birth	Date	1985-86 Club	G.	A.	Pts.
Bertuzzi, Brian	6:00	185	Vancouver, B.C.	1-24-66	New Westminster-Kalamazoo	26	24	50
Bruce, Dave	5:11	177	Thunder Bay, Ont.	10- 7-64	Fredericton-Vancouver	25	17	42
Coxe, Craig	6:04	195	Chula Vista, Calif.	1-21-64	Vancouver	3	5	8
Crawford, Marc	5:11	185	Belleville, Ont.	2-13-61	Fredericton-Vancouver	21	28	49
Hall, Taylor	5:11	185	Regina, Sask.	2-20-64	Vancouver-Fredericton	26	19	45
Hawkins, Todd	6:01	195	Kingston, Ont.	8- 2-66	Belleville	14	13	27
Kirton, Mark	5:10	170	Regina, Sask.	2- 3-58	Fredericton	23	36	59
Kulak, Stu	5:10	180	Edmonton, Alta.	3-10-63	Kalamazoo-Fredericton	15	8	23
Lanthier, Jean-Marc	6:02	195	Montreal, Que.	3-27-63	Fredericton-Vancouver	12	15	27
LeBlanc, John	6:01	190	Campellton, N.B.	2-21-64	Univ. New Bruns.-Team Canada	39	26	65
Lemay, Moe	5:11	185	Saskatoon, Sask.	2-18-62	Vancouver	16	15	31
Lowry, Dave	6:01	185	Sudbury, Ont.	1-14-65	Vancouver	10	8	18
MacIntyre, Dunc	5:08	167	Cornwall, Ont.	7- 3-64	Fredericton	23	22	45
Noble, Jeff	5:10	167	Mount Forest, Ont.	5-20-68	Kitchener	22	33	55
Pederson, Barry	5:11	185	Big River, Sask.	3-13-61	Boston	29	47	76
Peterson, Brent	6:00	190	Calgary, Alta.	2-15-58	Vancouver	8	23	31
Rohlicek, Jeff	6:00	180	Park Ridge, Ill.	1-27-66	Spokane	50	52	102
Sandlak, Jim	6:03	209	Kitchener, Ont.	12-12-66	Vancouver-London	9	17	26
Siska, Randy	6:02	195	Kitchener, Ont.	6- 1-67	Medicine Hat	11	13	24
Skriko, Petri	5:10	172	Lapeenranta, Finland	3-12-62	Vancouver	38	40	78
Smyl, Stan	5:08	185	Glendon, Alta.	1-28-58	Vancouver	27	35	62
Stern, Ronnie	6:00	195	St.-Agathe, Que.	1-11-67	Longueuil	39	33	72
Stevens, Mike	5:11	193	Kitchener, Ont.	12-30-65	Fredericton	12	19	31
Sundstrom, Patrik	6:02	203	Skelleftea, Sweden	12-14-61	Vancouver	18	48	66
Sutter, Rich	5:11	183	Viking, Alta.	12- 2-63	Philadelphia	14	25	39
Tambellini, Steve	6:00	184	Trail, B.C.	5-14-58	Vancouver	15	15	30
Tanti, Tony	5:09	185	Toronto, Ont.	9- 7-63	Vancouver	39	33	72
Taylor, Darren	6:02	173	Calgary, Alta.	5-28-67	Calgary Jrs.-Seattle	11	19	30
Tottle, Scott	5:11	180	Brantford, Ont.	1-30-65	Fredericton	15	22	37
Woodley, Dan	6:00	190	Oklahoma City, Okla.	12-29-67	Portland	45	47	92

DEFENSEMEN

Name	Hgt.	Wgt.	Place of Birth	Date	1985-86 Club	G.	A.	Pts.
Agnew, Jim	6:01	185	Hartney, Man.	3-21-66	Portland	6	30	36
Bartel, Robin	6:00	200	Drake, Sask.	5-16-61	Moncton-Calgary	4	21	25
Butcher, Garth	6:00	200	Regina, Sask.	1- 8-63	Vancouver	4	7	11
Cochrane, Glen	6:03	207	Kamloops, B.C.	1-29-58	Vancouver	0	3	3
Doyle, Shane	6:01	200	Lindsay, Ont.	4-26-67	Belleville-Cornwall	4	28	32
Dunbar, Dale	6:01	201	Winthrop, Mass.	10-14-61	Fredericton-Vancouver	2	10	12
Halward, Doug	6:01	197	Toronto, Ont.	11- 1-55	Vancouver	8	25	33
Herniman, Steve	6:03	199	Windsor, Ont.	6- 9-68	Cornwall	3	12	15
Hunt, Curtis	6:00	180	North Battleford, Sask.	1-28-67	Prince Albert	5	29	34
Lanz, Rick	6:02	193	Karlouyvary, Czech.	9-16-61	Vancouver	15	38	53
Lidster, Doug	6:01	195	Kamloops, B.C.	10-18-60	Vancouver	12	16	28
Lyons, Marc	6:01	201	Toronto, Ont.	1- 8-67	Kingston	4	11	15
MacDonald, Brett	6:01	200	Bothwell, Ont.	1- 5-66	Kitchener	10	33	43
Measures, Allan	6:00	170	Barrhead, Alta.	5- 8-65	Calgary	23	34	57
Petit, Michel	6:01	205	St. Malo, Que.	2-12-64	Fredericton-Vancouver	1	19	20
Richter, Dave	6:05	220	St. Boniface, Man.	4- 8-60	Minnesota-Philadelphia	0	5	5

GOALTENDERS

Name	Hgt.	Wgt.	Place of Birth	Date	1985-86 Club	Mins.	GA.	SO.
Brodeur, Richard	5:07	175	Longueil, Que.	9-15-52	Vancouver	3541	240	2
Caprice, Frank	5:09	160	Hamilton, Ont.	5- 2-62	Vancouver-Fredericton	1834	138	0
Gamble, Troy	5:11	178	New Glasgow, N.S.	4- 7-67	Medicine Hat	2264	142	0
Kilroy, Shawn	5:11	175	Ottawa, Ont.	8-22-64	Mohawk Valley	1922	159	1
Young, Wendell	5:08	185	Halifax, N.S.	8- 1-63	Fredericton-Vancouver	2480	139	0

Washington Capitals
Patrick Division

Chairman of the Board and Governor	Abe Pollin
President and Alternate Governor	Richard M. Patrick
Legal Counsel and Alternate Governors	Peter F. O'Malley, David M. Osnos
Vice-President and General Manager	David Poile
Comptroller	Ed Stelzer
Coach	Bryan Murray
Assistant Coaches	Terry Murray, Ron Lapointe
Goaltender Coach	Warren Strelow
Director of Player Personnel and Recruitment	Jack Button
Assistant Director of Player Recruitment	Sam McMaster
Scouts	Bob Carpenter Sr., Gilles Cote, Clare Rothermel, Bob Schmidt
Director of Marketing	Lew Strudler
Director of Public Relations	Lou Corletto
Director of Community Relations	Yvon Labre
Director of Promotions	Charles Copeland
Director of Season Subscriptions	Louise Robinson
Trainer	Dick Young
Assistant Trainer	Doug Shearer
Home Ice	Capital Centre
Address	Landover, Md. 20785
Seating Capacity	18,130
Club Colors	Red, White and Blue
Phone	(301) 386-7000

Abe Pollin

David Poile

Jack Button

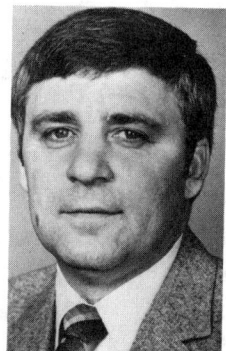

Bryan Murray

Washington Capitals 1986-87 Roster

FORWARDS

Name	Hgt.	Wgt.	Place of Birth	Date	1985-86 Club	G.	A.	Pts.
Adams, Greg	6:01	195	Victoria, B.C.	5-31-60	Washington	18	38	56
Carpenter, Bobby	6:00	190	Beverly, Mass.	7-13-63	Washington	27	29	56
Christian, Dave	5:11	175	Warroad, Minn.	5-12-59	Washington	41	42	83
Corriveau, Yvon	6:02	205	Welland, Ont.	2- 8-67	Toronto Jrs.-Washington	54	36	90
Cramarossa, Vito	6:02	205	Toronto, Ont.	3- 9-66	Toronto Jrs.	20	35	55
DeGagne, Rob	5:08	190	Ft. Frances, Ont.	2- 4-65	North Bay	24	72	96
Druce, John	6:01	187	Peterborough, Ont.	2-23-66	Peterborough	22	24	46
Duchesne, Gaetan	5:11	195	Les Saules, Que.	7-11-62	Washington	11	28	39
Dumas, Claude	6:01	175	Thetford-Mines, Que.	1-10-67	Granby-Binghamton	33	60	93
Franceschetti, Lou	6:00	190	Toronto, Ont.	3-28-58	Washington	7	14	21
Gartner, Mike	6:00	185	Barrie, Ont.	10-29-59	Washington	35	40	75
Gould, Bobby	5:11	195	Petrolia, Ont.	9- 2-57	Washington	19	19	38
Greenlaw, Jeff	6:02	215	Toronto, Ont.	2-28-68	Team Canada	3	16	19
Haworth, Alan	5:10	190	Drummondville, Que.	9- 1-60	Washington	34	39	73
Hollett, Steve	6:01	180	St. John's, Nfld.	6-12-67	Sault Ste. Marie	31	34	65
Hutton, Dwaine	5:11	185	Edmonton, Alta.	4-18-65	Spokane-Team Canada	13	25	38
Jensen, David A.	6:01	185	Needham, Mass.	8-19-65	Binghamton-Washington	18	14	32
Kastelic, Ed	6:02	215	Toronto, Ont.	1-29-64	Washington	0	0	0
King, Kris	5:11	189	Bracebridge, Ont.	2-18-66	Peterborough	19	40	59
Laughlin, Craig	5:11	198	Toronto, Ont.	9-14-57	Washington	30	45	75
Leach, Steve	5:11	190	Cambridge, Mass.	1-16-66	Univ. New Hamp.-Washington	23	9	32
Martin, Grant	5:10	190	Sm'th Rock Falls, Ont.	3-13-62	Binghamton-Washington	27	50	77
Pettersson, Jorgen	6:02	185	Gothenburg, Sweden	7-11-56	Hartford-Washington	13	21	34
Pivonka, Michal	6:02	192	Kladno, Czech.	1-28-66	Dukla-Jihlava	..	..	..
Purves, John	6:01	180	Toronto, Ont.	2-12-68	Hamilton	16	37	53
Sampson, Gary	6:00	190	Atikokan, Ont.	8-24-59	Washington-Binghamton	10	25	35
Schofield, Dwight	6:01	210	Waltham, Mass.	3-25-56	Washington	1	2	3
Seftel, Steve	6:01	183	Kitchener, Ont.	5-14-68	Kingston	11	16	27
Taylor, Mark	5:11	180	Vancouver, B.C.	6- 1-58	Washington-Binghamton	21	39	60

DEFENSEMEN

Name	Hgt.	Wgt.	Place of Birth	Date	1985-86 Club	G.	A.	Pts.
Babcock, Bob	5:11	196	Toronto, Ont.	8- 3-68	Sault Ste. Marie	1	7	8
Barrett, John	6:00	208	Ottawa, Ont.	7- 1-58	Detroit-Washington	2	15	17
Beaudoin, Yves	6:00	190	P'te-aux-Tr'mbl's, Que.	1- 7-65	Binghamton-Washington	5	12	17
Cavallini, Paul	6:02	202	Toronto, Ont.	10-13-65	Team Canada-Binghamton	4	15	19
Eakins, Dallas	6:02	195	Dade City, Fla.	1-20-67	Peterborough	6	16	22
Hatcher, Kevin	6:04	212	Detroit, Mich.	9- 9-66	Washington	9	10	19
Kellin, Tony	6:02	205	Grand Rapids, Minn.	3-19-63	Univ. of Minnesota	10	24	34
Langway, Rod	6:03	215	Taiwan, Formosa	5- 3-57	Washington	1	17	18
Murphy, Larry	6:02	206	Scarborough, Ont.	3- 8-61	Washington	21	44	65
Shaw, Larry	6:00	200	Guelph, Ont.	2-10-67	Peterborough	2	17	19
Smith, Greg	6:00	195	Ponoka, Alta.	7-18-55	Detroit-Washington	5	22	27
Stevens, Scott	6:01	210	Kitchener, Ont.	4- 1-64	Washington	15	38	53

GOALTENDERS

Name	Hgt.	Wgt.	Place of Birth	Date	1985-86 Club	Mins.	GA.	SO.
Jensen, Al	5:10	180	Hamilton, Ont.	11-27-58	Washington	2437	129	2
Mason, Bob	6:01	180	Int'l Falls, Minn.	4-22-61	Binghamton-Washington	1956	126	0
Peeters, Pete	6:01	207	Edmonton, Alta.	8-17-57	Boston-Washington	2506	144	1
Raymond, Alain	5:10	177	Rimouski, Que.	6-24-65	Team Canada	2571	151	4
Simpson, Shawn	5:11	180	Vancouver, B.C.	8-10-68	Sault Ste. Marie	2233	219	1

Winnipeg Jets

Smythe Division

President and Governor	Barry Shenkarow
Vice-President and General Manager	John Ferguson
Assistant G.M. and Director of Player Personnel	Mike Smith
Vice-President, Finance and Administration	Romeo Verrier
Coach	Dan Maloney
Assistant Coaches	Bill Sutherland, Rick Bowness
Chief Scout	Les Binkley
Eastern Scout	Tom Savage
Western Scout	Charlie Hodge
Special Assignments	Bill Lesuk
Scouts	Joe Yanetti, Ken Chisholm, John O'Flaherty, Bruce Southern
Director of Hockey and Media Information	Ralph Carter
Director of Corporate Marketing	Madeline Hanson
Athletic Therapist	Chuck Badcock
Equipment Manager	Jack Stouffer
Home Ice	Winnipeg Arena
Address	15-1430 Maroons Road, Winnipeg, Man. R3G 0L5
Seating Capacity	15,257
Club Colors	Red, White and Blue
Phone	(204) 772-9491

Barry Shenkarow

John Ferguson

Mike Smith

Dan Maloney

Winnipeg Jets 1986-87 Roster

FORWARDS

Name	Hgt.	Wgt.	Place of Birth	Date	1985-86 Club	G.	A.	Pts.
Acton, Al	5:10	190	Unity, Sask.	8-28-65	Regina	44	45	89
Antongiovanni, Patrick	6:03	220	Vancouver, B.C.	5-28-64	Auronzo	42	23	65
Baillargeon, Joel	6:02	215	Charlesbourg, Que.	10- 6-64	Sherbrooke	6	12	18
Boschman, Laurie	6:00	185	Major, Sask.	6- 4-60	Winnipeg	27	42	69
Cormier, Eric	6:02	201	Bathurst, N.B.	4-10-64	U. of Moncton	17	22	39
Derlago, Bill	5:10	195	Birtle, Man.	8-25-58	Tor-Bos-Winnipeg	10	21	31
Douris, Peter	6:01	192	Toronto, Ont.	2-19-66	Winnipeg	0	0	0
Elynuik, Pat	6:00	185	Foam Lake, Sask.	10-30-67	Prince Albert	53	53	106
Endean, Craig	5:11	175	Kamloops, B.C.	4-13-68	Seattle	58	70	128
Fleming, Gerry	6:05	225	Montreal, Que.	10-16-66	Montreal	22	28	50
Gilhen, Randy	5:10	190	Zw'br'cken, W. Ger.	6-13-63	Fort Wayne	44	40	84
Hamel, Gilles	6:00	185	Asbestos, Que.	3-18-60	Buffalo	19	25	44
Hawerchuk, Dale	5:11	185	Toronto, Ont.	4- 4-63	Winnipeg	46	59	105
Jarvenpaa, Hannu	6:00	193	Ilves, Finland	5-19-63	Karpat	26	9	35
Lapointe, Yves	6:03	210	Montreal, Que.	2- 2-64	U. of Quebec-Three Rivers	14	16	30
MacLean, Paul	6:00	205	Grostenquin, France	3- 9-58	Winnipeg	27	29	56
Martin, Tom	6:02	195	Victoria, B.C.	5-11-64	Sherbrooke	11	18	29
McBain, Andrew	6:01	195	Toronto, Ont.	2-18-65	Winnipeg	3	3	6
Moxam, Daran	5:10	180	Sudbury, Ont.	5-25-66	Belleville	21	35	56
Mullen, Brian	5:10	180	New York, N.Y.	3-16-62	Winnipeg	28	34	62
Neufeld, Ray	6:03	210	St. Boniface, Man.	4-15-59	Hartford-Winnipeg	25	38	63
Nielsen, Len	5:09	170	Moosejaw, Sask.	3-28-67	Regina	30	77	107
Nill, Jim	6:00	185	Hanna, Alta.	4-11-58	Winnipeg	6	8	14
Pooley, Paul	6:00	175	Exeter, Ont.	8- 2-60	Sherbrooke	20	21	41
Pooley, Perry	6:00	175	Exeter, Ont.	8- 2-60	Sherbrooke	12	19	31
Ray, Derek	5:11	200	Auburn, Wash.	10-30-63	Clarkson Univ.	8	6	14
Simard, Martin	6:03	210	Verdun, Que.	6-25-66	Hull	40	36	76
Smail, Doug	5:09	175	Moose Jaw, Sask.	9- 2-57	Winnipeg	16	26	42
Spencer, Michael	6:02	200	Weyburn, Sask.	4-12-63	N.A.I.T.	43	34	77
Steen, Thomas	5:10	195	Tockmark, Sweden	6- 8-60	Winnipeg	17	47	64
Stewart, Ryan	6:02	185	Prince George, B.C.	6- 1-67	Prince Albert	52	44	96
Turnbull, Perry	6:02	200	Bentley, Alta.	3- 9-59	Winnipeg	20	31	51
Vilgrain, Claude	6:01	195	Port-Au-Prince, Haiti	3- 1-63	U. of Moncton	17	20	37
Wilson, Ron	5:09	175	Toronto, Ont.	5-13-56	Winnipeg-Sherbrooke	15	15	30

DEFENSEMEN

Name	Hgt.	Wgt.	Place of Birth	Date	1985-86 Club	G.	A.	Pts.
Berry, Brad	6:02	190	Bashaw, Alta.	4- 1-65	U. of N. Dakota-Winnipeg	7	29	36
Campbell, Scott	6:02	210	Toronto, Ont.	6-22-54	Retired from Hockey			
Carlyle, Randy	5:10	200	Sudbury, Ont.	4-19-56	Winnipeg	16	33	49
Channell, Craig	5:11	190	Moncton, N.B.	4-24-62	Fort Wayne	7	28	35
Dollas, Bobby	6:02	215	Montreal, Que.	1-31-65	Winnipeg-Sherbrooke	4	12	16
Ellett, Dave	6:01	200	Cleveland, O.	3-30-64	Winnipeg	15	31	46
Krc, Pavol	6:02	175	B'nska Bystrica, Czech.	12- 5-60	Banska Bystrica	..	..	..
Kyte, Jim	6:05	210	Ottawa, Ont.	3-21-64	Winnipeg	1	3	4
Marois, Mario	5:11	190	Ancienne Lorette, Que.	12-15-57	Quebec-Winnipeg	5	40	45
McFall, Dan	6:00	192	Kenmore, N.Y.	4- 8-63	Sherbrooke-Winnipeg	2	11	13
Olausson, Frederik	6:02	200	Vaxsjo, Sweden	10- 5-66	Farjestad	5	12	17
Pessetti, Ron	5:11	190	Laval, Que.	5- 3-63	Western Michigan	8	20	28
Sambray, James	6:01	185	Thunder Bay, Ont.	3-30-64	Thunder Bay	10	27	37
Taglianetti, Peter	6:02	200	Framingham, Mass.	8-15-63	Winnipeg-Sherbrooke	1	8	9
Watters, Tim	5:11	180	Kamloops, B.C.	7-25-59	Winnipeg	6	8	14

GOALTENDERS

Name	Hgt.	Wgt.	Place of Birth	Date	1985-86 Club	Mins.	GA.	SO.
Behrend, Marc	6:01	185	Madison, Wis.	1-11-61	Sherbrooke-Winnipeg	2454	173	1
Berthiaume, Daniel	5:09	150	Longeuil, Que.	1-26-66	Chicoutimi	3718	286	3
Bouchard, Daniel	6:00	190	Val d'Or, Que.	12-12-50	Winnipeg	1696	107	2
Dyck, Larry	5:10	170	Winkler, Man.	12-15-65	Seattle	3096	264	2
Hayward, Brian	5:10	175	Georgetown, Ont.	6-25-60	Winnipeg-Sherbrooke	2906	222	0
Quigley, David	5:10	155	Cap-La M'd'l'ne, Que.	1-17-65	Univ. of Moncton	1142	60	0
Reddick, Pokey	5:08	170	Halifax, N.S.	10- 6-64	Fort Wayne	1811	92	3
Reimer, Mark	5:11	168	Calgary, Alta.	3-23-67	Saskatoon	2340	192	0
Robertson, Tim	6:02	195	Regina, Sask.	11-29-64	York University	..	..	..
Verstappen, Yannick	5:09	165	Geel, Belgium	9-30-67	HYC Herentals	..	..	..

Wayne Gretzky

Mike Bossy

Michel Goulet

The Sporting News
1985-86 NHL All-Star Team

First Team	Position	Second Team
Wayne Gretzky, Edmonton	Center	Mario Lemieux, Pittsburgh
Mike Bossy, N.Y. Islanders	Right Wing	Jari Kurri, Edmonton
Michel Goulet, Quebec	Left Wing	Mats Naslund, Montreal
Mark Howe, Philadelphia	Defense	Larry Robinson, Montreal
Paul Coffey, Edmonton	Defense	Ray Bourque, Boston
John Vanbiesbrouck, N.Y. Rangers	Goalie	Grant Fuhr, Edmonton

THE SPORTING NEWS NHL Player of the Year: Wayne Gretzky, Edmonton
THE SPORTING NEWS Rookie of the Year: Wendel Clark, Toronto
THE SPORTING NEWS Coach of the Year: Jacques Demers, St. Louis
THE SPORTING NEWS Executive of the Year: Emile Francis, Hartford
Note: THE SPORTING NEWS All-Star Team is selected by the NHL Players.

Mark Howe

Paul Coffey

John Vanbiesbrouck

Arguably the NHL's second-best player, Pittsburgh Penguins center Mario Lemieux finished second to Edmonton's Wayne Gretzky in the league scoring race and was named to The Sporting News' All-Star second team.

The Calgary Flames, led by sharp-shooting winger Joe Mullen (above) and goaltender Mike Vernon, upset defending Stanley Cup champion Edmonton in a seven-game Smythe Division final before bowing to Montreal in five games in the finals.

1985-86 FINAL NHL STANDINGS

Prince of Wales Conference

Charles F. Adams Division

	G.	W.	L.	T.	Pts.	GF.	GA.
Quebec Nordiques	80	43	31	6	92	330	289
Montreal Canadiens	80	40	33	7	87	330	280
Boston Bruins	80	37	31	12	86	311	288
Hartford Whalers	80	40	36	4	84	332	302
Buffalo Sabres	80	37	37	6	80	296	291

Lester Patrick Division

	G.	W.	L.	T.	Pts.	GF.	GA.
Philadelphia Flyers	80	53	23	4	110	335	241
Washington Capitals	80	50	23	7	107	315	272
New York Islanders	80	39	29	12	90	327	284
New York Rangers	80	36	38	6	78	280	276
Pittsburgh Penguins	80	34	38	8	76	313	305
New Jersey Devils	80	28	49	3	59	300	374

Clarence Campbell Conference

James Norris Division

	G.	W.	L.	T.	Pts.	GF.	GA.
Chicago Black Hawks	80	39	33	8	86	351	349
Minnesota North Stars	80	38	33	9	85	327	305
St. Louis Blues	80	37	34	9	83	302	291
Toronto Maple Leafs	80	25	48	7	57	311	386
Detroit Red Wings	80	17	57	6	40	266	415

Conn Smythe Division

	G.	W.	L.	T.	Pts.	GF.	GA.
Edmonton Oilers	80	56	17	7	119	426	310
Calgary Flames	80	40	31	9	89	354	315
Winnipeg Jets	80	26	47	7	59	295	372
Vancouver Canucks	80	23	44	13	59	282	333
Los Angeles Kings	80	23	49	8	54	284	389

Top 20 Scorers for the Art Ross Memorial Trophy

*Indicates league-leading figure.

	Games	G.	A.	Pts.	Pen.
1. Wayne Gretzky, Edmonton	80	52	*163	*215	46
2. Mario Lemieux, Pittsburgh	79	48	93	141	43
3. Paul Coffey, Edmonton	79	48	90	138	120
4. Jari Kurri, Edmonton	78	*68	63	131	22
5. Mike Bossy, New York Islanders	80	61	62	123	14
6. Peter Stastny, Quebec	76	41	81	122	60
7. Denis Savard, Chicago	80	47	69	116	111
8. Mats Naslund, Montreal	80	43	67	110	16
9. Dale Hawerchuk, Winnipeg	80	46	59	105	44
Neal Broten, Minnesota	80	29	76	105	47
11. Michel Goulet, Quebec	75	53	51	104	64
12. Glenn Anderson, Edmonton	72	54	48	102	90
Bernie Federko, St. Louis	80	34	68	102	34
14. Troy Murray, Chicago	80	45	54	99	94
15. Brian Propp, Philadelphia	72	40	57	97	47
Bernie Nicholls, Los Angeles	80	36	61	97	78
17. Bryan Trottier, New York Islanders	78	37	59	96	72
18. Marcel Dionne, Los Angeles	80	36	58	94	42
19. Joe Mullen, St. Louis-Calgary	77	44	46	90	21
20. Dino Ciccarelli, Minnesota	75	44	45	89	51

National Hockey League Team-by-Team Individual Scoring

*Indicates league-leading figure.

Boston Bruins

	Games	G.	A.	Pts	Pen.
Keith Crowder	78	38	46	84	177
Ken Linseman	64	23	58	81	97
Barry Pederson	79	29	47	76	60
Ray Bourque	74	19	57	76	68
Reed Larson, Detroit	67	19	41	60	109
Boston	13	3	4	7	8
Totals	80	22	45	67	117
Charlie Simmer	55	36	24	60	42
Rick Middleton	49	14	30	44	10
Randy Burridge	52	17	25	42	28
Steve Kasper	80	17	23	40	73
Gord Kluzak	70	8	31	39	155
Geoff Courtnall	64	21	16	37	61
Dave Pasin	71	18	19	37	50
Kraig Nienhuis	70	16	14	30	37
Michael Thelven	60	6	20	26	48
Nevin Markwart	65	7	15	22	207
Dave Reid	37	10	10	20	10
Dwight Foster, Detroit	55	6	12	18	48
Boston	13	0	0	0	4
Totals	68	6	12	18	52
John Blum	61	1	7	8	80
Mike Milbury	22	2	5	7	102
Brian Curran	43	2	5	7	192
Louis Sleigher	13	4	2	6	20
Alain Cote	32	0	6	6	14
Mats Thelin	31	2	3	5	29
Jay Miller	46	3	0	3	178
Lyndon Byers	5	0	2	2	9
Greg Johnston	20	0	2	2	0
Frank Simonetti	17	1	0	1	14
Doug Keans (Goalie)	30	0	1	1	12
Wade Campbell, Winnipeg	24	0	1	1	27
Boston	8	0	0	0	15
Totals	32	0	1	1	42
Cleon Daskalakis (Goalie)	2	0	0	0	0
John Carter	3	0	0	0	0
Bill Ranford (Goalie)	4	0	0	0	0
Dave Donnelly	8	0	0	0	17
Pat Riggin, Washington (Goalie)	7	0	0	0	2
Boston (Goalie)	39	0	0	0	4
Totals	46	0	0	0	0

Buffalo Sabres

	Games	G.	A.	Pts	Pen.
Dave Andreychuk	80	36	51	87	61
Mike Foligno	79	41	39	80	168
John Tucker	75	31	34	65	39
Phil Housley	79	15	47	62	54
Gilbert Perreault	72	21	39	60	28
Paul Cyr	71	20	31	51	120
Gilles Hamel	77	19	25	44	61
Doug Smith, Los Angeles	48	8	9	17	56
Buffalo	30	10	11	21	73
Totals	78	18	20	38	129
Lindy Ruff	54	20	12	32	158
Mike Ramsey	76	7	21	28	117
Hannu Virta	47	5	23	28	16
Gates Orlando	60	13	12	25	29

Buffalo Sabres center Dave Andreychuk.

	Games	G.	A.	Pts.	Pen.
Ric Seiling	69	12	13	25	74
Steve Dykstra	64	4	21	25	108
Brian Engblom, Los Angeles	49	3	13	16	61
Buffalo	30	1	4	5	16
Totals	79	4	17	21	77
Bill Hajt	58	1	16	17	25
Normand Lacombe	25	6	7	13	13
Pat Hughes	50	4	9	13	25
Phil Russell, New Jersey	30	2	3	5	51
Buffalo	12	2	3	5	12
Totals	42	4	6	10	63
Mikael Andersson	32	1	9	10	4
Bob Halkidis	37	1	9	10	115
Richie Dunn	29	4	5	9	25
Don Lever	29	7	1	8	6
Dave Fenyves	47	0	7	7	37
Jody Gage	7	3	2	5	0
Tom Barrasso (Goalie)	60	0	4	4	28
Chris Langevin	16	2	1	3	20
Mal Davis	7	2	0	2	4
Adam Creighton	19	1	1	2	2
Jacques Cloutier (Goalie)	15	0	2	2	2
Paul Gardner	2	0	0	0	0
Richard Hajdu	3	0	0	0	4
Joe Reekie	3	0	0	0	14
Jim Hofford	5	0	0	0	5
Daren Puppa (Goalie)	7	0	0	0	0

Calgary Flames

	Games	G.	A.	Pts.	Pen.
Joe Mullen, St. Louis	48	28	24	52	10
Calgary	29	16	22	38	11
Totals	77	44	46	90	21
Dan Quinn	78	30	42	72	44
Lanny McDonald	80	28	43	71	44
John Tonelli, N.Y. Islanders	65	20	41	61	50
Calgary	9	3	4	7	10
Totals	74	23	45	68	60
Gary Suter	80	18	50	68	141
Al MacInnis	77	11	57	68	76
Hakan Loob	68	31	36	67	36
Joel Otto	79	25	34	59	188
Jim Peplinski	77	24	35	59	214
Carey Wilson	76	29	29	58	24
Steve Bozek	64	21	22	43	24
Doug Risebrough	62	15	28	43	169
Perry Berezan	55	12	21	33	39
Paul Reinhart	32	8	25	33	15
Jamie Macoun	77	11	21	32	81
Colin Patterson	61	14	13	27	22
Neil Sheehy	65	2	16	18	271
Tim Hunter	66	8	7	15	291
Terry Johnson, St. Louis	49	0	4	4	87
Calgary	24	1	4	5	71
Totals	73	1	8	9	158
Paul Baxter	47	4	3	7	194
Rik Wilson, St. Louis	32	0	4	4	48
Calgary	2	0	0	0	0
Totals	34	0	4	4	48
Rejean Lemelin (Goalie)	60	0	4	4	10
Yves Courteau	4	1	1	2	0
Brian Bradley	5	0	1	1	0
Nick Fotiu	9	0	1	1	21
Mike Vernon (Goalie)	18	0	1	1	4
Robin Bartel	1	0	0	0	0
Dale Degray	1	0	0	0	0
Mark Lamb	1	0	0	0	0
Marc D'Amour (Goalie)	15	0	0	0	22

Calgary Flames center Dan Quinn.

Chicago Black Hawks

	Games	G.	A.	Pts.	Pen.
Denis Savard	80	47	69	116	111
Troy Murray	80	45	54	99	94
Ed Olczyk	79	29	50	79	47
Al Secord	80	40	36	76	201
Steve Larmer	80	31	45	76	47
Curt Fraser	61	29	39	68	84
Doug Wilson	79	17	47	64	80
Behn Wilson	69	13	38	51	113
Keith Brown	70	11	29	40	87
Bob Murray	80	9	29	38	75
Ken Yaremchuk	78	14	20	34	43
Darryl Sutter	50	17	10	27	44
Bill Watson	52	8	16	24	2
Jack O'Callahan	80	4	19	23	116
Tom Lysiak	51	2	19	21	14
Wayne Presley	38	7	8	15	38
Jerome Dupont	75	2	13	15	173
Marc Bergevin	71	7	7	14	60
Rick Paterson	70	9	3	12	24
Steve Ludzik	49	6	5	11	21
Murray Bannerman (Goalie)	48	0	2	2	6
Bruce Boudreau	7	1	0	1	2
Bob Sauve (Goalie)	38	0	1	1	27
Bruce Cassidy	1	0	0	0	0
Warren Skorodenski (Goalie)	1	0	0	0	0
Jeff Larmer	2	0	0	0	0
Mark LaVarre	2	0	0	0	0
Victor Posa	2	0	0	0	2
Tom McMurchy	4	0	0	0	2

Detroit Red Wings

	Games	G.	A.	Pts.	Pen.
Doug Shedden, Pittsburgh	67	32	34	66	32
Detroit	11	2	3	5	2
Totals	78	34	37	71	34
John Ogrodnick	76	38	32	70	18
Kelly Kisio	76	21	48	69	85
Petr Klima	74	32	24	56	16
Warren Young	79	22	24	46	161
Steve Yzerman	51	14	28	42	16
Gerard Gallant	52	20	19	39	106
Mike O'Connell, Boston	63	8	21	29	47
Detroit	13	1	7	8	16
Totals	76	9	28	37	63
Claude Loiselle	48	7	15	22	142
Chris Cichocki	59	10	11	21	21
Bob Probert	44	8	13	21	186
Adam Oates	38	9	11	20	10
Randy Ladouceur	78	5	13	18	196
Darren Veitch, Washington	62	3	9	12	27
Detroit	13	0	5	5	2
Totals	75	3	14	17	29
Danny Gare	57	7	9	16	102
Joey Kocur	59	9	6	15	*377
Jim Leavins	37	2	11	13	26
Billy Carroll, Edmonton	5	0	2	2	0
Detroit	21	2	4	6	11
Totals	26	2	6	8	11
Harold Snepsts	35	0	6	6	75
Lane Lambert	34	2	3	5	130
Steve Richmond, N.Y. Rangers	17	0	2	2	63
Detroit	29	1	2	3	82
Totals	46	1	4	5	145
Tim Friday	23	0	3	3	6
Ted Speers	4	1	1	2	0

Chicago Black Hawks center Troy Murray.

	Games	G.	A.	Pts.	Pen.
Glenn Merkosky	17	0	2	2	0
Greg Stefan (Goalie)	37	0	2	2	23
Ed Johnstone	3	1	0	1	2
Shawn Burr	5	1	0	1	4
Bruce Eakin	4	0	1	1	0
Ray Staszak	4	0	1	1	7
Rick Zombo	14	0	1	1	16
Ed Mio (Goalie)	18	0	1	1	17
Chris Pusey (Goalie)	1	0	0	0	0
Basil McRae	4	0	0	0	5
Doug Houda	6	0	0	0	4
Corrado Micalef (Goalie)	11	0	0	0	8
Barry Melrose	14	0	0	0	70
Mark Laforest (Goalie)	28	0	0	0	23

Edmonton Oilers

	Games	G.	A.	Pts.	Pen.
Wayne Gretzky	80	52	*163	*215	46
Paul Coffey	79	48	90	138	120
Jari Kurri	78	*68	63	131	22
Glenn Anderson	72	54	48	102	90
Mark Messier	63	35	49	84	68
Mark Napier	80	24	32	56	14
Craig MacTavish	74	23	24	47	70
Charlie Huddy	76	6	35	41	55
Mike Krushelnyski	54	16	24	40	22
Raimo Summanen	73	19	18	37	16
Dave Hunter	62	15	22	37	77
Kevin McClelland	79	11	25	36	266
Randy Gregg	64	2	26	28	47
Lee Fogolin	80	4	22	26	129
Steve Smith	55	4	20	24	166
Marty McSorley	59	11	12	23	265
Dave Lumley	46	11	9	20	35
Dave Semenko	69	6	12	18	141
Kevin Lowe	74	2	16	18	90
Esa Tikkanen	35	7	6	13	28
Don Jackson	45	2	8	10	93
Mike Rogers, N.Y. Rangers	9	1	3	4	2
Edmonton	8	1	0	1	0
Totals	17	2	3	5	2
Gord Sherven, Minnesota	13	0	2	2	11
Edmonton	5	1	1	2	4
Totals	18	1	3	4	15
Risto Jalo	3	0	3	3	0
Grant Fuhr (Goalie)	40	0	2	2	0
Andy Moog (Goalie)	47	0	2	2	8
Ken Solheim	6	1	0	1	5
Jeff Brubaker, Toronto	21	0	0	0	67
Edmonton	4	1	0	1	12
Totals	25	1	0	1	79
Dean Hopkins	1	0	0	0	0
Mike Moller	1	0	0	0	0
Selmar Odelein	4	0	0	0	0

Hartford Whalers

	Games	G.	A.	Pts.	Pen.
Sylvain Turgeon	76	45	34	79	88
Ray Ferraro	76	30	47	77	57
Ron Francis	53	24	53	77	24
John Anderson, Quebec	65	21	28	49	26
Hartford	14	8	17	25	2
Totals	79	29	45	74	28
Dave Babych, Winnipeg	19	4	12	16	14
Hartford	62	10	43	53	36
Totals	81	14	55	69	50

Hartford Whalers left wing Sylvain Turgeon.

	Games	G.	A.	Pts.	Pen.
Kevin Dineen	57	33	35	68	124
Stewart Gavin	76	26	29	55	51
Dean Evason	55	20	28	48	65
Wayne Babych, Pittsburgh	2	0	0	0	0
Quebec	15	6	5	11	18
Hartford	37	11	17	28	59
Totals	54	17	22	39	77
Paul Lawless	64	17	21	38	20
Torrie Robertson	76	13	24	37	358
Dave Tippett	80	14	20	34	18
Doug Jarvis, Washington	25	1	2	3	16
Hartford	57	8	16	24	20
Totals	82	9	18	27	36
Dana Murzyn	78	3	23	26	125
Joel Quenneville	71	5	20	25	83
Ulf Samuelsson	80	5	19	24	174
Paul MacDermid	74	13	10	23	160
Mike McEwen, Detroit	29	0	10	10	16
N.Y. Rangers	16	2	5	7	8
Hartford	10	3	2	5	6
Totals	55	5	17	22	30
Bill Gardner, Chicago	46	3	10	13	6
Hartford	18	1	8	9	4
Totals	64	4	18	22	10
Tim Bothwell	62	2	8	10	53
Scot Kleinendorst	41	2	7	9	62
Mike Hoffman	6	1	2	3	2
Brad Shaw	8	0	2	2	4
Mike Zuke	17	0	2	2	12
Mike Liut (Goalie)	57	0	2	2	0
Steve Weeks (Goalie)	27	0	1	1	9
Paul Fenton	1	0	0	0	0
Sylvain Cote	2	0	0	0	0
John Newberry	3	0	0	0	0
Mark Paterson	5	0	0	0	5
Jack Brownschidle	9	0	0	0	4

Los Angeles Kings

	Games	G.	A.	Pts.	Pen.
Bernie Nicholls	80	36	61	97	78
Marcel Dionne	80	36	58	94	42
Dave Taylor	76	33	38	71	110
Dave Williams	72	20	29	49	320
Phil Sykes	76	20	24	44	97
Bryan Erickson	55	20	23	43	36
Jay Wells	79	11	31	42	226
Grant Ledyard, N.Y. Rangers	27	2	9	11	20
Los Angeles	52	7	18	25	78
Totals	79	9	27	36	98
Jim Fox	39	14	17	31	2
Joe Paterson, Philadelphia	5	0	0	0	12
Los Angeles	47	9	18	27	153
Totals	52	9	18	27	165
Mark Hardy	55	6	21	27	71
Morris Lukowich, Boston	14	1	4	5	10
Los Angeles	55	11	9	20	51
Totals	69	12	13	25	61
Craig Redmond	73	6	18	24	57
Sean McKenna, Buffalo	45	6	12	18	28
Los Angeles	30	4	0	4	7
Totals	75	10	12	22	35
Garry Galley	49	9	13	22	46
John Paul Kelly	61	6	9	15	50
Brian Wilks	43	4	8	12	25
Dean Kennedy	78	2	10	12	132
Paul Guay	23	3	3	6	18
Len Hachborn	24	4	1	5	2

Los Angeles Kings center Bernie Nicholls.

	Games	G.	A.	Pts.	Pen.
Anders Hakansson	38	4	1	5	8
Bob Mongrain	11	2	3	5	2
Larry Playfair	47	1	2	3	100
Los Angeles	14	0	1	1	28
Totals	61	1	3	4	128
Rick LaPointe	20	0	4	4	18
Glen Currie	12	1	2	3	9
Bob Janecyk (Goalie)	38	0	2	2	11
Craig Duncanson	2	0	1	1	0
Ken Hammond	3	0	1	1	2
Dan Brennan	6	0	1	1	9
Lyle Phair	15	0	1	1	2
Darren Eliot (Goalie)	27	0	1	1	4
Roland Melanson, Minnesota (Goalie)	6	0	0	0	0
Los Angeles (Goalie)	22	0	1	1	8
Totals	28	0	1	1	8
Allan Tuer	45	0	1	1	150
Glenn Healy (Goalie)	1	0	0	0	0
Dave Gans	3	0	0	0	2

Minnesota North Stars

	Games	G.	A.	Pts.	Pen.
Neal Broten	80	29	76	105	47
Dino Ciccarelli	75	44	45	89	51
Brian Bellows	77	31	48	79	46
Scott Bjugstad	80	43	33	76	24
Kent Nilsson	61	16	44	60	10
Keith Acton	79	26	32	58	100
Dennis Maruk	70	21	37	58	67
Craig Hartsburg	75	10	47	57	127
Dirk Graham	80	22	33	55	87
Tony McKegney	70	15	25	40	48
Brian Lawton	65	18	17	35	36
Curt Giles	69	6	21	27	30
Tom McCarthy	25	12	12	24	12
Gordie Roberts	76	2	21	23	101
Willi Plett	59	10	7	17	231
Bob Rouse	75	1	14	15	151
Steve Payne	22	8	4	12	8
Dave Langevin	80	0	8	8	58
Ed Hospodar, Philadelphia	17	3	1	4	55
Minnesota	43	0	2	2	91
Totals	60	3	3	6	146
Mats Hallin	38	3	2	5	86
Marc Habscheid	6	2	3	5	0
Craig Levie	14	2	2	4	8
Tim Coulis	19	2	2	4	73
Ron Wilson	11	1	3	4	8
Bill Stewart	8	0	2	2	13
Paul Houck	3	1	0	1	0
Emanuel Viveiros	4	0	1	1	0
Chris Pryor	7	0	1	1	0
Larry DePalma	1	0	0	0	0
Randy Smith	1	0	0	0	0
Kari Takko (Goalie)	1	0	0	0	0
Dan Mandich	3	0	0	0	25
Dave Jensen	5	0	0	0	7
Jim Archibald	11	0	0	0	32
Jon Casey (Goalie)	26	0	0	0	6
Don Beaupre (Goalie)	52	0	0	0	34

Montreal Canadiens

	Games	G.	A.	Pts.	Pen.
Mats Naslund	80	43	67	110	16
Bobby Smith	79	31	55	86	55
Larry Robinson	78	19	63	82	39

Minnesota North Stars center Neal Broten.

	Games	G.	A.	Pts.	Pen.
Kjell Dahlin	77	32	39	71	4
Guy Carbonneau	80	20	36	56	57
Ryan Walter	69	15	34	49	45
Bob Gainey	80	20	23	43	20
Mike McPhee	70	19	21	40	69
Mario Tremblay	56	19	20	39	55
Stephane Richer	65	21	16	37	50
Chris Nilan	72	19	15	34	274
Chris Chelios	41	8	26	34	67
Lucien DeBlois	61	14	17	31	48
Tom Kurvers	62	7	23	30	36
Gaston Gingras	34	8	18	26	12
Brian Skrudland	65	9	13	22	57
Petr Svoboda	73	1	18	19	93
Sergio Momesso	24	8	7	15	46
Mike Lalor	62	3	5	8	56
Randy Bucyk	17	4	2	6	8
Craig Ludwig	69	2	4	6	63
Rick Green	46	3	2	5	20
Steve Rooney	38	2	3	5	114
Serge Boisvert	9	2	2	4	2
Claude Lemieux	10	1	2	3	22
Patrick Roy (Goalie)	47	0	3	3	4
John Kordic	5	0	1	1	12
Dom Campedelli	2	0	0	0	0
Alfie Turcotte	2	0	0	0	2
Shayne Corson	3	0	0	0	2
David Maley	3	0	0	0	0
Steve Penney (Goalie)	18	0	0	0	0
Doug Soetaert (Goalie)	23	0	0	0	6

New Jersey Devils

	Games	G.	A.	Pts.	Pen.
Greg Adams	78	35	42	77	30
Kirk Muller	77	25	41	66	45
Mel Bridgman	78	23	40	63	80
Mark Johnson	80	21	41	62	16
John MacLean	74	21	36	57	112
Pat Verbeek	76	25	28	53	79
Doug Sulliman	73	21	22	43	20
Peter McNab	71	19	24	43	14
Aaron Broten	66	18	25	43	26
Rich Preston	76	19	22	41	65
Paul Gagne	47	19	19	38	14
Joe Cirella	66	6	23	29	147
Tim Higgins	59	9	17	26	47
Uli Hiemer	50	8	16	24	61
Dave Pichette	33	7	12	19	22
Perry Anderson	51	7	12	19	91
Bruce Driver	40	3	15	18	32
Craig Wolanin	44	2	16	18	74
Dave Lewis	69	0	15	15	81
Jan Ludvig	42	5	9	14	63
Ken Daneyko	44	0	10	10	100
Randy Velischek	47	2	7	9	39
Bob Lorimer	46	2	2	4	52
Alain Chevrier (Goalie)	37	0	3	3	0
Dan Dorion	3	1	1	2	0
Pat Conacher	2	0	2	2	2
Don Dietrich	11	0	2	2	10
Craig Billington (Goalie)	18	0	1	1	0
Murray Brumwell	1	0	0	0	0
Alan Hepple	1	0	0	0	0
Kirk McLean (Goalie)	2	0	0	0	0
Sam St. Laurent (Goalie)	4	0	0	0	0
Allan Stewart	4	0	0	0	21

New Jersey Devils left wing Kirk Muller.

New York Islanders

	Games	G.	A.	Pts.	Pen.
Mike Bossy	80	61	62	123	14
Bryan Trottier	78	37	59	96	72
Denis Potvin	74	21	38	59	78
Brent Sutter	61	24	31	55	74
Pat LaFontaine	65	30	23	53	43
Duane Sutter	80	20	33	53	157
Pat Flatley	73	18	34	52	66
Tomas Jonsson	77	14	30	44	62
Rich Kromm, Calgary	63	12	17	29	31
N.Y. Islanders	14	7	7	14	4
Totals	77	19	24	43	35
Mikko Makela	58	16	20	36	28
Paul Boutilier	77	4	30	34	100
Bob Bourne	62	17	15	32	36
Steve Konroyd, Calgary	59	7	20	27	64
N.Y. Islanders	14	0	5	5	16
Totals	73	7	25	32	80
Greg Gilbert	60	9	19	28	82
Stefan Persson	56	1	19	20	40
Mark Hamway	49	5	12	17	9
Clark Gillies	55	4	10	14	55
Randy Boyd	55	2	12	14	79
Roger Kortko	52	5	8	13	19
Ken Morrow	69	0	12	12	22
Gord Dineen	57	1	8	9	81
Neal Coulter	16	3	4	7	4
Ari Haanpaa	18	0	7	7	20
Dale Henry	7	1	3	4	15
Bob Bassen	11	2	1	3	6
Gerald Diduck	10	1	2	3	2
Scott Howson	10	1	2	3	2
Billy Smith (Goalie)	41	0	3	3	49
Kelly Hrudey (Goalie)	45	0	3	3	14
Ken Leiter	9	1	1	2	6
Bob Nystrom	14	1	1	2	16
Brad Dalgarno	2	1	0	1	0
Alan Kerr	7	0	1	1	16
Glen Johannesen	2	0	0	0	0

New York Rangers

	Games	G.	A.	Pts.	Pen.
Mike Ridley	80	22	43	65	69
Reijo Ruotsalainen	80	17	42	59	47
Tomas Sandstrom	73	25	29	54	109
Ron Greschner	78	20	28	48	104
Brian MacLellan, Los Angeles	27	5	8	13	19
N.Y. Rangers	51	11	21	32	47
Totals	78	16	29	45	66
Bob Brooke	79	24	20	44	111
James Patrick	75	14	29	43	88
Mark Pavelich	59	20	20	40	82
Mark Osborne	62	16	24	40	80
Raimo Helminen	66	10	30	40	10
Bob Crawford, Hartford	57	14	20	34	16
N.Y. Rangers	11	1	2	3	10
Totals	68	15	22	37	26
Kelly Miller	74	13	20	33	52
Don Maloney	68	11	17	28	56
Pierre Larouche	28	20	7	27	4
Wilf Paiement, Quebec	44	7	12	19	145
N.Y. Rangers	8	1	6	7	13
Totals	52	8	18	26	158
Peter Sundstrom	53	8	15	23	12
Jan Erixon	31	2	17	19	4
Tom Laidlaw	68	6	12	18	103

New York Rangers defenseman Reijo Ruotsalainen.

	Games	G.	A.	Pts.	Pen.
Willie Huber	70	7	8	15	85
Mike Allison	28	2	13	15	22
Larry Melnyk, Edmonton	6	2	3	5	11
N.Y. Rangers	46	1	8	9	65
Totals	52	3	11	14	76
Barry Beck	25	4	8	12	24
Dave Gagner	32	4	6	10	19
George McPhee	30	4	4	8	63
Rob Whistle	32	4	2	6	10
Chris Jensen	9	1	3	4	0
Jim Wiemer	7	3	0	3	2
John Vanbiesbrouck (Goalie)	61	0	3	3	16
Randy Heath	1	0	1	1	0
Glen Hanlon (Goalie)	23	0	1	1	4
Terry Kleisinger (Goalie)	4	0	0	0	2
Ron Scott (Goalie)	4	0	0	0	0
Kjell Samuelsson	9	0	0	0	10
Tony Feltrin	10	0	0	0	21

Philadelphia Flyers

	Games	G.	A.	Pts.	Pen.
Brian Propp	72	40	57	97	47
Tim Kerr	76	58	26	84	79
Mark Howe	77	24	58	82	36
Ilkka Sinisalo	74	39	37	76	31
Dave Poulin	79	27	42	69	49
Per-Erik Eklund	70	15	51	66	12
Ron Sutter	75	18	41	59	159
Brad McCrimmon	80	13	43	56	85
Murray Craven	78	21	33	54	34
Peter Zezel	79	17	37	54	76
Doug Crossman	80	6	37	43	55
Rich Sutter	78	14	25	39	199
Rick Tocchet	69	14	21	35	284
Lindsay Carson	50	9	12	21	84
Dave Brown	76	10	7	17	277
Brad Marsh	79	0	13	13	123
Derrick Smith	69	6	6	12	57
Dave Richter, Minnesota	14	0	3	3	29
Philadelphia	50	0	2	2	138
Totals	64	0	5	5	167
Bo Berglund, Minnesota	3	2	0	2	2
Philadelphia	7	0	2	2	4
Totals	10	2	2	4	6
Thomas Eriksson	43	0	4	4	16
Don Nachbaur	5	1	1	2	7
Darryl Stanley	33	0	2	2	69
Mike Stothers	6	0	1	1	6
Darren Jensen (Goalie)	29	0	1	1	2
Bob Froese (Goalie)	51	0	1	1	8
Carl Mokosak	1	0	0	0	5
Ross Fitzpatrick	2	0	0	0	0
Scott Mellanby	2	0	0	0	0
Steve Smith	2	0	0	0	2
Kevin McCarthy	4	0	0	0	4
Pelle Lindbergh (Goalie)	8	0	0	0	0
Glenn Resch, New Jersey (Goalie)	31	0	0	0	14
Philadelphia (Goalie)	5	0	0	0	0
Totals	36	0	0	0	14

Pittsburgh Penguins

	Games	G.	A.	Pts.	Pen.
Mario Lemieux	79	48	93	141	43
Mike Bullard	77	41	42	83	69
Moe Mantha	78	15	52	67	102
Terry Ruskowski	73	26	37	63	162

Philadelphia Flyers left wing Brian Propp.

	Games	G.	A.	Pts.	Pen.
Ron Duguay, Detroit	67	19	29	48	26
Pittsburgh	13	6	7	13	6
Totals	80	25	36	61	32
Randy Cunneyworth	75	15	30	45	74
John Chabot	77	14	31	45	6
Doug Bodger	79	4	33	37	63
Dave Hannan	75	17	18	35	91
Willy Lindstrom	71	14	17	31	30
Mike Blaisdell	66	15	14	29	36
Norm Schmidt	66	15	14	29	57
Jim Johnson	80	3	26	29	115
Craig Simpson	76	11	17	28	49
Dan Frawley	69	10	11	21	174
Bob Errey	37	11	6	17	8
Ville Siren	60	4	8	12	32
Troy Loney	47	3	9	12	95
Rod Buskas	72	2	7	9	159
Jim McGeough	17	3	2	5	8
Chris Dahlquist	5	1	2	3	2
Tom O'Regan	9	1	2	3	2
Randy Hillier	28	0	3	3	53
Ted Nolan	18	1	1	2	34
Dwight Mathiason	4	1	0	1	2
Todd Charlesworth	2	0	1	1	0
Gilles Meloche (Goalie)	34	0	1	1	2
Roberto Romano (Goalie)	46	0	1	1	4
Denis Herron (Goalie)	3	0	0	0	0
Joe McDonnell	3	0	0	0	2
Mike Rowe	3	0	0	0	4
Phil Bourque	4	0	0	0	2
Tom Roulston	5	0	0	0	2

Quebec Nordiques

	Games	G.	A.	Pts.	Pen.
Peter Stastny	76	41	81	122	60
Michel Goulet	75	53	51	104	64
Anton Stastny	74	31	43	74	19
Dale Hunter	90	28	42	70	265
Brent Ashton	77	26	32	58	64
J.F. Sauve	75	16	40	56	20
Paul Gillis	80	19	24	43	203
Robert Picard, Winnipeg	20	2	5	7	17
Quebec	48	7	27	34	36
Totals	68	9	32	41	53
Risto Siltanen, Hartford	52	8	22	30	30
Quebec	13	2	5	7	6
Totals	65	10	27	37	36
Alain Cote	78	13	21	34	29
Peter Andersson, Washington	61	6	16	22	36
Quebec	12	1	8	9	4
Totals	73	7	24	31	40
David Shaw	73	7	19	26	78
Steve Patrick, N.Y. Rangers	28	4	3	7	37
Quebec	27	4	13	17	17
Totals	55	8	16	24	54
Mike Eagles	73	11	12	23	49
Randy Moller	69	5	18	23	141
Mark Kumpel	47	10	12	22	17
Greg Malone, Hartford	22	6	7	13	24
Quebec	27	3	5	8	18
Totals	49	9	12	21	42
Gilbert Delorme	64	2	18	20	51
Pat Price	54	3	13	16	82
Normand Rochefort	26	5	4	9	30
Daniel Poudrier	13	1	5	6	10
Jeff Brown	8	3	2	5	6
Gord Donnelly	36	2	2	4	85

Quebec Nordiques left wing Anton Stastny.

	Games	G.	A.	Pts.	Pen.
Mario Gosselin (Goalie)	31	0	3	3	2
Jimmy Mann	35	0	3	3	148
Clint Malarchuk (Goalie)	46	0	2	2	21
Jean Marc Gaulin	1	1	0	1	0
Trevor Stienburg	2	1	0	1	0
Claude Julien	13	0	1	1	25
Steven Finn	17	0	1	1	28
Dave Latta	1	0	0	0	0
Alain Lemieux	7	0	0	0	2
Richard Sevigny (Goalie)	11	0	0	0	8

St. Louis Blues

	Games	G.	A.	Pts.	Pen.
Bernie Federko	80	34	68	102	34
Mark Hunter	78	44	30	74	171
Ron Flockhart	79	22	45	67	26
Rob Ramage	77	10	56	66	171
Doug Gilmour	74	25	28	53	41
Dave Barr	72	13	38	51	70
Brian Sutter	44	19	23	42	87
Eddy Beers, Calgary	33	11	10	21	8
St. Louis	24	7	11	18	24
Totals	57	18	21	39	32
Kevin LaVallee	64	18	20	38	8
Mark Reeds	78	10	28	38	28
Greg Paslawski	56	22	11	33	18
Rick Meagher	79	11	19	30	28
Lee Norwood	71	5	24	29	134
Gino Cavallini, Calgary	27	7	7	14	26
St. Louis	30	6	5	11	36
Totals	57	13	12	25	62
Ric Nattress	78	4	20	24	52
Bruce Bell	75	2	18	20	43
Doug Wickenheiser	36	8	11	19	16
Charles Bourgeois, Calgary	29	5	5	10	128
St. Louis	31	2	7	9	116
Totals	60	7	12	19	244
Jim Pavese	69	4	7	11	116
Denis Cyr	31	3	4	7	2
Kent Carlson, Montreal	2	0	0	0	0
St. Louis	26	2	3	5	42
Totals	28	2	3	5	42
Normand Baron	23	2	0	2	39
Doug Evans	13	1	0	1	2
Darrell May (Goalie)	3	0	1	1	2
Greg Millen (Goalie)	36	0	1	1	8
Mike Posavad	6	0	0	0	0
Shawn Evans	7	0	0	0	2
Herb Raglan	7	0	0	0	5
Rick Wamsley (Goalie)	42	0	0	0	2

Toronto Maple Leafs

	Games	G.	A.	Pts.	Pen.
Miroslav Frycer	73	32	43	75	74
Tom Fergus	78	31	42	73	64
Rick Vaive	61	33	31	64	85
Russ Courtnall	73	22	38	60	52
Steve Thomas	65	20	37	57	36
Marian Stastny	70	23	30	53	21
Wendel Clark	66	34	11	45	227
Peter Ihnacak	63	18	27	45	16
Walt Poddubny	33	12	22	34	25
Al Iafrate	65	8	25	33	40
Greg Terrion	76	10	22	32	31
Gary Leeman	53	9	23	32	20
Brad Maxwell	52	8	18	26	108

St. Louis Blues right wing Mark Hunter.

	Games	G.	A.	Pts.	Pen.
Dan Hodgson	40	13	12	25	12
Jim Benning	52	4	21	25	71
Borje Salming	41	7	15	22	48
Brad Smith	42	5	17	22	84
Dan Daoust	80	7	13	20	88
Gary Nylund	79	2	16	18	180
Chris Kotsopoulos	61	6	11	17	83
Gary McAdam	15	1	6	7	0
Miroslav Ihnacak	21	2	4	6	27
Bob McGill	61	1	4	5	141
Jeff Jackson	5	1	2	3	2
Todd Gill	15	1	2	3	28
Wes Jarvis	2	1	0	1	2
Rich Costello	2	0	1	1	0
Craig Muni	6	0	1	1	4
Tim Bernhardt (Goalie)	23	0	1	1	0
Bill Root	27	0	1	1	29
Blake Wesley	27	0	1	1	21
Allan Bester (Goalie)	1	0	0	0	0
Rod Schutt	6	0	0	0	0
Ken Wregget (Goalie)	30	0	0	0	16
Don Edwards (Goalie)	38	0	0	0	4

Vancouver Canucks

	Games	G.	A.	Pts.	Pen.
Petri Skriko	80	38	40	78	34
Tony Tanti	77	39	33	72	85
Patrik Sundstrom	79	18	48	66	28
Stan Smyl	73	27	35	62	144
Rick Lanz	75	15	38	53	73
Thomas Gradin	71	14	27	41	34
Cam Neely	73	14	20	34	126
Doug Halward	70	8	25	33	111
Moe Lemay	48	16	15	31	92
Brent Peterson	77	8	23	31	94
Steve Tambellini	48	15	15	30	12
Jiri Bubla	43	6	24	30	30
Doug Lidster	78	12	16	28	56
J.J. Daigneault	64	5	23	28	45
Marc Crawford	54	11	14	25	92
Dave Lowry	73	10	8	18	143
Jean-Marc Lanthier	62	7	10	17	12
Garth Butcher	70	4	7	11	188
Taylor Hall	19	5	5	10	6
Craig Coxe	57	3	5	8	176
Michel Petit	32	1	6	7	27
Gary Lupul	19	4	1	5	12
Jim Sandlak	23	1	3	4	10
Neil Belland	7	1	2	3	4
Glen Cochrane	49	0	3	3	125
Richard Brodeur (Goalie)	64	0	2	2	16
Frank Caprice (Goalie)	7	0	1	1	0
David Bruce	12	0	1	1	14
Dale Dunbar	1	0	0	0	2
Wendell Young (Goalie)	22	0	0	0	0

Washington Capitals

	Games	G.	A.	Pts.	Pen.
Dave Christian	80	41	42	83	15
Mike Gartner	74	35	40	75	63
Craig Laughlin	75	30	45	75	43
Bengt Gustafsson	70	23	52	75	26
Alan Haworth	71	34	39	73	72
Larry Murphy	78	21	44	65	50
Bobby Carpenter	80	27	29	56	105
Greg Adams	78	18	38	56	152

Washington Capitals right wing Craig Laughlin.

	Games	G.	A.	Pts.	Pen.
Scott Stevens	73	15	38	53	165
Gaetan Duchesne	80	11	28	39	39
Bobby Gould	79	19	19	38	26
Jorgen Pettersson, Hartford	23	5	5	10	2
Washington	47	8	16	24	10
Totals	70	13	21	34	12
Greg Smith, Detroit	62	5	19	24	84
Washington	14	0	3	3	10
Totals	76	5	22	27	94
Lou Franceschetti	76	7	14	21	131
Kevin Hatcher	79	9	10	19	119
Rod Langway	71	1	17	18	61
John Barrett, Detroit	65	2	12	14	125
Washington	14	0	3	3	12
Totals	79	2	15	17	137
Gary Sampson	19	1	4	5	2
Mark Taylor	30	2	1	3	4
Dwight Schofield	50	1	2	3	127
Stephen Leach	11	1	1	2	2
Pete Peeters, Boston (Goalie)	8	0	2	2	4
Washington (Goalie)	34	0	0	0	8
Totals	42	0	2	2	12
Dave Jensen	5	1	0	1	0
Daryl Evans	6	0	1	1	0
Grant Martin	11	0	1	1	6
Al Jensen (Goalie)	44	0	1	1	4
Bob Mason (Goalie)	1	0	0	0	0
Yvon Corriveau	2	0	0	0	0
Yves Beaudoin	4	0	0	0	0
Ed Kastelic	15	0	0	0	73

Winnipeg Jets

	Games	G.	A.	Pts.	Pen.
Dale Hawerchuk	80	46	59	105	44
Laurie Boschman	77	27	42	69	241
Thomas Steen	78	17	47	64	76
Ray Neufeld, Hartford	16	5	10	15	40
Winnipeg	60	20	28	48	62
Totals	76	25	38	63	102
Brian Mullen	79	28	34	62	38
Paul MacLean	69	27	29	56	74
Perry Turnbull	80	20	31	51	183
Randy Carlyle	68	16	33	49	93
Dave Ellett	80	15	31	46	96
Mario Marois, Quebec	20	1	12	13	42
Winnipeg	56	4	28	32	110
Totals	76	5	40	45	152
Scott Arniel	80	18	25	43	40
Doug Smail	73	16	26	42	32
Bill Derlago, Toronto	1	0	0	0	0
Boston	39	5	16	21	15
Winnipeg	27	5	5	10	6
Totals	67	10	21	31	21
Tim Watters	56	6	8	14	97
Jim Nill	61	6	8	14	75
Ron Wilson	54	6	7	13	16
Bengt Lundholm	16	3	5	8	6
Andrew McBain	28	3	3	6	17
Dave Silk	32	2	4	6	63
Bobby Dollas	46	0	5	5	66
Jim Kyte	71	1	3	4	126
Anssi Melametsa	27	0	3	3	2
Brian Hayward (Goalie)	52	0	2	2	25
Ryan Stewart	3	1	0	1	0
Murray Eaves	4	1	0	1	0
Brad Berry	13	1	0	1	10
Paul Pooley	3	0	1	1	0

Winnipeg Jets center Laurie Boschman.

	Games	G.	A.	Pts.	Pen.
Dan McFall	7	0	1	1	0
Dan Bouchard (Goalie)	32	0	1	1	38
Tom Martin	5	0	0	0	0
Marc Behrend (Goalie)	9	0	0	0	0
Peter Douris	11	0	0	0	0
Peter Taglianetti	18	0	0	0	48

Complete Goaltending Records

	Games	Mins.	Goals	SO	Avg.
Bob Froese, Philadelphia	51	2728	116(1)	*5	*2.55
Pelle Lindbergh, Philadelphia	8	480	23	1	2.88
Glenn Resch, Philadelphia (a)	5	187	10	0	3.21
Darren Jensen, Philadelphia	29	1436	88(3)	2	3.68
PHILADELPHIA TOTALS	80	4831	241	8	2.99
Bob Mason, Washington	1	16	0	0	0.00
Al Jensen, Washington	44	2437	129(3)	2	3.18
Pete Peeters, Washington (b)	34	2021	113(3)	1	3.35
Pat Riggin, Washington (c)	7	369	23(1)	0	3.74
WASHINGTON TOTALS	80	4843	272	3	3.37
John Vanbiesbrouck, New York Rangers	61	3326	184(2)	3	3.32
Glen Hanlon, New York Rangers	23	1170	65	0	3.33
Ron Scott, New York Rangers	4	156	11	0	4.23
Terry Kleisinger, New York Rangers	4	191	14	0	4.40
NEW YORK RANGERS TOTALS	80	4843	276	3	3.42
Doug Soetaert, Montreal	23	1215	56(1)	3	2.77
Patrick Roy, Montreal	47	2651	148(3)	1	3.35
Steve Penney, Montreal	18	990	72	0	4.36
MONTREAL TOTALS	80	4856	280	4	3.46
Kelly Hrudey, New York Islanders	45	2563	137(2)	1	3.21
Billy Smith, New York Islanders	41	2308	143(2)	1	3.72
NEW YORK ISLANDERS TOTALS	80	4871	284	2	3.50
Bill Ranford, Boston	4	240	10	0	2.50
Pat Riggin, Boston (c)	39	2272	127(1)	1	3.35
Doug Keans, Boston	30	1757	107(1)	0	3.65
Pete Peeters, Boston (b)	8	485	31(1)	0	3.84
Cleon Daskalakis, Boston	2	120	10	0	5.00
BOSTON TOTALS	80	4874	288	1	3.55
Clint Malarchuk, Quebec	46	2657	142	4	3.21
Mario Gosselin, Quebec	31	1726	111(3)	2	3.86
Richard Sevigny, Quebec	11	468	33	0	4.23
QUEBEC TOTALS	80	4851	289	6	3.57
Rick Wamsley, St. Louis	42	2517	144	1	3.43
Greg Millen, St. Louis	36	2168	129(5)	1	3.57
Darrell May, St. Louis	3	184	13	0	4.24
ST. LOUIS TOTALS	80	4869	291	2	3.59
Daren Puppa, Buffalo	7	401	21	1	3.14
Jacques Cloutier, Buffalo	15	872	49(2)	1	3.37
Tom Barrasso, Buffalo	60	*3561	214(5)	2	3.61
BUFFALO TOTALS	80	4834	291	4	3.61
Mike Liut, Hartford	57	3282	198(3)	2	3.62
Steve Weeks, Hartford	27	1544	99(2)	1	3.85
HARTFORD TOTALS	80	4826	302	3	3.75
Kari Takko, Minnesota	1	60	3(1)	0	3.00
Don Beaupre, Minnesota	52	3073	182(2)	1	3.55
Jon Casey, Minnesota	26	1402	91(2)	0	3.89
Roland Melanson, Minnesota (d)	6	325	24	0	4.43
MINNESOTA TOTALS	80	4860	305	1	3.77
Roberto Romano, Pittsburgh	46	2684	159(6)	2	3.55
Gilles Meloche, Pittsburgh	34	1989	119(5)	0	3.59
Denis Herron, Pittsburgh	3	180	14(2)	0	4.67
PITTSBURGH TOTALS	80	4853	305	2	3.77

Flyers goalie Bob Froese helped pick up the pieces following Pelle Lindbergh's tragic death and led the league with five shutouts and a 2.55 goals-against average.

Player	GP	Min	GA	SO	Avg
Andy Moog, Edmonton	47	2664	164(2)	1	3.69
Grant Fuhr, Edmonton	40	2184	143(1)	0	3.93
EDMONTON TOTALS	80	4848	310	1	3.84
Mike Vernon, Calgary	18	921	52	1	3.39
Marc D'Amour, Calgary	15	560	32	0	3.43
Rejean Lemelin, Calgary	60	3369	229(2)	1	4.08
CALGARY TOTALS	80	4850	315	2	3.90
Wendell Young, Vancouver	22	1023	61(1)	0	3.58
Richard Brodeur, Vancouver	*64	3541	*240(3)	2	4.07
Frank Caprice, Vancouver	7	308	28	0	5.45
VANCOUVER TOTALS	80	4872	333	2	4.10
Bob Sauve, Chicago	38	2099	138(2)	0	3.94
Murray Bannerman, Chicago	48	2689	201(2)	1	4.48
Warren Skorodenski, Chicago	1	60	6	0	6.00
CHICAGO TOTALS	80	4848	349	1	4.32
Dan Bouchard, Winnipeg	32	1696	107(1)	2	3.79
Brian Hayward, Winnipeg	52	2721	217(5)	0	4.79
Marc Behrend, Winnipeg	9	422	41(1)	0	5.83
WINNIPEG TOTALS	80	4839	372	2	4.61
Sam St. Laurent, New Jersey	4	188	13	1	4.15
Glenn Resch, New Jersey (a)	31	1769	126(4)	0	4.27
Alain Chevrier, New Jersey	37	1863	143	0	4.61
Craig Billington, New Jersey	18	901	77	0	5.13
Kirk McLean, New Jersey	2	111	11	0	5.95
NEW JERSEY TOTALS	80	4832	374	1	4.64
Ken Wregget, Toronto	30	1566	113(3)	0	4.33
Don Edwards, Toronto	38	2009	160(1)	0	4.78
Tim Bernhardt, Toronto	23	1266	107	0	5.07
Allan Bester, Toronto	1	20	2	0	6.00
TORONTO TOTALS	80	4861	386	0	4.76
Roland Melanson, Los Angeles (d)	22	1246	87(8)	0	4.19
Bob Janecyk, Los Angeles	38	2083	162(2)	0	4.67
Darren Eliot, Los Angeles	27	1481	121(3)	0	4.90
Glenn Healy, Los Angeles	1	51	6	0	7.06
LOS ANGELES TOTALS	80	4861	389	0	4.80
Greg Stefan, Detroit	37	2068	155(3)	1	4.50
Chris Pusey, Detroit	1	40	3	0	4.50
Mark Laforest, Detroit	28	1383	114(5)	1	4.95
Corrado Micalef, Detroit	11	565	52	0	5.52
Ed Mio, Detroit	18	788	83	0	6.32
DETROIT TOTALS	80	4844	415	2	5.14

( )—Empty Net Goals. Do not count against an individual average.
(a)—Resch played for New Jersey and Philadelphia.
(b)—Peeters played for Boston and Washington.
(c)—Riggin played for Washington and Boston.
(d)—Melanson played for Minnesota and Los Angeles.

NHL Miscellaneous Statistics

(Players are listed alphabetically)

Player — Team	Games	Shots	Goals	Shooting Pct.	PPG	SHG	+/−
Keith Acton, Minnesota	79	169	26	15.4	5	0	− 11
Greg Adams, Washington	78	149	18	12.1	3	0	+ 24
Greg Adams, New Jersey	78	202	35	17.3	10	0	− 6
Mike Allison, N. Y. Rangers	28	26	2	7.7	0	0	+ 4
Glenn Anderson, Edmonton	72	243	54	22.2	18	2	+ 38
Mikael Andersson, Buffalo	33	13	1	7.7	0	0	Even
Perry Anderson, New Jersey	51	61	7	11.5	1	0	− 7
John Anderson, Quebec	65	190	21	11.1	8	3	− 1
Hartford	14	49	8	16.3	1	0	+ 17
Totals	79	239	29	12.1	9	3	+ 16
Peter Andersson, Washington	61	83	6	7.2	3	0	− 8
Quebec	12	16	1	6.3	1	0	+ 8
Totals	73	99	7	7.1	4	0	Even
Dave Andreychuk, Buffalo	80	225	36	16.0	12	0	+ 3
Jim Archibald, Minnesota	11	7	0	0.0	0	0	− 3
Scott Arniel, Winnipeg	80	125	18	14.4	3	0	− 8
Brent Ashton, Quebec	77	207	26	12.6	5	2	+ 7
Dave Babych, Winnipeg	19	53	4	7.5	2	0	− 1
Hartford	62	152	10	6.6	7	1	+ 1
Totals	81	205	14	6.8	9	1	Even
Wayne Babych, Pittsburgh	2	0	0	0.0	0	0	− 1
Quebec	15	32	6	18.8	1	0	Even
Hartford	37	65	11	16.9	2	0	+ 7
Totals	54	97	17	17.5	3	0	+ 6
Normand Baron, St. Louis	23	13	2	15.4	0	0	− 7
Dave Barr, St. Louis	75	106	13	12.3	0	0	+ 11
John Barrett, Detroit	65	60	2	3.3	0	0	− 29
Washington	14	7	0	0.0	0	0	+ 3
Totals	79	67	2	3.0	0	0	− 26
Robin Bartel, Calgary	1	0	0	0.0	0	0	− 1
Bob Bassen, N.Y. Islanders	11	5	2	40.0	0	0	Even
Paul Baxter, Calgary	47	41	4	9.8	0	1	+ 5
Yves Beaudoin, Washington	4	7	0	0.0	0	0	− 4
Barry Beck, N.Y. Rangers	25	53	4	7.5	3	0	+ 7
Eddy Beers, Calgary	33	83	11	13.3	4	0	− 3
St. Louis	24	53	7	13.2	4	0	− 3
Totals	57	136	18	13.2	8	0	− 6
Bruce Bell, St. Louis	75	96	2	2.1	2	0	+ 2
Neil Belland, Vancouver	7	10	1	10.0	1	0	− 2
Brian Bellows, Minnesota	77	256	31	12.1	11	0	+ 16
Jim Benning, Toronto	52	76	4	5.3	2	0	− 4
Perry Berezan, Calgary	55	117	12	10.3	0	2	+ 19
Marc Bergevin, Chicago	71	50	7	14.0	0	0	Even
Bo Berglund, Minnesota	3	6	2	33.3	1	0	Even
Philadelphia	7	5	0	0.0	0	0	Even
Totals	10	11	2	18.2	1	0	Even
Brad Berry, Winnipeg	13	2	1	50.0	0	0	+ 1
Scott Bjugstad, Minnesota	80	217	43	19.8	14	0	+ 5
Mike Blaisdell, Pittsburgh	66	125	15	12.0	0	0	+ 15
John Blum, Boston	61	34	1	2.9	0	0	+ 8
Doug Bodger, Pittsburgh	79	140	4	2.9	1	0	+ 3
Serge Boisvert, Montreal	9	18	2	11.1	0	0	+ 1
Laurie Boschman, Winnipeg	77	158	27	17.1	3	2	− 29
Mike Bossy, N.Y. Islanders	80	302	61	20.2	21	1	+ 30
Tim Bothwell, Hartford	62	50	2	4.0	0	0	+ 12
Bruce Boudreau, Chicago	7	3	1	33.3	0	0	+ 1
Charlie Bourgeois, Calgary	29	30	5	16.7	0	0	+ 9
St. Louis	31	34	2	5.9	1	0	+ 9
Totals	60	64	7	10.9	1	0	+ 18
Bob Bourne, N.Y. Islanders	62	100	17	17.0	2	0	− 7
Phil Bourque, Pittsburgh	4	0	0	0.0	0	0	− 2
Ray Bourque, Boston	74	289	19	6.6	11	0	+ 17
Paul Boutilier, N.Y. Islanders	77	124	4	3.2	0	0	− 5
Randy Boyd, N.Y. Islanders	55	52	2	3.8	0	0	+ 9
Steve Bozek, Calgary	64	146	21	14.4	5	4	+ 24
Brian Bradley, Calgary	5	4	0	0.0	0	0	− 3
Dan Brennan, Los Angeles	6	6	0	0.0	0	0	− 1

Player — Team	Games	Shots	Goals	Shooting Pct.	PPG	SHG	+/−
Mel Bridgman, New Jersey	78	136	23	16.9	5	1	+ 1
Bob Brooke, N.Y. Rangers	79	178	24	13.5	6	2	+ 6
Aaron Broten, New Jersey	66	157	19	12.1	4	0	+ 3
Neal Broten, Minnesota	80	193	29	15.0	6	0	+ 14
Dave Brown, Philadelphia	76	73	10	13.7	0	0	+ 7
Jeff Brown, Quebec	8	16	3	18.8	0	0	+ 5
Keith Brown, Chicago	70	151	11	7.3	1	1	− 6
Jack Brownschidle, Hartford	9	7	0	0.0	0	0	− 4
Jeff Brubaker, Toronto	21	8	0	0.0	0	0	Even
Edmonton	4	4	1	25.0	0	0	+ 1
Totals	25	12	1	8.3	0	0	+ 1
David Bruce, Vancouver	12	17	0	0.0	0	0	− 2
Murray Brumwell, New Jersey	1	3	0	0.0	0	0	− 1
Jiri Bubla, Vancouver	43	62	6	9.7	4	0	− 25
Randy Bucyk, Montreal	17	21	4	19.0	0	0	+ 5
Mike Bullard, Pittsburgh	77	213	41	19.2	16	2	− 16
Shawn Burr, Detroit	5	6	1	16.7	1	0	+ 1
Randy Burridge, Boston	52	90	17	18.9	1	0	+ 17
Rod Buskas, Pittsburgh	72	50	2	4.0	1	0	− 9
Garth Butcher, Vancouver	70	57	4	7.0	0	0	− 25
Lyndon Byers, Boston	5	1	0	0.0	0	0	+ 1
Wade Campbell, Winnipeg	24	13	0	0.0	0	0	− 12
Boston	8	0	0	0.0	0	0	+ 1
Totals	32	13	0	0.0	0	0	− 11
Dom Campedelli, Montreal	2	1	0	0.0	0	0	− 2
Guy Carbonneau, Montreal	80	147	20	13.6	1	2	+ 18
Kent Carlson, Montreal	2	0	0	0.0	0	0	Even
St. Louis	26	14	2	14.3	0	0	+ 2
Totals	28	14	2	14.3	0	0	+ 2
Randy Carlyle, Winnipeg	68	52	16	30.8	3	0	− 12
Bobby Carpenter, Washington	80	205	27	13.2	7	0	− 12
Billy Carroll, Edmonton	5	0	0	0.0	0	0	+ 2
Detroit	22	13	2	15.4	0	0	− 8
Totals	27	13	2	15.4	0	0	− 6
Lindsay Carson, Philadelphia	50	59	9	15.3	0	0	+ 10
John Carter, Boston	3	2	0	0.0	0	0	Even
Bruce Cassidy, Chicago	1	2	0	0.0	0	0	Even
Gino Cavallini, Calgary	27	51	7	13.7	4	0	− 7
St. Louis	30	44	6	13.6	1	0	− 2
Totals	57	95	13	13.7	5	0	− 9
John Chabot, Pittsburgh	77	89	14	15.7	1	2	− 1
Todd Charlesworth, Pittsburgh	2	1	0	0.0	0	0	− 1
Chris Chelios, Montreal	41	101	8	7.9	2	0	+ 4
Dave Christian, Washington	80	218	41	18.8	18	2	+ 3
Dino Ciccarelli, Minnesota	75	262	44	16.8	19	0	+ 12
Chris Cichocki, Detroit	59	76	10	13.2	1	1	− 8
Joe Cirella, New Jersey	66	89	6	6.7	2	0	− 12
Wendel Clark, Toronto	66	164	34	20.7	4	0	− 27
Glen Cochrane, Vancouver	49	24	0	0.0	0	0	− 5
Paul Coffey, Edmonton	79	307	48	15.6	9	9	+ 61
Pat Conacher, New Jersey	2	3	0	0.0	0	0	Even
Yvon Corriveau, Washington	2	3	0	0.0	0	0	− 1
Shayne Corson, Montreal	3	1	0	0.0	0	0	− 3
Rich Costello, Toronto	2	2	0	0.0	0	0	Even
Alain Cote, Quebec	78	120	13	10.8	0	3	− 3
Alain Cote, Boston	32	15	0	0.0	0	0	+ 5
Sylvain Cote, Hartford	2	0	0	0.0	0	0	+ 1
Tim Coulis, Minnesota	19	13	2	15.4	0	0	− 5
Neal Coulter, N.Y. Islanders	16	17	3	17.6	0	0	− 1
Yves Courteau, Calgary	4	7	1	14.3	0	0	+ 1
Geoff Courtnall, Boston	64	161	21	13.0	2	0	+ 1
Russ Courtnall, Toronto	73	203	22	10.8	3	1	Even
Craig Coxe, Vancouver	57	48	3	6.3	1	0	− 13
Murray Craven, Philadelphia	78	182	21	11.5	2	0	+ 24
Marc Crawford, Vancouver	54	80	11	13.8	0	0	− 7
Bobby Crawford, Hartford	57	110	14	12.7	4	0	− 16
N.Y. Rangers	11	15	1	6.7	0	0	+ 2
Totals	68	125	15	12.0	4	0	− 14
Adam Creighton, Buffalo	20	9	1	11.1	0	0	− 2
Doug Crossman, Philadelphia	80	134	6	4.5	2	0	− 5
Keith Crowder, Boston	78	184	38	20.7	20	0	+ 14

Player — Team	Games	Shots	Goals	Shooting Pct.	PPG	SHG	+/−
Randy Cunneyworth, Pittsburgh	75	134	15	11.2	2	2	+ 12
Brian Curran, Boston	43	23	2	8.7	0	0	+ 6
Glen Currie, Los Angeles	12	11	1	9.1	1	0	Even
Denis Cyr, St. Louis	31	21	3	14.3	0	0	− 11
Paul Cyr, Buffalo	71	151	20	13.2	4	1	+ 4
Kjell Dahlin, Montreal	77	172	32	18.6	14	0	+ 10
Chris Dahlquist, Pittsburgh	5	5	1	20.0	0	0	+ 1
J.J. Daigneault, Vancouver	64	114	5	4.4	4	0	− 20
Brad Dalgarno, N.Y. Islanders	2	3	1	33.3	0	0	+ 1
Ken Daneyko, New Jersey	44	48	0	0.0	0	0	+ 1
Dan Daoust, Toronto	80	92	7	7.6	1	0	− 21
Mal Davis, Buffalo	7	5	2	40.0	2	0	− 1
Lucien DeBlois, Montreal	61	102	14	13.7	2	0	+ 3
Dale Degray, Calgary	1	1	0	0.0	0	0	− 1
Gilbert Delorme, Quebec	65	102	2	2.0	1	0	− 1
Larry DePalma, Minnesota	1	0	0	0.0	0	0	Even
Bill Derlago, Toronto	1	35	0	0.0	0	0	Even
Boston	39	77	5	6.5	1	1	+ 4
Winnipeg	27	37	5	13.5	1	0	− 13
Totals	67	35	10	28.6	2	1	− 9
Gerald Diduck, N.Y. Islanders	10	6	1	16.7	0	0	+ 5
Don Dietrich, New Jersey	11	14	0	0.0	0	0	− 9
Gord Dineen, N.Y. Islanders	57	52	1	1.9	0	0	+ 15
Kevin Dineen, Hartford	57	167	33	19.8	6	0	+ 16
Marcel Dionne, Los Angeles	80	284	36	12.7	11	0	− 22
Bobby Dollas, Winnipeg	46	20	0	0.0	0	0	− 3
Dave Donnelly, Boston	8	8	0	0.0	0	0	Even
Gord Donnelly, Quebec	36	30	2	6.7	0	0	Even
Dan Dorion, New Jersey	3	6	1	16.7	0	0	− 1
Peter Douris, Winnipeg	11	0	0	0.0	0	0	− 1
Bruce Driver, New Jersey	40	64	3	4.7	1	0	+ 10
Gaetan Duchesne, Washington	80	119	11	9.2	0	1	+ 10
Ron Duguay, Detroit	67	153	19	12.4	8	0	− 30
Pittsburgh	13	33	6	18.2	3	0	− 14
Totals	80	186	25	13.4	11	0	− 44
Dale Dunbar, Vancouver	1	0	0	0.0	0	0	Even
Craig Duncanson, Los Angeles	2	0	0	0.0	0	0	− 1
Richie Dunn, Buffalo	29	55	4	7.3	4	0	− 5
Jerome Dupont, Chicago	75	69	2	2.9	0	0	− 17
Steve Dykstra, Buffalo	65	70	4	5.7	1	1	+ 1
Mike Eagles, Quebec	73	68	11	16.2	1	0	+ 3
Bruce Eakin, Detroit	4	1	0	0.0	0	0	− 4
Murray Eaves, Winnipeg	4	2	1	50.0	0	0	− 2
Per-Erik Eklund, Philadelphia	70	141	15	10.6	8	0	− 4
Dave Ellett, Winnipeg	80	121	15	12.4	2	0	− 38
Brian Engblom, Los Angeles	49	53	3	5.7	0	0	− 13
Buffalo	30	24	1	4.2	0	0	+ 3
Totals	79	77	4	5.2	0	0	− 10
Bryan Erickson, Los Angeles	55	108	20	18.5	6	0	+ 1
Thomas Eriksson, Philadelphia	43	32	0	0.0	0	0	− 12
Jan Erixon, N.Y. Rangers	31	33	2	6.1	0	0	+ 12
Bob Errey, Pittsburgh	37	57	11	19.3	1	0	+ 1
Daryl Evans, Washington	6	14	0	0.0	0	0	− 1
Doug Evans, St. Louis	13	12	1	8.3	0	0	Even
Shawn Evans, St. Louis	7	1	0	0.0	0	0	− 1
Dean Evason, Hartford	55	101	20	19.8	5	2	+ 4
Bernie Federko, St. Louis	80	167	34	20.4	16	0	+ 10
Tony Feltrin, N.Y. Rangers	10	8	0	0.0	0	0	− 3
Paul Fenton, Hartford	1	3	0	0.0	0	0	+ 1
Dave Fenyves, Buffalo	47	31	0	0.0	0	0	+ 12
Tom Fergus, Toronto	78	168	31	18.5	3	2	− 24
Ray Ferraro, Hartford	76	131	30	22.9	14	0	+ 12
Steven Finn, Quebec	17	8	0	0.0	0	0	Even
Ross Fitzpatrick, Philadelphia	2	0	0	0.0	0	0	− 1
Pat Flatley, N.Y. Islanders	73	120	18	15.0	6	0	+ 20
Ron Flockhart, St. Louis	79	199	22	11.1	5	2	+ 8
Lee Fogolin, Edmonton	80	71	4	5.6	0	0	+ 48
Mike Foligno, Buffalo	79	223	41	18.4	7	1	+ 25
Dwight Foster, Detroit	55	41	6	14.6	1	1	− 13
Boston	13	8	0	0.0	0	0	− 5
Totals	68	49	6	12.2	1	1	− 18

Player — Team	Games	Shots	Goals	Shooting Pct.	PPG	SHG	+/−
Nick Fotiu, Calgary	9	7	0	0.0	0	0	− 3
Jim Fox, Los Angeles	39	81	14	17.3	2	0	− 9
Lou Franceschetti, Washington	76	57	7	12.3	0	0	− 4
Ron Francis, Hartford	53	120	24	20.0	7	1	+ 8
Curt Fraser, Chicago	61	144	29	20.1	7	0	+ 11
Dan Frawley, Pittsburgh	69	79	10	12.7	4	0	− 19
Tim Friday, Detroit	23	13	0	0.0	0	0	− 9
Miroslav Frycer, Toronto	73	201	32	15.9	7	0	− 24
Jody Gage, Buffalo	7	18	3	16.7	3	0	− 3
Paul Gagne, New Jersey	47	91	19	20.9	4	0	− 14
Dave Gagner, N.Y. Rangers	32	41	4	9.8	0	0	+ 1
Bob Gainey, Montreal	80	135	20	14.8	0	2	+ 10
Gerard Gallant, Detroit	52	116	20	17.2	3	1	− 10
Garry Galley, Los Angeles	49	57	9	15.8	1	0	− 9
Dave Gans, Los Angeles	3	3	0	0.0	0	0	Even
Paul Gardner, Buffalo	2	4	0	0.0	0	0	− 3
Bill Gardner, Chicago	46	29	3	10.3	0	0	− 8
Hartford	18	12	1	8.3	0	0	− 6
Totals	64	41	4	9.8	0	0	− 14
Danny Gare, Detroit	57	108	7	6.5	1	0	− 19
Mike Gartner, Washington	74	279	35	12.5	11	2	− 5
Jean Marc Gaulin, Quebec	1	2	1	50.0	0	0	Even
Stewart Gavin, Hartford	76	161	26	16.1	3	3	+ 12
Greg Gilbert, N.Y. Islanders	60	58	9	15.5	1	0	− 5
Curt Giles, Minnesota	69	59	6	10.2	0	0	+ 19
Todd Gill, Toronto	15	9	1	11.1	0	0	Even
Clark Gillies, N.Y. Islanders	55	74	4	5.4	1	0	+ 8
Paul Gillis, Quebec	80	136	19	14.0	0	2	− 2
Doug Gilmour, St. Louis	74	183	25	13.7	2	1	− 3
Gaston Gingras, Montreal	34	77	8	10.4	7	0	− 10
Bob Gould, Washington	79	125	19	15.2	0	3	+ 7
Michel Goulet, Quebec	75	244	53	21.7	28	0	+ 6
Thomas Gradin, Vancouver	71	121	14	11.6	2	1	− 17
Dirk Graham, Minnesota	80	173	22	12.7	0	0	− 6
Rick Green, Montreal	46	45	3	6.7	0	0	− 9
Randy Gregg, Edmonton	64	55	2	3.6	0	0	+ 30
Ron Greschner, N.Y. Rangers	78	150	20	13.3	6	1	+ 9
Wayne Gretzky, Edmonton	80	350	52	14.9	11	3	+ 71
Paul Guay, Los Angeles	23	18	3	16.7	0	0	− 6
Bengt Gustafsson, Washington	70	113	23	20.4	8	4	+ 9
Ari Haanpaa, N.Y. Islanders	18	16	0	0.0	0	0	Even
Marc Habscheid, Minnesota	6	8	2	25.0	1	0	− 2
Len Hachborn, Los Angeles	24	14	4	28.6	1	0	− 9
Richard Hajdu, Buffalo	3	2	0	0.0	0	0	+ 1
Bill Hajt, Buffalo	58	42	1	2.4	0	0	+ 17
Anders Hakansson, Los Angeles	38	27	4	14.8	0	0	− 8
Bob Halkidis, Buffalo	37	19	1	5.3	0	0	− 3
Taylor Hall, Vancouver	19	30	5	16.7	1	0	− 11
Mats Hallin, Minnesota	38	29	3	10.3	0	0	− 3
Doug Halward, Vancouver	70	122	8	6.6	3	0	− 19
Gilles Hamel, Buffalo	77	158	19	12.0	4	3	− 27
Ken Hammond, Los Angeles	3	2	0	0.0	0	0	− 1
Mark Hamway, N.Y. Islanders	49	50	5	10.0	1	0	− 5
Dave Hannan, Pittsburgh	75	100	17	17.0	0	3	− 4
Mark Hardy, Los Angeles	55	113	6	5.3	2	1	− 11
Craig Hartsburg, Minnesota	75	185	10	5.4	4	0	+ 7
Kevin Hatcher, Washington	79	132	9	6.8	1	0	+ 6
Dale Hawerchuk, Winnipeg	80	313	46	14.7	18	2	− 27
Alan Haworth, Washington	71	194	34	17.5	7	0	+ 36
Randy Heath, N.Y. Rangers	1	1	0	0.0	0	0	+ 1
Raimo Helminen, N.Y. Rangers	66	125	10	8.0	4	0	− 1
Dale Henry, N.Y. Islanders	7	5	1	20.0	0	0	Even
Alan Hepple, New Jersey	1	0	0	0.0	0	0	Even
Uli Hiemer, New Jersey	50	100	8	8.0	6	0	+ 1
Tim Higgins, New Jersey	59	90	9	10.0	2	0	+ 7
Randy Hillier, Pittsburgh	28	22	0	0.0	0	0	− 3
Dan Hodgson, Toronto	40	54	13	24.1	2	0	− 5
Mike Hoffman, Hartford	6	7	1	14.3	0	0	− 2
Jim Hofford, Buffalo	5	3	0	0.0	0	0	− 1
Dean Hopkins, Edmonton	1	0	0	0.0	0	0	Even

Player — Team	Games	Shots	Goals	Shooting Pct.	PPG	SHG	+/-
Ed Hospodar, Philadelphia	17	11	3	27.3	0	0	Even
Minnesota	43	33	0	0.0	0	0	+ 8
Totals	60	44	3	6.8	0	0	+ 8
Paul Houck, Minnesota	3	3	1	33.3	0	0	+ 1
Doug Houda, Detroit	6	5	0	0.0	0	0	− 7
Phil Housley, Buffalo	79	180	15	8.3	7	0	− 9
Mark Howe, Philadelphia	77	193	24	12.4	4	7	+ 85
Scott Howson, N.Y. Islanders	10	8	1	12.5	0	0	+ 2
Willie Huber, N.Y. Rangers	70	124	7	5.6	1	0	− 11
Charlie Huddy, Edmonton	76	151	6	4.0	1	0	+ 30
Pat Hughes, Buffalo	50	51	4	7.8	0	0	− 6
Dale Hunter, Quebec	80	152	28	18.4	7	0	+ 6
Dave Hunter, Edmonton	62	110	15	13.6	0	0	+ 37
Mark Hunter, St. Louis	78	204	44	21.6	11	2	+ 15
Tim Hunter, Calgary	66	65	8	12.3	2	0	− 9
Al Iafrate, Toronto	65	94	8	8.5	2	0	− 10
Miroslav Ihnacak, Toronto	21	25	2	8.0	1	0	− 6
Peter Ihnacak, Toronto	63	96	18	18.8	5	0	− 9
Don Jackson, Edmonton	45	34	2	5.9	0	0	+ 2
Jeff Jackson, Toronto	5	2	1	50.0	0	0	+ 3
Risto Jalo, Edmonton	3	3	0	0.0	0	0	+ 2
Doug Jarvis, Washington	25	19	1	5.3	0	0	− 5
Hartford	57	55	8	14.5	0	3	+ 7
Totals	82	74	9	12.2	0	3	+ 2
Wes Jarvis, Toronto	2	2	1	50.0	0	0	− 1
Chris Jensen, N.Y. Rangers	9	18	1	5.6	0	0	+ 1
Dave Jensen, Washington	5	5	1	20.0	0	0	+ 1
Dave Jensen, Minnesota	5	1	0	0.0	0	0	− 2
Glen Johannesen, N.Y. Islanders	2	2	0	0.0	0	0	− 1
Jim Johnson, Pittsburgh	80	118	3	2.5	0	0	+ 12
Mark Johnson, New Jersey	80	167	21	12.6	6	0	− 13
Terry Johnson, St. Louis	49	21	0	0.0	0	0	− 6
Calgary	24	11	1	9.1	0	0	− 3
Totals	73	32	1	3.1	0	0	− 9
Greg Johnston, Boston	20	11	0	0.0	0	0	− 2
Ed Johnstone, Detroit	3	3	1	33.3	0	0	Even
Tomas Jonsson, N.Y. Islanders	77	119	14	11.8	5	1	+ 16
Claude Julien, Quebec	13	4	0	0.0	0	0	+ 2
Steve Kasper, Boston	80	149	17	11.4	1	3	− 10
Ed Kastelic, Washington	15	2	0	0.0	0	0	Even
John Paul Kelly, Los Angeles	61	38	6	15.8	0	0	− 17
Dean Kennedy, Los Angeles	78	59	2	3.4	0	0	− 10
Alan Kerr, N.Y. Islanders	7	9	0	0.0	0	0	+ 1
Tim Kerr, Philadelphia	76	285	58	20.4	34	0	− 5
Kelly Kisio, Detroit	76	140	21	15.0	7	3	− 21
Scot Kleinendorst, Hartford	41	26	2	7.7	0	0	+ 8
Petr Klima, Detroit	74	174	32	18.4	8	0	− 39
Gord Kluzak, Boston	70	114	8	7.0	3	0	+ 3
Joey Kocur, Detroit	59	65	9	13.8	2	0	− 24
Steve Konroyd, Calgary	59	111	7	6.3	1	0	+ 20
N.Y. Islanders	14	13	0	0.0	0	0	+ 4
Totals	73	124	7	5.6	1	0	+ 24
John Kordic, Montreal	5	0	0	0.0	0	0	+ 1
Roger Kortko, N.Y. Islanders	52	49	5	10.2	0	0	− 11
Chris Kotsopoulos, Toronto	61	69	6	8.7	0	0	− 5
Rich Kromm, Calgary	63	97	12	12.4	0	0	+ 9
N.Y. Islanders	14	23	7	30.4	0	0	+ 8
Totals	77	120	19	15.8	0	0	+ 17
Mike Krushelnyski, Edmonton	54	98	16	16.3	3	0	+ 11
Mark Kumpel, Quebec	47	76	10	13.2	0	0	+ 10
Jari Kurri, Edmonton	78	236	68	28.8	16	6	+ 45
Tom Kurvers, Montreal	62	69	7	10.1	3	0	+ 9
Jim Kyte, Winnipeg	71	0	1	0.0	0	0	− 21
Normand Lacombe, Buffalo	25	38	6	15.8	3	0	+ 9
Randy Ladouceur, Detroit	78	92	5	5.4	0	0	− 54
Pat LaFontaine, N.Y. Islanders	65	172	30	17.4	2	0	+ 16
Tom Laidlaw, N.Y. Rangers	68	50	6	12.0	0	1	− 3
Mike Lalor, Montreal	62	44	3	6.8	0	0	− 4
Mark Lamb, Calgary	1	0	0	0.0	0	0	Even
Lane Lambert, Detroit	34	32	2	6.3	0	0	− 11
Chris Langevin, Buffalo	16	10	2	20.0	0	0	+ 3

Defenseman Mark Howe was the NHL's plus-minus leader at plus 85 last season as well as Philadelphia's third-leading scorer.

Player — Team	Games	Shots	Goals	Shooting Pct.	PPG	SHG	+/−
Dave Langevin, Minnesota	80	54	0	0.0	0	0	− 17
Rod Langway, Washington	71	54	1	1.9	1	0	+ 28
Jean-Marc Lanthier, Vancouver	62	50	7	14.0	3	0	− 17
Rick Lanz, Vancouver	75	191	15	7.9	11	0	− 26
Rick LaPointe, Los Angeles	20	7	0	0.0	0	0	− 13
Jeff Larmer, Chicago	2	1	0	0.0	0	0	+ 1
Steve Larmer, Chicago	80	184	31	16.8	13	1	+ 9
Pierre Larouche, N.Y. Rangers	28	85	20	23.5	7	0	− 6
Reed Larson, Detroit	67	205	19	9.3	11	0	− 36
Boston	13	41	3	7.3	1	0	+ 5
Totals	80	246	22	8.9	12	0	− 31
Dave Latta, Quebec	1	1	0	0.0	0	0	Even
Craig Laughlin, Washington	75	114	30	26.3	10	0	+ 24
Kevin LaVallee, St. Louis	64	129	18	14.0	7	0	+ 8
Mark LaVarre, Chicago	2	2	0	0.0	0	0	− 2
Paul Lawless, Hartford	64	140	17	12.1	5	0	− 3
Brian Lawton, Minnesota	65	98	18	18.4	4	0	+ 10
Stephen Leach, Washington	11	4	1	25.0	0	0	Even
Jim Leavins, Detroit	37	63	2	3.2	1	0	− 23
Grant Ledyard, N.Y. Rangers	27	57	2	3.5	0	0	− 7
Los Angeles	52	113	7	6.2	4	0	− 22
Totals	79	170	9	5.3	4	8	− 29
Gary Leeman, Toronto	53	123	9	7.3	1	1	− 1
Ken Leiter, N.Y. Islanders	9	9	1	11.1	0	0	+ 1
Moe Lemay, Vancouver	48	112	16	14.3	6	0	− 14
Alain Lemieux, Quebec	7	1	0	0.0	0	0	− 1
Claude Lemieux, Montreal	10	16	1	6.3	1	0	− 6
Mario Lemieux, Pittsburgh	79	276	48	17.4	17	0	− 6
Don Lever, Buffalo	29	31	7	22.6	0	1	− 5
Craig Levie, Minnesota	14	22	2	9.1	0	0	− 5
Dave Lewis, New Jersey	69	38	0	0.0	0	0	Even
Doug Lidster, Vancouver	78	151	12	7.9	1	1	− 12
Willy Lindstrom, Pittsburgh	71	87	14	16.1	0	0	Even
Ken Linseman, Boston	64	132	23	17.4	8	0	+ 15
Claude Loiselle, Detroit	48	83	7	8.4	2	0	− 27
Troy Loney, Pittsburgh	47	50	3	6.0	0	0	− 8
Hakan Loob, Calgary	68	174	31	17.8	10	0	+ 22
Bob Lorimer, New Jersey	46	28	2	7.1	0	0	− 13
Kevin Lowe, Edmonton	74	57	2	3.5	0	0	+ 24
Dave Lowry, Vancouver	73	66	10	15.2	1	0	− 21
Jan Ludvig, New Jersey	42	74	5	6.8	0	0	− 16
Craig Ludwig, Montreal	69	58	2	3.4	0	0	+ 7
Steve Ludzik, Chicago	49	40	6	15.0	0	1	− 2
Morris Lukowich, Boston	14	25	1	4.0	0	0	+ 2
Los Angeles	55	85	11	12.9	0	0	− 19
Totals	69	110	12	10.9	0	0	− 17
Dave Lumley, Edmonton	46	33	11	33.3	1	0	+ 13
Bengt Lundholm, Winnipeg	16	30	3	10.0	0	1	− 4
Gary Lupul, Vancouver	19	17	4	23.5	0	0	Even
Tom Lysiak, Chicago	51	77	2	2.6	0	0	− 19
Paul MacDermid, Hartford	74	88	13	14.8	0	0	+ 1
Al MacInnis, Calgary	77	241	11	4.6	4	0	+ 39
John MacLean, New Jersey	74	138	21	15.2	1	0	− 2
Paul MacLean, Winnipeg	69	168	27	16.1	11	0	− 14
Brian MacLellan, Los Angeles	27	53	5	9.4	4	0	− 13
N.Y. Rangers	51	112	11	9.8	8	0	− 20
Totals	78	165	16	9.7	12	0	− 33
Craig MacTavish, Edmonton	74	121	23	19.0	4	1	+ 17
Jamie Macoun, Calgary	77	133	11	8.3	0	2	+ 14
Mikko Makela, N.Y. Islanders	58	68	16	23.5	2	0	+ 12
David Maley, Montreal	3	0	0	0.0	0	0	Even
Greg Malone, Hartford	22	35	6	17.1	1	0	− 5
Quebec	27	26	3	11.5	0	0	− 3
Totals	49	61	9	14.8	1	0	− 8
Don Maloney, N.Y. Rangers	68	89	11	12.4	0	0	+ 18
Dan Mandich, Minnesota	3	0	0	0.0	0	0	Even
Jimmy Mann, Quebec	35	4	0	0.0	0	0	− 2
Moe Mantha, Pittsburgh	78	224	15	6.7	11	2	− 4
Nevin Markwart, Boston	65	42	7	16.7	0	0	− 2

Player — Team	Games	Shots	Goals	Shooting Pct.	PPG	SHG	+/−
Mario Marois, Quebec	20	173	1	0.6	1	0	− 10
Winnipeg	56	125	4	3.2	0	0	− 22
Totals	76	150	5	3.3	1	0	− 32
Brad Marsh, Philadelphia	79	104	0	0.0	0	0	Even
Grant Martin, Washington	11	5	0	0.0	0	0	− 5
Tom Martin, Winnipeg	5	0	0	0.0	0	0	Even
Dennis Maruk, Minnesota	70	135	21	15.6	1	0	+ 13
Dwight Mathiason, Pittsburgh	4	4	1	25.0	0	0	− 4
Brad Maxwell, Toronto	52	93	8	8.6	4	0	− 27
Gary McAdam, Toronto	15	9	1	11.1	0	0	− 11
Andrew McBain, Winnipeg	28	50	3	6.0	0	0	− 11
Kevin McCarthy, Philadelphia	4	0	0	0.0	0	0	Even
Tom McCarthy, Minnesota	25	45	12	26.7	4	0	− 3
Kevin McClelland, Edmonton	79	104	11	10.6	0	0	+ 9
Brad McCrimmon, Philadelphia	80	162	13	8.0	2	0	+ 83
Lanny McDonald, Calgary	80	227	28	12.3	11	0	− 3
Joe McDonnell, Pittsburgh	3	1	0	0.0	0	0	− 3
Mike McEwen, Detroit	29	82	0	0.0	0	0	− 8
N.Y. Rangers	16	36	2	5.6	0	0	− 4
Hartford	10	18	3	16.7	0	0	+ 5
Totals	55	136	5	3.7	0	0	− 7
Dan McFall, Winnipeg	7	1	0	0.0	0	0	− 3
Jim McGeough, Pittsburgh	17	29	3	10.3	0	0	− 4
Bob McGill, Toronto	61	28	1	3.6	0	0	− 17
Tony McKegney, Minnesota	70	141	15	10.6	3	0	− 5
Sean McKenna, Buffalo	45	83	6	7.2	1	0	− 8
Los Angeles	30	47	4	8.5	0	1	− 15
Totals	75	130	10	7.7	1	1	− 23
Tom McMurchy, Chicago	4	2	0	0.0	0	0	− 1
Peter McNab, New Jersey	71	93	19	20.4	6	0	− 10
George McPhee, N.Y. Rangers	30	31	4	12.9	0	0	+ 5
Mike McPhee, Montreal	70	103	19	18.4	0	2	+ 8
Basil McRae, Detroit	4	3	0	0.0	0	0	− 4
Marty McSorley, Edmonton	59	72	11	15.3	0	0	+ 9
Rick Meagher, St. Louis	79	109	11	10.1	0	3	− 1
Anssi Melametsa, Winnipeg	27	5	0	0.0	0	0	− 5
Scott Mellanby, Philadelphia	2	0	0	0.0	0	0	− 1
Larry Melnyk, Edmonton	6	4	2	50.0	0	0	+ 8
N.Y. Rangers	46	33	1	3.0	0	0	+ 2
Totals	52	37	3	8.1	0	0	+ 10
Barry Melrose, Detroit	14	2	0	0.0	0	0	− 6
Glenn Merkosky, Detroit	17	18	0	0.0	0	0	− 12
Mark Messier, Edmonton	63	201	35	17.4	10	5	+ 36
Rick Middleton, Boston	49	100	14	14.0	4	2	+ 18
Mike Milbury, Boston	22	12	2	16.7	0	0	+ 1
Jay Miller, Boston	46	21	3	14.3	0	0	− 4
Kelly Miller, N.Y. Rangers	74	112	13	11.6	0	1	+ 3
Carl Mokosak, Philadelphia	1	0	0	0.0	0	0	Even
Mike Moller, Edmonton	1	2	0	0.0	0	0	Even
Randy Moller, Quebec	69	105	5	4.8	0	0	+ 9
Sergio Momesso, Montreal	24	37	8	21.6	3	0	− 4
Bob Mongrain, Los Angeles	11	10	2	20.0	0	0	− 3
Ken Morrow, N.Y. Islanders	69	55	0	0.0	0	0	+ 24
Brian Mullen, Winnipeg	79	211	28	13.3	13	0	− 17
Joe Mullen, St. Louis	48	142	28	19.7	9	0	− 7
Calgary	29	61	16	26.2	5	0	+ 3
Totals	77	203	44	21.7	14	0	− 4
Kirk Muller, New Jersey	77	168	25	14.9	5	1	− 19
Craig Muni, Toronto	6	2	0	0.0	0	0	− 3
Larry Murphy, Washington	78	180	21	11.7	8	1	+ 3
Bob Murray, Chicago	80	139	9	6.5	3	0	+ 6
Troy Murray, Chicago	80	198	45	22.7	9	5	+ 32
Dana Murzyn, Hartford	78	80	3	3.8	0	0	+ 1
Don Nachbaur, Philadelphia	5	4	1	25.0	0	0	+ 3
Mark Napier, Edmonton	80	117	24	20.5	3	1	+ 13
Mats Naslund, Montreal	80	223	43	19.3	19	0	+ 11
Ric Nattress, St. Louis	78	124	4	3.2	1	0	− 8
Cam Neely, Vancouver	73	113	14	12.4	6	0	− 30
Ray Neufeld, Hartford	16	35	5	14.3	3	0	− 3
Winnipeg	60	132	20	15.2	7	0	− 16
Totals	76	167	25	15.0	10	0	− 19

Player — Team	Games	Shots	Goals	Shooting Pct.	PPG	SHG	+/−
John Newberry, Hartford	3	4	0	0.0	0	0	− 4
Bernie Nichols, Los Angeles	80	281	36	12.8	10	4	− 5
Kraig Nienhuis, Boston	70	120	16	13.3	3	0	− 10
Chris Nilan, Montreal	72	120	19	15.8	2	0	+ 10
Jim Nill, Winnipeg	61	14	6	42.9	0	0	− 6
Kent Nilsson, Minnesota	61	122	16	13.1	8	0	+ 4
Ted Nolan, Pittsburgh	18	17	1	5.9	0	0	− 1
Lee Norwood, St. Louis	71	111	5	4.5	2	0	+ 7
Gary Nylund, Toronto	79	84	2	2.4	0	0	− 32
Bob Nystrom, N.Y. Islanders	14	17	1	5.9	0	0	− 4
Jack O'Callahan, Chicago	80	86	4	4.7	0	0	+ 5
Mike O'Connell, Boston	63	174	8	4.6	4	1	− 8
Detroit	13	38	1	2.6	0	1	− 6
Totals	76	212	9	4.2	4	2	− 14
Tom O'Regan, Pittsburgh	9	7	1	14.3	0	0	+ 1
Adam Oates, Detroit	38	49	9	18.4	1	0	− 24
Selmar Odelein, Edmonton	4	2	0	0.0	0	0	+ 1
John Ogrodnick, Detroit	76	208	38	18.3	15	1	− 30
Ed Olczyk, Chicago	79	218	29	13.3	8	1	+ 2
Gates Orlando, Buffalo	61	70	13	18.6	1	2	− 7
Mark Osborne, N.Y. Rangers	62	134	16	11.9	5	1	+ 5
Joel Otto, Calgary	79	147	25	17.0	9	0	+ 22
Wilf Paiement, Quebec	44	75	7	9.3	2	0	Even
N.Y. Rangers	8	14	1	7.1	0	0	+ 2
Totals	52	89	8	9.0	2	0	+ 2
Dave Pasin, Boston	71	116	18	15.5	4	0	− 1
Greg Paslawski, St. Louis	56	150	22	14.7	1	1	− 12
Mark Paterson, Hartford	5	0	0	0.0	0	0	− 5
Rick Paterson, Chicago	70	36	9	25.0	0	5	− 1
Joe Paterson, Philadelphia	5	4	0	0.0	0	0	+ 1
Los Angeles	47	75	9	12.0	2	0	− 7
Totals	52	79	9	11.4	2	0	− 6
James Patrick, N.Y. Rangers	75	131	14	10.7	2	1	+ 14
Steve Patrick, N.Y. Rangers	28	20	4	20.0	0	0	− 7
Quebec	27	29	4	13.8	1	0	+ 1
Totals	55	49	8	16.3	1	0	− 6
Colin Patterson, Calgary	61	84	14	16.7	0	0	+ 8
Mark Pavelich, N.Y. Rangers	59	104	20	19.2	8	0	− 3
Jim Pavese, St. Louis	69	51	4	7.8	1	0	− 3
Steve Payne, Minnesota	22	60	8	13.3	3	0	Even
Barry Pederson, Boston	79	192	29	15.1	12	0	+ 19
Jim Peplinski, Calgary	77	161	24	14.9	0	1	+ 32
Gilbert Perreault, Buffalo	72	164	21	12.8	5	1	− 10
Stefan Persson, N.Y. Islanders	56	46	1	2.2	1	0	− 3
Brent Peterson, Vancouver	77	86	8	9.3	0	3	− 10
Michel Petit, Vancouver	32	43	1	2.3	1	0	− 6
Jorgen Pettersson, Hartford	23	27	5	18.5	2	0	− 12
Washington	47	74	8	10.8	2	0	− 4
Totals	70	101	13	12.9	4	0	− 16
Lyle Phair, Los Angeles	15	11	0	0.0	0	0	− 12
Robert Picard, Winnipeg	20	40	2	5.0	0	0	− 2
Quebec	48	131	7	5.3	1	1	− 2
Totals	68	171	9	5.3	1	1	− 4
Dave Pichette, New Jersey	33	58	7	12.1	4	0	− 11
Larry Playfair, Buffalo	47	35	1	2.9	0	0	− 8
Los Angeles	14	6	0	0.0	0	0	− 14
Totals	61	41	1	2.4	0	0	− 22
Willi Plett, Minnesota	59	72	10	13.9	4	0	− 20
Walt Poddubny, Toronto	33	76	12	15.8	5	0	+ 6
Paul Pooley, Winnipeg	3	0	0	0.0	0	0	+ 1
Victor Posa, Chicago	2	1	0	0.0	0	0	Even
Mike Posavad, St. Louis	6	2	0	0.0	0	0	− 1
Denis Potvin, N.Y. Islanders	74	168	21	12.5	8	1	+ 34
Daniel Poudrier, Quebec	13	6	1	16.7	0	0	+ 2
Dave Poulin, Philadelphia	79	181	27	14.9	2	6	+ 20
Wayne Presley, Chicago	38	56	7	12.5	0	0	− 6
Rich Preston, New Jersey	76	117	19	16.2	3	0	+ 1
Pat Price, Quebec	53	49	3	6.1	0	0	Even
Bob Probert, Detroit	44	46	8	17.4	3	0	− 14
Brian Propp, Philadelphia	72	317	40	12.6	11	2	+ 24
Chris Pryor, Minnesota	7	8	0	0.0	0	0	Even

Player — Team	Games	Shots	Goals	Shooting Pct.	PPG	SHG	+/−
Joel Quenneville, Hartford	71	49	5	10.2	1	0	+ 20
Dan Quinn, Calgary	78	191	30	15.7	17	3	− 12
Herb Raglan, St. Louis	7	4	0	0.0	0	0	− 3
Rob Ramage, St. Louis	77	227	10	4.4	7	0	+ 18
Mike Ramsey, Buffalo	76	154	7	4.5	1	0	+ 1
Craig Redmond, Los Angeles	73	116	6	5.2	3	0	− 34
Mark Reeds, St. Louis	78	108	10	9.3	0	0	+ 11
Joe Reekie, Buffalo	3	1	0	0.0	0	0	− 2
Dave Reid, Boston	37	53	10	18.9	4	0	+ 2
Paul Reinhart, Calgary	32	58	8	13.8	4	0	+ 4
Stephane Richer, Montreal	65	112	21	18.8	5	0	+ 1
Steve Richmond, N.Y. Rangers	17	8	0	0.0	0	0	+ 2
Detroit	29	18	1	5.6	0	0	− 18
Totals	46	26	1	3.8	0	0	− 16
Dave Richter, Minnesota	14	5	0	0.0	0	0	− 6
Philadelphia	50	17	0	0.0	0	0	− 2
Totals	64	22	0	0.0	0	0	− 8
Mike Ridley, N.Y. Rangers	80	150	22	14.7	7	0	Even
Doug Risebrough, Calgary	62	92	15	16.3	0	3	+ 22
Gordie Roberts, Minnesota	76	66	2	3.0	0	0	+ 14
Torrie Robertson, Hartford	76	87	13	14.9	3	0	− 9
Larry Robinson, Montreal	78	167	19	11.4	10	0	+ 29
Normand Rochefort, Quebec	26	51	5	9.8	2	0	+ 9
Mike Rogers, N.Y. Rangers	9	20	1	5.0	1	0	+ 2
Edmonton	8	6	1	16.7	0	0	− 2
Totals	17	26	2	7.7	1	0	Even
Steve Rooney, Montreal	38	24	2	8.3	1	0	− 4
Bill Root, Toronto	27	34	0	0.0	0	0	− 8
Tom Roulston, Pittsburgh	5	6	0	0.0	0	0	− 2
Bob Rouse, Minnesota	75	91	1	1.1	0	0	+ 15
Mike Rowe, Pittsburgh	3	5	0	0.0	0	0	− 1
Lindy Ruff, Buffalo	54	131	20	15.3	5	1	+ 8
Reijo Ruotsalainen, N.Y. Rangers	80	228	17	7.5	6	0	+ 22
Terry Ruskowski, Pittsburgh	73	91	26	28.6	11	0	+ 10
Phil Russell, New Jersey	30	22	2	9.1	0	0	− 17
Buffalo	12	15	2	13.3	0	0	− 8
Totals	42	37	4	10.8	0	0	− 25
Borje Salming, Toronto	41	71	7	9.9	3	1	− 7
Gary Sampson, Washington	19	17	1	5.9	0	0	− 3
Kjell Samuelsson, N.Y. Rangers	9	7	0	0.0	0	0	− 1
Ulf Samuelsson, Hartford	80	71	5	7.0	0	1	+ 8
Jim Sandlak, Vancouver	23	34	1	2.9	0	0	− 4
Tomas Sandstrom, N.Y. Rangers	73	238	25	10.5	8	2	− 4
Jean Francois Sauve, Quebec	75	100	16	16.0	13	0	− 13
Denis Savard, Chicago	80	279	47	16.8	14	1	+ 7
Norm Schmidt, Pittsburgh	66	141	15	10.6	3	0	+ 7
Dwight Schofield, Washington	50	13	1	7.7	0	0	+ 5
Rod Schutt, Toronto	6	2	0	0.0	0	0	− 2
Al Secord, Chicago	80	210	40	19.0	12	0	+ 8
Ric Seiling, Buffalo	69	85	12	14.1	0	0	− 5
Dave Semenko, Edmonton	69	51	6	11.8	0	0	Even
Brad Shaw, Hartford	8	17	0	0.0	0	0	− 1
David Shaw, Quebec	73	126	7	5.6	2	0	+ 14
Doug Shedden, Pittsburgh	67	179	32	17.9	19	0	− 7
Detroit	11	33	2	6.1	2	0	− 1
Totals	78	212	34	16.0	21	0	− 8
Neil Sheehy, Calgary	65	59	2	3.4	1	0	− 1
Gord Sherven, Minnesota	13	8	0	0.0	0	0	+ 1
Edmonton	5	6	1	16.7	0	0	Even
Totals	18	14	1	7.1	0	0	+ 1
Dave Silk, Winnipeg	32	28	2	7.1	0	0	− 6
Risto Siltanen, Hartford	52	126	8	6.3	6	0	+ 2
Quebec	13	53	2	3.8	2	0	− 1
Totals	65	179	10	5.6	8	0	+ 1
Charlie Simmer, Boston	55	141	36	25.5	14	0	+ 12
Frank Simonetti, Boston	17	8	1	12.5	0	0	− 1
Craig Simpson, Pittsburgh	76	74	11	14.9	2	1	+ 1
Ilkka Sinisalo, Philadelphia	74	187	39	20.9	19	1	+ 17
Ville Siren, Pittsburgh	60	58	4	6.9	1	0	− 8
Petri Skriko, Vancouver	80	192	38	19.8	12	1	− 17

Player — Team	Games	Shots	Goals	Shooting Pct.	PPG	SHG	+/−
Brian Skrudland, Montreal	65	62	9	14.5	0	2	+ 3
Louis Sleigher, Boston	13	18	4	22.2	0	0	− 4
Doug Smail, Winnipeg	73	40	16	40.0	1	3	− 11
Bobby Smith, Montreal	79	202	31	15.3	5	0	+ 10
Brad Smith, Toronto	42	46	5	10.9	0	0	− 8
Derrick Smith, Philadelphia	69	108	6	5.6	0	0	+ 14
Doug Smith, Los Angeles	48	115	8	7.0	1	1	− 29
Buffalo	30	72	10	13.9	3	1	+ 2
Totals	78	187	18	9.6	4	2	− 27
Greg Smith, Detroit	62	53	5	9.4	0	0	− 14
Washington	14	6	0	0.0	0	0	+ 3
Totals	76	59	5	8.5	0	0	− 11
Randy Smith, Minnesota	1	0	0	0.0	0	0	Even
Steve Smith, Philadelphia	2	1	0	0.0	0	0	− 1
Steve Smith, Edmonton	55	74	4	5.4	1	0	+ 30
Stan Smyl, Vancouver	73	165	27	16.4	3	4	− 20
Harold Snepsts, Detroit	35	12	0	0.0	0	0	− 7
Ken Solheim, Edmonton	6	8	1	12.5	0	0	− 2
Ted Speers, Detroit	4	6	1	16.7	0	0	+ 2
Darryl Stanley, Philadelphia	33	7	0	0.0	0	0	− 5
Anton Stastny, Quebec	74	163	31	19.0	8	0	+ 8
Marian Stastny, Toronto	70	132	23	17.4	7	0	− 6
Peter Stastny, Quebec	76	207	41	19.8	15	0	+ 2
Ray Staszak, Detroit	4	5	0	0.0	0	0	− 3
Thomas Steen, Winnipeg	78	195	17	8.7	2	3	− 29
Scott Stevens, Washington	73	121	15	12.4	3	0	Even
Ryan Stewart, Winnipeg	3	16	1	6.3	0	0	Even
Allan Stewart, New Jersey	4	0	0	0.0	0	0	− 1
Bill Stewart, Minnesota	8	3	0	0.0	0	0	+ 2
Trevor Stienburg, Quebec	2	6	1	16.7	0	0	Even
Mike Stothers, Philadelphia	6	1	0	0.0	0	0	+ 1
Doug Sulliman, New Jersey	73	139	21	15.1	7	1	− 10
Raimo Summanen, Edmonton	73	83	19	22.9	1	0	+ 7
Patrik Sundstrom, Vancouver	79	155	18	11.6	6	1	− 8
Peter Sundstrom, N.Y. Rangers	53	63	8	12.7	0	0	+ 7
Gary Suter, Calgary	80	195	18	9.2	9	0	+ 11
Brent Sutter, N.Y. Rangers	61	135	24	17.8	10	0	+ 11
Brian Sutter, St. Louis	44	92	19	20.7	8	0	− 12
Darryl Sutter, Chicago	50	89	17	19.1	3	0	− 15
Duane Sutter, N.Y. Islanders	80	151	20	13.2	4	0	+ 15
Rich Sutter, Philadelphia	78	124	14	11.3	0	0	+ 28
Ron Sutter, Philadelphia	75	145	18	12.4	0	0	+ 26
Petr Svoboda, Montreal	73	63	1	1.6	0	0	+ 24
Phil Sykes, Los Angeles	76	132	20	15.2	1	2	− 26
Peter Taglianetti, Winnipeg	18	0	0	0.0	0	0	− 1
Steve Tambellini, Vancouver	48	89	15	16.9	6	0	− 18
Tony Tanti, Vancouver	77	213	39	18.3	17	0	− 7
Dave Taylor, Los Angeles	76	203	33	16.3	11	0	− 16
Mark Taylor, Washington	30	23	2	8.7	0	0	− 4
Greg Terrion, Toronto	76	105	10	9.5	0	2	− 5
Mats Thelin, Boston	31	29	2	6.9	1	0	+ 3
Michael Thelven, Boston	60	108	6	5.6	1	0	+ 7
Steve Thomas, Toronto	65	197	20	10.2	5	0	− 15
Esa Tikkanen, Edmonton	35	44	7	15.9	0	0	+ 5
Dave Tippett, Hartford	80	118	14	11.9	0	2	+ 10
Rick Tocchet, Philadelphia	69	108	14	13.0	3	0	+ 12
John Tonelli, N.Y. Islanders	65	139	20	14.4	3	0	+ 22
Calgary	9	18	3	16.7	1	0	Even
Totals	74	157	23	14.6	4	0	+ 22
Mario Tremblay, Montreal	56	119	19	16.0	3	0	+ 4
Bryan Trottier, N.Y. Islanders	78	185	37	20.0	5	1	+ 29
John Tucker, Buffalo	75	146	31	21.2	8	0	Even
Allan Tuer, Los Angeles	45	14	0	0.0	0	0	− 16
Alfie Turcotte, Montreal	2	0	0	0.0	0	0	Even
Sylvain Turgeon, Hartford	76	249	45	18.1	13	0	+ 3
Perry Turnbull, Winnipeg	80	168	20	11.9	6	0	− 18
Rick Vaive, Toronto	61	225	33	14.7	12	0	− 19
Darren Veitch, Washington	62	82	3	3.7	0	0	+ 21
Detroit	13	22	0	0.0	0	0	− 9
Totals	75	104	3	2.9	0	0	+ 12

Player — Team	Games	Shots	Goals	Shooting Pct.	PPG	SHG	+/−
Randy Velischek, New Jersey	47	24	2	8.3	0	0	− 19
Pat Verbeek, New Jersey	76	159	25	15.7	4	1	− 25
Hannu Virta, Buffalo	47	81	5	6.2	1	0	+ 2
Emanuel Viveiros, Minnesota	4	4	0	0.0	0	0	+ 2
Ryan Walter, Montreal	69	115	15	13.0	9	0	− 9
Bill Watson, Chicago	52	67	8	11.9	2	0	− 4
Tim Watters, Winnipeg	56	64	6	9.4	0	0	− 10
Jay Wells, Los Angeles	79	113	11	9.7	4	0	+ 7
Blake Wesley, Toronto	27	11	0	0.0	0	0	− 4
Rob Whistle, N.Y. Rangers	32	30	4	13.3	1	0	− 1
Doug Wickenheiser, St. Louis	36	53	8	15.1	0	0	+ 11
Jim Wiemer, N.Y. Rangers	7	22	3	13.6	0	0	Even
Brian Wilks, Los Angeles	43	31	4	12.9	0	0	− 7
Dave Williams, Los Angeles	72	138	20	14.5	5	0	− 6
Behn Wilson, Chicago	69	138	13	9.4	10	0	− 11
Carey Wilson, Calgary	76	150	29	19.3	5	0	+ 1
Doug Wilson, Chicago	79	243	17	7.0	3	0	+ 24
Rik Wilson, St. Louis	32	45	0	0.0	0	0	− 9
Calgary	2	3	0	0.0	0	0	+ 2
Totals	34	48	0	0.0	0	0	− 7
Ron Wilson, Winnipeg	54	24	6	25.0	0	2	− 2
Ron Wilson, Minnesota	11	21	1	4.8	1	0	− 2
Craig Wolanin, New Jersey	44	45	2	4.4	0	0	− 7
Ken Yaremchuk, Chicago	78	82	14	17.1	0	0	− 17
Warren Young, Detroit	79	95	22	23.2	9	0	− 34
Steve Yzerman, Detroit	51	132	14	10.6	3	0	− 24
Peter Zezel, Philadelphia	79	144	17	11.8	4	0	+ 27
Rick Zombo, Detroit	14	8	0	0.0	0	0	− 10
Mike Zuke, Hartford	17	2	0	0.0	0	0	− 2

NHL Departmental Leaders

Goals
1. Jari Kurri, Edmonton 68
2. Mike Bossy, N.Y. Islanders 61
3. Tim Kerr, Philadelphia 58
4. Glenn Anderson, Edmonton 54

Assists
1. Wayne Gretzky, Edmonton 163
2. Mario Lemieux, Pittsburgh 93
3. Paul Coffey, Edmonton 90
4. Peter Stastny, Quebec 81

Power-Play Goals
1. Tim Kerr, Philadelphia 34
2. Michel Goulet, Quebec 28
3. Mike Bossy, N.Y. Islanders 21
   Doug Shedden, Pittsburgh-Detroit 21
5. Keith Crowder, Boston 20

Shorthanded Goals
1. Paul Coffey, Edmonton 9
2. Mark Howe, Philadelphia 7
3. Jari Kurri, Edmonton 6
   Dave Poulin, Philadelphia 6

Game-Winning Goals
1. Glenn Anderson, Edmonton 9
   Mike Bossy, N.Y. Islanders 9
   Jari Kurri, Edmonton 9
4. Kevin Dineen, Hartford 8
   Tim Kerr, Philadelphia 8
   Joe Mullen, St. Louis-Calgary 8
   Denis Savard, Chicago 8
   Peter Stastny, Quebec 8

Shots on Goal
1. Wayne Gretzky, Edmonton 350
2. Brian Propp, Philadelphia 317
3. Dale Hawerchuk, Winnipeg 313
4. Paul Coffey, Edmonton 307
5. Mike Bossy, N.Y. Islanders 302

Shooting Percentage
1. Jari Kurri, Edmonton 28.6
2. Terry Ruskowski, Pittsburgh 28.6
3. Craig Laughlin, Washington 26.3
4. Charlie Simmer, Boston 25.5
5. Pierre Larouche, N.Y. Rangers 23.5

Miscellaneous Goaltending Statistics

	Games	W.	L.	T.	Goals	Saves	Sv. Pct.	Goal Interval
Murray Bannerman, Chicago	48	20	19	6	201	1337	86.9	13.38
Tom Barrasso, Buffalo	60	29	24	5	214	1564	88.0	16.64
Don Beaupre, Minnesota	52	25	20	6	182	1508	89.2	16.88
Marc Behrend, Winnipeg	9	2	5	0	41	179	81.4	10.29
Tim Bernhardt, Toronto	23	4	12	3	107	620	85.3	11.83
Allan Bester, Toronto	1	0	0	0	2	3	60.0	10.00
Craig Billington, New Jersey	18	4	9	1	77	405	84.0	11.71
Dan Bouchard, Winnipeg	32	11	14	2	107	683	86.5	15.85
Richard Brodeur, Vancouver	64	19	32	8	240	1484	86.1	14.75
Frank Caprice, Vancouver	7	0	3	2	28	127	81.9	11.00
Jon Casey, Minnesota	26	11	11	1	91	698	88.5	15.41
Alain Chevrier, New Jersey	37	11	18	2	143	808	85.0	13.02
Jacques Cloutier, Buffalo	15	5	9	1	49	379	88.6	17.86
Marc D'Amour, Calgary	15	2	4	2	32	278	89.7	17.50
Cleon Daskalakis, Boston	2	0	2	0	10	53	84.1	12.00
Don Edwards, Toronto	38	12	23	0	160	980	86.0	12.56
Darren Eliot, Los Angeles	27	5	17	3	121	680	84.9	12.24
Bob Froese, Philadelphia	51	31	10	3	116	1154	90.9	23.52
Grant Fuhr, Edmonton	40	29	8	0	143	1153	89.0	15.27
Mario Gosselin, Quebec	31	14	14	1	111	685	86.1	15.55
Glen Hanlon, N.Y. Rangers	23	5	12	1	65	543	89.3	18.00
Brian Hayward, Winnipeg	52	13	28	5	217	1156	84.2	12.54
Glenn Healy, Los Angeles	1	0	0	0	6	29	82.9	8.50
Denis Herron, Pittsburgh	3	0	3	0	14	78	84.8	12.86
Kelly Hrudey, N.Y. Islanders	45	19	15	8	137	1318	90.6	18.71
Bob Janecyk, Los Angeles	38	14	16	4	162	968	85.7	12.86
Al Jensen, Washington	44	29	9	3	129	1039	89.0	18.89
Darren Jensen, Philadelphia	29	15	9	1	88	668	88.4	16.32
Doug Keans, Boston	30	14	13	3	107	688	86.5	16.42
Terry Kleisinger, N.Y. Rangers	4	0	2	0	14	95	87.2	13.64
Mark Laforest, Detroit	28	4	21	0	114	630	84.7	12.13
Rejean Lemelin, Calgary	60	29	24	4	229	1558	87.2	14.71
Pelle Lindbergh, Philadelphia	8	6	2	0	23	176	88.4	20.87
Mike Liut, Hartford	57	27	23	4	197	1377	87.5	16.66
Clint Malarchuk, Quebec	46	26	12	4	142	1216	89.5	18.71
Bob Mason, Washington	1	1	0	0	0	5	100.0	....
Darrell May, St. Louis	3	1	2	0	13	73	84.9	14.15
Kirk McLean, New Jersey	2	1	1	0	11	48	81.4	10.09
Roland Melanson, Minnesota	6	2	1	2	24	151	86.3	13.54
Los Angeles	22	4	16	1	87	567	86.7	14.32
Totals	28	6	17	3	111	718	86.6	14.15
Gilles Meloche, Pittsburgh	34	13	15	5	119	884	88.1	16.71
Corrado Micalef, Detroit	11	1	9	1	52	290	84.8	10.87
Greg Millen, St. Louis	36	14	16	6	129	1011	88.7	16.81
Ed Mio, Detroit	18	2	7	0	83	357	81.1	9.49
Andy Moog, Edmonton	47	27	9	7	164	1316	88.9	16.24
Pete Peeters, Boston	8	3	4	1	31	214	87.3	15.65
Washington	34	19	11	3	113	797	87.6	17.88
Totals	42	22	15	4	144	1011	87.5	17.40
Steve Penney, Montreal	18	6	8	2	72	375	83.9	13.75
Daren Puppa, Buffalo	7	3	4	0	21	163	88.6	19.10
Chris Pusey, Detroit	1	0	0	0	3	9	75.0	13.33
Bill Ranford, Boston	4	3	1	0	10	96	90.6	24.00
Glenn Resch, New Jersey	31	10	20	0	126	759	85.8	14.04
Philadelphia	5	1	2	0	10	74	88.1	18.70
Totals	36	11	22	0	136	833	86.0	14.38
Pat Riggin, Washington	7	2	3	1	23	110	82.7	16.04
Boston	39	17	11	8	127	846	86.9	17.89
Totals	46	19	14	9	150	956	86.4	17.61
Roberto Romano, Pittsburgh	46	21	20	3	159	1235	88.6	16.88
Patrick Roy, Montreal	47	23	19	3	150	1041	87.4	17.67
Bob Sauve, Chicago	38	19	13	2	138	1072	88.6	15.21
Ron Scott, N.Y. Rangers	4	0	3	0	11	45	80.4	14.18
Richard Sevigny, Quebec	11	3	5	1	33	209	86.4	14.18
Warren Skorodenski, Chicago	1	0	1	0	6	39	86.7	10.00
Billy Smith, N.Y. Islanders	41	20	14	4	143	1061	88.1	16.14
Doug Soetaert, Montreal	23	11	6	2	54	473	89.8	22.50
Sam St. Laurent, New Jersey	4	2	1	0	13	98	88.3	14.46

	Games	W.	L.	T.	Goals	Saves	Sv. Pct.	Goal Interval
Greg Stefan, Detroit	37	10	20	5	155	923	85.6	13.34
Kari Takko, Minnesota	1	0	1	0	3	31	91.2	20.00
John Vanbiesbrouck, N.Y. Rangers	61	31	21	5	184	1442	88.7	18.08
Mike Vernon, Calgary	18	9	3	3	52	365	87.5	17.71
Rick Wamsley, St. Louis	42	22	16	3	144	1210	89.4	17.48
Steve Weeks, Hartford	27	13	13	0	99	624	86.3	15.60
Ken Wregget, Toronto	30	9	13	4	113	788	87.5	13.86
Wendell Young, Vancouver	22	4	9	3	61	475	88.6	16.77

NOTE: Goal Interval is the average amount of time between goals allowed. Empty Net Goals are not counted.

Goaltending Departmental Leaders

Games Played
1. Richard Brodeur, Vancouver 64
2. John Vanbiesbrouck, N.Y. Rangers 61
3. Tom Barrasso, Buffalo 60
   Rejean Lemelin, Calgary 60
5. Mike Liut, Hartford 57

Minutes Played
1. Tom Barrasso, Buffalo 3561
2. Richard Brodeur, Vancouver 3541
3. Rejean Lemelin, Calgary 3369
4. John Vanbiesbrouck, N.Y. Rangers 3326
5. Mike Liut, Hartford 3282

Win Leaders
1. Bob Froese, Philadelphia 31
   John Vanbiesbrouck, N.Y. Rangers 31
3. Tom Barrasso, Buffalo 29
   Rejean Lemelin, Calgary 29
   Grant Fuhr, Edmonton 29

Save Leaders
1. Rejean Lemelin, Calgary 1787
2. Tom Barrasso, Buffalo 1778
3. Richard Brodeur, Vancouver 1724
4. Don Beaupre, Minnesota 1690
5. John Vanbiesbrouck, N.Y. Rangers 1625

Save Percentage Leaders
1. Bob Froese, Philadelphia 90.9
2. Kelly Hrudey, N.Y. Islanders 90.6
3. Clint Malarchuk, Quebec 89.5
4. Rick Wamsley, St. Louis 89.4
5. Don Beaupre, Minnesota 89.2

Shutouts
1. Bob Froese, Philadelphia 5
2. Clint Malarchuk, Quebec 4
3. Doug Soetaert, Montreal 3
   John Vanbiesbrouck, N.Y. Rangers 3

1986 Stanley Cup Playoffs

Top 10 Playoff Scoring Leaders

	Games	G.	A.	Pts.	Pen.
Doug Gilmour, St. Louis	19	9	12	*21	25
Bernie Federko, St. Louis	19	7	14	*21	17
Joe Mullen, Calgary	21	*12	7	19	4
Wayne Gretzky, Edmonton	10	8	11	19	2
Mats Naslund, Montreal	20	8	11	19	4
Al MacInnis, Calgary	21	4	*15	19	30
Lanny McDonald, Calgary	22	11	7	18	30
Paul Reinhart, Calgary	21	5	13	18	4
Greg Paslawski, St. Louis	17	10	7	17	13
Pierre Larouche, N.Y. Rangers	16	8	9	17	2

*Indicates a league-leading figure.

Preliminary Rounds

(Division Semifinals)
(Best-of-five Series)

ADAMS DIVISION

	W.	L.	Pts.	GF.	GA.
Hartford Whalers	3	0	6	16	7
Quebec Nordiques	0	3	0	7	16

(Hartford won Adams Division semifinal, 3-0)
Wed. April 9—Hartford 3, at Quebec 2
Thur. April 10—Hartford 4, at Quebec 1
Sat. April 12—Quebec 4, at Hartford 9

	W.	L.	Pts.	GF.	GA.
Montreal Canadiens	3	0	6	10	6
Boston Bruins	0	3	0	6	10

(Montreal won Adams Division semifinal, 3-0)
Wed. April 9—Boston 1, at Montreal 3
Thur. April 10—Boston 2, at Montreal 3
Sat. April 12—Montreal 4, at Boston 3

PATRICK DIVISION

	W.	L.	Pts.	GF.	GA.
New York Rangers	3	2	6	18	15
Philadelphia Flyers	2	3	4	15	18

(New York Rangers won Patrick Division semifinal, 3-2)
Wed. April 9—N.Y. Rangers 6, at Philadelphia 2
Thur. April 10—N.Y. Rangers 1, at Philadelphia 2
Sat. April 12—Philadelphia 2, at N.Y. Rangers 5
Sun. April 13—Philadelphia 7, at N.Y. Rangers 1
Tues. April 15—N.Y. Rangers 5, at Philadelphia 2

	W.	L.	Pts.	GF.	GA.
Washington Capitals	3	0	6	11	4
New York Islanders	0	3	0	4	11

(Washington won Patrick Division semifinal, 3-0)
Wed. April 9—N.Y. Islanders 1, at Washington 3
Thur. April 10—N.Y. Islanders 2, at Washington 5
Sat. April 12—Washington 3, at N.Y. Islanders 1

NORRIS DIVISION

	W.	L.	Pts.	GF.	GA.
Toronto Maple Leafs	3	0	6	18	9
Chicago Black Hawks	0	3	0	9	18

(Toronto won Norris Division semifinal, 3-0)
Wed. April 9—Toronto 5, at Chicago 3
Thur. April 10—Toronto 6, at Chicago 4
Sat. April 12—Chicago 2, at Toronto 7

	W.	L.	Pts.	GF.	GA.
St. Louis Blues	3	2	6	18	20
Minnesota North Stars	2	3	4	20	18

(St. Louis won Norris Division semifinal, 3-2)
Wed. April 9—St. Louis 2, at Minnesota 1
Thur. April 10—St. Louis 2, at Minnesota 6
Sat. April 12—Minnesota 3, at St. Louis 4
Sun. April 13—Minnesota 7, at St. Louis 4
Tues. April 15—St. Louis 6, at Minnesota 3

SMYTHE DIVISION

	W.	L.	Pts.	GF.	GA.
Edmonton Oilers	3	0	6	17	5
Vancouver Canucks	0	3	0	5	17

(Edmonton won Smythe Division semifinal, 3-0)
Wed. April 9—Vancouver 3, at Edmonton 7
Thur. April 10—Vancouver 1, at Edmonton 5
Sat. April 12—Edmonton 5, at Vancouver 1

	W.	L.	Pts.	GF.	GA.
Calgary Flames	3	0	6	15	8
Winnipeg Jets	0	3	0	8	15

(Calgary won Smythe Division semifinal, 3-0)
Wed. April 9—Winnipeg 1, at Calgary 5
Thur. April 10—Winnipeg 4, at Calgary 6
Sat. April 12—Calgary 4, at Winnipeg 3 (a)

(a)—Lanny McDonald scored at 8:25 of overtime for Calgary.

Quarterfinal Rounds
(Division Finals)
(Best-of-seven series)

ADAMS DIVISION

	W.	L.	Pts.	GF.	GA.
Montreal Canadiens	4	3	8	16	13
Hartford Whalers	3	4	6	13	16

(Montreal won Division final, 4-3)

Thur. April 17—Hartford 4, at Montreal 1
Sat. April 19—Hartford 1, at Montreal 3
Mon. April 21—Montreal 4, at Hartford 1
Wed. April 23—Montreal 1, at Hartford 2 (b)
Fri. April 25—Hartford 3, at Montreal 5
Sun. April 27—Montreal 0, at Hartford 1
Tues. April 29—Hartford 1, at Montreal 2 (c)

(b)—Kevin Dineen scored at 1:07 of overtime for Hartford.

(c)—Claude Lemieux scored at 5:55 of overtime for Montreal.

NORRIS DIVISION

	W.	L.	Pts.	GF.	GA.
St. Louis Blues	4	3	8	24	22
Toronto Maple Leafs	3	4	6	22	24

(St. Louis won Division final, 4-3)

Fri. April 18—Toronto 1, at St. Louis 6
Sun. April 20—Toronto 3, at St. Louis 0
Tues. April 22—St. Louis 2, at Toronto 5
Thur. April 24—St. Louis 7, at Toronto 4
Sat. April 26—Toronto 3, at St. Louis 4 (f)
Mon. April 28—St. Louis 3, at Toronto 5
Wed. April 30—Toronto 1, at St. Louis 2

(f)—Mark Reeds scored at 7:11 of overtime for St. Louis.

PATRICK DIVISION

	W.	L.	Pts.	GF.	GA.
New York Rangers	4	2	8	20	25
Washington Capitals	2	4	4	25	20

(New York Rangers won Division final, 4-2)

Thur. April 17—N.Y. Rangers 4, at Washington 3 (d)
Sat. April 19—N.Y. Rangers 1, at Washington 8
Mon. April 21—Washington 6, at N.Y. Rangers 3
Wed. April 23—Washington 5, at N.Y. Rangers 6 (e)
Fri. April 25—N.Y. Rangers 4, at Washington 2
Sun. April 27—Washington 1, at N.Y. Rangers 2

(d)—Brian MacLellan scored at 1:16 of overtime for N.Y. Rangers.

(e)—Bob Brooke scored at 2:40 of overtime for N.Y. Rangers.

SMYTHE DIVISION

	W.	L.	Pts.	GF.	GA.
Calgary Flames	4	3	8	25	24
Edmonton Oilers	3	4	6	24	25

(Calgary won Division final, 4-3)

Fri. April 18—Calgary 4, at Edmonton 1
Sun. April 20—Calgary 5, at Edmonton 6 (g)
Tues. April 22—Edmonton 2, at Calgary 3
Thur. April 24—Edmonton 7, at Calgary 4
Sat. April 26—Calgary 4, at Edmonton 1
Mon. April 28—Edmonton 5, at Calgary 2
Wed. April 30—Calgary 3, at Edmonton 2

(g)—Glenn Anderson scored at 1:04 of overtime for Edmonton.

Semifinal Rounds
(Conference Championships)
(Best-of-seven series)

PRINCE OF WALES CONFERENCE

	W.	L.	Pts.	GF.	GA.
Montreal Canadiens	4	1	8	15	9
New York Rangers	1	4	2	9	15

(Montreal won Conference Title, 4-1)

Thur. May 1—N.Y. Rangers 1, at Montreal 2
Sat. May 3—N.Y. Rangers 2, at Montreal 6
Mon. May 5—Montreal 4, at N.Y. Rangers 3 (h)
Wed. May 7—Montreal 0, at N.Y. Rangers 2
Fri. May 9—N.Y. Rangers 1, at Montreal 3

(h)—Claude Lemieux scored at 9:41 of overtime for Montreal.

CLARENCE CAMPBELL CONFERENCE

	W.	L.	Pts.	GF.	GA.
Calgary Flames	4	3	8	28	22
St. Louis Blues	3	4	6	22	28

(Calgary won Conference Title, 4-3)

Fri. May 2—St. Louis 3, at Calgary 2
Sun. May 4—St. Louis 2, at Calgary 8
Tues. May 6—Calgary 5, at St. Louis 3
Thur. May 8—Calgary 2, at St. Louis 5
Sat. May 10—St. Louis 2, at Calgary 4
Mon. May 12—Calgary 5, at St. Louis 6 (i)
Wed. May 14—St. Louis 1, at Calgary 2

(i)—Doug Wickenheiser scored at 7:30 of overtime for St. Louis.

Finals for the Stanley Cup
(Best-of-seven series)

	W.	L.	Pts.	GF.	GA.
Montreal Canadiens	4	1	8	17	13
Calgary Flames	1	4	2	13	17

(Montreal Canadiens won Stanley Cup Championship Series, 4-1)

Fri. May 16—Montreal 2, at Calgary 5
Sun. May 18—Montreal 3, at Calgary 2 (j)
Tues. May 20—Calgary 3, at Montreal 5
Thur. May 22—Calgary 0, at Montreal 1
Sat. May 24—Montreal 4, at Calgary 3

(j)—Brian Skrudland scored at 0:09 of overtime for Montreal.

Game 1—Friday, May 16 at Calgary (Calgary won, 5-2)

```
Montreal ..................................... 1    0    1—2
Calgary ...................................... 2    0    3—5
```

FIRST PERIOD: 1. Montreal, Naslund (Smith, Robinson) PPG 6:04. 2. Calgary, Tonelli (MacInnis, Quinn) 12:08. 3. Calgary, Peplinski (Baxter, Otto) 19:11. Penalties: McPhee, Montreal 3:35; Bartel, Calgary, misconduct 3:35; Mullen, Calgary 4:14; Baxter, Calgary 10:16; Robinson, Montreal 11:57; Ludwig, Montreal 15:10; McDonald, Calgary 15:10; Nilan, Montreal 17:36; Hunter, Calgary 17:36; Roy, Montreal, misconduct (served by Kordic) 19:11.

SECOND PERIOD: No scoring. Penalties: Smith, Montreal 2:51; Loob, Calgary 2:51; Hunter, Calgary 4:57; Fotiu, Calgary 9:54; Maley, Montreal 18:03; Macoun, Calgary 18:03; Ludwig, Montreal 20:00; Nilan, Montreal, major-misconduct 20:00; Peplinski, Calgary 20:00; Hunter, Calgary, major-misconduct 20:00.

THIRD PERIOD: 4. Calgary, Quinn (unassisted) SHG 2:14; 5. Calgary, McDonald (Fotiu, Peplinski) 3:33; 6. Montreal Chelios (Maley, Naslund) 17:56; 7. Calgary, Risebrough (Peplinski) ENG 19:35. Penalties: Bozek, Calgary 1:04; Carbonneau, Montreal 3:43; Reinhart, Calgary 3:43; Peplinski, Calgary 6:16; Skrudland, Montreal 14:33.

Shots Against:
```
  Roy (Montreal) .................................................... 13    7    10 — 30
  Vernon (Calgary) ................................................. 10    9     5 — 24
```
Attendance: 16,762

Game 2—Sunday, May 18 at Calgary (Montreal won, 3-2)

```
Montreal ..................... 0    1    1    1—3
Calgary ...................... 1    1    0    0—2
```

FIRST PERIOD: 1. Calgary, Tonelli (Mullen, Quinn) 9:06. Penalties: MacInnis, Calgary 2:22; McPhee, Montreal, misconduct 6:08; Skrudland, Montreal 9:19; Macoun, Calgary 9:19; Gainey, Montreal 10:25; Nilan, Montreal, major 10:25; Peplinski, Calgary 10:25; Hunter, Calgary, major 10:25; Skrudland, Montreal 15:47; Carbonneau, Montreal 16:12; Smith, Montreal 19:21.

SECOND PERIOD: 2. Calgary, Reinhart (McDonald, Loob) PPG 0:15; 3. Montreal, Gingras (unassisted) 3:45. Penalties: Otto, Calgary 1:07; Ludwig, Montreal 4:41; Sheehy, Calgary 11:31; MacInnis, Calgary 17:01.

THIRD PERIOD: 4. Montreal, Maley (Carbonneau, Chelios) 3:30. Penalties: Ludwig, Montreal 1:11; Mullen, Calgary 8:24; Kordic, Montreal, misconduct 10:50; Sheehy, Calgary, misconduct 10:50; Carbonneau, Montreal 18:30; Peplinski, Calgary 18:30.

OVERTIME: 5. Montreal, Skrudland (McPhee, Lemieux) 0:09. Penalties: None.

Shots Against:
```
  Roy (Montreal) ........................................ 8     9     5     0 — 22
  Vernon (Calgary) .................................... 14    12    8     1 — 35
```
Attendance: 16,762

Game 3—Tuesday, May 20 at Montreal (Montreal won, 5-3)

```
Calgary ................................. 2    1    0—3
Montreal ............................... 4    1    0—5
```

FIRST PERIOD: 1. Calgary, Mullen (Otto, Loob) PPG 5:45; 2. Montreal, Naslund (Robinson, Smith) 6:50; 3. Calgary, Otto (MacInnis, Reinhart) PPG 17:59; 4. Montreal, Smith (Robinson, Naslund) 18:25; 5. Montreal, Naslund (Walter, Chelios) PPG 19:17; 6. Montreal, Gainey (Carbonneau, Chelios) 19:33. Penalties: Ludwig, Montreal 2:18; Lalor, Montreal 4:21; Johnson, Calgary, misconduct 6:32; Quinn, Calgary 7:30; Carbonneau, Montreal 11:20; Quinn, Calgary 13:04; Skrudland, Montreal 13:04; Lemieux, Montreal 16:41; Bartel, Calgary 19:09; McDonald, Calgary 19:39; Peplinski, Calgary 19:39; Sheehy, Calgary, major-misconduct 19:39; Ludwig, Montreal 19:39; Nilan, Montreal, major-misconduct 19:39.

SECOND PERIOD: 7. Calgary, McDonald (Quinn, MacInnis) PPG 7:13; 8. Montreal, Dahlin (Gingras, Carbonneau) 19:22. Penalties: Skrudland, Montreal 5:35; Hunter, Calgary, major 8:02; Kordic, Montreal, major 8:02; Peplinski, Calgary 9:04; MacInnis, Calgary 17:53; Walter, Montreal 17:53; Hunter, Calgary, major-misconduct 18:32; Otto, Calgary, misconduct 18:32; Nilan, Montreal, minor-misconduct 18:32; Skrudland, Montreal, misconduct 18:32.

THIRD PERIOD: No scoring. Penalties: MacInnis, Calgary 17:11.

Shots Against:
```
  Vernon and Lemelin (Calgary) ............................................... 16    8    5 — 29
  Roy (Montreal) .................................................................... 10    9    6 — 25
```
Attendance: 18,072

Game 4—Thursday, May 22 at Montreal (Montreal won, 1-0)

```
Calgary ................................. 0    0    0—0
Montreal ............................... 0    0    1—1
```

FIRST PERIOD: No scoring. Penalties: Johnson, Calgary 1:31; McPhee, Montreal 1:31; Chelios, Montreal 1:31; Berezan, Calgary 6:13; Sheehy, Calgary, double minor 8:25; Smith, Montreal, double minor 8:25; Berezan, Calgary 19:34; Lemieux, Montreal 19:34.

SECOND PERIOD: No scoring. Penalties: Bozek, Calgary 7:55; Eaves, Calgary 15:23.

THIRD PERIOD: 1. Montreal, Lemieux (unassisted) 11:10. Penalties: McPhee, Montreal, misconduct 17:38; Risebrough, Calgary 20:00; Peplinski, Calgary, major-misconduct-game misconduct 20:00; Baxter, Calgary, major-game misconduct 20:00; Bozek, Calgary, major-game misconduct 20:00; Tonelli, Calgary, major-game misconduct 20:00;

Lemieux, Montreal, major-misconduct-game misconduct 20:00; Carbonneau, Montreal, major-game misconduct 20:00; Chelios, Montreal, major-game misconduct 20:00, Lalor, Montreal, major-game misconduct 20:00.

Shots Against:
Vernon (Calgary) 6   8   10 — 24
Roy (Montreal) 7   2   6 — 15

Attendance: 18,076

Game 5—Saturday, May 24 at Calgary (Montreal won, 4-3)

Montreal 1   1   2—4
Calgary 0   1   2—3

FIRST PERIOD: 1. Montreal, Gingras (Lemieux, Naslund) PPG 6:53. Penalties: Fotiu, Calgary 2:43; McDonald, Calgary 5:53; Skrudland, Montreal 7:15; Skrudland, Montreal, misconduct 15:21; Riseborough, Calgary, misconduct 15:21; Fotiu, Calgary 18:26.

SECOND PERIOD: 2. Calgary, Bozek (Hunter, Peplinski) 7:17; 3. Montreal, Skrudland (McPhee, Lemieux) 10:49. Penalties: Lalor, Montreal 1:28; Chelios, Montreal 3:26; Fotiu, Calgary 14:40.

THIRD PERIOD: 4. Montreal, Green (Maley, Lalor) 10:11; 5. Montreal, Smith (Naslund) 10:30; 6. Calgary, Bozek (Macoun) 16:46; 7. Calgary, Mullen (Quinn, MacInnis) 19:14. Penalties: Ludwig, Montreal 6:31; Fotiu, Calgary 6:31; Lemieux, Montreal 13:01; Hunter, Calgary 13:01.

Shots Against:
Roy (Montreal) 7   12   14 — 33
Vernon (Calgary) 12   10   11 — 33

Attendance: 16,762

Team-by-Team Playoff Scoring

Boston Bruins
(Lost Adams Division semifinals to Montreal, 3-0)

	Games	G.	A.	Pts.	Pen.
Randy Burridge	3	0	4	4	12
Keith Crowder	3	2	0	2	21
Gord Kluzak	3	1	1	2	16
Dwight Foster	3	0	2	2	2
Steve Kasper	3	1	0	1	4
Reed Larson	3	1	0	1	6
Barry Pederson	3	1	0	1	0
Ken Linseman	3	0	1	1	17
Dave Pasin	3	0	1	1	0
Mike Milbury	1	0	0	0	17
Pat Riggin (Goalie)	1	0	0	0	2
Louis Sleigher	1	0	0	0	14
Brian Curran	2	0	0	0	4
Jay Miller	2	0	0	0	17
Kraig Nienhuis	2	0	0	0	14
Bill Ranford (Goalie)	2	0	0	0	0
John Blum	3	0	0	0	6
Ray Bourque	3	0	0	0	0
Geoff Courtnall	3	0	0	0	2
Charlie Simmer	3	0	0	0	4
Frank Simonetti	3	0	0	0	0
Michael Thelven	3	0	0	0	0

Calgary Flames
(Lost Stanley Cup finals to Montreal, 4-1)

	Games	G.	A.	Pts.	Pen.
Joe Mullen	21	12	7	19	4
Al MacInnis	21	4	15	19	30
Lanny McDonald	22	11	7	18	30
Paul Reinhart	21	5	13	18	4
Doug Riseborough	22	7	9	16	38
John Tonelli	22	7	9	16	49
Dan Quinn	18	8	7	15	10
Joel Otto	22	5	10	15	80
Jim Peplinski	22	5	9	14	107
Hakan Loob	22	4	10	14	6
Gary Suter	10	2	8	10	8
Colin Patterson	19	6	3	9	10
Steve Bozek	14	2	6	8	32
Jamie Macoun	22	1	6	7	23
Terry Johnson	17	0	3	3	64
Tim Hunter	19	0	3	3	108
Perry Berezan	8	1	1	2	6
Mike Eaves	8	1	1	2	8
Carey Wilson	9	0	2	2	2
Neil Sheehy	22	0	2	2	79
Rejean Lemelin (Goalie)	3	0	1	1	0
Nick Fotiu	11	0	1	1	34
Paul Baxter	13	0	1	1	55
Mike Vernon (Goalie)	21	0	1	1	0
Brian Bradley	1	0	0	0	0
Yves Courteau	1	0	0	0	0
Brett Hull	2	0	0	0	0
Robin Bartel	6	0	0	0	16

Chicago Black Hawks
(Lost Norris Division semifinals to Toronto, 3-0)

	Games	G.	A.	Pts.	Pen.
Denis Savard	3	4	1	5	6
Tom Lysiak	3	2	1	3	2
Darryl Sutter	3	1	2	3	0
Steve Larmer	3	0	3	3	4
Doug Wilson	3	1	1	2	2
Ken Yaremchuk	3	1	1	2	2
Al Secord	2	0	2	2	26
Bob Murray	3	0	2	2	0
Bill Watson	2	0	1	1	0
Keith Brown	3	0	1	1	9
Curt Fraser	3	0	1	1	12
Jack O'Callahan	3	0	1	1	4
Jerome Dupont	1	0	0	0	0
Murray Bannerman (G.)	2	0	0	0	4
Troy Murray	2	0	0	0	2
Bob Sauve (Goalie)	2	0	0	0	0
Behn Wilson	2	0	0	0	2
Marc Bergevin	3	0	0	0	0
Steve Ludzik	3	0	0	0	12
Ed Olczyk	3	0	0	0	2
Rick Paterson	3	0	0	0	0
Wayne Presley	3	0	0	0	0

Edmonton Oilers
(Lost Smythe Division finals to Calgary, 4-3)

	Games	G.	A.	Pts.	Pen.
Wayne Gretzky	10	8	11	19	2
Jari Kurri	10	2	10	12	4
Glenn Anderson	10	8	3	11	14
Mark Messier	10	4	6	10	18
Paul Coffey	10	1	9	10	30
Mike Krushelnyski	10	4	5	9	16
Craig MacTavish	10	4	4	8	11
Esa Tikkanen	8	3	2	5	7
Dave Hunter	10	2	3	5	23
Mark Napier	10	1	4	5	0
Kevin Lowe	10	1	3	4	15
Raimo Summanen	5	1	1	2	0
Dave Lumley	3	0	2	2	2
Charlie Huddy	7	0	2	2	0
Lee Fogolin	8	0	2	2	10
Marty McSorley	8	0	2	2	50
Randy Gregg	10	1	0	1	12
Kevin McClelland	10	1	0	1	32
Steve Smith	6	0	1	1	14
Grant Fuhr (Goalie)	9	0	1	1	0
Jeff Beukeboom	1	0	0	0	4
Andy Moog (Goalie)	1	0	0	0	0
Dave Semenko	6	0	0	0	32
Don Jackson	8	0	0	0	21

Hartford Whalers
(Lost Adams Division finals to Montreal, 4-3)

	Games	G.	A.	Pts.	Pen.
Kevin Dineen	10	6	7	13	18
John Anderson	10	5	8	13	0
Ray Ferraro	10	3	6	9	4
Stewart Gavin	10	4	1	5	13
Sylvain Turgeon	9	2	3	5	4
Dean Evason	10	1	4	5	10
Dave Tippett	10	2	2	4	4
Dave Babych	8	1	3	4	14
Mike McEwen	8	0	4	4	6
Paul MacDermid	10	2	1	3	20
Ron Francis	10	1	2	3	4
Ulf Samuelsson	10	1	2	3	38
Doug Jarvis	10	0	3	3	4
Joel Quenneville	10	0	2	2	12
Torrie Robertson	10	1	0	1	67
Wayne Babych	10	0	1	1	2
Scot Kleinendorst	10	0	1	1	18
Paul Lawless	1	0	0	0	0
Steve Weeks (Goalie)	3	0	0	0	0
Dana Murzyn	4	0	0	0	10
Mike Liut (Goalie)	8	0	0	0	0
Tim Bothwell	10	0	0	0	8

Minnesota North Stars
(Lost Norris Division semifinals to St. Louis, 3-2)

	Games	G.	A.	Pts.	Pen.
Dennis Maruk	5	4	9	13	4
Ron Wilson	5	2	4	6	4
Brian Bellows	5	5	0	5	16
Neal Broten	5	3	2	5	2
Kent Nilsson	5	1	4	5	0
Dirk Graham	5	3	1	4	2
Gordie Roberts	5	0	4	4	8
Tony McKegney	5	2	1	3	22
Keith Acton	5	0	3	3	6
Brian Lawton	3	0	1	1	2
Scott Bjugstad	5	0	1	1	0
Dino Ciccarelli	5	0	1	1	6
Curt Giles	5	0	1	1	10
Craig Hartsburg	5	0	1	1	2
Dave Langevin	5	0	1	1	9
Willi Plett	5	0	1	1	45
Mats Hallin	1	0	0	0	0
Marc Habscheid	2	0	0	0	0
Ed Hospodar	2	0	0	0	0
Bob Rouse	3	0	0	0	2
Don Beaupre (Goalie)	5	0	0	0	0

Montreal Canadiens
(Winners of 1986 Stanley Cup Playoffs)

	Games	G.	A.	Pts.	Pen.
Mats Naslund	20	8	11	19	4
Claude Lemieux	20	10	6	16	68
Bobby Smith	20	7	8	15	22
Larry Robinson	20	0	13	13	22
Guy Carbonneau	20	7	5	12	35
Chris Chelios	20	2	9	11	49
Bob Gainey	20	5	5	10	12
Mike McPhee	20	3	4	7	45
Brian Skrudland	20	2	4	6	76
Stephane Richer	16	4	1	5	23
Gaston Gingras	11	2	3	5	4
Kjell Dahlin	16	2	3	5	4
Rick Green	18	1	4	5	8
David Maley	7	1	3	4	2
Chris Nilan	18	1	2	3	141
Mike Lalor	17	1	1	2	29
Ryan Walter	5	0	1	1	2
Serge Boisvert	8	0	1	1	0
Craig Ludwig	20	0	1	1	48
Steve Rooney	1	0	0	0	0
Randy Bucyk	2	0	0	0	0
Petr Svoboda	8	0	0	0	21
Lucien DeBlois	11	0	0	0	7
John Kordic	18	0	0	0	53
Patrick Roy (Goalie)	20	0	0	0	10

New York Islanders
(Lost Patrick Division semifinals to Washington, 3-0)

	Games	G.	A.	Pts.	Pen.
Mike Bossy	3	1	2	3	4
Bryan Trottier	3	1	1	2	2
Clark Gillies	3	1	0	1	6
Pat LaFontaine	3	1	0	1	0
Bob Bassen	3	0	1	1	0
Tomas Jonsson	3	0	1	1	4
Rich Kromm	3	0	1	1	0
Denis Potvin	3	0	1	1	0
Brent Sutter	3	0	1	1	2
Mark Hamway	1	0	0	0	0
Alan Kerr	1	0	0	0	0
Billy Smith (Goalie)	1	0	0	0	0
Greg Gilbert	2	0	0	0	9
Kelly Hrudey (Goalie)	2	0	0	0	4
Ken Morrow	2	0	0	0	4
Bob Bourne	3	0	0	0	0
Paul Boutilier	3	0	0	0	2
Randy Boyd	3	0	0	0	2
Gord Dineen	3	0	0	0	2
Patrick Flatley	3	0	0	0	21
Steve Konroyd	3	0	0	0	6
Duane Sutter	3	0	0	0	16

New York Rangers
(Lost Prince of Wales Conference finals to Montreal, 4-1)

	Games	G.	A.	Pts.	Pen.
Pierre Larouche	16	8	9	17	2
Bob Brooke	16	6	9	15	28
Mike Ridley	16	6	8	14	26
Wilf Paiement	16	5	5	10	45
Tomas Sandstrom	16	4	6	10	20
Reijo Ruotsalainen	16	0	8	8	6
Kelly Miller	16	3	4	7	4
Brian MacLellan	16	2	4	6	15
James Patrick	16	1	5	6	34
Willie Huber	16	3	2	5	16
Mark Osborne	15	2	3	5	26
Ron Greschner	5	3	1	4	11
Don Maloney	16	2	1	3	31
Larry Melnyk	16	1	2	3	46
Tom Laidlaw	7	0	2	2	12
Mike Allison	16	0	2	2	38
John Vanbiesbrouck (G.)	16	0	2	2	2
Jim Wiemer	8	1	0	1	6
Bob Crawford	7	0	1	1	8
Kjell Samuelsson	9	0	1	1	8
Jan Erixon	12	0	1	1	4
Peter Sundstrom	1	0	0	0	2
Raimo Helminen	2	0	0	0	0
Glen Hanlon (Goalie)	3	0	0	0	0
Rob Whistle	3	0	0	0	2
George McPhee	11	0	0	0	32

Philadelphia Flyers
(Lost Patrick Division semifinals to N.Y. Rangers, 3-2)

	Games	G.	A.	Pts.	Pen.
Tim Kerr	5	3	3	6	8
Peter Zezel	5	3	1	4	4
Ilkka Sinisalo	5	2	2	4	2
Mark Howe	5	0	4	4	0
Rick Tocchet	5	1	2	3	26
Murray Craven	5	0	3	3	4
Brad McCrimmon	5	2	0	2	2
Dave Poulin	5	2	0	2	2
Rich Sutter	5	2	0	2	19
Per-Erik Eklund	5	0	2	2	0
Brian Propp	5	0	2	2	4
Ron Sutter	5	0	2	2	10
Doug Crossman	5	0	1	1	4
Bob Froese (Goalie)	5	0	1	1	0
Lindsay Carson	1	0	0	0	5
Glenn Resch (Goalie)	1	0	0	0	0
Darryl Stanley	1	0	0	0	2
Mike Stothers	3	0	0	0	4
Derrick Smith	4	0	0	0	10
Dave Brown	5	0	0	0	16
Brad Marsh	5	0	0	0	2
Dave Richter	5	0	0	0	21

Quebec Nordiques
(Lost Adams Division semifinals to Hartford, 3-0)

	Games	G.	A.	Pts.	Pen.
Brent Ashton	3	2	1	3	9
Alain Lemieux	1	1	2	3	0
Michel Goulet	3	1	2	3	10
Anton Stastny	3	1	1	2	0
Paul Gillis	3	0	2	2	14
Robert Picard	3	0	2	2	2
Mark Kumpel	2	1	0	1	0
Alain Cote	3	1	0	1	0
Peter Andersson	2	0	1	1	0
Pat Price	3	0	1	1	4
Risto Siltanen	3	0	1	1	2
Peter Stastny	3	0	1	1	2
Jeff Brown	1	0	0	0	0
Gord Donnelly	1	0	0	0	0
Mario Gosselin (Goalie)	1	0	0	0	0
Greg Malone	1	0	0	0	0
Trevor Stienburg	1	0	0	0	0
Gilbert Delorme	2	0	0	0	5
Jimmy Mann	2	0	0	0	19
J.F. Sauve	2	0	0	0	0
Mike Eagles	3	0	0	0	2
Dale Hunter	3	0	0	0	15
Clint Malarchuk (Goalie)	3	0	0	0	0
Randy Moller	3	0	0	0	26
Steve Patrick	3	0	0	0	6

St. Louis Blues
(Lost Campbell Conference finals to Calgary, 4-3)

	Games	G.	A.	Pts.	Pen.
Doug Gilmour	19	9	12	21	25
Bernie Federko	19	7	14	21	17
Greg Paslawski	17	10	7	17	13
Mark Hunter	19	7	7	14	48
Rob Ramage	19	1	10	11	66
Gino Cavallini	17	4	5	9	10
Lee Norwood	19	2	7	9	64
Rick Meagher	19	4	4	8	12
Mark Reeds	19	4	4	8	2
Eddy Beers	19	3	4	7	8
Doug Wickenheiser	19	2	5	7	12
Ric Nattress	18	1	4	5	24
Kevin LaVallee	13	2	2	4	6
Charles Bourgeois	19	2	2	4	116
Ron Flockhart	8	1	3	4	6
Brian Benning	6	1	2	3	13
Brian Sutter	9	1	2	3	22
Cliff Ronning	5	1	1	2	2
Herb Raglan	10	1	1	2	24
Dave Barr	11	1	1	2	14
Bruce Bell	14	0	2	2	13
Jim Pavese	19	0	2	2	51
Kent Carlson	5	0	0	0	11
Greg Millen (Goalie)	10	0	0	0	0
Rick Wamsley (Goalie)	10	0	0	0	0

Toronto Maple Leafs
(Lost Norris Division finals to St. Louis, 4-3)

	Games	G.	A.	Pts.	Pen.
Steve Thomas	10	6	8	14	9
Tom Fergus	10	5	7	12	6
Gary Leeman	10	2	10	12	2
Russ Courtnall	10	3	6	9	8
Rick Vaive	9	6	2	8	9
Borje Salming	10	1	6	7	14
Wendel Clark	10	5	1	6	47
Walt Poddubny	9	4	1	5	4
Peter Ihnacak	10	2	3	5	12
Dan Daoust	10	2	2	4	19
Miroslav Frycer	10	1	3	4	10
Brad Smith	6	2	1	3	20
Al Iafrate	10	0	3	3	4
Greg Terrion	10	0	3	3	17
Bill Root	7	0	2	2	13

	Games	G.	A.	Pts.	Pen.
Gary Nylund	10	0	2	2	25
Chris Kotsopoulos	10	1	0	1	14
Brad Maxwell	3	0	1	1	12
Todd Gill	1	0	0	0	0
Marian Stastny	3	0	0	0	0
Bob McGill	9	0	0	0	35
Ken Wregget (Goalie)	10	0	0	0	4

Vancouver Canucks

(Lost Smythe Division semifinals to Edmonton, 3-0)

	Games	G.	A.	Pts.	Pen.
Thomas Gradin	3	2	1	3	2
Brent Peterson	3	2	0	2	9
J.J. Daigneault	3	0	2	2	0
Patrik Sundstrom	3	1	0	1	0
Wendell Young (Goalie)	1	0	1	1	0
Marc Crawford	3	0	1	1	8
Doug Lidster	3	0	1	1	2
Jim Sandlak	3	0	1	1	0
Tony Tanti	3	0	1	1	11
David Bruce	1	0	0	0	0
Richard Brodeur (G.)	2	0	0	0	2
Glen Cochrane	2	0	0	0	5
Jiri Bubla	3	0	0	0	2
Garth Butcher	3	0	0	0	0
Craig Coxe	3	0	0	0	2
Doug Halward	3	0	0	0	4
Rick Lanz	3	0	0	0	0
Dave Lowry	3	0	0	0	0
Gary Lupul	3	0	0	0	0
Cam Neely	3	0	0	0	6
Petri Skriko	3	0	0	0	0

Washington Capitals

(Lost Patrick Division finals to N.Y. Rangers, 4-2)

	Games	G.	A.	Pts.	Pen.
Mike Gartner	9	2	10	12	4
Scott Stevens	9	3	8	11	12
Alan Haworth	9	4	6	10	11
Bob Carpenter	9	5	4	9	12
Dave Christian	9	4	4	8	0
Gaetan Duchesne	9	4	3	7	12
Bob Gould	9	4	3	7	11
Larry Murphy	9	1	5	6	6
Greg Adams	9	1	3	4	27
John Barrett	9	2	1	3	35
Greg Smith	9	2	1	3	9
Jorgen Pettersson	8	1	2	3	2
Rod Langway	9	1	2	3	6
Craig Laughlin	9	1	2	3	10
Yvon Corriveau	4	0	3	3	2
Kevin Hatcher	9	1	1	2	19
Stephen Leach	6	0	1	1	0
Dwight Schofield	3	0	0	0	14
Mark Taylor	3	0	0	0	0
Dave Jensen	4	0	0	0	0
Lou Franceschetti	8	0	0	0	15
Pete Peeters (Goalie)	9	0	0	0	2

Winnipeg Jets

(Lost Smythe Division semifinals to Calgary, 3-0)

	Games	G.	A.	Pts.	Pen.
Mario Marois	3	1	4	5	6
Brian Mullen	3	1	2	3	6
Dale Hawerchuk	3	0	3	3	0
Ray Neufeld	3	2	0	2	10
Thomas Steen	3	1	1	2	4
Paul MacLean	2	1	0	1	7
Bill Derlago	3	1	0	1	0
Doug Smail	3	1	0	1	0
Laurie Boschman	3	0	1	1	6
Dave Ellett	3	0	1	1	0
Perry Turnbull	3	0	1	1	11
Marc Behrend (Goalie)	1	0	0	0	0
Daniel Berthiaume (G.)	1	0	0	0	0
Dan Bouchard (Goalie)	1	0	0	0	2
Dave Silk	1	0	0	0	2
Ron Wilson	1	0	0	0	0
Brian Hayward (Goalie)	2	0	0	0	0
Bengt Lundholm	2	0	0	0	2
Scott Arniel	3	0	0	0	12
Brad Berry	3	0	0	0	0
Bobby Dollas	3	0	0	0	2
Jim Kyte	3	0	0	0	12
Jim Nill	3	0	0	0	4
Peter Taglianetti	3	0	0	0	2

Complete Stanley Cup Goaltending

	Games	Mins.	Goals	SO.	Avg.
Patrick Roy	20	1218	39(2)	1	1.92
Montreal Totals	20	1218	41	1	2.02
Mike Liut	8	441	14	1	*1.90
Steve Weeks	3	169	8(1)	0	2.84
Hartford Totals	10	610	23	1	2.26
Pete Peeters	9	544	24	0	2.65
Washington Totals	9	544	24	0	2.65
Andy Moog	1	60	1	0	1.00
Grant Fuhr	9	541	28(1)	0	3.11
Edmonton Totals	10	601	30	0	3.00
Mike Vernon	*21	*1229	*60(2)	0	2.93
Rejean Lemelin	3	109	7	0	3.85
Calgary Totals	22	1338	69	0	3.09
Ken Wregget	10	607	32(1)	1	3.16
Toronto Totals	10	607	33	1	3.26

	Games	Mins.	Goals	SO.	Avg.
Pat Riggin	1	60	3	0	3.00
Bill Ranford	2	120	7	0	3.50
Boston Totals	3	180	10	0	3.33
John Vanbiesbrouck	16	899	49	*1	3.27
Glen Hanlon	3	75	6	0	4.00
New York Rangers Totals	16	974	55	1	3.39
Don Beaupre	5	300	17(1)	0	3.40
Minnesota Totals	5	300	18	0	3.60
Bob Froese	5	293	15(2)	0	3.07
Glenn Resch	1	7	1	0	8.57
Philadelphia Totals	5	300	18	0	3.60
Greg Millen	10	586	29(3)	0	2.97
Rick Wamsley	10	569	37(1)	0	3.90
St. Louis Totals	19	1155	70	0	3.64
Kelly Hrudey	2	120	6	0	3.00
Billy Smith	1	60	4(1)	0	4.00
New York Islanders Totals	3	180	11	0	3.67
Marc Behrend	1	12	0	0	0.00
Daniel Berthiaume	1	68	4	0	3.53
Brian Hayward	2	68	6	0	5.29
Dan Bouchard	1	40	5	0	7.50
Winnipeg Totals	3	188	15	0	4.79
Clint Malarchuk	3	143	11	0	4.62
Mario Gosselin	1	40	5	0	7.50
Quebec Totals	3	183	16	0	5.25
Wendell Young	1	60	5	0	5.00
Richard Brodeur	2	120	12	0	6.00
Vancouver Totals	3	180	17	0	5.67
Bob Sauve	2	99	8(1)	0	4.85
Murray Bannerman	2	81	9	0	6.67
Chicago Totals	3	180	18	0	6.00

( )—Empty Net Goals. Not counted against an individual goalie's average.

Individual Stanley Cup Leaders

Goals	Joe Mullen, Calgary—	12
Assists	Al MacInnis, Calgary—	15
Points	Doug Gilmour, St. Louis—	21
	Bernie Federko, St. Louis—	21
Penalty Minutes	Chris Nilan, Montreal—	141
Goaltender's average (360 minutes)	Mike Liut, Hartford—	1.90
Shutouts	Mike Liut, Hartford—	1
	Patrick Roy, Montreal—	1
	John Vanbiesbrouck, New York Rangers—	1
	Ken Wregget, Toronto—	1

Individual 1985-86 NHL Trophy Winners

ART ROSS TROPHY (Scoring Leaders)	Wayne Gretzky, Edmonton
HART MEMORIAL TROPHY (Most Valuable)	Wayne Gretzky, Edmonton
JAMES NORRIS MEMORIAL TROPHY (Top Defensemen)	Paul Coffey, Edmonton
VEZINA TROPHY (Top Goaltender)	John Vanbiesbrouck, N.Y. Rangers
BILL JENNINGS TROPHY (Goaltending Trophy)	Bob Froese, Philadelphia
CALDER MEMORIAL TROPHY (Top Rookie)	Gary Suter, Calgary
LADY BYNG TROPHY (Most Gentlemanly)	Mike Bossy, N.Y. Islanders
CONN SMYTHE TROPHY (Playoff MVP)	Patrick Roy, Montreal
BILL MASTERTON MEMORIAL TROPHY (Perseverance, Sportsmanship and Dedication)	Charlie Simmer, Boston
FRANK J. SELKE TROPHY (Best Defensive Forward)	Troy Murray, Chicago
JACK ADAMS AWARD (Coach of the Year)	Glen Sather, Edmonton

Year-By-Year NHL Standings

From 1917-18 through the 1925-26 season, National Hockey League champions played against the Pacific Coast Hockey League for the Stanley Cup. So, only Stanley Cup championships are designated in the following club records for that period.

Key to standings: *—Missed playoffs. †—Eliminated in first round of new playoff format (1974-75). a—Eliminated in quarterfinal round. b—Eliminated in semifinal round. c—Eliminated in final round. xx—Stanley Cup champion.

NOTE: Records for Edmonton Oilers, Hartford Whalers, Quebec Nordiques and Winnipeg Jets include World Hockey Association results prior to their entrance into NHL in 1979-80. Key to WHA standings: *—Missed playoffs. †—Preliminary round (established for 1975-76 season). a—Eliminated in quarterfinal round. b—Eliminated in semifinal round. c—Eliminated in final round. xx—Avco World Cup champion.

Boston Bruins

Season	W.	L.	T.	Pts.	GF.	GA.	Position
1924-25	6	24	0	12	49	119	Sixth
1925-26	17	15	4	38	92	85	Fourth
1926-27	21	20	3	45	97	89	Second—c
1927-28	20	13	11	51	77	70	First—b
1928-29	26	13	5	57	89	52	First—xx
1929-30	38	5	1	77	179	98	First—c
1930-31	28	10	6	62	143	90	First—b
1931-32	15	21	12	42	122	117	Fourth—*
1932-33	25	15	8	58	124	88	First—b
1933-34	18	25	5	41	111	130	Fourth—*
1934-35	26	16	6	58	129	112	First—b
1935-36	22	20	6	50	92	83	Second—a
1936-37	23	18	7	53	120	110	Second—a
1937-38	30	11	7	67	142	89	First—b
1938-39	36	10	2	74	156	76	First—xx
1939-40	31	12	5	67	170	98	First—b
1940-41	27	8	13	67	168	102	First—xx
1941-42	25	17	6	56	160	118	Third—b
1942-43	24	17	9	57	195	176	Second—c
1943-44	19	26	5	43	223	268	Fifth—*
1944-45	16	30	4	36	179	219	Fourth—b
1945-46	24	18	8	56	167	156	Second—c
1946-47	26	23	11	63	190	175	Third—b
1947-48	23	24	13	59	167	168	Third—b
1948-49	29	23	8	66	178	163	Second—b
1949-50	22	32	16	60	198	228	Fifth—*
1950-51	22	30	18	62	178	197	Fourth—b
1951-52	25	29	16	66	162	176	Fourth—b
1952-53	28	29	13	69	152	172	Third—c
1953-54	32	28	10	74	177	181	Fourth—b
1954-55	23	26	21	67	169	188	Fourth—b
1955-56	23	34	13	59	147	185	Fifth—*
1956-57	34	24	12	80	195	174	Third—c
1957-58	27	28	15	69	199	194	Fourth—c
1958-59	32	29	9	73	205	215	Second—b
1959-60	28	34	8	64	220	241	Fifth—*
1960-61	15	42	13	43	176	254	Sixth—*
1961-62	15	47	8	38	177	306	Sixth—*
1962-63	14	39	17	45	198	281	Sixth—*
1963-64	18	40	12	48	170	212	Sixth—*
1964-65	21	43	6	48	166	253	Sixth—*
1965-66	21	43	6	48	174	275	Fifth—*
1966-67	17	43	10	44	182	253	Sixth—*
1967-68	37	27	10	84	259	216	Third—a
1968-69	42	18	16	100	303	221	Second—b
1969-70	40	17	19	99	277	216	Second—xx
1970-71	57	14	7	121	399	207	First—a
1971-72	54	13	11	119	330	204	First—xx
1972-73	51	22	5	107	330	235	Second—a
1973-74	52	17	9	113	349	221	First—c
1974-75	40	26	14	94	345	245	Second—†
1975-76	48	15	17	113	313	237	First—b
1976-77	49	23	8	106	312	240	First—c
1977-78	51	18	11	113	333	218	First—c
1978-79	43	23	14	100	316	270	First—b
1979-80	46	21	13	105	310	234	Second—a
1980-81	37	30	13	87	316	272	Second—†

Season	W.	L.	T.	Pts.	GF.	GA.	Position
1981-82	43	27	10	96	323	285	Second—a
1982-83	50	20	10	110	327	228	First—b
1983-84	49	25	6	104	336	261	First—†
1984-85	36	34	10	82	303	287	Fourth—†
1985-86	37	31	12	86	311	288	Third—†
	1874	1475	603	4351	12586	11621	

Buffalo Sabres

Season	W.	L.	T.	Pts.	GF.	GA.	Position
1970-71	24	39	15	63	217	291	Fifth—*
1971-72	16	43	19	51	203	289	Sixth—*
1972-73	37	27	14	88	257	219	Fourth—a
1973-74	32	34	12	76	242	250	Fifth—*
1974-75	49	16	15	113	354	240	First—c
1975-76	46	21	13	105	339	240	Second—a
1976-77	48	24	8	104	301	220	Second—a
1977-78	44	19	17	105	288	215	Second—a
1978-79	36	28	16	88	280	263	Second—†
1979-80	47	17	16	110	318	201	First—b
1980-81	39	20	21	99	327	250	First—a
1981-82	39	26	15	93	307	273	Third—†
1982-83	38	29	13	89	318	285	Third—a
1983-84	48	25	7	103	315	257	Second—†
1984-85	38	28	14	90	290	237	Third—†
1985-86	37	37	6	80	296	291	Fifth—*
	618	433	221	1447	4652	4021	

Calgary Flames

Season	W.	L.	T.	Pts.	GF.	GA.	Position
1972-73	25	38	15	65	191	239	Seventh—*
1973-74	30	34	14	74	214	238	Fourth—a
1974-75	34	31	15	83	243	233	Fourth—*
1975-76	35	33	12	82	262	237	Third—†
1976-77	34	34	12	80	264	265	Third—†
1977-78	34	27	19	87	274	252	Third—†
1978-79	41	31	8	90	327	280	Fourth—†
1979-80	35	32	13	83	282	269	Fourth—†
1980-81	39	27	14	92	329	298	Third—b
1981-82	29	34	17	75	334	345	Third—†
1982-83	32	34	14	78	321	317	Second—a
1983-84	34	32	14	82	311	314	Second—a
1984-85	41	27	12	94	363	302	Third—†
1985-86	40	31	9	89	354	315	Second—c
	483	445	188	1154	4069	3904	

Chicago Black Hawks

Season	W.	L.	T.	Pts.	GF.	GA.	Position
1926-27	19	22	3	41	115	116	Third—a
1927-28	7	34	3	17	68	134	Fifth—*
1928-29	7	29	8	22	33	85	Fifth—*
1929-30	21	18	5	47	117	111	Second—a
1930-31	24	17	3	51	108	78	Second—c
1931-32	18	19	11	47	86	101	Second—a
1932-33	16	20	12	44	88	101	Fourth—*
1933-34	20	17	11	51	88	83	Second—xx
1934-35	26	17	5	57	118	88	Second—a
1935-36	21	19	8	50	93	92	Third—a
1936-37	14	27	7	35	99	131	Fourth—*
1937-38	14	25	9	37	97	139	Third—xx
1938-39	12	28	8	32	91	132	Seventh—*
1939-40	23	19	6	52	112	120	Fourth—a
1940-41	16	25	7	39	112	139	Fifth—b
1941-42	22	23	3	47	145	155	Fourth—a
1942-43	17	18	15	49	179	180	Fifth—*
1943-44	22	23	5	49	178	187	Fourth—c
1944-45	13	30	7	33	141	194	Fifth—*
1945-46	23	20	7	53	200	178	Third—b

Season	W.	L.	T.	Pts.	GF.	GA.	Position
1946-47	19	37	4	42	193	274	Sixth—*
1947-48	20	34	6	46	195	225	Sixth—*
1948-49	21	31	8	50	173	211	Fifth—*
1949-50	22	38	10	54	203	244	Sixth—*
1950-51	13	47	10	36	171	280	Sixth—*
1951-52	17	44	9	43	158	241	Sixth—*
1952-53	27	28	15	69	169	175	Fourth—b
1953-54	12	51	7	31	133	242	Sixth—*
1954-55	13	40	17	43	161	235	Sixth—*
1955-56	19	39	12	50	155	216	Sixth—*
1956-57	16	39	15	47	169	225	Sixth—*
1957-58	24	39	7	55	163	202	Fifth—*
1958-59	28	29	13	69	197	208	Third—b
1959-60	28	29	13	69	191	180	Third—b
1960-61	29	24	17	75	198	180	Third—xx
1961-62	31	26	13	75	217	186	Third—c
1962-63	32	21	17	81	194	178	Second—b
1963-64	36	22	12	84	218	169	Second—b
1964-65	34	28	8	76	224	176	Third—c
1965-66	37	25	8	82	240	187	Second—b
1966-67	41	17	12	94	264	170	First—b
1967-68	32	26	16	80	212	222	Fourth—b
1968-69	34	33	9	77	280	246	Sixth—*
1969-70	45	22	9	99	250	170	First—b
1970-71	49	20	9	107	277	184	First—c
1971-72	46	17	15	107	256	166	First—b
1972-73	42	27	9	93	284	225	First—c
1973-74	41	14	23	105	272	164	Second—b
1974-75	37	35	8	82	268	241	Third—a
1975-76	32	30	18	82	254	261	First—a
1976-77	26	43	11	63	240	298	Third—†
1977-78	32	29	19	83	230	220	First—a
1978-79	29	36	15	73	244	277	First—a
1979-80	34	27	19	87	241	250	First—a
1980-81	31	33	16	78	304	315	Second—†
1981-82	30	38	12	72	332	363	Fourth—b
1982-83	47	23	10	104	338	268	First—b
1983-84	30	42	8	68	277	311	Fourth—†
1984-85	38	35	7	83	309	299	Second—b
1985-86	39	33	8	86	351	349	First—†
	1568	1701	618	3753	11473	11777	

Detroit Red Wings

Season	W.	L.	T.	Pts.	GF.	GA.	Position
1926-27	12	28	4	28	76	105	Fifth—*
1927-28	19	19	6	44	88	79	Fourth—*
1928-29	19	16	9	47	72	63	Third—a
1929-30	14	24	6	34	117	133	Fourth—*
1930-31	16	21	7	39	102	105	Fourth—*
1931-32	18	20	10	46	95	108	Third—a
1932-33	25	15	8	58	111	93	Second—b
1933-34	24	14	10	58	113	98	First—c
1934-35	19	22	7	45	127	114	Fourth—*
1935-36	24	16	8	56	124	103	First—xx
1936-37	25	14	9	59	128	102	First—xx
1937-38	12	25	11	35	99	133	Fourth—*
1938-39	18	24	6	42	107	128	Fifth—b
1939-40	16	26	6	38	90	126	Fifth—b
1940-41	21	16	11	53	112	102	Third—c
1941-42	19	25	4	42	140	147	Fifth—c
1942-43	25	14	11	61	169	124	First—xx
1943-44	26	18	6	58	214	177	Second—b
1944-45	31	14	5	67	218	161	Second—c
1945-46	20	20	10	50	146	159	Fourth—b
1946-47	22	27	11	55	190	193	Fourth—b
1947-48	30	18	12	72	187	148	Second—c
1948-49	34	19	7	75	195	145	First—c
1949-50	37	19	14	88	229	164	First—xx
1950-51	44	13	13	101	236	139	First—b
1951-52	44	14	12	100	215	133	First—xx

Season	W.	L.	T.	Pts.	GF.	GA.	Position
1952-53	36	16	18	90	222	133	First—b
1953-54	37	19	14	88	191	132	First—xx
1954-55	42	17	11	95	204	134	First—xx
1955-56	30	24	16	76	183	148	Second—c
1956-57	38	20	12	88	198	157	First—b
1957-58	29	29	12	70	176	207	Third—b
1958-59	25	37	8	58	167	218	Sixth—*
1959-60	26	29	15	67	186	197	Fourth—b
1960-61	25	29	16	66	195	215	Fourth—c
1961-62	23	33	14	60	184	219	Fifth—*
1962-63	32	25	13	77	200	194	Fourth—c
1963-64	30	29	11	71	191	204	Fourth—c
1964-65	40	23	7	87	224	175	First—b
1965-66	31	27	12	74	221	194	Fourth—c
1966-67	27	39	4	58	212	241	Fifth—*
1967-68	27	35	12	66	245	257	Sixth—*
1968-69	33	31	12	78	239	221	Fifth—*
1969-70	40	21	15	95	246	199	Third—a
1970-71	22	45	11	55	209	308	Seventh—*
1971-72	33	35	10	76	261	262	Fifth—*
1972-73	37	29	12	86	265	243	Fifth—*
1973-74	29	39	10	68	255	319	Sixth—*
1974-75	23	45	12	58	259	335	Fourth—*
1975-76	26	44	10	62	226	300	Fourth—*
1976-77	16	55	9	41	183	309	Fifth—*
1977-78	32	34	14	78	252	266	Second—a
1978-79	23	41	16	62	252	295	Fifth—*
1979-80	26	43	11	63	268	306	Fifth—*
1980-81	19	43	18	56	252	339	Fifth—*
1981-82	21	47	12	54	270	351	Sixth—*
1982-83	21	44	15	57	263	344	Fifth—*
1983-84	31	42	7	69	298	323	Third—†
1984-85	27	41	12	66	313	357	Third—†
1985-86	17	57	6	40	266	415	Fifth—*
	1588	1668	630	3806	11476	11799	

Edmonton Oilers

Season	W.	L.	T.	Pts.	GF.	GA.	Position
1972-73	38	37	3	79	269	256	Fifth—*
1973-74	38	37	3	79	268	269	Third—a
1974-75	36	38	4	76	279	279	Fifth—*
1975-76	27	49	5	59	268	345	Fourth—a
1976-77	34	43	4	72	243	304	Fourth—a
1977-78	38	39	3	79	309	307	Fifth—a
1978-79	48	30	2	98	340	266	First—c
1979-80	28	39	13	69	301	322	Fourth—†
1980-81	29	35	16	74	328	327	Fourth—a
1981-82	48	17	15	111	417	295	First—†
1982-83	47	21	12	106	424	315	First—c
1983-84	57	18	5	119	446	314	First—xx
1984-85	49	20	11	109	401	298	First—xx
1985-86	56	17	7	119	426	310	First—a
	573	440	103	1249	4719	4207	

Hartford Whalers

Season	W.	L.	T.	Pts.	GF.	GA.	Position
1972-73	46	30	2	94	318	263	First—xx
1973-74	43	31	4	90	291	260	First—a
1974-75	43	30	5	91	274	279	First—a
1975-76	33	40	7	73	255	290	Third—b
1976-77	35	40	6	76	275	290	Fourth—a
1977-78	44	31	5	93	335	269	Second—c
1978-79	37	34	9	83	298	287	Fourth—b
1979-80	27	34	19	73	303	312	Fourth—†
1980-81	21	41	18	60	292	372	Fourth—*
1981-82	21	41	18	60	264	351	Fifth—*
1982-83	19	54	7	45	261	403	Fifth—*
1983-84	28	42	10	66	288	320	Fifth—*
1984-85	30	41	9	69	268	318	Fifth—*
1985-86	40	36	4	84	332	302	Fourth—a
	467	525	123	1057	4059	4316	

Los Angeles Kings

Season	W.	L.	T.	Pts.	GF.	GA.	Position
1967-68	31	33	10	72	200	224	Second—a
1968-69	24	42	10	58	185	260	Fourth—b
1969-70	14	52	10	38	168	290	Sixth—*
1970-71	25	40	13	63	239	303	Fifth—*
1971-72	20	49	9	49	206	305	Seventh—*
1972-73	31	36	11	73	232	245	Sixth—*
1973-74	33	33	12	78	233	231	Third—a
1974-75	42	17	21	105	269	185	Second—†
1975-76	38	33	9	85	263	265	Second—a
1976-77	34	31	15	83	271	241	Second—a
1977-78	31	34	15	77	243	245	Third—†
1978-79	34	34	12	80	292	286	Third—†
1979-80	30	36	14	74	290	313	Second—†
1980-81	43	24	13	99	337	290	Second—†
1981-82	24	41	15	63	314	369	Fourth—a
1982-83	27	41	12	66	308	365	Fifth—*
1983-84	23	44	13	59	309	376	Fifth—*
1984-85	34	32	14	82	339	326	Fourth—†
1985-86	23	49	8	54	284	389	Fifth—†
	561	601	236	1358	4982	5508	

Minnesota North Stars

Season	W.	L.	T.	Pts.	GF.	GA.	Position
1967-68	27	32	15	69	191	226	Fourth—b
1968-69	18	43	15	51	189	270	Sixth—*
1969-70	19	35	22	60	224	257	Third—a
1970-71	28	34	16	72	191	223	Fourth—b
1971-72	37	29	12	86	212	191	Second—a
1972-73	37	30	11	85	254	230	Third—a
1973-74	23	38	17	63	235	275	Seventh—*
1974-75	23	50	7	53	221	341	Fourth—*
1975-76	20	53	7	47	195	303	Fourth—*
1976-77	23	39	18	64	240	310	Second—†
1977-78	18	53	9	45	218	325	Fifth—*
1978-79	28	40	12	68	257	289	Fourth—*
1979-80	36	28	16	88	311	253	Third—b
1980-81	35	28	17	87	291	263	Third—c
1981-82	37	23	20	94	346	288	First—†
1982-83	40	24	16	96	321	290	Second—a
1983-84	39	31	10	88	345	344	First—b
1984-85	25	43	12	62	268	321	Fourth—a
1985-86	38	33	9	85	327	305	Second—†
	551	686	261	1363	4836	5304	

Montreal Canadiens

Season	W.	L.	T.	Pts.	GF.	GA.	Position
1917-18	13	9	0	26	115	84	First and Third
1918-19	10	8	0	20	88	78	Second
1919-20	13	11	0	26	129	113	Second
1920-21	13	11	0	26	112	99	Third
1921-22	12	11	1	25	88	94	Third
1922-23	13	9	2	28	73	61	Second
1923-24	13	11	0	26	59	48	Second—xx
1924-25	17	11	2	36	93	56	Third
1925-26	11	24	1	23	79	108	Seventh
1926-27	28	14	2	58	99	67	Second—c
1927-28	26	11	7	59	116	48	First—b
1928-29	22	7	15	59	71	43	First—b
1929-30	21	14	9	51	142	114	Second—xx
1930-31	26	10	8	60	129	89	First—xx
1931-32	25	16	7	57	128	111	First—b
1932-33	18	25	5	41	92	115	Third—a
1933-34	22	20	6	50	99	101	Second—a
1934-35	19	23	6	44	110	145	Third—a
1935-36	11	26	11	33	82	123	Fourth—*
1936-37	24	18	6	54	115	111	First—b
1937-38	18	17	13	49	123	128	Third—a
1938-39	15	24	9	39	115	146	Sixth—a
1939-40	10	33	5	25	90	167	Seventh—*
1940-41	16	26	6	38	121	147	Sixth—a

Season	W.	L.	T.	Pts.	GF.	GA.	Position
1941-42	18	27	3	39	134	173	Sixth—a
1942-43	19	19	12	50	181	191	Fourth—b
1943-44	38	5	7	83	234	109	First—xx
1944-45	38	8	4	80	228	121	First—b
1945-46	28	17	5	61	172	134	First—xx
1946-47	34	16	10	78	189	138	First—c
1947-48	20	29	11	51	147	169	Fifth—*
1948-49	28	23	9	65	152	126	Third—b
1949-50	29	22	19	77	172	150	Second—b
1950-51	25	30	15	65	173	184	Third—c
1951-52	34	26	10	78	195	164	Second—c
1952-53	28	23	19	75	155	148	Second—xx
1953-54	35	24	11	81	195	141	Second—c
1954-55	41	18	11	93	228	157	Second—c
1955-56	45	15	10	100	222	131	First—xx
1956-57	35	23	12	82	210	155	Second—xx
1957-58	43	17	10	96	250	158	First—xx
1958-59	39	18	13	91	258	158	First—xx
1959-60	40	18	12	92	255	178	First—xx
1960-61	41	19	10	92	254	188	First—b
1961-62	42	14	14	98	259	166	First—b
1962-63	28	19	23	79	225	183	Third—b
1963-64	36	21	13	85	209	167	First—b
1964-65	36	23	11	83	211	185	Second—xx
1965-66	41	21	8	90	239	173	First—xx
1966-67	32	25	13	77	202	188	Second—c
1967-68	42	22	10	94	236	167	First—xx
1968-69	46	19	11	103	271	202	First—xx
1969-70	38	22	16	92	244	201	Fifth—*
1970-71	42	23	13	97	291	216	Third—xx
1971-72	46	16	16	108	307	205	Third—a
1972-73	52	10	16	120	329	184	First—xx
1973-74	45	24	9	99	293	240	Second—a
1974-75	47	14	19	113	374	225	First—b
1975-76	58	11	11	127	337	174	First—xx
1976-77	60	8	12	132	387	171	First—xx
1977-78	59	10	11	129	359	183	First—xx
1978-79	52	17	11	115	337	204	First—xx
1979-80	47	20	13	107	328	240	First—a
1980-81	45	22	13	103	332	232	First—†
1981-82	46	17	17	109	360	223	First—†
1982-83	42	24	14	98	350	286	Second—†
1983-84	35	40	5	75	286	295	Fourth—b
1984-85	41	27	12	94	309	262	First—a
1985-86	40	33	7	87	330	280	Second—xx
	2172	1288	652	4996	13877	10721	

New Jersey Devils

Season	W.	L.	T.	Pts.	GF.	GA.	Position
1974-75	15	54	11	41	184	328	Fifth—*
1975-76	12	56	12	36	190	351	Fifth—*
1976-77	20	46	14	54	226	307	Fifth—*
1977-78	19	40	21	59	257	305	Second—†
1978-79	15	53	12	42	210	331	Fourth—*
1979-80	20	48	13	51	234	308	Sixth—*
1980-81	22	45	13	57	258	344	Fifth—*
1981-82	18	49	13	49	241	362	Fifth—*
1982-83	17	49	14	48	230	338	Fifth—*
1983-84	17	56	7	41	231	350	Fifth—*
1984-85	22	48	10.	54	263	346	Fifth—*
1985-86	28	49	3	59	300	374	Fifth—*
	225	593	143	591	2824	4047	

New York Islanders

Season	W.	L.	T.	Pts.	GF.	GA.	Position
1972-73	12	60	6	30	170	347	Eighth—*
1973-74	19	41	18	56	182	247	Eighth—*
1974-75	33	25	22	88	264	221	Third—b
1975-76	42	21	17	101	297	190	Second—b
1976-77	47	21	12	106	288	193	Second—b

Season	W.	L.	T.	Pts.	GF.	GA.	Position
1977-78	48	17	15	111	334	210	First—a
1978-79	51	15	14	116	358	214	First—b
1979-80	39	28	13	91	281	247	Second—xx
1980-81	48	18	14	110	355	260	First—xx
1981-82	54	16	10	118	385	250	First—xx
1982-83	42	26	12	96	302	226	Second—xx
1983-84	50	26	4	104	357	269	First—c
1984-85	40	34	6	86	345	312	Third—a
1985-86	39	29	12	90	327	284	Third—†
	564	377	175	1303	4245	3470	

New York Rangers

Season	W.	L.	T.	Pts.	GF.	GA.	Position
1926-27	25	13	6	56	95	72	First—a
1927-28	19	16	9	47	94	79	Second—xx
1928-29	21	13	10	52	72	65	Second—c
1929-30	17	17	10	44	136	143	Third—b
1930-31	19	16	9	47	106	87	Third—b
1931-32	23	17	8	54	134	112	First—c
1932-33	23	17	8	54	135	107	Third—xx
1933-34	21	19	8	50	120	113	Third—a
1934-35	22	20	6	50	137	139	Third—b
1935-36	19	17	12	50	91	96	Fourth—*
1936-37	19	20	9	47	117	106	Third—c
1937-38	27	15	6	60	149	96	Second—a
1938-39	26	16	6	58	149	105	Second—b
1939-40	27	11	10	64	136	77	Second—xx
1940-41	21	19	8	50	143	125	Fourth—a
1941-42	29	17	2	60	177	143	First—b
1942-43	11	31	8	30	161	253	Sixth—*
1943-44	6	39	5	17	162	310	Sixth—*
1944-45	11	29	10	32	154	247	Sixth—*
1945-46	13	28	9	35	144	191	Sixth—*
1946-47	22	32	6	50	167	186	Fifth—*
1947-48	21	26	13	55	176	201	Fourth—b
1948-49	18	31	11	47	133	172	Sixth—*
1949-50	28	31	11	67	170	189	Fourth—c
1950-51	20	29	21	61	169	201	Fifth—*
1951-52	23	34	13	59	192	219	Fifth—*
1952-53	17	37	16	50	152	211	Sixth—*
1953-54	29	31	10	68	161	182	Fifth—*
1954-55	17	35	18	52	150	210	Fifth—*
1955-56	32	28	10	74	204	203	Third—b
1956-57	26	30	14	66	184	227	Fourth—b
1957-58	32	25	13	77	195	188	Second—b
1958-59	26	32	12	64	201	217	Fifth—*
1959-60	17	38	15	49	187	247	Sixth—*
1960-61	22	38	10	54	204	248	Fifth—*
1961-62	26	32	12	64	195	207	Fourth—b
1962-63	22	36	12	56	211	233	Fifth—*
1963-64	22	38	10	54	186	242	Fifth—*
1964-65	20	38	12	52	179	246	Fifth—*
1965-66	18	41	11	47	195	261	Sixth—*
1966-67	30	28	12	72	188	189	Fourth—b
1967-68	39	23	12	90	226	183	Second—a
1968-69	41	26	9	91	231	196	Third—a
1969-70	38	22	16	92	246	189	Fourth—a
1970-71	49	18	11	109	259	177	Second—b
1971-72	48	17	13	109	317	192	Second—c
1972-73	47	23	8	102	297	208	Third—b
1973-74	40	24	14	94	300	251	Third—b
1974-75	37	29	14	88	319	276	Second—†
1975-76	29	42	9	67	262	333	Fourth—*
1976-77	29	37	14	72	272	310	Fourth—*
1977-78	30	37	13	73	279	280	Fourth—†
1978-79	40	29	11	91	316	292	Third—c
1979-80	38	32	10	86	308	284	Third—a
1980-81	30	36	14	74	312	317	Fourth—b
1981-82	39	27	14	92	316	306	Second—a
1982-83	35	35	10	80	306	287	Fourth—a
1983-84	42	29	9	93	314	304	Fourth—†

Season	W.	L.	T.	Pts.	GF.	GA.	Position
1984-85	26	44	10	62	295	345	Fourth—†
1985-86	36	38	6	78	280	276	Fourth—b
	1600	1648	638	3838	11866	12151	

Philadelphia Flyers

Season	W.	L.	T.	Pts.	GF.	GA.	Position
1967-68	31	32	11	73	173	179	First—a
1968-69	20	35	21	61	174	225	Third—a
1969-70	17	35	24	58	197	225	Fifth—*
1970-71	28	33	17	73	207	225	Third—a
1971-72	26	38	14	66	200	236	Fifth—*
1972-73	37	30	11	85	296	256	Second—b
1973-74	50	16	12	112	273	164	First—xx
1974-75	51	18	11	113	293	181	First—xx
1975-76	51	13	16	118	348	209	First—c
1976-77	48	16	16	112	323	213	First—b
1977-78	45	20	15	105	296	200	Second—b
1978-79	40	25	15	95	281	248	Second—a
1979-80	48	12	20	116	327	254	First—c
1980-81	41	24	15	97	313	249	Second—a
1981-82	38	31	11	87	325	313	Third—†
1982-83	49	23	8	106	326	240	First—†
1983-84	44	26	10	98	350	290	Third—†
1984-85	53	20	7	113	348	240	First—c
1985-86	53	23	4	110	335	241	First—†
	770	470	258	1798	5385	4488	

Pittsburgh Penguins

Season	W.	L.	T.	Pts.	GF.	GA.	Position
1967-68	27	34	13	67	195	216	Fifth—*
1968-69	20	45	11	51	189	252	Fifth—*
1969-70	26	38	12	64	182	238	Second—b
1970-71	21	37	20	62	221	240	Sixth—*
1971-72	26	38	14	66	220	258	Fourth—a
1972-73	32	37	9	73	257	265	Fifth—*
1973-74	28	41	9	65	242	273	Fifth—*
1974-75	37	28	15	89	326	289	Third—a
1975-76	35	33	12	82	339	303	Third—†
1976-77	34	33	13	81	240	252	Third—†
1977-78	25	37	18	68	254	321	Fourth—*
1978-79	36	31	13	85	281	279	Second—a
1979-80	30	37	13	73	251	303	Third—†
1980-81	30	37	13	73	302	345	Third—†
1981-82	31	36	13	75	310	337	Fourth—†
1982-83	18	53	9	45	257	394	Sixth—*
1983-84	16	58	6	38	254	390	Sixth—*
1984-85	24	51	5	53	276	385	Fifth—*
1985-86	34	38	8	76	313	305	Fifth—*
	530	742	226	1286	4667	5645	

Quebec Nordiques

Season	W.	L.	T.	Pts.	GF.	GA.	Position
1972-73	33	40	5	71	276	313	Fifth—*
1973-74	38	36	4	80	306	280	Fifth—*
1974-75	46	32	0	92	331	299	First—c
1975-76	50	27	4	104	371	316	Second—a
1976-77	47	31	3	97	353	295	First—xx
1977-78	40	37	3	83	349	347	Fourth—b
1978-79	41	34	5	87	288	271	Second—b
1979-80	25	44	11	61	248	313	Fifth—*
1980-81	30	32	18	78	314	318	Fourth—†
1981-82	33	31	16	82	356	345	Fourth—b
1982-83	34	34	12	80	343	336	Fourth—†
1983-84	42	28	10	94	360	278	Third—†
1984-85	41	30	9	91	323	275	Second—b
1985-86	43	31	6	92	330	289	First—†
	543	464	106	1192	4548	4275	

St. Louis Blues

Season	W.	L.	T.	Pts.	GF.	GA.	Position
1967-68	27	31	16	70	177	191	Third—c
1968-69	37	25	14	88	204	157	First—c
1969-70	37	27	12	86	224	179	First—c
1970-71	34	25	19	87	223	208	Second—a
1971-72	28	39	11	67	208	247	Third—b
1972-73	32	34	12	76	233	251	Fourth—a
1973-74	26	40	12	64	206	248	Sixth—*
1974-75	35	31	14	84	269	267	Second—†
1975-76	29	37	14	72	249	290	Third—†
1976-77	32	39	9	73	239	276	First—a
1977-78	20	47	13	53	195	304	Fourth—*
1978-79	18	50	12	48	249	348	Third—*
1979-80	34	34	12	80	266	278	Second—†
1980-81	45	18	17	107	352	281	First—a
1981-82	32	40	8	72	315	349	Third—a
1982-83	25	40	15	65	285	316	Fourth—†
1983-84	32	41	7	71	293	316	Second—a
1984-85	37	31	12	86	299	288	First—†
1985-86	37	34	9	83	302	291	Third—b
	597	663	238	1432	4788	5085	

Toronto Maple Leafs

Season	W.	L.	T.	Pts.	GF.	GA.	Position
1917-18	13	9	0	26	108	109	Second, First
1918-19	5	13	0	10	64	92	Third
1919-20	12	12	0	24	119	106	Third
1920-21	15	9	0	30	105	100	First
1921-22	13	10	1	27	98	97	Second—xx
1922-23	13	10	1	27	82	88	Third
1923-24	10	14	0	20	59	85	Third
1924-25	19	11	0	38	90	84	Second
1925-26	12	21	3	27	92	114	Sixth
1926-27	15	24	5	35	79	94	Fifth—*
1927-28	18	18	8	44	89	88	Fourth—*
1928-29	21	18	5	47	85	69	Third—b
1929-30	17	21	6	40	116	124	Fourth—*
1930-31	22	13	9	53	118	99	Second—a
1931-32	23	18	7	53	155	127	Second—xx
1932-33	24	18	6	54	119	111	First—c
1933-34	26	13	9	61	174	119	First—b
1934-35	30	14	4	64	157	111	First—c
1935-36	23	19	6	52	126	106	Second—c
1936-37	22	21	5	49	119	115	Third—a
1937-38	24	15	9	57	151	127	First—c
1938-39	19	20	9	47	114	107	Third—c
1939-40	25	17	6	56	134	110	Third—c
1940-41	28	14	6	62	145	99	Second—b
1941-42	27	18	3	57	158	136	Second—xx
1942-43	22	19	9	53	198	159	Third—b
1943-44	23	23	4	50	214	174	Third—b
1944-45	24	22	4	52	183	161	Third—xx
1945-46	19	24	7	45	174	185	Fifth—*
1946-47	31	19	10	72	209	172	Second—xx
1947-48	32	15	13	77	182	143	First—xx
1948-49	22	25	13	57	147	161	Fourth—xx
1949-50	31	27	12	74	176	173	Third—b
1950-51	41	16	13	95	212	138	Second—xx
1951-52	29	25	16	74	168	157	Third—b
1952-53	27	30	13	67	156	167	Fifth—*
1953-54	32	24	14	78	152	131	Third—b
1954-55	24	24	22	70	147	135	Third—b
1955-56	24	33	13	61	153	181	Fourth—b
1956-57	21	34	15	57	174	192	Fifth—*
1957-58	21	38	11	53	192	226	Sixth—*
1958-59	27	32	11	65	189	201	Fourth—c
1959-60	35	26	9	79	199	195	Second—c
1960-61	39	19	12	90	234	176	Second—b
1961-62	37	22	11	85	232	180	Second—xx
1962-63	35	23	12	82	221	180	First—xx
1963-64	33	25	12	78	192	172	Third—xx

Season	W.	L.	T.	Pts.	GF.	GA.	Position
1964-65	30	26	14	74	204	173	Fourth—b
1965-66	34	25	11	79	208	187	Third—b
1966-67	32	27	11	75	204	211	Third—xx
1967-68	33	31	10	76	209	176	Fifth—*
1968-69	35	26	15	85	234	217	Fourth—a
1969-70	29	34	13	71	222	242	Sixth—*
1970-71	37	33	8	82	248	211	Fourth—a
1971-72	33	31	14	80	209	208	Fourth—a
1972-73	27	41	10	64	247	279	Sixth—*
1973-74	35	27	16	86	274	230	Fourth—a
1974-75	31	33	16	78	280	309	Third—a
1975-76	34	31	15	83	294	276	Third—b
1976-77	33	32	15	81	301	285	Third—a
1977-78	41	29	10	92	271	237	Third—b
1978-79	34	33	13	81	267	252	Third—a
1979-80	35	40	5	75	304	327	Fourth—†
1980-81	28	37	15	71	322	367	Fifth—†
1981-82	20	44	16	56	298	380	Fifth—*
1982-83	28	40	12	68	293	330	Third—†
1983-84	26	45	9	61	303	387	Fifth—*
1984-85	20	52	8	48	253	358	Fifth—*
1985-86	25	48	7	57	311	386	Fourth—a
	1785	1700	627	4197	12716	12404	

Vancouver Canucks

Season	W.	L.	T.	Pts.	GF.	GA.	Position
1970-71	24	46	8	56	229	296	Sixth—*
1971-72	20	50	8	48	203	297	Seventh—*
1972-73	22	47	9	53	233	339	Seventh—*
1973-74	24	43	11	59	224	296	Seventh—*
1974-75	38	32	10	86	271	254	First—a
1975-76	33	32	15	81	271	272	Second—†
1976-77	25	42	13	63	235	294	Fourth—*
1977-78	20	43	17	57	239	320	Third—*
1978-79	25	42	13	63	217	291	Second—†
1979-80	27	37	16	70	256	281	Third—†
1980-81	28	32	20	76	289	301	Third—†
1981-82	30	33	17	77	290	286	Second—c
1982-83	30	35	15	75	303	309	Third—†
1983-84	32	39	9	73	306	328	Third—†
1984-85	25	46	9	59	284	401	Fifth—*
1985-86	23	44	13	59	282	333	Fourth—†
	426	643	203	1055	4132	4898	

Washington Capitals

Season	W.	L.	T.	Pts.	GF.	GA.	Position
1974-75	8	67	5	21	181	446	Fifth—*
1975-76	11	59	10	32	224	394	Fifth—*
1976-77	24	42	14	62	221	307	Fourth—*
1977-78	17	49	14	48	195	321	Fifth—*
1978-79	24	41	15	63	273	338	Fourth—*
1979-80	27	40	13	67	261	293	Fifth—*
1980-81	26	36	18	70	286	317	Fifth—*
1981-82	26	41	13	65	319	338	Fifth—*
1982-83	39	25	16	94	306	283	Third—†
1983-84	48	27	5	101	308	226	Second—a
1984-85	46	25	9	101	322	240	Second—†
1985-86	50	23	7	107	315	272	Second—a
	346	475	139	831	3211	3775	

Winnipeg Jets

Season	W.	L.	T.	Pts.	GF.	GA.	Position
1972-73	43	31	4	90	285	249	First—c
1973-74	34	39	5	73	264	296	Fourth—a
1974-75	38	35	5	81	322	293	Third—*
1975-76	52	27	2	106	345	254	First—xx
1976-77	46	32	2	94	366	291	Second—c
1977-78	50	28	2	102	381	270	First—xx
1978-79	39	35	6	84	307	306	Third—xx
1979-80	20	49	11	51	214	314	Fifth—*

Toronto left winger Wendel Clark, the NHL's top draft pick of 1985, capped last season by being named The Sporting News' NHL Rookie of the Year.

Season	W.	L.	T.	Pts.	GF.	GA.	Position
1980-81	9	57	14	32	246	400	Sixth—*
1981-82	33	33	14	80	319	332	Second—†
1982-83	33	39	8	74	311	333	Fourth—†
1983-84	31	38	11	73	340	374	Third—†
1984-85	43	27	10	96	358	332	Second—a
1985-86	26	47	7	59	295	372	Third—†
	497	517	101	1095	4353	4416	

NHL Stanley Cup Winners

SEASON	TEAM	COACH
1917-18	Toronto Arenas	Dick Carroll
1919-20	Ottawa Senators	Pete Green
1920-21	Ottawa Senators	Pete Green
1921-22	Toronto St. Pats	Eddie Powers
1922-23	Ottawa Senators	Pete Green
1923-24	Montreal Canadiens	Leo Dandurand
1924-25	Victoria Cougars	Lester Patrick
1925-26	Montreal Maroons	Eddie Gerard
1926-27	Ottawa Senators	Dave Gill
1927-28	New York Rangers	Lester Patrick
1928-29	Boston Bruins	Cy Denneny
1929-30	Montreal Canadiens	Cecil Hart
1930-31	Montreal Canadiens	Cecil Hart
1931-32	Toronto Maple Leafs	Dick Irvin
1932-33	New York Rangers	Lester Patrick
1933-34	Chicago Black Hawks	Tommy Gorman
1934-35	Montreal Maroons	Tommy Gorman
1935-36	Detroit Red Wings	Jack Adams
1936-37	Detroit Red Wings	Jack Adams
1937-38	Chicago Black Hawks	Bill Stewart
1938-39	Boston Bruins	Art Ross
1939-40	New York Rangers	Frank Boucher
1940-41	Boston Bruins	Cooney Weiland
1941-42	Toronto Maple Leafs	Hap Day
1942-43	Detroit Red Wings	Jack Adams
1943-44	Montreal Canadiens	Dick Irvin
1944-45	Toronto Maple Leafs	Hap Day
1945-46	Montreal Canadiens	Dick Irvin
1946-47	Toronto Maple Leafs	Hap Day
1947-48	Toronto Maple Leafs	Hap Day
1948-49	Toronto Maple Leafs	Hap Day
1949-50	Detroit Red Wings	Tommy Ivan
1950-51	Toronto Maple Leafs	Joe Primeau
1951-52	Detroit Red Wings	Tommy Ivan
1952-53	Montreal Canadiens	Dick Irvin
1953-54	Detroit Red Wings	Tommy Ivan
1954-55	Detroit Red Wings	Jimmy Skinner
1955-56	Montreal Canadiens	Toe Blake
1956-57	Montreal Canadiens	Toe Blake
1957-58	Montreal Canadiens	Toe Blake
1958-59	Montreal Canadiens	Toe Blake
1959-60	Montreal Canadiens	Toe Blake
1960-61	Chicago Black Hawks	Rudy Pilous
1961-62	Toronto Maple Leafs	Punch Imlach
1962-63	Toronto Maple Leafs	Punch Imlach
1963-64	Toronto Maple Leafs	Punch Imlach
1964-65	Montreal Canadiens	Toe Blake
1965-66	Montreal Canadiens	Toe Blake
1966-67	Toronto Maple Leafs	Punch Imlach
1967-68	Montreal Canadiens	Toe Blake
1968-69	Montreal Canadiens	Claude Ruel
1969-70	Boston Bruins	Harry Sinden
1970-71	Montreal Canadiens	Al MacNeil
1971-72	Boston Bruins	Tom Johnson
1972-73	Montreal Canadiens	Scotty Bowman
1973-74	Philadelphia Flyers	Fred Shero
1974-75	Philadelphia Flyers	Fred Shero
1975-76	Montreal Canadiens	Scotty Bowman
1976-77	Montreal Canadiens	Scotty Bowman
1977-78	Montreal Canadiens	Scotty Bowman
1978-79	Montreal Canadiens	Scotty Bowman
1979-80	New York Islanders	Al Arbour
1980-81	New York Islanders	Al Arbour
1981-82	New York Islanders	Al Arbour
1982-83	New York Islanders	Al Arbour
1983-84	Edmonton Oilers	Glen Sather
1984-85	Edmonton Oilers	Glen Sather
1985-86	Montreal Canadiens	Jean Perron

NOTE: 1918-19 series between Montreal and Seattle cancelled after five games because of influenza epidemic.

Stanley Cup Playoff Records

Team

1—Most Stanley Cup Championships: Montreal Canadiens (21).
2—Most Final Series Appearances: Montreal Canadiens (27).
3—Most Years in Playoffs: Montreal Canadiens (56).
4—Most Consecutive Stanley Cup Championships: Montreal Canadiens (5).
5—Most Consecutive Playoff Appearances: Montreal Canadiens (21).
6—Most Goals, One Team, One Game: Montreal Canadiens (11) vs. Toronto, March 30, 1944; Edmonton Oilers (11) vs. Chicago, May 4, 1985.
7—Most Goals, One Team, One Period: Montreal Canadiens (7) vs. Toronto, March 30, 1944—3rd period.
8—Most Consecutive Playoff Game Victories: Edmonton Oilers (12).

Individual

1—Most Years in Playoffs: Gordie Howe (Detroit 19, Hartford 1)—20.
2—Most Consecutive Years in Playoffs: Brad Park (N.Y. Rangers, Boston, Detroit)—17.
3—Most Playoff Games: Henri Richard (Montreal)—180.
4—Most Points in Playoffs: Jean Beliveau (Montreal)—176.
5—Most Goals in Playoffs: Mike Bossy (N.Y. Islanders)—83.
6—Most Assists in Playoffs: Denis Potvin (N.Y. Islanders)—101.
7—Most Shutouts in Playoffs: Jacques Plante (Montreal, St. Louis)—14.
8—Most Games Played by Goaltender: Bill Smith (N.Y. Islanders)—129.
9—Most Points One Year: Wayne Gretzky (Edmonton)—47 in 1984-85.
10—Most Goals One Year:
    Reggie Leach (Philadelphia)—19 in 1975-76.
    Jari Kurri (Edmonton)—19 in 1984-85.
11—Most Assists One Year: Wayne Gretzky (Edmonton)—30 in 1984-85.
12—Most Points By Defenseman One Year: Paul Coffey (Edmonton)—37 in 1984-85.
13—Most Goals By Defenseman One Year: Paul Coffey (Edmonton)—12 in 1984-85.
14—Most Assists By Defenseman One Year: Paul Coffey (Edmonton)—25 in 1984-85.
15—Most Penalty Minutes One Year: Chris Nilan (Montreal)—141 in 1985-86.
16—Most Shutouts One Year:
    Clint Benedict (Montreal Maroons)—4 in 1927-28.
    Dave Kerr (N.Y. Rangers)—4 in 1936-37.
    Frank McCool (Toronto)—4 in 1944-45.
    Terry Sawchuk (Detroit)—4 in 1951-52.
    Bernie Parent (Philadelphia)—4 in 1974-75.
    Ken Dryden (Montreal)—4 in 1976-77.
17—Most Consecutive Shutouts: Frank McCool (Toronto)—3 in 1944-45.
18—Most Points One Game:
    Wayne Gretzky (Edmonton)—7 vs. Calgary, April 17, 1983.
                             7 vs. Winnipeg, April 25, 1985.
19—Most Goals One Game:
    Maurice Richard (Montreal)—5 vs. Toronto, March 23, 1944.
    Darryl Sittler (Toronto)—5 vs. Philadelphia, April 22, 1976.
    Reggie Leach (Philadelphia)—5 vs. Boston, May 6, 1976.
20—Most Assists One Game:
    Mikko Leinonen (N.Y. Rangers)—6 vs. Philadelphia, April 8, 1982.
21—Most Penalty Minutes in Playoffs: Dave (Tiger) Williams (Toronto, Vancouver, Los Angeles)—425.

Individual Awards

Art Ross Trophy
(Leading Scorer—Regular Season)

Season	Player, Team	Games	G.	A.	Pts.
1917-18	Joe Malone, Montreal	20	44	**	44
1918-19	Newsy Lalonde, Montreal	17	23	9	32
1919-20	Joe Malone, Quebec Bulldogs	24	39	6	45
1920-21	Newsy Lalonde, Montreal	24	33	8	41
1921-22	Punch Broadbelt, Ottawa	24	32	14	46
1922-23	Babe Dye, Toronto	22	26	11	37
1923-24	Cy Denneny, Ottawa	21	22	1	23
1924-25	Babe Dye, Toronto	29	38	6	44
1925-26	Nels Stewart, Montreal Maroons	36	34	8	42
1926-27	Bill Cook, New York Rangers	44	33	4	37
1927-28	Howie Morenz, Montreal	43	33	18	51
1928-29	Ace Bailey, Toronto	44	22	10	32
1929-30	Cooney Weiland, Boston	44	43	30	73
1930-31	Howie Morenz, Montreal	39	28	23	51
1931-32	Harvey Jackson, Toronto	48	28	25	53
1932-33	Bill Cook, New York Rangers	48	28	22	50
1933-34	Charlie Conacher, Toronto	42	32	20	52
1934-35	Charlie Conacher, Toronto	48	36	21	57
1935-36	Dave Schriner, New York Americans	48	19	26	45
1936-37	Dave Schriner, New York Americans	48	21	25	46
1937-38	Gordie Drillon, Toronto	48	26	26	52
1938-39	Toe Blake, Montreal	48	24	23	47
1939-40	Milt Schmidt, Boston	48	22	30	52
1940-41	Bill Cowley, Boston	46	17	45	62
1941-42	Bryan Hextall, New York Rangers	48	24	32	56
1942-43	Doug Bentley, Chicago	50	33	40	73
1943-44	Herbie Cain, Boston	48	36	46	82
1944-45	Elmer Lach, Montreal	50	26	54	80
1945-46	Max Bentley, Chicago	47	31	30	61
1946-47	Max Bentley, Chicago	60	29	43	72
1947-48	Elmer Lach, Montreal	60	30	31	61
1948-49	Roy Conacher, Chicago	60	26	42	68
1949-50	Ted Lindsay, Detroit	69	23	55	78
1950-51	Gordie Howe, Detroit	70	43	43	86
1951-52	Gordie Howe, Detroit	70	47	39	86
1952-53	Gordie Howe, Detroit	70	49	46	95
1953-54	Gordie Howe, Detroit	70	33	48	81
1954-55	Bernie Geoffrion, Montreal	70	38	37	75
1955-56	Jean Beliveau, Montreal	70	47	41	88
1956-57	Gordie Howe, Detroit	70	44	45	89
1957-58	Dickie Moore, Montreal	70	36	48	84
1958-59	Dickie Moore, Montreal	70	41	55	96
1959-60	Bobby Hull, Chicago	70	39	42	81
1960-61	Bernie Geoffrion, Montreal	64	50	45	95
1961-62	Bobby Hull, Chicago	70	50	34	84
1962-63	Gordie Howe, Detroit	70	38	48	86
1963-64	Stan Mikita, Chicago	70	39	50	89
1964-65	Stan Mikita, Chicago	70	28	59	87
1965-66	Bobby Hull, Chicago	65	54	43	97
1966-67	Stan Mikita, Chicago	70	35	62	97
1967-68	Stan Mikita, Chicago	72	40	47	87
1968-69	Phil Esposito, Boston	74	49	77	126
1969-70	Bobby Orr, Boston	76	33	87	120
1970-71	Phil Esposito, Boston	78	76	76	152
1971-72	Phil Esposito, Boston	76	66	67	133
1972-73	Phil Esposito, Boston	78	55	75	130
1973-74	Phil Esposito, Boston	78	68	77	145
1974-75	Bobby Orr, Boston	80	46	89	135
1975-76	Guy Lafleur, Montreal	80	56	69	125
1976-77	Guy Lafleur, Montreal	80	56	80	136
1977-78	Guy Lafleur, Montreal	78	60	72	132
1978-79	Bryan Trottier, New York Islanders	76	47	87	134
1979-80	Marcel Dionne, Los Angeles	80	53	84	137
1980-81	Wayne Gretzky, Edmonton	80	55	109	164
1981-82	Wayne Gretzky, Edmonton	80	92	120	212
1982-83	Wayne Gretzky, Edmonton	80	71	125	196

	Games	G.	A.	Pts.
1983-84—Wayne Gretzky, Edmonton	74	87	118	205
1984-85—Wayne Gretzky, Edmonton	80	73	135	208
1985-86—Wayne Gretzky, Edmonton	80	52	163	215

**—Number of assists not recorded.
(Originally Leading Scorer Trophy. Present trophy presented to NHL by Art Ross, former manager-coach of Boston Bruins, in 1947. In event of tie, player with most goals receives the award.)

Hart Memorial Trophy
(Most Valuable Player)

1923-24—Frank Nighbor, Ottawa
1924-25—Billy Burch, Hamilton
1925-26—Nels Stewart, Montreal Maroons
1926-27—Herb Gardiner, Montreal
1927-28—Howie Morenz, Montreal
1928-29—Roy Worters, N.Y. Americans
1929-30—Nels Stewart, Montreal Maroons
1930-31—Howie Morenz, Montreal
1931-32—Howie Morenz, Montreal
1932-33—Eddie Shore, Boston
1933-34—Aurel Joliat, Montreal
1934-35—Eddie Shore, Boston
1935-36—Eddie Shore, Boston
1936-37—Babe Siebert, Montreal
1937-38—Eddie Shore, Boston
1938-39—Toe Blake, Montreal
1939-40—Ebbie Goodfellow, Detroit
1940-41—Bill Cowley, Boston
1941-42—Tom Anderson, N.Y. Americans
1942-43—Bill Cowley, Boston
1943-44—Babe Pratt, Toronto
1944-45—Elmer Lach, Montreal
1945-46—Max Bentley, Chicago
1946-47—Maurice Richard, Montreal
1947-48—Buddy O'Connor, N.Y. Rangers
1948-49—Sid Abel, Detroit
1949-50—Chuck Rayner, N.Y. Rangers
1950-51—Milt Schmidt, Boston
1951-52—Gordie Howe, Detroit
1952-53—Gordie Howe, Detroit
1953-54—Al Rollins, Chicago
1954-55—Ted Kennedy, Toronto
1955-56—Jean Beliveau, Montreal
1956-57—Gordie Howe, Detroit
1957-58—Gordie Howe, Detroit
1958-59—Andy Bathgate, N.Y. Rangers
1959-60—Gordie Howe, Detroit
1960-61—Bernie Geoffrion, Montreal
1961-62—Jacques Plante, Montreal
1962-63—Gordie Howe, Detroit
1963-64—Jean Beliveau, Montreal
1964-65—Bobby Hull, Chicago
1965-66—Bobby Hull, Chicago
1966-67—Stan Mikita, Chicago
1967-68—Stan Mikita, Chicago
1968-69—Phil Esposito, Boston
1969-70—Bobby Orr, Boston
1970-71—Bobby Orr, Boston
1971-72—Bobby Orr, Boston
1972-73—Bobby Clarke, Philadelphia
1973-74—Phil Esposito, Boston
1974-75—Bobby Clarke, Philadelphia
1975-76—Bobby Clarke, Philadelphia
1976-77—Guy Lafleur, Montreal
1977-78—Guy Lafleur, Montreal
1978-79—Bryan Trottier, N.Y. Islanders
1979-80—Wayne Gretzky, Edmonton
1980-81—Wayne Gretzky, Edmonton
1981-82—Wayne Gretzky, Edmonton
1982-83—Wayne Gretzky, Edmonton
1983-84—Wayne Gretzky, Edmonton
1984-85—Wayne Gretzky, Edmonton
1985-86—Wayne Gretzky, Edmonton

Penalty Leaders

	Games	Penalty Minutes
1926-27—Nels Stewart, Montreal Maroons	44	133
1927-28—Eddie Shore, Boston	44	165
1928-29—Merv "Red" Dutton, Montreal Maroons	44	139
1929-30—Joe Lamb, Ottawa Senators	44	119
1930-31—Harvey Rockburn, Detroit	42	118
1931-32—Merv "Red" Dutton, N.Y. Americans	47	107
1932-33—Red Horner, Toronto	47	144
1933-34—Red Horner, Toronto	42	126*
1934-35—Red Horner, Toronto	46	125
1935-36—Red Horner, Toronto	43	167
1936-37—Red Horner, Toronto	48	124
1937-38—Red Horner, Toronto	47	82*
1938-39—Red Horner, Toronto	48	85
1939-40—Red Horner, Toronto	30	87
1940-41—Jimmy Orlando, Detroit	48	99
1941-42—Jimmy Orlando, Detroit	48	81**
1942-43—Jimmy Orlando, Detroit	40	89*
1943-44—Mike McMahon, Montreal Canadiens	42	98
1944-45—Pat Egan, Boston	48	86
1945-46—Jack Stewart, Detroit	47	73
1946-47—Gus Mortson, Toronto	60	133
1947-48—Bill Barilko, Toronto	57	147
1948-49—Bill Ezinicki, Toronto	52	145
1949-50—Bill Ezinicki, Toronto	67	144
1950-51—Gus Mortson, Toronto	60	142

Season	Player, Team	GP	PIM
1951-52	Walter "Gus" Kyle, Boston	69	127
1952-53	Maurice Richard, Montreal Canadiens	70	112
1953-54	Gus Mortson, Chicago	68	132
1954-55	Fernie Flaman, Boston	70	150
1955-56	Lou Fontinato, N.Y. Rangers	70	202
1956-57	Gus Mortson, Chicago	70	147
1957-58	Lou Fontinato, N.Y. Rangers	70	152
1958-59	Ted Lindsay, Chicago	70	184
1959-60	Carl Brewer, Toronto	67	150
1960-61	Pierre Pilote, Chicago	70	165
1961-62	Lou Fontinato, Montreal Canadiens	54	167
1962-63	Howie Young, Detroit	64	273
1963-64	Vic Hadfield, N.Y. Rangers	69	151
1964-65	Carl Brewer, Toronto	70	177
1965-66	Reg Fleming, N.Y. Rangers	69	166
1966-67	John Ferguson, Montreal Canadiens	67	177
1967-68	Barclay Plager, St. Louis Blues	49	153
1968-69	Forbes Kennedy, Philadelphia-Toronto	77	219
1969-70	Keith Magnuson, Chicago	76	213
1970-71	Keith Magnuson, Chicago	76	291
1971-72	Bryan Watson, Pittsburgh Penguins	75	212
1972-73	Dave Schultz, Philadelphia Flyers	76	259
1973-74	Dave Schultz, Philadelphia Flyers	73	348
1974-75	Dave Schultz, Philadelphia Flyers	76	472
1975-76	Steve Durbano, Pittsburgh-Kansas City	69	370
1976-77	Dave Williams, Toronto	77	338
1977-78	Dave Schultz, Los Angeles-Pittsburgh	74	405
1978-79	Dave Williams, Toronto	77	298
1979-80	Jimmy Mann, Winnipeg	72	287
1980-81	Dave Williams, Vancouver	77	333
1981-82	Paul Baxter, Pittsburgh	76	407
1982-83	Randy Holt, Washington	70	275
1983-84	Chris Nilan, Montreal	76	338
1984-85	Chris Nilan, Montreal	77	358
1985-86	Joey Kocur, Detroit	59	377

*—Match Misconduct penalty not included in total minutes.
**—Three Match misconduct penalties not included in total minutes. 1946-47 was first season that Match penalties were automatically included in penalty totals.

James Norris Memorial Trophy
(Outstanding Defenseman)

1953-54—Red Kelly, Detroit
1954-55—Doug Harvey, Montreal
1955-56—Doug Harvey, Montreal
1956-57—Doug Harvey, Montreal
1957-58—Doug Harvey, Montreal
1958-59—Tom Johnson, Montreal
1959-60—Doug Harvey, Montreal
1960-61—Doug Harvey, Montreal
1961-62—Doug Harvey, N.Y. Rangers
1962-63—Pierre Pilote, Chicago
1963-64—Pierre Pilote, Chicago
1964-65—Pierre Pilote, Chicago
1965-66—Jacques Laperriere, Montreal
1966-67—Harry Howell, N.Y. Rangers
1967-68—Bobby Orr, Boston
1968-69—Bobby Orr, Boston
1969-70—Bobby Orr, Boston
1970-71—Bobby Orr, Boston
1971-72—Bobby Orr, Boston
1972-73—Bobby Orr, Boston
1973-74—Bobby Orr, Boston
1974-75—Bobby Orr, Boston
1975-76—Denis Potvin, N.Y. Islanders
1976-77—Larry Robinson, Montreal
1977-78—Denis Potvin, N.Y. Islanders
1978-79—Denis Potvin, N.Y. Islanders
1979-80—Larry Robinson, Montreal
1980-81—Randy Carlyle, Pittsburgh
1981-82—Doug Wilson, Chicago
1982-83—Rod Langway, Washington
1983-84—Rod Langway, Washington
1984-85—Paul Coffey, Edmonton
1985-86—Paul Coffey, Edmonton

Vezina Trophy

(Awarded to goalkeeper(s) having played a minimum 25 games for the team with fewest goals scored against. Beginning with 1981-82 season, awarded to outstanding goaltender.)

Season	Goaltender, Team	Games	Goals	SO.	Avg.
1926-27	George Hainsworth, Montreal	44	67	14	1.52
1927-28	George Hainsworth, Montreal	44	48	13	1.09
1928-29	George Hainsworth, Montreal	44	43	22	0.98

Season		Games	Goals	SO.	Avg.
1929-30	Tiny Thompson, Boston	44	98	3	2.23
1930-31	Roy Worters, New York Americans	44	74	8	1.68
1931-32	Charlie Gardiner, Chicago	48	101	4	2.10
1932-33	Tiny Thompson, Boston	48	88	11	1.83
1933-34	Charlie Gardiner, Chicago	48	83	10	1.73
1934-35	Lorne Chabot, Chicago	48	88	8	1.83
1935-36	Tiny Thompson, Boston	48	82	10	1.71
1936-37	Normie Smith, Detroit	48	102	6	2.13
1937-38	Tiny Thompson, Boston	48	89	7	1.85
1938-39	Frank Brimsek, Boston	43	69	10	1.60
1939-40	Dave Kerr, New York Rangers	48	77	8	1.60
1940-41	Turk Broda, Toronto	48	99	4	2.06
1941-42	Frank Brimsek, Boston	47	112	3	2.38
1942-43	Johnny Mowers, Detroit	50	124	6	2.48
1943-44	Bill Durnan, Montreal	50	109	2	2.18
1944-45	Bill Durnan, Montreal	50	121	1	2.42
1945-46	Bill Durnan, Montreal	40	104	4	2.60
1946-47	Bill Durnan, Montreal	60	138	4	2.30
1947-48	Turk Broda, Toronto	60	143	5	2.38
1948-49	Bill Durnan, Montreal	60	126	10	2.10
1949-50	Bill Durnan, Montreal	64	141	8	2.20
1950-51	Al Rollins, Toronto	40	70	5	1.75
1951-52	Terry Sawchuk, Detroit	70	139	11	1.98
1952-53	Terry Sawchuk, Detroit	70	133	12	1.94
1953-54	Harry Lumley, Toronto	69	128	13	1.85
1954-55	Terry Sawchuk, Detroit	68	132	12	1.94
1955-56	Jacques Plante, Montreal	64	119	7	1.86
1956-57	Jacques Plante, Montreal	61	123	9	2.02
1957-58	Jacques Plante, Montreal	57	119	9	2.09
1958-59	Jacques Plante, Montreal	67	144	9	2.15
1959-60	Jacques Plante, Montreal	69	175	3	2.54
1960-61	John Bower, Toronto	58	145	2	2.50
1961-62	Jacques Plante, Montreal	70	166	4	2.37
1962-63	Glenn Hall, Chicago	66	166	5	2.51
1963-64	Charlie Hodge, Montreal	62	140	8	2.26
1964-65	Terry Sawchuk, Toronto	36	92	1	2.56
	John Bower, Toronto	34	81	3	2.38
1965-66	Lorne Worsley, Montreal	48	114	2	2.36
	Charlie Hodge, Montreal	21	56	1	2.58
1966-67	Glenn Hall, Chicago	32	66	2	2.38
	Denis DeJordy, Chicago	44	104	4	2.46
1967-68	Lorne Worsley, Montreal	40	73	6	1.98
	Rogatien Vachon, Montreal	39	92	4	2.48
1968-69	Glenn Hall, St. Louis	41	85	8	2.17
	Jacques Plante, St. Louis	37	70	5	1.96
1969-70	Tony Esposito, Chicago	63	136	15	2.17
1970-71	Ed Giacomin, New York Rangers	45	95	8	2.15
	Gilles Villemure, N.Y. Rangers	34	78	4	2.29
1971-72	Tony Esposito, Chicago	48	82	9	1.76
	Gary Smith, Chicago	28	62	5	2.41
1972-73	Ken Dryden, Montreal	54	119	6	2.26
1973-74	Bernie Parent, Philadelphia	73	136	12	1.89
	Tony Esposito, Chicago	70	141	10	2.04
1974-75	Bernie Parent, Philadelphia	68	137	12	2.03
1975-76	Ken Dryden, Montreal	62	121	8	2.03
1976-77	Ken Dryden, Montreal	56	117	10	2.14
	Michel Larocque, Montreal	26	53	4	2.09
1977-78	Ken Dryden, Montreal	52	105	5	2.05
	Michel Larocque, Montreal	30	77	1	2.67
1978-79	Ken Dryden, Montreal	47	108	5	2.30
	Michel Larocque, Montreal	34	94	3	2.84
1979-80	Bob Sauve, Buffalo	32	74	4	2.36
	Don Edwards, Buffalo	49	125	4	2.57
1980-81	Richard Sevigny, Montreal	33	71	2	2.40
	Michel Larocque, Montreal	28	82	1	3.03
	Denis Herron, Montreal	25	67	1	3.50
1981-82	Bill Smith, New York Islanders	46	133	0	2.97
1982-83	Pete Peeters, Boston	62	142	8	2.36
1983-84	Tom Barrasso, Buffalo	42	117	2	2.84
1984-85	Pelle Lindbergh, Philadelphia	65	194	2	3.02
1985-86	John Vanbiesbrouck, N.Y. Rangers	61	184	3	3.32

Bill Jennings Trophy

(Awarded to goalkeeper(s) having played a minimum of 25 games for the team with fewest goals scored against, beginning with 1981-82 season.)

		Games	Goals	SO.	Avg.
1981-82	Denis Herron, Montreal	27	68	3	2.64
	Rick Wamsley, Montreal	38	101	2	2.75
1982-83	Roland Melanson, N.Y. Islanders	44	109	1	2.66
	Billy Smith, N.Y. Islanders	41	112	1	2.87
1983-84	Pat Riggin, Washington	41	102	4	2.66
	Al Jensen, Washington	43	117	4	2.91
1984-85	Tom Barrasso, Buffalo	54	144	5	2.66
	Bob Sauve, Buffalo	27	84	0	3.22
1985-86	Bob Froese, Philadelphia	51	116	5	2.55
	Darren Jensen, Philadelphia	29	88	2	3.68

Calder Memorial Trophy
(Rookie of the Year)

1932-33—Carl Voss, Detroit
1933-34—Russ Blinco, Montreal Maroons
1934-35—Dave Schriner, N.Y. Americans
1935-36—Mike Karakas, Chicago
1936-37—Syl Apps, Toronto
1937-38—Cully Dahlstrom, Chicago
1938-39—Frank Brimsek, Boston
1939-40—Kilby Macdonald, N.Y. Rangers
1940-41—John Quilty, Montreal
1941-42—Grant Warwick, N.Y. Rangers
1942-43—Gaye Stewart, Toronto
1943-44—Gus Bodnar, Toronto
1944-45—Frank McCool, Toronto
1945-46—Edgar Laprade, N.Y. Rangers
1946-47—Howie Meeker, Toronto
1947-48—Jim McFadden, Detroit
1948-49—Pentti Lund, N.Y. Rangers
1949-50—Jack Gelineau, Boston
1950-51—Terry Sawchuk, Detroit
1951-52—Bernie Geoffrion, Montreal
1952-53—Lorne Worsley, N.Y. Rangers
1953-54—Camille Henry, N.Y. Rangers
1954-55—Ed Litzenberger, Chicago
1955-56—Glenn Hall, Detroit
1956-57—Larry Regan, Boston
1957-58—Frank Mahovlich, Toronto
1958-59—Ralph Backstrom, Montreal
1959-60—Bill Hay, Chicago
1960-61—Dave Keon, Toronto
1961-62—Bobby Rousseau, Montreal
1962-63—Kent Douglas, Toronto
1963-64—Jacques Laperriere, Montreal
1964-65—Roger Crozier, Detroit
1965-66—Brit Selby, Toronto
1966-67—Bobby Orr, Boston
1967-68—Derek Sanderson, Boston
1968-69—Danny Grant, Minnesota
1969-70—Tony Esposito, Chicago
1970-71—Gilbert Perreault, Buffalo
1971-72—Ken Dryden, Montreal
1972-73—Steve Vickers, N.Y. Rangers
1973-74—Denis Potvin, N.Y. Islanders
1974-75—Eric Vail, Atlanta
1975-76—Bryan Trottier, N.Y. Islanders
1976-77—Willi Plett, Atlanta
1977-78—Mike Bossy, N.Y. Islanders
1978-79—Bobby Smith, Minnesota
1979-80—Ray Bourque, Boston
1980-81—Peter Stastny, Quebec
1981-82—Dale Hawerchuk, Winnipeg
1982-83—Steve Larmer, Chicago
1983-84—Tom Barrasso, Buffalo
1984-85—Mario Lemieux, Pittsburgh
1985-86—Gary Suter, Calgary

(Award was originally Leading Rookie Award. Named Calder Trophy in 1936-37 and became Calder Memorial Trophy when NHL President Frank Calder passed away—1942-43 season.)

Lady Byng Memorial Trophy
(Most Gentlemanly Player)

1924-25—Frank Nighbor, Ottawa
1925-26—Frank Nighbor, Ottawa
1926-27—Billy Burch, N.Y. Americans
1927-28—Frank Boucher, N.Y. Rangers
1928-29—Frank Boucher, N.Y. Rangers
1929-30—Frank Boucher, N.Y. Rangers
1930-31—Frank Boucher, N.Y. Rangers
1931-32—Joe Primeau, Toronto
1932-33—Frank Boucher, N.Y. Rangers
1933-34—Frank Boucher, N.Y. Rangers
1934-35—Frank Boucher, N.Y. Rangers
1935-36—Doc Romnes, Chicago
1936-37—Marty Barry, Detroit
1937-38—Gordie Drillon, Toronto
1938-39—Clint Smith, N.Y. Rangers
1939-40—Bobby Bauer, Boston
1940-41—Bobby Bauer, Boston
1941-42—Syl Apps, Toronto
1942-43—Max Bentley, Chicago
1943-44—Clint Smith, Chicago
1944-45—Bill Mosienko, Chicago
1945-46—Toe Blake, Montreal
1946-47—Bobby Bauer, Boston
1947-48—Buddy O'Connor, N.Y. Rangers
1948-49—Bill Quackenbush, Detroit
1949-50—Edgar Laprade, N.Y. Rangers
1950-51—Red Kelly, Detroit
1951-52—Sid Smith, Toronto
1952-53—Red Kelly, Detroit
1953-54—Red Kelly, Detroit
1954-55—Sid Smith, Toronto
1955-56—Earl Reibel, Detroit
1956-57—Andy Hebenton, N.Y. Rangers
1957-58—Camille Henry, N.Y. Rangers
1958-59—Alex Delvecchio, Detroit
1959-60—Don McKenney, Boston
1960-61—Red Kelly, Toronto
1961-62—Dave Keon, Toronto
1962-63—Dave Keon, Toronto
1963-64—Ken Wharram, Chicago

1964-65—Bobby Hull, Chicago
1965-66—Alex Delvecchio, Detroit
1966-67—Stan Mikita, Chicago
1967-68—Stan Mikita, Chicago
1968-69—Alex Delvecchio, Detroit
1969-70—Phil Goyette, St. Louis
1970-71—John Bucyk, Boston
1971-72—Jean Ratelle, N.Y. Rangers
1972-73—Gil Perreault, Buffalo
1973-74—John Bucyk, Boston
1974-75—Marcel Dionne, Detroit
1975-76—Jean Ratelle, N.Y. R.-Boston
1976-77—Marcel Dionne, Los Angeles
1977-78—Butch Goring, Los Angeles
1978-79—Bob MacMillan, Atlanta
1979-80—Wayne Gretzky, Edmonton
1980-81—Butch Goring, N.Y. Islanders
1981-82—Rick Middleton, Boston
1982-83—Mike Bossy, N.Y. Islanders
1983-84—Mike Bossy, N.Y. Islanders
1984-85—Jari Kurri, Edmonton
1985-86—Mike Bossy, N.Y. Islanders

(Originally Lady Byng Trophy. After winning award seven times, Frank Boucher received permanent possession and a new trophy was donated to NHL in 1936. After Lady Byng's death in 1949, NHL changed name to Lady Byng Memorial Trophy.)

Conn Smythe Trophy
(Most Valuable Player in Playoffs)

1964-65—Jean Beliveau, Montreal
1965-66—Roger Crozier, Detroit
1966-67—Dave Keon, Toronto
1967-68—Glenn Hall, St. Louis
1968-69—Serge Savard, Montreal
1969-70—Bobby Orr, Boston
1970-71—Ken Dryden, Montreal
1971-72—Bobby Orr, Boston
1972-73—Yvan Cournoyer, Montreal
1973-74—Bernie Parent, Philadelphia
1974-75—Bernie Parent, Philadelphia
1975-76—Reggie Leach, Philadelphia
1976-77—Guy Lafleur, Montreal
1977-78—Larry Robinson, Montreal
1978-79—Bob Gainey, Montreal
1979-80—Bryan Trottier, N.Y. Islanders
1980-81—Butch Goring, N.Y. Islanders
1981-82—Mike Bossy, N.Y. Islanders
1982-83—Billy Smith, N.Y. Islanders
1983-84—Mark Messier, Edmonton
1984-85—Wayne Gretzky, Edmonton
1985-86—Patrick Roy, Montreal

Bill Masterton Memorial Trophy

(Presented by Professional Hockey Writers' Association to player who best exemplifies the qualities of perseverance, sportsmanship and dedication to hockey.)

1967-68—Claude Provost, Montreal
1968-69—Ted Hampson, Oakland
1969-70—Pit Martin, Chicago
1970-71—Jean Ratelle, N.Y. Rangers
1971-72—Bobby Clarke, Philadelphia
1972-73—Lowell MacDonald, Pittsburgh
1973-74—Henri Richard, Montreal
1974-75—Don Luce, Buffalo
1975-76—Rod Gilbert, N.Y. Rangers
1976-77—Ed Westfall, N.Y. Islanders
1977-78—Butch Goring, Los Angeles
1978-79—Serge Savard, Montreal
1979-80—Al MacAdam, Minnesota
1980-81—Blake Dunlop, St. Louis
1981-82—Glenn Resch, Colorado
1982-83—Lanny McDonald, Calgary
1983-84—Brad Park, Detroit
1984-85—Anders Hedberg, N.Y. Rangers
1985-86—Charlie Simmer, Boston

Frank J. Selke Trophy
(Best Defensive Forward)

1977-78—Bob Gainey, Montreal
1978-79—Bob Gainey, Montreal
1979-80—Bob Gainey, Montreal
1980-81—Bob Gainey, Montreal
1981-82—Steve Kasper, Boston
1982-83—Bobby Clarke, Philadelphia
1983-84—Doug Jarvis, Washington
1984-85—Craig Ramsay, Buffalo
1985-86—Troy Murray, Chicago

Jack Adams Award
(Coach of the Year)

1973-74—Fred Shero, Philadelphia
1974-75—Bob Pulford, Los Angeles
1975-76—Don Cherry, Boston
1976-77—Scotty Bowman, Montreal
1977-78—Bobby Kromm, Detroit
1978-79—Al Arbour, N.Y. Islanders
1979-80—Pat Quinn, Philadelphia
1980-81—Red Berenson, St. Louis
1981-82—Tom Watt, Winnipeg
1982-83—Orval Tessier, Chicago
1983-84—Bryan Murray, Washington
1984-85—Mike Keenan, Philadelphia
1985-86—Glen Sather, Edmonton

NHL Entry Draft—June 21, 1986

First Round

NHL Club	PLAYER	(Pos)	1985-86 CLUB (League)
1—Detroit	Joe Murphy	(C)	Michigan State Univ.
2—Los Angeles	Jimmy Carson	(C)	Verdun (QHL)
3—New Jersey	Neil Brady	(C)	Medicine Hat (WHL)
4—Pittsburgh	Zarley Zalapski	(D)	Team Canada
5—Buffalo	Shawn Anderson	(D)	Team Canada
6—Toronto	Vincent Damphousse	(LW)	Laval (QHL)
7—Vancouver	Dan Woodley	(C)	Portland (WHL)
8—Winnipeg	Pat Elynuik	(RW)	Prince Albert (WHL)
9—New York Rangers	Brian Leetch	(D)	Avon Old Farms Prep (Ct.)
10—St. Louis	Jocelyn Lemieux	(RW)	Laval (QHL)
11—Hartford	Scott Young	(RW)	Boston University
12—Minnesota	Warren Babe	(LW)	Lethbridge (WHL)
13—Boston	Craig Janney	(F)	Boston College
14—Chicago	Everett Sanipass	(LW)	Verdun (QHL)
15—Montreal	Mark Pederson	(LW)	Medicine Hat (WHL)
16—Calgary	George Pelawa	(RW)	Bemidji H.S. (Minn.)
17—New York Islanders	Tom Fitzgerald	(C)	Austin Prep (Mass.)
18—Quebec	Ken McRae	(C)	Sudbury (OHL)
19—Washington	Jeff Greenlaw	(LW)	Team Canada
20—Philadelphia	Kerry Huffman	(D)	Guelph (OHL)
21—Edmonton	Kim Issel	(RW)	Prince Albert (WHL)

Second Round

NHL Club	PLAYER	(Pos)	1985-86 CLUB (League)
22—Detroit	Adam Graves	(C)	Windsor (OHL)
23—Philadelphia (from L.A.)	Jukka Seppa	(W)	Vasa Sport, Finland
24—New Jersey	Todd Copeland	(D)	Belmont Hill H.S. (Mass.)
25—Pittsburgh	Dave Capuano	(C)	Mt. St. Charles H.S. (R.I.)
26—Buffalo	Greg Brown	(D)	St. Mark's H.S. (Mass.)
27—Montreal (from Toronto)	Benoit Brunet	(LW)	Hull (QHL)
28—Philadelphia (from Vancouver)	Kent Hawley	(C)	Ottawa (OHL)
29—Winnipeg	Teppo Numminen	(D)	Tappara, Finland
30—Minnesota (from N.Y. Rangers)	Neil Wilkinson	(D)	Selkirk (Winn. Tier II)
31—St. Louis	Mike Posma	(D)	Buffalo Jr. Sabres
32—Hartford	Marc Laforge	(D)	Kingston (OHL)
33—Minnesota	Dean Kolstad	(D)	Prince Albert (WHL)
34—Boston	Pekka Tirkkonen	(C)	Sapko, Finland
35—Chicago	Mark Kurzawski	(D)	Windsor (OHL)
36—Toronto (from Montreal)	Darryl Shannon	(D)	Windsor (OHL)
37—Calgary	Brian Glynn	(D)	Saskatoon (WHL)
38—New York Islanders	Dennis Vaske	(D)	Armstrong H.S. (Minn.)
39—Quebec	Jean Mark Routhier	(RW)	Hull (QHL)
40—Washington	Steve Seftel	(LW)	Kingston (OHL)
41—Quebec (from Philadelphia)	Stephane Guerard	(D)	Shawinigan (QHL)
42—Edmonton	Jamie Nichols	(LW)	Portland (WHL)

Third Round

NHL Club	PLAYER	(Pos)	1985-86 CLUB (League)
43—Detroit	Derek Mayer	(D)	University of Denver
44—Los Angeles	Denis Larocque	(D)	Guelph (OHL)
45—New Jersey	Janne Ojanen	(C)	Tappara, Finland
46—Pittsburgh	Brad Aitken	(LW)	Sault Ste. Marie (OHL)
47—Buffalo	Bob Corkum	(F)	University of Maine
48—Toronto	Sean Boland	(D)	Toronto (OHL)
49—Vancouver	Don Gibson	(D)	Winkler (Man. Tier II)
50—Winnipeg	Esa Palosaari	(RW)	Karpat, Finland
51—New York Rangers	Bret Walter	(C)	University of Alberta
52—St. Louis	Tony Hejna	(LW)	Nichols H.S. (Buff.)
53—N.Y. Rangers (from Hartford)	Shawn Clouston	(RW)	University of Alberta
54—Minnesota	Eric Bennett	(LW)	Wilbraham Monson H.S. (Mass.)
55—Minnesota (from Boston)	Rob Zettler	(D)	Sault Ste. Marie (OHL)
56—Buffalo (from Chicago)	Kevin Kerr	(RW)	Windsor (OHL)
57—Montreal	Jyrkki Lumme	(D)	Ilves, Finland
58—Minnesota (from Calgary)	Brad Turner	(D)	Calgary Canucks (Tier II)
59—New York Islanders	Bill Berg	(D)	Toronto (OHL)
60—Washington (from Quebec)	Shawn Simpson	(G)	Sault Ste. Marie (OHL)
61—Washington	Jim Hrivnak	(G)	Merrimack College
62—New Jersey (from Phila.)	Marc Laniel	(D)	Oshawa (OHL)
63—Edmonton	Ron Shudra	(D)	Kamloops (WHL)

Fourth Round

NHL Club	PLAYER	(Pos)	1985-86 CLUB (League)
64—Detroit	Tim Cheveldae	(G)	Saskatoon (WHL)
65—Los Angeles	Sylvain Couturier	(LW)	Laval (QHL)
66—New Jersey	Anders Carlsson	(C)	Sodertalje, Sweden
67—Pittsburgh	Rob Brown	(C)	Kamloops (WHL)
68—Buffalo	David Baseggio	(D)	Yale University
69—Toronto	Kent Hulst	(C)	Windsor (OHL)
70—Vancouver	Ronnie Stern	(RW)	Longueuil (QHL)
71—Winnipeg	Hannu Jarvenpaa	(RW)	Karpat, Finland
72—New York Rangers	Mark Janssens	(C)	Regina (WHL)
73—St. Louis	Glen Featherstone	(D)	Windsor (OHL)
74—Hartford	Brian Chapman	(D)	Belleville (OHL)
75—Minnesota	Kirk Tomlinson	(C)	Hamilton (OHL)
76—Boston	Dean Hall	(C)	St. James (Man. Tier II)
77—Chicago	Kucera Frantisek	(D)	Sparta Praha, Czech.
78—Montreal	Brent Bobyck	(LW)	Notre Dame H.S. (Sask.)
79—Calgary	Tom Quinlan	(RW)	Hill Murray H.S. (Minn.)
80—New York Islanders	Shawn Byram	(LW)	Regina (WHL)
81—Quebec	Ron Tugnutt	(G)	Peterborough (OHL)
82—Washington	Erin Ginnell	(C)	Calgary (WHL)
83—Philadelphia	Mark Bar	(D)	Peterborough (OHL)
84—Edmonton	Dan Currie	(LW)	Sault Ste. Marie (OHL)

Fifth Round

NHL Club	PLAYER	(Pos)	1985-86 CLUB (League)
85—Detroit	Johan Garpenlov	(F)	Nacka, Sweden
86—Los Angeles	Dave Guden	(LW)	Roxbury Latin H.S. (Mass.)
87—St. Louis (from New Jersey)	Michael Wolak	(C)	Kitchener (OHL)
88—Pittsburgh	Sandy Smith	(C)	Brainerd H.S. (Minn.)
89—Buffalo	Larry Rooney	(F)	Thayer H.S. (Mass.)
90—Toronto	Scott Taylor	(D)	Kitchener (OHL)
91—Vancouver	Eric Murano	(C)	Calgary Canucks (Tier II)
92—Winnipeg	Craig Endean	(LW)	Seattle (WHL)
93—New York Rangers	Jeff Bloemberg	(D)	North Bay (OHL)
94—Montreal (from St. Louis)	Eric Aubertin	(LW)	Granby (QHL)
95—Hartford	Bill Horn	(G)	Western Michigan Univ.
96—Minnesota	Jari Gronstand	(D)	Tappara, Finland
97—Boston	Matt Pesklewis	(LW)	St. Albert (Alta. Tier II)
98—Chicago	Lonnie Loach	(LW)	Guelph (OHL)
99—Montreal	Mario Milani	(RW)	Verdun (QHL)
100—Calgary	Scott Bloom	(LW)	Burnsville H.S. (Minn.)
101—New York Islanders	Dean Sexsmith	(C)	Brandon (WHL)
102—Quebec	Gerald Bzdel	(D)	Regina (WHL)
103—Washington	John Purves	(RW)	Hamilton (OHL)
104—N.Y. Islanders (from Phila.)	Todd McLellan	(C)	Saskatoon (WHL)
105—Edmonton	David Haas	(LW)	London (OHL)

Sixth Round

NHL Club	PLAYER	(Pos)	1985-86 CLUB (League)
106—Detroit	Jay Stark	(D)	Portland (WHL)
107—Los Angeles	Robb Stauber	(G)	Duluth Denfield H.S. (Minn.)
108—New Jersey	Troy Crowder	(RW)	Hamilton (OHL)
109—Pittsburgh	Jeff Daniels	(D)	Oshawa (OHL)
110—Buffalo	Miguel Baldris	(D)	Shawinigan (QHL)
111—Toronto	Stephane Giguere	(LW)	St. Jean (QHL)
112—Vancouver	Steve Herniman	(D)	Cornwall (OHL)
113—Winnipeg	Robertson Bateman	(RW)	St. Laurent H.S. (Que.)
114—New York Rangers	Darren Turcotte	(C)	North Bay (OHL)
115—St. Louis	Mike O'Toole	(RW)	Markham (Ont. Tier II)
116—Hartford	Joe Quinn	(RW)	Calgary Canucks (Tier II)
117—Quebec (from Minnesota)	Scott White	(D)	Michigan Tech
118—Boston	Garth Premak	(D)	New Westminster (WHL)
119—Chicago	Mario Doyon	(D)	Drummondville (QHL)
120—Montreal	Steve Bisson	(D)	Sault Ste. Marie (OHL)
121—Calgary	John Parker	(C)	White Bear Lake H.S. (Minn.)
122—New York Islanders	Tony Schmalzbauer	(D)	Hill Murray H.S. (Minn.)
123—Quebec	Morgan Samuelsson	(F)	Boden, Sweden
124—Washington	Stefan Nilsson	(C)	Lulea, Sweden
125—Philadelphia	Steve Scheifele	(RW)	Stratford Jr. B (Ont.)
126—Edmonton	Jim Ennis	(D)	Boston University

Seventh Round

NHL Club	PLAYER	(Pos)	1985-86 CLUB (League)
127—Detroit	Per Djoos	(D)	Mora, Sweden
128—Los Angeles	Sean Krakiwsky	(RW)	Calgary (WHL)
129—New Jersey	Kevin Todd	(C)	Prince Albert (WHL)
130—Pittsburgh	Doug Hobson	(D)	Prince Albert (WHL)
131—Buffalo	Mike Hartman	(RW)	North Bay (OHL)
132—Toronto	Danny Hie	(C)	Ottawa (OHL)
133—Vancouver	Jon Helgeson	(C)	Rosseau H.S. (Minn.)
134—Quebec (from Winnipeg)	Mark Vermette	(RW)	Lake Superior State
135—New York Rangers	Robb Graham	(RW)	Guelph (OHL)
136—St. Louis	Andy May	(C)	Bramalea Jr. B. (Ont.)
137—Hartford	Steve Torrel	(C)	Hibbing H.S. (Minn.)
138—New York Islanders	Will Anderson	(D)	Victoria (WHL)
139—Boston	Paul Beraldo	(C)	Sault Ste. Marie (OHL)
140—Chicago	Mike Hudson	(LW)	Sudbury (OHL)
141—Montreal	Lyle Odelin	(D)	Moose Jaw (WHL)
142—Calgary	Rick Lessard	(D)	Ottawa (OHL)
143—New York Islanders	Richard Pilon	(D)	Prince Albert AAA (Tier II)
144—Quebec	Jean-Francois Nault	(C)	Granby (QHL)
145—Washington	Peter Choma	(RW)	Belleville (OHL)
146—Philadelphia	Sami Wahlsten	(LW)	TPS, Finland
147—Edmonton	Ivan Matulik	(LW)	Slovan Bratislava, Czech.

Eighth Round

NHL Club	PLAYER	(Pos)	1985-86 CLUB (League)
148—Detroit	Dean Morton	(D)	Oshawa (OHL)
149—Los Angeles	Rene Chapdelaine	(D)	Lake Superior State
150—New Jersey	Ryan Pardoski	(LW)	Calgary Canucks (Tier II)
151—Pittsburgh	Steve Rohlik	(LW)	Hill Murray H.S. (Minn.)
152—Buffalo	Francois Guay	(LW)	Laval (QHL)
153—Toronto	Stephen Brennan	(RW)	New Prep (Mass.)
154—Vancouver	Jeff Noble	(C)	Kitchener (OHL)
155—Winnipeg	Frank Furlan	(G)	Sherwood Park (B.C. Tier II)
156—New York Rangers	Barry Chyzowski	(C)	St. Albert (Alta. Tier II)
157—St. Louis	Randy Skarda	(D)	St. Thomas H.S. (Minn.)
158—Hartford	Ron Hoover	(C)	Western Michigan Univ.
159—Minnesota	Scott Mathias	(C)	University of Denver
160—Boston	Brian Ferreira	(RW)	Falmouth H.S. (Mass.)
161—Chicago	Marty Nanne	(RW)	Univ. of Minnesota
162—Montreal	Rick Hayward	(D)	Hull (QHL)
163—Calgary	Mark Olsen	(D)	Colorado College
164—New York Islanders	Peter Harris	(G)	Haverhill H.S. (Mass.)
165—Quebec	Keith Miller	(LW)	Guelph (OHL)
166—Washington	Lee Davidson	(C)	Penticton (B.C. Tier II)
167—Philadelphia	Murray Baron	(D)	Vernon (B.C. Tier II)
168—Edmonton	Nicolas Beaulieu	(LW)	Drummondville (QHL)

Ninth Round

NHL Club	PLAYER	(Pos)	1985-86 CLUB (League)
169—Detroit	Marc Potvin	(RW)	Stratford Jr. B (Ont.)
170—Los Angeles	Trevor Pochipinski	(D)	Penticton (B.C. Tier II)
171—New Jersey	Scott McCormack	(D)	St. Paul's Prep (Mass.)
172—Pittsburgh	Dave McIlwain	(RW)	North Bay (OHL)
173—Buffalo	Shawn Whitham	(D)	Providence College
174—Toronto	Brian Bellefeuille	(LW)	Canterbury H.S. (Ct.)
175—Vancouver	Matt Merton	(G)	Stratford Jr. B (Ont.)
176—Winnipeg	Mark Green	(C)	New Hampton (Mass.)
177—New York Rangers	Pat Scanlon	(C)	Cretin H.S. (Minn.)
178—St. Louis	Martyn Ball	(LW)	St. Michael's Jr. B. (Ont.)
179—Hartford	Robert Glasgow	(RW)	Sherwood Park (Alta. Tier II)
180—Minnesota	Lance Pitlick	(D)	Cooper H.S. (Minn.)
181—Boston	Jeff Flaherty	(RW)	Weymouth H.S. (Mass.)
182—Chicago	Geoff Benic	(LW)	Windsor (OHL)
183—Montreal	Antonin Routa	(D)	Czechoslovakia
184—Calgary	Warren Sharples	(G)	Penticton (B.C. Tier II)
185—New York Islanders	Jeff Jablonski	(LW)	London Diamonds (Ont. Jr. B)
186—Quebec	Pierre Millier	(D)	Chicoutimi (QHL)
187—Washington	Tero Toivola	(W)	Tappara, Finland
188—Philadelphia	Blaine Rude	(RW)	Fergus Falls H.S. (N.D.)
189—Edmonton	Mike Greenlay	(G)	Calgary Midgets AAA

Tenth Round

NHL Club	PLAYER	(Pos)	1985-86 CLUB (League)
190—Detroit	Scott King	(G)	Vernon (B.C. Tier II)
191—Los Angeles	Paul Kelly	(D)	Guelph (OHL)
192—New Jersey	Frederic Chabot	(D)	St. Foy Midget AAA (Que.)
193—Pittsburgh	Kelly Cain	(C)	London (OHL)
194—Buffalo	Kenton Rein	(G)	Prince Albert (WHL)
195—Toronto	Sean Davidson	(RW)	Toronto (OHL)
196—Vancouver	Marc Lyons	(D)	Kingston (OHL)
197—Winnipeg	John Blue	(G)	Univ. of Minnesota
198—New York Rangers	Joe Ranger	(D)	London (OHL)
199—St. Louis	Rod Thacker	(D)	Hamilton (OHL)
200—Hartford	Sean Evoy	(G)	Cornwall (OHL)
201—Minnesota	Dan Keczmer	(D)	Detroit Lit. Caesars
202—Boston	Greg Hawgood	(D)	Kamloops (WHL)
203—Chicago	Glen Lowes	(LW)	Toronto (OHL)
204—Montreal	Eric Bohemier	(G)	Hull (QHL)
205—Calgary	Doug Pickell	(LW)	Kamloops (WHL)
206—New York Islanders	Kerry Clark	(RW)	Saskatoon (WHL)
207—Quebec	Chris Lappin	(D)	Canterbury H.S. (Ct.)
208—Washington	Bobby Babcock	(D)	Sault Ste. Marie (OHL)
209—Philadelphia	Shawn Sabol	(D)	St. Paul Vulcans (USHL)
210—Edmonton	Matt Lanza	(D)	Winthrop H.S. (Mass.)

Eleventh Round

NHL Club	PLAYER	(Pos)	1985-86 CLUB (League)
211—Detroit	Tom Bissett	(C)	Michigan Tech
212—Los Angeles	Russ Mann	(D)	St. Lawrence Univ.
213—New Jersey	John Andersen	(LW)	Oshawa (OHL)
214—Pittsburgh	Stan Drulia	(RW)	Belleville (OHL)
215—Buffalo	Troy Arndt	(D)	Portland (WHL)
216—Toronto	Mark Holick	(RW)	Saskatoon (WHL)
217—Vancouver	Todd Hawkins	(RW)	Belleville (OHL)
218—Winnipeg	Matt Cote	(D)	Lake Superior State
219—New York Rangers	Russell Parent	(D)	South Winnipeg Blues (Tier II)
220—St. Louis	Terry MacLean	(C)	Longueuil (QHL)
221—Hartford	Cal Brown	(D)	Penticton (B.C. Tier II)
222—Minnesota	Garth Joy	(D)	Hamilton (OHL)
223—Boston	Steffan Malmquist	(D)	Leksand, Sweden
224—Chicago	Chris Thayer	(C)	Kent School (Ct.)
225—Montreal	Charlie Moore	(LW)	Belleville (OHL)
226—Calgary	Anders Lindstrom	(C)	Timra, Sweden
227—New York Islanders	Dan Beaudette	(C)	St. Thomas Academy (Minn.)
228—Quebec	Martin Latreille	(D)	Laval (QHL)
229—Washington	John Schratz	(D)	Amherst Jr. B. (Buff.)
230—Philadelphia	Brett Lawrence	(RW)	Rochester Jr. Americans
231—Edmonton	Mojmir Bozik	(D)	Kosice, Czech.

Twelfth Round

NHL Club	PLAYER	(Pos)	1985-86 CLUB (League)
232—Detroit	Peter Ekroth	(D)	Sodertalje, Sweden
233—Los Angeles	Brian Hayton	(LW)	Guelph (OHL)
234—St. Louis (from New Jersey)	Bill Butler	(LW)	Northwood Prep (N.Y.)
235—Pittsburgh	Rob Wilson	(D)	Sudbury (OHL)
236—New Jersey (from Buffalo)	Doug Kirton	(W)	Orillia Tier II (Ont.)
237—Toronto	Brian Hoard	(D)	Hamilton (OHL)
238—Vancouver	Vladimir Krutov	(W)	Zska Moscow, U.S.S.R.
239—Winnipeg	Arto Blomsten	(D)	Djurgarden, Sweden
240—New York Rangers	Soren True	(W)	Skobakken, Denmark
241—St. Louis	David O'Brien	(RW)	Northeastern Univ.
242—Hartford	Brian Verbeek	(C)	Kingston (OHL)
243—Minnesota	Kurt Stahura	(LW)	Williston Academy (Mass.)
244—Boston	Joel Gardner	(C)	Sarnia (Ont. Jr. B.)
245—Chicago	Sean Williams	(C)	Oshawa (OHL)
246—Montreal	Karel Svoboda	(W)	Czechoslovakia
247—Calgary	Antonin Stavjana	(D)	Czech. Nat. Team
248—New York Islanders	Paul Thompson	(D)	Northern Manitoba AAA
249—Quebec	Sean Boudreault	(F)	Mt. St. Charles H.S. (R.I.)
250—Washington	Scott McCrory	(C)	Oshawa (OHL)
251—Philadelphia	Daniel Stephano	(G)	Northwood School (N.Y.)
252—Edmonton	Tony Hand	(C)	Murrayfield Racers (Scotland)

The NHL's top two draft picks got together on draft day: No. 1 pick Joe Murphy of Detroit (right) and No. 2 pick Jimmy Carson of Los Angeles. Murphy played at Michigan State last season while Carson played for Verdun of the Quebec Hockey League.

INDIVIDUAL RECORDS

SINGLE SEASON RECORDS

1—GOALS
  NHL—Wayne Gretzky, Edmonton Oilers—92 (1981-82 season).
  WHA—Bobby Hull, Winnipeg Jets—77 (1974-75 season).
  CHL—Alain Caron, St. Louis Braves—77 (1963-64 season).
  AHL—Paul Gardner, Rochester Americans—61 (1985-86 season).
  IHL—Dan Lecours, Milwaukee Admirals—75 (1982-83 season).

2—ASSISTS
  NHL—Wayne Gretzky, Edmonton Oilers—163 (1985-86 season).
  WHA—Andre Lacroix, San Diego Mariners—106 (1974-75 season).
  CHL—Richie Hansen, Salt Lake Golden Eagles—81 (1981-82 season).
  AHL—George "Red" Sullivan, Hershey Bears—89 (1953-54 season).
  IHL—Dale Yakiwchuk, Milwaukee Admirals—100 (1982-83 season).

3—POINTS
  NHL—Wayne Gretzky, Edmonton Oilers—215 (1985-86 season).
  WHA—Marc Tardif, Quebec Nordiques—154 (1977-78 season).
  CHL—Alain Caron, St. Louis Braves—125 (1963-64 season).
  AHL—Paul Gardner, Binghamton—130 (1984-85 season).
  IHL—Gary Ford, Muskegon Mohawks—141 (1972-73 season).

4—PENALTY MINUTES
  NHL—Dave Schultz, Philadelphia Flyers—472 (1974-75 season).
  WHA—Curt Brackenbury, Minnesota Fighting Saints and Quebec Nordiques—365 (1975-76 season).
  CHL—Randy Holt, Dallas Black Hawks—411 (1974-75 season).
  AHL—Steve Martinson, Hershey Bears—432 (1985-86 season).
  IHL—Mark Toffolo, Saginaw Gears—557 (1978-79 season).

5—SHUTOUTS
  NHL—George Hainsworth, Montreal Canadiens—22 (1928-29 season).

  Modern Era
  NHL—Tony Esposito, Chicago Black Hawks—15 (1969-70 season).
  WHA—Gerry Cheevers, Cleveland Crusaders—5 (1972-73 season).
    Joe Daley, Winnipeg Jets—5 (1975-76 season).
  CHL—Marcel Pelletier, St. Paul Rangers—9 (1963-64 season).
  AHL—Gordie Bell, Buffalo Bisons—9 (1942-43 season).
  IHL—Charlie Hodge, Cincinnati Mohawks—10 (1953-54 season).

6—GOALS AGAINST AVERAGE
  NHL—George Hainsworth, Montreal Canadiens—0.98 (1928-29 season).
  WHA—Don McLeod, Houston Aeros—2.57 (1973-74 season).
  CHL—Russ Gillow, Oklahoma City Blazers—2.16 (1967-68 season).
  AHL—Frank Brimsek, Providence Reds—1.79 (1937-38 season).
  IHL—Glenn Ramsay, Cincinnati Mohawks—1.88 (1956-57 season).

CAREER (Regular Season Only)
(No WHA Records Listed for Most Seasons Played.)

1—MOST SEASONS
  NHL—Gordie Howe, Detroit Red Wings and Hartford Whalers—26 (1946-47 through 1970-71 and 1979-80).
  CHL—Richie Hansen, Fort Worth Texans, Salt Lake Golden Eagles, Wichita Wind—9 (1975-76 through 1983-84 seasons).
  AHL—Fred Glover, Indianapolis Caps, St. Louis Flyers, Cleveland Barons—20.
    Willie Marshall, Pittsburgh Hornets, Rochester Americans, Hershey Bears, Providence Reds, Baltimore Clippers—20.
  IHL—Glenn Ramsay, Cincinnati Mohawks, Fort Wayne Komets, Troy Bruins, Toledo Blades, St. Paul Saints, Omaha Knights, Des Moines Oak Leafs, Toledo Hornets, Port Huron Flags—18 (1956-57 through 1973-74).

2—GAMES PLAYED
  NHL—Gordie Howe, Detroit Red Wings and Hartford Whalers—1,767 (26 seasons).
  WHA—Andre Lacroix, Philadelphia Blazers, New York Golden Blades, Jersey Knights, San Diego Mariners, Houston Aeros and New England Whalers—551 (7 seasons).
  CHL—Richie Hansen, Fort Worth Texans, Salt Lake Golden Eagles, Wichita Wind—575 (9 seasons).
  AHL—Willie Marshall, Pittsburgh Hornets, Rochester Americans, Hershey Bears, Providence Reds, Baltimore Clippers—1,205 (20 seasons).
  IHL—Glenn Ramsay, Cincinnati Mohawks, Fort Wayne Komets, Troy Bruins, Toledo Blades, St. Paul Saints, Omaha Knights, Des Moines Oak Leafs, Toledo Hornets, Port Huron Flags—1,053 (18 seasons).

3—GOALS SCORED
NHL—Gordie Howe, Detroit Red Wings, Hartford Whalers—801 (26 seasons).
WHA—Marc Tardif, Quebec Nordiques—316 (6 seasons).
CHL—Richie Hansen, Fort Worth Texans, Salt Lake Golden Eagles, Wichita Wind—204 (9 seasons).
AHL—Willie Marshall, Pittsburgh Hornets, Rochester Americans, Hershey Bears, Providence Reds, Baltimore Clippers—523 (20 seasons).
IHL—Joe Kastelic, Fort Wayne Komets, Troy Bruins, Louisville Rebels, Muskegon Zephyrs, Muskegon Mohawks—526 (15 seasons).

4—ASSISTS
NHL—Gordie Howe, Detroit Red Wings, Hartford Whalers—1,049.
WHA—Andre Lacroix, Philadelphia Blazers, Jersey Knights, San Diego Mariners, Houston Aeros, New England Whalers—547 (7 seasons).
CHL—Richie Hansen, Fort Worth Texans, Salt Lake Golden Eagles, Wichita Wind—374 (9 seasons).
AHL—Willie Marshall, Pittsburgh Hornets, Hershey Bears, Rochester Americans, Providence Reds, Baltimore Clippers—852 (20 seasons).
IHL—Len Thornson, Huntington Hornets, Indianapolis Chiefs, Fort Wayne Komets—826 (13 seasons).

5—TOTAL POINTS
NHL—Gordie Howe, Detroit Red Wings, Hartford Whalers—1,850 (26 seasons).
WHA—Andre Lacroix, Philadelphia Blazers, Jersey Knights, San Diego Mariners, Houston Aeros, New England Whalers—798 (7 seasons).
CHL—Richie Hansen, Fort Worth Texans, Salt Lake Golden Eagles, Wichita Wind—578 (9 seasons).
AHL—Willie Marshall, Pittsburgh Hornets, Hershey Bears, Rochester Americans, Providence Reds, Baltimore Clippers—1,375 (20 seasons).
IHL—Len Thornson, Huntington Hornets, Indianapolis Chiefs, Fort Wayne Komets—1,252 (13 seasons).

6—PENALTY MINUTES
NHL—Dave (Tiger) Williams, Toronto Maple Leafs, Vancouver Canucks, Detroit Red Wings, Los Angeles Kings—3,515 (11 seasons).
WHA—Paul Baxter, Cleveland Crusaders, Quebec Nordiques—962 (5 seasons).
CHL—Brad Gassoff, Tulsa Oilers, Dallas Black Hawks—899 (5 seasons).
AHL—Fred Glover, Indianapolis Caps, St. Louis Flyers, Cleveland Barons—2,402 (20 seasons).
IHL—Gord Malinoski, Dayton Gems, Saginaw Gears—2,175 (9 seasons).

7—SHUTOUTS
NHL—Terry Sawchuk, Detroit Red Wings, Boston Bruins, Los Angeles Kings, New York Rangers, Toronto Maple Leafs—103 (21 seasons).
WHA—Ernie Wakely, Winnipeg Jets, San Diego Mariners, Houston Aeros—16 (6 seasons).
CHL—Michel Dumas, Dallas Black Hawks—12 (4 seasons).
Mike Veisor, Dallas Black Hawks—12 (5 seasons).
AHL—Johnny Bower, Cleveland Barons, Providence Reds—45 (11 seasons).
IHL—Glenn Ramsay, Cincinnati Mohawks, Fort Wayne Komets, Troy Bruins, Toledo Blades, St. Paul Saints, Omaha Knights, Des Moines Oak Leafs, Toledo Hornets, Port Huron Flags—45 (18 seasons).

SINGLE GAME RECORDS

1—GOALS
NHL—Joe Malone, Quebec Bulldogs (January 31, 1920 vs. Toronto St. Pats)—7.

Modern Era
NHL—Syd Howe, Detroit Red Wings (Feb. 3, 1944 vs. N.Y. Rangers)—6.
Gordon Berenson, St. Louis Blues (Nov. 7, 1968 vs. Philadelphia)—6.
Darryl Sittler, Toronto Maple Leafs (Feb. 7, 1976 vs. Boston Bruins)—6.
WHA—Ron Ward, New York Raiders (January 4, 1973 vs. Ottawa)—5.
Ron Climie, Edmonton Oilers (vs. N.Y. Golden Blades, November 6, 1973)—5.
Andre Hinse, Houston Aeros (Jan. 16, 1975 vs. Edmonton)—5.
Vaclav Nedomansky, Toronto Toros (Nov. 13, 1975 vs. Denver Spurs)—5.
Wayne Connelly, Minnesota Fighting Saints (Nov. 27, 1975 vs. Cincinnati Stingers)—5.
Ron Ward, Cleveland Crusaders (Nov. 30, 1975 vs. Toronto Toros)—5.
Real Cloutier, Quebec Nordiques (Oct. 26, 1976 vs. Phoenix Roadrunners)—5.
CHL—Jim Mayer, Dallas Black Hawks (February 23, 1979)—6.
AHL—Bob Heron, Pittsburgh Hornets (1941-42)—6.
Harry Pidhirny, Springfield Indians (1953-54)—6.
Camille Henry, Providence Reds (1955-56)—6.
IHL—Pierre Brillant, Indianapolis Chiefs (Feb. 18, 1959)—6.
Bryan McLay, Muskegon Zephyrs (Mar. 8, 1961)—6.
Elliott Chorley, St. Paul Saints (Jan. 17, 1962)—6.
Joe Kastelic, Muskegon Zephyrs (Mar. 1, 1962)—6.
Tom St. James, Flint Generals (Mar. 15, 1985)—6.

2—ASSISTS
NHL—Billy Taylor, Detroit Red Wings (Mar. 16, 1947 vs. Chicago)—7.
Wayne Gretzky, Edmonton Oilers (Feb. 15, 1980 vs. Washington)—7.
WHA—Jim Harrison, Alberta Oilers (January 30, 1973 vs. New York)—7.
Jim Harrison, Cleveland Crusaders (Nov. 30, 1975 vs. Toronto Toros)—7.

CHL—Art Stratton, St. Louis Braves (1966-67)—6.
  Ron Ward, Tulsa Oilers (1967-68)—6.
  Bill Hogaboam, Omaha Knights, January 15, 1972—6.
  Jim Wiley, Tulsa Oilers, (1974-75)—6.
AHL—Art Stratton, Buffalo Bisons (Mar. 17, 1963 vs. Pittsburgh)—9.
IHL—Jean-Paul Denis, St. Paul Saints (Jan. 17, 1962)—9.

3—POINTS
  NHL—Darryl Sittler, Toronto Maple Leafs (Feb. 7, 1976 vs. Boston Bruins)—10.
  WHA—Jim Harrison, Alberta Oilers (January 30, 1973 vs. New York)—10.
  CHL—Steve Vickers, Omaha Knights (Jan. 15, 1972 vs. Kansas City)—8.
  AHL—Art Stratton, Buffalo Bisons (Mar. 17, 1963 vs. Pittsburgh)—9.
  IHL—Elliott Chorley, St. Paul Saints (Jan. 17, 1962)—11.
    Jean-Paul Denis, St. Paul Saints (Jan. 17, 1962)—11.

4—PENALTY MINUTES
  NHL—Randy Holt, Los Angeles Kings (March 11, 1979 vs. Philadelphia)—67.
  WHA—Dave Hanson, Birmingham Bulls (Feb. 5, 1978 vs. Indianapolis)—46.
  CHL—Gary Rissling, Birmingham Bulls (Dec. 5, 1980 vs. Salt Lake)—49.
  AHL—Wally Weir, Rochester Americans (Jan. 16, 1981 vs. New Brunswick)—54.
  IHL—Willie Prognitz, Dayton Gems (Oct. 29, 1977)—63.

DEFENSEMEN'S RECORDS
SINGLE SEASON

1—GOALS
  NHL—Paul Coffey, Edmonton Oilers (1985-86 season)—48.
  WHA—Kevin Morrison, Jersey Knights (1973-74 season)—24.
  CHL—Dan Poulin, Nashville South Stars (1981-82 season)—29.
  AHL—Greg Tebbutt, Baltimore Skipjacks (1982-83 season)—28.
  IHL—Roly McLenahan, Cincinnati Mohawks (1955-56 season)—34.

2—ASSISTS
  NHL—Bobby Orr, Boston Bruins (1970-71 season)—102.
  WHA—J. C. Tremblay, Quebec Nordiques (1975-76 season)—77.
  CHL—Barclay Plager, Omaha Knights (1963-64 season)—61.
  AHL—Craig Levie, Nova Scotia Voyageurs (1980-81 season)—62.
  IHL—Gerry Glaude, Muskegon Zephyrs (1962-63 season)—86.

3—POINTS
  NHL—Bobby Orr, Boston Bruins (1970-71 season)—139.
  WHA—J. C. Tremblay, Quebec Nordiques (1972-73 and 1975-76 seasons)—89.
  CHL—Dan Poulin, Nashville South Stars (1981-82 season)—85.
  AHL—Greg Tebbutt, Baltimore Skipjacks (1982-83 season)—84.
  IHL—Gerry Glaude, Muskegon Zephyrs (1962-63 season)—101.

American Hockey League

218 Memorial Avenue, West Springfield, Mass. 01089
Phone— (413) 781-2030

Chairman of the Board—Robert W. Clarke
President and Treasurer—Jack Butterfield
Vice-President and General Counsel—Richard F. Canning
Vice-President, Secretary—Gordon C. Anziano

Board Of Governors

Adirondack—Jim Devellano
Baltimore—John M. Haas
Binghamton—Robert Carr
Fredericton—Gilles Leger
Hershey—Frank Mathers
Maine—Ed Anderson
Moncton—Gary O'Neill
New Haven—Macgregor Kilpatrick
Nova Scotia—Bruce McGregor
Rochester—George Bergantz
St. Catharines—Gerry McNamara
Sherbrooke—Serge Savard
Springfield—Peter Cooney
Honorary Governors—Edward W. Shore, Sr.,
George Sage

Adirondack Red Wings

President—Michael Ilitch
Executive Vice President—Jim Lites
General Manager—Neil Smith
Dir. of Operations—Jack Kelley
Business Manager—Stu Mayer
Coach—Bill Dineen
Dir. of Public Relations—Nancy Owen
Dir. of Marketing and Promotions—Tim Connor
Trainer—David Casey
Home Ice—Glens Falls Civic Center
Address—1 Civic Center Plaza,
Glens Falls, N.Y. 12801
Capacity—4,770
NHL Affiliation—Detroit Red Wings
Phone— (518) 798-0366

Baltimore Skipjacks

President—Barton S. Mitchell
Governor—John M. Haas
Alternate Governor—Ken Schinkel
Vice-President—William Sullivan
Secretary—James S. Watson
Treasurer—Gary Fisher
Exec. Vice-Pres.—Walter R. "Bud" Freeman, Jr.
Director of Media Relations and Community Affairs—
  Patricia A. Eberle
Director of Marketing and Promotions—Mike Naused
Coach—Gene Ubriaco
Trainer—Tim Ringler
Home Ice—Baltimore Civic Center
Address—Civic Center-Suite 412,
  201 W. Baltimore St.
  Baltimore, Md. 21201
Seating Capacity—11,025
NHL Affiliation—Pittsburgh Penguins
Phone— (301) 727-0703

Binghamton Whalers

General Partners—Bob Carr, Jim McCoy,
  Tom Mitchell
Coach, Dir. of Hockey Operations—Larry Pleau
Business Manager—Bob Ohralbo
Director of Broadcasting—Phil Jacobs
Director of Marketing—Dave Armstrong
Trainer—Jon R. Smith
Executive Assistant—Kim Anderson
Home Ice—Broome County
  Veterans Memorial Arena
Address—1 Stuart Street
  Binghamton, N.Y. 13901
Seating Capacity—4,855
NHL Affiliations—Hartford Whalers and
  Washington Capitals
Phone— (607) 723-8937

Fredericton Express

President—Gilles Leger
Director of Operations—Michael Doyle
General Manager/Coach—Andre Savard
Comptroller—Mary Lifford
Dir. Media Relations—Ernie Fitzsimmons
Trainer—Marty Flynn
Assistant Comptroller—Cathy Belmore
Equipment Manager—Scott Beckingham
Executive Secretary—Janice Wilson
Home Ice—Aitken Center, University
  of New Brunswick
Seating Capacity—3,548
NHL Affiliations—Quebec Nordiques
  and Vancouver Canucks
Address—Aitken Center, Box 9900
  Fredericton, N.B. E3B 5G4
Phone— (506) 458-9929

Hershey Bears

Board Chairman—Edward R. Book
President—J. Bruce McKinney
President & Gen. Mgr.—Frank Mathers
Coach—John Paddock
Trainer—Dan Stuck
Publicity and Marketing—Doug Yingst
Home Ice—Hersheypark Arena
Address—P.O. Box 866
  Hershey, Pa. 17033
Seating Capacity—7,286
NHL Affiliation—Philadelphia Flyers
Phone— (717) 534-3380

Maine Mariners

Chairman—John J. McMullen
President—Ed Anderson
Director of Hockey Oper.—Max McNab
General Manager—Ed Anderson
Coach—Tom McVie
V.P., Media—Dale Arnold
Bus. Manager-Controller—Gordon Corkum
Marketing Director—Dale Arnold
Home Ice—Cumberland County
  Civic Center
Address—P.O. Box 1219
  Portland, Me. 04104
Seating Capacity—6,734
NHL Affiliation—New Jersey Devils
Phone— (207) 775-3411

Moncton Golden Flames

Governor—Gary O'Neill
General Manager/Coach—Terry Crisp
Business Manager—Brian Foster
Director of Marketing, Media Relations
  and Public Relations—Bill Riley
Accountant—Darlene Weir
Home Ice—Moncton Coliseum
Address—Moncton, N.B.
  E1C 8P2

Seating Capacity—6,904
NHL Affiliations—Calgary Flames
and Boston Bruins
Phone—(506) 857-4000

New Haven Nighthawks

Governor—Macgregor Kilpatrick
President—Ken Doi
General Manager—Roy Mlakar
Coach—Robbie Ftorek
Dir. of Press Relations—Jan MacDonald
Trainer—To be named
Office Manager—Henry Bradbury
Home Ice—Veterans Mem. Coliseum
Address—P.O. Box 1444,
New Haven, Conn. 06506
Seating Capacity—5,636
NHL Affiliations—New York Rangers and
Los Angeles Kings
Phone—(203) 787-0101

Newmarket Saints

Chairman of the Board—Harold Ballard
Governor—Gerry McNamara
Coach—To be announced
Trainer—Ken Garrett
Dir. of Public Relations—Roy Green
Home Ice—Newmarket Recreation Complex
Address—Eagle Street
Newmarket, Que., Ont., L3Y 4W3
Seating Capacity—2,700
NHL Affiliation—Toronto Maple Leafs
Phone—(416) 895-7078

Nova Scotia Oilers

Chairman—R.F. "Tiny" Titus
President—Glen Sather
Governor/Vice President—Bruce McGregor
Director of Operations—John Blackwell
General Manager/Coach—Larry Kish
Controller—Warner Baum
Media Relations and Dir. of Marketing—Larry Haley
Dir. of Player Personnel—Barry Fraser
Director of Admin. and Tickets—Pamela Rudolph
Trainer—Kevin Duguay
Home Ice—Halifax Metro-Centre
Address—5284 Duke Street
Halifax, N.S. B3J 3L2
Seating Capacity—9,549
NHL Affiliations—Edmonton Oilers and
Chicago Black Hawks
Phone—(902) 429-7600

Rochester Americans

Board Chairman—R. Bruce Davey
Governor and General Manager—George Bergantz
Coach—John Van Boxmeer
P.R. Director—John Gurtler
Asst. Dir. of P.R.—Mike Tedesco
Dir. of Marketing/Sales—Randy Scott
Executive Assistant—Cheryl Barz
Administrative Asst.—Donna Arengi
Trainer—Kent Weisback
Home Ice—War Memorial Auditorium
Address—War Memorial Auditorium,
100 Exchange Street
Rochester, N.Y. 14614
Seating Capacity—7,357
NHL Affiliation—Buffalo Sabres
Phone—(716) 454-5335

Sherbrooke Canadiens

President—George Guilbault
Governor—Serge Savard
General Manager-Coach—Pierre Creamer
Director of Marketing—Alain Trehout
Public Relations Director—Claude Larose
Trainer—Pierre Gervais
Home Ice—Sherbrooke Sports Palace
Address—360 Park Street
Sherbrooke, Que. J1E 2J9
Seating Capacity—4,321
NHL Affiliations—Montreal Canadiens and
Winnipeg Jets
Phone—(819) 566-2114

Springfield Indians

President—Peter R. Cooney
Governor—James J. Coogan
Alternate Governor—Bill Torrey, Lou Nanne
General Manager—Bruce Landon
Business Manager—Martha Dailey
Broadcaster/Publicity Dir.—John Forslund
Coach—Fred Creighton
Trainer—Ed Tyburski
Home Ice—Springfield Civic Center
Address—58 Dwight St.,
Springfield, Mass. 01103
Seating Capacity—7,602
NHL Affiliations—New York Islanders and
Minnesota North Stars
Phone—(413) 736-4546

1985-86 Final AHL Standings

North Division

	G.	W.	L.	T.	Pts.	GF.	GA.
Adirondack Red Wings	80	41	31	8	90	339	298
Maine Mariners	80	40	31	9	89	274	285
Moncton Alpines	80	34	34	12	80	294	307
Fredericton Express	80	35	37	8	78	319	311
Sherbrooke Canadiens	80	33	38	9	75	340	341
Nova Scotia Oilers	80	29	43	8	66	314	353

South Division

	G.	W.	L.	T.	Pts.	GF.	GA.
Hershey Bears	80	48	29	3	99	346	292
Binghamton Whalers	80	41	34	5	87	316	290
St. Catharines Saints	80	38	37	5	81	304	308
New Haven Nighthawks	80	36	37	7	79	340	343
Springfield Indians	80	36	39	5	77	301	309
Rochester Americans	80	34	39	7	75	320	337
Baltimore Skipjacks	80	28	44	8	64	271	304

Top 20 Scorers for the John B. Sollenberger Trophy

	Games	G.	A.	Pts.	Pen.
1. Paul Gardner, Rochester	71	**61	51	*112	16
2. Jody Gage, Rochester	73	42	57	99	56
3. Ross Fitzpatrick, Hershey	77	50	47	97	28
Tim Tookey, Hershey	69	35	*62	97	66
5. Wes Jarvis, St. Catharines	74	36	60	96	38
6. Daryl Evans, Binghamton	69	40	52	92	50
Geordie Robertson, Adirondack	79	36	56	92	99
8. Paul Fenton, Binghamton	75	53	35	88	87
Serge Boisvert, Sherbrooke	69	40	48	88	18
10. Tom Roulston, Baltimore	73	38	49	87	38
Larry Floyd, Maine	80	29	58	87	25
12. Steve Tsujiura, Maine	80	31	55	86	34
13. David Gans, New Haven	17	11	12	23	14
Hershey	56	24	32	56	88
Totals	73	35	44	79	102
14. Ray Allison, Hershey	77	32	46	78	131
15. Claude Larose, Sherbrooke	65	38	39	77	2
16. Grant Martin, Binghamton	54	27	49	76	97
Mark Lamb, Moncton	79	26	50	76	51
18. Tony Currie, Fredericton	75	35	40	75	23
19. Randy Heath, New Haven	77	36	38	74	53
Alain Lemieux, Fredericton	64	29	45	74	54

**Established new record, breaking old record of 57 set in 1982-83 by Mitch Lamoureux of Baltimore.

Adirondack Red Wings

	Games	G.	A.	Pts.	Pen.
Geordie Robertson	79	36	56	92	99
Ted Speers	74	32	35	67	20
Eddie Johnstone	62	29	31	60	74
Pierre Aubry	66	28	31	59	124
Glenn Merkosky	59	24	33	57	22
Larry Trader	64	10	46	56	77
Basil McRae	69	22	30	52	259
Dale Krentz	79	19	27	46	27
Adam Oates	34	18	28	46	4
Gary Yaremchuk	60	12	32	44	90
Lane Lambert	45	16	25	41	69
Rick Zombo	69	7	34	41	94
Tim Friday	43	2	31	33	23
Bob Probert	32	12	15	27	152
Claude Loiselle	21	15	11	26	32
Jim Leavins	36	4	21	25	19
Greg Joly	65	0	22	22	68
Ray Staszak	26	13	8	21	41
Wayne Thompson	19	9	8	17	4
Steve Richmond, N.H.	11	2	6	8	32
Adirondack	20	1	7	8	23
Totals	31	3	13	16	55
Dave Korol	74	3	9	12	56
Joe Kocur	9	6	2	8	34
Chris Cichocki	9	4	4	8	6
Barry Melrose	57	4	4	8	204
Ted Huesing	57	0	8	8	26
Brian Shaw	23	3	1	4	14
Shawn Burr	3	2	2	4	2
Brett Callighen	11	0	2	2	6
Mark Laforest (Goalie)	19	0	1	1	14
Chris Pusey (Goalie)	22	0	1	1	8
Ed Mio (Goalie)	8	0	0	0	0
Corrado Micalef (G.)	25	0	0	0	0

Baltimore Skipjacks

	Games	G.	A.	Pts.	Pen.
Tom Roulston	73	38	49	87	38
Tom O'Regan	61	23	31	54	65
Mitch Lamoureux	75	22	31	53	129
Gary Rissling	76	19	34	53	340
Colin Chin	78	17	28	45	38
Roger Belanger	69	17	21	38	61
Dean Defazio	75	14	24	38	171
Steve Carlson	66	9	27	36	56
Steve Gatzos	53	25	8	33	34
Dave Simpson	79	13	19	32	56
Greg Hotham	78	2	26	28	94
Jim McGeough	38	14	13	27	20
Phil Bourque	74	8	18	26	226
Chris Dahlquist	65	4	21	25	64
Troy Loney	33	12	11	23	84
Wally Weir	67	5	12	17	300
Dave Goertz	74	1	15	16	76
Bob Errey	18	8	7	15	28
Joe McDonnell	31	1	13	14	20
Rob Geale	21	5	7	12	9
Fred Perlini	25	6	4	10	6
Ted Nolan	10	4	4	8	19
Randy Hillier	8	0	5	5	14
Mike Rowe	67	0	5	5	107
Todd Charlesworth	19	1	3	4	10
Tony Fiore	15	2	1	3	6
John DelCol	26	1	2	3	16
Glen Sharpley	7	0	3	3	4
Brian Ford (Goalie)	39	0	1	1	8
Jeff Cooper (Goalie)	23	0	0	0	4
Denis Herron (Goalie)	27	0	0	0	6

Binghamton Whalers

	Games	G.	A.	Pts.	Pen.
Daryl Evans	69	40	52	92	50
Paul Fenton	75	53	35	88	87
Grant Martin	54	27	49	76	97
Mark Taylor	43	19	38	57	27
Brad Shaw	64	10	44	54	33
Mike Siltala	50	25	22	47	36
Andre Hidi	66	19	24	43	104
David Jensen	41	17	14	31	4
Jack Brownschidle	58	5	26	31	18
Gary Sampson	49	9	21	30	16
Mike Hoffman	40	14	14	28	79
Dean Evason	26	9	17	26	29
Jim Thomson	59	15	9	24	195
Timo Blomqvist	71	6	18	24	76
Mark Paterson	67	2	16	18	121
Yves Beaudoin	48	5	12	17	36
Ed Kastelic	23	7	9	16	76
Bruce Shoebottom, N.H.	6	2	0	2	12
Binghamton	62	7	5	12	249
Totals	68	9	5	14	261
Shane Churla	52	4	10	14	306
Chris Brant	73	7	6	13	45
John Mokosak	64	0	9	9	196
Paul Cavallini	15	3	4	7	20
Claude Dumas	7	2	2	4	0
Grant Jennings	51	0	4	4	109
Bob Mason (Goalie)	34	0	3	3	6
John Hutchings	6	0	2	2	0
Pierre Rioux, Moncton	5	0	0	0	0
Binghamton	6	0	2	2	0
Totals	11	0	2	2	0

	Games	G.	A.	Pts.	Pen.
Rick Heinz (Goalie)	1	0	0	0	2
Mike O'Neill	1	0	0	0	0
Steve Hollett	8	0	0	0	2
Dave MacLean	23	0	0	0	7
Peter Sidorkiewicz (G.)	49	0	0	0	7

Fredericton Express

	Games	G.	A.	Pts.	Pen.
Tony Currie	75	35	40	75	23
Alain Lemieux	64	29	45	74	54
Mark Kirton	77	23	36	59	33
Mike Hough	74	21	33	54	68
Dunc MacIntyre	80	23	22	45	31
Jean Marc Gaulin	58	16	26	42	66
Dave Bruce	66	25	16	41	151
Scott Tottle	69	15	22	37	12
Ken Quiney	61	11	26	37	34
Taylor Hall	45	21	14	35	28
Gary Lupul	43	13	22	35	76
Mike Stevens	79	12	19	31	208
Daniel Poudrier	65	5	26	31	9
Marc Crawford	26	10	14	24	55
Neil Belland	36	6	18	24	10
Yves Heroux	31	12	10	22	42
Claude Julien	49	3	18	21	74
Jere Gillis	29	4	14	18	21
Scott Clements, St.Cath.	53	1	10	11	43
Fredericton	20	0	2	2	4
Totals	73	1	12	13	47
Michel Petit	25	0	13	13	79
Tom Karalis	51	4	8	12	106
Andy Schliebener	73	3	9	12	60
Dale Dunbar	32	2	10	12	26
Richard Zemlack	58	6	5	11	305
Jean Lanthier	7	5	5	10	2
Gord Donnelly	37	3	5	8	103
Wayne Groulx	15	2	6	8	12
Mark Kumpel	7	4	2	6	4
Jim Collucci	10	1	4	5	2
Al MacAdam	11	0	4	4	5
Tony Stiles, Moncton	20	0	2	2	18
Fredericton	9	0	1	1	9
Totals	29	0	3	3	27
Stu Kulak	3	1	0	1	0
Dave Latta	3	1	0	1	0
John Garrett (Goalie)	3	0	0	0	2
Mario Gosselin (Goalie)	5	0	0	0	0
Richard Sevigny (Goalie)	6	0	0	0	7
Luc Guenette (Goalie)	20	0	0	0	2
Wendell Young (Goalie)	24	0	0	0	2
Frank Caprice (Goalie)	26	0	0	0	4

Hershey Bears

	Games	G.	A.	Pts.	Pen.
Ross Fitzpatrick	77	50	47	97	28
Tim Tookey	69	35	*62	97	66
David Gans, N.H.	17	11	12	23	14
Hershey	56	24	32	56	88
Totals	73	35	44	79	102
Ray Allison	77	32	46	78	131
Carl Mokosak	79	30	42	72	312
Al Hill	80	17	40	57	129
Kevin McCarthy	64	15	40	55	157
Steve Seguin	75	25	29	54	91
Don Nachbaur	74	23	24	47	301

	Games	G.	A.	Pts.	Pen.
Bo Berglund, Spring.	3	0	1	1	2
Hershey	43	17	28	45	40
Totals	46	17	29	46	42
Pierre Larouche	32	22	17	39	16
Andre Dore	65	10	18	28	124
Dave Farrish	74	5	17	22	78
Joe Paterson	20	5	10	15	68
Mike Stothers	66	4	9	13	221
Steve Smith	49	1	11	12	96
Lance Nethery	13	5	6	11	2
Bernie Johnston	15	2	9	11	6
Florent Robidoux	47	6	3	9	81
Steve Martinson	69	3	6	9	*32
Andre Villeneuve	33	2	7	9	18
Brent Loney	59	0	8	8	113
Ian Armstrong	66	0	8	8	42
Daryl Stanley	27	0	4	4	88
Ron Hextall (Goalie)	53	0	2	2	54
Brian Dobbin	2	1	0	1	0
Greg Smith	2	0	1	1	5
Bill Schafhauser	8	0	1	1	2
Tom Gorence	1	0	0	0	0
Bob Dailey	5	0	0	0	8
John Kemp (Goalie)	8	0	0	0	0
Shawn MacKenzie (G.)	10	0	0	0	0
Darren Jensen (Goalie)	14	0	0	0	0

Maine Mariners

	Games	G.	A.	Pts.	Pen.
Larry Floyd	80	29	58	87	25
Steve Tsujiura	80	31	55	86	34
Bud Stefanski	68	32	39	71	70
Andy Brickley	60	26	34	60	20
Rich Chernomaz	78	21	28	49	82
Pat Conacher	69	15	30	45	83
Murray Brumwell	66	9	28	37	35
Luc Dufour	75	15	20	35	57
Kevin Maxwell	49	14	17	31	77
Rocky Trottier	66	12	19	31	42
Tim Army	68	11	16	27	10
Alan Hepple	69	4	21	25	104
Gordie Mark	77	9	13	22	134
Don Dietrich	68	9	11	20	33
Alan Stewart	58	7	12	19	181
Dave Pichette	25	4	15	19	28
Rob Palmer	73	2	10	12	18
Bruce Driver	15	4	7	11	16
Archie Henderson	57	4	6	10	172
Uli Hiemer	15	5	2	7	19
Mitch Wilson	64	4	3	7	217
Greg Evtushevski	21	3	4	7	60
Michel Bolduc	66	1	6	7	29
Ken Daneyko	21	3	2	5	75
Hector Marini	6	0	5	5	17
Randy Velischek	21	0	4	4	4
Karl Friesen (Goalie)	35	0	1	1	2
Sam St. Laurent (Goalie)	50	0	1	1	8
Neil Davey	7	0	0	0	8
Kevin Foster	7	0	0	0	0
Bob Hoffmeyer	8	0	0	0	6

Moncton Alpines

	Games	G.	A.	Pts.	Pen.
Mark Lamb	79	26	50	76	51
Brian Bradley	59	23	42	65	40
Benoit Doucet	79	26	34	60	18
Tom McMurchy, N.S.	49	26	21	47	73
Moncton	16	7	3	10	27
Totals	65	33	24	57	100
Doug Kostynski	72	18	36	54	24
Peter Bakovic	80	18	36	54	349
John Newberry, Bing.	21	6	11	17	38
Moncton	44	10	24	34	31
Totals	65	16	35	51	69
Yves Courteau	70	26	22	48	19
Greg Johnston	60	19	26	45	56
Bob Bodak, Springfield	4	0	0	0	4
Moncton	58	27	15	42	114
Totals	62	27	15	42	118
Dale Degray	76	10	31	41	128
Tom Thornbury, Fred.	24	0	15	15	30
Moncton	40	6	12	18	38
Totals	64	6	27	33	68
Dave Reid	26	14	18	32	4
George White	73	16	12	28	24
Robin Bartel	74	4	21	25	100
Kevan Guy	73	4	20	24	56
Peter Dineen, Bing.	11	0	1	1	35
Moncton	55	5	13	18	136
Totals	66	5	14	19	171
Geoff Courtnall	12	8	8	16	6
Rob Kivell	41	7	3	10	85
Jay Miller	18	4	6	10	113
Al Pedersen	59	1	8	9	39
Lyndon Byers	14	2	4	6	26
Wade Campbell, Sher.	9	0	2	2	26
Moncton	17	2	2	4	21
Totals	26	2	4	6	47
John Blum	12	1	5	6	37
Gino Cavallini	4	3	2	5	7
John Meulenbroeks	51	1	4	5	51
Jim Buettgen	37	2	1	3	38
Neil Sheehy	4	1	1	2	21
Ali Butorac	11	0	2	2	42
Lou Kiriakou	11	0	2	2	9
Darwin McCutcheon	12	0	2	2	31
Mats Thelin	2	0	1	1	0
Cleon Daskalakis (G.)	41	0	1	1	23
Claude Lefebvre	2	0	0	0	0
Robert MacInnis	2	0	0	0	0
Alain Cote	3	0	0	0	0
Ken Sabourin	3	0	0	0	0
Frank Simonetti	5	0	0	0	2
Al Larochelle (Goalie)	6	0	0	0	0
Dave Meszaros (Goalie)	6	0	0	0	2
Mike Vernon (Goalie)	6	0	0	0	0
Rick Kosti (Goalie)	15	0	0	0	6
Marc D'Amour (Goalie)	21	0	0	0	10

New Haven Nighthawks

	Games	G.	A.	Pts.	Pen.
Randy Heath	77	36	38	74	53
Jim Wiemer	73	24	49	73	108
Mark Lofthouse	70	32	35	67	56
Marty Dallman	69	23	33	56	92
Steve Moria	74	19	37	56	29
Paul Guay	57	15	36	51	101
Steve Duchesne	75	14	35	49	76
Len Hachborn, Hershey	23	12	22	34	34
New Haven	12	5	8	13	21
Totals	35	17	30	47	55
Dave Nicholls	64	21	19	40	146

	Games	G.	A.	Pts.	Pen.
Gordie Walker	46	11	28	39	66
Dan Brennan	62	8	22	30	76
Kjell Samuelsson	56	6	21	27	87
Bill O'Dwyer	41	10	15	25	41
Chris Kontos	21	8	15	23	12
Dave Gagner	16	10	11	21	11
Bryan Erickson, Bing.	7	5	3	8	2
New Haven	14	8	3	11	11
Totals	21	13	6	19	13
Lyle Phair	35	9	9	18	15
Dan McCarthy	33	7	9	16	46
Ken Hammond	67	4	12	16	96
Bobby Crawford	27	7	8	15	6
Mike Allison	9	6	6	12	4
Jim Andonoff	38	5	7	12	25
Jim Dobson	29	5	6	11	12
Darcy Roy	38	1	10	11	43
Peter Sundstrom	8	3	6	9	4
Garry Galley	4	2	6	8	6
Brock Tredway	39	2	6	8	0
Simo Saarinen	13	3	4	7	11
Nick Fotiu	9	4	2	6	21
Jay Caufield	42	2	3	5	40
Don Waddell	6	1	4	5	9
Rob Whistle	20	1	4	5	5
Glenn Currie	8	0	4	4	2
Peter Sawkins	7	1	2	3	14
Dan Clark	10	1	2	3	35
Mike McEwen	2	0	3	3	2
Tom Price	8	0	2	2	8
Steve Tuite	14	0	2	2	6
Ron Scott (Goalie)	19	0	2	2	7
Tony Feltrin	22	0	2	2	38
Glenn Healy (Goalie)	43	0	2	2	18
Al Tuer	8	1	0	1	53
Guy Benoit	9	1	0	1	0
Bob Bergloff	7	0	1	1	7
Robbie Ftorek	1	0	0	0	0
Bill Grum	1	0	0	0	0
Andy Otto	1	0	0	0	0
Mark Decola	2	0	0	0	0
Dave Hainsworth (G.)	2	0	0	0	0
Greg Hickey	2	0	0	0	0
Brian Paton	2	0	0	0	0
Darren Eliot (Goalie)	3	0	0	0	2
John Franzosa (Goalie)	3	0	0	0	0
Roland Melanson (G.)	3	0	0	0	0
Mike Backman	4	0	0	0	4
Scott Smith	5	0	0	0	7
Terry Kleisinger (Goalie)	10	0	0	0	2
Glen Hanlon, Adir. (G.)	10	0	0	0	2
New Haven (G.)	5	0	0	0	0
Totals	15	0	0	0	2

Nova Scotia Voyageurs

	Games	G.	A.	Pts.	Pen.
Mike Rogers, N.H.	20	9	15	24	28
Nova Scotia	33	15	28	43	14
Totals	53	24	43	67	42
Bruce Boudreau	65	30	36	66	36
Jeff Larmer	77	20	44	64	46
Don Biggs, Spring.	28	15	16	31	46
Nova Scotia	47	6	23	29	36
Totals	75	21	39	60	82
Dean Hopkins	60	23	32	55	131
Mickey Volcan	66	12	36	48	114

	Games	G.	A.	Pts.	Pen.
Ken Solheim	71	19	27	46	45
John Miner	79	10	33	43	90
Gord Sherven, Spring.	11	3	7	10	8
Nova Scotia	38	14	17	31	4
Totals	49	17	24	41	12
John Ollson	60	19	21	40	10
Steve Graves	78	19	18	37	22
Bruce Eakin, Adir.	25	8	10	18	23
Nova Scotia	14	6	12	18	12
Totals	39	14	22	36	35
Mark LaVarre	62	15	19	34	32
Mike Moller	62	16	15	31	24
Jeff Beukeboom	77	9	20	29	175
Bill Carroll	26	7	18	25	15
Lou Crawford	78	8	11	19	214
Dwayne Boettger	64	2	15	17	103
Rik Wilson, Monc.	8	3	3	6	2
Nova Scotia	13	4	5	9	11
Totals	21	7	8	15	13
Wayne Presley	29	6	9	15	22
Jim Playfair	73	2	12	14	160
Esa Tikkanen	15	4	8	12	17
Dean Dachyshyn	55	2	9	11	148
Ray Cote	20	7	3	10	17
Larry Melnyk	19	2	8	10	72
Jeff Brubaker	19	4	3	7	41
Darin Sceviour	31	4	3	7	6
Marty McSorley	9	2	4	6	34
Kent Paynter	23	1	2	3	36
Steve Smith	4	0	2	2	11
Daryl Reaugh (Goalie)	38	0	2	2	4
Dave Michayluk	3	0	1	1	0
Bruce Gillies (Goalie)	1	0	0	0	2
Brian Noonan	2	0	0	0	0
Jim Camazzola	3	0	0	0	0
Bruce Cassidy	4	0	0	0	0
Ron Low (Goalie)	6	0	0	0	0
Jim Ralph (Goalie)	9	0	0	0	0
W. Skorodenski (G.)	32	0	0	0	10

Rochester Americans

	Games	G.	A.	Pts.	Pen.
Paul Gardner	71	*61	51	*112	16
Jody Gage	73	42	57	99	56
Doug Trapp	75	21	42	63	86
Claude Verret	52	19	32	51	14
Warren Harper	80	18	30	48	83
Jim Jackson	65	16	32	48	10
Adam Creighton	32	17	21	38	27
Richard Hajdu	54	10	27	37	95
Mal Davis	38	21	15	36	23
Jason Meyer	76	7	28	35	74
Jeff Hamilton	74	19	10	29	48
Joe Reekie	77	3	25	28	178
Normand Lacombe	32	10	13	23	56
Richie Dunn	34	6	17	23	12
Don Lever	29	6	11	17	16
Mark Ferner	63	3	14	17	87
Taras Zytynsky	65	2	15	17	78
Heikki Leime	53	0	17	17	51
Mikael Andersson	20	10	4	14	6
Ross Yates	22	4	8	12	4
Brian McKinnon	51	4	7	11	14
Jay Fraser	20	4	5	9	61
Jim Hofford	40	2	7	9	148
Tim Hoover	49	2	5	7	34

	Games	G.	A.	Pts	Pen.
Pat Hughes	10	3	3	6	7
Gates Orlando	3	4	0	4	10
Mike Anderson	25	3	1	4	2
Jim Aldred	10	1	3	4	4
Andy Ristau	46	1	2	3	170
Mike Lay	10	1	1	2	6
Ken Priestlay	4	0	2	2	0
Tom Cronin	14	0	2	2	9
Mike Craig (Goalie)	47	0	2	2	4
Kevin Beaton	6	0	1	1	4
Daren Puppa (Goalie)	20	0	1	1	0
Randy Irving	6	0	0	0	4
Bob McNamara (Goalie)	8	0	0	0	0
Jacques Cloutier (G.)	14	0	0	0	4

St. Catharines Saints

	Games	G.	A.	Pts	Pen.
Wes Jarvis	74	36	60	96	38
John Goodwin	78	21	35	56	37
Walt Poddubny	37	28	27	55	52
Rod Schutt	70	21	28	49	44
Jeff Jackson	74	17	28	45	122
Brad Smith	31	13	29	42	79
Ken Strong	33	16	25	41	14
Rich Costello	76	18	22	40	87
Bill Kitchen	72	7	32	39	109
Craig Muni	73	3	34	37	91
Greg Britz	72	17	19	36	52
Gary McAdam	27	15	18	33	16
Todd Gill	58	8	25	33	90
Steve Thomas	19	18	14	32	35
Dan Hodgson	22	13	16	29	15
Gary Leeman	25	15	13	28	6
Cam Plante	49	6	15	21	28
Leigh Verstraete	75	8	12	20	300
Kevin Maguire	61	6	9	15	161
Bill Root	14	7	4	11	11
Garry Lariviere	52	0	9	9	10
Miroslav Ihnacak	13	4	4	8	2
Blake Wesley	37	3	4	7	56
Mark Botell	11	1	3	4	17
Val James	80	0	3	3	162
Chris McRae	59	1	1	2	233
Ken Wregget (Goalie)	18	0	2	2	8
Rod Isbester	6	1	0	1	0
Cliff Albrecht	1	0	1	1	0
Derek Laxdal	7	0	1	1	15
Tim Bernhardt (Goalie)	14	0	1	1	2
Allan Bester (Goalie)	50	0	1	1	6
Bruce Dowie (Goalie)	5	0	0	0	0
Ken Spangler	7	0	0	0	16
Todd Petkovich	8	0	0	0	5

Sherbrooke Canadiens

	Games	G.	A.	Pts	Pen.
Serge Boisvert	69	40	48	88	18
Claude Larose	65	38	39	77	2
Murray Eaves	68	22	51	73	26
Alfie Turcotte	75	29	36	65	60
Perry Ganchar	75	25	29	54	42
Claude Lemieux	58	21	32	53	145
Randy Bucyk	43	18	33	51	22
Paul Pooley	70	20	21	41	31
Gilles Thibaudeau	61	15	21	36	20
Steve Smith	63	5	31	36	37
Perry Pooley	67	12	19	31	15
Gaston Gingras	42	11	20	31	14
Rejean Cloutier	67	7	23	30	142
Tom Martin	69	11	18	29	227
Tom Anastos	55	9	18	27	8
Kent Carlson	35	11	15	26	79
Dave Silk	18	5	14	19	18
Joel Baillargeon	56	6	12	18	115
Ron Wilson	10	9	8	17	9
John Kordic	68	3	14	17	238
Bill Campbell, Hershey	37	0	8	8	18
Sherbrooke	22	1	6	7	25
Totals	59	1	14	15	43
Dominic Campedelli	38	4	10	14	27
Steven Fletcher	64	2	12	14	293
Anssi Melametsa	14	7	5	12	6
Dan McFall	50	2	10	12	16
Bobby Dollas	25	4	7	11	29
Peter Taglianetti	24	1	8	9	75
Graham Herring	24	0	9	9	19
Remi Gagne	16	2	2	4	4
Scott Sandelin	6	0	2	2	2
Brian Hayward (Goalie)	3	0	1	1	0
Jim Nesich	4	0	1	1	0
Mark Behrend (Goalie)	35	0	1	1	6
Yves Lavoie (Goalie)	3	0	0	0	0
Mark Holden (Goalie)	12	0	0	0	4
Paul Pageau (Goalie)	31	0	0	0	4

Springfield Indians

	Games	G.	A.	Pts	Pen.
Alan Kerr	71	35	36	71	127
Ron Handy	79	31	30	61	66
Marc Habschid	41	18	32	50	21
Terry Martin	72	19	22	41	17
Dale Henry	64	14	26	40	162
Scott Howson	53	15	19	34	10
Bob Bassen	54	13	21	34	111
Ken Leiter	68	7	27	34	51
Paul Houck	61	15	17	32	27
Terry Tait	62	11	19	30	34
Glenn Johannesen	78	8	21	29	187
Craig Levie	36	5	23	28	82
Neil Coulter	60	17	9	26	92
Bill Stewart	59	7	19	26	135
Gary Lacey	52	12	11	23	41
Dave Jensen	40	4	18	22	31
Gerald Diduck	61	6	14	20	175
Chris Pryor	55	4	16	20	104
George Servinis	30	2	14	16	19
Vern Smith	55	3	11	14	83
Mark Hamway	14	5	8	13	7
Jim Koudys	40	3	10	13	32
Tim Coulis	13	5	7	12	42
Roger Kortko	12	2	10	12	10
Ed Lee, Fredericton	6	3	1	4	2
Springfield	24	3	4	7	26
Totals	30	6	5	11	28
Bob Lakso	17	3	6	9	2
Jim Archibald	12	1	7	8	34
Steve Jensen	4	3	3	6	2
Gord Dineen	11	2	3	5	20
Earl Ingarfield Jr.	18	2	3	5	27
Ari Haanpaa	20	3	1	4	13
Mats Hallin	2	1	1	2	0
Mikko Makela	2	1	1	2	0
Gord Paddock	20	1	1	2	52

	Games	G.	A.	Pts.	Pen.
Mike Neill	8	0	2	2	11
Pat Micheletti	2	1	0	1	0
Mike Walsh	2	1	0	1	0
Greg Gilbert	2	0	0	0	2
Dan Mandich	3	0	0	0	4
Rob Holland (Goalie)	8	0	0	0	0
Jon Casey (Goalie)	9	0	0	0	6
Mike Sands (Goalie)	27	0	0	0	24
Karri Takko (Goalie)	43	0	0	0	6

Complete AHL Goaltending

	Games	Mins.	Goals	SO.	Avg.
Glen Hanlon (a)	10	605	33	0	3.27
Mark Laforest	19	1142	57(1)	0	2.99
Chris Pusey	22	1171	76(4)	1	3.89
Ed Mio	8	487	32	0	3.94
Corrado Micalef	25	1436	93(2)	0	3.89
Adirondack Totals	84	4841	298	1	3.69
Jeff Cooper	23	1099	77(1)	2	4.20
Brian Ford	39	2230	136(4)	1	3.66
Denis Herron	27	1510	86	0	3.42
Baltimore Totals	89	4839	304	3	3.77
Bob Mason	34	1940	126	0	3.90
Peter Sidorkiewicz	49	2819	150(5)	2	*3.19
Rick Heinz	1	60	9	0	9.00
Binghamton Totals	84	4819	290	2	3.61
Luc Guenette	20	1021	76	0	4.47
Wendell Young	24	1457	78	0	3.21
Frank Caprice	26	1526	109(3)	0	4.29
John Garrett	3	179	9	0	3.02
Richard Sevigny	6	362	21	0	3.48
Mario Gosselin	5	304	15	0	2.96
Fredericton Totals	84	4849	311	0	3.85
Ron Hextall	*53	*3061	174(3)	*5	3.41
Darren Jensen	14	795	38	1	2.87
Shawn MacKenzie	10	521	36(1)	0	4.15
John Kemp	8	440	40	0	5.45
Hershey Totals	85	4817	292	6	3.64
Karl Friesen	35	1983	115(2)	2	3.48
Sam St. Laurent	50	2862	161(7)	1	3.38
Maine Totals	85	4845	285	3	3.53
Cleon Daskalakis	41	2343	141(3)	0	3.61
Rick Kosti	15	705	44(1)	1	3.74
Dave Meszaros	6	105	7	0	4.00
Al Larochelle	6	216	17	0	4.72
Mike Vernon	6	374	21	0	3.37
Marc D'Amour	21	1129	72(1)	0	3.83
Moncton Totals	95	4872	307	1	3.78
John Franzosa	3	180	22(1)	0	7.33
Glenn Healy	43	2410	160(2)	0	3.98
Ron Scott	19	1069	66(2)	1	3.70
Dave Hainsworth	2	29	1	0	2.07
Terry Kleisinger	10	497	34(1)	0	4.10
Glen Hanlon (a)	5	279	22	0	4.73
Roland Melanson	3	179	13	0	4.36
Darren Eliot	3	180	19	0	6.33
New Haven Totals	88	4823	343	1	4.27
Bruce Gillies	1	60	4	0	4.00
Jim Ralph	9	549	46(1)	0	5.03
Daryl Reaugh	38	2205	156(5)	0	4.24
Ron Low	6	299	24(1)	0	4.82
Warren Skorodenski	32	1716	109(7)	0	3.81
Nova Scotia Totals	86	4829	353	0	4.39
Mike Craig	47	2573	*183(4)	0	4.27
Bob McNamara	8	335	31(1)	0	5.55
Daren Puppa	20	1092	79(1)	0	4.34
Jacques Cloutier	14	835	38	1	2.73
Rochester Totals	89	4835	337	1	4.18

	Games	Mins.	Goals	SO.	Avg.
Allan Bester	50	2855	173(5)	1	3.64
Bruce Dowie	5	139	14	0	6.04
Ken Wregget	18	1058	78	1	4.42
Tim Bernhardt	14	776	38	1	2.94
St. Catharines Totals	87	4828	308	3	3.83
Paul Pageau	31	1767	132(2)	0	4.48
Yves Lavoie	3	160	16	0	6.00
Mark Behrend	35	2028	132(1)	1	3.91
Brian Hayward	3	185	5	0	1.62
Mark Holden	12	696	52(1)	0	4.48
Sherbrooke Totals	84	4836	341	1	4.23
Mike Sands	27	1490	94(1)	0	3.79
Karri Takko	43	2386	161	1	4.05
Jon Casey	9	464	30	0	3.88
Rob Holland	8	479	23	0	2.88
Springfield Totals	87	4819	309	1	3.85

( )—Empty Net Goals. Do not count against a Goaltender's average.
(a)—Hanlon played for Adirondack and New Haven.

Individual 1985-86 Leaders

Goals	Paul Gardner, Rochester—	61
Assists	Tim Tookey, Hershey—	62
Points	Paul Gardner, Rochester—	112
Penalty Minutes	Steve Martinson, Hershey—	432
Goaltending Average (25 Games)	Peter Sidorkiewicz, Binghamton—	3.19
Shutouts	Ron Hextall, Hershey—	5

1986 Calder Cup Playoffs
(All series best of seven)

Quarterfinals

Series "A"
	W.	L.	Pts.	GF.	GA.
Adirondack	4	2	8	28	28
Fredericton	2	4	4	28	28

(Adirondack wins series, 4 games to 2)

Series "C"
	W.	L.	Pts.	GF.	GA.
Hershey	4	1	8	23	15
New Haven	1	4	2	15	23

(Hershey wins series, 4 games to 1)

Series "B"
	W.	L.	Pts.	GF.	GA.
Moncton	4	1	8	14	11
Maine	1	4	2	11	14

(Moncton wins series, 4 games to 1)

Series "D"
	W.	L.	Pts.	GF.	GA.
St. Catharines	4	2	8	23	20
Binghamton	2	4	4	20	23

(St. Catharines wins series, 4 games to 2)

Semifinals

Series "E"
	W.	L.	Pts.	GF.	GA.
Adirondack	4	1	8	22	15
Moncton	1	4	2	15	22

(Adironidack wins series, 4 games to 1)

Series "F"
	W.	L.	Pts.	GF.	GA.
Hershey	4	3	8	22	22
St. Catharines	3	4	6	22	22

(Hershey wins series, 4 games to 3)

Finals—For the Calder Cup

Series "G"
	W.	L.	Pts.	GF.	GA.
Adirondack	4	2	8	26	19
Hershey	2	4	4	19	26

(Adirondack wins series, and Calder Cup, 4 games to 2)

Top 10 Playoff Scorers

	Games	G.	A.	Pts.	Pen.
1. Larry Trader, Adirondack	17	6	*16	*22	14
2. Adam Oates, Adirondack	17	7	14	21	4
3. Tim Tookey, Hershey	18	*11	8	19	10
4. Bo Berglund, Hershey	16	7	10	17	17
5. Ross Fitzpatrick, Hershey	17	9	7	16	10
6. Pierre Aubry, Adirondack	16	*11	4	15	20
David Gans, Hershey	18	10	5	15	60
Brian Bradley, Moncton	10	6	9	15	4
Claude Loiselle, Adirondack	16	5	10	15	38
10. Wes Jarvis, St. Catharines	13	5	8	13	12
Lance Nethery, Hershey	18	4	9	13	2

Team-by-Team Playoff Scoring

Adirondack Red Wings
(Winners of 1986 Calder Cup Playoffs)

	Games	G.	A.	Pts.	Pen.
Larry Trader	17	6	*16	*22	14
Adam Oates	17	7	14	21	4
Pierre Aubry	16	*11	4	15	20
Claude Loiselle	16	5	10	15	38
Ted Speers	15	7	5	12	9
Shawn Burr	17	5	7	12	32
Eddie Johnstone	17	5	7	12	4
Glenn Merkosky	17	5	7	12	15
Steve Richmond	17	2	9	11	34
Lane Lambert	16	5	5	10	9
Geordie Robertson	15	4	6	10	25
Basil McRae	17	5	4	9	101
Ted Huesing	17	2	7	9	6
Dale Krentz	13	2	6	8	9
Tim Friday	16	0	6	6	6
Bob Probert	10	2	3	5	68
Ray Staszak	16	2	3	5	70
Greg Joly	16	0	4	4	38
Rick Zombo	17	0	4	4	40
Gary Yaremchuk	1	1	0	1	0
Dave Korol	3	0	1	1	4
Chris Pusey (Goalie)	1	0	0	0	0
Mark Laforest (Goalie)	17	0	0	0	2

Binghamton Whalers
(Lost quarterfinals to St. Catharines, 4-2)

	Games	G.	A.	Pts.	Pen.
Daryl Evans	5	6	2	8	0
David Jensen	4	2	4	6	0
Andre Hidi	6	1	4	5	13
Gary Sampson	6	2	2	4	4
Grant Martin	6	1	3	4	14
Timo Blomqvist	6	0	4	4	6
Mike Siltala	2	3	0	3	0
Yves Beaudoin	6	1	2	3	0
Jack Brownschidle	6	0	3	3	0
Paul Fenton	6	2	0	2	0
Jim Thomson	6	1	1	2	20
Brad Shaw	5	0	2	2	6
Paul Cavallini	6	0	2	2	56
Mike Hoffman	2	1	0	1	2
Chris Brant	6	0	1	1	19
Steve Hollett	4	0	0	0	0
Claude Dumas	5	0	0	0	0
Vito Cramarossa	4	0	0	0	0
Shane Churla	3	0	0	0	22

	Games	G.	A.	Pts.	Pen.
Bob Mason (Goalie)	3	0	0	0	0
John Mokosak	6	0	0	0	6
Peter Sidorkiewicz (G.)	4	0	0	0	0
Mark Paterson	6	0	0	0	6

Fredericton Express
(Lost quarterfinals to Adirondack, 4-2)

	Games	G.	A.	Pts.	Pen.
Tony Currie	6	5	2	7	4
Alain Lemieux	5	5	2	7	5
Neil Belland	6	1	6	7	2
Dunc MacIntyre	6	3	3	6	4
Jean Marc Gaulin	6	2	3	5	31
Claude Julien	6	1	4	5	19
Mark Kirton	6	2	2	4	4
Ken Quiney	6	2	2	4	9
Stu Kulak	6	2	1	3	0
Scott Clements	6	1	2	3	2
Mike Hough	6	0	3	3	8
Daniel Poudrier	6	0	3	3	0
Dave Latta	5	0	3	3	0
Gary Lupul	3	2	0	2	4
Mike Stevens	6	1	1	2	35
Scott Tottle	3	1	1	2	0
Dave Bruce	2	0	1	1	12
Andy Schliebener	6	0	1	1	10
Yves Heroux	2	0	1	1	7
Jeff Brown	1	0	1	1	0
Gord Donnelly	5	0	0	0	33
Luc Guenette (Goalie)	2	0	0	0	0
Richard Zemlack	3	0	0	0	49
Frank Caprice (Goalie)	6	0	0	0	0
Taylor Hall	1	0	0	0	0

Hershey Bears
(Lost finals to Adirondack, 4-2)

	Games	G.	A.	Pts.	Pen.
Tim Tookey	18	*11	8	19	10
Bo Berglund	16	7	10	17	17
Ross Fitzpatrick	17	9	7	16	10
David Gans	18	10	5	15	60
Lance Nethery	18	4	9	13	2
Kevin McCarthy	17	1	10	11	12
Brian Dobbin	18	5	5	10	21
Ray Allison	18	4	6	10	28

	Games	G.	A.	Pts.	Pen.
Don Nachbaur	18	5	4	9	70
Al Hill	18	2	6	8	52
Steve Smith	16	2	4	6	43
Andre Dore	18	0	6	6	35
Bernie Johnston	18	2	3	5	11
Carl Mokosak	16	0	4	4	111
Dave Farrish	18	0	4	4	24
Mike Stothers	13	0	3	3	88
Steve Seguin	15	2	0	2	22
Andre Villeneuve	14	0	1	1	11
Jeff Chychrun	4	0	1	1	9
Ron Hextall (Goalie)	14	0	1	1	37
Darren Jensen (Goalie)	7	0	1	1	0
Steve Martinson	3	0	0	0	56
Florent Robidoux	3	0	0	0	15
Brent Loney	1	0	0	0	0
Greg Smyth	8	0	0	0	60
Ian Armstrong	1	0	0	0	0

Maine Mariners
(Lost quarterfinals to Moncton, 4-1)

	Games	G.	A.	Pts.	Pen.
Larry Floyd	5	3	3	6	0
Steve Tsujiura	5	2	3	5	2
Dan Dorion	5	2	2	4	0
Andy Brickley	5	0	4	4	0
Kevin Maxwell	5	2	1	3	9
Murray Brumwell	5	0	3	3	2
Pat Conacher	5	1	1	2	11
Tim Army	4	1	0	1	0
Michel Bolduc	5	0	1	1	6
Gordie Mark	5	0	1	1	9
Rich Chernomaz	5	0	0	0	2
Don Dietrich	3	0	0	0	0
Luc Dufour	5	0	0	0	8
Karl Friesen (Goalie)	5	0	0	0	0
Archie Henderson	5	0	0	0	24
Alan Hepple	5	0	0	0	11
Rob Palmer	5	0	0	0	0
Bud Stefanski	2	0	0	0	6
Mitch Wilson	3	0	0	0	2
Bob Hoffmeyer	5	0	0	0	6
Todd Ewen	3	0	0	0	7

Moncton Alpines
(Lost semifinals to Adirondack, 4-1)

	Games	G.	A.	Pts.	Pen.
Brian Bradley	10	6	9	15	4
Greg Johnston	10	4	6	10	4
Mark Lamb	10	2	6	8	17
Yves Courteau	10	4	2	6	5
Bob Bodak	10	3	3	6	0
Benoit Doucet	10	3	2	5	7
John Newberry	9	1	4	5	2
Doug Kostynski	8	3	1	4	9
Peter Bakovic	10	2	2	4	30
Kevan Guy	10	0	2	2	6
Tom Thornbury	7	0	2	2	10
Randy Burridge	3	0	2	2	2
Peter Dineen	9	1	0	1	9
Dale Degray	6	0	1	1	0
Tom McMurchy	2	0	1	1	6
Ken Sabourin	6	0	1	1	2
Rob Kivell	7	0	0	0	5
Robin Bartel	3	0	0	0	0
Cleon Daskalakis (G.)	6	0	0	0	0

	Games	G.	A.	Pts.	Pen.
John Meulenbroeks	8	0	0	0	11
George White	9	0	0	0	6
Al Pedersen	3	0	0	0	0
Wade Campbell	10	0	0	0	16
Marc D'Amour (Goalie)	5	0	0	0	2
Darwin McCutcheon	9	0	0	0	9

New Haven Nighthawks
(Lost quarterfinals to Hershey, 4-1)

	Games	G.	A.	Pts.	Pen.
Chris Kontos	5	4	2	6	4
Randy Heath	5	3	2	5	7
Marty Dallman	5	0	4	4	4
Paul Guay	5	3	0	3	11
Mark Lofthouse	5	2	1	3	0
Dave Gagner	4	1	2	3	2
Don Waddell	5	1	2	3	4
Bob Bergloff	4	0	2	2	2
Steve Duchesne	5	0	2	2	9
Dave Nicholls	2	1	0	1	2
Steve Moria	5	0	1	1	4
Len Hachborn	3	0	1	1	26
Bill O'Dwyer	5	0	1	1	2
Lyle Phair	2	0	1	1	0
Dan Brennan	2	0	0	0	10
Kjell Samuelsson	3	0	0	0	10
Glenn Currie	2	0	0	0	10
Jim Andonoff	5	0	0	0	19
Bobby Crawford	5	0	0	0	2
Jay Caufield	1	0	0	0	0
Craig Duncanson	2	0	0	0	5
Glenn Healy (Goalie)	2	0	0	0	2
Jim Dobson	1	0	0	0	0
Chris McSorley	2	0	0	0	12
Scott Smith	3	0	0	0	0
Ron Scott (Goalie)	2	0	0	0	0
Darren Eliot (Goalie)	1	0	0	0	0
Ken Hammond	4	0	0	0	7

St. Catharines Saints
(Lost semifinals to Hershey, 4-3)

	Games	G.	A.	Pts.	Pen.
Wes Jarvis	13	5	8	13	12
John Goodwin	13	5	7	12	11
Dan Hodgson	13	3	9	12	14
Miroslav Ihnacak	13	8	3	11	10
Rod Schutt	13	7	4	11	18
Rich Costello	13	3	6	9	30
Jeff Jackson	13	5	2	7	30
Todd Gill	10	1	6	7	17
Greg Britz	13	3	3	6	17
Leigh Verstraete	11	2	3	5	*114
Craig Muni	13	0	5	5	16
Mark Botell	12	1	3	4	8
Blake Wesley	13	0	3	3	41
Cam Plante	5	0	3	3	2
Val James	13	1	1	2	53
Derek Laxdal	12	1	1	2	24
Bill Kitchen	12	0	2	2	19
Garry Lariviere	6	0	1	1	6
Chris McRae	11	0	1	1	65
Ken Strong	3	0	1	1	0
Tim Bernhardt (Goalie)	3	0	0	0	0
Todd Petkovich	6	0	0	0	17
Allan Bester (Goalie)	11	0	0	0	0
Kevin Maguire	1	0	0	0	0
Ken Spangler	2	0	0	0	15

Complete Calder Cup Goaltending

	Games	Mins.	Goals	SO.	Avg.
Cleon Daskalakis, Moncton	6	372	13	0	*2.10
Karl Friesen, Maine	5	340	14	0	2.47
Allan Bester, St. Catharines	11	637	27(3)	0	2.54
Peter Sidorkiewicz, Binghamton	4	235	12(2)	0	3.06
Darren Jensen, Hershey	7	365	19	0	3.12
Ron Hextall, Hershey	13	780	42(2)	*1	3.23
Mark Laforest, Adirondack	*17	*1075	*58	0	3.24
Ron Scott, New Haven	2	143	8	0	3.36
Frank Caprice, Fredericton	6	333	22	0	3.96
Darren Eliot, New Haven	1	60	4	0	4.00
Marc D'Amour, Moncton	5	296	20	0	4.05
Bob Mason, Binghamton	3	124	9	0	4.35
Tim Bernhardt, St. Catharines	3	140	12	0	5.14
Glenn Healy, New Haven	2	119	11	0	5.55
Chris Pusey, Adirondack	1	27	4	0	8.89
Luc Guenette, Fredericton	2	32	6	0	11.25

( )—Empty Net Goals. Do not count against a Goaltender's average.

Individual AHL Playoff Leaders

Goals	Tim Tookey, Hershey—	11
	Pierre Aubry, Adirondack—	11
Assists	Larry Trader, Adirondack—	16
Points	Larry Trader, Adirondack—	22
Penalty Minutes	Leigh Verstraete, St. Catharines—	114
Goaltender's Average	Cleon Daskalakis, Moncton—	2.10
Shutouts	Ron Hextall, Hershey—	1

★★★

AHL 1985-86 ALL-STARS

First Team	Position	Second Team
Ron Hextall, Hershey	Goal	Sam St. Laurent, Maine
Jim Wiemer, New Haven	Defense	Larry Trader, Adirondack
Kevin McCarthy, Hershey	Defense	Jack Brownschidle, Bing.
Paul Gardner, Rochester	Center	Tim Tookey, Hershey
Jody Gage, Rochester	Right Wing	Serge Boisvert, Sherbrooke
Paul Fenton, Binghamton	Left Wing	Ross Fitzpatrick, Hershey

★★★

AHL 1985-86 TROPHY WINNERS

John B. Sollenberger Trophy (Leading Scorer)	Paul Gardner, Rochester
Les Cunningham Plaque (Most Valuable Player)	Paul Gardner, Rochester
Harry (Hap) Holmes Memorial Trophy (Top Team Goaltending)	Sam St. Laurent and Karl Friesen, Maine
Dudley (Red) Garrett Memorial Trophy (Top Rookie)	Ron Hextall, Hershey
Eddie Shore Plaque (Outstanding Defenseman)	Jim Wiemer, New Haven
Fred Hunt Memorial Award (Sportsmanship, Determination, Dedication)	Steve Tsujiura, Maine
Louis A.R. Pieri Memorial Award (Top AHL Coach)	Bill Dineen, Adirondack
Baz Bastien Trophy (Coaches pick as top AHL Goalie)	Sam St. Laurent, Maine
Jack Butterfield Trophy (Calder Cup Playoffs MVP)	Tim Tookey, Hershey

AHL All-Time Trophy Winners

John B. Sollenberger Trophy
Leading Scorer

(Originally called Wally Kilrea Trophy, later changed to Carl Liscombe Trophy and during summer of 1955 given current name)

	Games	G.	A.	Pts.	Pen.
1936-37—Jack Markle, Syracuse	48	21	39	60	2
1937-38—Jack Markle, Syracuse	48	22	32	54	8
1938-39—Don Deacon, Pittsburgh	46	24	41	65	41
1939-40—Norm Locking, Syracuse	55	31	32	63	12
1940-41—Les Cunningham, Cleveland	56	22	42	64	10
1941-42—Pete Kelly, Springfield	46	34	44	78	11
1942-43—Wally Kilrea, Hershey	56	31	68	99	8
1943-44—Tommy Burlington, Cleveland	52	33	49	82	17
1944-45—Bob Gracie, Pittsburgh	58	40	55	95	4
Bob Walton, Pittsburgh	58	37	58	95	17
1945-46—Les Douglas, Indianapolis	62	44	46	90	35
1946-47—Phil Hergesheimer, Philadelphia	64	48	44	92	20
1947-48—Carl Liscombe, Providence	68	50	68	118	10
1948-49—Sid Smith, Pittsburgh	68	55	57	112	4
1949-50—Les Douglas, Cleveland	67	32	68	100	27
1950-51—Ab DeMarco, Buffalo	64	37	76	113	35
1951-52—Ray Powell, Providence	67	35	62	97	6
1952-53—Eddie Olson, Cleveland	61	32	54	86	33
1953-54—George Sullivan, Hershey	69	30	89	119	54
1954-55—Eddie Olson, Cleveland	60	41	47	88	48
1955-56—Zellio Toppazzini, Providence	64	42	71	113	44
1956-57—Fred Glover, Cleveland	64	42	57	99	111
1957-58—Willie Marshall, Hershey	68	40	64	104	56
1958-59—Bill Hicke, Rochester	69	41	56	97	41
1959-60—Fred Glover, Cleveland	72	38	69	107	143
1960-61—Bill Sweeney, Springfield	70	40	68	108	26
1961-62—Bill Sweeney, Springfield	70	40	61	101	14
1962-63—Bill Sweeney, Springfield	69	38	65	103	16
1963-64—Gerry Ehman, Rochester	66	36	49	85	26
1964-65—Art Stratton, Buffalo	71	25	84	109	32
1965-66—Dick Gamble, Rochester	71	47	51	98	22
1966-67—Gordon Labossiere, Quebec	72	40	55	95	71
1967-68—Simon Nolet, Quebec	70	44	52	96	45
1968-69—Jeannot Gilbert, Hershey	71	35	65	100	13
1969-70—Jude Drouin, Montreal	65	37	69	106	88
1970-71—Fred Speck, Baltimore	72	31	61	92	40
1971-72—Don Blackburn, Providence	76	34	65	99	12
1972-73—Yvon Lambert, Nova Scotia	76	52	52	104	84
1973-74—Steve West, New Haven	76	50	60	110	41
1974-75—Doug Gibson, Rochester	75	44	72	116	81
1975-76—Jean-Guy Gratton, Hershey	73	35	58	93	38
1976-77—Andre Peloffy, Springfield	79	42	57	99	106
1977-78—Gord Brooks, Philadelphia	81	42	56	98	40
Rick Adduono, Rochester	76	38	60	98	34
1978-79—Bernie Johnston, Maine	70	29	66	95	40
1979-80—Norm Dube, Nova Scotia	77	40	61	101	51
1980-81—Mark Lofthouse, Hershey	74	48	55	103	131
1981-82—Mike Kaszycki, New Brunswick	80	36	82	118	67
1982-83—Ross Yates, Binghamton	77	41	84	125	28
1983-84—Claude Larose, Sherbrooke	80	53	67	120	6
1984-85—Paul Gardner, Binghamton	64	51	79	130	10
1985-86—Paul Gardner, Rochester	71	61	51	112	16

Les Cunningham Plaque
Most Valuable Player

1947-48—Carl Liscombe, Providence
1948-49—Carl Liscombe, Providence
1949-50—Les Douglas, Cleveland
1950-51—Ab DeMarco, Buffalo
1951-52—Ray Powell, Providence

1952-53—Eddie Olson, Cleveland
1953-54—George "Red" Sullivan, Hershey
1954-55—Ross Lowe, Springfield
1955-56—Johnny Bower, Providence
1956-57—Johnny Bower, Providence

1957-58—Johnny Bower, Cleveland
1958-59—Bill Hicke, Rochester
 Rudy Migay, Rochester (tie)
1959-60—Fred Glover, Cleveland
1960-61—Phil Maloney, Buffalo
1961-62—Fred Glover, Cleveland
1962-63—Denis DeJordy, Buffalo
1963-64—Fred Glover, Cleveland
1964-65—Art Stratton, Buffalo
1965-66—Dick Gamble, Rochester
1966-67—Mike Nykoluk, Hershey
1967-68—Dave Creighton, Providence
1968-69—Gilles Villemure, Buffalo
1969-70—Gilles Villemure, Buffalo
1970-71—Fred Speck, Baltimore
1971-72—Garry Peters, Boston
1972-73—Billy Inglis, Cincinnati
1973-74—Art Stratton, Rochester
1974-75—Doug Gibson, Rochester
1975-76—Ron Andruff, Nova Scotia
1976-77—Doug Gibson, Rochester
1977-78—Blake Dunlop, Maine
1978-79—Rocky Saganiuk, New Brunswick
1979-80—Norm Dube, Nova Scotia
1980-81—Pelle Lindbergh, Maine
1981-82—Mike Kasczyki, New Brunswick
1982-83—Ross Yates, Binghamton
1983-84—Mal Davis, Rochester
 Garry Lariviere, St. Catharines (tie)
1984-85—Paul Gardner, Binghamton
1985-86—Paul Gardner, Rochester

Harry (Hap) Holmes Memorial Trophy
Outstanding Goaltender

	Games	Goals	SO.	Avg.
1936-37—Bert Gardiner, Philadelphia	47	108	4	2.29
1937-38—Frank Brimsek, Providence	48	86	5	1.79
1938-39—Alfie Moore, Hershey	53	105	7	1.98
1939-40—Moe Roberts, Cleveland	56	130	5	2.32
1940-41—Chuck Rayner, Springfield	36	87	6	2.42
1941-42—Bill Beveridge, Cleveland	31	73	8	2.35
1942-43—Gordie Bell, Buffalo	52	125	9	2.40
1943-44—Nick Damore, Hershey	54	133	4	2.46
1944-45—Yves Nadon, Buffalo	30	87	3	2.90
1945-46—Connie Dion, St. Louis-Buffalo	42	124	1	2.95
1946-47—Baz Bastien, Pittsburgh	40	140	7	2.60
1947-48—Baz Bastien, Pittsburgh	68	170	5	2.50
1948-49—Baz Bastien, Pittsburgh	68	175	6	2.57
1949-50—Gil Mayer, Pittsburgh	50	142	4	2.84
1950-51—Gil Mayer, Pittsburgh	71	174	6	2.45
1951-52—Johnny Bower, Cleveland	68	165	3	2.43
1952-53—Gil Mayer, Pittsburgh	62	146	6	2.35
1953-54—Jacques Plante, Buffalo	55	148	3	2.69
1954-55—Gil Mayer, Pittsburgh	64	179	3	2.80
1955-56—Gil Mayer, Pittsburgh	56	151	5	2.70
1956-57—Johnny Bower, Providence	57	138	4	2.42
1957-58—Johnny Bower, Cleveland	64	140	8	2.19
1958-59—Bob Perreault, Hershey	50	134	6	2.68
1959-60—Ed Chadwick, Rochester	67	184	4	2.75
1960-61—Marcel Paille, Springfield	67	188	8	2.81
1961-62—Marcel Paille, Springfield	45	115	2	2.56
1962-63—Denis DeJordy, Buffalo	67	187	6	2.79
1963-64—Roger Crozier, Pittsburgh	44	103	4	2.34
1964-65—Gerry Cheevers, Rochester	72	195	5	2.68
1965-66—Les Binkley, Cleveland	66	192	2	2.93
1966-67—Andre Gill, Hershey	56	161	4	2.90
1967-68—Bob Perreault, Rochester	57	149	6	2.88
1968-69—Gilles Villemure, Buffalo	62	148	6	2.41
1969-70—Gilles Villemure, Buffalo	65	156	8	2.52
1970-71—Gary Kurt, Cleveland	42	101	3	2.67
1971-72—Dan Bouchard, Boston	50	122	4	2.51
Ross Brooks, Boston	30	65	1	2.38
1972-73—Michel Larocque, Nova Scotia	47	114	1	2.50
1973-74—Jim Shaw, Nova Scotia	41	104	3	2.68
Dave Elenbaas, Nova Scotia	39	109	3	2.96
1974-75—Ed Walsh, Nova Scotia	46	128	2	2.77
Dave Elenbaas, Nova Scotia	30	93	1	3.15
1975-76—Dave Elenbaas, Nova Scotia	48	114	5	2.42
Ed Walsh, Nova Scotia	31	91	2	3.06
1976-77—Ed Walsh, Nova Scotia	40	115	3	2.86
Dave Elenbaas, Nova Scotia	31	81	5	2.61
1977-78—Bob Holland, Nova Scotia	38	120	1	3.17
Maurice Barrette, Nova Scotia	39	107	2	2.74
1978-79—Pete Peeters, Maine	35	100	2	2.90
Robbie Moore, Maine	26	84	1	3.38
1979-80—Rick St. Croix, Maine	46	132	1	2.90
Robbie Moore, Maine	32	106	1	3.48

	Games	Goals	SO.	Avg.
1980-81—Pelle Lindbergh, Maine	51	165	1	3.26
Robbie Moore, Maine	25	92	1	3.86
1981-82—Bob Janecyk, New Brunswick	53	153	2	2.85
Warren Skorodenski, New Brunswick	28	70	3	2.55
1982-83—Brian Ford, Fredericton	27	84	0	3.49
Clint Malarchuk, Fredericton	25	78	1	3.11
1983-84—Brian Ford, Fredericton	36	105	2	2.94
1984-85—Jon Casey, Baltimore	46	116	4	2.63
1985-86—Sam St. Laurent, Maine	50	161	1	3.38
Karl Friesen, Maine	35	115	2	3.48

Dudley (Red) Garrett Memorial Trophy
Outstanding Rookie Player

1947-48—Bob Solinger, Cleveland Barons
1948-49—Terry Sawchuk, Indianapolis Caps
1949-50—Paul Meger, Buffalo Bisons
1950-51—Wally Hergesheimer, Cleveland Barons
1951-52—Earl "Dutch" Reibel, Indianapolis Caps
1952-53—Guyle Fielder, St. Louis Flyers
1953-54—Don Marshall, Buffalo Bisons
1954-55—Jimmy Anderson, Springfield Indians
1955-56—Bruce Cline, Providence Reds
1956-57—Boris "Bo" Elik, Cleveland Barons
1957-58—Bill Sweeney, Providence Reds
1958-59—Bill Hicke, Rochester Americans
1959-60—Stan Baluik, Providence Reds
1960-61—Ronald "Chico" Maki, Buffalo Bisons
1961-62—Les Binkley, Cleveland Barons
1962-63—Doug Robinson, Buffalo Bisons
1963-64—Roger Crozier, Pittsburgh Hornets
1964-65—Ray Cullen, Buffalo Bisons
1965-66—Mike Walton, Rochester Americans
1966-67—Bob Rivard, Quebec Aces
1967-68—Gerry Desjardins, Cleveland Barons
1968-69—Ron Ward, Rochester Americans
1969-70—Jude Drouin, Montreal Voyageurs
1970-71—Fred Speck, Baltimore Clippers
1971-72—Terry Caffery, Cleveland Barons
1972-73—Ron Anderson, Boston Braves
1973-74—Rick Middleton, Providence Reds
1974-75—Jerry Holland, Providence Reds
1975-76—Greg Holst, Providence (tie)
  Pierre Mondou, Nova Scotia
1976-77—Rod Schutt, Nova Scotia
1977-78—Norm Dupont, Nova Scotia
1978-79—Mike Meeker, Binghamton
1979-80—Daryl Sutter, New Brunswick
1980-81—Pelle Lindbergh, Maine
1981-82—Bob Sullivan, Binghamton
1982-83—Mitch Lamoureux, Baltimore
1983-84—Claude Verret, Rochester
1984-85—Steve Thomas, St. Catharines
1985-86—Ron Hextall, Hershey

Eddie Shore Plaque
Outstanding Defenseman

1958-59—Steve Kraftcheck, Rochester
1959-60—Larry Hillman, Providence
1960-61—Bob McCord, Springfield
1961-62—Kent Douglas, Springfield
1962-63—Marc Reaume, Hershey
1963-64—Ted Harris, Cleveland
1964-65—Al Arbour, Rochester
1965-66—Jim Morrison, Quebec
1966-67—Bob McCord, Pittsburgh
1967-68—Bill Needham, Cleveland
1968-69—Bob Blackburn, Buffalo
1969-70—Noel Price, Springfield
1970-71—Marshall Johnston, Cleveland
1971-72—Noel Price, Nova Scotia
1972-73—Ray McKay, Cincinnati
1973-74—Gordon Smith, Springfield
1974-75—Joe Zanussi, Providence
1975-76—Noel Price, Nova Scotia
1976-77—Brian Engblom, Nova Scotia
1977-78—Terry Murray, Maine
1978-79—Terry Murray, Maine
1979-80—Rick Vasko, Adirondack
1980-81—Craig Levie, Nova Scotia
1981-82—Dave Farrish, New Brunswick
1982-83—Greg Tebbutt, Baltimore
1983-84—Garry Lariviere, St. Catharines
1984-85—Richie Dunn, Binghamton
1985-86—Jim Wiemer, New Haven

Louis A. R. Pieri Memorial Award
Outstanding Coach

1967-68—Vic Stasiuk, Quebec
1968-69—Frank Mathers, Hershey
1969-70—Fred Shero, Buffalo
1970-71—Terry Reardon, Baltimore
1971-72—Al MacNeil, Nova Scotia
1972-73—Floyd Smith, Cincinnati
1973-74—Don Cherry, Rochester
1974-75—John Muckler, Providence
1975-76—Chuck Hamilton, Hershey
1976-77—Al MacNeil, Nova Scotia
1977-78—Bob McCammon, Maine
1978-79—Parker MacDonald, New Haven
1979-80—Doug Gibson, Hershey
1980-81—Bob McCammon, Maine
1981-82—Orval Tessier, New Brunswick
1982-83—Jacques Demers, Fredericton
1983-84—Gene Ubriaco, Baltimore
1984-85—Bill Dineen, Adirondack
1985-86—Bill Dineen, Adirondack

Fred Hunt Memorial Award
AHL Coaches' MVP

1977-78—Blake Dunlop, Maine
1978-79—Bernie Johnston, Maine
1979-80—Norm Dube, Nova Scotia
1980-81—Tony Cassolato, Hershey
1981-82—Mike Kasczyki, New Brunswick
1982-83—Ross Yates, Binghamton
1983-84—Claude Larose, Sherbrooke
1984-85—Paul Gardner, Binghamton
1985-86—Steve Tsujiura, Maine

AHL All-Time Championship Teams

REGULAR SEASON		PLAYOFFS (Calder Cup)	
Div.	Championship Team (Coach)	Year	Championship Team (Coach)
E	Philadelphia (Herb Gardiner)	1936-37	Syracuse Stars (E. Powers)
W	Syracuse (Eddie Powers)		
E	Providence (Bun Cook)	1937-38	Providence Reds (Bun Cook)
W	Cleveland (Bill Cook)		
E	Philadelphia (Herb Gardiner)	1938-39	Cleveland Barons (Bill Cook)
W	Hershey (Herb Mitchell)		
E	Providence (Bun Cook)	1939-40	Providence Reds (Bun Cook)
W	Indianapolis (Herb Lewis)		
E	Providence (Bun Cook)	1940-41	Cleveland Barons (Bill Cook)
W	Cleveland (Bill Cook)		
E	Springfield (Johnny Mitchell)	1941-42	Indianapolis Caps (Herb Lewis)
W	Indianapolis (Herb Lewis)		
	Hershey (Cooney Weiland)	1942-43	Buffalo Bisons (Art Chapman)
E	Hershey (Cooney Weiland)	1943-44	Buffalo Bisons (Art Chapman)
W	Cleveland (Bun Cook)		
E	Buffalo (Art Chapman)	1944-45	Cleveland Barons (Bun Cook)
W	Cleveland (Bun Cook)		
E	Buffalo (Frank Beisler)	1945-46	Buffalo Bisons (Frank Beisler)
W	Indianapolis (Earl Seibert)		
E	Hershey (Don Penniston)	1946-47	Hershey Bears (Don Penniston)
W	Cleveland (Bun Cook)		
E	Providence (Terry Reardon)	1947-48	Cleveland Barons (Bun Cook)
W	Cleveland (Bun Cook)		
E	Providence (Terry Reardon)	1948-49	Providence Reds (Terry Reardon)
W	St. Louis (Ebbie Goodfellow)		
E	Buffalo (Roy Goldsworthy)	1949-50	Indianapolis Caps (Ott Heller)
W	Cleveland (Bun Cook)		
E	Buffalo (Roy Goldsworthy)	1950-51	Cleveland Barons (Bun Cook)
W	Cleveland (Bun Cook)		
E	Hershey (John Crawford)	1951-52	Pittsburgh Hornets (King Clancy)
W	Pittsburgh (King Clancy)		
	Cleveland (Bun Cook)	1952-53	Cleveland Barons (Bun Cook)
	Buffalo (Frank Eddolls)	1953-54	Cleveland Barons (Bun Cook)
	Pittsburgh (Howie Meeker)	1954-55	Pittsburgh Hornets (Howie Meeker)
	Providence (John Crawford)	1955-56	Providence Reds (John Crawford)
	Providence (John Crawford)	1956-57	Cleveland Barons (Jack Gordon)
	Hershey (Frank Mathers)	1957-58	Hershey Bears (Frank Mathers)
	Buffalo (Bobby Kirk)	1958-59	Hershey Bears (Frank Mathers)
	Springfield (Pat Egan)	1959-60	Springfield Indians (Pat Egan)
	Springfield (Pat Egan)	1960-61	Springfield Indians (Pat Egan)
E	Springfield (Pat Egan)	1961-62	Springfield Indians (Pat Egan)
W	Cleveland (Jack Gordon)		
E	Providence (Fern Flaman)	1962-63	Buffalo Bisons (Billy Reay)
W	Buffalo (Billy Reay)		
E	Quebec (Floyd Curry)	1963-64	Cleveland Barons (Fred Glover)
W	Pittsburgh (Vic Stasiuk)		
E	Quebec (Bernie Geoffrion)	1964-65	Rochester Americans (Joe Crozier)
W	Rochester (Joe Crozier)		
E	Quebec (Bernie Geoffrion)	1965-66	Rochester Americans (Joe Crozier)
W	Rochester (Joe Crozier)		
E	Hershey (Frank Mathers)	1966-67	Pittsburgh Hornets (Baz Bastien)
W	Pittsburgh (Baz Bastien)		
E	Hershey (Frank Mathers)	1967-68	Rochester Americans (Joe Crozier)
W	Rochester (Joe Crozier)		

REGULAR SEASON		PLAYOFFS (Calder Cup)	
Div.	Championship Team (Coach)	Year	Championship Team (Coach)
E	Hershey (Frank Mathers)	1968-69	Hershey Bears (Frank Mathers)
W	Buffalo (Fred Shero)		
E	Montreal (Al MacNeil)	1969-70	Buffalo Bisons (Fred Shero)
W	Buffalo (Fred Shero)		
E	Providence (Larry Wilson)	1970-71	Springfield Kings (John Wilson)
W	Baltimore (Terry Reardon)		
E	Boston (Armond Guidolin)	1971-72	Nova Scotia Voyageurs (Al MacNeil)
W	Baltimore (Terry Reardon)		
E	Nova Scotia (Al MacNeil)	1972-73	Cincinnati Swords (Floyd Smith)
W	Cincinnati (Floyd Smith)		
N	Rochester (Don Cherry)	1973-74	Hershey Bears (Chuck Hamilton)
S	Baltimore (Terry Reardon)		
N	Providence (John Muckler)	1974-75	Springfield Indians (Ron Stewart)
S	Virginia (Doug Barkley)		
N	Nova Scotia (Al MacNeil)	1975-76	Nova Scotia Voyageurs (Al MacNeil)
S	Hershey (Chuck Hamilton)		
	Nova Scotia (Al MacNeil)	1976-77	Nova Scotia Voyageurs (Al MacNeil)
N	Maine (Bob McCammon)	1977-78	Maine Mariners (Bob McCammon)
S	Rochester (Duane Rupp)		
N	Maine (Bob McCammon)	1978-79	Maine Mariners (Bob McCammon)
S	New Haven (Parker MacDonald)		
N	New Brunswick (Crozier-Angotti)	1979-80	Hershey Bears (Doug Gibson)
S	New Haven (Parker MacDonald)		
N	Maine (Bob McCammon)	1980-81	Adirondack Red Wings (Tom Webster, J. P. LeBlanc)
S	Hershey (Bryan Murray)		
N	New Brunswick (Orval Tessier)	1981-82	New Brunswick (Orval Tessier)
S	Binghamton (Larry Kish)		
N	Fredericton (Jacques Demers)	1982-83	Rochester (Mike Keenan)
S	Rochester (Mike Keenan)		
N	Fredericton (Earl Jessiman)	1983-84	Maine (John Paddock)
S	Baltimore (Gene Ubriaco)		
N	Maine (McVie-Paddock)	1984-85	Sherbrooke (Pierre Creamer)
S	Binghamton (Larry Pleau)		
N	Adirondack (Bill Dineen)	1985-86	Adirondack (Bill Dineen)
S	Hershey (John Paddock)		

International Hockey League

(Organized, December 21, 1945)

8650 Commerce Park Place
Suite D
Indianapolis, Ind. 46268
(317) 872-1524
TWX 510-600-2072
Commissioner—Bud Poile

Mike Meyers—Director of Information

Flint Spirits
Governor and General Manager—Bob Perani
Alternate Governor—C. J. Shelley
Manager/Coach—Rick Dudley
Director of Public Relations—To be announced
Director of Sales—To be announced
Home Ice—I.M.A. Sports Arena (4,021)
Address—3501 Lapeer Road
Flint, Mich. 48503
Affiliation—Buffalo Sabres
Phone—(313) 743-1870

Fort Wayne Komets
Governor and General Manager—Bob Britt
Alternate Governor—Colin Lister
Manager and Coach—Rob Laird
Director of Public Relations—Phil Schultz
Director of Marketing—Bill Falsing
Home Ice—Allen County Memorial (8,022)
Address—4000 Parnell Ave.,
Fort Wayne, Ind. 46805
Affiliations—Washington Capitals and Winnipeg Jets
Phone—(219) 484-2581

Indianapolis Checkers
Governor—Larry Woods
Alt. Gov./Gen. Man./Coach—Ron Ullyot
Asst. Gen. Man.—Amy Rosencrans
Director of Sales—Sheila Bedell
Home Ice—Market Square Arena (15,822)
Address—54 Monument Circle
Suite 800
Indianapolis, Ind. 46204
Affiliations—New Jersey Devils and Minnesota North Stars
Phone—(317) 637-8425

Kalamazoo Wings
Governor—Ted Parfet
Alt. Gov./Gen. Man./Coach—Bill Inglis
Director of Public Relations—Steve Doherty
Director of Broadcasting—Mike Miller
Home Ice—Wings Stadium (5,121)
Address—3620 Van Rick Dr.,
Kalamazoo, Mich. 49002
Affiliations—Detroit Red Wings, Philadelphia Flyers and Vancouver Canucks
Phone—(616) 349-9772

Milwaukee Admirals
Governor—Joseph E. Tierney Jr.
Alt. Gov./Gen. Man./Coach—Phil Wittlif
Director of Public Relations—Mike Wojciechowski
Director of Broadcasting—Doug Petitt
Home Ice—Mecca Arena (8,946)
Address—320 E. Michigan St.
Milwaukee, Wis. 53202
Affiliations—Boston Bruins and Toronto Maple Leafs
Phone—(414) 278-7711

Muskegon Lumberjacks
Governor and General Manager—Larry Gordon
Alternate Governor—John Snider
Coach—Rick Ley
Director of Public Relations—Bob Heethuis
Director of Sales—Leo Hunstiger
Home Ice—L.C. Walker Sports Arena (5,061)
Address—470 W. Western Ave.
Muskegon, Mich. 49440
Affiliations—Edmonton Oilers, Quebec Nordiques and Pittsburgh Penguins
Phone—(616) 726-5058

Peoria Rivermen
Governor—Harold Hansen
Alt. Gov./Gen. Man./Coach—Pat Kelly
Director of Public Relations—Stephanie Bussey
Business Manager—Scott Wilson
Home Ice—Peoria Civic Center (9,228)
Address—201 S. W. Jefferson
Peoria, Ill. 61602
Affiliation—St. Louis Blues
Phone—(309) 673-8900

Saginaw Generals
Governor—Eugene Chardoul, M.D.
Alt. Gov./Gen. Man./Coach—Dennis Desrosiers
Director of Public Relations—Mike Bublitz
Director of Sales—To be announced
Home Ice—Saginaw Civic Center (5,463)
Address—118 North Washington
Saginaw, Mich. 48607
Affiliations—Montreal Canadiens and Chicago Black Hawks
Phone—(517) 754-3940

Salt Lake Golden Eagles
Governor—Art Teece
Alt. Gov./Gen. Man.—Marc Amicone
Coach—Wayne Thomas
Dir. of P.R. and Broadcasting—Don Stevens
Home Ice—Salt Palace (10,594)
Address—100 S.W. Temple
Salt Lake City, Utah 84101
Affiliations—Hartford Whalers and Calgary Flames
Phone—(801) 521-6120

1985-86 Final IHL Standings

East Division

	G.	W.	L.	T.	Pts.	GF.	GA.
Muskegon Lumberjacks	82	50	32	0(5)	105	376	290
Kalamazoo Wings	82	47	35	0(6)	100	341	310
Saginaw Generals	82	41	41	0(8)	90	318	285
Toledo Goaldiggers	82	24	58	0(10)	58	293	421
Flint Spirits	82	16	66	0(6)	38	270	495

West Division

	G.	W.	L.	T.	Pts.	GF.	GA.
Fort Wayne Komets	82	52	30	0(8)	112	345	263
Milwaukee Admirals	82	48	33	1(5)	102	368	306
Peoria Rivermen	82	46	36	0(5)	97	338	297
Salt Lake Golden Eagles	82	44	38	0(2)	90	340	325
Indianapolis Checkers	82	41	40	1(5)	88	296	303

NOTE: IHL teams are awarded a point for going into overtime. They collect a second point if they win. Overtime losses are added to the loss column and indicated by the bracketed figure in the ties column. This number must be added to wins and ties to calculate points.

Top 20 Scorers for the Leo P. Lamoureux Memorial Trophy

	Games	G.	A.	Pts.	Pen.
1. Scott MacLeod, Salt Lake	77	54	*80	*134	93
2. Brent Sapergia, Salt Lake	80	58	65	123	127
3. Jock Callander, Muskegon	82	39	72	111	121
4. Scott Gruhl, Muskegon	82	*59	50	109	178
Bill Terry, Kalamazoo	78	43	66	109	28
Jeff Pyle, Saginaw	80	39	70	109	49
7. Guy Benoit, Toledo	55	40	46	86	8
Muskegon	13	7	12	19	16
Totals	68	47	58	105	24
8. Dave Michayluk, Muskegon	77	52	52	104	73
9. Wayne Crawford, Kalamazoo	77	51	51	102	83
Jim Egerton, Flint	76	46	56	102	226
11. Daniel Lecours, Milwaukee	81	57	44	101	46
Dale Yakiwchuk, Milwaukee	82	33	68	101	265
13. Doug Evans, Peoria	69	46	51	97	179
14. Jim Burton, Fort Wayne	82	30	64	94	47
15. Charlie Skjodt, Indianapolis	80	28	65	93	94
16. John Vecchiarelli, Flint	81	40	52	92	89
17. Wally Schreiber, Fort Wayne	72	37	52	89	38
Fred Berry, Milwaukee	81	31	58	89	51
19. Mike Prestidge, Peoria	81	31	56	87	16
20. Randy Gilhen, Fort Wayne	82	44	40	84	48

Flint Generals

	Games	G.	A.	Pts.	Pen.
Jim Egerton	76	46	56	102	226
John Vecchiarelli	81	40	52	92	89
Tom Searle	61	15	41	56	66
Carmine Vani, Milw.	3	1	0	1	4
Flint	58	27	26	53	100
Totals	61	28	26	54	104
Scot Birnie, Toledo	45	11	19	30	65
Flint	31	8	13	21	29
Totals	76	19	32	51	94
Glenn Oliver	82	12	30	42	41
Scott Robins	67	18	23	41	10
Mike Opre	56	16	17	33	49
Rene Breton	73	8	24	32	19
Tom Rothstein, Ind.	25	11	10	21	19
Flint	13	5	4	9	2
Totals	38	16	14	30	21
Wray Brimmer	64	5	24	29	66
Dave Nicholls	56	11	14	25	72
Jim Andonoff, Salt Lake	10	1	2	3	10
Flint	39	9	12	21	17
Totals	49	10	14	24	27
Scott Brydges	61	7	15	22	52
Kelly Hubbard	65	4	18	22	186
Mike Bycina	28	12	8	20	15
Paul Stone	48	8	9	17	8
Normand Baron, Peoria	17	4	4	8	61
Flint	11	1	7	8	43
Totals	28	5	11	16	104
Chris DeLabbio, Sag.	13	4	3	7	10
Flint	22	4	3	7	16
Totals	35	8	6	14	26
Brian Bell	30	5	8	13	48
Fred Boimistruck	17	3	6	9	15
Nick Manych	32	0	6	6	49
Brad Walcot	8	2	2	4	2
Tim Maracle	15	0	4	4	12

	Games	G.	A.	Pts.	Pen.
Kurt Wickenheiser, Mus.	6	0	0	0	0
Flint	13	2	1	3	0
Totals	19	2	1	3	0
Bill Audycki	5	1	1	2	2
Michel Lanquette	3	0	2	2	16
Adam Lewis	11	0	2	2	0
Greg Hudas	23	0	2	2	35
Jeff Eatough	4	1	0	1	2
Don DeLabbio	3	0	1	1	5
Howie Young	4	0	1	1	2
Tom Gibson	5	0	1	1	0
Michel Valliere (Goalie)	41	0	1	1	9
Dave Parro (Goalie)	46	0	1	1	8
Dave Moffitt (Goalie)	3	0	0	0	0
Dan Olson (Goalie)	3	0	0	0	0
Tom Christiano	10	0	0	0	7
Todd Smith	11	0	0	0	26

Fort Wayne Komets

	Games	G.	A.	Pts.	Pen.
Jim Burton	82	30	64	94	47
Wally Schreiber	72	37	52	89	38
Randy Gilhen	82	44	40	84	48
Doug Rigler	73	33	48	81	57
David Anderson	75	33	41	74	156
Steve Salvucci	61	27	42	69	129
Lee Blossom, Toledo	58	26	29	55	33
Fort Wayne	14	7	4	11	8
Totals	72	33	33	66	41
Russ Adam	48	24	37	61	36
Dale Baldwin	78	20	36	56	226
Ron Leef	47	17	30	47	23
Rick Hendricks, Peoria	37	5	16	21	44
Fort Wayne	26	3	18	21	39
Totals	63	8	34	42	83
Dan Ryder	76	5	34	39	35
Paul Kobylarz	76	21	17	38	70
Craig Channell	69	7	28	35	116
Rob Tudor	13	6	8	14	7
Jay Johnson	78	1	13	14	176
Tony Camazzola	54	5	7	12	144
Kevin Foster	11	1	3	4	10
Rick St. Croix (Goalie)	42	0	3	3	6
Hector Marini	7	1	1	2	5
George Kotsopoulos	4	0	2	2	0
Lawrence Duke	9	1	0	1	7
Rob Laird	2	0	0	0	15
Al Chatlin	6	0	0	0	0
Mark Holden (Goalie)	9	0	0	0	0
Derek Ray	9	0	0	0	17
Pokey Reddick (Goalie)	32	0	0	0	6

Indianapolis Checkers

	Games	G.	A.	Pts.	Pen.
Charlie Skjodt	80	28	65	93	94
Bob Lakso	58	41	35	76	4
Gerry Minor	72	28	46	74	108
Monty Trottier	81	27	38	65	106
Kurt Kleinendorst, S.L.	24	5	12	17	21
Indianapolis	45	11	22	33	22
Totals	69	16	34	50	43
Phil DeGaetano	80	9	39	48	107
Mel Hewitt, Saginaw	17	6	4	10	49
Indianapolis	54	18	16	34	210
Totals	71	24	20	44	259

	Games	G.	A.	Pts.	Pen.
Darren McKay, Musk.	36	4	22	26	62
Indianapolis	30	4	14	18	42
Totals	66	8	36	44	104
Mark Magnan	69	15	22	37	279
Mike Nepi	80	9	24	33	109
Pat Ribble	52	6	21	27	45
Paul Skjodt	32	12	14	26	36
Tom D'Andrea	29	8	10	18	10
Earl Ingarfield	20	11	6	17	17
Jim Koudys	32	4	13	17	23
Dan Miele	55	5	11	16	68
Doug Moffitt, Salt Lake	9	1	2	3	0
Indianapolis	27	3	7	10	6
Totals	36	4	9	13	6
Mike Neill	71	2	11	13	117
Steve Lyons	15	6	6	12	9
Byron Lomow	9	8	3	11	10
Tim Thomas	10	3	5	8	15
Yvon Joly	17	1	6	7	28
Andy Cozzi	14	4	1	5	2
Todd Bjorkstrand, Sag.	10	0	0	0	6
Indianapolis	14	1	2	3	2
Totals	24	1	2	3	8
Rory Cava	12	0	3	3	9
Frank Janicek	4	1	0	1	2
John McDonald	4	0	1	1	6
Ron Dreger	8	0	1	1	2
Brian Johnson	13	0	1	1	57
Ed Lee	2	0	0	0	0
Scott Thomas	2	0	0	0	2
Tim Lockridge	7	0	0	0	2
Rob Holland (Goalie)	40	0	0	0	4
Mike Zanier (Goalie)	47	0	0	0	4

Kalamazoo Wings

	Games	G.	A.	Pts.	Pen.
Bill Terry	78	43	66	109	28
Wayne Crawford	77	51	51	102	83
Rob Nichols	73	38	41	79	406
Brent Jarrett	71	18	48	66	97
Claude Noel, Toledo	12	1	7	8	4
Kalamazoo	71	15	38	53	18
Totals	83	16	45	61	22
Neil Hawryliw, Musk.	14	4	1	5	10
Kalamazoo	68	32	23	55	67
Totals	82	36	24	60	77
Bill Schafhauser	75	9	45	54	46
Brian Tutt	82	11	39	50	129
Lawrie Nisker	49	22	21	43	51
John Beukeboom	78	7	36	43	244
Rob Davies	51	14	18	32	18
John Flesch	48	15	15	30	33
Neil Meadmore	37	12	17	29	118
Grant Anderson	71	8	18	26	149
Stu Kulak	30	14	8	22	38
Brian McDavid	68	3	16	19	89
Scott McMichael, F.W.	11	1	1	2	24
Kalamazoo	30	4	12	16	87
Totals	41	5	13	18	111
Paul Moore, Salt Lake	1	0	0	0	0
Kalamazoo	51	7	8	15	93
Totals	52	7	8	15	93
Kevin Evans	11	3	5	8	97
Brian Rorabeck	7	2	5	7	0
Don Shaw	9	1	3	4	0
Georges Gagnon (G.)	64	0	4	4	22

	Games	G.	A.	Pts.	Pen.
Brian Bertuzzi	4	2	0	2	2
Dave Ross, Toledo (G.)	9	0	1	1	14
Kalamazoo (G.)	17	0	1	1	29
Totals	26	0	2	2	43
Bob Curtis	3	0	1	1	2
John Stevens	6	0	1	1	8
Bill Campbell	1	0	0	0	0
Bill Gilliam	1	0	0	0	0
Mike Bloski (Goalie)	2	0	0	0	0
Tim Bratner	2	0	0	0	2
Shawn MacKenzie (G.)	6	0	0	0	4
Corrado Micalef (G.)	7	0	0	0	2

Milwaukee Admirals

	Games	G.	A.	Pts.	Pen.
Daniel Lecours	81	57	44	101	46
Dale Yakiwchuk	82	33	68	101	265
Fred Berry	81	31	58	89	51
Kevin Schamehorn	82	47	34	81	101
Gord Stafford	82	20	57	77	40
Greg Tebbutt	77	20	49	69	226
Bill McCreary	80	30	31	61	83
Mario Belanger	73	31	25	56	14
Alan Graves, Salt Lake	16	4	1	5	61
Milwaukee	63	25	21	46	105
Totals	79	29	22	51	166
Blaine Peerless	80	10	39	49	110
Tim Molle	80	12	35	47	165
Kevin Willison	77	9	29	38	57
Marc Damphousse	50	14	23	37	58
Doug Kyle	63	18	17	35	15
Derek Davis	77	5	18	23	328
Brian Byrnes	42	3	10	13	37
Jim Buettgen	19	4	5	9	4
Craig Homola	12	2	2	4	2
L. Middlebrook (G.)	56	0	3	3	6
Michel Therrien	2	1	1	2	0
Lyndon Byers	8	0	2	2	22
Mark Plantery	1	0	0	0	0
Bob Laforest	3	0	0	0	0
Todd Lumbard (Goalie)	6	0	0	0	0
Allan LaRochelle (G.)	8	0	0	0	0
Jim Ralph (Goalie)	14	0	0	0	4

Muskegon Lumberjacks

	Games	G.	A.	Pts.	Pen.
Jock Callander	82	39	72	111	121
Scott Gruhl	82	*59	50	109	178
Guy Benoit, Toledo	55	40	46	86	8
Muskegon	13	7	12	19	16
Totals	68	47	58	105	24
Dave Michayluk	77	52	52	104	73
Dennis Polonich	78	32	36	68	222
Todd Strueby	58	25	40	65	191
Dan Naud	80	13	52	65	34
Jiri Poner, Indianapolis	3	0	0	0	2
Muskegon	70	17	43	60	118
Totals	73	17	43	60	120
Wayne Groulx	55	22	27	49	56
Dave Allison	66	7	30	37	247
Todd Charlesworth	51	9	27	36	78
Don Keller, Peoria	31	8	4	12	80
Muskegon	38	9	12	21	108
Totals	69	17	16	33	188
Roy Sommer, Ind.	37	9	10	19	118
Muskegon	27	5	8	13	109
Totals	64	14	18	32	227

	Games	G.	A.	Pts.	Pen.
Gord Paddock, Ind.	11	1	1	2	11
Muskegon	47	1	20	21	87
Totals	58	2	21	23	98
Yves Heroux	42	14	8	22	41
Pat Mayer, Toledo	61	1	13	14	216
Muskegon	13	1	2	3	17
Totals	74	2	15	17	233
Tom Karalis	21	5	8	13	84
Mike Forbes	14	1	7	8	13
Tom Thornbury	9	0	8	8	8
Pat Rabbitt	17	0	6	6	11
John DePalma, Toledo	6	1	1	2	7
Muskegon	19	1	2	3	9
Totals	25	2	3	5	16
Richard Zemlak	3	1	2	3	36
Marc Zeitlin	14	0	3	3	10
Rod McGillis	7	1	1	2	0
Brian Ford (Goalie)	9	0	2	2	2
Jack Irving	5	0	1	1	4
Bruce Gillies (Goalie)	29	0	1	1	2
Michel Dufour (Goalie)	52	0	1	1	12
Larry Beck	4	0	0	0	0
Danny Lane	4	0	0	0	0
Peter Hermes	5	0	0	0	2

Peoria Rivermen

	Games	G.	A.	Pts.	Pen.
Doug Evans	69	46	51	97	179
Mike Prestidge	81	31	56	87	16
Grant Rezansoff	80	30	47	77	23
Brian Shaw	54	41	23	64	139
Glen Sharpley	50	26	37	63	32
Don Edwardson, Musk.	36	17	10	27	41
Peoria	38	20	15	35	23
Totals	74	37	25	62	64
Tony Curtale	70	7	51	58	116
Bob Fleming	78	21	35	56	140
Dave MacQueen	74	24	25	49	21
Denis Cyr	34	15	26	41	15
Paul Adey, Fort Wayne	39	13	11	24	44
Peoria	14	8	7	15	7
Totals	53	21	18	39	51
Bruce Holloway, Kala.	38	7	11	18	45
Peoria	29	4	13	17	47
Totals	67	11	24	35	92
Brad Kempthorne	45	9	26	35	27
Shawn Evans	55	8	26	34	36
Pat Ethier, Milwaukee	10	0	2	2	18
Toledo	41	5	8	13	78
Peoria	21	1	11	12	35
Totals	72	6	21	27	131
Mark Cupolo	60	9	14	23	87
Dennis Smith	70	5	15	20	102
Dan Wood	33	8	10	18	24
Mike Posavad	72	1	17	18	75
Graham Herring	34	1	9	10	22
Marty Ruff	44	3	6	9	34
Brian Cross	5	1	3	4	4
David McDonald	8	1	2	3	12
Brian Clark	8	1	1	2	25
Don Einwechter (G.)	23	0	2	2	2
Rob Brownlie	2	0	0	0	0
Carey Walker (Goalie)	5	0	0	0	2
John Deasey	7	0	0	0	0
Ron Choules	8	0	0	0	14
Darrell May (Goalie)	56	0	0	0	20

Saginaw Generals

	Games	G.	A.	Pts.	Pen.
Jeff Pyle	80	39	70	109	49
Brian Noonan	76	39	39	78	69
Kevin Robinson	81	34	36	70	43
Bernie Gallant	45	24	29	53	36
Peter Horachek	79	21	32	53	16
Tom St. James	53	16	34	50	36
Guy Jacob	67	24	16	40	142
Jim Camazzola	42	16	22	38	10
Luc Gauthier	66	9	29	38	165
Warren Holmes	65	17	20	37	88
Wade Dawson	80	7	20	27	101
Greg Lynott	67	3	23	26	96
Richard Adolfi, Ind.	21	2	2	4	36
Saginaw	43	6	12	18	55
Totals	64	8	14	22	91
Darin Sceviour	24	9	11	20	7
Bruce Howes	45	3	16	19	39
Dwayne Robinson, Mus.	12	1	2	3	0
Saginaw	46	6	9	15	11
Totals	58	7	11	18	11
Dave Russell	32	8	9	17	29
Jeff Eisley, Indianapolis	5	0	1	1	0
Saginaw	26	1	15	16	18
Totals	31	1	16	17	18
Daniel Letendre	40	8	7	15	2
John Ollson	13	6	6	12	9
Michel Caron	27	3	8	11	41
Garnet McKechney, Ind.	3	0	1	1	2
Milwaukee	15	0	2	2	11
Saginaw	8	2	2	4	2
Totals	26	2	5	7	15
Mike Brown	11	0	3	3	7
Darren Pang (Goalie)	44	0	2	2	4
Neil Jones	2	0	1	1	0
Kent Paynter	4	0	1	1	2
Ed Considine	9	0	1	1	24
Dave Westner	1	0	0	0	0
Rejean Cloutier	2	0	0	0	4
Dean Miller	2	0	0	0	0
Todd Francis	3	0	0	0	0
Joey Collins, Muskegon	2	0	0	0	0
Saginaw	2	0	0	0	0
Totals	4	0	0	0	0
Rick Knickle (Goalie)	39	0	0	0	6

Salt Lake Golden Eagles

	Games	G.	A.	Pts.	Pen.
Scott MacLeod	77	54	*80	*134	93
Brent Sapergia	80	58	65	123	127
Bobby Francis	82	32	44	76	163
Steve Harrison	77	17	53	70	48
Doug Morrison	80	27	34	61	30
Gary Burns	78	23	35	58	85
Ted Pearson	77	28	27	55	68
Glenn Hicks	82	14	40	54	75
Bobby Simpson	74	6	38	44	37
Todd Hooey	80	15	23	38	95
Kelly Elcombe, Ind.	35	2	11	13	42
Salt Lake	37	5	20	25	62
Totals	72	7	31	38	104
Gary DeGrio	59	19	14	33	18
Gary Stewart	82	6	27	33	233
Roger Dube, Saginaw	28	7	15	22	22
Salt Lake	10	1	2	3	4
Totals	38	8	17	25	26

	Games	G.	A.	Pts.	Pen.
Dave MacLean	41	9	14	23	14
Randy Turnbull	77	6	14	20	236
Randy Pierce	20	5	5	10	25
Len Frig	18	0	5	5	24
Jim Laing	20	0	4	4	8
Chris Brant	5	2	1	3	4
Ali Butorac	5	2	1	3	7
Rick Heinz (Goalie)	52	0	3	3	12
Mike Vernon (Goalie)	10	0	2	2	2
Neil Trineer	2	0	1	1	0
Rick Kosti (Goalie)	25	0	1	1	2
Kraeg Korinek (Goalie)	2	0	0	0	2
Rob Grillo	5	0	0	0	2
Mike Guentzel	6	0	0	0	2

Toledo Goaldiggers

	Games	G.	A.	Pts.	Pen.
Dave Falkenberg	80	32	51	83	117
Tim Hrynewich, Musk.	67	25	26	51	110
Toledo	13	8	13	21	25
Totals	80	33	39	72	135
Don Waddell	63	19	50	69	113
Steve Driscoll, Kala.	11	3	4	7	4
Toledo	68	26	28	54	8
Totals	79	29	32	61	12
Chris McSorley	75	27	28	55	*545
Don Murdoch, Musk.	12	4	4	8	0
Indianapolis	11	4	3	7	4
Toledo	37	15	23	38	8
Totals	60	23	30	53	12
Steve Tuite	47	5	31	36	36
John Hutchings, F.W.	56	1	25	26	79
Toledo	13	1	6	7	19
Totals	69	2	31	33	98
Paul Couture, F.W.	7	4	3	7	0
Toledo	13	11	13	24	2
Totals	20	15	16	31	2
Jim Aldred	51	9	17	26	110
John Baldassari, Musk.	63	2	17	19	132
Toledo	13	0	5	5	12
Totals	76	2	22	24	144
Barry Scully	23	9	9	18	10
Mark Salvucci, F.W.	35	2	7	9	165
Toledo	11	4	3	7	38
Totals	46	6	10	16	203
Kurt Kalweit	20	7	7	14	10
Peter Mahovlich	23	4	10	14	50
Mike Lauen	27	4	10	14	16
John Del Col, Muskegon	5	0	0	0	0
Toledo	33	6	7	13	23
Totals	38	6	7	13	23
Neil Davey	49	5	8	13	35
Joe Lunney	9	4	9	13	9
Peter Sawkins	25	4	8	12	25
Jim Hunter	32	2	9	11	33
Peter DeArmas	18	0	9	9	2
Jay Caufield	30	5	3	8	54
Darryl Moise	24	2	6	8	41
Bob Hodge	20	1	3	4	10
Bob Moise	17	3	0	3	14
Don McCoy	2	1	1	2	0
Venci Sebek	16	1	1	2	33
Bill King	18	1	1	2	16
Brian Walker	12	0	2	2	11
Billy Grum	3	1	0	1	0
Todd McCauley	5	1	0	1	2
Kevin Petendra	5	0	1	1	2

	Games	G.	A.	Pts.	Pen.		Games	G.	A.	Pts.	Pen.
Todd Morgan	9	0	1	1	28	Brian Paton	4	0	0	0	0
Dave Lundmark	12	0	1	1	7	Mark Chiamp, F.W. (G.)	3	0	0	0	2
T. Kleisinger, Flint (G.)	5	0	0	0	19	Toledo (Goalie)	2	0	0	0	0
Toledo (Goalie)	15	0	1	1	14	Totals	5	0	0	0	2
Totals	20	0	1	1	33	Glenn Healy (Goalie)	7	0	0	0	0
Jac Ostrander (Goalie)	1	0	0	0	0	Mario Proulx (Goalie)	23	0	0	0	12
Darcey Roy	3	0	0	0	4	John Franzosa (Goalie)	36	0	0	0	9

Individual IHL Goaltending

	Games	Mins.	Goals	SO.	Avg.
Jac Ostrander, Toledo	1	4	0	0	0.00
Pokey Reddick, Fort Wayne	32	1811	92(3)	*3	3.05
Michel Dufour, Muskegon	52	2935	151(2)	0	*3.09
Mark Holden, Fort Wayne	9	496	26	1	3.14
Rick St. Croix, Fort Wayne	42	2474	132(1)	2	3.20
Darrell May, Peoria	56	3321	179(1)	1	3.23
Mike Zanier, Indianapolis	47	2727	151(3)	0	3.32
Darren Pang, Saginaw	44	2638	148(2)	2	3.37
Mike Vernon, Salt Lake	10	601	34	1	3.39
Georges Gagnon, Kalamazoo	63	3718	211(3)	*3	3.40
Lindsay Middlebrook, Milwaukee	56	3318	191	*3	3.45
Rick Knickle, Saginaw	39	2235	135	2	3.62
Rick Heinz, Salt Lake City	52	3000	185(4)	1	3.70
Carey Walker, Peoria	5	299	19	0	3.81
Mark Chiamp, Fort Wayne	3	180	10	0	3.33
Toledo	2	119	9	0	4.54
Totals	5	299	19	0	3.82
Brian Ford, Muskegon	9	513	33	0	3.86
Rob Holland, Indianapolis	41	2246	146(3)	0	3.90
Bruce Gilles, Muskegon	29	1501	104(1)	0	4.16
Glenn Healy, Toledo	7	402	28	0	4.18
Jim Ralph, Milwaukee	14	819	58	1	4.25
Don Einwechter, Peoria	23	1318	95(1)	2	4.32
Corrado Micalef, Kalamazoo	7	398	29(1)	0	4.37
Rick Kosti, Salt Lake City	25	1330	99	0	4.47
Shawn MacKenzie, Kalamazoo	6	362	27	0	4.48
Allan LaRochelle, Milwaukee	8	455	34	0	4.48
Todd Lumbard, Milwaukee	6	305	23	0	4.52
Kraeg Korinek, Salt Lake	2	38	3	0	4.74
John Franzosa, Toledo	36	2021	160(5)	0	4.75
Dave Ross, Toledo	9	489	40(1)	0	4.91
Kalamazoo	8	406	31	0	4.58
Totals	17	895	71(1)	0	4.76
Mario Proulx, Toledo	22	1140	93(2)	1	4.90
Dan Olson, Flint	3	132	11	0	5.00
Dave Parro, Flint	46	2527	235(2)	0	5.58
Mike Bloski, Kalamazoo	2	83	8	0	5.78
Michel Valliere, Flint	41	2004	205	0	6.14
Terry Kleisinger, Flint	4	200	25	0	7.50
Toledo	14	786	76	0	5.80
Totals	18	986	101	0	6.15
Dave Moffitt, Flint	3	77	15	0	11.69

Individual IHL Playoff Leaders

Goals	Jock Callander, Muskegon—	12
Assists	Scott Gruhl, Muskegon—	13
	Russ Adams, Fort Wayne—	13
Points	Jock Callander, Muskegon—	23
Penalty Minutes	Roy Sommer, Muskegon—	92
Goaltending Average	Brian Ford, Muskegon—	3.10
Shutouts	Pokey Reddick, Fort Wayne—	2

1985-86 Turner Cup Playoffs

(All series best of seven)

Quarterfinals

West Division

Series "A"

	W.	L.	Pts.	GF.	GA.
Fort Wayne	4	1	8	28	24
Salt Lake	1	4	2	24	28

(Fort Wayne wins series, 4 games to 1)

Series "C"

	W.	L.	Pts.	GF.	GA.
Peoria	4	1	8	19	15
Milwaukee	1	4	2	15	19

(Peoria wins series, 4 games to 1)

East Division

Series "B"

	W.	L.	Pts.	GF.	GA.
Muskegon	4	1	8	24	18
Indianapolis	1	4	2	18	24

(Muskegon wins series, 4 games to 1)

Series "D"

	W.	L.	Pts.	GF.	GA.
Saginaw	4	2	8	29	24
Kalamazoo	2	4	4	24	29

(Saginaw wins series, 4 games to 2)

Semifinals

West Division

Series "E"

	W.	L.	Pts.	GF.	GA.
Fort Wayne	4	2	8	25	22
Peoria	2	4	4	22	25

(Fort Wayne wins series, 4 games to 2)

East Division

Series "F"

	W.	L.	Pts.	GF.	GA.
Muskegon	4	1	8	20	18
Saginaw	1	4	2	18	20

(Muskegon wins series, 4 games to 1)

Finals for the Turner Cup

Series "G"

	W.	L.	Pts.	GF.	GA.
Muskegon	4	0	8	23	11
Fort Wayne	0	4	0	11	23

(Muskegon wins series, and Turner Cup, 4 games to 0)

Top 10 Playoff Scorers

	Games	G.	A.	Pts.	Pen.
1. Jock Callander, Muskegon	14	*12	11	*23	12
2. Steve Salvucci, Fort Wayne	14	10	10	20	37
Scott Gruhl, Muskegon	14	7	*13	20	22
Russ Adam, Fort Wayne	14	7	*13	20	9
5. Guy Benoit, Muskegon	14	7	12	19	6
6. Randy Gilhen, Fort Wayne	15	10	8	18	6
Dennis Polonich, Muskegon	14	8	10	18	36
Wally Schreiber, Fort Wayne	15	8	10	18	14
9. Jim Burton, Fort Wayne	15	6	10	16	34
Jeff Pyle, Saginaw	11	4	12	16	2

Team-by-Team Playoff Scoring

Fort Wayne Komets

(Lost finals to Muskegon, 4-0)

	Games	G.	A.	Pts.	Pen.
Steve Salvucci	14	10	10	20	37
Russ Adam	14	7	*13	20	9
Randy Gilhen	15	10	8	18	6
Wally Schreiber	15	8	10	18	14
Jim Burton	15	6	10	16	34
Craig Channell	15	3	12	15	41
Doug Rigler	12	2	12	14	12
David Anderson	15	4	7	11	55
Dale Baldwin	12	2	5	7	43
Tony Camazzola	14	6	0	6	17
Rob Tudor	15	4	2	6	35
Rick Hendricks	15	0	3	3	31
Paul Kobylarz	5	1	1	2	4
Dan Ryder	15	0	2	2	2
Lee Blossom	6	1	0	1	0
Derek Ray	12	0	1	1	22
Jay Johnston	15	0	1	1	47
Pokey Reddick (Goalie)	9	0	1	1	0
Rick St. Croix (Goalie)	8	0	0	0	0

Indianapolis Checkers

(Lost quarterfinals to Muskegon, 4-1)

	Games	G.	A.	Pts.	Pen.
Gerry Minor	5	3	4	7	8
Charlie Skjodt	5	2	5	7	8
Mike Nepi	5	0	7	7	6
Bob Lakso	5	4	2	6	0
Earl Ingarfield	5	2	3	5	11

	Games	G.	A.	Pts.	Pen.
Mel Hewitt	5	2	2	4	48
Byron Lomow	5	2	1	3	2
Phil DeGaetano	5	2	1	3	15
Monty Trottier	5	1	2	3	17
Tim Thomas	5	0	2	2	2
Darren McKay	4	0	1	1	17
Marc Magnan	5	0	1	1	48
Jim Koudys	5	0	1	1	0
Pat Ribble	2	0	1	1	2
Paul Skjodt	5	0	0	0	15
Mike Neill	3	0	0	0	4
Kurt Kleinendorst	1	0	0	0	0
Rob Holland (Goalie)	4	0	0	0	0
Mike Zanier (Goalie)	2	0	0	0	10

Kalamazoo Wings
(Lost quarterfinals to Saginaw, 4-2)

	Games	G.	A.	Pts.	Pen.
Bill Terry	6	6	4	10	8
Brian Tutt	6	1	6	7	11
Claude Noel	6	2	4	6	2
Wayne Crawford	6	2	4	6	2
Brent Jarrett	6	1	5	6	4
Rob Nichols	5	4	1	5	28
Neil Hawryliw	6	1	3	4	17
Kevin Evans	6	3	0	3	56
Bill Schafhauser	6	1	2	3	2
John Flesch	6	0	3	3	2
John Stevens	6	0	3	3	9
Stu Kulak	2	2	0	2	0
Jeff Chychrun	3	1	0	1	0
Grant Anderson	6	0	1	1	24
Lawrie Nisker	1	0	1	1	4
John Beukeboom	6	0	1	1	6
Paul Moore	4	0	0	0	0
Brian McDavid	2	0	0	0	0
Bob Curtis	1	0	0	0	0
Georges Gagnon (G.)	6	0	0	0	2

Milwaukee Admirals
(Lost quarterfinals to Peoria, 4-1)

	Games	G.	A.	Pts.	Pen.
Fred Berry	5	3	2	5	2
Alan Graves	5	2	2	4	0
Kevin Schamehorn	5	1	3	4	4
Dale Yakiwchuk	4	0	4	4	20
Bill McCreary	5	3	0	3	6
Daniel Lecours	5	2	1	3	2
Gord Stafford	5	1	2	3	2
Greg Tebbutt	5	0	3	3	8
Blaine Peerless	5	0	3	3	2
Doug Kyle	5	2	0	2	0
Tim Molle	5	1	1	2	11
Marc Damphousse	4	0	2	2	5
Kevin Willison	5	0	0	0	2
Derek Davis	3	0	0	0	24
Mario Belanger	3	0	0	0	0
Jim Buettgen	2	0	0	0	0
Brian Byrnes	2	0	0	0	0
L. Middlebrook (G.)	5	0	0	0	0

Muskegon Lumberjacks
(Winners of 1986 Turner Cup Playoffs)

	Games	G.	A.	Pts.	Pen.
Jock Callander	14	*12	11	*23	12
Scott Gruhl	14	7	*13	20	22

	Games	G.	A.	Pts.	Pen.
Guy Benoit	14	7	12	19	6
Dennis Polonich	14	8	10	18	36
Dave Michayluk	14	6	9	15	12
Todd Strueby	14	7	5	12	51
Dan Naud	14	2	10	12	10
Todd Charlesworth	14	3	8	11	14
Dave Allison	14	2	9	11	46
Jiri Poner	9	5	3	8	6
Wayne Groulx	12	4	4	8	26
Roy Sommer	12	2	4	6	*92
Don Keller	14	1	5	6	57
Tom Karalis	11	1	3	4	32
Pat Mayer	13	0	2	2	37
Mike Forbes	13	0	2	2	19
Brian Ford (Goalie)	13	0	0	0	4
Michel Dufour (Goalie)	1	0	0	0	0

Peoria Rivermen
(Lost semifinals to Fort Wayne, 4-2)

	Games	G.	A.	Pts.	Pen.
Doug Evans	10	4	6	10	32
Denis Cyr	11	5	4	9	2
Paul Adey	11	5	4	9	6
Grant Rezansoff	11	3	5	8	2
Mike Prestidge	10	1	7	8	7
Brian Shaw	10	3	4	7	32
Dave MacQueen	7	3	2	5	2
Bruce Holloway	7	2	3	5	2
Brad Kempthorne	10	1	3	4	8
Tony Curtale	11	1	3	4	57
Bob Fleming	11	2	1	3	46
Dan Wood	11	1	2	3	32
Pat Ethier	11	0	3	3	17
Dennis Smith	10	0	2	2	18
Philippe Bozon	5	1	0	1	0
Marty Ruff	5	1	0	1	2
Mike Posavad	11	0	1	1	13
Mark Cupolo	3	0	0	0	2
Darrell May (Goalie)	11	0	0	0	4
Don Einwechter (Goalie)	2	0	0	0	0

Saginaw Generals
(Lost semifinals to Muskegon, 4-1)

	Games	G.	A.	Pts.	Pen.
Jeff Pyle	11	4	12	16	2
Darren Sceviour	11	8	5	13	5
John Ollson	11	6	5	11	4
Brian Noonan	11	6	3	9	8
Kevin Robinson	11	5	4	9	32
Luc Gauthier	11	1	7	8	12
Michel Caron	11	0	9	9	42
Dave Russell	11	5	3	8	14
Tom St. James	11	1	5	6	8
Greg Lynott	9	1	5	6	10
Bruce Howes	8	5	0	5	8
Guy Jacob	11	3	1	4	68
Dwayne Robinson	7	1	3	4	4
Wade Dawson	6	0	4	4	4
Peter Horachek	11	1	2	3	2
Jim Camazzola	8	0	3	3	15
Richard Adolfi	3	0	0	0	27
Neil Jones	2	0	0	0	0
Rick Knickle (Goalie)	3	0	0	0	7
Darren Pang (Goalie)	8	0	0	0	2

Salt Lake Golden Eagles

(Lost quarterfinals to Fort Wayne, 4-1)

	Games	G.	A.	Pts.	Pen.
Scott MacLeod	5	3	8	11	7
Doug Morrison	5	7	3	10	14
Ted Pearson	5	2	4	6	0
Gary DeGrio	5	2	3	5	2
Bobby Simpson	5	2	3	5	8
Steve Harrison	5	1	4	5	4
Bobby Francis	5	0	4	4	10
Glenn Hicks	5	0	4	4	6
Gary Stewart	5	2	1	3	9
Kelly Elcombe	5	1	2	3	15
Todd Hooey	5	1	1	2	9
Ali Butorac	4	1	1	2	19
Dave MacLean	5	1	1	2	8
Gary Burns	4	1	0	1	6
Randy Turnbull	5	0	1	1	15
Brent Sapergia	1	0	1	1	2
Roger Dube	1	0	0	0	10
Rick Heinz (Goalie)	5	0	0	0	6

Complete Turner Cup Goaltending

	Games	Mins.	Goals	SO.	Avg.
Brian Ford, Muskegon	13	*793	*41(1)	0	*3.10
Pokey Reddick, Fort Wayne	9	489	29(1)	*2	3.56
Darrell May, Peoria	11	634	38(1)	1	3.60
Lindsay Middlebrook, Milwaukee	5	298	18(1)	1	3.62
Rick Knickle, Saginaw	3	193	12	0	3.73
Darren Pang, Saginaw	8	492	32	0	3.90
Rick St. Croix, Fort Wayne	8	411	30	0	4.38
Mike Zanier, Indianapolis	2	120	9	0	4.50
Georges Gagnon, Kalamazoo	6	371	28(1)	0	4.53
Michel Dufour, Muskegon	1	65	5	0	4.62
Don Einwechter, Peoria	2	26	2	0	4.62
Rob Holland, Indianapolis	4	182	15	0	4.94
Rick Heinz, Salt Lake	5	299	26(2)	0	5.22

( )—Empty Net Goals. Do not count against a Goaltender's average.

Individual 1985-86 Leaders

Goals	Scott Gruhl, Muskegon—	59
Assists	Scott MacLeod, Salt Lake—	80
Points	Scott MacLeod, Salt Lake—	134
Penalty Minutes	Chris McSorley, Toledo—	545
Goaltending Average (2,000 Minutes)	Michael Dufour, Muskegon—	3.09
Shutouts	Pokey Reddick, Fort Wayne—	3
	Georges Gagnon, Kalamazoo—	3
	Lindsay Middlebrook, Milwaukee—	3

★★★

IHL 1985-86 All-Stars

First Team	Position	Second Team
Darrell May, Peoria	Goal	Rich St. Croix, Fort Wayne
		Michel Dufour, Muskegon
Jim Burton, Fort Wayne	Defense	Dan Naud, Muskegon
Don Waddell, Toledo	Defense	Tony Curtale, Peoria
Scott MacLeod, Salt Lake	Center	Bill Terry, Kalamazoo
Brent Sapergia, Salt Lake	Right Wing	Wally Schreiber, Fort Wayne
Doug Evans, Peoria	Left Wing	Scott Gruhl, Muskegon

★★★

IHL 1985-86 Trophy Winners

James Gatschene Memorial Trophy (Most Valuable Player)	Darrell May, Peoria
Leo P. Lamoureux Memorial Trophy (Leading Scorer)	Scott MacLeod, Salt Lake
James Norris Memorial Trophy (Outstanding Goaltender)	Pokey Reddick, Fort Wayne
	Rick St. Croix, Fort Wayne
Governors Trophy (Outstanding Defenseman)	Jim Burton, Fort Wayne
Garry F. Longman Memorial Trophy (Outstanding Rookie)	Guy Benoit, Muskegon
Ken McKenzie Trophy (Outstanding American-Born Rookie)	Brian Noonan, Saginaw
Commissioner's Trophy (Coach of the Year)	Rob Laird, Fort Wayne
Turner Cup Playoff MVP	Jock Callander, Muskegon
Fred A. Huber Trophy (Regular Season Champion)	Fort Wayne Komets
Joseph Turner Memorial Cup Winner (Playoff Champion)	Muskegon Lumberjacks

IHL All-Time Trophy Winners

James Gatschene Memorial Trophy
Most Valuable Player

1946-47—Herb Jones, Det. Auto Club
1947-48—Lyle Dowell, Det. Bright's Goodyears
1948-49—Bob McFadden, Det. Jerry Lynch
1949-50—Dick Kowcinak, Sarnia
1950-51—John McGrath, Toledo
1951-52—Ernie Dick, Chatham
1952-53—Donnie Marshall, Cincinnati
1953-54—No award given
1954-55—Phil Goyette, Cincinnati
1955-56—George Hayes, Grand Rapids
1956-57—Pierre Brillant, Indianapolis
1957-58—Pierre Brillant, Indianapolis
1958-59—Len Thornson, Fort Wayne
1959-60—Billy Reichart, Minneapolis
1960-61—Len Thornson, Fort Wayne
1961-62—Len Thornson, Fort Wayne
1962-63—Len Thornson, Fort Wayne
          Eddie Lang, Fort Wayne (tie)
1963-64—Len Thornson, Fort Wayne
1964-65—Chick Chalmers, Toledo
1965-66—Gary Schall, Muskegon
1966-67—Len Thornson, Fort Wayne
1967-68—Len Thornson, Fort Wayne
          Don Westbrooke, Dayton (tie)
1968-69—Don Westbrooke, Dayton
1969-70—Cliff Pennington, Des Moines
1970-71—Lyle Carter, Muskegon
1971-72—Len Fontaine, Port Huron
1972-73—Gary Ford, Muskegon
1973-74—Pete Mara, Des Moines
1974-75—Gary Ford, Muskegon
1975-76—Len Fontaine, Port Huron
1976-77—Tom Mellor, Toledo
1977-78—Dan Bonar, Fort Wayne
1978-79—Terry McDougall, Fort Wayne
1979-80—Al Dumba, Fort Wayne
1980-81—Marcel Comeau, Saginaw
1981-82—Brent Jarrett, Kalamazoo
1982-83—Claude Noel, Toledo
1983-84—Darren Jensen, Fort Wayne
1984-85—Scott Gruhl, Muskegon
1985-86—Darrell May, Peoria

Leo P. Lamoureux Memorial Trophy
Leading Scorer

(Originally called George H. Wilkinson Trophy
from 1946-47 through 1959-60.)

1946-47—Harry Marchand, Windsor
1947-48—Dick Kowcinak, Det. Auto Club
1948-49—Leo Richard, Toledo
1949-50—Dick Kowcinak, Sarnia
1950-51—Herve Parent, Grand Rapids
1951-52—George Parker, Grand Rapids
1952-53—Alex Irving, Milwaukee
1953-54—Don Hall, Johnstown
1954-55—Phil Goyette, Cincinnati
1955-56—Max Mekilok, Cincinnati
1956-57—Pierre Brillant, Indianapolis
1957-58—Warren Hynes, Cincinnati
1958-59—George Ranieri, Louisville
1959-60—Chick Chalmers, Louisville
1960-61—Ken Yackel, Minneapolis
1961-62—Len Thornson, Fort Wayne
1962-63—Moe Bartoli, Minneapolis
1963-64—Len Thornson, Fort Wayne
1964-65—Lloyd Maxfield, Port Huron
1965-66—Bob Rivard, Fort Wayne
1966-67—Len Thornson, Fort Wayne
1967-68—Gary Ford, Muskegon
1968-69—Don Westbrooke, Dayton
1969-70—Don Westbrooke, Dayton
1970-71—Darrel Knibbs, Muskegon
1971-72—Gary Ford, Muskegon
1972-73—Gary Ford, Muskegon
1973-74—Pete Mara, Des Moines
1974-75—Rick Bragnalo, Dayton
1975-76—Len Fontaine, Port Huron
1976-77—Jim Koleff, Flint
1977-78—Jim Johnston, Flint
1978-79—Terry McDougall, Fort Wayne
1979-80—Al Dumba, Fort Wayne
1980-81—Marcel Comeau, Saginaw
1981-82—Brent Jarrett, Kalamazoo
1982-83—Dale Yakiwchuk, Milwaukee
1983-84—Wally Schreiber, Fort Wayne
1984-85—Scott MacLeod, Salt Lake
1985-86—Scott MacLeod, Salt Lake

James Norris Memorial Trophy
Outstanding Goaltender

1955-56—Bill Tibbs, Troy
1956-57—Glenn Ramsey, Cincinnati
1957-58—Glenn Ramsey, Cincinnati
1958-59—Don Rigazio, Louisville
1959-60—Rene Zanier, Fort Wayne
1960-61—Ray Mikulan, Minneapolis
1961-62—Glenn Ramsey, Omaha
1962-63—Glenn Ramsey, Omaha
1963-64—Glenn Ramsey, Toledo
1964-65—Chuck Adamson, Fort Wayne
1965-66—Bob Sneddon, Port Huron
1966-67—Glenn Ramsey, Toledo
1967-68—Tim Tabor, Muskegon
          Bob Perani, Muskegon
1968-69—Pat Rupp, Dayton
          John Adams, Dayton
1969-70—Gaye Cooley, Des Moines
          Bob Perreault, Des Moines

1970-71—Lyle Carter, Muskegon
1971-72—Glenn Resch, Muskegon
1972-73—Robbie Irons, Fort Wayne
  Don Atchison, Fort Wayne
1973-74—Bill Hughes, Muskegon
1974-75—Bob Volpe, Flint
  Merlin Jenner, Flint
1975-76—Don Cutts, Muskegon
1976-77—Terry Richardson, Kalamazoo
1977-78—Lorne Molleken, Saginaw
  Pierre Chagnon, Saginaw
1978-79—Gord Laxton, Grand Rapids
1979-80—Larry Lozinski, Kalamazoo
1980-81—Claude Legris, Kalamazoo
  Georges Gagnon, Kalamazoo
1981-82—Lorne Molleken, Toledo
  Dave Tardich, Toledo
1982-83—Lorne Molleken, Toledo
1983-84—Darren Jensen, Fort Wayne
1984-85—Rick Heinz, Peoria
1985-86—Rick St. Croix, Fort Wayne
  Pokey Reddick, Fort Wayne

Governors Trophy
Outstanding Defenseman

1964-65—Lionel Repka, Fort Wayne
1965-66—Bob Lemieux, Muskegon
1966-67—Larry Mavety, Port Huron
1967-68—Carl Brewer, Muskegon
1968-69—Al Breaule, Dayton
  Moe Benoit, Dayton (tie)
1969-70—John Gravel, Toledo
1970-71—Bob LaPage, Des Moines
1971-72—Rick Pagnutti, Fort Wayne
1972-73—Bob McCammon, Port Huron
1973-74—Dave Simpson, Dayton
1974-75—Murry Flegel, Muskegon
1975-76—Murry Flegel, Muskegon
1976-77—Tom Mellor, Toledo
1977-78—Michel LaChance, Milwaukee
1978-79—Guido Tenesi, Grand Rapids
1979-80—John Gibson, Saginaw
1980-81—Larry Goodenough, Saginaw
1981-82—Don Waddell, Saginaw
1982-83—Jim Burton, Fort Wayne
  Kevin Willison, Milwaukee (tie)
1983-84—Kevin Willison, Milwaukee
1984-85—Lee Norwood, Peoria
1985-86—Jim Burton, Fort Wayne

Garry F. Longman Memorial Trophy
Outstanding Rookie

1961-62—Dave Richardson, Fort Wayne
1962-63—John Gravel, Omaha
1963-64—Don Westbrooke, Toledo
1964-65—Bob Thomas, Toledo
1965-66—Frank Golembrowsky, Port Huron
1966-67—Kerry Bond, Columbus
1967-68—Gary Ford, Muskegon
1968-69—Doug Volmar, Columbus
1969-70—Wayne Zuk, Toledo
1970-71—Corky Agar, Flint
  Herb Howdle, Dayton (tie)
1971-72—Glenn Resch, Muskegon
1972-73—Danny Gloor, Des Moines
1973-74—Frank DeMarco, Des Moines
1974-75—Rick Bragnalo, Dayton
1975-76—Sid Veysey, Fort Wayne
1976-77—Ron Zanussi, Fort Wayne
  Garth MacGuigan, Muskegon (tie)
1977-78—Dan Bonar, Fort Wayne
1978-79—Wes Jarvis, Port Huron
1979-80—Doug Robb, Milwaukee
1980-81—Scott Vanderburgh, Kalamazoo
1981-82—Scott Howson, Toledo
1982-83—Tony Fiore, Flint
1983-84—Darren Jensen, Fort Wayne
1984-85—Gilles Thibaudeau, Flint
1985-86—Guy Benoit, Muskegon

Ken McKenzie Trophy
Outstanding American-born Rookie

1977-78—Mike Eruzione, Toledo
1978-79—Jon Fontas, Saginaw
1979-80—Bob Janecyk, Fort Wayne
1980-81—Mike Labianca, Toledo
  Steve Janaszak, Fort Wayne (tie)
1981-82—Steve Salvucci, Saginaw
1982-83—Paul Fenton, Peoria
1983-84—Mike Krensing, Muskegon
1984-85—Bill Schafhauser, Kalamazoo
1985-86—Brian Noonan, Saginaw

Commissioner's Trophy
Coach of the Year

1984-85—Rick Ley, Muskegon
  Pat Kelly, Peoria (tie)
1985-86—Rob Laird, Fort Wayne

Turner Cup Playoff MVP

1984-85—Denis Cyr, Peoria
1985-86—Jock Callander, Muskegon

IHL All-Time Championship Teams

(Regular season championship award originally called
J.P. McGuire Trophy from 1946-47 through 1953-54.)

Fred A. Huber Trophy Regular Season Champion			Joseph Turner Memorial Cup Winner Playoff Champion	
Championship Team	(Coach)	Year	Championship Team	(Coach)
No Trophy Awarded		1945-46	Detroit Auto Club	(Jack Ward)
Windsor Staffords	(Jack Ward)	1946-47	Windsor Spitfires	(Ebbie Goodfellow)
Windsor Spitfires	(Dent-Goodfellow)	1947-48	Toledo Mercurys	(Andy Mulligan)
Toledo Mercurys	(Andy Mulligan)	1948-49	Windsor Hettche Spitfires	(Jimmy Skinner)
Sarnia Sailors	(Dick Kowcinak)	1949-50	Chatham Maroons	(Bob Stoddart)
Grand Rapid Rockets	(Lou Trudell)	1950-51	Toledo Mercurys	(Alex Wood)
Grand Rapid Rockets	(Lou Trudell)	1951-52	Toledo Mercurys	(Alex Wood)
Cincinnati Mohawks	(Buddy O'Conner)	1952-53	Cincinnati Mohawks	(Buddy O'Conner)
Cincinnati Mohawks	(Roly McLenahan)	1953-54	Cincinnati Mohawks	(Roly McLenahan)
Cincinnati Mohawks	(Roly McLenahan)	1954-55	Cincinnati Mohawks	(Roly McLenahan)
Cincinnati Mohawks	(Roly McLenahan)	1955-56	Cincinnati Mohawks	(Roly McLenahan)
Cincinnati Mohawks	(Roly McLenahan)	1956-57	Cincinnati Mohawks	(Roly McLenahan)
Cincinnati Mohawks	(Bill Gould)	1957-58	Indianapolis Chiefs	(Leo Lamoureux)
Louisville Rebels	(Leo Gasparini)	1958-59	Louisville Rebels	(Leo Gasparini)
Fort Wayne Komets	(Ken Ullyot)	1959-60	St. Paul Saints	(Fred Shero)
Minneapolis Millers	(Ken Yackel)	1960-61	St. Paul Saints	(Fred Shero)
Muskegon Zephyrs	(Moose Lallo)	1961-62	Muskegon Zephyrs	(Moose Lallo)
Fort Wayne Komets	(Ken Ullyot)	1962-63	Fort Wayne Komets	(Ken Ullyot)
Toledo Blades	(Moe Benoit)	1963-64	Toledo Blades	(Moe Benoit)
Port Huron Flags	(Lloyd Maxfield)	1964-65	Fort Wayne Komets	(Eddie Long)
Muskegon Mohawks	(Moose Lallo)	1965-66	Port Huron Flags	(Lloyd Maxfield)
Dayton Gems	(Warren Back)	1966-67	Toledo Blades	(Terry Slater)
Muskegon Mohawks	(Moose Lallo)	1967-68	Muskegon Mohawks	(Moose Lallo)
Dayton Gems	(Larry Wilson)	1968-69	Dayton Gems	(Larry Wilson)
Muskegon Mohawks	(Moose Lallo)	1969-70	Dayton Gems	(Larry Wilson)
Muskegon Mohawks	(Moose Lallo)	1970-71	Port Huron Flags	(Ted Garvin)
Muskegon Mohawks	(Moose Lallo)	1971-72	Port Huron Flags	(Ted Garvin)
Fort Wayne Komets	(Marc Boileau)	1972-73	Fort Wayne Komets	(Marc Boileau)
Des Moines Capitals	(Dan Belisle)	1973-74	Des Moines Capitols	(Dan Belisle)
Muskegon Mohawks	(Moose Lallo)	1974-75	Toledo Goaldiggers	(Ted Garvin)
Dayton Gems	(Ivan Prediger)	1975-76	Dayton Gems	(Ivan Prediger)
Saginaw Gears	(Don Perry)	1976-77	Saginaw Gears	(Don Perry)
Fort Wayne Komets	(Gregg Pilling)	1977-78	Toledo Goaldiggers	(Ted Garvin)
Grand Rapids Owls	(Moe Bartoli)	1978-79	Kalamazoo Wings	(Bill Purcell)
Kalamazoo Wings	(Doug McKay)	1979-80	Kalamazoo Wings	(Doug McKay)
Kalamazoo Wings	(Doug McKay)	1980-81	Saginaw Gears	(Don Perry)
Toledo Goaldiggers	(Bill Inglis)	1981-82	Toledo Goaldiggers	(Bill Inglis)
Toledo Goaldiggers	(Bill Inglis)	1982-83	Toledo Goaldiggers	(Bill Inglis)
Fort Wayne Komets	(Ron Ullyot)	1983-84	Flint Generals	(Dennis Desrosier)
Peoria Rivermen	(Pat Kelly)	1984-85	Peoria Rivermen	(Pat Kelly)
Fort Wayne Komets	(Rob Laird)	1985-86	Muskegon Lumberjacks	(Rick Ley)

Atlantic Coast Hockey League

Commissioner—Ray Miron
800 W. Glendale, Broken Arrow, Okla. 74011
Phone—(918) 451-1849
TWX 62906124

President—William B. Coffey
Vice President—Henry Brabham
Secretary/Treasurer—Steven Stroul
Supervisor of Officials—Dick Brinkman

Carolina Thunderbirds
Owners—William B. Coffey, Brad Thomas
Coach and General Manager—To be announced
Director of Public Relations—Jim Riggs
Home Ice—Winston-Salem Memorial Coliseum
Address—P.O. Box N-13 Winston-Salem, N.C. 27115-4513
Seating Capacity—5,937
Phone—(919) 748-0919

Erie Golden Blades
Owners—Steven Stroul, Jim Mikol
General Manager—Jim Mikol
Coach and Business Manager—Ron Hansis
Director of Public Relations—Bill Miller
Home Ice—Tullio Convention Center
Address—P.O. Box 6116 Erie, Pa. 16512
Seating Capacity—5,506
Phone—(814) 455-3936

Mohawk Valley Comets
President—Frank DuRoss
Vice President—Dr. Reynold Golden
Secretary/Treasurer—James Moselle Jr.
Coach and General Manager—Bill Horton
Director of Public Relations—Scott Martin
Home Ice—Utica Memorial Coliseum
Address—400 Oriskany Street, West Utica, N.Y. 13502
Seating Capacity—4,059
Phone—(315) 724-2126

Troy Slapshots
Chairman of the Board—Rudy Slucker
Coach and General Manager—Joe Selinski
Operations Manager—Al Shibley
Home Ice—R.P.I. Field House
Address—Peoples & Burdett Avenue, Troy, N.Y. 12180
Seating Capacity—5,500
Phone—(518) 274-0095

Virginia Lancers
President—Henry Brabham IV
Secretary/Treasurer—Gail Brabham
Coach—John Tortorella
Director of Public Relations—To be announced
Home Ice—Vinton Sports Complex
Address—P.O. Box 218, Vinton, Va. 24179
Seating Capacity—3,400
Phone—(703) 345-3557

1985-86 Final ACHL Standings

	G.	W.	L.	T.	Pts.	GF.	GA.
Carolina Thunderbirds	63	49	14	0	104	397	227
Erie Golden Blades	64	34	30	0	76	369	321
Virginia Lancers	62	28	34	0	61	299	340
Mohawk Valley Comets	62	23	39	0	49	259	332
New York Slapshots	59	21	38	0	43	260	367

NOTE: In ACHL games in 1985-86, if a game remained tied after an overtime, the two teams would take alternating penalty shots to determine a winner.

Top 10 ACHL Scorers

	Games	G.	A.	Pts.	Pen.
1. David Herbst, Erie	63	*74	52	*126	186
2. Joe Curran, Carolina	61	42	*82	124	102
3. Paul Mancini, Erie	64	51	72	123	20
4. Todd Bjorkstrand	49	58	52	110	112
5. John Hill, Carolina	12	5	6	11	6
Virginia	46	43	42	85	34
Totals	58	48	48	96	40
6. John Tortorella, Virginia	60	37	59	96	153
7. Don McCoy, Virginia	62	50	44	94	33
8. Brian Carroll, Carolina	61	41	53	94	216
9. John Torchetti, Carolina	61	51	42	93	55
10. Dan Lane, Mohawk Valley	56	55	37	92	180

Carolina Thunderbirds

	Games	G.	A.	Pts.	Pen.
Joe Curran	61	42	*82	124	102
Brian Carroll	61	41	53	94	216
John Torchetti	61	51	42	93	55
Andy Cozzi	43	52	31	83	26
Bob Hagan	63	17	56	73	81
Kim Elliott	61	28	44	72	137
Matt Winnicki	62	10	58	68	42
Doug McCarthy	38	16	43	59	35
Michel Lanouette	44	26	23	49	150
Don Shaw	36	25	22	47	20
Randy Irving	54	9	33	42	111
Jay Fraser	21	13	14	27	127
Ed Christian	22	8	17	25	42
Bob Dore	36	7	14	21	33
Brian Johnson	22	8	11	19	167
Mark Huglen	19	9	9	18	64
Kermit Salfi	19	5	10	15	2
Andy Ristau	15	10	4	14	148
Louis Finocchiaro	14	5	9	14	6
Kurt Steinbergs	14	1	10	11	19
Dave Watson	9	3	3	6	21
Bill Audycki	7	0	6	6	52
Dan Vlaisavljevich	10	1	4	5	37
Ray LeBlanc (Goalie)	42	0	5	5	4
Bill King	3	2	0	2	6
Mile Albano	2	0	2	2	4
Mark Liska (Goalie)	23	0	2	2	2
Craig Chamberlain	1	0	1	1	0
Darren Hunter	4	0	0	0	6

Erie Golden Blades

	Games	G.	A.	Pts.	Pen.
Dave Herbst	63	*74	52	*126	186
Paul Mancini	64	51	72	123	20
Todd Bjorkstrand	49	58	52	110	112
Jim Cowell	64	36	54	90	111
Ron Hansis	57	25	59	84	126
Mike Hoar	64	23	58	81	47
Darryl Moise	48	9	48	57	110
Sylvain Cote	45	28	16	44	319
Terry Shook	60	3	41	44	194
Bob Moise	50	16	25	41	68
Bob Van Biesbrouck	64	6	35	41	194
Dave Barry	45	6	15	21	44
Bob Bennett	13	4	9	13	11
Steve Szydlowski	33	1	10	11	2
Scott Willman	17	2	6	8	2
Ray Jacques	5	2	3	5	2
Scott Hansis	13	3	1	4	2
Brad McClintock	6	2	1	3	2
Jim Morris	7	1	2	3	6
Pierre Legace	5	1	1	2	2
Jay Ziedel	2	0	2	2	4
David Howell (Goalie)	22	0	2	2	16
Peter Barbagallo	5	1	0	1	2
Greg Vaughan	13	1	0	1	10
Steve McLarnon	1	0	1	1	0
Adolph Brink (Goalie)	22	0	1	1	2
Todd Lumbard (Goalie)	24	0	1	1	2
Marc Straub, Carolina	4	0	0	0	2
Erie	4	0	0	0	0
Totals	8	0	0	0	2

Mohawk Valley Comets

	Games	G.	A.	Pts.	Pen.
Dan Lane	56	55	37	92	180
Dick Popiel	62	19	61	80	79
Ron Carter, Virginia	20	14	13	27	2
Mohawk Valley	32	34	18	52	4
Totals	52	48	31	79	6
Larry Rusconi	54	32	33	65	57
Mark Blizzard	60	15	32	47	102
Kurt Rugenius	55	9	34	43	155
Jay Ness	61	8	35	43	42
Andy Skop	54	14	27	41	106
Jeffrey Eatough	27	18	19	37	43
Bruce Horvath, Carolina	4	3	0	3	4
New York	17	13	5	18	64
Mohawk Valley	24	3	8	11	162
Totals	45	19	13	32	230
Barry Smith, Erie	33	9	6	15	172
Mohawk Valley	23	4	8	12	58
Totals	56	13	14	27	230
Dennis Laing	55	4	20	24	71
Steve Atwell	29	7	11	18	8
Mike Tompkins	28	9	3	12	54
Jim Beaton	39	2	9	11	252
Peter Clement	11	1	4	5	12
Mike Kuzmich	15	1	4	5	26
Sylvain Lajunesse	6	2	2	4	0
Shawn Kilroy (Goalie)	35	0	4	4	12
Greg Dey	6	0	3	3	7
Jeff Fortier	11	1	1	2	8
Stuart Frye (Goalie)	32	0	2	2	22
John Depalma, N.Y.	1	0	0	0	0
Mohawk Valley	1	0	0	0	0
Totals	2	0	0	0	0
Dan Moskal	2	0	0	0	0
Al Maio (Goalie)	2	0	0	0	2
Craig Thomas	3	0	0	0	4
Dave Moffit (Goalie)	3	0	0	0	0

New York Slapshots

	Games	G.	A.	Pts.	Pen.
Dan Potter	58	35	51	86	93
Bobby Williams	40	45	18	63	28
Joe DeMitchell	58	33	27	60	63
Scott Rettew	56	16	32	48	79
Rich Kelly, Mo. Val.	50	13	30	43	26
New York	7	0	4	4	4
Totals	57	13	34	47	30
Bill Gillam	49	18	27	45	31
Bryan Walker	50	12	29	41	181
Paul Castron	19	11	27	38	7
Kevin Foster	25	6	28	34	15
Don Herczeg	39	10	23	33	190
Kurt Dade	24	17	10	27	40
Jeff Salzbrunn	32	11	14	25	46
Gasper Paul, Mo. Val.	31	6	12	18	50
New York	16	1	4	5	21
Totals	47	7	16	23	71
Dave Litz, Erie	2	0	0	0	7
Mohawk Valley	23	2	4	6	36
New York	28	5	11	16	30
Totals	53	7	15	22	73
Dan Griffin	25	3	17	20	34
Robert David	35	5	13	18	25
Brad Hammett	19	2	12	14	35
Dwight Boss	18	5	6	11	9
Gregg Anderson	9	2	8	10	9

	Games	G.	A.	Pts.	Pen.
Jay Swist, Carolina	1	0	0	0	0
New York	11	2	7	9	13
Totals	12	2	7	9	13
Doug Brown	29	1	8	9	55
Garth Fraser	18	3	4	7	6
Karl Goupil	4	2	2	4	7
Joe Vrtik	6	1	2	3	29
Ward Komonosky (G.)	39	0	3	3	23
Mike Bloski (Goalie)	27	0	2	2	60
Todd McCauley	8	0	2	2	32
Mike Rauch	9	0	2	2	2
Dave Boudreau	3	1	0	1	2
Ken Grabeldinger	1	1	0	1	2
Chuck Aikens	3	0	1	1	0
Dean Miller	2	0	1	1	0
Kurt Therres	2	0	1	1	7
Kurt Wickenheiser	2	0	1	1	18
Howie Young	7	0	1	1	18
Nick Cecere, Mo. Val.	3	0	0	0	0
New York	5	0	0	0	0
Totals	8	0	0	0	0
Joey Collins	2	0	0	0	14
Chris Cyr	2	0	0	0	10
Paul Litz	1	0	0	0	0
Kevin McGovern	8	0	0	0	4
John Mundy (Goalie)	1	0	0	0	0
Joe Selinski	1	0	0	0	2

Virginia Lancers

	Games	G.	A.	Pts.	Pen.
John Hill, Carolina	12	5	6	11	6
Virginia	46	43	42	85	34
Totals	58	48	48	96	40

	Games	G.	A.	Pts.	Pen.
John Tortorella	60	37	59	96	153
Don McCoy	62	50	44	94	33
Paul O'Neil	57	34	38	72	18
Pete DeArmas	49	27	39	66	8
Scott Crowther	59	20	28	48	77
Rob Clavette	35	20	27	47	32
Steve Doll	53	13	22	35	*436
Jerry Kiser, Erie	17	6	8	14	26
Virginia	25	4	17	21	25
Totals	42	10	25	35	51
Scott Lauder	60	7	25	32	53
Frank Perkins	41	7	23	30	139
Tom Madson	56	3	15	18	62
Ed Considine	44	2	16	18	174
John O'Sullivan	10	7	7	14	24
Scott Weibolt	27	2	10	12	32
Billy Keane	18	3	4	7	8
Bob Smith	16	1	6	7	46
Darryl McLeod	1	3	1	4	0
Steve Arnold	5	0	3	3	2
John O'Connor	3	1	1	2	27
Mark Weikroski	5	0	2	2	0
Bill Grumm	9	1	0	1	0
Mark Salvucci	3	1	0	1	73
Joe Zambito, Mo. Val.	2	0	0	0	4
Erie	4	1	0	1	2
Virginia	6	0	0	0	0
Totals	12	1	0	1	6
Keith Houghton (Goalie)	29	0	1	1	0
Keith Knight (Goalie)	3	0	1	1	0
Carey Walker (Goalie)	32	0	1	1	28
Mark Chiamp (Goalie)	11	0	0	0	0
Vinnie Pumilio	1	0	0	0	0

Individual ACHL Goaltending

	Games	Mins.	Goals	SO.	Avg.
Ray LeBlanc, Carolina	*42	*2505	133	*3	*3.18
Mark Liska, Carolina	23	1298	91	0	4.20
Todd Lumbard, Erie	24	1446	102	0	4.23
Shawn Kilroy, Mohawk Valley	35	1926	157	1	4.89
David Howell, Erie	22	1247	102	0	4.91
Stuart Frye, Mohawk Valley	32	1638	140	0	5.13
Keith Knight, Virginia	3	127	11	0	5.21
Carey Walker, Virginia	32	1865	166	0	5.34
Keith Houghton, Virginia	21	1084	99	0	5.48
Mike Bloski, New York	28	1455	138	0	5.69
Adolph Brink, Erie	22	1185	115	0	5.82
Mark Chiamp, Virginia	11	664	67	1	6.05
Ward Komonosky, New York	39	2066	*216	0	6.27
Dave Moffit, Mohawk Valley	3	133	15	0	6.77
John Mundy, New York	1	60	9	0	9.00
Al Maio, Mohawk Valley	2	61	11	0	10.82

Individual 1985-86 Leaders

Goals	David Herbst, Erie— 74*
Assists	Joe Curran, Carolina— 82*
Points	David Herbst, Erie— 126
Penalty Minutes	Steve Doll, Virginia— 436*
Goaltending Average	Ray LeBlanc, Carolina— 3.18
Shutouts	Ray LeBlanc, Carolina— 3*

*Established new league record.

1985-86 ACHL Playoffs

(All series best of seven)

Semifinals

Series "A"
	W.	L.	Pts.	GF.	GA.
Carolina	4	2	8	32	22
Mohawk Valley	2	4	4	22	32

(Carolina wins series, 4 games to 2)

Series "B"
	W.	L.	Pts.	GF.	GA.
Erie	4	1	8	32	17
Virginia	1	4	2	17	32

(Erie wins series, 4 games to 1)

Finals

Series "C"
	W.	L.	Pts.	GF.	GA.
Carolina	4	1	8	28	20
Erie	1	4	2	20	28

(Carolina wins series, and Bob Payne Trophy, 4 games to 1)

Top 10 Playoff Scorers

	Games	G.	A.	Pts.	Pen.
1. Paul Mancini, Erie	10	8	*18	*26	4
2. Bob Bennett, Erie	10	7	15	22	8
3. Andy Cozzi, Carolina	11	10	11	21	11
4. Joe Curran, Carolina	11	*12	7	19	18
5. John Torchetti, Carolina	11	5	13	18	16
6. Brian Carroll, Carolina	11	7	9	16	24
Todd Bjorkstrand, Erie	10	5	11	16	16
8. Dave Herbst, Erie	8	7	7	14	49
9. Jeff Eatough, Mohawk Valley	6	5	8	13	4
Bob Hagan, Carolina	11	3	10	13	12

Team-by-Team Playoff Scoring

Carolina Thunderbirds
(Winners of 1986 ACHL Playoffs)

	Games	G.	A.	Pts.	Pen.
Andy Cozzi	11	10	11	21	11
Joe Curran	11	*12	7	19	18
John Torchetti	11	5	13	18	16
Brian Carroll	11	7	9	16	24
Bob Hagan	11	3	10	13	12
Randy Irving	11	1	11	12	42
Kim Elliott	11	4	6	10	11
Matt Winnicki	11	3	7	10	9
Doug McCarthy	11	3	6	9	6
Don Shaw	11	4	4	8	9
Michel Lanouette	11	4	4	8	25
Bob Dore	11	2	3	5	36
Dave Watson	10	1	4	5	16
Dan Vlaisavljevich	9	1	1	2	13
Mark Huglen	2	0	0	0	4
Ray LeBlanc (Goalie)	11	0	0	0	0

Erie Golden Blades
(Lost finals to Carolina, 4-1)

	Games	G.	A.	Pts.	Pen.
Paul Mancini	10	8	*18	*26	4
Bob Bennett	10	7	15	22	8
Todd Bjorkstrand	10	5	11	16	16
Dave Herbst	8	7	7	14	49
Mike Hoar	10	6	5	11	2
Sylvain Cote	9	5	6	11	*74
Dave Barry	10	2	6	8	23
Jim Cowell	10	4	3	7	59
Ron Hansis	10	3	4	7	36
Darryl Moise	10	1	6	7	16
Bob Van Biesbrouck	10	0	5	5	12
Bob Moise	9	3	1	4	43
Terry Shook	10	0	3	3	40
Steve Szydlowski	10	1	0	1	5
Todd Lumbard (Goalie)	10	0	1	1	8

Mohawk Valley Comets
(Lost semifinals to Carolina, 4-2)

	Games	G.	A.	Pts.	Pen.
Jeffrey Eatough	6	5	8	13	4
Dan Lane	6	5	5	10	4
Dick Popiel	6	3	5	8	11
Ron Carter	6	2	5	7	0
Kurt Rugenius	6	3	2	5	13
Jay Ness	6	2	2	4	2
Mark Blizzard	6	1	2	3	18
Larry Rusconi	6	1	2	3	12
Steve Atwell	6	0	2	2	4
Jim Beaton	6	0	2	2	29
Dennis Laing	6	0	1	1	10
Greg Dey	6	0	1	1	5
Andy Skop	6	0	1	1	4
Barry Smith	6	0	0	0	18
Shawn Kilroy (Goalie)	4	0	0	0	0
Stuart Frye (Goalie)	2	0	0	0	0

Virginia Lancers
(Lost semifinals to Erie, 4-1)

	Games	G.	A.	Pts.	Pen.
Pete DeArmas	5	5	3	8	0
John Hill	5	2	4	6	0
Don McCoy	5	3	2	5	0
Steve Arnold	5	3	1	4	2
Paul O'Neil	5	2	2	4	2
John Tortorella	5	1	3	4	60
Ed Considine	5	1	2	3	28
Tom Madson	5	0	3	3	0
Frank Perkins	5	0	1	1	50
Darryl McLeod	5	0	1	1	6
Steve Doll	5	0	1	1	28
Jerry Kiser	5	0	0	0	16
Bob Smith	3	0	0	0	15
Scott Lauder	5	0	0	0	4
Carey Walker (Goalie)	5	0	0	0	0

Complete ACHL Playoff Goaltending

	Games	Mins.	Goals	SO.	Avg.
Ray LeBlanc, Carolina	*11	*669	42	0	*3.77
Shawn Kilroy, Mohawk Valley	4	248	17	*1	4.11
Todd Lumbard, Erie	10	599	*45	0	4.50
Carey Walker, Virginia	5	299	32	0	6.44
Stuart Frye, Mohawk Valley	2	119	14	0	7.08

Individual ACHL Playoff Leaders

Goals	Joe Curran, Carolina—	12
Assists	Paul Mancini, Erie—	18
Points	Paul Mancini, Erie—	26
Penalty Minutes	Sylvain Cote, Erie—	74
Goaltending Average	Ray LeBlanc, Carolina—	3.77
Shutouts	Shawn Kilroy, Mohawk Valley—	1

★★

ACHL 1985-86 All-Stars

First Team	Position	Second Team
Ray LeBlanc, Carolina	Goal	Shawn Kilroy, Mohawk Valley
Bob Hagan, Carolina	Defense	Randy Irving, Carolina
Bryan Walker, New York	Defense	Kurt Rugenius, Mohawk Valley
David Herbst, Erie	Center	Joe Curran, Carolina
Andy Cozzi, Carolina	Right Wing	John Hill, Virginia
Paul Mancini, Erie	Left Wing	John Tortorella, Virginia
		Jim Cowell, Erie

ACHL 1985-86 Trophy Winners

Most Valuable Player	Joe Curran, Carolina
Rookie of the Year	Bobby Williams, New York
Top Goaltender	Ray LeBlanc, Carolina
Most Valuable Player in ACHL Playoffs	Bob Dore, Carolina

★★

MEMORIAL CUP WINNERS

Season	Team
1918-19—	University of Toronto Schools
1919-20—	Toronto Canoe Club
1920-21—	Winnipeg Falcons
1921-22—	Fort William War Veterans
1922-23—	Univ. of Manitoba-Winnipeg
1923-24—	Owen Sound Greys
1924-25—	Regina Pats
1925-26—	Calgary Canadians
1926-27—	Owen Sound Greys
1927-28—	Regina Monarchs
1928-29—	Toronto Marlboros
1929-30—	Regina Pats
1930-31—	Winnipeg Elmwoods
1931-32—	Sudbury Wolves
1932-33—	Newmarket
1933-34—	Toronto St. Michael's
1934-35—	Winnipeg Monarchs
1935-36—	West Toronto Redmen
1936-37—	Winnipeg Monarchs
1937-38—	St. Boniface Seals
1938-39—	Oshawa Generals
1939-40—	Oshawa Generals
1940-41—	Winnipeg Rangers
1941-42—	Portage la Prairie
1942-43—	Winnipeg Rangers
1943-44—	Oshawa Generals
1944-45—	Toronto St. Michael's
1945-46—	Winnipeg Monarchs
1946-47—	Toronto St. Michael's
1947-48—	Port Arthur West End Bruins
1948-49—	Montreal Royals
1949-50—	Montreal Jr. Canadiens
1950-51—	Barrie Flyers
1951-52—	Guelph Biltmores
1952-53—	Barrie Flyers
1953-54—	St. Catharines Tee Pees
1954-55—	Toronto Marlboros
1955-56—	Toronto Marlboros
1956-57—	Flin Flon Bombers
1957-58—	Ottawa-Hull Jr. Canadiens
1958-59—	Winnipeg Braves
1959-60—	St. Catharines Tee Pees
1960-61—	Toronto St. Michael's Majors
1961-62—	Hamilton Red Wings
1962-63—	Edmonton Oil Kings
1963-64—	Toronto Marlboros
1964-65—	Niagara Falls Flyers
1965-66—	Edmonton Oil Kings
1966-67—	Toronto Marlboros
1967-68—	Niagara Falls Flyers
1968-69—	Montreal Jr. Canadiens
1969-70—	Montreal Jr. Canadiens
1970-71—	Quebec Remparts
1971-72—	Cornwall Royals
1972-73—	Toronto Marlboros
1973-74—	Regina Pats
1974-75—	Toronto Marlboros
1975-76—	Hamilton Fincups
1976-77—	New Westminster Bruins
1977-78—	New Westminster Bruins
1978-79—	Peterborough Petes
1979-80—	Cornwall Royals
1980-81—	Cornwall Royals
1981-82—	Kitchener Rangers
1982-83—	Portland Winter Hawks
1983-84—	Ottawa 67's
1984-85—	Prince Albert Raiders
1985-86—	Guelph Platers

Ontario Hockey League

Commissioner—David E. Branch
Chairman of the Board—Dr. Robert Vaughan
655 Dixon Rd., Rexdale, Ontario M9W 1J4
Phone—(416) 243-3100
Director of Information and Statistics—Herb Morrell
Director of Officiating—Ken Bodendistel
Director of Central Scouting—Jack Ferguson
Director of Public Relations and Marketing—John Sop

1985-86 Final OHL Standings

Matt Leyden Division

	G.	W.	L.	T.	Pts.	GF.	GA.
Peterborough Petes	66	45	19	2	92	298	190
Belleville Bulls	66	37	27	2	76	305	268
Oshawa Generals	66	37	27	2	76	285	257
Kingston Canadians	66	35	28	3	73	297	257
Cornwall Royals	66	28	36	2	58	307	356
Toronto Marlboros	66	22	41	3	47	297	345
Ottawa 67's	66	18	46	2	38	274	352

Hap Emms Division

	G.	W.	L.	T.	Pts.	GF.	GA.
North Bay Centennials	66	41	21	4	86	330	240
Guelph Platers	66	41	23	2	84	297	235
Windsor Compuware Spitfires	66	34	26	6	74	280	259
Kitchener Rangers	66	35	27	4	74	318	309
Sudbury Wolves	66	29	33	4	62	293	330
London Knights	66	28	33	5	61	271	292
Hamilton Steelhawks	66	26	36	4	56	268	306
Sault Ste. Marie Greyhounds	66	15	48	3	33	263	387

Top 10 Scorers for the Eddie Powers Memorial Trophy

	Games	G.	A.	Pts.	Pen.
1. Ray Sheppard, Cornwall	63	*81	61	*142	25
2. Scott McCrory, Oshawa	66	52	80	132	40
Jason Lafreniere, Hamilton	14	12	10	22	2
Belleville	48	37	73	110	2
Totals	62	49	83	132	4
Ron Sanko, North Bay	14	9	12	21	55
Kitchener	53	34	77	111	83
Totals	67	43	*89	132	138
5. Shawn Burr, Kitchener	59	60	67	127	83
6. Jack MacKeigan, Toronto	66	53	59	112	64
7. Craig Duncanson, Sudbury	21	12	17	29	55
Cornwall	40	31	50	81	135
Totals	61	43	67	110	190
8. Gary McColgan, Oshawa	57	49	55	104	22
Mike Stapleton, Cornwall	56	39	65	104	74
Tim Armstrong, Toronto	64	35	69	104	36

Belleville Bulls

	Games	G.	A.	Pts.	Pen.		Games	G.	A.	Pts.	Pen.
Jason Lafreniere, Ham...	14	12	10	22	2	Keith Gretzky, Windsor	43	24	36	60	10
Belleville	48	37	73	110	2	Belleville	18	3	11	14	2
Totals	62	49	83	132	4	Totals	61	27	47	74	12
Brian MacDonald, Ham.	14	5	3	8	25	Dan Gratton, Oshawa...	10	3	5	8	15
Belleville	54	32	43	75	41	Ottawa	25	18	18	36	19
Totals	68	37	46	83	66	Belleville	20	12	14	26	11
Stan Drulia	66	43	37	80	73	Totals	55	33	37	70	45

	Games	G.	A.	Pts.	Pen.
Marc West, Hamilton	14	4	5	9	6
Belleville	54	10	32	42	18
Totals	68	14	37	51	24
Daran Moxam	56	21	29	50	93
Gary Callaghan	53	29	16	45	42
Mike Vellucci	64	11	32	43	154
Brian Chapman	66	6	31	37	168
Steve Ewing, North Bay	4	1	3	4	9
Belleville	61	12	15	27	42
Totals	65	13	18	31	51
Todd Hawkins	60	14	13	27	172
Peter Choma, Hamilton	18	2	3	5	13
Belleville	46	9	11	20	25
Totals	64	11	14	25	38
Bryan Marchment	57	5	15	20	225
John Tamer	59	3	14	17	37
Tony Crisp	48	6	4	10	8
Charlie Moore	47	4	4	8	100
Lawrence Hinch, Corn.	18	1	0	1	44
Belleville	37	1	6	7	52
Totals	55	2	6	8	96
Peter Hughes, Hamilton	2	0	0	0	0
Belleville	36	1	5	6	29
Totals	38	1	5	6	29
Greg Snyder	11	2	3	5	8
Mark Ragot	7	1	1	2	4
Mike Arthur	4	0	2	2	0
Mike Bishop (Goalie)	34	0	2	2	0
Jim Way	34	0	2	2	25
Mike King	2	1	0	1	0
P. Henriques, N.B. (G.)	19	0	1	1	2
Belleville (G.)	8	0	0	0	2
Totals	27	0	1	1	4
Saverio Manzo (Goalie)	2	0	0	0	0
Craig Billington (Goalie)	3	0	0	0	0

Cornwall Royals

	Games	G.	A.	Pts.	Pen.
Ray Sheppard	63	*81	61	*142	25
Craig Duncanson, Sud.	21	12	17	29	55
Cornwall	40	31	50	81	135
Totals	61	43	67	110	190
Mike Stapleton	56	39	65	104	74
Bill Bennett, Belleville	11	6	9	15	7
Cornwall	49	31	42	73	46
Totals	60	37	51	88	53
Mike Bukowski	63	39	35	74	103
John Copple	66	5	48	53	55
Shane Doyle, Belleville	13	1	5	6	41
Hamilton	10	0	7	7	24
Cornwall	32	3	16	19	139
Totals	55	4	28	32	204
Bruno Lapensee, N.B.	30	3	7	10	98
Cornwall	28	6	11	17	62
Totals	58	9	18	27	160
Paul Wilkinson	44	9	16	25	16
Paul Cain	62	11	12	23	21
Ken Sabourin, S.S.M.	25	1	5	6	77
Cornwall	37	3	12	15	94
Totals	62	4	17	21	171
Dean Guitard	38	11	9	20	67
Robert Ray	53	6	13	19	253
Pat Malone, Sudbury	15	1	2	3	8
Cornwall	46	1	14	15	37
Totals	61	2	16	18	45

	Games	G.	A.	Pts.	Pen.
Neil Jones, Sudbury	16	0	2	2	17
Cornwall	43	1	15	16	11
Totals	59	1	17	18	28
Steve Herniman	55	3	12	15	128
Dan Nowak	19	5	7	12	7
Paul Reynolds	29	4	8	12	20
Mark Evans	63	2	8	10	52
Sean Evoy, Sudbury (G.)	21	0	2	2	8
Cornwall (G.)	27	0	3	3	4
Totals	48	0	5	5	12
Jim Hutchins, Hamilton	10	3	0	3	7
Cornwall	11	0	0	0	5
Totals	21	3	0	3	12
Glen Leslie, London	27	0	1	1	19
Cornwall	28	0	2	2	20
Totals	55	0	3	3	39
Steve Titus (Goalie)	33	0	2	2	8
Rod MacKenzie	8	1	0	1	0
Frank Sinfield	3	0	1	1	9
Robert Emond	11	0	1	1	4
Doug Senior	16	0	1	1	0
Kent Trolley	18	0	1	1	16
Gary Theoret	1	0	0	0	0
Marty Goeree	2	0	0	0	2

Guelph Platers

	Games	G.	A.	Pts.	Pen.
Gary Roberts, Ottawa	24	26	25	51	83
Guelph	23	18	15	33	65
Totals	47	44	40	84	148
Lonnie Loach	65	41	42	83	63
Mike Murray	56	27	38	65	19
Paul Kelly	59	26	32	58	95
Paul Brydges	62	17	40	57	88
Jamie McKinley	66	23	30	53	48
Marc Tournier	58	8	42	50	93
Keith Miller	61	32	17	49	30
Steve Chiasson	54	12	29	41	126
Allan MacIsaac	63	12	23	35	92
Tom Nickolau	39	6	26	32	81
Robb Graham	62	10	18	28	78
Kerry Huffman	56	3	24	27	35
Luciano Fagioli	60	7	15	22	34
Luc Sabourin	40	7	14	21	37
Denis Larocque	66	2	16	18	144
Rob Arabski	54	9	8	17	13
Brian Hayton	56	6	11	17	99
John McIntyre	30	4	6	10	25
Bill Loshaw	60	1	7	8	196
Steve Guenette (Goalie)	50	0	2	2	16
Tim Kaiser	1	0	0	0	0
Kevin O'Brien	3	0	0	0	4
Gerry Iuliano (Goalie)	10	0	0	0	2
Andy Helmuth, Ott. (G.)	20	0	0	0	12
Guelph (Goalie)	12	0	0	0	8
Totals	32	0	0	0	20

Hamilton Steelhawks

	Games	G.	A.	Pts.	Pen.
Shayne Corson	47	41	57	98	153
Brad Dalgarno	54	22	43	65	79
John Purves, Belleville	16	3	9	12	6
Hamilton	36	13	28	41	36
Totals	52	16	37	53	42
Kirk Tomlinson	58	28	23	51	230

	Games	G.	A.	Pts.	Pen.
Jamie Nadjiwan, Sud.	16	11	7	18	8
Cornwall	9	2	7	9	2
Hamilton	24	10	14	24	12
Totals	49	23	28	51	22
Brent Thompson, Corn.	24	6	4	10	33
Hamilton	37	20	20	40	37
Totals	61	26	24	50	70
Steve Hedington	64	17	32	49	27
Ron Bernacci	66	21	26	47	155
Brad Belland, Sudbury	7	0	6	6	0
Hamilton	52	20	20	40	40
Totals	59	20	26	46	40
Garth Joy	50	6	31	37	64
Angelo Catenaro, Belle.	3	0	0	0	4
Hamilton	51	4	28	32	86
Totals	54	4	28	32	90
Guy Girouard	66	6	24	30	126
Mike Ware	44	8	11	19	155
Brad Hyatt, Cornwall	28	1	5	6	20
Hamilton	37	5	6	11	59
Totals	65	6	11	17	79
Jordan Fois, Pete.	5	0	1	1	0
Hamilton	53	3	8	11	55
Totals	58	3	9	12	55
Don Pancoe	57	1	11	12	108
Rod Thacker	58	2	9	11	60
Troy Crowder	55	4	4	8	178
Brian Hoard	34	2	2	4	69
Dennis Vial	31	1	1	2	66
Peter Richards (Goalie)	54	0	2	2	31
Matt Leonard	44	0	1	1	20
Mike Rosati (Goalie)	1	0	0	0	0
Chris French (Goalie)	2	0	0	0	0
Joey Stefan	4	0	0	0	0
Wayne Schrapp	7	0	0	0	0
Willie Popp (Goalie)	26	0	0	0	4

Kingston Canadians

	Games	G.	A.	Pts.	Pen.
Brian Verbeek	62	50	40	90	132
Scott Metcalfe	66	36	43	79	213
Daril Holmes	66	25	37	62	97
Mike Maurice	58	25	32	57	60
Barry Burkholder	58	17	35	52	90
Peter Viskovich	64	18	31	49	17
Wayne Erskine	59	21	25	46	31
Ted Linseman	66	22	22	44	53
Mike Fiset	65	15	25	40	24
Scott Pearson	63	16	23	39	56
Todd Clarke	58	7	21	28	123
Steve Seftel	42	11	16	27	53
Jeff Chychrun	61	4	21	25	127
Troy MacNevin	62	4	17	21	14
Bryan Fogarty	47	2	19	21	14
Herb Raglan	28	10	9	19	88
Jeff Cornelius	59	2	17	19	143
Marc Lyons	58	4	11	15	78
Marc Laforge	60	1	13	14	248
Chris Clifford (Goalie)	50	1	7	8	16
Jeff Sirkka	34	1	6	7	51
Terry Collett	1	1	0	1	0
Brad Wood	1	0	1	1	0
Darcy Cahill	3	0	1	1	0
John Knight	2	0	0	0	0
John Thornton	2	0	0	0	0
Andy Pearson (Goalie)	6	0	0	0	0

	Games	G.	A.	Pts.	Pen.
Brian Tessier, N.B. (G.)	5	0	0	0	4
Kingston (G.)	13	0	0	0	4
Totals	18	0	0	0	8

Kitchener Rangers

	Games	G.	A.	Pts.	Pen.
Ron Sanko, North Bay	14	9	12	21	55
Kitchener	53	34	77	111	83
Totals	67	43	*89	132	138
Shawn Burr	59	60	67	127	83
Mike Morrison, Belleville	4	1	4	5	2
Kitchener	55	33	63	96	75
Totals	59	34	67	101	77
David Latta	55	36	34	70	60
Mike Wolak	62	24	44	68	48
Jeff Noble	58	22	33	55	65
Ken Alexander	62	12	31	43	80
Brett MacDonald, N.B.	15	0	6	6	42
Kitchener	53	10	27	37	52
Totals	68	10	33	43	94
Peter Lisy, N.B.	14	6	6	12	4
Kitchener	48	10	20	30	9
Totals	62	16	26	42	13
Ron Goodall	54	14	20	34	21
Steve Marcolini	41	4	19	23	172
Brad Sparkes	34	10	11	21	44
Scott Taylor	59	4	13	17	211
Kevin Grant	63	2	15	17	204
Ian Pound	63	2	12	14	87
Greg Hankkio	62	4	7	11	43
Doug Jones	46	5	4	9	4
Kent Falby	15	4	3	7	22
Craig Booker	49	4	3	7	70
Blair MacPherson	54	3	4	7	81
Shawn Tyers	26	2	3	5	14
Sean Wallington	13	0	4	4	4
Kevin Moore	11	2	1	3	50
Richard Hawkins, Tor.	5	0	0	0	5
North Bay	2	0	1	1	2
Kitchener	16	1	0	1	2
Totals	23	1	1	2	9
Paul Penelton	24	1	0	1	21
Mike Volpe (Goalie)	36	0	1	1	11
Jim David	2	0	0	0	0
Jamie Hicks	2	0	0	0	0
Paul Porter (Goalie)	2	0	0	0	4
Rob Dopson (Goalie)	8	0	0	0	2
David Weiss (Goalie)	29	0	0	0	9

London Knights

	Games	G.	A.	Pts.	Pen.
Greg Puhalski	58	38	63	101	59
Kelly Cain	62	46	51	97	87
Brian Dobbin	59	38	55	93	113
Brendan Shanahan	59	28	34	62	70
Greg Smyth	46	12	42	54	197
Murray Nystrom	58	21	25	46	86
Garnet McKechney	27	16	14	30	50
Trevor Stienburg	31	12	18	30	88
Jim Sandlak	16	7	13	20	36
Tom Allen	60	7	13	20	112
Mike Zombo	64	3	17	20	81
Ed Kister	39	2	18	20	44
Rob Coutts, Ottawa	9	0	1	1	2
London	45	9	9	18	17
Totals	54	9	10	19	19

	Games	G.	A.	Pts.	Pen.
Peter McLeod	18	6	12	18	63
David Haas	62	4	13	17	91
Brad Schlegel	62	2	13	15	35
Don Martin, North Bay	7	0	0	0	21
London	55	7	6	13	112
Totals	62	7	6	13	133
Joe Ranger	36	0	8	8	54
Matt Smyth	47	3	2	5	151
Jamie Groke	33	2	3	5	36
Ray Gallagher	43	2	3	5	26
Tim Horvat	10	1	4	5	2
Denis Hebert	39	1	4	5	38
Patrick Vachon	42	1	0	1	52
Rod Gerow	11	0	1	1	2
Jeff Reese (Goalie)	57	0	1	1	25
Dean Derrigan	1	0	0	0	0
Peter McMenemy	1	0	0	0	0
Ernie Thompson	2	0	0	0	5
Lyle Jonathan	4	0	0	0	7
Andy Doxtator	5	0	0	0	0
Jamie Ward	7	0	0	0	0
Frank Tremblay	8	0	0	0	0
Scott Cumming (Goalie)	16	0	0	0	0

North Bay Centennials

	Games	G.	A.	Pts.	Pen.
Nick Kypreos	64	62	35	97	112
Rob DeGagne	57	24	72	96	46
David McLlwain, Kit.	13	7	7	14	12
North Bay	51	30	28	58	25
Totals	64	37	35	72	37
Darren Turcotte	62	35	37	72	35
Tim Bean	66	32	34	66	129
Len Soccio	66	20	43	63	79
Doug Stromback, Kit.	13	7	10	17	13
North Bay	50	19	22	41	50
Totals	63	26	32	58	63
Kevin Vescio	51	12	38	50	70
Todd Elik	40	12	34	46	20
Wayne MacPhee	57	5	38	43	135
Mike Hartman, Belleville	4	2	1	3	5
North Bay	53	19	16	35	205
Totals	57	21	17	38	210
Darin Smith, London	9	2	5	7	23
North Bay	45	7	24	31	131
Totals	54	9	29	38	154
Mike Gillies	56	9	28	37	11
Bill Houlder	59	5	30	35	97
John Keller, Kitchener	13	1	2	3	0
North Bay	29	5	9	14	28
Totals	42	6	11	17	28
Larry Van Herzele, Belle.	33	1	5	6	32
North Bay	26	3	5	8	15
Totals	59	4	10	14	47
Dean Haig	24	5	8	13	17
Jeff Bloemberg	60	2	11	13	76
Brent Bywater	46	1	10	11	69
Adam Burt	49	0	11	11	81
Shawn Roy	26	0	4	4	7
Chad Gleason	36	0	4	4	35
Tom Warden	12	1	2	3	27
David Burt	5	2	0	2	0
Jeff McClenaghan	5	0	2	2	2
Mike Ricci (Goalie)	22	0	1	1	8
John Reid, Belle. (G.)	24	0	0	0	5
North Bay (G.)	23	0	0	0	6
Totals	47	0	0	0	11

Oshawa Generals

	Games	G.	A.	Pts.	Pen.
Scott McCrory	66	52	80	132	40
Gary McColgan	57	49	55	104	22
Craig Morrison	52	25	43	68	78
Lee Giffin	54	29	37	66	28
Petri Matikainen	53	14	42	56	27
Derek King, S.S.M.	25	12	17	29	33
Oshawa	19	8	13	21	15
Totals	44	20	30	50	48
Sean Williams	55	15	23	38	23
Joel Curtis	55	6	30	36	35
Marc Laniel	66	9	25	34	27
Jeff Daniels	62	13	19	32	23
Jim Buwalda, Hamilton	4	1	2	3	15
Belleville	5	0	2	2	28
Oshawa	30	7	16	23	108
Totals	39	8	20	28	151
Jim Paek	64	5	21	26	122
John Andersen	60	13	11	24	15
Gordon Murphy	64	7	15	22	56
Ian Ferguson	48	6	10	16	43
Greg Watson	53	7	6	13	189
Dean Morton, Ottawa	16	3	1	4	32
Oshawa	48	2	6	8	92
Totals	64	5	7	12	124
Scott MacDonald	52	5	6	11	21
John Stevens	65	1	7	8	146
Darren Colbourne	46	4	3	7	16
Tony Joseph	41	3	1	4	28
Dennis Wigle, Ottawa	8	0	2	2	47
Oshawa	3	0	1	1	5
Totals	11	0	3	3	52
Brian Hunt	16	0	1	1	2
Bob Carroll	1	0	0	0	0
Chuck Petahtegoose	1	0	0	0	0
Dave Sankey	2	0	0	0	0
Mark Gowans (Goalie)	25	0	0	0	0
Kirk McLean (Goalie)	51	0	0	0	8

Ottawa 67's

	Games	G.	A.	Pts.	Pen.
Guy Larose, Guelph	37	12	36	48	55
Ottawa	28	19	25	44	63
Totals	65	31	61	92	118
Frank DiMuzio, Belleville	46	22	16	38	96
Ottawa	17	7	10	17	9
Totals	63	29	26	55	105
David Rowbotham	63	17	35	52	25
Kent Hawley	64	21	30	51	96
Steve Simoni	65	22	28	50	44
Warren Rychel, Guelph	38	14	5	19	119
Ottawa	29	11	18	29	54
Totals	67	25	23	48	173
John English, Hamilton	12	2	10	12	57
Ottawa	43	8	28	36	120
Totals	55	10	38	48	177
Brent Battistelli, Pete.	4	1	0	1	7
Ottawa	58	19	20	39	93
Totals	62	20	20	40	100
Steve Hrynewich	59	18	19	37	65
Brian Therrien	55	12	23	35	8
Mike Griffith	59	14	13	27	38
Graydon Almstedt	64	3	24	27	32
Tim Helmer	28	13	12	25	29
Danny Hie	55	7	18	25	75
Rick Lessard	64	1	20	21	231

	Games	G.	A.	Pts	Pen.
Mike Rutherford	60	3	14	17	59
Chris Vickers	40	3	9	12	60
Bob Giffin	21	2	6	8	37
Ransome Drcar	66	3	3	6	70
David Gibbons	39	0	5	5	84
Chris Glover	8	1	2	3	0
Jeff Stanton, S.S.M.	8	0	3	3	2
Ottawa	2	0	0	0	0
Totals	10	0	3	3	2
Mike Larouche	8	1	1	2	0
Darren Beals (Goalie)	45	0	2	2	17
Dan Levasseur	2	0	1	1	0
Allan Thompson (Goalie)	1	0	0	0	0
Don MacDonald	2	0	0	0	0
Kevin Smith	2	0	0	0	0
Brent Almstedt	3	0	0	0	0
Bill Kuchma	3	0	0	0	0
Marty Abrams (Goalie)	4	0	0	0	0

Peterborough Petes

	Games	G.	A.	Pts.	Pen.
Graeme Bonar, S.S.M.	38	33	25	58	21
Peterborough	18	20	15	35	20
Totals	56	53	40	93	41
John Hanna, Ottawa	40	22	57	79	33
Peterborough	15	7	7	14	10
Totals	55	29	64	93	43
Mark Teevens	50	31	50	81	106
Darren Treloar	66	28	53	81	29
Kris King	58	19	40	59	254
Bill McMillan	56	16	31	47	67
John Druce	49	22	24	46	84
Mark Freer	65	16	28	44	24
Terry Carkner	54	12	32	44	106
Jody Hull	61	20	22	42	29
Greg Vey	61	14	20	34	49
Rob Murray	52	14	18	32	125
Todd Gregory	59	14	18	32	55
Randy Burridge	17	15	11	26	23
Mark Bar	56	2	24	26	98
Luke Richardson	63	6	18	24	57
Dallas Eakins	60	6	16	22	134
Glen Seabrooke	19	8	12	20	33
Kevin MacDonald	51	4	15	19	132
Larry Shaw	66	2	17	19	106
Darren Gani	25	5	7	12	19
Mike Dagenais	45	1	3	4	40
Jamie Batley	5	1	2	3	0
Kay Whitmore (Goalie)	41	0	3	3	14
Bill Huard	7	1	1	2	2
Todd Clayton	4	1	0	1	0
Scott McCullough	1	0	0	0	0
Ron Tugnutt (Goalie)	26	0	0	0	4

Sault Ste. Marie Greyhounds

	Games	G.	A.	Pts.	Pen.
Mike Oliverio	64	26	56	82	45
Steve Hollett	63	31	34	65	81
Brad Aitken, Pete.	48	9	28	37	77
Sault Ste. Marie	20	8	19	27	11
Totals	68	17	47	64	88
Tyler Larter	60	15	40	55	137
Jean Marc MacKenzie	64	28	26	54	10
Dan Currie	66	21	22	43	37
Scott Green	64	17	21	38	48

	Games	G.	A.	Pts	Pen.
Dan Mahon, Windsor	12	4	3	7	19
Sault Ste. Marie	28	6	22	28	31
Totals	40	10	25	35	50
Mike Glover	61	14	19	33	133
Paul Beraldo	61	15	13	28	48
Rob Zettler	57	5	23	28	92
Mark Haarmann, Osh.	20	1	4	5	22
Sault Ste. Marie	36	6	16	22	37
Totals	56	7	20	27	59
Steve Bisson	66	3	23	26	44
Ed Smith, Windsor	9	2	5	7	17
Sault Ste. Marie	26	5	8	13	43
Totals	35	7	13	20	60
Tom Roman, Windsor	15	0	1	1	10
Sault Ste. Marie	49	3	12	15	66
Totals	64	3	13	16	76
Peter Turko	56	3	6	9	29
Bob Babcock	50	1	7	8	185
Peter Fiorentino	58	1	6	7	87
Hal Turner, Oshawa	18	1	1	2	10
Sault Ste. Marie	1	0	2	2	0
Totals	19	1	3	4	10
Doug Crandall	12	0	3	3	16
Rick Mitchell	13	1	1	2	4
Bob Jones	10	0	1	1	0
Jamie Jardine	6	0	0	0	2
Terry Zoryk	7	0	0	0	8
Rob Watson (Goalie)	8	0	0	0	2
Dan Gatenby (Goalie)	33	0	0	0	18
Shawn Simpson (Goalie)	42	0	0	0	6

Sudbury Wolves

	Games	G.	A.	Pts.	Pen.
Max Middendorf	61	40	42	82	71
Mike Hudson, Hamilton	7	3	2	5	4
Sudbury	59	35	42	77	20
Totals	66	38	44	82	24
Glenn Greenough	64	30	41	71	34
Ken McRae	66	25	40	65	127
Mario Chitaroni	45	20	37	57	127
Jeff Brown	45	22	28	50	24
Todd Lalonde	57	17	30	47	43
Mark Turner	59	17	20	37	38
Dave Moylan	52	10	25	35	87
Jeff N. Smith, Cornwall	6	3	0	3	8
Sudbury	40	9	21	30	20
Totals	46	12	21	33	28
Brad Walcot	64	5	28	33	34
Alec Haidy, Hamilton	21	1	11	12	31
Sudbury	25	9	10	19	48
Totals	46	10	21	31	79
Keith Van Rooyen, Ham.	7	0	1	1	24
Sudbury	58	9	15	24	93
Totals	65	9	16	25	117
Brent Daugherty	64	2	12	14	129
Robin Rubic, Kitchener	1	0	0	0	2
Toronto	5	0	1	1	13
Sudbury	45	4	6	10	57
Totals	51	4	7	11	72
Andy Paquette	34	3	5	8	9
Mike Rouleau, Cornwall	22	2	4	6	32
Sudbury	11	0	1	1	24
Totals	33	2	5	7	56
Costa Papista	63	2	5	7	102

	Games	G.	A.	Pts.	Pen.
Morgan Watts, London..	13	1	2	3	23
North Bay...............	5	1	1	2	0
Sudbury	14	0	1	1	2
Totals	32	2	4	6	25
Rob Wilson	61	1	5	6	93
Vance Henson	9	2	3	5	0
Jeff J. Smith	39	2	3	5	44
Jeff Dobish	7	2	0	2	10
Guy Mathias................	1	1	0	1	0
Scott Mohns................	7	1	0	1	0
Ross Wilson	2	0	1	1	2
Wayne Venedam	3	0	1	1	0
Matt Taylor	10	0	1	1	0
Ed Lemaire	11	0	1	1	2
Chris Fillator	1	0	0	0	0
Norm Krumpschmid.......	1	0	0	0	0
Mike Lauzon	1	0	0	0	0
Greg Levert	1	0	0	0	0
Keith Whitmore	2	0	0	0	0
Piero Greco (Goalie)	3	0	0	0	0
Jim Kennedy	3	0	0	0	2
Dan Melanson	3	0	0	0	0
Mike Patrick, Corn. (G.)..	14	0	0	0	6
Sudbury (G.)	25	0	0	0	9
Totals	39	0	0	0	15
Bill White (Goalie).........	39	0	0	0	9

Toronto Marlboros

	Games	G.	A.	Pts.	Pen.
Jack MacKeigan	66	53	59	112	64
Tim Armstrong..............	64	35	69	104	36
Yvon Corriveau	59	54	36	90	75
Mike Richard	63	32	48	80	28
Victor Posa	48	28	34	62	116
Vito Cramarossa...........	51	20	35	55	77
Sean Davidson	65	18	34	52	23
Bill Berg	64	3	35	38	143
Brian Melanson	66	6	24	30	87
Paul Giusto	65	10	15	25	20
Jamie Henckel..............	52	14	9	23	8
Darren Wright, Kingston	38	4	9	13	35
Toronto.................	27	5	4	9	14
Totals	65	9	13	22	49
Glen Lowes.................	64	8	14	22	134
Dennis Tester, Pete........	7	3	4	7	0
Hamilton...............	5	1	2	3	0
Toronto.................	25	1	5	6	0
Totals	37	5	11	16	0
John Blessman	64	2	13	15	116
Sean Boland................	52	2	10	12	85
Brian Merko, S.S.M.	30	2	6	8	30
Toronto.................	27	0	4	4	9
Totals	57	2	10	12	39

	Games	G.	A.	Pts.	Pen.
Mike Flanagan	58	2	5	7	69
Sean Burke (Goalie)	47	0	5	5	32
Dave Nesbitt.................	15	1	2	3	0
David Kunda	61	1	2	3	38
Kevin Hunter	32	1	1	2	11
Allan Sadowy, Sudbury	3	1	0	1	2
Toronto.................	2	0	0	0	2
Totals	5	1	0	1	4
Ian Rand	11	1	0	1	0
Dave Dmytrow..............	6	0	1	1	2
Todd Hermes	1	0	0	0	0
Cole Sefc....................	2	0	0	0	0
Brad Adams.................	3	0	0	0	0
John Caranci, London....	2	0	0	0	5
Toronto.................	8	0	0	0	7
Totals	10	0	0	0	12
Paul Stafford...............	14	0	0	0	6
Nick Vitucci (Goalie)......	20	0	0	0	4

Windsor Compuware Spitfires

	Games	G.	A.	Pts.	Pen.
Brian Martin	60	42	41	83	115
Kevin Kerr....................	59	21	51	72	*266
Adam Graves................	62	27	37	64	35
Wilf Payne...................	64	31	31	62	44
Ian O'Rear	65	21	37	58	53
Brit Peer, S.S.M.	17	6	9	15	34
Windsor................	28	16	24	40	58
Totals	45	22	33	55	92
Jean-Paul Gorley	58	15	26	41	4
Kent Hulst, Belleville......	43	6	17	23	20
Windsor................	17	6	10	16	9
Totals	60	12	27	39	29
Shane Whelan	64	9	29	38	69
Mark Kurzawski.............	66	11	26	37	66
John Urbanic................	40	18	12	30	69
Darryl Shannon	57	6	21	27	52
Paul Hampton, Cornwall	15	0	7	7	16
Windsor................	37	0	18	18	33
Totals	52	0	25	25	49
Frank Melone	65	13	11	24	74
Paul Maurice	56	3	10	13	89
Rich Kokila	57	2	11	13	28
Brian Blad	56	2	9	11	195
Geoff Benic	59	3	7	10	80
Peter DeBoer	55	3	6	9	20
Glen Featherstone........	49	0	6	6	135
Pat Jablonski (Goalie)....	29	0	3	3	4
Alan Perry (Goalie)	42	0	2	2	18
Steve Cote	5	1	0	1	2
Mike Siefker	7	0	1	1	17
Jim MacPherson............	1	0	0	0	0
Darrin McClusky (G.)......	1	0	0	0	0
Terry McDonnell	1	0	0	0	0

Complete OHL Goaltending

	Games	Mins.	Goals	SO.	Avg.
Kay Whitmore	41	2467	114(2)	*3	*2.77
Ron Tugnutt	26	1543	74	1	2.88
Peterborough Totals	66	4010	190	4	2.84
Steve Guenette	50	2910	165(2)	*3	3.40
Gerry Iuliano	10	466	29	0	3.73
Andy Helmuth (a)	12	620	39	0	3.77
Guelph Totals	66	3994	235	3	3.53

	Games	Mins.	Goals	SO.	Avg.
John Reid (b)	23	1318	64	1	2.91
Paul Henriques (c)	19	1132	62(3)	0	3.29
Mike Ricci	22	1297	82(2)	0	3.79
Brian Tessier (d)	5	271	27	0	5.98
North Bay Totals	66	4019	240	1	3.58
Kirk McLean	51	2830	169(3)	1	3.58
Mark Gowans	25	1187	84(1)	0	4.25
Oshawa Totals	66	4017	257	1	3.84
Alan Perry	42	2424	131(2)	*3	3.24
Pat Jablonski	29	1600	119(4)	1	4.46
Darrin McClusky	1	20	3	0	9.00
Windsor Totals	66	4043	259	4	3.84
Chris Clifford	50	2988	178(1)	1	3.57
Brian Tessier (d)	13	780	55	0	4.23
Andy Pearson	6	241	23	0	5.73
Kingston Totals	66	4007	257	1	3.85
Mike Bishop	34	1921	111	2	3.47
Craig Billington	3	180	11	0	3.67
Paul Henriques (c)	9	502	36	0	4.30
John Reid (b)	24	1309	100(2)	0	4.58
Saverio Manzo	2	94	8	0	5.11
Belleville Totals	66	4005	268	2	4.01
Jeff Reese	*57	*3281	215(3)	0	3.93
Scott Cumming	16	765	73(1)	0	5.73
London Totals	66	4046	292	0	4.33
Willie Popp	26	1146	75	0	3.93
Mike Rosati	1	70	5	0	4.29
Peter Richards	54	2748	214(4)	0	4.67
Chris French	2	57	8	0	8.42
Hamilton Totals	66	4021	306	0	4.57
Mike Volpe	36	1926	137(1)	0	4.27
Paul Porter	2	115	9	0	4.70
Rob Dopson	8	403	32	0	4.76
David Weiss	29	1574	128(2)	0	4.88
Kitchener Totals	66	4018	309	0	4.61
Sean Evoy (e)	21	1212	69	0	3.42
Bill White	39	1789	156(2)	0	5.23
Mike Patrick (f)	25	970	92(3)	0	5.69
Piero Greco	3	61	8	0	7.87
Sudbury Totals	66	4030	330	0	4.91
Sean Burke	47	2840	*233(4)	0	4.92
Nick Vitucci	20	1203	108	0	5.39
Toronto Totals	66	4043	345	0	5.12
Marty Abrams	4	202	16	0	4.75
Andy Helmuth (a)	20	1175	97	0	4.95
Darren Beals	45	2622	*233(2)	1	5.33
Allan Thompson	1	15	4	0	16.00
Ottawa Totals	66	4012	352	1	5.26
Steve Titus	33	1846	161(3)	0	5.23
Sean Evoy (e)	27	1391	122	1	5.26
Mike Patrick (f)	14	774	69(1)	0	5.35
Cornwall Totals	66	4010	356	1	5.33
Dan Gatenby	33	1519	125(3)	1	4.94
Shawn Simpson	42	2233	219(5)	1	5.88
Rob Watson	8	251	35	0	8.37
Sault Ste. Marie Totals	66	4002	387	2	5.80

( )—Empty Net Goals. Do not count against a Goaltender's average.
(a)—Helmuth played for Guelph and Ottawa.
(b)—Reid played for North Bay and Belleville.
(c)—Henriques played for North Bay and Belleville.
(d)—Tessier played for North Bay and Kingston.
(e)—Evoy played for Sudbury and Cornwall.
(f)—Patrick played for Sudbury and Cornwall.

Individual 1985-86 Leaders

Goals	Ray Sheppard, Cornwall—	81
Assists	Ron Sanko, Kitchener—	89
Points	Ray Sheppard, Cornwall—	142
Penalty Minutes	Kevin Kerr, Windsor—	266
Goaltender's Average	Kay Whitmore, Peterborough—	2.77
Shutouts	Kay Whitmore, Peterborough—	3
	Steve Guenette, Guelph—	3
	Alan Perry, Windsor—	3

1986 J. Ross Robertson Cup Playoffs
Division Quarterfinals
(Eight point series)

Leyden Division

Series "A"

	W.	L.	T.	Pts.	GF.	GA.
Peterborough	4	0	0	8	24	6
Toronto	0	4	0	0	6	24

(Peterborough wins series, 8 points to 0)

Series "B"

	W.	L.	T.	Pts.	GF.	GA.
Belleville	4	1	1	9	36	26
Cornwall	1	4	1	3	26	36

(Belleville wins series, 9 points to 3)

Series "C"

	W.	L.	T.	Pts.	GF.	GA.
Kingston	4	2	0	8	31	25
Oshawa	2	4	0	4	25	31

(Kingston wins series, 8 points to 4)

Emms Division

Series "A"

	W.	L.	T.	Pts.	GF.	GA.
North Bay	4	0	1	9	25	16
London	0	4	1	1	16	25

(North Bay wins series, 9 points to 1)

Series "B"

	W.	L.	T.	Pts.	GF.	GA.
Guelph	4	0	0	8	25	12
Sudbury	0	4	0	0	12	25

(Guelph wins series, 8 points to 0)

Series "C"

	W.	L.	T.	Pts.	GF.	GA.
Windsor	4	1	0	8	22	23
Kitchener	1	4	0	2	23	22

(Windsor wins series, 8 points to 2)

Division Semifinals
(Round-robin series)

Leyden Division

Series "D"

	W.	L.	T.	Pts.	GF.	GA.
Peterborough	3	1	0	6	15	12
Belleville	2	2	0	4	14	19
Kingston	1	3	0	2	15	13

(Peterborough and Belleville advance to Division Finals)

Emms Division

Series "D"

	W.	L.	T.	Pts.	GF.	GA.
Guelph	4	0	0	8	25	8
Windsor	2	3	0	4	16	23
North Bay	1	4	0	2	13	23

(Guelph and Windsor advance to Division Finals)

Division Finals
(Eight point series)

Leyden Division

Series "E"

	W.	L.	T.	Pts.	GF.	GA.
Belleville	4	3	1	9	29	24
Peterborough	3	4	1	7	24	29

(Belleville wins series, 9 points to 7)

Emms Division

Series "E"

	W.	L.	T.	Pts.	GF.	GA.
Guelph	4	2	0	8	27	22
Windsor	2	4	0	4	22	27

(Guelph wins series, 8 points to 4)

OHL Final Series For the J. Ross Robertson Cup
(Eight point series)

Series "F"

	W.	L.	T.	Pts.	GF.	GA.
Guelph	3	1	2	8	25	17
Belleville	1	3	2	4	17	25

(Guelph wins series, and Robertson Cup, 8 points to 4)

Top 10 Playoff Scorers

	Games	G.	A.	Pts.	Pen.
1. Jason Lafreniere, Belleville	23	10	*22	*32	6
2. Gary Roberts, Guelph	20	18	13	31	43
3. Dan Gratton, Belleville	24	*20	9	29	16
4. Paul Brydges, Guelph	19	10	15	25	22
Mark Teevens, Peterborough	16	4	21	25	19
6. Jamie McKinley, Guelph	20	9	15	24	12
Brian MacDonald, Belleville	24	9	15	24	6
Keith Miller, Guelph	20	8	16	24	6
9. Marc Tournier, Guelph	14	3	20	23	28
10. Graeme Bonar, Peterborough	16	11	10	21	15
Keith Gretzky, Belleville	24	8	13	21	2

Team-by-Team Playoff Scoring

Belleville Bulls
(Lost league finals to Guelph, 8 points to 4)

	Games	G.	A.	Pts.	Pen.
Jason Lafreniere	23	10	*22	*32	6
Dan Gratton	24	*20	9	29	16
Brian MacDonald	24	9	15	24	6
Keith Gretzky	24	8	13	21	2
Todd Hawkins	24	9	7	16	60
Daran Moxam	25	10	5	15	65
Stan Drulia	24	4	11	15	15
Marc West	24	7	7	14	10
Gary Callaghan	24	4	6	10	28
Steve Ewing	24	4	6	10	26
Brian Chapman	24	2	6	8	54
John Tamer	24	2	6	8	11
Mike Vellucci	24	2	5	7	45
Bryan Marchment	21	0	7	7	*83
Peter Choma	24	2	4	6	8
Charlie Moore	23	1	2	3	28
Peter Hughes	24	1	2	3	17
Tony Crisp	17	1	1	2	4
Jim Way	1	0	0	0	0
Mike Bishop (Goalie)	8	0	0	0	2
Lawrence Hinch	10	0	0	0	4
Craig Billington (G.)	20	0	0	0	2

Guelph Platers
(Winners of 1986 J. Ross Robertson Cup Playoffs)

	Games	G.	A.	Pts.	Pen.
Gary Roberts	20	18	13	31	43
Paul Brydges	19	10	15	25	22
Jamie McKinley	20	9	15	24	12
Keith Miller	20	8	16	24	6
Marc Tournier	14	3	20	23	28
Steve Chiasson	18	10	10	20	37
Mike Murray	20	7	13	20	0
Paul Kelly	20	10	7	17	19
Rob Arabski	20	8	9	17	4
Lonnie Loach	20	7	8	15	16
Luciano Fagioli	20	2	12	14	18
Kerry Huffman	20	1	10	11	10
Luc Sabourin	19	1	6	7	8
Robb Graham	20	4	2	6	24
John McIntyre	20	1	5	6	31
Denis Larocque	20	1	4	5	44
Brian Hayton	10	1	3	4	27
Allan MacIsaac	20	1	2	3	22
Bill Loshaw	20	0	3	3	46
Steve Guenette (Goalie)	20	0	2	2	6
Andy Helmuth (Goalie)	1	0	0	0	0

Kingston Canadians
(Lost division semifinals to Peterborough and Belleville)

	Games	G.	A.	Pts.	Pen.
Barry Burkholder	10	9	10	19	14
Mike Maurice	10	9	9	18	10
Scott Metcalfe	10	3	6	9	21
Herb Raglan	10	5	2	7	30
Brian Verbeek	10	3	4	7	34
Mike Fiset	10	2	4	6	2
Jeff Cornelius	10	1	5	6	22
Wayne Erskine	6	2	3	5	2
Ted Linseman	10	1	4	5	4
Peter Viskovich	10	0	5	5	0
Daril Holmes	10	2	2	4	4
Bryan Fogarty	10	1	3	4	4
Jeff Chychrun	10	2	1	3	17
Todd Clarke	10	2	1	3	6
Steve Seftel	10	2	1	3	14
Tony MacNevin	10	0	2	2	2
Marc Lyons	4	1	0	1	0
Scott Pearson	8	1	0	1	2
Marc Laforge	10	0	1	1	30
Jeff Sirkka	2	0	0	0	0
Brian Tessier (Goalie)	2	0	0	0	0
Chris Clifford (Goalie)	10	0	0	0	6

Cornwall Royals
(Lost division quarterfinals to Belleville, 9 points to 3)

	Games	G.	A.	Pts.	Pen.
Ray Sheppard	6	7	4	11	0
Craig Duncanson	6	4	7	11	4
Bill Bennett	6	3	4	7	12
John Copple	6	1	6	7	8
Mike Bukowski	6	3	2	5	8
Mike Stapleton	6	2	3	5	2
Paul Wilkinson	6	2	3	5	0
Bruno Lapensee	6	1	3	4	0
Neil Jones	6	0	4	4	7
Ken Sabourin	6	1	2	3	6
Paul Cain	6	1	1	2	5
Shane Doyle	6	1	0	1	17
Mark Evans	6	0	1	1	0
Steve Titus (Goalie)	1	0	0	0	0
Sean Evoy (Goalie)	5	0	0	0	0
Steve Herniman	6	0	0	0	2
Glen Leslie	6	0	0	0	0
Pat Malone	6	0	0	0	2
Rob Ray	6	0	0	0	26

Kitchener Rangers

(Lost division quarterfinals to Windsor, 8 points to 2)

	Games	G.	A.	Pts.	Pen.
Brett MacDonald	5	3	7	10	6
Mike Wolak	5	0	9	9	2
David Latta	5	7	1	8	15
Ron Sanko	5	3	4	7	20
Shawn Burr	5	2	3	5	8
Jeff Noble	5	2	2	4	11
Ron Goodall	4	2	1	3	0
Mike Morrison	4	1	2	3	12
Ken Alexander	5	1	2	3	2
Brad Sparkes	3	0	2	2	0
Peter Lisy	5	0	2	2	4
Ian Pound	3	1	0	1	6
Scott Taylor	4	1	0	1	6
Blair MacPherson	2	0	1	1	0
Sean Wallington	3	0	1	1	7
Kevin Grant	5	0	1	1	11
Steve Marcolini	5	0	1	1	9
Paul Penelton	1	0	0	0	0
Mike Volpe (Goalie)	1	0	0	0	0
Rob Dopson (Goalie)	2	0	0	0	0
Doug Jones	2	0	0	0	0
David Weiss (Goalie)	3	0	0	0	0
Greg Hankkio	4	0	0	0	0
Craig Booker	5	0	0	0	6
Kent Falby	5	0	0	0	0

London Knights

(Lost division quarterfinals to North Bay, 9 points to 1)

	Games	G.	A.	Pts.	Pen.
Brendan Shanahan	5	5	5	10	5
Murray Nystrom	5	3	3	6	4
Jim Sandlak	5	2	3	5	24
Brian Dobbin	5	2	1	3	9
Greg Smyth	4	1	2	3	28
Tom Allen	5	0	3	3	14
Greg Puhalski	5	0	3	3	0
Mike Zombo	5	0	3	3	4
Kelly Cain	5	1	0	1	7
Don Martin	5	1	0	1	14
Garnet McKechney	5	1	0	1	2
Denis Hebert	3	0	1	1	0
Dave Haas	5	0	1	1	0
Scott Cumming (Goalie)	1	0	0	0	0
Jamie Groke	1	0	0	0	0
Ed Kister	2	0	0	0	0
Patrick Vachon	2	0	0	0	4
Matt Smyth	3	0	0	0	14
Rob Coutts	5	0	0	0	7
Ray Gallagher	5	0	0	0	0
Jeff Reese (Goalie)	5	0	0	0	0
Brad Schlegel	5	0	0	0	4
Trevor Stienburg	5	0	0	0	20

North Bay Centennials

(Lost division semifinals to Guelph and Windsor)

	Games	G.	A.	Pts.	Pen.
Rob DeGagne	10	5	9	14	5
Todd Elik	10	7	6	13	0
Tim Bean	10	5	5	10	22
David McIlwain	10	4	4	8	2
Wayne MacPhee	10	0	8	8	26
Mike Gillies	10	5	2	7	4
Darren Turcotte	10	3	4	7	8
Bill Houlder	10	1	6	7	12
Mike Hartman	10	2	4	6	34
Len Soccio	10	1	5	6	11
Darin Smith	10	3	2	5	16
Kevin Vescio	10	0	5	5	4
Jeff Bloemberg	8	1	2	3	9
Brent Bywater	10	0	3	3	6
Dean Haig	10	1	1	2	9
Mike Ricci (Goalie)	1	0	0	0	10
Larry Van Herzele	3	0	0	0	4
John Keller	9	0	0	0	0
Adam Burt	10	0	0	0	24
John Reid (Goalie)	10	0	0	0	0
Doug Stromback	10	0	0	0	14

Oshawa Generals

(Lost division quarterfinals to Kingston, 8 points to 4)

	Games	G.	A.	Pts.	Pen.
Scott McCrory	6	5	8	13	0
Gary McColgan	6	7	4	11	2
Craig Morrison	6	2	6	8	10
Derek King	6	3	2	5	13
Marc Laniel	6	2	3	5	6
Sean Williams	6	2	3	5	4
Petri Matikainen	6	1	4	5	13
Lee Giffin	6	0	5	5	8
Gordon Murphy	6	1	1	2	6
John Stevens	6	0	2	2	14
John Andersen	6	1	0	1	4
Jim Buwalda	6	1	0	1	28
Scott MacDonald	3	0	1	1	0
Jeff Daniels	6	0	1	1	0
Jim Paek	6	0	1	1	9
Darren Colbourne	2	0	0	0	0
Mark Gowans (Goalie)	3	0	0	0	0
Ian Ferguson	4	0	0	0	2
Kirk McLean (Goalie)	4	0	0	0	0
Joel Curtis	5	0	0	0	0
Dean Morton	5	0	0	0	9
Greg Watson	5	0	0	0	13

Peterborough Petes

(Lost division finals to Belleville, 9 points to 7)

	Games	G.	A.	Pts.	Pen.
Mark Teevens	16	4	21	25	19
Graeme Bonar	16	11	10	21	15
Darren Treloar	16	8	10	18	8
Glen Seabrooke	14	9	7	16	14
John Hanna	16	6	9	15	13
Terry Carkner	16	1	7	8	17
Mark Freer	14	3	4	7	13
Todd Gregory	16	3	4	7	21
Greg Vey	10	5	1	6	12
Darren Gani	14	2	4	6	9
Jody Hull	16	1	5	6	4
John Druce	16	0	5	5	34
Kevin MacDonald	16	0	5	5	24
Kris King	8	4	0	4	21
Randy Burridge	3	1	3	4	2
Mark Bar	11	0	4	4	9
Luke Richardson	16	2	1	3	18
Rob Murray	16	1	2	3	50
Bill McMillan	6	1	1	2	4
Larry Shaw	16	1	1	2	24
Dallas Eakins	16	0	1	1	30
Ron Tugnutt (Goalie)	3	0	0	0	0
Kay Whitmore (Goalie)	14	0	0	0	4

Sudbury Wolves

(Lost division quarterfinals to Guelph, 8 points to 0)

	Games	G.	A.	Pts.	Pen.
Mike Hudson	4	2	5	7	7
Max Middendorf	4	4	2	6	11
Ken McRae	4	2	1	3	12
Mario Chitaroni	4	1	2	3	8
Glenn Greenough	4	0	3	3	12
Jeff N. Smith	4	1	1	2	2
Mark Turner	4	1	1	2	0
Brad Walcot	4	1	1	2	6
Jeff Brown	4	0	2	2	11
Rob Wilson	4	0	2	2	10
Todd Lalonde	4	0	1	1	8
Keith Van Rooyen	4	0	1	1	6
Bill White (Goalie)	2	0	0	0	2
Robin Rubic	3	0	0	0	0
Brent Daugherty	4	0	0	0	7
Alec Haidy	4	0	0	0	5
Dave Moylan	4	0	0	0	15
Costa Papista	4	0	0	0	7
Mike Patrick (Goalie)	4	0	0	0	0
Jeff J. Smith	4	0	0	0	0

Toronto Marlboros

(Lost division quarterfinals to Peterborough, 8 points to 0)

	Games	G.	A.	Pts.	Pen.
Tim Armstrong	4	1	3	4	9
Jack MacKeigan	4	2	0	2	4
Yvon Corriveau	4	1	1	2	0
Mike Richard	4	1	1	2	2
Mike Flanagan	4	1	0	1	5
Vito Cramarossa	4	0	1	1	0
Sean Davidson	4	0	1	1	0
Jamie Henckel	4	0	1	1	7
Brian Merko	4	0	1	1	0

	Games	G.	A.	Pts.	Pen.
David Kunda	1	0	0	0	0
Nick Vitucci (Goalie)	1	0	0	0	0
Cole Sefc	2	0	0	0	0
Glenn Lowes	3	0	0	0	0
Bill Berg	4	0	0	0	19
John Blessman	4	0	0	0	11
Sean Boland	4	0	0	0	13
Sean Burke (Goalie)	4	0	0	0	2
Paul Giusto	4	0	0	0	0
Brian Melanson	4	0	0	0	4
Darren Wright	4	0	0	0	2

Windsor Compuware Spitfires

(Lost division finals to Guelph, 8 points to 4)

	Games	G.	A.	Pts.	Pen.
Brit Peer	16	6	13	19	6
Ian O'Rear	16	3	14	17	4
Adam Graves	16	5	11	16	10
Wilf Payne	16	7	8	15	9
Kevin Kerr	16	6	8	14	55
Kent Hulst	16	5	8	13	13
Brian Martin	12	7	4	11	23
Darryl Shannon	16	5	6	11	22
Mark Kurzawski	16	3	5	8	23
Frank Melone	16	3	1	4	8
John Urbanic	15	1	3	4	35
Rich Kokila	16	2	1	3	6
Jean Paul Gorley	10	1	2	3	2
Shane Whelan	12	1	2	3	33
Brian Blad	13	1	1	2	34
Glen Featherstone	14	1	1	2	23
Paul Hampton	11	0	2	2	8
Paul Maurice	16	0	2	2	8
Peter DeBoer	11	1	0	1	0
Geoff Benic	14	0	1	1	10
Pat Jablonski (Goalie)	6	0	0	0	0
Alan Perry (Goalie)	13	0	0	0	6

Complete Robertson Cup Goaltending

	Games	Mins.	Goals	SO.	Avg.
Steve Guenette	*20	*1167	54	*2	*2.78
Andy Helmuth	1	33	3	0	5.45
Guelph Totals	20	1200	57	2	2.85
Ron Tugnutt	3	133	6	0	2.71
Kay Whitmore	14	837	40(1)	0	2.87
Peterborough Totals	16	970	47	0	2.90
Chris Clifford	10	564	31(1)	1	3.30
Brian Tessier	2	48	6	0	7.50
Kingston Totals	10	612	38	1	3.73
Craig Billington	*20	1133	*68	0	3.60
Mike Bishop	8	322	25(1)	0	4.66
Belleville Totals	24	1455	94	0	3.87
Mike Ricci	1	23	0(1)	0	0.00
John Reid	10	577	37(1)	0	3.85
North Bay Totals	10	600	39	0	3.90
David Weiss	3	161	11	1	4.10
Rob Dopson	2	79	6	0	4.56
Mike Volpe	1	60	5	0	5.00
Kitchener Totals	5	300	22	1	4.40
Alan Perry	13	697	51(1)	0	4.39
Pat Jablonski	6	263	20(1)	0	4.56
Windsor Totals	16	960	73	0	4.56

	Games	Mins.	Goals	SO.	Avg.
Scott Cumming	1	1	0	0	0.00
Jeff Reese	5	299	25	0	5.02
London Totals	5	300	25	0	5.00
Mark Gowans	3	159	12	0	4.53
Kirk McLean	4	201	18(1)	0	5.37
Oshawa Totals	6	360	31	0	5.17
Sean Evoy	5	300	27	0	5.40
Steve Titus	1	60	9	0	9.00
Cornwall Totals	6	360	36	0	6.00
Nick Vitucci	1	2	0	0	0.00
Sean Burke	4	238	24	0	6.05
Toronto Totals	4	240	24	0	6.00
Bill White	2	91	5(1)	0	3.30
Mike Patrick	4	149	18(1)	0	7.25
Sudbury Totals	4	240	25	0	6.25

( )—Empty Net Goals. Do not count against a Goaltender's average.

Individual OHL Playoff Leaders

Goals	Dan Gratton, Belleville —	20
Assists	Jason Lafreniere, Belleville —	22
Points	Jason Lafreniere, Belleville —	32
Penalty Minutes	Bryan Marchment, Belleville —	83
Goaltender's average	Steve Guenette, Guelph —	2.78
Shutouts	Steve Guenette, Guelph —	2

★★★

OHL 1985-86 All-Stars

First Team	Position	Second Team
Kay Whitmore, Peterborough	Goal	Steve Guenette, Guelph
Terry Carkner, Peterborough	Defense	Petri Matikainen, Oshawa
Jeff Brown, Sudbury	Defense	Greg Smyth, London
Jason Lafreniere, Belleville	Center	Shawn Burr, Kitchener
Ray Sheppard, Cornwall	Right Wing	Graeme Bonar, Peterborough
Nick Kypreos, North Bay	Left Wing	Gary Roberts, Guelph

★★★

OHL 1985-86 Trophy Winners

Red Tilson Trophy (Outstanding Player)	Ray Sheppard, Cornwall
Max Kaminsky Trophy (Outstanding Defenseman)	Terry Carkner, Peterborough
	Jeff Brown, Sudbury
William Hanley Trophy (Most Gentlemanly)	Jason Lafreniere, Belleville
Emms Family Award (Rookie of the Year)	Lonnie Loach, Guelph
Matt Leyden Trophy (Coach of the Year)	Jacques Martin, Guelph
Eddie Powers Memorial Trophy (Scoring Champion)	Ray Sheppard, Cornwall
Jim Mahon Memorial Trophy (Top scoring Right Wing)	Ray Sheppard, Cornwall
Dave Pinkney Trophy (Top Team Goaltending)	Kay Whitmore, Peterborough
	Ron Tugnutt, Peterborough
F.W. Dinty Moore Trophy (Lowest average by a rookie goalie)	Paul Henriques, Belleville

Historical OHL Trophy Winners

Red Tilson Trophy
(Outstanding Player)

Season	Player	Club
1944-45	Doug McMurdy, St. Catharines
1945-46	Tod Sloan, St. Michael's
1946-47	Ed Sanford, St. Michael's
1947-48	George Armstrong, Stratford
1948-49	Gil Mayer, Barrie
1949-50	George Armstrong, Marlboros
1950-51	Glenn Hall, Windsor
1951-52	Bill Harrington, Kitchener
1952-53	Bob Attersley, Oshawa
1953-54	Brian Cullen, St. Catharines
1954-55	Hank Ciesla, St. Catharines
1955-56	Ron Howell, Guelph
1956-57	Frank Mahovlich, St. Michael's
1957-58	Murray Oliver, Hamilton
1958-59	Stan Mikita, St. Catharines
1959-60	Wayne Connelly, Peterborough
1960-61	Rod Gilbert, Guelph
1961-62	Pit Martin, Hamilton
1962-63	Wayne Maxner, Niagara Falls
1963-64	Yvan Cournoyer, Montreal
1964-65	Andre Lacroix, Peterborough
1965-66	Andre Lacroix, Peterborough
1966-67	Mickey Redmond, Peterborough
1967-68	Walt Tkaczuk, Kitchener
1968-69	Rejean Houle, Montreal
1969-70	Gilbert Perreault, Montreal
1970-71	Dave Gardner, Marlboros
1971-72	Don Lever, Niagara Falls
1972-73	Rick Middleton, Oshawa
1973-74	Jack Valiquette, Sault Ste. Marie
1974-75	Dennis Maruk, London
1975-76	Peter Lee, Ottawa
1976-77	Dale McCourt, St. Catharines
1977-78	Bobby Smith, Ottawa
1978-79	Mike Foligno, Sudbury
1979-80	Jim Fox, Ottawa
1980-81	Ernie Godden, Windsor
1981-82	Dave Simpson, London
1982-83	Doug Gilmour, Cornwall
1983-84	John Tucker, Kitchener
1984-85	Wayne Groulx, Sault Ste. Marie
1985-86	Ray Sheppard, Cornwall

Eddie Powers Memorial Trophy
(Scoring Champion)

Season	Player	Club
1933-34	J. Groboski, Oshawa
1934-35	J. Good, Toronto Lions
1935-36	John O'Flaherty, West Toronto
1936-37	Billy Taylor, Oshawa
1937-38	Hank Goldup, Tor. Marlboros
1938-39	Billy Taylor, Oshawa
1939-40	Jud McAtee, Oshawa
1940-41	Gaye Stewart, Tor. Marlboros
1941-42	Bob Wiest, Brantford
1942-43	Norman "Red" Tilson, Oshawa
1943-44	Ken Smith, Oshawa
1944-45	Leo Gravelle, St. Michael's
1945-46	Tod Sloan, St. Michael's
1946-47	Fleming Mackell, St. Michael's
1947-48	George Armstrong, Stratford
1948-49	Bert Giesebrecht, Windsor
1949-50	Earl Reibel, Windsor
1950-51	Lou Jankowski, Oshawa
1951-52	Ken Laufman, Guelph
1952-53	Jim McBurney, Galt
1953-54	Brian Cullen, St. Catharines
1954-55	Hank Ciesla, St. Catharines
1955-56	Stan Baliuk, Kitchener
1956-57	Bill Sweeney, Guelph
1957-58	John McKenzie, St. Catharines
1958-59	Stan Mikita, St. Catharines
1959-60	Chico Maki, St. Catharines
1960-61	Rod Gilbert, Guelph
1961-62	Andre Boudrias, Montreal
1962-63	Wayne Maxner, Niagara Falls
1963-64	Andre Boudrias, Montreal
1964-65	Ken Hodge, St. Catharines
1965-66	Andre Lacroix, Peterborough
1966-67	Derek Sanderson, Niagara Falls
1967-68	Tom Webster, Niagara Falls
1968-69	Rejean Houle, Montreal
1969-70	Marcel Dionne, St. Catharines
1970-71	Marcel Dionne, St. Catharines
1971-72	Bill Harris, Toronto
1972-73	Blake Dunlop, Ottawa
1973-74	Jack Valiquette, Sault Ste. Marie
	Rick Adduono, St. Catharines
1974-75	Bruce Boudreau, Toronto
1975-76	Mike Kaszycki, Sault Ste. Marie
1976-77	Dwight Foster, Kitchener
1977-78	Bobby Smith, Ottawa
1978-79	Mike Foligno, Sudbury
1979-80	Jim Fox, Ottawa
1980-81	John Goodwin, Sault Ste. Marie
1981-82	Dave Simpson, London
1982-83	Doug Gilmour, Cornwall
1983-84	Tim Salmon, Kingston
1984-85	Dave MacLean, Belleville
1985-86	Ray Sheppard, Cornwall

Dave Pinkney Trophy
(Top Team Goaltending)

Season	Player	Club
1948-49	Gil Mayer, Barrie
1949-50	Don Lockhart, Marlboros
1950-51	Don Lockhart, Marlboros
	Lorne Howes, Barrie
1951-52	Don Head, Marlboros
1952-53	John Henderson, Marlboros
1953-54	Dennis Riggin, Hamilton
1954-55	John Albani, Marlboros
1955-56	Jim Crockett, Marlboros
1956-57	Len Broderick, Marlboros
1957-58	Len Broderick, Marlboros
1958-59	Jacques Caron, Peterborough
1959-60	Gerry Cheevers, St. Michael's
1960-61	Bud Blom, Hamilton
1961-62	George Holmes, Montreal
1962-63	Chuck Goddard, Peterborough
1963-64	Bernie Parent, Niagara Falls
1964-65	Bernie Parent, Niagara Falls
1965-66	Ted Quimet, Montreal
1966-67	Peter MacDuffe, St. Catharines
1967-68	Bruce Mullet, Montreal
1968-69	Wayne Wood, Montreal
1969-70	John Garrett, Peterborough
1970-71	John Garrett, Peterborough
1971-72	Michel Larocque, Ottawa
1972-73	Mike Palmateer, Toronto
1973-74	Don Edwards, Kitchener
1974-75	Greg Millen, Peterborough
1975-76	Jim Bedard, Sudbury
1976-77	Pat Riggin, London
1977-78	Al Jensen, Hamilton
1978-79	Nick Ricci, Niagara Falls
1979-80	Rick LaFerriere, Peterborough

Season	Player	Club
1980-81	Jim Ralph, Ottawa	
1981-82	Marc D'Amour, Sault Ste. Marie	
1982-83	Peter Sidorkiewicz, Oshawa	
	Jeff Hogg, Oshawa	
1983-84	Darren Pang, Ottawa	
	Greg Coram, Ottawa	
1984-85	Scott Mosey, Sault Ste. Marie	
	Marty Abrams, Sault Ste. Marie	
1985-86	Kay Whitmore, Peterborough	
	Ron Tugnutt, Peterborough	

Max Kaminsky Trophy
(Outstanding Defenseman)

Season	Player	Club
1969-70	Ron Plumb, Peterborough	
1970-71	Jocelyn Guevremont, Montreal	
1971-72	Denis Potvin, Ottawa	
1972-73	Denis Potvin, Ottawa	
1973-74	Jim Turkiewicz, Peterborough	
1974-75	Mike O'Connell, Kingston	
1975-76	Rick Green, London	
1976-77	Craig Hartsburg, S. Ste. Marie	
1977-78	Brad Marsh, London	
	Rob Ramage, London	
1978-79	Greg Theberge, Peterborough	
1979-80	Larry Murphy, Peterborough	
1980-81	Steve Smith, Sault Ste. Marie	
1981-82	Ron Meighan, Niagara Falls	
1982-83	Allan MacInnis, Kitchener	
1983-84	Brad Shaw, Ottawa	
1984-85	Bob Halkidis, London	
1985-86	Terry Carkner, Peterborough	
	Jeff Brown, Sudbury	

William Hanley Trophy
(Most Gentlemanly)

Season	Player	Club
1960-61	Bruce Draper, St. Michael's	
1961-62	Lowell MacDonald, Hamilton	
1962-63	Paul Henderson, Hamilton	
1963-64	Fred Stanfield, St. Catharines	
1964-65	Jimmy Peters, Hamilton	
1965-66	Andre Lacroix, Peterborough	
1966-67	Mickey Redmond, Peterborough	
1967-68	Tom Webster, Niagara Falls	
1968-69	Rejean Houle, Montreal	
1969-74	No award presented	
1974-75	Doug Jarvis, Peterborough	
1975-76	Dale McCourt, Hamilton	
1976-77	Dale McCourt, St. Catharines	
1977-78	Wayne Gretzky, S.S. Marie	
1978-79	Sean Simpson, Ottawa	
1979-80	Sean Simpson, Ottawa	
1980-81	John Goodwin, Sault Ste. Marie	
1981-82	Dave Simpson, London	
1982-83	Kirk Muller, Guelph	
1983-84	Kevin Conway, Kingston	
1984-85	Scott Tottle, Peterborough	
1985-86	Jason Lafreniere, Belleville	

Emms Family Award
(Rookie of the Year)

Season	Player	Club
1972-73	Dennis Maruk, London	
1973-74	Jack Valiquette, Sault Ste. Marie	
1974-75	Danny Shearer, Hamilton	
1975-76	John Travella, Sault Ste. Marie	
1976-77	Yvan Joly, Ottawa	
1977-78	Wayne Gretzky, S. S. Marie	
1978-79	John Goodwin, Sault Ste. Marie	
1979-80	Bruce Dowie, Toronto	
1980-81	Tony Tanti, Oshawa	
1981-82	Pat Verbeek, Sudbury	
1982-83	Bruce Cassidy, Ottawa	
1983-84	Shawn Burr, Kitchener	
1984-85	Derek King, Sault Ste. Marie	
1985-86	Lonnie Loach, Guelph	

Matt Leyden Trophy
(Coach of the Year)

Season	Coach	Club
1971-72	Gus Bodnar, Oshawa	
1972-73	George Armstrong, Toronto	
1973-74	Jack Bownass, Kingston	
1974-75	Bert Templeton, Hamilton	
1975-76	Jerry Toppazzini, Sudbury	
1976-77	Bill Long, London	
1977-78	Bill White, Oshawa	
1978-79	Gary Green, Peterborough	
1979-80	Dave Chambers, Toronto	
1980-81	Brian Kilrea, Ottawa	
1981-82	Brian Kilrea, Ottawa	
1982-83	Terry Crisp, Sault Ste. Marie	
1983-84	Tom Barrett, Kitchener	
1984-85	Terry Crisp, Sault Ste. Marie	
1985-86	Jacques Martin, Guelph	

Jim Mahon Memorial Trophy
(Top Scoring Right Wing)

Season	Player	Club
1971-72	Bill Harris, Toronto	
1972-73	Dennis Ververgaert, London	
1973-74	Dave Gorman, St. Catharines	
1974-75	Mark Napier, Toronto	
1975-76	Peter Lee, Ottawa	
1976-77	John Anderson, Toronto	
1977-78	Dino Ciccarelli, London	
1978-79	Mike Foligno, Sudbury	
1979-80	Jim Fox, Ottawa	
1980-81	Tony Tanti, Oshawa	
1981-82	Tony Tanti, Oshawa	
1982-83	Ian MacInnis, Cornwall	
1983-84	Wayne Presley, Kitchener	
1984-85	Dave MacLean, Belleville	
1985-86	Ray Sheppard, Cornwall	

F.W. Dinty Moore Trophy
(Lowest Average by a Rookie Goalie)

Season	Player	Club
1975-76	Mark Locken, Hamilton	
1976-77	Barry Heard, London	
1977-78	Ken Ellacott, Peterborough	
1978-79	Nick Ricci, Niagara Falls	
1979-80	Mike Vezina, Ottawa	
1980-81	John Vanbiesbrouck, Sault Ste. Marie	
1981-82	Shawn Kilroy, Peterborough	
1982-83	Dan Burrows, Belleville	
1983-84	Jerry Iuliano, Sault Ste. Marie	
1984-85	Ron Tugnutt, Peterborough	
1985-86	Paul Henriques, Belleville	

Western Hockey League

(Known as Western Canada Hockey League prior to 1978-79)

President—Ed Chynoweth
Vice-President—Richard Doerksen
Executive Assistant—Norman Dueck
616-5920 Macleod Trail S., Calgary, Alberta T2H 0K2
Phone—(403) 253-8113

Final 1985-86 WHL Standings

East Division

	G.	W.	L.	T.	Pts.	GF.	GA.
Medicine Hat Tigers	72	54	17	1	109	384	245
Prince Albert Raiders	72	52	17	3	107	424	257
Regina Pats	72	45	26	1	91	384	295
Saskatoon Blades	72	38	28	6	82	381	360
Lethbridge Broncos	72	27	42	3	57	314	379
Moose Jaw Warriors	72	25	44	3	53	294	375
Brandon Wheat Kings	72	24	46	2	50	324	438
Calgary Wranglers	72	23	47	2	48	288	378

West Division

	G.	W.	L.	T.	Pts.	GF.	GA.
Kamloops Blazers	72	49	19	4	102	449	299
Portland Winter Hawks	72	47	24	1	95	438	348
Spokane Chiefs	72	30	41	1	61	373	413
Seattle Thunderbirds	72	27	43	2	56	330	406
New Westminster Bruins	72	25	45	2	52	276	373
Victoria Cougars	72	22	49	1	45	346	439

Top 20 Scorers for the Bob Brownridge Memorial Trophy

	Games	G.	A.	Pts.	Pen.
1. Rob Brown, Kamloops	69	58	*115	*173	171
2. Simon Wheeldon, Victoria	70	61	96	157	85
3. Ken Morrison, Prince Albert	15	14	13	27	6
Kamloops	57	69	54	123	59
Totals	72	*83	67	150	65
4. Randy Smith, Saskatoon	70	60	86	146	44
5. Ken Priestlay, Victoria	72	73	72	145	45
6. Rod Matechuk, Saskatoon	72	57	78	135	93
7. Ray Podloski, Portland	66	59	75	134	68
8. Mike Nottingham, Kamloops	70	61	70	131	101
9. Craig Endean, Seattle	70	58	70	128	34
10. Dave Waldie, Portland	72	68	58	126	63
11. Tim Iannone, Regina	71	65	57	122	36
12. Byron Lomow, Brandon	72	52	67	119	77
Greg Hawgood, Kamloops	71	34	85	119	86
14. Terry Perkins, Portland	6	5	4	9	9
Spokane	63	66	42	108	65
Totals	69	71	46	117	74
15. Larry DePalma, Saskatoon	65	61	51	112	232
16. Steve Nemeth, Lethbridge	70	42	69	111	47
17. Troy Vollhoffer, Saskatoon	72	55	55	110	118
18. Theoren Fleury, Moose Jaw	72	43	65	108	124
19. Len Nielsen, Regina	66	30	77	107	49
20. Pat Elynuik, Prince Albert	68	53	53	106	62
Dale McFee, Prince Albert	72	47	59	106	104

Team-by-Team Breakdown of WHL Scoring

Brandon Wheat Kings

	Games	G.	A.	Pts.	Pen.
Byron Lomow	72	52	67	119	77
Shane Eirickson	68	3	61	64	40
Terry Yake	72	26	26	52	49
Dave Thomlinson	53	25	20	45	116
Jason Phillips	66	20	20	40	17
Jeff Waver	68	16	23	39	171
Dean Sexsmith	65	13	23	36	34
Trent Ciprick	52	13	19	32	82
Darin Kimble, Calgary	37	14	8	22	93
New Westminster	11	1	1	2	22
Brandon	15	1	6	7	39
Totals	63	16	15	31	154
Brent Mireau	60	12	19	31	29
Mike Morin	34	10	21	31	62
Brian McFarlane, Seattle	35	9	7	16	20
Brandon	19	4	5	9	4
Totals	54	13	12	25	24
Boyd Lomow	38	10	15	25	103
Lee Trim	72	0	23	23	176
Kirk Phare, Seattle	41	5	11	16	70
Brandon	18	2	2	4	20
Totals	59	7	13	20	90
Al Cherniwchan, Spo.	8	0	0	0	2
Brandon	50	9	8	17	29
Totals	58	9	8	17	31
Murray Rice	62	4	8	12	149
Trevor Semeniuk, Vic.	38	1	7	8	190
Brandon	25	1	3	4	45
Totals	63	2	10	12	235
Kevin Mayo	30	4	6	10	22
Dave German, M.J.	44	2	2	4	35
Brandon	15	0	4	4	18
Totals	59	2	6	8	53
Brad McGinnis	18	3	4	7	6
Kevin Yellowaga	8	2	1	3	0
Kevin Clayton	12	0	3	3	18
Randy Hoffart	40	0	2	2	143
Kelly Hitchens (Goalie)	48	0	1	1	8
Curtis Bateman	1	0	0	0	0
Brian Gilroy	1	0	0	0	0
Jeff Klassen	7	0	0	0	0
Gary Johnson (Goalie)	13	0	0	0	33

Calgary Wranglers

	Games	G.	A.	Pts.	Pen.
Terry Zaporzan	70	28	38	66	46
Dale Brisco	70	26	32	58	32
Al Measures	46	23	34	57	50
Ron Bonora	71	26	30	56	75
Ken Spangler	66	19	36	55	237
Erin Ginnell, New West.	22	17	13	30	14
Calgary	22	6	11	17	14
Totals	44	23	24	47	28
Mitch Cornett	70	20	22	42	82
Sean Krakiwsky	39	9	32	41	27
Mike Van Slooten	61	17	20	37	25
Cam Lazoruk	59	20	14	34	180
Rich Wiest, Lethbridge	31	5	13	18	111
Seattle	2	0	0	0	2
Calgary	23	8	3	11	74
Totals	56	13	16	29	187
Bob Wilkie	63	8	19	27	56
Kurt Lackten, M.J.	6	0	3	3	16
Medicine Hat	27	2	5	7	51
Calgary	28	3	12	15	45
Totals	61	5	20	25	112
John Heasty	72	9	14	23	93
Ed Brost	62	3	18	21	53
Kurt Woolf, P.A.	2	0	0	0	0
Seattle	12	0	1	1	14
New Westminster	32	3	4	7	31
Calgary	20	2	6	8	21
Totals	66	5	11	16	66
Terry Baustad	20	3	9	12	17
Craig Penner, M.H.	29	1	9	10	68
Calgary	11	0	2	2	16
Totals	40	1	11	12	84
Roby Goodwin	48	3	8	11	25
Roger Mulvenna	10	1	5	6	12
Doug Barber	29	2	3	5	34
Mike Dyck	69	2	3	5	79
Ray Andrews	29	2	2	4	35
Len Barrie	32	3	0	3	18
Chris Churchill	46	0	3	3	14
Bryan Bosch	6	2	0	2	5
Andrew Huculak	33	0	1	1	4
Grant McPhail (Goalie)	37	0	1	1	29
Jeff Ferguson (Goalie)	1	0	0	0	0
David Aldred	2	0	0	0	0

Kamloops Blazers

	Games	G.	A.	Pts.	Pen.
Rob Brown	69	58	*115	*173	171
Ken Morrison, P.A.	15	14	13	27	6
Kamloops	57	69	54	123	59
Totals	72	*83	67	150	65
Mike Nottingham	70	61	70	131	101
Greg Hawgood	71	34	85	119	86
Greg Evtushevski	34	29	47	76	100
Robin Bawa	63	29	43	72	78
Mark Kachowski	61	21	31	52	182
Ron Shudra	72	10	40	50	81
Len Mark	70	23	25	48	20
Doug Pickell, M.H.	8	2	4	6	11
Kamloops	62	25	16	41	101
Totals	70	27	20	47	112
Lonnie Spink	69	15	29	44	68
Troy Kennedy, M.J.	24	5	10	15	6
Kamloops	45	4	19	23	21
Totals	69	9	29	38	27
Chris Tarnowski, Victoria	41	2	16	18	80
Kamloops	25	4	6	10	26
Totals	66	6	22	28	106
Todd Carnelley	44	3	23	26	63
Peter Soberlak	55	10	11	21	46
Rudy Poeschek	32	3	13	16	92
Don Schmidt, P.A.	14	0	2	2	48
Kamloops	29	2	5	7	168
Totals	43	2	7	9	216
David Marcinyshyn	57	2	7	9	111
Pat Bingham	44	4	3	7	43
Troy Bakogeorge, M.J.	24	2	1	3	31
Kamloops	10	2	0	2	7
Totals	34	4	1	5	38
Rob McKinley (Goalie)	54	0	5	5	27
Mike Ragot	20	0	2	2	22

	Games	G.	A.	Pts.	Pen.
Randy Hansch, Vic. (G.).	26	0	2	2	6
Kamloops (G.)	5	0	0	0	0
Totals	31	0	2	2	6
Darren Stolk	33	1	1	2	9
Willie Popp (Goalie)	2	0	1	1	0
Pat Nogier (Goalie)	29	0	1	1	17
Jason Proulx	1	0	0	0	0
Darren Kwiatkowski	6	0	0	0	0
Todd Sawtell, Brandon	2	0	0	0	2
Kamloops	4	0	0	0	2
Totals	6	0	0	0	4

Lethbridge Broncos

	Games	G.	A.	Pts.	Pen.
Steve Nemeth	70	42	69	111	47
Terry Houlder	71	43	62	105	33
Dwight Mullins	72	52	37	89	99
Mario Desjardins, Sea.	41	17	30	47	64
Lethbridge	28	10	12	22	17
Totals	69	27	42	69	81
Trent Kaese	67	24	41	65	67
Warren Babe	63	33	24	57	125
Darcy Norton	69	19	25	44	69
Doug Quinn, New West.	10	1	5	6	31
Lethbridge	58	7	27	34	63
Totals	68	8	32	40	94
Mark Tinordi	58	8	30	38	139
Todd Sceviour	66	14	19	33	52
Dale Marquette	64	12	14	26	83
Matt Hervey	60	9	17	26	110
Jayson More	61	7	18	25	155
Paul More	34	8	12	20	67
Landis Chaulk, Spokane	22	6	6	12	40
Lethbridge	22	2	4	6	39
Totals	44	8	10	18	79
Ryan McGill	64	5	10	15	171
Ian Herbers, Spokane	29	1	6	7	85
Lethbridge	32	1	4	5	109
Totals	61	2	10	12	194
Terry Black	61	5	5	10	25
Gord Green	57	1	7	8	179
Mike Swanson	30	3	4	7	35
Rob Krauss	12	0	2	2	15
Jaako Pulli	17	0	2	2	2
Glen Seymour, Sea. (G.)	5	0	0	0	2
Portland (G.)	7	0	2	2	4
Lethbridge (G.)	7	0	0	0	0
Totals	19	0	2	2	6
D. Schrapp, Reg. (G.)	28	0	1	1	18
Lethbridge (G.)	15	0	1	1	28
Totals	43	0	2	2	46
Grant Thomlinson (G.)	3	0	1	1	0
Joe Sakic	3	0	0	0	0
Jeff Dobish	4	0	0	0	7
Mike Sutherland (G.)	13	0	0	0	6

Medicine Hat Tigers

	Games	G.	A.	Pts.	Pen.
Mark Pederson	72	46	60	106	46
Al Conroy	61	41	60	101	141
Guy Phillips	72	38	55	93	66
Neil Brady	72	21	60	81	104
Darren Cota	59	34	37	71	258
Dave Mackey, Kamloops	9	3	4	7	13
Medicine Hat	60	25	32	57	167
Totals	69	28	36	64	180
Craig Berube, Kamloops	32	17	14	31	119
Medicine Hat	34	14	16	30	95
Totals	66	31	30	61	214
Gord Hynes	58	22	39	61	45
Rob Dimaio, Kamloops	6	1	0	1	0
Medicine Hat	55	20	30	50	82
Totals	61	21	30	51	82
Wayne Hynes	67	26	24	50	48
Jeff Wenaas	65	20	26	46	57
Doug Houda, Calgary	16	4	10	14	60
Medicine Hat	35	9	23	32	80
Totals	51	13	33	46	140
Dale Kushner	66	25	19	44	218
Scott McGrady	65	8	25	33	114
Randy Siska	41	11	13	24	19
Mike Claringbull	69	2	15	17	123
Dean Chynoweth	69	3	12	15	208
Wayne McBean	67	1	14	15	73
Mark Kuntz	58	5	9	14	77
Steve Risling	21	2	4	6	7
Troy Gamble (Goalie)	45	0	3	3	29
Trevor Linden	5	2	0	2	0
Mike Schwengler	2	1	1	2	0
Tim Flanagan	2	0	1	1	0
Trevor Ellerman	5	0	1	1	0
Corey Cheyney	6	0	1	1	0
Mark Fitzpatrick (G.)	41	0	1	1	6
Derek Babe (Goalie)	1	0	0	0	0
Kalvin Knibbs	1	0	0	0	0
Jeff Cox	2	0	0	0	0
Brad Neumier	2	0	0	0	0

Moose Jaw Warriors

	Games	G.	A.	Pts.	Pen.
Theoren Fleury	72	43	65	108	124
Kent Hayes	72	50	42	92	39
Mike Keane	67	34	49	83	162
Troy Edwards	72	29	29	58	35
Jay Johnson	70	15	34	49	105
Garth Lamb, M.H.	6	0	4	4	15
Moose Jaw	66	13	31	44	67
Totals	72	13	35	48	82
Lyle Odelein	67	9	37	46	117
Kevin Herom	66	22	18	40	103
Kelly Buchberger	72	14	22	36	206
Trevor Hendry, Kam.	19	4	7	11	26
Moose Jaw	21	3	11	14	28
Totals	40	7	18	25	54
Garnet Kazuik	59	14	8	22	39
Neil Pogany, New West.	33	1	6	7	22
Moose Jaw	31	3	10	13	8
Totals	64	4	16	20	30
Neil Pilon	59	2	18	20	112
Robert Oberrech, Kam.	13	2	5	7	22
Seattle	17	2	1	3	36
Moose Jaw	11	4	5	9	22
Totals	41	8	11	19	80
Sean Pass, Medicine Hat	8	2	0	2	17
Kamloops	7	1	1	2	11
Moose Jaw	47	6	7	13	31
Totals	62	9	8	17	59
Pat Beauchesne, M.H.	4	0	0	0	10
Moose Jaw	64	3	13	16	116
Totals	68	3	13	16	126
Tim Logan	70	5	9	14	106
Kevin Green	43	10	3	13	13

	Games	G.	A.	Pts.	Pen.
Brent Kilpatrick, Seattle	22	2	7	9	66
Spokane	5	0	0	0	5
Moose Jaw	22	1	1	2	41
Totals	49	3	8	11	112
Corey Bealieu	68	3	1	4	111
Larry Rusconi	10	2	1	3	0
Artie Feher, Bran. (G.)	24	0	3	3	4
Moose Jaw (G.)	8	0	0	0	5
Totals	32	0	3	3	9
Jim MacKenzie	3	0	2	2	0
Chad Fleck	25	0	2	2	11
Darryl Gilmour (Goalie)	62	0	2	2	4
Todd Crowther, M.H.	5	0	1	1	0
Moose Jaw	2	0	0	0	0
Totals	7	0	1	1	0
Stacey Borger	1	0	0	0	0
Taras Diakiwski	2	0	0	0	0
Dan Pahl	3	0	0	0	4
Jerome Bechard	4	0	0	0	0
Chad Lutz	4	0	0	0	0
Dean Antos	5	0	0	0	0
Dan McKersie	5	0	0	0	0
Steve Thorne (Goalie)	14	0	0	0	0

New Westminster Bruins

	Games	G.	A.	Pts.	Pen.
Derek Laxdal, Brandon	42	34	35	69	62
New Westminster	18	9	6	15	14
Totals	60	43	41	84	76
Brent Hughes	71	28	52	80	180
Mark Recchi	72	21	40	61	55
Glenn Mulvenna	65	24	31	55	55
Todd Ewen	60	28	24	52	289
Brian Bertuzzi	47	24	24	48	58
Stuart Sage, Seattle	52	14	11	25	48
New Westminster	18	2	7	9	0
Totals	70	16	18	34	48
Gary Moscaluk	49	6	26	32	51
Tim Brantner, Lethbridge	13	0	2	2	62
New Westminster	50	6	22	28	183
Totals	63	6	24	30	245
Gerry Johannson	65	6	24	30	227
Perry Fafard, Brandon	5	0	2	2	9
New Westminster	63	17	10	27	41
Totals	68	17	12	29	50
Garth Premak	72	10	18	28	55
Mike Bafaro	35	14	11	25	85
Dean Ewen	61	7	15	22	154
R.J. Dundas	19	9	12	21	47
Alan May, Medicine Hat	6	1	0	1	25
New Westminster	32	8	9	17	81
Totals	38	9	9	18	106
Jamie Leach	58	8	7	15	20
Mike MacWilliam	52	8	6	14	98
Darwin McPherson	63	2	8	10	149
Rene Vinopal	20	2	4	6	17
Dan Baker	25	4	2	6	57
Cal Zankowski	15	3	1	4	5
Randy Wong	32	2	2	4	31
Mike Pawlenchuk	16	1	3	4	80
Gary Ruff, Lethbridge	9	1	1	2	25
New Westminster	5	1	0	1	12
Totals	14	2	1	3	37
Tony Bobbit	6	0	3	3	2
Paul Rajotte	24	0	2	2	17
Scott Farrell	4	1	0	1	9

	Games	G.	A.	Pts.	Pen.
Al Marin	4	1	0	1	18
Ron Bhala	5	1	0	1	0
Jeff Brooks	3	0	1	1	0
Doneau Menard	7	0	1	1	5
Drago Adam, Leth. (G.)	1	0	0	0	0
New West. (G.)	29	0	1	1	6
Totals	30	0	1	1	6
Bill Ranford (Goalie)	53	0	1	1	23
Mike Catchpole	1	0	0	0	7
Brad Moore	1	0	0	0	0
Darryl Regier	1	0	0	0	0
Scott Thomas	1	0	0	0	0
Reid Simpson	2	0	0	0	0
Chris Marcil	3	0	0	0	0
Wayne Labrie (Goalie)	4	0	0	0	7
Chris Weseen	4	0	0	0	5
Chris Furey	9	0	0	0	0

Portland Winter Hawks

	Games	G.	A.	Pts.	Pen.
Ray Podloski	66	59	75	134	68
Dave Waldie	72	68	58	126	63
Dan Woodley	62	45	47	92	100
Glen Wesley	69	16	75	91	96
Dave McLay	70	37	49	86	219
Blaine Chrest	71	29	57	86	7
Jeff Finley	70	11	59	70	83
Bob Fogliotta	57	36	32	68	49
Dave Archibald	70	29	35	64	56
Walter Shutter	71	25	31	56	130
Jamie Nicolls	65	15	37	52	60
Ron Jones	71	22	26	48	113
Jim Agnew	70	6	30	36	386
James Latos, Saskatoon	40	4	7	11	111
Portland	21	6	7	13	80
Totals	61	10	14	24	191
Troy Arndt	63	3	20	23	288
Doug Wieck	37	5	14	19	40
Brian Gerrits	40	8	7	15	24
Jay Stark, Spokane	8	0	2	2	13
Portland	61	2	11	13	102
Totals	69	2	13	15	115
Jeff Sharples, Spokane	3	0	0	0	4
Portland	19	2	6	8	44
Totals	22	2	6	8	48
Troy Mick	6	2	5	7	2
Tye Cameron	52	0	6	6	102
Dennis Holland	1	3	2	5	0
Bruce Basken	47	1	4	5	32
Lance Carlsen (Goalie)	40	0	1	1	28
Tyler Sunday	3	0	0	0	9
Chris Eisenhart (Goalie)	36	0	0	0	33

Prince Albert Raiders

	Games	G.	A.	Pts.	Pen.
Pat Elynuik	68	53	53	106	62
Dale McFee	72	47	59	106	104
Scott Kruger	72	26	80	106	22
Steve Gotaas	61	40	61	101	31
Ryan Stewart, Kamloops	10	7	11	18	27
Prince Albert	52	45	33	78	55
Totals	62	52	44	96	82
Emanuel Viveiros	57	22	70	92	30
Tony Grenier	52	42	37	79	16
Kim Issel	68	29	39	68	41

	Games	G.	A.	Pts.	Pen.
David Manson	70	14	34	48	177
Rod Dallman	59	20	21	41	198
Collin Feser	71	17	22	39	119
Kevin Todd	55	14	25	39	19
Curtis Hunt	72	5	29	34	108
Dean Braham	63	16	17	33	158
Ken Baumgartner	70	4	23	27	277
Dean Kolstad, N. West.	16	0	5	5	19
Prince Albert	54	2	15	17	80
Totals	70	2	20	22	99
Doug Hobson	66	2	17	19	70
Gord Kruppke	62	1	8	9	81
Maurizio Scudier	9	4	3	7	10
Andy Kenning	44	1	6	7	18
Rod Kavanaugh	26	4	1	5	13
Roydon Gunn (Goalie)	51	0	5	5	6
Kenton Rein (Goalie)	23	0	3	3	4
Wayde Bucsis	7	1	1	2	0
George Bodnar	3	1	0	1	5
Allan Wonitowy	1	0	1	1	0
Scott Frizzell	5	0	1	1	2
Randy Lewis	2	0	0	0	5
Paul Sutcliffe	2	0	0	0	0
Todd Nelson	4	0	0	0	0
Richard Pilon	6	0	0	0	0
Joey Johannson	7	0	0	0	2

Regina Pats

	Games	G.	A.	Pts.	Pen.
Tim Iannone	71	65	57	122	36
Len Nielsen	66	30	77	107	49
Allan Acton	62	44	45	89	52
Bryan Wells	62	22	63	85	283
Robert Dirk	72	19	60	79	140
Brent Fedyk	50	43	34	77	47
Brad Lauer	57	36	38	74	69
Mark Janssens	71	25	38	63	146
Kevin Clemens	71	26	32	58	70
Selmar Odelein	36	13	28	41	57
Brad Hornung	64	17	18	35	42
Kevin Ekdahl	65	8	18	26	40
Kevin Kuntz	64	5	12	17	34
Terry Lloyd	51	4	13	17	132
Gerald Bzdel	72	2	15	17	107
Brad Miller	71	2	14	16	99
Ken McIntyre	60	4	10	14	82
Shawn Byram	46	7	6	13	45
Frank Joo	22	1	8	9	39
Lawrence Siccia	61	4	2	6	186
Gary Dickie	26	3	3	6	10
Bob Heeney, Brandon	31	1	5	6	139
Regina	6	0	0	0	29
Totals	37	1	5	6	168
Greg Hubert, Leth. (G.)	44	0	2	2	21
Regina (G.)	14	0	0	0	2
Totals	58	0	2	2	23
Jamie Dubberley (G.)	14	0	1	1	0
Stacey Nickel, Spo. (G.)	10	0	0	0	4
Regina (G.)	22	0	1	1	6
Totals	32	0	1	1	10
Scott Smith	1	0	0	0	0
Troy Frederick	2	0	0	0	0
Kirby Lindal	3	0	0	0	7
Kelly Handy	10	0	0	0	13

Saskatoon Blades

	Games	G.	A.	Pts.	Pen.
Randy Smith	70	60	86	146	44
Rod Matechuk	72	57	78	135	93
Larry DePalma	65	61	51	112	232
Troy Vollhoffer	72	55	55	110	118
Duncan MacPherson	70	10	54	64	147
Mike Bukta, Seattle	30	5	29	34	34
Saskatoon	28	4	25	29	36
Totals	58	9	54	63	70
Tracey Katelnikoff, Vic.	4	1	0	1	2
Saskatoon	60	25	25	50	63
Totals	64	26	25	51	65
Grant Tkachuk	52	18	27	45	82
Jack Bowkus	56	10	31	41	54
Bryan Larkin	66	8	24	32	94
Brian Glynn	66	7	25	32	131
Kelly Chase	57	7	18	25	172
Shawn Van Allen	55	12	11	23	43
Kerry Clark, Regina	23	4	4	8	58
Saskatoon	39	5	8	13	104
Totals	62	9	12	21	162
Todd McLellan	27	9	10	19	13
Curtis Chamberlin	60	7	10	17	119
Mark Holick	60	6	11	17	137
Devon Oleniuk	70	4	12	16	104
Trent Kachur	63	0	16	16	124
Blair Atcheynum	19	1	4	5	22
Marty Prazma	33	2	2	4	53
Blaine Gusdal	34	0	4	4	50
Mark Reimer (Goalie)	41	0	4	4	31
Kevin Kaminski	4	1	1	2	35
Dean Holoien	1	1	0	1	0
Tim Cheveldae (Goalie)	36	0	1	1	8
Curtis Leschyshyn	1	0	0	0	0
Greg Nelson	1	0	0	0	0

Seattle Thunderbirds

	Games	G.	A.	Pts.	Pen.
Craig Endean	70	58	70	128	34
John Dzikowski, Bran.	44	35	20	55	72
Seattle	25	18	15	33	38
Totals	69	53	35	88	110
Brad Melin	42	23	53	76	14
Darryl Daignault, Cal.	43	16	23	39	74
Seattle	29	12	17	29	36
Totals	72	28	40	68	110
Kelly Para	66	21	44	65	60
Ray Savard	71	32	22	54	180
Dave Curry, Brandon	31	16	24	40	12
Seattle	15	7	6	13	2
Totals	46	23	30	53	14
Larry Bernard	54	17	25	42	72
Glen Goodall	65	13	28	41	53
Brent Severyn, Sask.	9	1	4	5	38
Seattle	33	11	20	31	164
Totals	42	12	24	36	202
Jim Bechtold	63	16	19	35	183
Darren Taylor, Calgary	41	9	11	20	83
Seattle	27	2	8	10	54
Totals	68	11	19	30	137
Jamie Huscroft	66	6	20	26	394
Scott Neely	31	10	12	22	4
Kevin Lowalchuk, Sask.	14	1	9	10	6
Seattle	31	5	7	12	8
Totals	45	6	16	22	14

	Games	G.	A.	Pts.	Pen.
Rod Taylor, Saskatoon ..	22	5	5	10	53
Seattle	23	4	5	9	87
Totals	45	9	10	19	140
Rob Dumas	68	4	11	15	121
Chris Joseph	72	4	8	12	50
Lloyd Cox	56	2	6	8	51
Cy Laflamme	16	3	4	7	27
Dennis Carignan	41	2	5	7	40
Rick Fry	6	2	1	3	2
Troy Kaye	18	2	1	3	27
Gary Grant	20	1	2	3	50
Larry Dyck (Goalie)	56	0	3	3	4
Darryl Mitchell, N. W. ...	2	0	0	0	0
Seattle	12	0	2	2	5
Totals	14	0	2	2	5
Mickey Doner	5	1	0	1	0
Scott Peace (Goalie)	15	0	1	1	4
Mike Behm (Goalie)	1	0	0	0	0
Victor Gervais	1	0	0	0	0
Dan Lorenz	1	0	0	0	0
Randy Zulinick	1	0	0	0	0
Shawn Ramstead	2	0	0	0	0
Jim Richards, Brandon ...	1	0	0	0	0
Seattle	1	0	0	0	0
Totals	2	0	0	0	0
Don Henderson	3	0	0	0	0

Spokane Chiefs

	Games	G.	A.	Pts.	Pen.
Terry Perkins, Portland ..	6	5	4	9	9
Spokane	63	66	42	108	65
Totals	69	71	46	117	74
Jeff Rohlicek	57	50	52	102	39
Rocky Dundas	71	31	70	101	160
Brent Gilchrist	52	45	45	90	57
Grant Delcourt	67	39	51	90	154
Marc Zeitlin	54	8	48	56	50
Mark Wingerter	61	23	30	53	83
Mike Berger, Lethbridge	21	2	9	11	39
Spokane	36	7	31	38	36
Totals	57	9	40	49	75
Tony Horacek	64	19	28	47	129
Dan Holden	52	21	21	42	32
Rick Herbert, Portland ...	42	2	19	21	60
Spokane	29	2	18	20	72
Totals	71	4	37	41	132
Mick Vukota	64	19	14	33	369
Dwaine Hutton	20	10	21	31	35
Judson Innes	66	7	17	24	7
Todd Voshell, Portland ..	5	1	1	2	22
Spokane	61	2	18	20	174
Totals	66	3	19	22	196
Skot Jorgenson	70	1	19	20	128
Sean Lebrun	70	6	11	17	41
Pat Seely	47	2	13	15	40
Mike Wegleitner	13	0	8	8	12
Trevor Jobe, Calgary ...	7	0	2	2	2
Lethbridge	5	1	0	1	0
Spokane	11	1	4	5	0
Totals	23	2	6	8	2
Greg Delcourt	66	3	5	8	48
Pat Loyer	6	1	5	6	8
Darcy Loewen	8	2	1	3	19
W. Flaherty, Sea. (G.) ...	9	0	1	1	0
Spokane (G.)	5	0	0	0	0
Totals	14	0	1	1	0
Jerry Iuliano (Goalie)	15	0	1	1	0
Kelly Kozack, M. J.	4	0	0	0	10
Spokane	8	0	1	1	8
Totals	12	0	1	1	18
J. Degirolamo, Vic. (G.) .	9	0	0	0	0
Spokane (G.)	9	0	0	0	0
Totals	18	0	0	0	0
Ross Elm	3	0	0	0	0
Bob MacKenzie	5	0	0	0	13

Victoria Cougars

	Games	G.	A.	Pts.	Pen.
Simon Wheeldon	70	61	96	157	85
Ken Priestlay	72	73	72	145	45
Adam Morrison	53	35	53	88	56
Korey Sundstrom	72	22	44	66	65
Chris Calverley	66	21	37	58	81
Kevin Evans	66	16	39	55	*441
Greg Batters	71	27	26	53	164
Ron Viglasi, Spokane	15	1	18	19	8
Victoria	27	9	15	24	14
Totals	42	10	33	43	22
Will Anderson, Kam.	42	1	18	19	69
Victoria	29	4	18	22	44
Totals	71	5	36	41	113
Jim Kambeitz, Kamloops	34	4	11	15	115
Victoria	26	12	12	24	32
Totals	60	16	23	39	147
Rod Williams, N. W.	1	0	0	0	0
Brandon	37	8	18	26	55
Victoria	29	7	6	13	88
Totals	67	15	24	39	143
Bill Gregoire	41	13	19	32	122
Tim Maracle	60	10	21	31	219
Dan Sexton	66	4	20	24	87
Marty Volcan	50	4	15	19	144
Dan Logan	57	5	9	14	19
Bruce Courtnall	44	5	7	12	51
Aaron Nosky, Spokane .	32	0	7	7	15
Victoria	30	1	3	4	11
Totals	62	1	10	11	26
Peter Schmid	64	2	8	10	29
Mike Aivazoff	27	3	4	7	25
Darryl Williams	38	3	2	5	66
Richard Lindstrom	30	1	3	4	74
Greg Davies	3	2	0	2	2
Bruce Pritchard	4	0	2	2	0
Sean Stotts	6	0	2	2	2
Peter Fry, Spokane (G.) .	1	0	0	0	0
Victoria (G.)	14	0	2	2	2
Totals	15	0	2	2	2
Kodie Nelson	22	1	1	2	48
Steve Hamilton	2	0	1	1	2
Jamie Barnett	3	0	1	1	0
Russ Goglin	6	1	0	1	10
Jody Gonek	7	0	1	1	28
Daryn Sivertson, Kam. ...	3	0	1	1	2
Victoria	8	0	0	0	2
Totals	11	0	1	1	4
Mike Doyle (Goalie)	33	0	1	1	4
Sean Crowther	1	0	0	0	0
Darren Matias	3	0	0	0	2
Dean Cook (Goalie)	3	0	0	0	0
Mika Hamalainen	15	0	0	0	20

Complete WHL Individual Goaltending

	Games	Mins.	Goals	SO.	Avg.
Gary Johnson	13	553	44(1)	0	4.77
Kelly Hitchins	48	2605	266	0	6.13
Artie Feher (a)	24	1191	126(1)	0	6.35
Brandon Totals	72	4349	438	0	6.04
Chris Churchill	46	2549	192(2)	0	4.52
Grant McPhail	37	1788	178(1)	0	5.97
Jeff Ferguson	1	40	5	0	7.50
Calgary Totals	72	4377	378	0	5.18
Willie Popp	2	72	3	0	2.50
Rob McKinley	54	2817	184(2)	*2	3.92
Randy Hansch (b)	5	298	20(2)	0	4.02
Pat Nogier	29	1179	86(2)	1	4.38
Kamloops Totals	72	4366	299	3	4.11
Dennis Schrapp (c)	15	814	59	0	4.35
Greg Hubert (d)	44	2518	197(2)	1	4.69
Glen Seymour (e)	7	320	35	0	6.57
Mike Sutherland	13	529	62	0	7.03
Grant Thomlinson	3	160	19	0	7.13
Drago Adam (f)	1	36	5	0	8.33
Lethbridge Totals	72	4377	379	1	5.20
Derek Babe	1	1	0	0	0.00
Mark Fitzpatrick	41	2074	99(4)	1	*2.86
Troy Gamble	45	2264	142	0	3.76
Medicine Hat Totals	72	4339	245	1	3.39
Darryl Gilmour	*62	*3482	*276(3)	1	4.76
Artie Feher (a)	8	424	40	0	5.66
Steve Thorne	14	459	55(1)	0	7.19
Moose Jaw Totals	72	4365	375	1	5.15
Bill Ranford	53	2791	225(1)	1	4.84
Drago Adam (f)	29	1489	137	0	5.52
Wayne Labrie	4	86	10	0	6.98
New Westminster Totals	72	4366	373	1	5.13
Lance Carlsen	40	2129	159(4)	0	4.48
Chris Eisenhart	36	1831	147(2)	0	4.82
Glen Seymour (e)	7	383	36	0	5.64
Portland Totals	72	4343	348	0	4.81
Kenton Rein	23	1302	71(2)	0	3.27
Roydon Gunn	51	3051	183(1)	*2	3.60
Prince Albert Totals	72	4353	257	2	3.54
Stacey Nickel (g)	22	1268	74(3)	1	3.50
Greg Hubert (d)	14	799	49(1)	0	3.68
Dennis Schrapp (c)	28	1568	113	0	4.32
Jamie Dubberley	14	710	54(1)	0	4.56
Regina Totals	72	4345	295	1	4.07
Mark Reimer	41	2362	192(2)	0	4.88
Tim Cheveldae	36	2030	165(1)	0	4.88
Saskatoon Totals	72	4392	360	0	4.92
Mike Behm	1	47	3	0	3.83
Larry Dyck	56	3096	264(4)	*2	5.12
Glen Seymour (e)	5	208	18	0	5.19
Scott Peace	15	746	81	0	6.51
Wade Flaherty (j)	9	271	36	0	7.97
Seattle Totals	72	4368	406	2	5.58
Darcy Wakaluk	47	2562	224	1	5.25
Jerry Iuliano	15	800	72(3)	0	5.40
Peter Fry (h)	1	60	6	0	6.00
Stacey Nickel (g)	10	447	45	0	6.04
Joe Degirolamo (i)	9	315	41	0	7.81
Wade Flaherty (j)	5	161	21(1)	0	7.84
Spokane Totals	72	4345	413	1	5.70
Mike Doyle	33	1679	151(1)	0	5.40
Randy Hansch (b)	26	1523	152(2)	0	5.99
Peter Fry (h)	14	610	63(2)	0	6.19
Joe Degirolamo (i)	9	382	45	0	7.07
Dean Cook	3	145	23	0	9.52
Victoria Totals	72	4339	439	0	6.07

( )—Empty Net Goals. Do not count against a goaltender's average.
(a)—Feher went from Brandon to Moose Jaw.
(b)—Hansch went from Victoria to Kamloops.
(c)—Schrapp went from Regina to Lethbridge.
(d)—Hubert went from Lethbridge to Regina.
(e)—Seymour went from Seattle to Portland to Lethbridge.
(f)—Adam went from Lethbridge to New Westminster.
(g)—Nickel went from Spokane to Regina.
(h)—Fry went from Spokane to Victoria.
(i)—Degirolano went from Victoria to Spokane.
(j)—Flaherty went from Seattle to Spokane.

Individual WHL Regular-Season Leaders

Goals	Ken Morrison, Kamloops—	83
Assists	Rob Brown, Kamloops—	115
Points	Rob Brown, Kamloops—	173
Penalty Minutes	Kevin Evans, Victoria—	441
Goaltender's Average	Mark Fitzpatrick, Medicine Hat—	2.86
Shutouts	Roydon Gunn, Prince Albert—	2

1986 WHL Playoffs

East Division Quarterfinal Round-Robin Standings
(Top four teams advance to semifinals)

	G.	W.	L.	T.	Pts.	GF.	GA.
Prince Albert	10	9	1	0	18	59	22
Medicine Hat	10	8	2	0	16	47	33
Saskatoon	10	7	3	0	14	56	39
Moose Jaw	10	4	6	0	8	47	58
Lethbridge	10	1	9	0	2	34	63
Regina	10	1	9	0	2	31	59

West Division Semifinals
(Best-of-nine series)

Series "A"

	W.	L.	Pts.	GF.	GA.
Portland	5	4	10	45	43
Spokane	4	5	8	43	45

(Portland wins series, 5 games to 4)

Series "B"

	W.	L.	Pts.	GF.	GA.
Kamloops	5	0	10	39	17
Seattle	0	5	0	17	39

(Kamloops wins series, 5 games to 0)

East Division Semifinals
(Best-of-five series)

Series "C"

	W.	L.	Pts.	GF.	GA.
Prince Albert	3	0	6	15	3
Saskatoon	0	3	0	3	15

(Prince Albert wins series, 3 games to 0)

Series "D"

	W.	L.	Pts.	GF.	GA.
Medicine Hat	3	0	6	20	8
Moose Jaw	0	3	0	8	20

(Medicine Hat wins series, 3 games to 0)

West Division Finals
(Best-of-nine series)

Series "E"

	W.	L.	Pts.	GF.	GA.
Kamloops	5	1	10	39	17
Portland	1	5	2	17	39

(Kamloops wins series, 5 games to 1)

East Division Finals
(Best-of-seven series)

Series "F"

	W.	L.	Pts.	GF.	GA.
Medicine Hat	4	3	8	22	25
Prince Albert	3	4	6	25	22

(Medicine Hat wins series, 4 games to 3)

Western Hockey League Playoff Finals
(Best-of-seven series)

Series "G"

	W.	L.	Pts.	GF.	GA.
Kamloops	4	1	8	25	13
Medicine Hat	1	4	2	13	25

(Kamloops wins WHL Playoffs, 4 games to 1)

Top 10 WHL Playoff Scorers

	Games	G.	A.	Pts.	Pen.
1. Rob Brown, Kamloops	16	*18	*28	*46	14
2. Ken Morrison, Kamloops	16	12	25	37	15
3. Al Conroy, Medicine Hat	25	11	20	31	54
Greg Hawgood, Kamloops	16	9	22	31	16
5. Greg Evtushevski, Kamloops	16	11	18	29	53
6. Emanuel Viveiros, Prince Albert	20	4	24	28	4
7. Rod Matechuk, Saskatoon	13	11	13	24	10
8. Tony Grenier, Prince Albert	19	14	9	23	20
Guy Phillips, Medicine Hat	25	10	13	23	7
Gord Hynes, Medicine Hat	25	8	15	23	32
Scott Kruger, Prince Albert	20	5	18	23	16
Doug Houda, Medicine Hat	25	4	19	23	64

Team-by-Team Playoff Scoring

Kamloops Blazers
(Winners of 1986 WHL Playoffs)

	Games	G.	A.	Pts.	Pen.
Rob Brown	16	*18	*28	*46	14
Ken Morrison	16	12	25	37	15
Greg Hawgood	16	9	22	31	16
Greg Evtushevski	16	11	18	29	53
Mike Nottingham	13	11	9	20	10
Robin Bawa	16	5	13	18	4
Mark Kachowski	16	7	8	15	57
Len Mark	16	9	4	13	0
Ron Shudra	16	1	11	12	11
Rudy Poeschek	16	3	7	10	40
Todd Carnelley	16	3	6	9	20
Troy Kennedy	16	3	5	8	9
Barry Kress	15	5	2	7	23
Doug Pickell	16	1	6	7	25
Lonnie Spink	16	2	4	6	13
Chris Tarnowski	16	1	4	5	19
Don Schmidt	12	0	4	4	57
David Marcinyshyn	16	1	2	3	12
Peter Soberlak	3	1	1	2	9
Randy Hansch (Goalie)	14	0	2	2	0
Pat Bingham	1	0	0	0	4
Rob McKinley (Goalie)	3	0	0	0	0
Mike Ragot	4	0	0	0	6

Medicine Hat Tigers
(Lost WHL finals to Kamloops, 4 games to 1)

	Games	G.	A.	Pts.	Pen.
Al Conroy	25	11	20	31	54
Guy Phillips	25	10	13	23	7
Gord Hynes	25	8	15	23	32
Doug Houda	25	4	19	23	64
Neil Brady	21	9	11	20	23
Mark Pederson	25	12	6	18	25
Jeff Wenaas	25	7	10	17	20
Darren Cota	20	8	8	16	52
Craig Berube	25	7	8	15	102
Rob Dimaio	22	6	6	12	39
Dave Mackey	25	6	3	9	72
Mike Claringbull	24	1	8	9	65
Wayne Hynes	24	4	4	8	11
Scott McCrady	25	0	7	7	67
Randy Siska	22	3	3	6	12
Wayne McBean	25	1	5	6	36
Dean Chynoweth	17	3	2	5	52
Dale Kushner	25	0	5	5	*114
Mark Kuntz	17	1	1	2	2
Trevor Linden	6	1	0	1	0
Troy Gamble (Goalie)	11	0	1	1	2
Mark Fitzpatrick (G.)	19	0	1	1	14
Byron Witkowski	2	0	0	0	8

Lethbridge Broncos
(Was eliminated in round-robin play)

	Games	G.	A.	Pts.	Pen.
Steve Nemeth	10	5	5	10	6
Darcy Norton	10	2	7	9	0
Trent Kaese	10	5	3	8	9
Terry Houlder	10	3	5	8	8
Dale Marquette	10	4	3	7	12
Matt Hervey	10	3	4	7	30
Dwight Mullins	10	3	4	7	12
Todd Sceviour	10	3	4	7	10
Mario Desjardins	8	2	3	5	2
Mark Tinordi	8	1	3	4	15
Dennis Schrapp (Goalie)	9	0	4	4	2
Terry Black	10	1	2	3	12
Doug Quinn	10	0	3	3	9
Rob Krauss	10	1	1	2	6
Jayson More	9	0	2	2	36
Ian Herbers	10	1	0	1	37
Ryan McGill	10	0	1	1	9
M. Sutherland (Goalie)	2	0	0	0	0
Mike Swainson	4	0	0	0	4
Gord Green	8	0	0	0	28

Moose Jaw Warriors
(Lost East Division semifinals to Medicine Hat, 3 games to 0)

	Games	G.	A.	Pts.	Pen.
Theoren Fleury	13	7	13	20	16
Kent Hayes	13	6	10	16	2
Kelly Buchberger	13	11	4	15	37
Mike Keane	13	6	8	14	8
Garth Lamb	13	2	9	11	7
Troy Edwards	13	5	5	10	11
Neil Pogany	13	1	7	8	0
Garnet Kazuik	11	4	3	7	7
Lyle Odelein	13	1	6	7	34
Kevin Herom	13	3	3	6	19
Robert Oberrech	13	3	3	6	23
Jay Johnson	12	2	3	5	8
Sean Pass	12	1	1	2	7
Corey Beaulieu	13	1	1	2	13
Neil Pilon	13	1	1	2	19
Pat Beauchesne	13	0	2	2	23

	Games	G.	A.	Pts.	Pen.
Kevin Green	6	1	0	1	7
Brent Kilpatrick	7	0	1	1	10
Tim Logan	13	0	1	1	26
Dan McKersie	4	0	0	0	0
Artie Feher (Goalie)	6	0	0	0	0
Darryl Gilmour (Goalie)	9	0	0	0	0

Portland Winter Hawks

(Lost West Division finals to Kamloops, 5 games to 1)

	Games	G.	A.	Pts.	Pen.
Dave Waldie	15	13	6	19	8
Glen Wesley	15	3	11	14	29
Dave Archibald	15	6	7	13	11
Bob Foglietta	15	7	5	12	8
Jamie Nicolls	15	2	10	12	7
Dennis Holland	11	3	8	11	2
Ray Podloski	7	1	9	10	8
Dave McLay	15	6	3	9	30
Walter Shutter	15	5	3	8	34
Blaine Chrest	8	4	4	8	0
Jeff Sharples	15	2	6	8	6
Jeff Finley	15	1	7	8	16
Dan Woodley	12	0	8	8	31
Troy Mick	15	4	3	7	0
Ron Jones	15	2	4	6	40
Jay Stark	15	1	5	6	10
James Latos	9	1	1	2	32
Tye Cameron	6	1	0	1	2
Chris Eisenhart (Goalie)	7	0	1	1	0
Jim Agnew	9	0	1	1	48
Troy Arndt	9	0	1	1	49
Brian Gerrits	9	0	1	1	7
Bruce Basken	1	0	0	0	0
Sean Clouston	1	0	0	0	0
Doug Wieck	8	0	0	0	0
Lance Carlsen (Goalie)	13	0	0	0	14

Regina Pats

(Was eliminated in round-robin play)

	Games	G.	A.	Pts.	Pen.
Tim Iannone	10	5	7	12	0
Brad Lauer	10	4	5	9	2
Len Nielsen	10	4	4	8	6
Robert Dirk	10	3	5	8	8
Selmar Odelein	8	5	2	7	24
Bryan Wells	10	4	3	7	63
Kevin Clemens	9	1	4	5	6
Brad Hornung	10	2	2	4	11
Lawrence Siccia	9	1	2	3	26
Gerald Bzdel	10	0	3	3	14
Ken McIntyre	9	1	1	2	25
Brad Miller	10	1	1	2	4
Mark Janssens	9	0	2	2	17
Brent Fedyk	5	0	1	1	0
Shawn Byram	9	0	1	1	11
Gary Dickie	10	0	1	1	7
Frank Joo	10	0	1	1	19
Kevin Ekdahl	6	0	0	0	4
Greg Hubert (Goalie)	6	0	0	0	0
Kelly Handy	7	0	0	0	11
Stacey Nickel (Goalie)	7	0	0	0	0
Terry Lloyd	8	0	0	0	15

Prince Albert Raiders

(Lost East Division finals to Medicine Hat, 4 games to 3)

	Games	G.	A.	Pts.	Pen.
Emanuel Viveiros	20	4	24	28	4
Tony Grenier	19	14	9	23	20
Scott Kruger	20	5	18	23	16
Steve Gotaas	20	8	14	22	8
Pat Elynuik	20	7	9	16	17
Ryan Stewart	15	7	8	15	21
Dean Braham	20	7	6	13	53
Kevin Todd	20	7	6	13	29
Kim Issel	19	6	7	13	6
Collin Feser	20	4	8	12	37
Ken Baumgartner	20	3	9	12	112
Rod Dallman	20	6	4	10	105
Curtis Hunt	18	2	8	10	28
David Manson	20	1	8	9	63
Dean Kolstad	20	5	3	8	26
Gord Kruppke	20	4	4	8	22
Dale McFee	5	4	1	5	4
Scott Frizzell	5	2	2	4	7
Wayde Bucsis	9	2	1	3	2
Doug Hobson	20	1	1	2	31
Rod Kavanaugh	4	0	2	2	5
Andy Kenning	1	0	1	1	0
Richard Pilon	5	0	1	1	10
Kenton Rein (Goalie)	6	0	1	1	4
Roydon Gunn (Goalie)	15	0	0	0	8

Saskatoon Blades

(Lost East Division semifinals to Prince Albert, 3 games to 0)

	Games	G.	A.	Pts.	Pen.
Rod Matechuk	13	11	13	24	10
Troy Vollhoffer	13	8	10	18	20
Larry DePalma	13	7	9	16	58
Randy Smith	9	4	9	13	4
Todd McLellan	13	9	3	12	8
Shawn Van Allen	13	4	8	12	28
Duncan MacPherson	13	3	8	11	38
Jack Bowkus	12	0	8	8	2
Kelly Chase	10	3	4	7	37
Tracey Katelnikoff	13	3	4	7	7
Mike Bukta	11	2	4	6	14
Bryan Larkin	11	0	5	5	12
Kerry Clark	13	2	2	4	33
Grant Tkachuk	12	1	3	4	15
Marty Prazma	12	0	4	4	11
Curtis Chamberlin	12	2	1	3	19
Trent Kachur	12	0	3	3	30
Brian Glynn	13	0	3	3	30
Devon Oleniuk	6	0	2	2	2
Mark Holick	7	0	1	1	14
Kevin Kaminski	2	0	0	0	5
Mark Reimer (Goalie)	5	0	0	0	0
Tim Cheveldae (Goalie)	8	0	0	0	2

Seattle Thunderbirds

(Lost West Division semifinals to Kamloops, 5 games to 0)

	Games	G.	A.	Pts.	Pen.
Craig Endean	5	5	1	6	0
Kelly Para	5	3	1	4	4

	Games	G.	A.	Pts.	Pen.
Jim Bechtold	5	1	3	4	14
Larry Bernard	5	1	3	4	10
Dave Curry	5	1	3	4	4
Brent Severyn	5	0	4	4	4
Scott Neely	5	2	1	3	0
Ray Savard	5	1	2	3	6
Chris Joseph	5	0	3	3	12
John Dzikowski	5	2	0	2	4
Glen Goodall	4	1	1	2	0
Brad Melin	2	0	1	1	0
Dennis Carignan	4	0	1	1	2
Darryl Daignault	4	0	1	1	11
Jamie Huscroft	5	0	1	1	18
Lloyd Cox	1	0	0	0	0
Darryl Mitchell	2	0	0	0	2
Scott Peace (Goalie)	2	0	0	0	0
Rick Fry	3	0	0	0	0
Robert Dumas	5	0	0	0	24
Larry Dyck (Goalie)	5	0	0	0	0
Kevin Kowalchuk	5	0	0	0	0
Darren Taylor	5	0	0	0	8

Spokane Chiefs

(Lost West Division semifinals to Portland, 5 games to 4)

	Games	G.	A.	Pts.	Pen.
Brent Gilchrist	9	6	7	13	19
Grant Delcourt	9	8	2	10	34
Mick Vukota	9	6	4	10	68
Tony Horacek	9	4	5	9	29
Jeff Rohlicek	9	6	2	8	16
Mark Wingerter	9	3	4	7	2
Rocky Dundas	9	2	5	7	28
Terry Perkins	9	2	5	7	24
Dan Holden	9	1	6	7	6
Judson Innes	9	3	3	6	4
Mike Berger	9	1	5	6	14
Marc Zeitlin	9	1	4	5	8
Skot Jorgenson	9	0	3	3	16
Sean Lebrun	9	0	3	3	7
Pat Seely	9	0	3	3	6
Todd Voshell	9	0	3	3	18
Rick Herbert	9	0	1	1	8
Jerry Iuliano (Goalie)	2	0	0	0	0
Darcy Wakaluk (Goalie)	7	0	0	0	0
Greg Delcourt	9	0	0	0	9

Complete WHL Playoff Goaltending

	Games	Mins.	Goals	SO.	Avg.
Randy Hansch	14	820	36	1	2.63
Rob McKinley	3	189	11	0	3.49
Kamloops Totals	17	1009	47	1	2.79
Dennis Schrapp	9	523	51(1)	0	5.85
Mike Sutherland	2	80	11	0	8.25
Lethbridge Totals	11	603	63	0	6.27
Troy Gamble	11	530	31(1)	0	3.51
Mark Fitzpatrick	*19	986	58(1)	0	3.53
Medicine Hat	30	1516	91	0	3.60
Artie Feher	6	317	30	0	5.68
Darryl Gilmour	9	490	48	0	5.88
Moose Jaw Totals	15	807	78	0	5.80
Lance Carlsen	13	649	57(2)	0	5.27
Chris Eisenhart	7	249	23	0	5.54
Portland Totals	20	898	82	0	5.48
Kenton Rein	6	308	4	2	*0.78
Roydon Gunn	15	*915	43	0	2.82
Prince Albert Totals	21	1223	47	2	2.31
Greg Hubert	6	269	24(1)	0	5.35
Stacey Nickel	7	330	34	0	6.18
Regina Totals	13	599	59	0	5.91
Tim Cheveldae	8	480	29	0	3.63
Mark Reimer	5	300	25	0	5.00
Saskatoon Totals	13	780	54	0	4.15
Scott Peace	2	93	9	0	5.81
Larry Dyck	5	238	30	0	7.56
Seattle Totals	7	331	39	0	7.07
Jerry Iuliano	2	120	7	0	3.50
Darcy Wakaluk	7	419	37(1)	0	5.30
Spokane Totals	9	539	45	0	5.01

( )—Empty Net Goals. Do not count against a goaltender's average.

Individual WHL Playoff Leaders

Goals	Rob Brown, Kamloops—	18
Assists	Rob Brown, Kamloops—	18
Points	Rob Brown, Kamloops—	46
Penalty Minutes	Dale Kushner, Medicine Hat—	114
Goaltender's Average (60 minutes)	Kenton Rein, Prince Albert—	0.78
Shutouts	Kenton Rein, Prince Albert—	2

★★★

1985-86 WHL All-Star Teams

East Division		West Division
First Team	Position	Second Team
Darryl Gilmour, Moose Jaw	Goal	Larry Dyck, Seattle
Emanuel Viveiros, Prince Albert	Defense	Glen Wesley, Portland
Ken Spangler, Calgary	Defense	Jim Agnew, Portland
		Greg Hawgood, Kamloops
Al Conroy, Medicine Hat	Center	Rob Brown, Kamloops
Tim Iannone, Regina	Left Wing	Dave Waldie, Portland
Pat Elynuik, Prince Albert	Right Wing	Ken Morrison, Kamloops

★★★

1986 WHL Trophy Winners

Top Defenseman	Emanuel Viveiros, Prince Albert (East Division)
	Glen Wesley, Portland (West Division)
Frank Boucher Memorial Trophy (Most Gentlemanly)	Randy Smith, Saskatoon (East Division)
	Ken Morrison, Kamloops (West Division)
Bob Brownridge Memorial Trophy (Top Scorer)	Rob Brown, Kamloops
Top Defenseman	Emanuel Viveiros, Prince Albert (East Division)
	Glen Wesley, Portland (West Division)
Top Goaltender	Mark Fitzpatrick, Medicine Hat
Top Rookie	Neil Brady, Medicine Hat (East Division)
	Ron Shudra, Kamloops (West Division)
Coach of the Year	Terry Simpson, Prince Albert

Historical WHL Trophy Winners

(Canadian Major Junior Hockey League in 1966-67, renamed the Western Canadian Hockey League from 1967-68 to 1976-77. Has been named the Western Hockey League since 1977-78 season).

Most Valuable Player Trophy

Gerry Pinder, Saskatoon	1966-67
Jim Harrison Estevan	1967-68
Bobby Clarke, Flin Flon	1968-69
Reggie Leach, Flin Flon	1969-70
Ed Dyck, Calgary	1970-71
John Davidson, Calgary	1971-72
Dennis Sobchuk, Regina	1972-73
Ron Chipperfield, Brandon	1973-74
Bryan Trottier, Lethbridge	1974-75
Bernie Federko, Saskatoon	1975-76
Barry Beck, New Westminster	1976-77
Ryan Walter, Seattle	1977-78
Perry Turnbull, Portland	1978-79
Doug Wickenheiser, Regina	1979-80
Steve Tsujiura, Medicine Hat	1980-81
Mike Vernon, Calgary	1981-82
Mike Vernon, Calgary	1982-83
Ray Ferraro, Brandon	1983-84
Cliff Ronning, New Westminster	1984-85
Emanuel Viveiros, Prince Albert (East Division)	1985-86
Rob Brown, Kamloops (West Division)	

Bob Brownridge Mem. Trophy (Leading Scorer)

1966-67	Gerry Pinder, Saskatoon (140 pts)
1967-68	Bobby Clarke, Flin Flon (168 pts)
1968-69	Bobby Clarke, Flin Flon (137 pts)
1969-70	Reggie Leach, Flin Flon (111 pts)
1970-71	Chuck Arnason, Flin Flon (163 pts)
1971-72	Tom Lysiak, Medicine Hat (143 pts)
1972-73	Tom Lysiak, Medicine Hat (154 pts)
1973-74	Ron Chipperfield, Brandon (162 pts)
1974-75	Mel Bridgman, Victoria (157 pts)
1975-76	Bernie Federko, Saskatoon (187 pts)
1976-77	Bill Derlago, Brandon (178 pts)
1977-78	Brian Propp, Brandon (182 pts)
1978-79	Brian Propp, Brandon (194 pts)
1979-80	Doug Wickenheiser, Regina (170 pts)
1980-81	Brian Varga, Regina (187 pts)
1981-82	Jock Callander, Regina (190 pts)
1982-83	Dale Derkatch, Regina (179 pts)
1983-84	Ray Ferraro, Brandon (192 pts)
1984-85	Cliff Ronning, New Westminster (197 pts)
1985-86	Rob Brown, Kamloops (173 pts)

Stewart Paul Memorial Trophy (Rookie of the Year)

Ron Garwasiuk, Regina	1966-67
Ron Fairbrother, Saskatoon	1967-68
Ron Williams, Edmonton	1968-69
Gene Carr, Flin Flon	1969-70
Stan Weir, Medicine Hat	1970-71
Dennis Sobchuk, Regina	1971-72
Rick Blight, Brandon	1972-73
Cam Connor, Flin Flon	1973-74
Don Murdoch, Medicine Hat	1974-75
Steve Tambellini, Lethbridge	1975-76
Brian Propp, Brandon	1976-77
John Ogrodnick, N.W.-Keith Brown, Port.	1977-78
Kelly Kisio, Calgary	1978-79
Grant Fuhr, Victoria	1979-80
Dave Michayluk, Regina	1980-81
Dale Derkatch, Regina	1981-82
Dan Hodgson, Prince Albert	1982-83
Cliff Ronning, New Westminster	1983-84
Mark Mackay, Moose Jaw	1984-85
Neil Brady, Medicine Hat (East Division)	1985-86
Ron Shudra, Kamloops (West Division)	

Frank Boucher Memorial Trophy (Most Gentlemanly Player)

1966-67	Morris Stefaniw, Estevan
1967-68	Bernie Blanchette, Saskatoon
1968-69	Bob Liddington, Calgary
1969-70	Randy Rota, Calgary
1970-71	Lorne Henning, Estevan
1971-72	Ron Chipperfield, Brandon
1972-73	Ron Chipperfield, Brandon
1973-74	Mike Rogers, Calgary
1974-75	Danny Arndt, Saskatoon
1975-76	Blair Chapman, Saskatoon
1976-77	Steve Tambellini, Lethbridge
1977-78	Steve Tambellini, Lethbridge
1978-79	Errol Rausse, Seattle
1979-80	Steve Tsujiura, Medicine Hat
1980-81	Steve Tsujiura, Medicine Hat
1981-82	Mike Moller, Lethbridge
1982-83	Darren Boyko, Winnipeg
1983-84	Mark Lamb, Medicine Hat
1984-85	Cliff Ronning, New Westminster
1985-86	Randy Smith, Saskatoon (East Division)
	Ken Morrison, Kamloops (West Division)

Top Defenseman Trophy

Barry Gibbs, Estevan	1966-67
Gerry Hart, Flin Flon	1967-68
Dale Hoganson, Estevan	1968-69
Jim Hargreaves, Winnipeg	1969-70
Ron James, Edmonton	1970-71
Jim Watson, Calgary	1971-72
George Pesut, Saskatoon	1972-73
Pat Price, Saskatoon	1973-74
Rick LaPointe, Victoria	1974-75
Kevin McCarthy, Winnipeg	1975-76
Barry Beck, New Westminster	1976-77
Brad McCrimmon, Brandon	1977-78
Keith Brown, Portland	1978-79
David Babych, Portland	1979-80
Jim Benning, Portland	1980-81
Gary Nylund, Portland	1981-82
Gary Leeman, Regina	1982-83
Bob Rouse, Lethbridge	1983-84
Wendel Clark, Saskatoon	1984-85
Emanuel Viveiros, Prince Albert (East Division)	1985-86
Glen Wesley, Portland (West Division)	

Top Goaltender Trophy

1966-67	Ken Brown, Moose Jaw
1967-68	Chris Worthy, Flin Flon
1968-69	Ray Martyniuk, Flin Flon
1969-70	Ray Martyniuk, Flin Flon
1970-71	Ed Dyck, Calgary
1971-72	John Davidson, Calgary
1972-73	Ed Humphreys, Saskatoon
1973-74	Garth Malarchuk, Calgary
1974-75	Bill Oleschuk, Calgary
1975-76	Carey Walker, New Westminster
1976-77	Glen Hanlon, Brandon
1977-78	Bart Hunter, Portland
1978-79	Rick Knickle, Brandon
1979-80	Kevin Eastman, Victoria
1980-81	Grant Fuhr, Victoria
1981-82	Mike Vernon, Calgary
1982-83	Mike Vernon, Calgary
1983-84	Ken Wregget, Lethbridge
1984-85	Troy Gamble, Medicine Hat
1985-86	Mark Fitzpatrick, Medicine Hat

Quebec Hockey League
(Formerly the Quebec Major Junior Hockey League)
President and Executive Director—Gilles Courteau
Vice-President—John Horman
Statistician—Jacques Dion
4635 1st Avenue, Room 240
Charlesbourg, Quebec G1G 5W5
Phone—(418) 623-1508

Final 1985-86 QHL Standings

Frank Dilio Division

	G.	W.	L.	T.	Pts.	GF.	GA.
Drummondville Voltigeurs	72	40	28	4	84	342	308
Trois-Rivieres Draveurs	72	36	34	2	74	343	331
Chicoutimi Sagueneens	72	34	34	4	72	393	351
Shawinigan Cataracts	72	32	38	2	66	353	361
Granby Bisons	72	23	46	3	49	333	444

Robert Lebel Division

	G.	W.	L.	T.	Pts.	GF.	GA.
Hull Olympiques	72	54	18	0	108	423	262
Verdun Junior Canadiens	72	38	31	3	79	358	364
Laval Titans	72	37	34	1	75	406	386
St. Jean Castors	72	35	33	4	74	350	377
Longueuil Chevaliers	72	18	51	3	39	302	419

Top 10 Scorers for the Jean Beliveau Trophy

	Games	G.	A.	Pts.	Pen.
1. Guy Rouleau, Hull	62	*92	99	*191	72
Luc Robitaille, Hull	63	68	*123	*191	93
3. Michel Mongeau, Laval	72	71	109	180	45
4. Patrick Emond, Chicoutimi	71	69	98	167	32
5. Vincent Damphousse, Laval	69	45	110	155	70
6. Jimmy Carson, Verdun	69	70	83	153	46
7. Stephan Lebeau, Shawinigan	72	69	77	146	22
8. Patrice Lefebvre, Shawinigan	69	38	98	136	146
9. Marc Fortier, Chicoutimi	71	47	86	133	49
10. Jocelyn Lemieux, Laval	71	57	68	125	131

Team-by-Team Regular Season QHL Scoring

Chicoutimi Sagueneens

	Games	G.	A.	Pts.	Pen.
Patrick Emond	71	69	98	167	32
Marc Fortier	71	47	86	133	49
Jean Marc Richard	72	19	88	107	111
Marc Bureau	63	36	62	98	69
Luc Duval	60	39	45	84	24
Steven Latour	66	47	36	83	292
Peter Kasper	59	24	42	66	79
Gregory Choules	65	20	32	52	118
Eric Pinard	70	20	32	52	15
Pierre Millier	67	22	15	37	69
Daniel Maurice	67	6	22	28	41
Patrice Tremblay	65	10	17	27	8
Chris Duperron	70	0	26	26	149
Daniel Bock	68	7	13	20	56
Carl Larouche	66	5	15	20	40
Carl Cleary	56	4	14	18	71
Serge Lauzon	72	2	15	17	125
Michel Therrien	58	5	11	16	111
Serge Lanthier	69	1	6	7	25
Alain Jobin	49	0	7	7	99
D. Berthiaume (Goalie)	66	0	2	2	12
Andre Lapensee (Goalie)	27	0	1	1	20
Evens Larouche	27	0	0	0	19

Drummondville Voltigeurs

	Games	G.	A.	Pts.	Pen.
Steve Pepin	52	47	56	103	110
Mario De Benedictis	72	41	62	103	34
Jose Charbonneau	57	44	45	89	158
Dan Vincelette	70	37	47	84	234
Simon Massie	72	33	41	74	123
Alain Charland	66	32	38	70	67
Denis Gosselin	68	16	48	64	196
Jean Guy Bergeron	61	12	52	64	40
James Gasseau	46	20	31	51	155
Martin Bergeron	71	14	34	48	65
Eric Tremblay	72	9	36	45	132

	Games	G.	A.	Pts.	Pen.
Martin Fecteau	71	9	34	43	172
Nicolas Beaulieu	70	11	20	31	93
Donald Gagnon	70	9	22	31	84
Regis Chouinard	50	3	25	28	333
Bernard Carrier	68	3	24	27	77
Eric Demers	55	13	10	23	243
Martin Lefebvre	58	8	12	20	57
Eric Latreille	58	11	8	19	74
Mario Doyon	71	5	14	19	129
Jean Fortin	61	2	4	6	140
Vincent Riendeau (G.)	57	0	3	3	40
Patrice Cote (Goalie)	18	0	0	0	4

Granby Bisons

	Games	G.	A.	Pts.	Pen.
Pierre Turgeon	69	47	67	114	31
Claude Dumas	64	31	58	89	78
Stephane Roy	61	33	52	85	68
Eric Aubertin	68	37	47	84	61
Sylvain Hurteau	71	28	47	75	100
Norman Desjardins	69	23	46	69	67
Jari Korpisalo	60	22	27	49	73
J. Francois Neault	39	13	20	33	20
Eric Gravel	70	6	26	32	117
Mario Barbe	70	5	25	30	261
Steve Pinard	42	9	19	28	164
Martin Lamoureux	64	9	12	21	46
Stephane Quintal	67	2	17	19	144
Alain Cote	22	4	12	16	48
Martin Olivier	69	4	12	16	34
Daniel Charbonneau	68	2	13	15	46
Andre Carbonneau	40	4	9	13	35
Benoit Adam	59	3	10	13	107
Robert Plante	48	7	5	12	45
Benoit Giroux	1	0	2	2	0
Stephane Cote	6	0	2	2	4
Yves Plourde	32	0	2	2	32
Stephane Gauthier (G.)	18	0	1	1	0
Alain Plante (Goalie)	35	0	0	0	2

Hull Olympiques

	Games	G.	A.	Pts.	Pen.
Guy Rouleau	62	*92	99	*191	72
Luc Robitaille	63	68	*123	*191	93
Joe Foglietta	59	39	78	117	73
Patrice Brisson	59	37	46	83	73
Martin Simard	68	40	36	76	184
Benoit Brunet	71	33	37	70	81
Stephane Richer	71	14	52	66	166
Shane MacEachern	70	20	45	65	128
Michel Carbonneau	54	24	28	52	61
Sylvain Cote	26	10	33	43	14
Rick Hayward	59	3	40	43	354
Doug Honneger	71	4	32	36	105
Jean Marc Routhier	71	18	16	34	111
Sam Lang	31	10	18	28	33
Michel Beaucaire	45	8	14	22	8
Bob Coyle	68	8	14	22	107
Luc Chenier	57	4	12	16	84
Stephane Matteau	60	6	8	14	19
Jeff Stanton	32	2	11	13	39
Cam Russell	56	3	4	6	24
Robert Desjardins (G.)	43	0	1	1	0
Eric Bohemier (Goalie)	32	0	0	0	17

Laval Titans

	Games	G.	A.	Pts.	Pen.
Michel Mongeau	72	71	109	180	45
Vincent Damphousse	69	45	110	155	70
Jocelyn Lemieux	71	57	68	125	131
Luc Beausoleil	70	57	56	113	40
Francois Guay	71	19	55	74	46
Alain Varennes	71	25	36	61	25
Sylvain Couturier	68	21	37	58	64
Tommy Paradis	67	23	22	45	233
Marcello Vespa	63	15	21	36	72
Gilles Charbonneau	31	9	24	33	27
Simon Gagne	71	15	16	31	150
Marc Dumont	56	14	12	26	65
Sylvain Lefebvre	71	8	17	25	48
Stuart Marston	32	7	18	25	63
Derrick Ivall	41	11	13	24	69
Bernard Morin	72	3	17	20	32
Steven Finn	29	4	15	19	111
Martin Latreille	65	1	11	12	48
Dem. Stefanopolos	72	3	8	11	49
Mario Brunetta (Goalie)	63	0	3	3	34
Daniel Stennett	6	0	0	0	0
J. Bernard Cardinal (G.)	14	0	0	0	0

Longueuil Chevaliers

	Games	G.	A.	Pts.	Pen.
Marc Saumier	72	28	55	83	*401
Terry MacLean	70	36	45	81	18
Ronnie Stern	70	39	33	72	317
Roger Dube	44	37	32	69	72
Michel Couvrette	58	25	39	64	48
Eric Couvrette	61	13	30	43	27
Mario Lanthier	70	13	27	40	22
Yves Gaucher	65	14	18	32	274
Eric Courchesne	71	3	23	26	74
Martin Vezina	50	9	16	25	25
Gaetan Sarrault	38	12	11	23	22
Daniel Jomphe	45	5	16	21	119
Rene Corriveau	58	5	16	21	155
Marc Andre Duclos	34	10	8	18	21
Andre Brassard	61	3	15	18	70
Stephane Guilbault	49	8	9	17	42
Serge Savard Jr.	64	2	12	14	68
Michel Thibodeau	34	2	8	10	54
Guy Darveau	55	0	8	8	139
Serge Pepin	42	0	5	5	24
Denis Desbiens (Goalie)	37	0	1	1	0
Steve Averill (Goalie)	43	0	1	1	21
Danny Seguin (Goalie)	16	0	0	0	0

St. Jean Castors

	Games	G.	A.	Pts.	Pen.
Phillippe Bozon	65	59	52	111	72
Benoit Hogue	65	54	54	108	115
Stephan Figliuzzi	69	35	53	88	47
Ghislain Provencher	61	26	55	81	63
Michael McCollough	69	18	57	75	88
Brook Kelly	62	30	35	65	102
Dominic Lavoie	70	12	37	49	99
Eric Germain	66	5	38	43	183
Stephane Brochu	63	14	27	41	121
Sylvain Harvey	58	13	21	34	68
Eric Boisvert	68	19	14	33	89
Stephane Giguere	71	13	20	33	110
Serge Richard	71	14	17	31	18

	Games	G.	A.	Pts.	Pen.
Robert Oullet	72	8	17	25	25
Alain Bedard	65	4	21	25	287
Sylvain Venne	28	9	13	22	4
Richard Linteau	66	9	9	18	151
Tom Gibbons	41	1	6	7	159
Dominic Boudreau	38	2	2	4	5
Martin Mercier	51	1	3	4	14
Sylvain Mayer	28	1	2	3	44
Francois Gravel (Goalie)	42	0	2	2	8
Joel Drolet (Goalie)	31	0	0	0	8

Shawinigan Cataracts

	Games	G.	A.	Pts.	Pen.
Stefan Lebeau	72	69	77	146	22
Patrice Lefebvre	69	38	98	136	146
Denis Paul	69	60	63	123	100
Jean Bois	69	31	64	95	111
Jean Bergeron	70	39	46	85	110
Daniel Shank	51	34	38	72	184
Robert Page	72	28	42	70	104
Mike Marcinkiewicz	59	27	33	60	101
Frederic Vernette	71	17	32	49	284
Sylvain Le Du	50	7	29	36	16
Miguel Baldris	67	2	30	32	101
Steeve Masse	67	8	18	26	337
Danny Gauvin	70	13	11	24	36
Alex Deviault	52	7	16	23	233
Stephane Guerard	59	4	16	20	167
Gilbert Poulin	52	1	18	19	265
Stephane Lavigne	67	2	5	7	113
Stephane Briand	62	2	3	5	26
Eric Lamontagne	7	1	1	2	2
J. Claude Bergeron (G.)	33	0	2	2	17
Stephane Carrier	66	0	2	2	58
Denis Brousseau (Goalie)	16	0	0	0	2
Bruno Guillemette (G.)	42	0	0	0	13

Trois-Rivieres Draveurs

	Games	G.	A.	Pts.	Pen.
Martin Desjardins	71	49	69	118	103
Claude Gagnon	69	48	68	116	16
Serge Poudrier	55	29	38	67	61
Steve Bargone	69	23	37	60	86
Benoit Gosselin	64	25	33	58	36

	Games	G.	A.	Pts.	Pen.
Christian Pouget	66	22	35	57	93
Claude Lapointe	72	19	38	57	74
Mike Gober	57	27	23	50	151
Donald Dufresne	63	8	32	40	160
Benoit Picard	71	12	27	39	106
Richard Charette	66	13	16	29	16
Denis Gaudreau	61	7	22	29	155
Francis Breault	60	15	13	28	73
Jean-Claude Latour	65	7	18	25	286
Eric Martin	68	8	14	22	60
Steve Veilleux	67	1	20	21	132
Ralf Di Fiore	41	0	21	21	110
Dominic Emond	61	4	7	11	8
Gaetan Legault	45	1	5	6	37
Andre Marois Jr.	35	2	2	4	8
Stephane Robinson (G.)	23	0	2	2	12
Martin Plante (Goalie)	50	0	1	1	10

Verdun Junior Canadiens

	Games	G.	A.	Pts.	Pen.
Jimmy Carson	69	70	83	153	46
Everett Sanipass	67	28	66	94	320
Jim Nesich	71	26	55	81	114
Gerry Peach	68	14	60	74	58
Richard Little	72	25	42	67	110
Eric Collin	69	33	33	66	134
Eric Legros	62	22	29	51	36
Mario Milani	71	16	31	47	74
Gerry Fleming Jr.	47	15	21	36	339
Franco De Santis	66	9	22	31	94
Luc Martineau	40	6	18	24	10
Scott MacTavish	50	7	14	21	145
Jocelyn Joly	62	13	7	20	139
Steve Chelios	65	2	18	20	76
Stephane Provost	56	2	13	15	37
Eric Bedard	32	4	9	13	8
Martin Lauzon	72	2	10	12	114
Don McGrath	66	4	6	10	249
Don Nowak	15	2	3	5	26
Garry Talis	17	0	2	2	6
Robert Emond	14	0	1	1	11
James Blanchard (G.)	25	0	1	1	2
Eric Pedneault (Goalie)	18	0	0	0	2
Yves Lavoie (Goalie)	36	0	0	0	4

Complete QHL Goaltending

	Games	Mins.	Goals	SO.	Avg.
Robert Desjardins, Hull	43	2493	138	1	*3.32
Vincent Riendeau, Drummondville	57	3336	215	*2	3.87
Eric Bohemier, Hull	32	1838	121	*2	3.95
Martin Plante, Trois-Rivieres	50	2944	208	0	4.24
Bruno Guillemette, Shawinigan	42	2286	169	1	4.44
Daniel Berthiaume, Chicoutimi	*66	*3718	*286	1	4.62
Yves Lavoie, Verdun	36	2125	164	0	4.63
Denis Vaillancourt, Trois-Rivieres	6	230	18	0	4.70
Stephane Robinson, Trois-Rivieres	23	1179	94	0	4.78
James Blanchard, Verdun	25	1238	102	0	4.94
Mario Brunetta, Laval	63	3383	279	0	4.95
Joel Drolet, St. Jean	31	1827	151	0	4.96
Andree Lapensee, Chicoutimi	27	1325	114	0	5.16
Denis Desbiens, Longueuil	37	1996	272	0	5.17
Francois Gravel, St. Jean	42	2450	212	0	5.19
J. Claude Bergeron, Shawinigan	33	1796	156	0	5.21
Patrice Cote, Drummondville	18	892	78	0	5.25
Eric Pedneault, Verdun	18	988	89	0	5.40
Steve Averill, Longueuil	43	2253	204	1	5.43

	Games	Mins.	Goals	SO.	Avg.
J. Bernard Cardinal, Laval	14	485	45	0	5.57
Francois Gauthier, Drummondville	2	100	10	0	6.00
Francois Toupin, Granby	1	60	6	0	6.00
Roberto Scanza, Chicoutimi	1	20	2	0	6.00
Alain Plante, Granby	35	1756	182	0	6.22
Stephane Gauthier, Granby	18	875	92	0	6.31
Jude Labilois, St. Jean	3	123	13	0	6.34
Carl Parker, Granby	13	550	66	0	7.20
Danny Seguin, Longueuil	16	636	77	0	7.26
Denis Brousseau, Shawinigan	16	608	74	0	7.30
Eric Maguire, Trois-Rivieres	2	54	9	0	10.00
Bill White, Verdun	2	26	5	0	11.54
Mario Boily, Chicoutimi	2	24	6	0	15.00
Donald Fougeres, Trois-Rivieres	1	30	9	0	18.00

Individual 1985-86 Leaders

Goals	Guy Rouleau, Hull —	92
Assists	Luc Robitaille, Hull —	123
Points	Guy Rouleau, Hull —	191
	Luc Robitaille, Hull —	191
Penalty Minutes	Marc Saumier, Longueuil —	401
Goaltending Average	Robert Desjardins, Hull —	3.32
Shutouts	Vincent Riendeau, Drummondville —	2
	Eric Bohemier, Hull —	2

1986 QHL President Cup Playoffs
(All series best of nine)

Quarterfinals

Series "A"
	W.	L.	Pts.	GF.	GA.
Hull	5	0	10	37	11
Shawinigan	0	5	0	11	37

(Hull wins series, 5 games to 0)

Series "C"
	W.	L.	Pts.	GF.	GA.
St. Jean	5	0	10	25	17
Verdun	0	5	0	17	25

(St. Jean wins series, 5 games to 0)

Series "B"
	W.	L.	Pts.	GF.	GA.
Drummondville	5	4	10	37	32
Chicoutimi	4	5	8	32	37

(Drummondville wins series, 5 games to 4)

Series "D"
	W.	L.	Pts.	GF.	GA.
Laval	5	0	10	30	19
Trois-Rivieres	0	5	0	19	30

(Laval wins series, 5 games to 0)

Semifinals

Series "E"
	W.	L.	Pts.	GF.	GA.
Hull	5	0	10	49	10
St. Jean	0	5	0	10	49

(Hull wins series, 5 games to 0)

Series "F"
	W.	L.	Pts.	GF.	GA.
Drummondville	5	4	10	42	52
Laval	4	5	8	52	42

(Drummondville wins series, 5 games to 4)

Finals

Series "G"
	W.	L.	Pts.	GF.	GA.
Hull	5	0	10	39	12
Drummondville	0	5	0	12	39

(Hull wins series, and President Cup, 5 games to 0)

Top 10 Playoff Scorers

	Games	G.	A.	Pts.	Pen.
1. Luc Robitaille, Hull	15	17	27	*44	28
2. Guy Rouleau, Hull	15	*23	20	43	21
3. Jose Charbonneau, Drummondville	23	16	20	36	40
Vincent Damphousse, Laval	14	9	27	36	12
5. Michel Mongeau, Laval	14	14	20	34	12
Sylvain Cote, Hull	13	6	*28	34	22
7. Patrice Brisson, Hull	15	14	18	32	37
8. Michel Carbonneau, Hull	15	15	15	30	11
Alain Charland, Drummondville	23	12	18	30	22
10. Martin Simard, Hull	14	8	19	27	19

Team-by-Team Playoff Scoring

Chicoutimi Sagueneens
(Lost quarterfinals to Drummondville, 5-4)

	Games	G.	A.	Pts.	Pen.
Manl Fortner	9	2	14	16	12
Steven Latour	9	6	6	12	39
Patrick Emond	9	7	4	11	6
Marc Bureau	9	3	7	10	10
Jean Marc Richard	9	3	5	8	14
Luc Duval	9	3	3	6	2
Patrice Tremblay	9	2	4	6	6
Christian Duperron	9	1	3	4	12
Alain Jobin	9	1	2	3	12
Pierre Millier	9	1	2	3	8
Daniel Maurice	9	0	2	2	4
Peter Kasper	4	1	0	1	2
Carl Larouche	9	1	0	1	4
Eric Pinard	9	1	0	1	2
Greg Choules	9	0	1	1	21
Serge Lauzon	9	0	1	1	2
Daniel Bock	5	0	0	0	2
Daniel Berthiaume (G.)	9	0	0	0	4
Serge Lanthier	9	0	0	0	8
Evens Larouche	9	0	0	0	0

Drummondville Voltigeurs
(Lost finals to Hull, 5-0)

	Games	G.	A.	Pts.	Pen.
Jose Charbonneau	23	16	20	36	40
Alain Charland	23	12	18	30	22
Daniel Vincelette	22	11	14	25	35
Steve Pepin	23	9	16	25	52
Simon Massie	23	11	11	22	40
Mario De Benedictis	23	9	9	18	26
James Gasseau	23	1	13	14	18
Denis Gosselin	20	1	12	13	28
Martin Fecteau	22	6	6	12	44
Eric Demers	15	4	6	10	43
Jean Guy Bergeron	23	3	7	10	10
Mario Doyon	23	5	4	9	32
Eric Tremblay	15	0	7	7	25
Donald Gagnon	17	0	5	5	6
Bernard Carrier	23	0	5	5	8
Martin Lefebvre	11	1	2	3	4
Eric Latreille	14	1	0	1	8
Nicolas Beaulieu	23	0	1	1	11
Martin Bergeron	23	0	1	1	25
Vincent Riendeau (G.)	23	0	1	1	14
Francois Gauthier (G.)	2	0	0	0	0
Patrice Cote (Goalie)	3	0	0	0	0
Giovanni Iasenza	4	0	0	0	6
Jean Fortin	23	0	0	0	49

Hull Olympiques
(Winners of 1986 President Cup Playoffs)

	Games	G.	A.	Pts.	Pen.
Luc Robitaille	15	17	27	*44	28
Guy Rouleau	15	*23	20	43	21
Sylvain Cote	13	6	*28	34	22
Patrice Brisson	15	14	18	32	37
Michel Carbonneau	15	15	15	30	11
Martin Simard	14	8	19	27	19
Joe Foglietta	13	6	17	23	4
Shane MacEachern	15	11	11	22	17
Benoit Brunet	15	5	14	19	33
Luc Chenier	15	5	11	16	33
Rick Hayward	15	2	11	13	*98
Doug Honegger	15	3	9	12	2
Jean Marc Routhier	15	3	6	9	27
Stephane Richer	15	1	7	8	17
Michel Beaucaire	13	3	4	7	0
Bob Coyle	15	2	3	5	13
Michel Charbonneau	15	1	2	3	60
Cam Russell	15	0	2	2	4
Jeff Stanton	3	0	0	0	0
Eric Bohemier (Goalie)	4	0	0	0	2
Stephane Matteau	4	0	0	0	0
Robert Desjardins (G.)	13	0	0	0	0

Laval Titans
(Lost semifinals to Drummondville, 5-4)

	Games	G.	A.	Pts.	Pen.
Vincent Damphousse	14	9	27	36	12
Michel Mongeau	14	14	20	34	12
Jocelyn Lemieux	14	9	15	24	37
Steven Finn	14	6	16	22	57
Luc Beausoleil	14	8	12	20	12
Gilles Charbonneau	14	10	8	18	10
Francois Guay	14	5	6	11	15
Alain Varennes	14	5	4	9	11
Marc Dumont	14	2	7	9	17
Stuart Lee Martson	12	4	4	8	16
Sylvain Couturier	14	1	7	8	28
Simon Gagne	14	2	5	7	37
Eddy Courtenay	8	2	4	6	2
Stephane Dufresne	8	2	3	5	14
Tommy Paradis	13	0	5	5	38
Dem. Stefanopolos	9	1	1	2	21
Martin Latreille	13	0	2	2	19
Marcello Vespa	7	1	0	1	14
Sylvain Lefebvre	14	1	0	1	25
Bernard Morin	14	0	1	1	14
J. Bernard Cardinal (G.)	1	0	0	0	0
Mario Brunetta (G.)	14	0	0	0	8

St. Jean Castors
(Lost semifinals to Hull, 5-0)

	Games	G.	A.	Pts.	Pen.
Phillippe Bozon	10	10	6	16	16
Stefan Figliuzzl	10	5	9	14	4
Ghislain Provencher	10	3	9	12	26
Benoit Hogue	9	6	4	10	26
Brook Kelly	10	4	5	9	12
Sylvain Harvey	8	1	7	8	8
Eric Germain	10	0	6	6	56
Dominique Lavoie	10	2	3	5	20
Michael McCullough	10	1	4	5	11
Richard Linteau	10	2	1	3	22
Stephane Brochu	3	1	0	1	2
Alain Bedard	10	0	1	1	47
Eric Boisvert	10	0	1	1	2
Tom Gibbons	10	0	1	1	37
Martin Mercier	10	0	1	1	4
Robert Ouellet	10	0	1	1	0
Dominic Boudreau	3	0	0	0	0
Joel Drolet (Goalie)	5	0	0	0	2
Francois Gravel (Goalie)	5	0	0	0	0

	Games	G.	A.	Pts.	Pen.
Stephane Giguere	8	0	0	0	7
Sylvain Mayer	8	0	0	0	11
Serge Richard	10	0	0	0	14

Shawinigan Cataracts
(Lost quarterfinals to Hull, 5-0)

	Games	G.	A.	Pts.	Pen.
Patrice Lefebvre	5	2	5	7	14
Stephan Lebeau	5	4	2	6	4
Denis Paul	5	0	5	5	12
Sylvain Le Du	5	1	3	4	2
Jean Bergeron	5	2	0	2	2
Stephane Guerard	3	1	1	2	0
Robert Page	5	1	1	2	8
Mike Marcinkiewick	5	0	2	2	2
Stephane Lavigne	5	0	1	1	0
Jean Cl. Bergeron (G.)	3	0	0	0	0
Bruno Guillemette (G.)	4	0	0	0	0
Steeve Masse	4	0	0	0	33
Miguel Baldris	5	0	0	0	0
Jean Bois	5	0	0	0	9
Dany Gauvin	5	0	0	0	0
Stephane Carrier	5	0	0	0	4
Alex Daviault	5	0	0	0	2
Stephane Briand	5	0	0	0	2
Carl Vermette	5	0	0	0	17

Trois-Rivieres Draveurs
(Lost quarterfinals to Laval, 5-0)

	Games	G.	A.	Pts.	Pen.
Claude Gagnon	5	3	8	11	0
Denis Gaudreau	5	3	3	6	6
Martin Desjardins	4	2	4	6	4
Claude Lapointe	5	2	4	6	14
Richard Charette	5	4	1	5	0
Benoit Gosselin	5	1	2	3	11
Christian Pouget	3	0	3	3	6

	Games	G.	A.	Pts.	Pen.
Serge Poudrier	3	1	1	2	2
Benoit Picard	5	1	1	2	12
Mike Gober	5	0	2	2	34
Ralf Di Fiore	5	1	0	1	4
Jean Claude Latour	5	1	0	1	31
Eric Martin	4	0	1	1	0
Dominic Emond	5	0	1	1	0
Francis Breault	5	0	1	1	18
Gaetan Legault	5	0	1	1	2
Donald Dufresne	1	0	0	0	0
Guy Lefebvre	3	0	0	0	0
Stephane Robinson (G.)	3	0	0	0	0
Martin Plante (Goalie)	4	0	0	0	0
Steve Bergone	5	0	0	0	15
Steve Veilleux	5	0	0	0	13

Verdun Junior Canadiens
(Lost quarterfinals to St. Jean, 5-0)

	Games	G.	A.	Pts.	Pen.
Gerry Peach	5	5	3	8	0
Jimmy Carson	5	2	6	8	0
Eric Collin	5	1	6	7	4
Daniel Marois	5	4	2	6	6
Eric Legros	5	2	2	4	14
Scott MacTavish	5	1	3	4	22
Richard Little	5	2	1	3	8
Stephane Provost	5	0	2	2	8
Everett Sanipass	5	0	2	2	16
Gerry Fleming Jr.	4	0	1	1	18
Martin Lauzon	5	0	1	1	6
Robert Emond	1	0	0	0	0
Steve Chelios	5	0	0	0	12
Franco De Santis	5	0	0	0	8
Jocelyn Joly	5	0	0	0	23
Yves Lavoie (Goalie)	5	0	0	0	0
Don McGrath	5	0	0	0	2
Mario Milani	5	0	0	0	4
Jim Nesish	5	0	0	0	8
Gary Talis	5	0	0	0	0

Complete 1985 President Cup Goaltending

	Games	Mins.	Goals	SO.	Avg.
J. Bernard Cardinal, Laval	1	13	0	0	0.00
Robert Desjardins, Hull	13	754	25	*2	*1.99
Eric Bohemier, Hull	4	146	8	0	3.29
Daniel Berthiaume, Chicoutimi	9	580	36	0	3.72
Francois Gauthier, Drummondville	2	15	1	0	4.00
Mario Brunetta, Laval	14	834	60(1)	0	4.32
Yves Lavoie, Verdun	5	312	25	0	4.81
Bruno Guillemette, Shawinigan	4	159	13(1)	0	4.91
Vincent Riendeau, Drummondville	*23	*1271	*106	1	5.00
Martin Plante, Trois-Rivieres	4	243	21(1)	0	5.19
Joel Drolet, St. Jean	5	305	28	0	5.31
Stephane Robinson, Trois-Rivieres	3	64	7(1)	0	6.56
Francois Gravel, St. Jean	5	307	38	0	7.42
Jean Claude Bergeron, Shawinigan	3	140	23	0	9.86
Patrice Cote, Drummondville	3	53	10	0	11.32

( )—Empty net goals. Do not count against a goaltender's average.

Individual President Cup Playoff Leaders

Goals	Guy Rouleau, Hull—	23
Assists	Sylvain Cote, Hull—	28
Points	Luc Robitaille, Hull—	44
Penalty Minutes	Rick Hayward, Hull—	98
Goaltender's Average	Robert Desjardins, Hull—	1.99
Shutouts	Robert Desjardins, Hull—	2

1985-86 QHL All-Star Teams

First Team	Position	Second Team
Robert Desjardins, Hull	Goal	V. Riendeau, Drummondville
Jean Marc Richard, Chicoutimi	Defense	Donald Dufresne, Trois-Rivieres
Sylvain Cote, Hull	Defense	J. Gasseau, Drummondville
Luc Robitaille, Hull	Left Wing	Phillippe Bozon, St. Jean
		Vincent Damphousse, Laval
Guy Rouleau, Hull	Center	Jimmy Carson, Verdun
		Michel Mongeau, Laval
Jocelyn Lemieux, Laval	Right Wing	Patrice Lefebvre, Shawinigan

1985-86 QHL Trophy Winners

Frank Selke Trophy (Most Gentlemanly) .... Jimmy Carson, Verdun
Michel Bergeron Trophy (Top Rookie Forward) .... Pierre Turgeon, Granby
Raymond Lagace Trophy (Top Rookie Defenseman or Goaltender) .... Stephane Guerard, Shawinigan
Michel Briere Trophy (Regular Season MVP) .... Guy Rouleau, Hull
Jean Beliveau Trophy (Leading Scorer) .... Guy Rouleau, Hull
Marcel Robert Trophy (Top Scholastic/Athletic Performer) .... Bernard Morin, Laval
Mike Bossy Trophy (Top Pro Prospect) .... Jimmy Carson, Verdun
Emile "Butch" Bouchard Trophy (Top Defenseman) .... Sylvain Cote, Hull
Jacque Plante Trophy (Best Goalie) .... Robert Desjardins, Hull
Guy Lafleur Trophy (Playoff MVP) .... Sylvain Cote, Hull
                                                                                                                    Luc Robitaille, Hull
Robert LeBel Trophy (Best Team Defensive Average) .... Hull Olympiques
John Rougeau Trophy (Regular Season Champions) .... Hull Olympiques
President Cup (Playoff Champions) .... Hull Olympiques

Historical QHL Trophy Winners

Frank Selke Trophy
(Most Gentlemanly Player)

1970-71—Norm Dube, Sherbrooke
1971-72—Gerry Teeple, Cornwall
1972-73—Claude Larose, Drummondville
1973-74—Gary MacGregor, Cornwall
1974-75—Jean-Luc Phaneuf, Montreal
1975-76—Norm Dupont, Montreal
1976-77—Mike Bossy, Laval
1977-78—Kevin Reeves, Montreal
1978-79—Ray Bourque, Verdun
        Jean Francois Sauve, Trois Rivieres
1979-80—Jean Francois Sauve, Trois Rivieres
1980-81—Claude Verret, Trois Rivieres
1981-82—Claude Verret, Trois Rivieres
1982-83—Pat LaFontaine, Verdun
1983-84—Jerome Carrier, Verdun
1984-85—Patrick Emond, Chicoutimi
1985-86—Jimmy Carson, Verdun

Michel Bergeron Trophy
(Top Rookie Forward)
(Prior to 1980-81 season, award was given to QMJHL Rookie-of-the-Year.)

1969-70—Serge Martel, Verdun
1970-71—Bob Murphy, Cornwall
1971-72—Bob Murray, Cornwall
1972-73—Pierre Larouche, Sorel
1973-74—Mike Bossy, Laval
1974-75—Dennis Pomerleau, Hull
1975-76—Jean-Marc Bonamie, Shawinigan
1976-77—Rick Vaive, Sherbrooke
1977-78—Norm Rochefort, Trois Rivieres
        Denis Savard, Montreal
1978-79—Alan Grenier, Laval
1979-80—Dale Hawerchuk, Cornwall
1980-81—Claude Verret, Trois Rivieres
1981-82—Sylvain Turgeon, Hull
1982-83—Pat LaFontaine, Verdun
1983-84—Stephane Richer, Granby
1984-85—Jimmy Carson, Verdun
1985-86—Pierre Turgeon, Granby

Raymond Lagace Trophy
(Top Rookie Defenseman or Goaltender)

1980-81—Billy Campbell, Montreal
1981-82—Michel Petit, Sherbrooke
1982-83—Bobby Dollas, Laval
1983-84—James Gasseau, Drummondville
1984-85—Robert Desjardins, Shawinigan
1985-86—Stephane Guerard, Shawinigan

Jean Beliveau Trophy
(Leading Point Scorer)

1969-70—Luc Simard, Trois Rivieres
1970-71—Guy Lafleur, Quebec
1971-72—Jacques Richard, Quebec
1972-73—Andre Savard, Quebec
1973-74—Pierre Larouche, Sorel
1974-75—Norm Dupont, Montreal
1975-76—Richard Dalpe, Trois Rivieres
        Sylvain Locas, Chicoutimi
1976-77—Jean Savard, Quebec
1977-78—Ron Carter, Sherbrooke
1978-79—Jean-Francois Sauve, Trois Rivieres
1979-80—Jean-Francois Sauve, Trois Rivieres
1980-81—Dale Hawerchuk, Cornwall
1981-82—Claude Verret, Trois Rivieres
1982-83—Pat LaFontaine, Verdun
1983-84—Mario Lemieux, Laval
1984-85—Guy Rouleau, Longueuil
1985-86—Guy Rouleau, Hull

Michael Briere Trophy
(Regular Season Most Valuable Player)

1972-73—Andre Savard, Quebec
1973-74—Gary MacGregor, Cornwall
1974-75—Mario Viens, Cornwall
1975-76—Peter Marsh, Sherbrooke
1976-77—Lucien DeBlois, Sorel
1977-78—Kevin Reeves, Montreal
1978-79—Pierre Lacroix, Trois Rivieres
1979-80—Denis Savard, Montreal
1980-81—Dale Hawerchuk, Cornwall
1981-82—John Chabot, Sherbrooke
1982-83—Pat LaFontaine, Verdun
1983-84—Mario Lemieux, Laval
1984-85—Daniel Berthiaune, Chicoutimi
1985-86—Guy Rouleau, Hull

Marcel Robert Trophy
(Top Scholastic/Athletic Performer)

1981-82—Jacques Sylvestre, Granby
1982-83—Claude Gosselin, Quebec
1983-84—Gilbert Paiement, Chicoutimi
1984-85—Claude Gosselin, Longueuil
1985-86—Bernard Morin, Laval

Mike Bossy Trophy
(Top Pro Prospect)
(Originally called Association of Journalism of Hockey Trophy from 1980-81 through 1982-83.)

1980-81—Dale Hawerchuk, Cornwall
1981-82—Michel Petit, Sherbrooke
1982-83—Pat LaFontaine, Verdun
        Sylvain Turgeon, Hull (tie)
1983-84—Mario Lemieux, Laval
1984-85—Jose Charbonneau, Drummondville
1985-86—Jimmy Carson, Verdun

Emile "Butch" Bouchard Trophy
(Top QHL Defenseman)

1975-76—Jean Gagnon, Quebec
1976-77—Robert Picard, Montreal
1977-78—Mark Hardy, Montreal
1978-79—Ray Bourque, Verdun
1979-80—Gaston Therrien, Quebec
1980-81—Fred Boimistruck, Cornwall
1981-82—Paul Andre Boutilier, Sherbrooke
1982-83—Jean-Jacques Daigneault, Longueuil
1983-84—Billy Campbell, Verdun
1984-85—Yves Beaudoin, Shawinigan
1985-86—Sylvain Cote, Hull

Jacques Plante Trophy
(Best Goalie)

1969-70—Michael Deguise, Sorel
1970-71—Reynald Fortier, Quebec
1971-72—Richard Brodeur, Cornwall
1972-73—Pierre Perusse, Quebec
1973-74—Claude Legris, Sorel
1974-75—Nick Sanza, Sherbrooke
1975-76—Tim Bernhardt, Cornwall

1976-77—Tim Bernhardt, Cornwall
1977-78—Tim Bernhardt, Cornwall
1978-79—Jacques Cloutier, Trois Rivieres
1979-80—Corrado Micalef, Sherbrooke
1980-81—Michel Dufour, Sorel
1981-82—Jeff Barratt, Montreal
1982-83—Tony Haladuick, Laval
1983-84—Tony Haladuick, Laval
1984-85—Daniel Berthiaume, Chicoutimi
1985-86—Robert Desjardins, Hull

Guy Lafleur Trophy
(Most Valuable Player During Playoffs)

1977-78—Richard David, Trois Rivieres
1978-79—Jean-Francois Sauve, Trois Rivieres
1979-80—Dale Hawerchuk, Cornwall
1980-81—Alain Lemieux, Trois Rivieres
1981-82—Michel Morissette, Sherbrooke
1982-83—Pat LaFontaine, Verdun
1983-84—Mario Lemieux, Laval
1984-85—Claude Lemieux, Verdun
1985-86—Sylvain Cote, Hull
        Luc Robitaille, Hull (tie)

Robert LeBel Trophy
(Best Team Defensive Average)

1977-78—Trois-Rivieres Draveurs
1978-79—Trois-Rivieres Draveurs
1979-80—Sherbrooke Beavers
1980-81—Sorel Black Hawks
1981-82—Montreal Juniors
1982-83—Shawinigan Cataracts
1983-84—Shawinigan Cataracts
1984-85—Shawinigan Cataracts
1985-86—Hull Olympiques

John Rougeau Trophy
(Regular Season Champions)
(Originally called Governors Trophy from 1969-70 through 1982-83.)

1969-70—Quebec Remparts
1970-71—Quebec Remparts
1971-72—Cornwall Royals
1972-73—Quebec Remparts
1973-74—Sorel Black Hawks
1974-75—Sherbrooke Beavers
1975-76—Sherbrooke Beavers
1976-77—Quebec Remparts
1977-78—Trois Rivieres Draveurs
1978-79—Trois Rivieres Draveurs
1979-80—Sherbrooke Beavers
1980-81—Cornwall Royals
1981-82—Sherbrooke Beavers
1982-83—Laval Voisins
1983-84—Laval Voisins
1984-85—Shawinigan Cataracts
1985-86—Hull Olympiques

President Cup
(Playoff Champions)

1969-70—Quebec Remparts
1970-71—Quebec Remparts
1971-72—Cornwall Royals
1972-73—Quebec Remparts
1973-74—Quebec Remparts
1974-75—Sherbrooke Beavers
1975-76—Quebec Remparts
1976-77—Sherbrooke Beavers
1977-78—Trois Rivieres Draveurs
1978-79—Trois Rivieres Draveurs
1979-80—Cornwall Royals
1980-81—Cornwall Royals
1981-82—Sherbrooke Beavers
1982-83—Verdun Juniors
1983-84—Laval Voisins
1984-85—Verdun Junior Canadiens
1985-86—Hull Olympiques

National Collegiate Athletic Association

Year	Champion	Coach	Runner-Up
1948	Michigan	Vic Heyliger	Dartmouth
1949	Boston College	John Kelley	Dartmouth
1950	Colorado College	Cheddy Thompson	Boston University
1951	Michigan	Vic Heyliger	Brown
1952	Michigan	Vic Heyliger	Colorado College
1953	Michigan	Vic Heyliger	Minnesota
1954	Rensselaer Poly	Ned Harkness	Minnesota
1955	Michigan	Vic Heyliger	Colorado College
1956	Michigan	Vic Heyliger	Michigan Tech
1957	Colorado College	Thomas Bedecki	Michigan
1958	Denver	Murray Armstrong	North Dakota
1959	North Dakota	Bob May	Michigan State
1960	Denver	Murray Armstrong	Michigan Tech
1961	Denver	Murray Armstrong	St. Lawrence
1962	Michigan Tech	John MacInnes	Clarkson
1963	North Dakota	Barry Thorndycraft	Denver
1964	Michigan	Al Renfrew	Denver
1965	Michigan Tech	John MacInnes	Boston College
1966	Michigan State	Amo Bessone	Clarkson
1967	Cornell	Ned Harkness	Boston University
1968	Denver	Murray Armstrong	North Dakota
1969	Denver	Murray Armstrong	Cornell
1970	Cornell	Ned Harkness	Clarkson
1971	Boston University	Jack Kelley	Minnesota
1972	Boston University	Jack Kelley	Cornell
1973	Wisconsin	Bob Johnson	Denver
1974	Minnesota	Herb Brooks	Michigan Tech
1975	Michigan Tech	John MacInnes	Minnesota
1976	Minnesota	Herb Brooks	Michigan Tech
1977	Wisconsin	Bob Johnson	Michigan
1978	Boston University	Jack Parker	Boston College
1979	Minnesota	Herb Brooks	North Dakota
1980	North Dakota	John Gasparini	Northern Michigan
1981	Wisconsin	Bob Johnson	Minnesota
1982	North Dakota	John Gasparini	Wisconsin
1983	Wisconsin	Jeff Sauer	Harvard
1984	Bowling Green	Jerry York	Minnesota-Duluth
1985	Rensselaer Polytechnic Inst.	Mike Addesa	Providence College
1986	Michigan State	Ron Mason	Harvard

Western Collegiate Hockey Association

	W.	L.	T.	GF.	GA.	Pct.
Denver (34-13-1)	25	9	0	170	115	.735
Minnesota (35-13-0)	24	10	0	179	116	.706
Wisconsin (27-13-0)	23	11	0	172	136	.676
Minnesota-Duluth (26-13-3)	21	12	1	153	118	.632
Northern Michigan (23-14-2)	21	13	0	168	151	.618
North Dakota (24-16-1)	19	14	1	156	137	.574
Colorado College (12-26-2)	11	21	2	131	155	.353
Michigan Tech (10-26-4)	9	22	3	118	164	.309

1985-86 WCHA All-Stars

First Team	Position	Second Team
John Blue, Minnesota	Goalie	Tom Allen, Denver
Norm Maciver, Minnesota-Duluth	Defenseman	Rob Doyle, Colorado
Scott Sandelin, North Dakota	Defenseman	Marty Wiitala, Wisconsin
Dallas Gaume, Denver	Forward	Dwight Mathiasen, Denver
Gary Emmons, Northern Michigan	Forward	Pat Micheletti, Minnesota
Brett Hull, Minnesota-Duluth	Forward	Corey Millen, Minnesota

WCHA PLAYOFFS
Quarterfinals
(Two-Game, Total Goal Series)
Minnesota defeated Colorado College, 14-7.
Minnesota-Duluth defeated Northern Michigan, 12-8.
Denver defeated Michigan Tech, 9-6.
Wisconsin defeated North Dakota, 12-7.

Semifinals
(Two-Game, Total Goal Series)
Denver defeated Minnesota-Duluth, 13-7.
Minnesota defeated Wisconsin, 11-4.

Championship
(Two-Game, Total Goal Series)
Denver defeated Minnesota, 6-2.

Central Collegiate Hockey Association

	W.	L.	T.	GF.	GA.	Pct.
Michigan State (34-9-2)	23	7	2	177	124	.750
Bowling Green (26-14-0)	23	9	0	179	129	.719
Western Michigan (32-12-0)	23	9	0	188	138	.719
Lake Superior State (24-18-1)	17	14	1	133	124	.547
Ohio State (23-19-1)	16	15	1	157	177	.516
Ferris State (17-19-2)	13	17	2	152	174	.438
Illinois-Chicago (25-14-1)	12	20	0	137	161	.375
Michigan (12-26-0)	10	22	0	151	184	.313
Miami (O.) (8-28-2)	3	27	2	113	177	.125

Overall record in parentheses.

1985-86 CCHA All-Stars

First Team	Position	Second Team
Gary Kruzich, Bowling Green	Goalie	Bob Essensa, Michigan State
Don McSween, Michigan State	Defenseman	Brian McKee, Bowling Green
Wayne Gagne, Western Michigan	Defenseman	Chris MacDonald, W. Mich.
Mike Donnelly, Michigan State	Forward	Paul Ysebaert, Bowling Green
Jamie Wansbrough, Bowling Green	Forward	Brad Jones, Michigan
Dan Dorion, Western Michigan	Forward	Stuart Burnie, Western Mich.

CCHA PLAYOFFS
Quarterfinals
(All series were best-of-three)
Michigan State defeated Michigan, 2-0.
Bowling Green defeated Illinois-Chicago, 2-0.
Western Michigan defeated Ferris State, 2-0.
Lake Superior State defeated Ohio State, 2-1.

Semifinals
Western Michigan defeated Bowling Green, 4-3 (3 OT).
Michigan State defeated Lake Superior State, 3-2.

Championship
Western Michigan defeated Michigan State, 3-1.

Eastern Collegiate Athletic Conference

	W.	L.	T.	GF.	GA.	Pct.
Harvard (25-8-1)	18	3	0	129	53	.857
Yale (21-10-0)	15	6	0	104	72	.714
Cornell (21-7-4)	13	6	2	101	74	.667
RPI (20-11-1)	13	7	1	100	88	.643
Clarkson (12-6-3)	12	6	3	101	70	.643
Vermont (17-13-1)	11	10	0	64	63	.524
St. Lawrence (16-15-0)	10	11	0	92	92	.476
Colgate (15-15-2)	9	11	1	82	109	.452
Princeton (11-17-2)	7	13	1	76	82	.357
Dartmouth (7-18-0)	4	17	0	59	121	.190
Brown (4-19-0)	3	18	0	63	127	.143

Overall record in parentheses.

1985-86 ECAC All-Stars

First Team	Position	Second Team
Tom Draper, Vermont	Goalie	Doug Dadswell, Cornell
Cliff Albrecht, Princeton	Defenseman	Chris Norton, Cornell
Mike Dark, RPI	Defenseman	Mark Benning, Harvard
		Randy Taylor, Harvard
Randy Wood, Yale	Forward	Tim Smith, Harvard
Joe Nieuwendyk, Cornell	Forward	Bob Logan, Yale
Scott Fusco, Harvard	Forward	Gerald Waslen, Colgate

ECAC PLAYOFFS

Semifinal Games
Cornell defeated Yale, 3-2 (2 OT).
Clarkson defeated Harvard, 4-2.

Championship Game
Cornell defeated Clarkson, 3-2 (2 OT).

HOCKEY EAST

	W.	L.	T.	GF.	GA.	Pct.
Boston College (26-13-3)	23	9	2	158	123	.706
Boston University (25-14-4)	20	11	3	147	127	.632
Northeastern (20-17-2)	18	14	2	165	158	.559
Providence (14-24-1)	11	22	1	105	140	.338
Maine (11-28-1)	8	25	1	118	177	.250
Lowell (7-25-2)	7	25	2	118	166	.235
New Hampshire (5-29-3)	5	27	2	114	118	.176

Overall record in parentheses.

1985-86 Hockey East All-Stars

First Team	Position	Second Team
Scott Gordon, Boston College	Goalie	Terry Taillefer, Boston Univ.
Scott Shaunessy, Boston University	Defenseman	Bob Emery, Boston College
Claude Lodin, Northeastern	Defenseman	Paul Fitzsimmons, Northeastern
David Quinn, Boston University		
Scott Harlow, Boston College	Forward	Gord Cruickshank, Providence
John Cullen, Boston University	Forward	Doug Brown, Boston College
Jay Heinbuck, Northeastern	Forward	Clark Donatelli, Boston Univ.

HOCKEY EAST PLAYOFFS

Quarterfinals
(Two-Game, Total Goal Series)
Lowell defeated Northeastern, 7-6.
Boston University defeated New Hampshire, 5-4.
Providence defeated Maine, 10-6.

Semifinal Games
Boston University defeated Providence, 3-2.
Boston College defeated Lowell, 5-2.

Championship Game
Boston University defeated Boston College, 9-4.

1986 NCAA TOURNAMENT

Quarterfinal Series
(Two-game, Total Goal Series)
Minnesota 6, Boston University 4
Minnesota 5, Boston University 3
(Minnesota wins series, 11-7)
Michigan State 6, Boston College 4
Michigan State 4, Boston College 2
(Michigan State wins series, 10-6)
Denver 4, Cornell 2
Cornell 4, Denver 3
(Denver wins series, 7-6)
Harvard 4, Western Michigan 2
Harvard 7, Western Michigan 2
(Harvard wins series, 11-4)

Semifinal Series
Played at Providence, Rhode Island
Michigan State 6, Minnesota 4
Harvard 5, Denver 2

Consolation Game
Minnesota 6, Denver 4

Championship Game
Michigan State 6, Harvard 5
1986 NCAA Champion: Michigan State University

1986 NCAA All-Tournament Team

Position	Player	College
Goalie	Norm Foster	Michigan State
Defenseman	Mark Benning	Harvard
Defenseman	Don McSween	Michigan State
Forward	Allen Bourbeau	Harvard
Forward	Mike Donnelly	Michigan State
Forward	Jeff Parker	Michigan State
NCAA Tournament MVP	Mike Donnelly	Michigan State

1985-86 College Hockey All-America Teams

FIRST TEAM
WEST

Position	Player	College
Goalie	Gary Kruzich	Bowling Green State
Defenseman	Wayne Gagne	Western Michigan
Defenseman	Norm Maciver	Minnesota-Duluth
Forward	Mike Donnelly	Michigan State
Forward	Dan Dorian	Western Michigan
Forward	Dallas Gaume	Denver

EAST

Position	Player	College
Goalie	Doug Dadswell	Cornell
Defenseman	Cliff Albrecht	Princeton
Defenseman	Mike Dark	RPI
Forward	Scott Fusco	Harvard
Forward	Scott Harlow	Boston College
Forward	Joe Nieuwendyk	Cornell

SECOND TEAM
WEST

Position	Player	College
Goalie	Chris Olson	Denver
Goalie	Bill Horn	Western Michigan
Defenseman	Don McSween	Michigan State
Defenseman	Scott Sandelin	North Dakota
Defenseman	Jim Smith	Denver
Forward	Dwight Mathiasen	Denver
Forward	Corey Millen	Minnesota
Forward	Matt Christensen	Minnesota-Duluth
Forward	Jamie Wansbrough	Bowling Green State

EAST

Position	Player	College
Goalie	Grant Blair	Harvard
Goalie	Chris Terreri	Providence
Defenseman	Mark Benning	Harvard
Defenseman	Jay Octeau	Boston University
Defenseman	Andy Otto	Clarkson
Forward	John Cullen	Boston University
Forward	Randy Wood	Yale
Forward	Doug Brown	Boston College
Forward	Clark Donatelli	Boston University

All-Time NCAA Tournament Records and Finishes

	Visits	W.	L.	GF	GA	Pct.	1st	2nd
Michigan	13	21	6	173	91	.778	7	2
Wisconsin	8	15	5	90	52	.750	4	1
Minnesota	12	19	10	138	115	.655	3	5
Denver	11	17	9	121	73	.654	5	2
North Dakota	11	17	9	102	78	.654	4	3
*Northeastern	1	2	1	17	14	.625	0	0
*Bowling Green State	5	6	4	38	42	.591	1	0
Michigan Tech	10	13	9	118	85	.591	3	4
†Michigan State	8	11	8	81	68	.579	2	1
#RPI	6	8	6	52	50	.567	2	0
Boston University	15	16	16	136	151	.500	3	2
Cornell	8	8	8	54	52	.500	2	2
Yale	1	1	1	7	5	.500	0	0
Providence	4	5	6	31	30	.455	0	1
Dartmouth	5	4	5	38	37	.444	0	2
Minnesota-Duluth	3	4	5	33	34	.444	0	1
Clarkson	8	7	9	48	67	.438	0	3
Colorado College	9	6	10	76	84	.375	2	2
Brown	3	2	4	28	38	.333	0	1
†Harvard	11	7	18	90	126	.280	0	2
Northern Michigan	2	1	3	10	19	.250	0	1
Boston College	15	7	22	101	70	.241	1	2
New Hampshire	4	2	8	35	56	.200	0	0
St. Lawrence	8	3	14	51	92	.176	0	1
#Lake Superior State	1	0	1	6	10	.025	0	0
Western Michigan	1	0	2	4	11	.000	0	0

Denver also participated in 1973 tournament but its record was voided by the NCAA in 1977 upon discovery of violations by the University. The team had finished second in '73.)
  *Bowling Green and Northeastern played to a 2-2 tie in 1981-82.
  †Harvard and Michigan State played to a 3-3 tie in 1982-83.
  #Lake Superior State and RPI played to a 3-3 tie in 1984-85.
  HOBEY BAKER MEMORIAL TROPHY (Top College hockey player in U.S.): Scott Fusco, Harvard.

Air Force Academy
Overall: 15-13

	Pos.	Class	Games	G.	A.	Pts.	Pen.
Frank Daldine	F	Sr.	28	18	26	44	22
Tim Hartje	F	Sr.	28	19	21	40	8
John Klimek	F	Jr.	28	16	22	38	26
Jay Mosley	F	Sr.	28	9	15	24	26
Jim Andersen	F	Sr.	28	14	4	18	58
Tom Zupancich	D	So.	28	3	15	18	36
Joe Chapman	F	Jr.	28	7	9	16	42
Keith Nightingale	D	Jr.	12	6	9	15	26
John Anzelc	D	Fr.	28	4	10	14	26
John Manney	F	So.	25	8	5	13	14
Mark Bucki	D	Sr.	28	3	9	12	26
Jim Brunkow	D	Jr.	28	0	12	12	10
Neil Sauve	F	Sr.	27	5	6	11	26
Joe Doyle	F	Fr.	27	4	6	10	18
Joe Delich	F	Fr.	27	6	3	9	6
Jeff Banks	D	Fr.	21	4	3	7	10
Brian Lloyd	F	Sr.	27	2	0	2	0
Kevin McManaman	D	Fr.	22	0	2	2	14
Jack Sundstrom	G	Jr.	9	0	2	2	0
Mike Mason	F	Fr.	1	1	0	1	0
T.J. O'Shaughnessy	G	Sr.	14	0	1	1	2
Jim Jirele	F	Fr.	1	0	1	1	0
Jeff Verville	F	So.	25	0	1	1	8
Darren Maturi	F	Fr.	1	0	1	1	0
Greg Gutterman	F	Fr.	1	0	0	0	0
Jay Ducharme	G	Sr.	11	0	0	0	2
John Thomas	D	Fr.	2	0	0	0	0
Brian Raduenz	F	So.	4	0	0	0	0

U.S. Military Academy (Army)
Overall: 18-11-1; ECAC: 2-9-0

	Pos.	Class	Games	G.	A.	Pts.	Pen.
Matt Wilson	F	Jr.	29	22	28	50	22
Rob Brenner	F	Jr.	30	19	31	50	10
Kevin Keenan	F	Jr.	30	19	29	48	8
Ted Moran	D	Sr.	30	10	27	37	48
Mike Curran	F	Sr.	29	12	23	35	49
Bob Nabb	F	Sr.	30	11	24	35	18
Darryl MacDonald	F	Sr.	30	18	11	29	14
Ted Hanley	F	Sr.	30	10	9	19	60
Vinny Bono	D	So.	30	4	12	16	12
Brian Cox	F	Fr.	14	5	10	15	2
Scott Custer	D	So.	30	4	10	14	40
Vince McDermott	F	Fr.	11	5	7	12	8
Dave Regan	F	Sr.	21	6	5	11	8
Mark Hudak	D	Fr.	30	1	9	10	32
Dan McCormick	F	Jr.	22	3	5	8	6
Bob Ness	D	Sr.	30	0	7	7	30
Mark Hill	D	So.	29	2	4	6	36
Ed Melanson	F	So.	8	3	0	3	2
Mike Chenette	F	So.	8	2	1	3	2
Tim McWain	F	Fr.	18	1	2	3	2
Chris Kohlbeck	F	So.	11	0	3	3	6
John Schoeppach	F	So.	14	0	1	1	6
Dave Cauble	F	Jr.	8	0	1	1	2
Matt Cantele	F	Fr.	2	0	1	1	0
Chris Pietrzak	F	So.	7	0	0	0	6
Scott Thornton	F	Fr.	1	0	0	0	0
Paul Kapsner	F	Sr.	3	0	0	0	2
Mark Kremer	F	Fr.	1	0	0	0	0
John Knieriem	F	Fr.	1	0	0	0	0
Paul DeGironimo	G	Jr.	21	0	0	0	7
Brian Drinkwine	G	Sr.	13	0	0	0	10

Boston College

Overall: 26-13-3; Hockey East: 23-9-2

	Pos.	Class	Games	G.	A.	Pts.	Pen.
Scott Harlow	LW	Sr.	42	38	41	79	48
Doug Brown	RW	Sr.	38	16	40	56	16
Kevin Stevens	LW	Jr.	42	17	27	44	56
Bob Sweeney	C	Sr.	41	15	24	39	52
Dan Shea	LW	So.	40	11	25	36	44
Neil Shea	RW	Sr.	41	12	18	30	52
Ken Hodge	C	So.	21	11	17	28	16
Craig Janney	C	Fr.	34	13	14	27	8
Chris Stapleton	RW	So.	37	12	10	22	10
John McNamara	D	Sr.	42	3	19	22	24
Kevin Houle	RW	Sr.	41	11	9	20	20
John McLean	D	Jr.	41	5	13	18	20
Bob Emery	D	Sr.	39	2	15	17	48
John Devereaux	C	So.	41	8	6	14	24
Tim Sweeney	LW	Fr.	32	8	4	12	8
Paul Marshall	D	Fr.	40	0	12	12	28
Michael Barron	D	Sr.	40	4	6	10	54
Richard Braccia	LW	Fr.	9	0	3	3	20
Mike Mullowney	D	Fr.	26	0	2	2	20
David Buckley	D	Fr.	22	0	2	2	4
Mike Gervasi	LW/D	So.	24	1	0	1	26
Shawn Kennedy	LW	Fr.	2	1	0	1	0
Scott Gordon	G	Sr.	32	0	1	1	14
David Littman	G	Fr.	9	0	1	1	0
Ed McCarthy	RW	Fr.	6	0	1	1	0
David Whyte	RW	Jr.	2	0	1	1	0
John Orr	RW	Sr.	9	0	0	0	0
Mike Connolly	D	Fr.	1	0	0	0	0

Boston University

Overall: 25-14-4; Hockey East: 20-11-3

	Pos.	Class	Games	G.	A.	Pts.	Pen.
John Cullen	C	Jr.	43	25	49	74	54
Clark Donatelli	LW	So.	43	28	34	62	30
Ed Lowney	RW	Jr.	43	18	20	38	14
Jay Octeau	D	Jr.	41	8	27	35	47
Scott Young	RW	Fr.	38	16	13	29	31
Chris Matchett	LW	Sr.	42	5	23	28	50
Mike Kelfer	C	Fr.	39	13	14	27	40
Scott Shaunessy	D	Jr.	38	4	22	26	60
Peter Marshall	C	Sr.	39	15	10	25	37
Scott Sanders	C	So.	36	11	14	25	19
Jeff Sveen	C	So	35	15	8	23	18
David Quinn	D	So.	37	2	20	22	58
Brad MacGregor	LW	Sr.	43	4	11	15	20
Paul Gerlitz	RW	Sr.	34	6	7	13	17
Eric Labrosse	LW	So.	30	4	7	11	28
Brian Foreman	C	So.	22	2	8	10	0
Tom Ryan	D	So.	42	2	8	10	22
Tony Majkozak	LW	Sr.	31	3	6	9	12
David Thiesing	D	Sr.	39	2	5	7	12
Jim Ennis	D	Fr.	40	1	4	5	22
Kris Werner	D	So.	10	0	3	3	2
Bob Deraney	G	So.	16	0	0	0	2
Peter Fish	G	So.	1	0	0	0	0
Terry Taillefer	G	Jr.	29	0	0	0	0
Peter Headon	LW	Fr.	2	0	0	0	0
Ian Wood	C	Fr.	1	0	0	0	0

Bowling Green State University

Overall: 26-14; CCHA: 23-9

	Pos.	Class	Games	G.	A.	Pts.	Pen.
Jamie Wansbrough	RW	Sr.	42	33	44	77	28
Paul Ysebaert	C	So.	42	23	45	68	50
Iain Duncan	LW	Jr.	41	26	26	52	124

	Pos.	Class	Games	G.	A.	Pts.	Pen.
Brian McKee	D	So.	42	19	33	52	120
Brian Maharry	C	So.	41	15	32	47	39
Don Barber	LW	So.	35	21	22	43	64
Greg Parks	C	Fr.	41	16	26	42	43
Clarke Pineo	RW	Fr.	36	16	14	30	12
Andy Gribble	RW	So.	40	6	17	23	8
Scott Paluch	LW/D	So.	34	10	11	21	44
Rob Urban	C	Jr.	34	9	10	19	62
Todd Flichel	D	Jr.	42	3	10	13	84
Geoff Williams	LW	So.	36	4	6	10	44
Doug Claggett	D	Jr.	19	4	4	8	12
Mike Natyshak	RW	Jr.	40	3	5	8	62
Chad Arthur	RW	Fr.	35	3	4	7	50
Thad Rusiecki	D	Fr.	36	0	6	6	38
Brent Regan	D	So.	32	4	2	6	28
Mark Lori	RW	Jr.	9	2	3	5	29
Tom Pratt	D	Jr.	38	1	4	5	74
Alan Leggett	D	Fr.	36	0	5	5	18
Gary Kruzich	G	Fr.	35	0	1	1	20
Steve Dickinson	C	Jr.	1	0	0	0	0
Dan Kwilas	G	Fr.	8	0	0	0	0

Brown University
Overall: 4-19; ECAC: 3-18

	Pos.	Class	Games	G.	A.	Pts.	Pen.
Steve Climo	LW	Jr.	23	7	14	21	14
Dan Allen	C	Jr.	23	4	14	18	2
Mike Rechan	C	Jr.	21	5	10	15	53
Bobby Jones	C	Sr.	17	5	9	14	28
Gordie Ernst	C	Fr.	22	4	10	14	6
Karl Burns	LW	So.	19	7	2	9	20
Joe Kuzneski	RW	Sr.	12	6	3	9	12
Pat Davis	D	Sr.	23	2	7	9	16
Kelly Burns	RW	So.	20	2	6	8	22
Steve Crozier	C	Jr.	18	2	6	8	10
Mark Rechan	LW	Jr.	16	4	4	8	6
Bruce McColl	D	So.	20	2	6	8	14
Sean McNamara	D	So.	19	1	6	7	26
Mark LaChance	D	Fr.	23	3	4	7	50
Mike Langton	RW	Fr.	16	1	5	6	4
Mike Girouard	D	Jr.	18	3	3	6	34
John Caragliano	D	So.	21	2	4	6	16
John McEvoy	RW	Sr.	15	2	4	6	6
Tom Wallack	RW	Sr.	7	3	2	5	20
Rob Hardy	RW	Fr.	9	2	3	5	6
Al Randaccio	LW	Sr.	13	3	2	5	4
Rod Pritchard	LW	Fr.	6	2	1	3	8
Sean Flanagan	RW	So.	4	1	1	2	0
Bob Ernst	F	Fr.	3	0	2	2	0
Mike Fanning	LW	Sr.	2	0	1	1	10
Mark Stonich	D	So.	10	0	0	0	10
Bob Naegele	G	So.	10	0	0	0	0
Michel Bayard	G	So.	15	0	0	0	2
Dave Schwartz	D	Fr.	3	0	0	0	0
Dominic Alfonso	G	So.	3	0	0	0	0
Rick Bonine	LW	Fr.	3	0	0	0	2
Ross Bonine	C	Fr.	3	0	0	0	0
Mike Perner	F	So.	3	0	0	0	4
Mike Hall	D	Fr.	1	0	0	0	0
Jim Lombardi	D	Fr.	1	0	0	0	4
Matt Parker	D/F	So.	2	0	0	0	0

Clarkson University
Overall: ECAC: 12-6-3

	Pos.	Class	Games	G.	A.	Pts.	Pen.
Charlie Meitner	LW	Sr.	28	18	23	41	42
Mike Harvey	C	Sr.	27	20	15	35	28
Luciano Borsato	C	So.	28	14	17	31	44

	Pos.	Class	Games	G.	A.	Pts.	Pen.
Steve Williams	RW	So.	28	13	17	30	18
Al Hill	C	Jr.	26	12	16	28	26
Andy Otto	D	Sr.	28	4	24	28	20
Mike Morrison	LW	Fr.	26	8	15	23	42
Bruce Tillotson	LW	Sr.	18	6	11	17	54
Jean Rouleau	RW	Fr.	19	4	13	17	12
Shawn LaVoy	C	Fr.	28	7	7	14	32
Derek Ray	RW	Sr.	28	8	4	12	142
Dan O'Brien	RW	Fr.	19	2	6	8	26
Brad James	D	Fr.	25	1	6	7	12
Jay Rose	D	So.	28	0	7	7	34
Jeff Korchinski	D	Jr.	25	2	4	6	18
Bob Lenney	C	Sr.	24	3	2	5	6
Chris Mills	D	So.	28	2	3	5	32
Rodger Huiatt	RW	So.	24	1	4	5	4
Michael Ashe	D	Fr.	28	1	2	3	20
Matt Lalonde	C	Fr.	6	2	0	2	4
Jamie Falle	G	Sr.	27	0	1	1	4
Jim Zabelny	D	Fr.	2	0	0	0	2
David Mellen	LW	Fr.	11	0	0	0	5

Colgate University
Overall: 15-15-2; ECAC: 9-11-1

	Pos.	Class	Games	G.	A.	Pts.	Pen.
Gerard Waslen	RW	Sr.	32	28	36	64	68
Rejean Boivin	RW	So.	32	26	20	46	6
Greg Drechsel	LW	So.	31	12	24	36	53
Gary Mitchell	C	So.	32	10	21	31	37
Brad Martel	LW	So.	32	8	15	23	14
Doug Davis	C	Jr.	32	6	17	23	14
Lowell MacDonald	LW	Jr.	32	6	15	21	12
Paul Jenkins	D	Jr.	31	4	16	20	66
Mike Bishop	D	Fr.	25	9	8	17	63
Mark Holmes	RW	So.	30	11	5	16	20
Harold Duvall	LW	Jr.	26	8	7	15	24
Scott Young	D	Fr.	28	5	6	11	88
Scott Reston	C	Jr.	28	3	7	10	29
Peter Webb	D	Fr.	17	1	5	6	8
Rick Russell	D	Jr.	29	0	6	6	6
Don Taylor	D	Jr.	14	1	2	3	24
Kelly Mills	LW	Fr.	17	1	2	3	4
Lou Wagar	RW	Sr.	20	2	0	2	4
John McCarthy	C	So.	9	0	2	2	0
Todd Wolf	D	Fr.	32	0	2	2	22
Gerry Brockman	C	Sr.	4	0	1	1	0
Joe Tetzlaff	LW	Sr.	7	0	1	1	0
Wayne Cowley	G	Fr.	7	0	0	0	2
Dan Delianedis	G	Sr.	28	0	0	0	2

Colorado College
Overall: 12-26-2; WCHA: 11-21-2

	Pos.	Class	Games	G.	A.	Pts.	Pen.
Rick Boh	C	Jr.	40	30	29	59	14
Rob Doyle	D	Jr.	40	18	41	59	73
Dan Brennan	C	Sr.	39	18	23	41	45
Brent Gropp	RW	Sr.	40	13	26	39	66
Scott Schneider	RW	Jr.	40	16	22	38	32
Gord Whitaker	RW	Jr.	34	14	16	30	53
Keith Hoppe	LW	So.	40	11	10	21	22
Scott Campbell	D	Jr.	40	0	18	18	30
Tim Budy	LW	Fr.	40	9	8	17	30
Marty Ketola	RW	Jr.	40	5	12	17	89
Tom Pederson	D	So.	40	7	8	15	10
Dave Hardie	D	Sr.	36	0	13	13	40
Ken Filbey	C	Sr.	20	5	7	12	34
Guy Gadowsky	RW	Fr.	38	5	7	12	6
Mark Krois	RW	Jr.	29	0	7	7	24
Mark Olsen	D	Fr.	39	2	4	6	48

	Pos.	Class	Games	G.	A.	Pts.	Pen.
Paul Markovich	D	So.	31	0	5	5	4
Doug Wieck	LW	Fr.	6	3	0	3	2
Dave Baker	D	Sr.	22	1	2	3	8
Dean French	C	Fr.	15	0	3	3	2
Steve Grumley	D	So.	14	1	1	2	12
Derek Pizzey	G	Sr.	19	0	2	2	4
Marty Wakelyn	G	Fr.	24	0	1	1	2
John Crawford	D	Fr.	3	0	0	0	0
Dion McClellan	RW	Fr.	5	0	0	0	4
Tim Sheridan	RW	So.	1	0	0	0	0

Cornell University
Overall: 21-7-4; ECAC: 13-6-2

	Pos.	Class	Games	G.	A.	Pts.	Pen.
Joe Nieuwendyk	C	So.	21	21	21	42	45
Duanne Moeser	W	Sr.	16	13	20	33	20
Peter Natyshak	W	Sr.	21	12	21	33	40
Chris Norton	D	So.	21	8	15	23	56
Mike Schafer	D	Sr.	21	2	20	22	65
Dave Hunter	W	Jr.	21	5	12	17	55
Pete Marcov	W	Sr.	21	3	14	17	18
Chris Grenier	C	Fr.	13	5	7	12	4
Andy Craig	D	Jr.	20	3	9	12	14
Mark Major	D	Jr.	21	5	6	11	6
Dave Crombeen	W	Fr.	20	6	4	10	45
Dave Shippel	W	Jr.	21	6	4	10	16
Mark Canduro	C	Sr.	20	4	5	9	14
Stewart Smith	C	So.	15	3	5	8	16
Keith Howie	W	Jr.	8	2	3	5	4
John Perry	D	Fr.	21	0	5	5	8
Alan Tigert	D	Jr.	17	0	5	5	4
Rob Levasseur	C	Fr.	17	2	2	4	12
Darren Snyder	D	Fr.	20	1	1	2	15
Mike Moberg	D	So.	3	0	2	2	2
Keith Donovan	D	Sr.	1	0	1	1	0
Pat Heaphy	W	Fr.	1	0	0	0	0
Tom Jackson	W	So.	1	0	0	0	0
Craig Donovan	D	Fr.	14	0	0	0	0
Doug Dadswell	G	So.	21	0	0	0	2

Dartmouth College
Overall: 7-18-0; ECAC: 4-17-0

	Pos.	Class	Games	G.	A.	Pts.	Pen.
Tom Finks	C	Fr.	25	9	15	24	20
Paul Rai	W	So.	23	7	13	20	40
Andy Donahue	C	Fr.	25	12	7	19	14
Brien Jacobson	D	Sr.	22	4	12	16	36
Ned Desmond	D	Fr.	23	4	12	16	4
Dan Nugent	W	Sr.	24	6	7	13	42
Brett Burlock	W	So.	25	5	7	12	18
Mark Glover	C	Fr.	19	5	6	11	14
Paul O'Hern	W	So.	25	2	8	10	26
Derek Tweddell	W	Fr.	25	2	7	9	2
Marty Sims	W	Sr.	21	5	3	8	4
Kevin McCann	C	Jr.	18	4	4	8	20
Doug Weiss	W	So.	25	2	6	8	28
Bill McInerny	W	So.	18	4	2	6	22
Rob Goulet	D	Fr.	22	1	4	5	32
Butch Coughlin	D	Fr.	17	3	1	4	10
Doug Bowman	D	Fr.	4	0	4	4	2
Paul Dion	D	Sr.	20	0	4	4	16
Don Raftery	D	So.	13	2	0	2	8
Tom Earle	W	Fr.	12	1	1	2	25
Jack Bohn	D	Jr.	20	0	2	2	41
Pat Kendall	D	Fr.	6	0	1	1	14
Tim Osby	G	Fr.	16	0	0	0	2
Jeff Bower	G	Jr.	10	0	0	0	2
Ed Cepuran	W	Fr.	2	0	0	0	4
Sal Tiano	W	So.	1	0	0	0	0

University of Denver
Overall: 34-13-1; WCHA: 25-9

	Pos.	Class	Games	G.	A.	Pts.	Pen.
Dallas Gaume	C	Sr.	47	32	67	99	18
Dwight Mathiasen	W	Jr.	48	40	49	89	48
John McMillan	C	Jr.	38	16	40	56	30
Jeff Lamb	C	Jr.	45	23	31	54	75
Jim Smith	D	Sr.	47	10	40	50	37
Tom Weiss	W	Sr.	48	22	26	48	50
Grant Dion	D	Sr.	47	10	23	33	14
Kermit Ecklebarger	W	Sr.	46	16	15	31	38
David Hanson	W	So.	45	12	14	26	45
Scott Mathias	W	Fr.	48	12	12	24	18
Jim Onstad	W	Jr.	44	8	15	23	8
Bruce Hill	W	So.	24	7	13	20	20
Ed Cristofoli	W	Fr.	46	10	9	19	32
David Gourlie	D	Jr.	48	5	11	16	43
Don Mercier	D	So.	48	3	10	13	60
Eric Johnson	D	Sr.	34	0	11	11	30
Derik Sheers	W	Sr.	19	5	5	10	12
Derek Mayer	D	Fr.	44	2	7	9	42
Thomas Moore	W/D	Fr.	25	1	4	5	4
Doug Menzies	D	So.	25	1	2	3	20
Tom Allen	G	Sr.	24	0	2	2	10
Chris Olson	G	Jr.	27	0	0	0	2

Ferris State College
Overall: 17-19-2; CCHA: 13-17-2

	Pos.	Class	Games	G.	A.	Pts.	Pen.
Paul Lowden	RW	Jr.	38	32	39	71	20
Peter Lowden	C	Jr.	37	28	40	68	25
Murray Winnicki	LW	Fr.	38	19	40	59	60
Gary Sweetnam	D	Fr.	38	6	40	46	76
Dean Cowling	RW	Fr.	37	16	23	39	49
Gilles Grondin	C	Fr.	35	10	14	24	33
Dean Davies	D	Fr.	38	8	16	24	50
Paul Couture	LW	Sr.	29	8	13	21	24
Darin Fridgen	C	So.	35	12	8	20	68
Andy Black	C	Fr.	33	10	8	18	6
Kevin MacIsaac	LW	Fr.	33	11	6	17	77
Phil Kaske	LW	Fr.	26	7	9	16	34
Rod Schluter	C	So.	8	6	8	14	8
Serge Poulin	C	Fr.	21	2	9	11	4
Doug McLeod	D	Fr.	22	2	7	9	35
Mike Chighisola	RW	Fr.	10	4	4	8	8
Mike Reidy	D	Fr.	36	2	6	8	51
Joey Edwards	C	Fr.	10	2	6	8	12
Dave DeSalo	D	So.	21	1	5	6	18
Mike Sparago	RW	Jr.	21	1	4	5	22
Jeff Lindsay	D	So.	20	1	3	4	21
Doug Edgar	D	So.	22	1	2	3	26
Dave Issel	LW	Fr.	18	2	0	2	10
Ron Johnston	D	Fr.	14	0	2	2	14
Gary Robertson	D	Fr.	22	0	2	2	28
Glenn Raeburn	G	Fr.	30	0	1	1	0
Dave Sharpe	G	Fr.	12	0	1	1	6
Yvon Prefontaine	D	Fr.	10	0	0	0	2
Scott Cowie	LW	Fr.	4	0	0	0	4
Phil Bryant	G	So.	5	0	0	0	0

Harvard University
Overall: 25-8-1; ECAC: 18-3

	Pos.	Class	Games	G.	A.	Pts.	Pen.
Scott Fusco	C	Sr.	31	24	44	68	37
Tim Smith	RW	Sr.	34	28	29	57	24
Tim Barakett	RW	Jr.	34	19	31	50	14
Lane MacDonald	LW	So.	30	22	24	46	45
Allen Bourbeau	C	So.	25	24	19	43	26
Mark Benning	D	Sr.	32	2	36	38	20

	Pos.	Class	Games	G.	A.	Pts.	Pen.
Ed Krayer	LW	Fr.	34	9	22	31	4
Randy Taylor	D	Jr.	33	5	20	25	30
Jerry Pawlowski	D	So.	34	3	19	22	22
Rob Ohno	C	So.	34	7	12	19	18
Steve Armstrong	LW	So.	33	10	7	17	38
Pete Chiarelli	RW	Jr.	31	4	11	15	16
Nick Carone	F	So.	33	7	7	14	36
Greg Chalmers	C	Sr.	18	7	6	13	18
Pete Follows	RW	Sr.	26	4	7	11	4
Andy Janfaza	LW	So.	27	4	5	9	32
Don Sweeney	D	So.	31	4	5	9	12
Chris Biotti	D	Fr.	15	3	5	8	18
Butch Cufone	D	Jr.	23	0	5	5	2
Josh Caplan	D	Fr.	30	1	3	4	10
Garry Green	RW	So.	8	0	3	3	2
Craig Taucher	C/LW	Fr.	2	0	2	2	0
Grant Blair	G	Sr.	31	0	2	2	12
Rick Haney	C/LW	Jr.	8	0	1	1	0
Dickie McEvoy	G	Sr.	4	0	1	1	0

University of Illinois-Chicago
Overall: 25-14-1; CCHA: 22-12

	Pos.	Class	Games	G.	A.	Pts.	Pen.
Jeff Nelson	C	So.	40	26	28	54	18
Mike Rucinski	W	Jr.	37	16	31	47	18
Scott Knutson	W	Sr.	39	19	21	40	34
Paul Tory	C	So.	40	21	14	35	45
Sheldon Gorski	W	Fr.	37	18	11	29	48
Trent Rees	C	Fr.	40	7	20	27	4
Rob Klenk	W	So.	34	10	15	25	64
Scott Seaver	W	Sr.	40	10	13	23	30
Mike Mersch	D	Jr.	36	4	19	23	30
Harry Armstrong	D	Jr.	34	6	13	19	21
Tom Almquist	W	Jr.	32	6	13	19	70
Shawn Cronin	D	Sr.	35	3	8	11	70
Steve Huglen	D	Jr.	38	2	8	10	40
Jeff Simmer	D	Fr.	31	1	9	10	18
Paul Pulis	W	Jr.	28	7	2	9	14
Terry Majich	W	Sr.	35	1	8	9	43
Darin Alexander	D	So.	39	1	8	9	97
Jamie Husgen	D	Jr.	29	2	5	7	51
Scott Shoffstall	C	Fr.	16	2	2	4	0
Henry Reimer	W	Fr.	31	2	1	3	10
John Mynatt	D	Jr.	15	0	2	2	18
Jim Hickey	G	Jr.	..	0	0	0	2
Brad Ryan	G	So.	..	0	0	0	12

Lake Superior State College
Overall: 24-18-1; CCHA: 17-14-1

	Pos.	Class	Games	G.	A.	Pts.	Pen.
Scott Johnson	LW	Sr.	38	21	24	45	55
Keith Martin	C	Sr.	40	20	23	43	97
Jim Roque	C	Jr.	39	14	23	37	12
Dean Dixon	C	Jr.	39	13	24	37	49
Nick Palumbo	LW	Sr.	40	23	12	35	30
Mike de Carle	RW	Fr.	36	12	21	33	40
Craig Hewson	C	So.	41	10	22	32	32
Paul Jerrard	RW	Jr.	38	13	11	24	34
Matt Cote	D	Jr.	40	4	18	22	42
Kim McIvor	LW	So.	39	7	13	20	18
Mark Vichorek	D	Sr.	39	9	11	20	38
Anthony Palumbo	C	Fr.	26	5	7	12	4
Mike Warus	RW	Jr.	38	5	6	11	85
Ken Martel	D	Fr.	39	3	8	11	29
Grant Clark	D	So.	41	1	8	9	14
Rene Chapdelaine	D	Fr.	38	2	7	9	24
Terry Hossack	D	So.	33	0	9	9	34
Vic Stynsky	C	Fr.	20	3	2	5	6

	Pos.	Class	Games	G.	A.	Pts.	Pen.
Mark Vermette	RW	Fr.	30	1	4	5	45
Brian Michaud	D	So.	13	0	4	4	4
Jeff Dicaire	D	So.	15	1	2	3	6
Steve Hurt	RW	So.	12	1	1	2	4
Randy Exelby	G	Jr.	27	0	2	2	2
Joe Shawhan	G	Jr.	20	0	1	1	2

University of Lowell

Overall: 11-29-2; Hockey East: 7-25-2

	Pos.	Class	Games	G.	A.	Pts.	Pen.
Jon Morris	C	So.	39	25	31	56	52
Tony LoPilato	RW	So.	35	18	19	37	73
Jim Newhouse	LW	So.	39	20	13	33	32
Bill Dohaney	C	So.	36	15	18	33	64
Paul Ames	D	Jr.	41	7	20	27	39
Rob Badger	LW	So.	36	8	17	25	27
Tom Evangelista	RW	Sr.	35	10	13	23	44
Mike Rawnsley	D	Sr.	35	6	13	19	26
John Borrell	RW	Fr.	41	3	15	18	12
Gary Valimont	C	So.	37	10	7	17	34
Tim Foley	D	So.	41	8	8	16	36
Dennis McCarroll	C	Sr.	38	6	10	16	69
Fred Allard	RW	Fr.	35	4	8	12	79
Peter Heinze	D	So.	36	1	11	12	62
Jim O'Brien	LW	Sr.	37	3	7	10	16
Carl Valimont	D	So.	26	1	9	10	12
Scott Drevitch	D	Fr.	32	1	8	9	10
Gary Murphy	D	So.	27	0	9	9	32
Scott Messina	C	Fr.	17	5	3	8	14
John Shumski	RW	Sr.	16	1	6	7	10
Doug Burns	LW	So.	18	1	5	6	16
George Dupont	C	Fr.	12	0	4	4	8
Jyrki Maki	D	So.	26	1	2	3	9
Dana Janis	LW	Fr.	11	1	0	1	4
Paul Mahan	RW	Jr.	6	0	1	1	2
Tom Healy	D	Fr.	1	0	0	0	0
Dave Delfino	G	So.	10	0	0	0	0
Dana Demole	G	Sr.	34	0	0	0	4

University of Maine

Overall: 11-28-1; Hockey East: 8-25-1

	Pos.	Class	Games	G.	A.	Pts.	Pen.
John McDonald	RW	Sr.	39	11	24	35	76
Bob Corkum	RW	Fr.	39	7	26	33	53
Dave Wensley	C	So.	40	13	18	31	30
Mike Golden	C	So.	24	13	16	29	10
Bruce Major	LW	Fr.	38	14	14	28	39
Jack Capuano	D	Fr.	39	9	18	27	51
Ron Hellen	LW	Sr.	39	12	12	24	48
Scott Smith	D	Sr.	39	6	15	21	102
Mike McHugh	LW	So.	38	9	10	19	24
Steve Santini	RW	Jr.	35	8	10	18	10
Chris Cambio	LW	Fr.	35	10	7	17	10
Eric Weinrich	D	Fr.	34	0	15	15	26
Todd Jenkins	C	Fr.	28	7	7	14	14
Shawn Anderson	D	Fr.	16	5	8	13	22
Dave Nonis	D	So.	40	3	10	13	22
Jay Mazur	LW	Jr.	34	5	7	12	18
Todd Studnicka	C	So.	33	6	5	11	31
Neil Johnson	D	Sr.	37	1	7	8	55
Rob Braccia	RW	Fr.	23	2	3	5	15
Todd McComb	D	So.	21	0	4	4	6
Duane Wahlin	D	So.	12	0	3	3	14
John Baker	D	Jr.	17	1	0	1	0
Vince Guidotti	LW	Fr.	16	0	0	0	8
Al Loring	G	Fr.	29	0	0	0	4
Jean Lacoste	G	Jr.	10	0	0	0	0
Ray Roy	G	Sr.	9	0	0	0	0
Rich Horrigan	D	Fr.	1	0	0	0	0

Miami (O.) University
Overall: 8-28-2; CCHA: 3-27-2

	Pos.	Class	Games	G.	A.	Pts.	Pen.
Todd Channell	RW	Sr.	38	27	27	54	18
John O'Connor	C	Jr.	38	13	20	33	8
Bill Easdale	RW	Sr.	38	18	14	32	38
Mike Orn	C	So.	31	13	19	32	58
Greg Dornbach	C	So.	35	13	18	31	42
Jeff Sisto	RW	Fr.	38	10	14	24	22
Tim Moore	D	Sr	38	5	17	22	68
Boyd Sutton	LW	Fr.	33	8	13	21	24
Nate Kondo	C	Fr.	32	6	14	20	14
Mike Martinec	C	Jr.	25	7	10	17	14
Chris Archer	RW	Fr.	33	7	10	17	23
Ron Saatzer	C	Fr.	23	7	9	16	16
Ron Renner	D	Sr.	38	7	8	15	20
Brian Wilkie	RW	Fr.	19	5	6	11	20
Steve Benson	D	So.	34	2	9	11	24
Rob Robinson	D	Fr.	38	1	9	10	24
Craig Pestell	RW	So.	23	2	6	8	28
Don Harkins	RW	Jr.	11	3	3	6	10
Tim Huettl	RW	Jr.	33	2	4	6	43
Mike Macoun	D	Jr.	33	0	6	6	42
Tom Terwilliger	D	So.	32	1	3	4	35
Jeff Johnson	LW	Fr.	8	1	0	1	6
Mike Garibaldi	C	Fr.	8	0	1	1	8
Bill Suhanek	G	So.	13	0	1	1	6
Brent Smith	G	Jr.	25	0	1	1	2
Tim Hall	G	Jr.	7	0	0	0	2
Dean Garnett	G	Fr.	1	0	0	0	0

University of Michigan
Overall: 12-26-0; CCHA: 10-22-0

	Pos.	Class	Games	G.	A.	Pts.	Pen.
Brad Jones	C	Jr.	36	28	39	67	40
Brad McCaughey	RW	So.	32	24	26	50	51
Jeff Norton	D	So.	37	15	30	45	99
Billy Powers	RW	So.	38	15	28	43	10
Tom Stiles	LW	Sr.	34	13	29	42	60
Chris Seyche	LW	Sr.	26	12	26	38	47
Todd Brost	C	Fr.	38	9	26	35	30
Frank Downing	RW	Sr.	38	20	9	29	20
Todd Carlile	D	Sr.	38	6	20	26	84
Myles O'Connor	D	Fr.	37	6	19	25	73
Bruce Macnab	C	Jr.	35	5	14	19	24
Jeff Urban	LW	Fr.	36	9	6	15	23
Pat Goff	D	Sr.	38	2	12	14	30
Joe Lockwood	RW	So.	38	7	6	13	45
Mike Cusack	RW	Fr.	37	8	2	10	51
Sean Baker	D	So.	32	1	7	8	24
Paul Rossi	C	So.	26	0	5	5	6
Bill Brauer	D	Sr.	28	1	2	3	22
Gary Lorden	D	So.	18	0	2	2	6
Arnold Morrison	D	Fr.	9	1	0	1	14
Dan Capuano	D	Fr.	4	0	1	1	2
Bob Lindgren	G	Fr.	13	0	1	1	0
Tim Makris	G	So.	29	0	0	0	17
Mike Rossi	G	So.	10	0	0	0	7
John Bjorkman	LW	Jr.	7	0	0	0	6

Michigan State University
Overall: 34-9-2; CCHA: 23-7-2

	Pos.	Class	Games	G.	A.	Pts.	Pen.
Mike Donnelly	LW	Sr.	44	59	38	97	65
Kevin Miller	C	So.	45	19	52	71	112
Mitch Messier	RW	Jr.	38	24	40	64	36
Joe Murphy	C	Fr.	35	24	37	61	50
Bill Shibicky	C	Jr.	44	17	39	56	104
Brian McReynolds	C	Fr.	45	14	24	38	78

	Pos.	Class	Games	G.	A.	Pts.	Pen.
Don McSween	D	Jr.	45	9	29	38	18
Jeff Parker	RW	Jr.	41	15	20	35	88
Tom Tilley	D	So.	42	9	25	34	48
Bruce Rendall	LW	Fr.	45	14	18	32	68
Danton Cole	RW	Fr.	43	11	10	21	22
Bobby Reynolds	LW	Fr.	45	9	10	19	26
Brad Beck	D	Sr.	41	3	15	18	40
Geir Hoff	LW	Fr.	39	3	11	14	14
Brad Hamilton	D	Fr.	43	3	10	13	52
Rick Tosto	C	So.	30	4	8	12	10
Sean Clement	D	So.	40	4	7	11	40
Chris Luongo	D	Fr.	38	1	5	6	29
Dee Rizzo	D	Sr.	28	0	5	5	12
Rick Fernandez	LW	Sr.	12	0	3	3	6
Dave Arkeilpane	RW	Jr.	19	2	0	2	14

Michigan Technological University
Overall: 10-26-4; WCHA: 9-22-3

	Pos.	Class	Games	G.	A.	Pts.	Pen.
John Archibald	C	So.	37	19	19	38	26
Randy McKay	RW	So.	40	12	22	34	46
Tom Bissett	C	Fr.	40	12	21	33	18
Geordie Hamilton	C	Sr.	39	15	17	32	43
Doug Harris	RW	Sr.	40	13	17	30	58
Richard Novak	RW	So.	38	9	20	29	20
Don Porter	LW	Jr.	40	17	10	27	28
Ally Cook	LW	Jr.	40	11	16	27	18
Dave Reierson	D	Sr.	39	7	16	23	51
Scott White	D	Fr.	40	3	15	18	56
Randy Oswald	D	Jr.	30	4	9	13	58
Kevin Fritz	LW	Jr.	39	5	7	12	33
Kelly Murphy	D	So.	40	0	11	11	20
Tim Flanagan	RW	So.	20	2	3	5	36
Scott Compton	LW	Sr.	40	0	5	5	108
Marc Colvin	RW	So.	25	2	2	4	27
Steve Wendorf	D	Fr.	37	1	1	2	23
Brian Hannon	LW	Jr.	4	1	1	2	2
Russ Becker	D	So.	33	0	2	2	51
Dave Roach	G	Jr.	23	0	1	1	4
Tiger Pierce	G	Sr.	21	0	0	0	7
Graham Hamilton	C	So.	13	0	0	0	6
Brad Mattson	RW	Fr.	3	0	0	0	4

University of Minnesota
Overall: 35-13; WCHA: 24-10

	Pos.	Class	Games	G.	A.	Pts.	Pen.
Corey Millen	C	Jr.	48	41	42	83	64
Pat Micheletti	W	Sr.	48	32	48	80	113
Steve MacSwain	W	Jr.	48	26	35	61	61
Wally Chapman	W	Sr.	47	29	29	58	35
Jay Cates	C	So.	47	20	33	53	50
Todd Okerlund	W	Jr.	48	17	32	49	58
Gary Shopek	D	Jr.	47	6	35	41	58
Tony Kellin	D	Jr.	44	10	24	34	61
Dave Snuggerud	C	Fr.	42	14	18	32	47
Todd Richards	D	Fr.	38	6	23	29	38
Tim Bergland	W	Jr.	48	11	16	27	26
Paul Broten	C	So.	38	6	16	22	24
Craig Mack	D	Jr.	45	2	15	17	32
Steve Orth	C	So.	38	6	7	13	4
David Grannis	W	So.	25	5	7	12	14
Eric Dornfeld	D	Jr.	43	3	8	11	29
Tom Chorske	W	Fr.	39	6	4	10	16
Marty Nanne	W	Fr.	20	5	5	10	20
Barry Nelson	D	Jr.	23	1	7	8	14
David Espe	W/D	Fr.	27	0	6	6	18
Chris May	C	Fr.	11	2	4	6	11
John Blue	G	So.	29	0	1	1	4

	Pos.	Class	Games	G.	A.	Pts.	Pen.
Frank Pietrangelo	G	Sr.	23	0	1	1	0
Frank Gersich	D	Sr.	22	1	0	1	22
Jon Brekken	G	So.	1	0	0	0	0
John Labatt	W	Jr.	1	0	0	0	0
Mike Luckraft	D	Fr.	1	0	0	0	0
Brian Golden	W	Fr.	1	0	0	0	0

University of Minnesota-Duluth
Overall: 26-13-3; WCHA: 21-12-1

	Pos.	Class	Games	G.	A.	Pts.	Pen.
Brett Hull	RW	So.	42	52	32	84	46
Skeeter Moore	LW	Jr.	42	28	41	69	52
Norm Maciver	D	Sr.	42	11	51	62	36
Matt Christensen	C	Sr.	33	16	41	57	36
Brian Johnson	LW/D	Sr.	42	11	37	48	18
Mark Odnokon	LW	Sr.	40	16	29	45	88
Sean Toomey	RW	Jr.	33	23	11	34	10
Dave Cowan	C	Jr.	41	9	16	25	8
Jim Toninato	C	Sr.	40	6	16	22	37
Guy Gosselin	D	Sr.	39	2	16	18	53
Jim Sprenger	D	Jr.	42	6	11	17	24
Darin Illikainen	LW	So.	31	6	6	12	6
Joe Delisle	RW	So.	39	4	6	10	32
Mike DeAngelis	D	So.	34	1	4	5	10
Bruce Fishback	RW	Jr.	37	2	3	5	4
Tom Lorentz	C	Fr.	17	4	1	5	6
Sean Krakiwsky	RW	Fr.	10	0	4	4	2
Tom Hanson	D	Fr.	28	1	2	3	6
Pat Janostin	D	Fr.	26	1	2	3	4
Brian Nelson	C	So.	14	1	2	3	2
Bob Alexander	RW	So.	6	1	1	2	4
Wayne Smith	C	Fr.	11	2	0	2	4
Terry Shold	LW	Fr.	18	1	1	2	2
Brian Durand	C	Jr.	11	1	0	1	6
Dan Tousignant	C	Fr.	17	1	0	1	4
Rob Pallin	D	Fr.	19	0	1	1	8
John Hyduke	G	Fr.	24	0	1	1	0
Rick Hayko	G	Fr.	1	0	0	0	0
Mike Cortes	G	Fr.	18	0	0	0	0

University of New Hampshire
Overall: 5-29-3; Hockey East: 5-27-2

	Pos.	Class	Games	G.	A.	Pts.	Pen.
Peter Herms	D	Sr.	37	13	29	42	22
Shane Skidmore	RW	Sr.	34	10	28	38	26
Mike Rossetti	C	So.	34	16	16	32	54
James Richmond	LW	Jr.	27	9	22	31	22
Steve Leach	C	So.	25	22	6	28	30
Tim Hanley	RW	So.	29	9	13	22	22
Quintin Brickley	RW	So.	26	8	10	18	4
Rick Lambert	LW	So.	37	9	7	16	39
Chris Laganas	C	Jr.	34	2	11	13	8
Kevin Thurston	RW	So.	26	3	6	9	10
Steve Horner	RW	Fr.	30	3	5	8	14
Steve Smith	C	Fr.	24	5	2	7	4
Scott Brown	LW	So.	31	3	4	7	10
Allister Brown	LW	Jr.	36	2	5	7	28
Peter Wotton	D	Jr.	25	1	6	7	34
Jeff Cournoyer	D	Fr.	34	2	4	6	26
Mark Babcock	D	Fr.	21	0	5	5	10
Mike Glennon	LW	So.	20	2	2	4	6
Greg Boudreau	D	Fr.	24	1	2	3	20
Tim Shields	C	Fr.	20	0	3	3	22
Mike Roth	D	Fr.	27	0	3	3	20
Dan Prachar	RW	Fr.	21	0	2	2	4
Kevin Schrader	D	Fr.	32	1	0	1	22
Greg Rota	D	Sr.	23	0	1	1	2
Rich Burchill	G	Fr.	15	0	0	0	0
John Olevitz	D	So.	2	0	0	0	0
Mark Dorval	RW	Fr.	5	0	0	0	0

University of North Dakota
Overall: 24-16-1; WCHA: 19-14-1

	Pos.	Class	Games	G.	A.	Pts.	Pen.
Chris Jensen	W	Sr.	34	25	40	65	53
Brian Williams	C	Sr.	40	22	40	62	61
Bob Joyce	W	So.	38	31	28	59	40
Scott Sandelin	D	Sr.	40	7	31	38	38
Mickey Krampotich	W	Jr.	34	18	17	35	14
Brad Berry	D	Jr.	40	6	29	35	26
Glen Klotz	D	Sr.	39	6	28	34	33
Steve Johnson	C	So.	38	8	20	28	18
Scott Dub	W	So.	40	11	13	24	82
Ian Kidd	D	Fr.	37	6	16	22	65
Perry Nakonechny	W	Jr.	38	8	12	20	28
Malcolm Parks	W	Jr.	39	6	14	20	38
Scott Koberinski	C	Fr.	31	5	9	14	6
Bill Claviter	W	Jr.	35	4	10	14	34
Jeff Bowen	C	So.	38	9	4	13	40
Tarek Howard	D/W	Jr.	32	2	11	13	28
Rick Forst	W	So.	32	7	4	11	22
Tom Benson	D	So.	31	1	6	7	55
Todd Norman	C	So.	19	4	1	5	32
Mike LaMoine	D	Fr.	13	0	4	4	10
Grant Paranica	W	Fr.	6	2	0	2	0
Tim Loven	D	Sr.	16	0	1	1	4
Greg Strome	G	Jr.	21	0	1	1	2
Jim Steen	W	Fr.	8	0	0	0	2
Scott Brower	G	So.	20	0	0	0	0

Northeastern University
Overall: 20-17-2; Hockey East: 18-14-2

	Pos.	Class	Games	G.	A.	Pts.	Pen.
Jay Heinbuck	C	Sr.	39	30	40	70	12
Rod Isbister	C	Sr.	39	27	29	56	28
Stew Emerson	RW	Sr.	38	18	23	41	54
David O'Brien	LW	So.	39	23	16	39	18
Greg Neary	RW	Sr.	39	12	18	30	22
Rico Rossi	LW	Fr.	38	12	18	30	83
Kevin Heffernan	C	So.	35	8	21	29	12
Claude Lodin	D	So.	33	4	25	29	61
Greg Pratt	LW	Jr.	39	14	12	26	8
Marty Raus	D	Sr.	38	4	21	25	30
Roman Kinal	LW	Jr.	31	8	15	23	14
Paul Fitzsimmons	D	So.	38	3	18	21	44
John Ridpath	D	Jr.	28	1	10	11	34
Bill Whitfield	D	Jr.	39	1	8	9	4
Brian Dowd	D	Fr.	24	1	8	9	36
Dave Buda	C	Sr.	39	4	4	8	39
Scott Marshall	RW	Sr.	24	3	5	8	6
Joe MacInnis	LW	So.	20	4	3	7	10
Gerry Kiley	D	So.	25	2	4	6	22
Peter Massey	LW	Jr.	36	4	0	4	22
Mike McDougall	RW	Fr.	11	1	2	3	0
Bruce Racine	G	So.	37	0	3	3	0
Greg Polak	RW	Fr.	4	1	1	2	6
Chris Long	G	Fr.	3	0	0	0	0

Northern Michigan University
Overall: 23-14-2; WCHA: 21-13

	Pos.	Class	Games	G.	A.	Pts.	Pen.
Gary Emmons	C	Jr.	36	45	30	75	34
Joe West	W	Jr.	36	20	33	53	111
Ralph Vos	W	Jr.	39	12	36	48	42
Ron Chyzowski	W	Jr.	38	20	19	39	12
Dave Moree	D	Jr.	39	7	31	38	48
Bob Curtis	C	Sr.	39	16	21	37	24
Jeff Grade	W	Sr.	36	8	23	31	76
Rod Poindexter	W	So.	39	9	19	28	50

	Pos.	Class	Games	G.	A.	Pts.	Pen.
Dave Randall	D	Sr.	39	6	21	27	52
Darryl Olsen	D	Fr.	37	5	20	25	46
Troy Jacobsen	C	Fr.	39	6	17	23	22
Kory Wright	W	Jr.	36	12	7	19	16
Glen Hartley	W	Jr.	30	5	9	14	26
Ron Brodeur	W	Sr.	37	6	8	14	38
Kevin Trach	C	Sr.	23	4	8	12	6
John Goode	D	Fr.	39	2	6	8	41
Mark Lanigan	D	So.	38	1	7	8	18
Phil Berger	W	Fr.	21	5	2	7	20
Tony Savarin	D	So.	31	0	7	7	24
Wayne Opsahl	D	Fr.	8	2	1	3	4
Dave Purmal	D	Sr.	15	0	2	2	10
Dennis Jiannaras	G	Sr.	27	0	1	1	0
Mike Jeffrey	G	So.	15	0	0	0	2

University of Notre Dame
Overall: 12-21-1

	Pos.	Class	Games	G.	A.	Pts.	Pen.
Mike McNeill	C	So.	34	18	29	47	32
Tim Reilly	RW	Sr.	34	21	23	44	54
Bob Thebeau	D	Sr.	30	16	22	38	45
Tom Mooney	C	So.	32	16	21	37	48
Brent Chapman	LW	Sr.	26	14	18	32	66
Rich Sobilo	RW	Jr.	23	14	9	23	14
Dave Waldbillig	LW	Sr.	34	14	8	22	8
Mark Anquillare	C	So.	28	7	13	20	22
Steve Whitmore	RW	Sr.	34	8	6	14	34
Roy Bemiss	D	Fr.	32	2	8	10	54
Bob Herber	RW	Fr.	12	4	5	9	2
Greg Duncan	D	Sr.	33	0	9	9	14
Jeff Badalich	RW	Sr.	28	3	5	8	37
Pat Foley	D	So.	34	1	7	8	54
Lance Patten	D	So.	33	0	8	8	60
Matt Hanzel	LW	Fr.	28	2	5	7	10
Brian Montgomery	C	Fr.	30	5	1	6	2
John Nickodemus	LW	Jr.	27	3	3	6	22
Bob Bilton	C	Fr.	8	3	3	6	0
Frank O'Brien	D	So.	26	0	5	5	52
John Welsch	RW	So.	26	2	2	4	2
Rob Bankoske	RW	Fr.	2	0	1	1	0
Jeff Henderson	G	So.	2	0	1	1	0
Marc Guay	G	Sr.	18	0	1	1	8
John Tiberi	LW	Sr.	22	0	0	0	8
Ray Markovich	D	So.	14	0	0	0	2
Tim Lukenda	G	Jr.	21	0	0	0	4

Ohio State University
Overall: 23-19-1; CCHA: 16-15-1

	Pos.	Class	Games	G.	A.	Pts.	Pen.
Rick Brebant	C	So.	40	25	35	60	86
Jeff Madill	W	So.	41	32	25	57	65
Dave Beaudin	C	Jr.	42	23	33	56	64
Joe Tracy	W	Jr.	42	20	34	54	32
Darcy Gryba	C	So.	43	10	39	49	34
Mark Anderson	W	So.	43	19	25	44	36
Andy Forcey	W	Fr.	42	18	25	43	99
Don Perkins	D	Sr.	42	12	29	41	69
Mark Shortt	D	Sr.	39	8	20	28	62
Dave Doyon	W	Fr.	41	9	16	25	46
Kevin Burden	C	Sr.	40	10	13	23	61
Bob Napierals	W	Sr.	37	9	12	21	54
Bob Gruhl	D	Sr.	41	5	13	18	84
Dan Wilhelm	C	Fr.	35	8	6	14	24
Scott Syring	D	Jr.	40	2	10	12	48
Eric Furland	D	Fr.	38	2	7	9	14
*Doug Claggett	D	So.	11	2	4	6	2
Mike Wurst	W	Jr.	15	1	3	4	16

	Pos.	Class	Games	G.	A.	Pts.	Pen.
Bill Brown	C	So.	23	1	3	4	12
Don Rothgery	W	Jr.	30	2	1	3	26
Sean Clifford	D	Fr.	12	0	2	2	18
Rick Brown	C	So.	11	0	1	1	6
Keith Rathbun	D	So.	11	0	1	1	27

*Also played at Bowling Green State University.

Princeton University

Overall: 11-17-2; ECAC: 7-13-1

	Pos.	Class	Games	G.	A.	Pts.	Pen.
Cliff Abrecht	D	Sr.	30	15	26	41	42
John Messuri	C	Fr.	30	14	27	41	42
Pat Brodeur	LW	Sr.	30	13	16	29	32
Tim Driscoll	RW	Jr.	28	10	11	21	43
Dave Umland	RW	So.	30	10	9	19	24
Allan Gray	RW	Jr.	22	9	9	18	50
Dan Titus	LW	Sr.	30	7	10	17	50
Tim Oshier	RW	Sr.	28	11	6	17	14
John Rocco	C	Jr.	30	4	11	15	28
Jaimie MacPherson	D	Jr.	28	3	11	14	24
Bill Brady	LW	Jr.	20	3	6	9	14
Scott Howe	D	Jr.	30	0	8	8	88
Kelly Szautner	C	So.	29	3	5	8	22
Todd Ladda	LW	Fr.	24	2	5	7	6
Len Quesnelle	D	So.	28	1	4	5	16
Tom Shustarich	LW	Sr.	15	1	3	4	0
Joe Ross	LW	Jr.	27	1	2	3	20
Fred Hnat	D	Sr.	18	2	1	3	8
Chris Hughes	LW	Fr.	24	0	2	2	10
John Allen	D	So.	26	0	2	2	32
David Downing	RW	Jr.	9	0	0	0	2
Mike Farrell	LW	Fr.	4	..	..	..	....
Joe Mickelson	D	So.	1	..	..	..	....

Providence College

Overall: 14-24-1; Hockey East: 11-22-1

	Pos.	Class	Games	G.	A.	Pts.	Pen.
Gord Cruickshank	C	So.	38	33	17	50	80
Rene Boudreault	LW	Sr.	39	10	24	34	30
Jim Robbins	RW	Sr.	39	10	19	29	16
Tim Sullivan	C	Sr.	36	10	15	25	54
Shawn Whitham	D	So.	38	11	13	24	89
Artie Yeomelakis	RW	Sr.	38	9	14	23	68
Steve Bianchi	C	Sr.	39	5	18	23	30
Jim Hughes	D	Fr.	36	3	19	22	18
Luke Vitale	LW	Fr.	39	9	7	16	16
Lance Nelson	RW	Jr.	29	3	9	12	16
Andy Calcione	C	Jr.	24	3	8	11	8
John DeVoe	D	Sr.	39	1	9	10	34
Perry Florio	D	Fr.	39	4	5	9	90
Terry Sullivan	RW	Jr.	30	4	3	7	12
Mike Koenig	LW	Fr.	27	0	7	7	16
Brad McClocklin	D	Fr.	15	2	2	4	8
Michael Flanagan	D	Jr.	33	0	4	4	45
John Ferguson	LW	Fr.	18	1	2	3	2
Neven Kardum	C	Fr.	12	1	0	1	0
Mike Brill	D	Sr.	37	0	0	0	24
Tom Lyons	C	Fr.	7	0	0	0	0
Chris Terreri	G	Sr.	26	0	0	0	4

Rensselaer Polytechnic Institute

Overall: 20-11-1; ECAC: 13-7-1

	Pos.	Class	Games	G.	A.	Pts.	Pen.
Mark Jooris	F	Sr.	31	34	26	60	36
John Carter	F	Sr.	27	23	18	41	68
Neil Hernberg	F	Jr.	32	16	25	41	34

	Pos.	Class	Games	G.	A.	Pts.	Pen.
Terry Butryn	F	Jr.	32	16	23	39	40
Maurice Mansi	F	So.	31	16	21	37	35
Michael Dark	D	Sr.	32	7	29	36	58
Trini Iturralde	F	Jr.	32	15	19	34	6
John Tiano	F	Sr.	32	6	19	25	22
Bill Kopecky	F	So.	29	9	15	24	26
Mike Robinson	D	Jr.	31	4	14	18	56
Bob DiPronio	F	Jr.	24	9	8	17	14
Marc Foland	D	Jr.	29	2	6	8	14
Graeme Townshend	F	Fr.	29	1	7	8	52
Steve Moore	D	Fr.	24	4	3	7	32
Jeff Prendergast	D	Sr.	31	0	7	7	18
Rod Brescia	D	Fr.	26	2	4	6	46
Rob Schena	D	Fr.	32	0	6	6	63
Ryan Kummu	D	Fr.	30	2	2	4	40
Jim Kropp	F	Fr.	12	0	3	3	8
Brian Jopling	G	Jr.	28	0	2	2	2
Dave Sette-Ducati	F	So.	8	0	1	1	8
Tony Martino	G	So.	15	0	0	0	8
Steve Tenney	F/D	Fr.	12	0	0	0	0
John Haley	G	Fr.	6	0	0	0	0

St. Lawrence University
Overall: 16-15; ECAC: 10-11

	Pos.	Class	Games	G.	A.	Pts.	Pen.
Pete Lappin	F	So.	30	20	26	46	64
Tim Lappin	F	So.	29	19	23	42	49
Dave Saunders	F	So.	29	15	19	34	26
Scott Nickerson	F	Jr.	30	11	21	32	41
Todd Petkowski	F	Sr.	31	12	17	29	54
Pete McGeough	D	So.	27	9	18	27	83
Jamie Baker	F	Fr.	31	9	16	25	52
Brian McColgan	D	Fr.	24	10	13	23	26
Chris Gunnarson	F	Sr.	31	3	17	20	40
Hank Lammens	D	So.	30	3	14	17	60
Pete Buckeridge	F	So.	28	6	10	16	56
Rick Mulligan	F	Jr.	28	3	11	14	12
Mike Pelletier	D	Fr.	27	4	8	12	24
Gary Robertson	F	Fr.	29	4	8	12	20
Mike Hurlbut	D	Fr.	25	2	10	12	40
Andre Dalbec	F	Jr.	25	5	5	10	23
Ross Mann	D	Fr.	31	3	4	7	44
Dave Witherell	F	Fr.	27	4	2	6	2
Brad McKee	F	So.	25	3	2	5	52
Scott Yearwood	G	So.	24	0	2	2	2
Rich Stewart	D	Fr.	4	0	0	0	0
Paul Cohen	G	So.	9	0	0	0	2
Kurt Schroeder	D	So.	9	0	0	0	0

United States International University
Overall: 20-13

	Pos.	Class	Games	G.	A.	Pts.	Pen.
Jeff Dobek	C	So.	33	25	31	56	18
Gordie Stewart	RW	Sr.	33	28	25	53	24
Kevin Poirier	C	Jr.	31	18	28	46	14
Gary Bernard	LW	Jr.	33	18	17	35	28
Darren Clarkin	D	Jr.	33	6	23	29	22
John Christofilos	RW	So.	32	9	16	25	24
Doug Hannesson	LW	Sr.	31	11	13	24	8
Mike McGrath	D	Jr.	33	5	19	24	49
Mike Castellano	D	Fr.	32	3	21	24	40
Matt Shaw	D	Fr.	32	6	16	22	48
David Nash	RW	So.	33	7	11	18	20
Leo Hanna	LW	Sr.	30	8	4	12	12
Peter Stensgard	C	So.	31	2	9	11	4
Matt Lundgren	C	So.	33	7	3	10	12
Tom Genz	LW	So.	20	3	6	9	4
Jim Plankers	D	Jr.	33	1	7	8	48

	Pos.	Class	Games	G.	A.	Pts.	Pen.
Craig Shepherd	LW	Fr.	27	3	2	5	18
Jack Grone	RW	So.	18	2	3	5	0
Chris Sonnesyn	D	Fr.	23	1	4	5	16
Dana Orent	G	So.	30	0	3	3	8
Brian Clark	D	So.	8	1	1	2	2
Alfred Shropshire	RW	Fr.	4	0	0	0	0
Richie Dusevic	C	Fr.	2	0	0	0	0
Steve Glassel	D	Fr.	1	0	0	0	0
Ben Duffey	G	So.	6	0	0	0	0
Rob Watson	G	So.	6	0	0	0	4

University of Vermont
Overall: 17-13-1; ECAC: 11-10

	Pos.	Class	Games	G.	A.	Pts.	Pen.
Kyle McDonough	C	Fr.	31	13	13	26	26
Jeff Capello	LW	Jr.	31	9	17	26	36
Ian Boyce	C	Fr.	30	10	11	21	21
Shannon Deegan	C	Jr.	28	9	9	18	30
Richard LaPlante	C	So.	28	1	17	18	14
Toby Ducolon	RW	So.	30	10	6	16	48
Bill McCormack	LW	Jr.	30	8	7	15	36
Dan Lambert	C	Fr	31	8	6	14	16
Duke Stump	RW	So.	28	7	7	14	14
Jim Purcell	LW	Jr.	30	6	8	14	51
Marc Lebreux	D	Fr.	28	3	10	13	38
Dennis Miller	D	Fr.	31	1	11	12	39
Mike Maher	LW	Sr.	26	6	4	10	12
Scott Ferguson	D	Jr.	31	5	5	10	39
Jim Walsh	LW	Fr.	28	3	6	9	11
Paul Seguin	D	So.	29	0	6	6	44
Tom Maher	RW	Sr.	13	2	3	5	6
Jeff Schulman	D	Fr.	12	1	3	4	0
Jerry Tarrant	D	Fr.	23	0	4	4	22
Craig Staff	RW	Jr.	5	0	2	2	6
Kevin Finnerty	D	So.	19	0	2	2	12
Brian McLaughlin	RW	Fr.	4	0	1	1	0
Tom Draper	G	Jr.	29	0	1	1	0
Joe Gervais	D	So.	12	0	0	0	2

Western Michigan University
Overall: 32-12; CCHA: 23-9

	Pos.	Class	Games	G.	A.	Pts.	Pen.
Dan Dorion	RW	Sr.	42	42	62	104	48
Troy Thrun	C	Sr.	44	33	51	84	20
Stuart Burnie	RW	Sr.	42	43	36	79	78
Wayne Gagne	D	Jr.	43	17	59	76	37
Rob Bryden	LW	Jr.	44	23	28	51	85
Chris MacDonald	D	Sr.	42	12	38	50	54
Ron Hoover	C	Fr.	43	10	23	33	36
Jeff Crossman	LW	Sr.	39	13	19	32	154
Henry Fung	RW	Jr.	44	13	19	32	36
Rob Adams	C	Sr.	44	15	15	30	12
Ron Pesetti	D	Sr.	42	8	20	28	62
Jim Culhane	D	Jr.	40	1	21	22	61
Pat Ryan	LW	Jr.	40	7	14	21	12
Chuck Chiatto	C	Jr.	31	4	10	14	12
Bob Worden	LW/C	Fr.	40	6	4	10	41
Jeff Wenninger	LW	Fr.	20	4	4	8	30
Scott Howe	D	So.	41	1	6	7	48
Lee Brodeur	RW	So.	20	1	4	5	22
Dave Lobdell	D	So.	25	1	3	4	26
Dave Bina	RW	Sr.	14	1	2	3	8
Kevin McCaffrey	G	So.	16	0	2	2	0
Jeff Kick	C/W	So.	10	1	0	1	4
John McCormick	D	Fr.	8	0	1	1	6
Bill Horn	G	Fr.	30	0	1	1	14
Dave Bramble	F	Fr.	8	0	0	0	2
Darrin Grava	D	Fr.	2	0	0	0	2

University of Wisconsin
Overall: 27-13; WCHA: 23-11

	Pos.	Class	Games	G.	A.	Pts.	Pen.
David Maley	F	Sr.	40	19	39	58	135
Marty Wiitala	D	Sr.	40	15	38	53	20
Tony Granato	F	Jr.	32	25	24	49	36
Tom Ryan	F	Sr.	39	24	24	48	18
Tim Thomas	D	Jr.	40	10	38	48	112
Scott Mellanby	F	So.	32	21	23	44	89
Ernie Vargas	F	Sr.	39	20	23	43	67
Pat Ford	F	So.	39	10	27	37	48
Paul Ranheim	F	So.	31	16	17	33	34
Jim Johannson	F	Sr.	28	18	12	30	42
Matt Walsh	D	Sr.	39	5	20	25	55
Ken MacKenzie	D	So.	36	0	13	13	42
Steve Tuttle	F	So.	30	2	10	12	2
Paul Stanton	D	Fr.	34	4	6	10	14
Steve Tschipper	F	Sr.	39	4	6	10	20
Paul Graveline	F	Jr.	34	5	4	9	16
Todd Geisness	F	Jr.	32	1	4	5	2
Garry Bunz	D	So.	40	1	3	4	38
Glenn Revak	F	So.	23	1	1	2	2
Andy Akervik	F	Fr.	20	1	0	1	5
Dean Anderson	G	So.	20	0	1	1	4
Kurt Semandel	D	Fr.	19	0	0	0	2
Mike Richter	G	Fr.	22	0	0	0	0
Tony Scheid	F	So.	7	0	0	0	2
Greg Poss	D	Fr.	3	0	0	0	0
Eric Faust	D	Jr.	1	0	0	0	0

Yale University
Overall: 21-10; ECAC: 15-6-0

	Pos.	Class	Games	G.	A.	Pts.	Pen.
Randy Wood	F	Sr.	31	25	30	55	26
Bob Logan	W	Sr.	31	21	23	44	24
Darren Acheson	C	Sr.	28	18	23	41	16
Bob Kudelski	C	Jr.	31	18	23	41	48
Eric Borg	W	Sr.	31	14	25	39	32
Ken Bielski	D	Sr.	31	10	21	31	14
Sean Neely	W	Sr.	31	13	17	30	40
David Tanner	F	So.	24	6	20	26	11
Dave Baseggio	D	So.	30	7	17	24	54
Tom Rzeszut	D	Sr.	26	5	17	22	10
Paul Marcotte	D	Sr.	31	1	20	21	60
Adam Snow	F	Jr.	30	6	7	13	16
Rich Geist	F	Jr.	31	3	7	10	34
Mike Griak	W	Sr.	29	3	7	10	12
Scott Webster	D	Sr.	31	1	8	9	26
Rob Baseggio	D	So.	24	3	5	8	22
Gary Davidson	D	Sr.	31	0	7	7	22
Andy Deiss	C	Sr.	19	3	3	6	16
Bill Zito	W	Jr.	7	1	3	4	4
Scott Sarbacker	D	So.	5	0	2	2	6
Rick Fossier	F	So.	8	1	0	1	0
Ralph Russo	D	So.	19	1	0	1	12
Michael Schwalb	G	Jr.	21	0	1	1	2
Mickey Kappele	G	Sr.	7	0	0	0	2
Michael O'Neill	G	Fr.	6	0	0	0	0

COLLEGIATE GOALTENDING RECORDS

	G.	W.	L.	T.	Min.	Goals	Avg.
AIR FORCE ACADEMY							
T.J. O'Shaughnessy	14	8	4	0	720	40	3.33
Jay Ducharme	11	6	4	0	600	47	4.70
Jack Sundstrom	9	1	5	0	440	44	6.00
(ARMY) U.S. MILITARY ACADEMY	G.	W.	L.	T.	Min.	Goals	Avg.
Paul DeGironimo	21	11	8	1	1169	73	3.75
Brian Drinkwine	13	7	3	0	653	44	4.04

	G.	W.	L.	T.	Min.	Goals	Avg.
BOSTON COLLEGE							
David Littman	9	5	0	2	442	22	2.98
Scott Gordon	32	19	12	1	1851	112	3.63
Shaun Real	7	2	1	0	262	19	4.35
BOSTON UNIVERSITY							
Tony Taillefer	29	16	8	3	1651	93	3.38
Bob Deraney	16	8	6	1	913	53	3.48
Peter Fish	1	1	0	0	60	5	5.00
BOWLING GREEN STATE UNIVERSITY							
D. Charbonneau	1	0	0	0	25	1	2.39
Gary Kruzich	35	23	11	0	2090	124	3.56
Dan Kwilas	8	5	3	0	473	33	4.19
BROWN UNIVERSITY							
Michel Bayard	15	3	10	0	767	66	5.16
Bob Naegele	10	1	8	0	502	50	5.96
Dominic Alfonso	3	0	1	0	105	13	7.43
CLARKSON UNIVERSITY							
Scott Domingos	2	0	0	0	32	1	1.90
Jamie Falle	31	18	10	3	1881	101	3.22
Sander Neumann	1	0	1	0	60	7	7.00
COLGATE UNIVERSITY							
Wayne Cowley	7	2	2	0	313	23	4.42
Dan Delianedis	26	13	12	2	1470	110	4.49
Mitch Murphy	1	0	0	0	31	5	9.84
COLORADO COLLEGE							
Marty Wakelyn	23	8	14	1	1380	100	4.34
Derek Pizzey	18	4	12	1	1062	87	4.90
CORNELL UNIVERSITY							
Darin McInnis	2	1	0	1	97	3	1.86
Doug Dadswell	30	20	7	3	1815	92	3.01
Jim Emands	4	0	0	0	81	9	6.67
DARTMOUTH COLLEGE							
Tim Osby	16	4	8	0	772	61	4.74
Mark Hoppe	6	1	4	0	291	28	5.77
Jeff Bower	10	2	6	0	432	45	6.25
UNIVERSITY OF DENVER							
Chris Olson	27	17	8	1	1576	82	3.12
Tom Allen	22	17	5	0	1303	74	3.41
FERRIS STATE COLLEGE							
Phil Bryant	5	2	0	0	125	6	2.88
Dave Sharpe	12	5	5	0	573	44	4.60
Glenn Raeburn	30	10	14	2	1589	149	5.62
HARVARD UNIVERSITY							
Dickie McEvoy	4	1	1	0	153	6	2.35
Grant Blair	31	24	6	1	1812	82	2.72
John Devin	4	0	1	0	90	6	4.00
UNIVERSITY OF ILLINOIS-CHICAGO							
Brad Ryan	23	7	13	1	1272	95	4.48
Jim Hickey	22	7	12	0	1158	98	5.08
LAKE SUPERIOR STATE COLLEGE							
Joe Shawhan	21	10	6	0	987	50	3.03
Randy Exelby	28	14	12	1	1626	98	3.61
UNIVERSITY OF LOWELL							
Dana Demole	34	9	22	2	2016	148	4.40
Dave Delfino	10	2	7	0	532	52	5.86
UNIVERSITY OF MAINE							
Jean Lacoste	9	2	6	0	495	36	4.33
Al Loring	25	6	18	1	1500	118	5.03
Ray Roy	8	0	1	0	236	19	6.82
MIAMI (O.) UNIVERSITY							
Brent Smith	25	4	14	2	1272	102	4.81
Bill Suhanek	13	3	8	0	718	67	5.59
Tim Hall	7	1	5	0	282	28	5.95
Dean Garrett	1	0	1	0	20	3	9.00
UNIVERSITY OF MICHIGAN							
Tim Markis	29	7	16	0	1423	130	5.46
Bob Lindgren	13	4	6	0	598	61	6.12
Mike Rossi	10	1	4	0	254	27	6.37

	G.	W.	L.	T.	Min.	Goals	Avg.
MICHIGAN STATE UNIVERSITY							
Bob Essensa	23	17	4	1	1333	74	3.33
Norm Foster	24	17	5	1	1414	87	3.69
MICHIGAN TECHNOLOGICAL UNIV.							
Tiger Pierce	21	5	11	2	1212	87	4.31
Dave Roach	23	5	15	2	1265	104	4.93
UNIVERSITY OF MINNESOTA							
Jon Brekken	1	0	0	0	20	0	0.00
John Blue	29	20	6	0	1588	80	3.02
Frank Pietrangelo	23	15	7	0	1284	76	3.55
UNIVERSITY OF MINNESOTA-DULUTH							
John Hyduke	24	14	7	3	1401	84	3.60
Mike Cortes	18	11	6	0	1074	65	3.63
Rick Hayko	1	1	0	0	60	7	7.00
UNIVERSITY OF NEW HAMPSHIRE							
Greg Rota	23	5	16	1	1352	117	5.19
Rich Burchill	16	0	13	2	900	82	5.46
UNIVERSITY OF NORTH DAKOTA							
Scott Brower	20	11	6	0	1096	67	3.47
Greg Strome	20	9	9	1	1189	78	3.90
Craig Perry	2	1	1	0	120	10	5.00
NORTHEASTERN UNIVERSITY							
Shawn O'Sullivan	1	0	0	1	70	4	3.43
Chris Long	3	1	0	0	100	6	3.60
Bruce Racine	37	19	17	1	1015	171	4.64
NORTHERN MICHIGAN UNIVERSITY							
Dennis Jiannaras	27	17	8	2	1556	103	3.97
Mike Jeffrey	15	5	6	0	743	58	4.69
John Corrigan	2	1	0	0	66	6	5.42
UNIVERSITY OF NOTRE DAME							
Tim Lukenda	21	7	9	1	1079	103	5.72
Marc Guay	18	5	11	0	891	93	6.26
Jeff Henderson	2	0	1	0	80	14	10.50
OHIO STATE UNIVERSITY							
Roger Beedon	27	12	11	0	1393	115	4.95
Bob Krautsak	22	10	8	1	1165	104	5.35
Hank Horn	2	1	0	0	40	5	7.50
PRINCETON UNIVERSITY							
Tony Manory	5	1	0	0	95	2	1.27
Dave Marotta	25	9	13	0	1353	79	3.50
Dave Shea	9	1	4	2	369	26	4.22
PROVIDENCE COLLEGE							
Chris Terreri	26	9	17	0	1539	96	3.74
Ed Walsh	12	4	6	1	685	50	4.38
Larry Crosby	3	1	1	0	132	11	5.00
RENSSELAER POLYTECHNIC INSTITUTE							
Brian Jopling	28	16	9	1	1471	99	4.04
Tony Martino	15	4	2	0	442	33	4.48
John Haley	6	0	0	0	36	5	8.36
UNITED STATES INTERNATIONAL U.							
Ben Duffey	6	1	1	0	180	11	3.67
Dana Orent	30	17	11	0	1607	118	4.41
Rob Watson	6	2	1	0	203	20	5.91
VERMONT UNIVERSITY							
Tom Draper	29	15	13	0	1697	87	3.08
Elias Delany	7	2	1	0	165	11	4.00
WESTERN MICHIGAN UNIV.							
Bill Horn	30	25	5	0	1797	114	3.81
Kevin McCaffrey	16	7	7	0	879	61	4.16
UNIVERSITY OF WISCONSIN							
Mike Richter	22	14	7	0	1280	81	3.80
Dean Anderson	20	13	6	0	1128	80	4.25
YALE UNIVERSITY							
Mickey Kappele	6	4	2	0	364	20	3.30
Mike O'Neill	6	3	1	0	289	17	3.53
Michael Schwalb	20	14	7	0	1218	78	3.84

NATIONAL HOCKEY LEAGUE SCHEDULE
1986-87

*Denotes afternoon game.

THURSDAY, OCTOBER 9
Calgary at Boston
Buffalo at Winnipeg
Montreal at Toronto
Detroit at Quebec
New York Islanders at Chicago
New Jersey at New York Rangers
Edmonton at Philadelphia
Washington at Pittsburgh
St. Louis at Los Angeles

SATURDAY, OCTOBER 11
Boston at New Jersey
Calgary at Hartford
Buffalo at Toronto
Edmonton at Montreal
Minnesota at Quebec
New York Islanders at Los Angeles
New York Rangers at Pittsburgh
Philadelphia at Washington
Chicago at Detroit
St. Louis at Vancouver

SUNDAY, OCTOBER 12
Hartford at Boston
Calgary at Buffalo
Pittsburgh at Chicago
Edmonton at Winnipeg

MONDAY, OCTOBER 13
Minnesota at Montreal
Quebec at Vancouver
Washington at New York Rangers

TUESDAY, OCTOBER 14
Boston at Winnipeg
Los Angeles at Pittsburgh
St. Louis at Toronto

WEDNESDAY, OCTOBER 15
Montreal at Buffalo
Quebec at Edmonton
New York Rangers at Chicago
Vancouver at New Jersey
Los Angeles at Detroit

THURSDAY, OCTOBER 16
Boston at Minnesota
Winnipeg at Hartford
Quebec at Calgary
Washington at New York Islanders
Vancouver at Philadelphia

FRIDAY, OCTOBER 17
Pittsburgh at Buffalo
Toronto at New Jersey
Detroit at Edmonton

SATURDAY, OCTOBER 18
Boston at Los Angeles
Philadelphia at Hartford
Buffalo at Washington
Winnipeg at Montreal
Quebec at St. Louis
N. York Rangers at N. York Islanders
New Jersey at Pittsburgh
Chicago at Toronto
Detroit at Calgary
Vancouver at Minnesota

SUNDAY, OCTOBER 19
N. York Islanders at N. York Rangers
Winnipeg at Philadelphia
Minnesota at Chicago
Edmonton at Los Angeles

MONDAY, OCTOBER 20
Washington at Montreal

TUESDAY, OCTOBER 21
Washington at Quebec
New Jersey at New York Islanders
Chicago at Edmonton

WEDNESDAY, OCTOBER 22
Boston at Vancouver
Buffalo at Pittsburgh
Montreal at Detroit
Quebec at Toronto
Los Angeles at New York Rangers
Minnesota at St. Louis
Edmonton at Calgary

THURSDAY, OCTOBER 23
Los Angeles at New Jersey
Pittsburgh at Philadelphia

FRIDAY, OCTOBER 24
Boston at Edmonton
Hartford at Buffalo
Minnesota at Washington
St. Louis at Detroit
Chicago at Vancouver
Calgary at Winnipeg

SATURDAY, OCTOBER 25
Buffalo at Hartford
New York Rangers at Montreal
Toronto at Quebec
Los Angeles at New York Islanders
New Jersey at Washington
Philadelphia at Pittsburgh
Detroit at St. Louis

SUNDAY, OCTOBER 26
Boston at Calgary
Toronto at New York Rangers
Minnesota at Philadelphia
Chicago at Winnipeg
Vancouver at Edmonton

MONDAY, OCTOBER 27
Los Angeles at Montreal

TUESDAY, OCTOBER 28
Pittsburgh at Hartford
Los Angeles at Quebec
Philadelphia at New York Islanders
Washington at Vancouver
Chicago at Toronto
Calgary at Minnesota

WEDNESDAY, OCTOBER 29
Buffalo at Montreal
New York Rangers at St. Louis
New Jersey at Pittsburgh
Washington at Edmonton
Chicago at Detroit
Calgary at Winnipeg

THURSDAY, OCTOBER 30
Montreal at Boston
Hartford at Toronto
Quebec at Philadelphia
New York Islanders at New Jersey
Detroit at Minnesota

FRIDAY, OCTOBER 31
Edmonton at Vancouver

SATURDAY, NOVEMBER 1
Boston at Philadelphia
Quebec at Hartford
Buffalo at New Jersey
Winnipeg at New York Islanders
Pittsburgh at St. Louis
Washington at Calgary
Detroit at Toronto
Chicago at Minnesota

SUNDAY, NOVEMBER 2
Buffalo at Boston
Hartford at Quebec
Montreal at Vancouver
Winnipeg at New York Rangers
Chicago at St. Louis
Los Angeles at Edmonton

MONDAY, NOVEMBER 3
Los Angeles at Calgary

TUESDAY, NOVEMBER 4
Winnipeg at Quebec
Washington at New York Islanders
New Jersey at Philadelphia
Vancouver at Pittsburgh

WEDNESDAY, NOVEMBER 5
Boston at Buffalo
New York Islanders at Hartford
New York Rangers at Detroit
Vancouver at Washington
St. Louis at Toronto
Minnesota at Chicago
Calgary at Edmonton

THURSDAY, NOVEMBER 6
Montreal at Los Angeles
Philadelphia at New Jersey
Toronto at Minnesota

FRIDAY, NOVEMBER 7
Vancouver at Buffalo
St. Louis at Winnipeg
Edmonton at Calgary

SATURDAY, NOVEMBER 8
Boston at Quebec
Hartford at Los Angeles
Montreal at Edmonton
Detroit at New York Islanders
*New York Rangers at Philadelphia
Pittsburgh at Minnesota
Chicago at Washington
Vancouver at Toronto

SUNDAY, NOVEMBER 9
New York Islanders at Buffalo
Montreal at Calgary
New York Rangers at Quebec
New Jersey at Winnipeg
Pittsburgh at Detroit
St. Louis at Chicago

TUESDAY, NOVEMBER 11
Edmonton at New York Islanders
Washington at Minnesota
Winnipeg at Los Angeles
Vancouver at Calgary

WEDNESDAY, NOVEMBER 12
Boston at Pittsburgh
Hartford at Vancouver
Buffalo at New York Rangers
Quebec at Montreal
Detroit at New Jersey
Washington at Chicago
Toronto at St. Louis

THURSDAY, NOVEMBER 13
Edmonton at Boston

— 233 —

Hartford at Calgary
Detroit at Philadelphia
Winnipeg at Los Angeles

FRIDAY, NOVEMBER 14
Quebec at Washington
Philadelphia at New York Rangers
Pittsburgh at New Jersey
Winnipeg at Vancouver

SATURDAY, NOVEMBER 15
New Jersey at Boston
Edmonton at Hartford
Buffalo at Montreal
Quebec at Pittsburgh
New York Islanders at Minnesota
Detroit at Toronto
Chicago at St. Louis
Calgary at Los Angeles

SUNDAY, NOVEMBER 16
New York Islanders at Winnipeg
Edmonton at New York Rangers
Washington at Philadelphia
Toronto at Chicago

MONDAY, NOVEMBER 17
Boston at Montreal
New York Rangers at New Jersey

TUESDAY, NOVEMBER 18
New York Islanders at Quebec
Pittsburgh at Winnipeg
Los Angeles at Washington
St. Louis at Minnesota
Calgary at Vancouver

WEDNESDAY, NOVEMBER 19
Boston at Buffalo
Montreal at Hartford
New York Rangers at Edmonton
New Jersey at Detroit
Philadelphia at Toronto
Los Angeles at Chicago
Minnesota at St. Louis

THURSDAY, NOVEMBER 20
Montreal at Boston
Toronto at New York Islanders
Chicago at Philadelphia
Pittsburgh at Calgary

FRIDAY, NOVEMBER 21
St. Louis at Hartford
Quebec at Buffalo
New York Rangers at Vancouver
Washington at Detroit
Los Angeles at Winnipeg

SATURDAY, NOVEMBER 22
St. Louis at Boston
Hartford at New York Islanders
Buffalo at Quebec
Detroit at Montreal
New York Rangers at Calgary
New Jersey at Minnesota
Toronto at Philadelphia
Pittsburgh at Washington
Vancouver at Edmonton

SUNDAY, NOVEMBER 23
New Jersey at Chicago
Los Angeles at Winnipeg

MONDAY, NOVEMBER 24
Boston at Toronto
Edmonton at Calgary

TUESDAY, NOVEMBER 25
Montreal at Quebec
Pittsburgh at New York Islanders
Los Angeles at Vancouver

WEDNESDAY, NOVEMBER 26
Boston at Washington

Buffalo at Hartford
Montreal at Philadelphia
Quebec at New York Rangers
New York Islanders at Pittsburgh
New Jersey at St. Louis
Toronto at Detroit
Chicago at Minnesota
Winnipeg at Edmonton
Vancouver at Los Angeles

THURSDAY, NOVEMBER 27
Winnipeg at Calgary

FRIDAY, NOVEMBER 28
Boston at Buffalo
Philadelphia at Washington
Toronto at Minnesota
St. Louis at Detroit
Chicago at Edmonton

SATURDAY, NOVEMBER 29
Buffalo at Boston
Hartford at Montreal
Washington at Quebec
Philadelphia at New York Islanders
New York Rangers at Pittsburgh
New Jersey at Los Angeles
Minnesota at Toronto
Detroit at St. Louis
Chicago at Calgary
Winnipeg at Vancouver

SUNDAY, NOVEMBER 30
Pittsburgh at N.Y. Rangers

MONDAY, DECEMBER 1
Hartford at Quebec
Washington at Montreal

TUESDAY, DECEMBER 2
Minnesota at Buffalo
N.Y. Islanders at Calgary
N.Y. Rangers at New Jersey
St. Louis at Philadelphia
Detroit at Los Angeles
Chicago at Vancouver

WEDNESDAY, DECEMBER 3
Quebec at Hartford
St. Louis at Montreal
N.Y. Islanders at Edmonton
Washington at Winnipeg

THURSDAY, DECEMBER 4
Quebec at Boston
Hartford at Philadelphia
Minnesota at New Jersey
Toronto at Los Angeles
Chicago at Calgary

FRIDAY, DECEMBER 5
St. Louis at Buffalo
Montreal at Detroit
N.Y. Islanders at Vancouver
N.Y. Rangers at Winnipeg
Edmonton at Pittsburgh

SATURDAY, DECEMBER 6
*Philadelphia at Boston
Detroit at Hartford
Buffalo at New Jersey
Montreal at Washington
Calgary at Quebec
Minnesota at Pittsburgh
Chicago at Los Angeles

SUNDAY, DECEMBER 7
N.Y. Islanders at Boston
Edmonton at Philadelphia
Toronto at St. Louis
Vancouver at Winnipeg

MONDAY, DECEMBER 8
Calgary at Montreal

TUESDAY, DECEMBER 9
Buffalo at Detroit
St. Louis at Quebec
Los Angeles at N.Y. Islanders
New Jersey at Washington
Vancouver at Philadelphia
Edmonton at Minnesota

WEDNESDAY, DECEMBER 10
St. Louis at Hartford
Buffalo at Chicago
Los Angeles at N.Y. Rangers
Calgary at Pittsburgh
Washington at Toronto
Edmonton at Winnipeg

THURSDAY, DECEMBER 11
Vancouver at Boston
N.Y. Rangers at Montreal
N.Y. Islanders at New Jersey
Calgary at Philadelphia
Minnesota at Detroit

FRIDAY, DECEMBER 12
Toronto at Pittsburgh
Winnipeg at Edmonton

SATURDAY, DECEMBER 13
Boston at Montreal
Vancouver at Hartford
Buffalo at Quebec
New Jersey at N.Y. Islanders
*N.Y. Rangers at Washington
Philadelphia at Minnesota
Pittsburgh at Toronto
Chicago at St. Louis
Calgary at Los Angeles

SUNDAY, DECEMBER 14
Boston at Quebec
Hartford at Buffalo
Montreal at New Jersey
Vancouver at Chicago
Philadelphia at Winnipeg
Edmonton at Los Angeles

MONDAY, DECEMBER 15
Minnesota at N.Y. Rangers

TUESDAY, DECEMBER 16
Montreal at St. Louis
Minnesota at N.Y. Islanders
Detroit at Calgary

WEDNESDAY, DECEMBER 17
Buffalo at Hartford
Quebec at Edmonton
Washington at N.Y. Rangers
Toronto at New Jersey
Pittsburgh at Los Angeles
Detroit at Vancouver
Winnipeg at Chicago

THURSDAY, DECEMBER 18
Hartford at Boston
Quebec at Calgary
N.Y. Islanders at Philadelphia
Minnesota at Toronto
Winnipeg at St. Louis

FRIDAY, DECEMBER 19
Montreal at Buffalo
Washington at New Jersey
Vancouver at Edmonton

SATURDAY, DECEMBER 20
Chicago at Boston
Hartford at Detroit
Buffalo at Toronto
New Jersey at Montreal
Quebec at Minnesota
N.Y. Rangers at N.Y. Islanders
Philadelphia at Pittsburgh
St. Louis at Washington

Calgary at Vancouver
Los Angeles at Edmonton

SUNDAY, DECEMBER 21
Hartford at N.Y. Rangers
Quebec at Winnipeg
St. Louis at Philadelphia
Detroit at Chicago

MONDAY, DECEMBER 22
Pittsburgh at Montreal
Los Angeles at Calgary

TUESDAY, DECEMBER 23
Boston at Hartford
Philadelphia at Buffalo
Pittsburgh at N.Y. Islanders
New Jersey at N.Y. Rangers
Toronto at Minnesota
Chicago at Detroit
Winnipeg at Edmonton
Los Angeles at Vancouver

FRIDAY, DECEMBER 26
Montreal at Hartford
Pittsburgh at Buffalo
N.Y. Islanders at Washington
N.Y. Rangers at New Jersey
Toronto at Detroit
St. Louis at Chicago
Winnipeg at Minnesota

SATURDAY, DECEMBER 27
Boston at Los Angeles
Hartford at Montreal
New Jersey at Quebec
N.Y. Islanders at Pittsburgh
N.Y. Rangers at St. Louis
Philadelphia at Vancouver
Detroit at Toronto

SUNDAY, DECEMBER 28
Calgary at Buffalo
Philadelphia at Edmonton
Washington at Chicago
Minnesota at Winnipeg

TUESDAY, DECEMBER 30
Boston at St. Louis
Hartford at Washington
Montreal at Quebec
Chicago at N.Y. Islanders
N.Y. Rangers at Pittsburgh
Calgary at New Jersey
Philadelphia at Los Angeles
Edmonton at Vancouver

WEDNESDAY, DECEMBER 31
Hartford at Minnesota
Chicago at Buffalo
Quebec at Montreal
N.Y. Islanders at N.Y. Rangers
Winnipeg at Toronto
Calgary at Detroit

THURSDAY, JANUARY 1
*Pittsburgh at Washington

FRIDAY, JANUARY 2
Boston at New Jersey
Winnipeg at Buffalo
Minnesota at Detroit
Los Angeles at Vancouver

SATURDAY, JANUARY 3
Boston at N.Y. Islanders
*Chicago at Hartford
Montreal at Pittsburgh
N.Y. Rangers at Quebec
New Jersey at Toronto
Philadelphia at Washington
Detroit at Minnesota
Calgary at St. Louis
Edmonton at Los Angeles

SUNDAY, JANUARY 4
Toronto at Hartford
Quebec at Buffalo
Calgary at Chicago
Vancouver at Winnipeg

MONDAY, JANUARY 5
Montreal at Boston
Minnesota at N.Y. Rangers
Washington at St. Louis

TUESDAY, JANUARY 6
Vancouver at Quebec
Minnesota at N.Y. Islanders
New Jersey at Philadelphia
Toronto at Detroit

WEDNESDAY, JANUARY 7
Hartford at St. Louis
Buffalo at Winnipeg
Vancouver at Montreal
Philadelphia at N.Y. Rangers
Washington at Pittsburgh
Toronto at Chicago
Los Angeles at Edmonton

THURSDAY, JANUARY 8
Detroit at Boston
Buffalo at Minnesota
Quebec at New Jersey
Los Angeles at Calgary

FRIDAY, JANUARY 9
Hartford at Winnipeg
N.Y. Islanders at N.Y. Rangers
Pittsburgh at Washington
St. Louis at Edmonton

SATURDAY, JANUARY 10
*Philadelphia at Boston
Hartford at Minnesota
Buffalo at Los Angeles
Quebec at Montreal
Toronto at N.Y. Islanders
*Vancouver at New Jersey
Winnipeg at Detroit
St. Louis at Calgary

SUNDAY, JANUARY 11
Vancouver at N.Y. Rangers
Washington at Philadelphia
Detroit at Chicago
Calgary at Edmonton

MONDAY, JANUARY 12
N.Y. Rangers at Boston
Hartford at New Jersey
Toronto at Montreal
St. Louis at Minnesota

TUESDAY, JANUARY 13
Pittsburgh at N.Y. Islanders
Winnipeg at Washington
Edmonton at Detroit

WEDNESDAY, JANUARY 14
Boston at Hartford
Montreal at Buffalo
N.Y. Rangers at Calgary
New Jersey at Chicago
Winnipeg at Pittsburgh
Minnesota at Toronto
Vancouver at Los Angeles

THURSDAY, JANUARY 15
Hartford at Boston
Montreal at Philadelphia
Edmonton at Quebec
Washington at N.Y. Islanders
Toronto at Detroit

FRIDAY, JANUARY 16
Winnipeg at New Jersey
Los Angeles at St. Louis
Calgary at Vancouver

SATURDAY, JANUARY 17
*Pittsburgh at Boston
Washington at Hartford
Buffalo at Montreal
Quebec at Detroit
Philadelphia at N.Y. Islanders
Edmonton at Toronto
Chicago at Minnesota
Los Angeles at St. Louis
Vancouver at Calgary

SUNDAY, JANUARY 18
Edmonton at Buffalo
Quebec at Chicago
N.Y. Islanders at Philadelphia
Washington at New Jersey
Detroit at Pittsburgh
Minnesota at Winnipeg

MONDAY, JANUARY 19
Hartford at Montreal
N.Y. Rangers at Los Angeles
Vancouver at Winnipeg

TUESDAY, JANUARY 20
Boston at Quebec
Buffalo at Minnesota
Calgary at N.Y. Islanders
New Jersey at Washington

WEDNESDAY, JANUARY 21
Montreal at Hartford
N.Y. Islanders at Detroit
N.Y. Rangers at Vancouver
Philadelphia at Chicago
Pittsburgh at Los Angeles
St. Louis at Toronto
Edmonton at Winnipeg

THURSDAY, JANUARY 22
Montreal at Boston
Calgary at New Jersey

FRIDAY, JANUARY 23
Quebec at Hartford
Washington at Buffalo
N.Y. Rangers at Edmonton
Chicago at Philadelphia
Pittsburgh at Vancouver
Toronto at Winnipeg
St. Louis at Detroit
Minnesota at Los Angeles

SATURDAY, JANUARY 24
*Calgary at Boston
Hartford at Toronto
Buffalo at Washington
Chicago at Montreal
N.Y. Islanders at Quebec
Philadelphia at New Jersey
Pittsburgh at Edmonton
Detroit at St. Louis

MONDAY, JANUARY 26
Buffalo at Boston
Montreal at Chicago
New Jersey at N.Y. Rangers
Calgary at Toronto

TUESDAY, JANUARY 27
Hartford at Quebec
Montreal at St. Louis
Winnipeg at N.Y. Islanders
Washington at Pittsburgh
Edmonton at Vancouver

WEDNESDAY, JANUARY 28
Philadelphia at Buffalo
Winnipeg at N.Y. Rangers
New Jersey at Los Angeles
Washington at Detroit
Toronto at Chicago
Vancouver at Edmonton

THURSDAY, JANUARY 29
Hartford at Boston
Pittsburgh at Philadelphia
Toronto at St. Louis
Minnesota at Calgary

FRIDAY, JANUARY 30
Quebec at Buffalo
N.Y. Islanders at Washington
New Jersey at Vancouver
Minnesota at Edmonton

SATURDAY, JANUARY 31
*Winnipeg at Boston
Hartford at N.Y. Islanders
Los Angeles at Montreal
*N.Y. Rangers at Philadelphia
New Jersey at Calgary
Detroit at Toronto
Chicago at St. Louis

SUNDAY, FEBRUARY 1
Boston at N.Y. Rangers
Hartford at Pittsburgh
Detroit at Buffalo
Los Angeles at Quebec
*Winnipeg at Washington
Edmonton at Chicago
Minnesota at Vancouver

MONDAY, FEBRUARY 2
Philadelphia at Toronto

TUESDAY, FEBRUARY 3
Montreal at Quebec
Edmonton at St. Louis
Vancouver at Calgary

WEDNESDAY, FEBRUARY 4
Buffalo at Hartford
Quebec at Montreal
N.Y. Islanders at Vancouver
Washington at N.Y. Rangers
Philadelphia at Winnipeg
Los Angeles at Toronto
Detroit at Chicago
Edmonton at Minnesota

THURSDAY, FEBRUARY 5
Pittsburgh at Boston
St. Louis at Calgary

FRIDAY, FEBRUARY 6
Hartford at Washington
N.Y. Islanders at Edmonton
Minnesota at Detroit
St. Louis at Vancouver
Los Angeles at Winnipeg

SATURDAY, FEBRUARY 7
*Toronto at Boston
Montreal at Hartford
*Buffalo at Quebec
N.Y. Islanders at Calgary
N.Y. Rangers at Washington
*Philadelphia at New Jersey
Chicago at Pittsburgh
Detroit at Minnesota

SUNDAY, FEBRUARY 8
*Quebec at Boston
Chicago at Buffalo
Toronto at N.Y. Rangers
Pittsburgh at New Jersey
St. Louis at Edmonton
*Los Angeles at Winnipeg
Calgary at Vancouver

TUESDAY, FEBRUARY 10
All-Stars vs. Soviets

THURSDAY, FEBRUARY 12
All-Stars vs. Soviets

SATURDAY, FEBRUARY 14
Boston at Toronto

Hartford at Los Angeles
Buffalo at N.Y. Islanders
Winnipeg at Montreal
*New Jersey at Detroit
Philadelphia at St. Louis
Vancouver at Pittsburgh
Calgary at Minnesota

SUNDAY, FEBRUARY 15
*Quebec at Chicago
Pittsburgh at N.Y. Rangers
Washington at Edmonton
St. Louis at Minnesota

MONDAY, FEBRUARY 16
Boston at Montreal
*Calgary at Philadelphia
*Toronto at Los Angeles

TUESDAY, FEBRUARY 17
Hartford at Chicago
Winnipeg at Quebec
Philadelphia at N.Y. Islanders
Detroit at N.Y. Rangers
Calgary at Pittsburgh
Vancouver at St. Louis

WEDNESDAY, FEBRUARY 18
Boston at Buffalo
Hartford at New Jersey
N.Y. Islanders at Montreal
Washington at Los Angeles
Toronto at Edmonton
Winnipeg at Detroit
Vancouver at Minnesota

THURSDAY, FEBRUARY 19
N.Y. Rangers at Chicago
Pittsburgh at Philadelphia
Minnesota at St. Louis

FRIDAY, FEBRUARY 20
Boston at Winnipeg
Buffalo at N.Y. Rangers
Quebec at Detroit
Washington at Vancouver
Toronto at Calgary

SATURDAY, FEBRUARY 21
Boston at Minnesota
Chicago at Hartford
Montreal at N.Y. Islanders
Quebec at St. Louis
New Jersey at Pittsburgh
Philadelphia at Los Angeles

SUNDAY, FEBRUARY 22
Hartford at Buffalo
N.Y. Islanders at New Jersey
Pittsburgh at N.Y. Rangers
Washington at Calgary
Toronto at Vancouver
Detroit at Chicago
*Edmonton at Winnipeg

MONDAY, FEBRUARY 23
Minnesota at Montreal

TUESDAY, FEBRUARY 24
N.Y. Rangers at Buffalo
Minnesota at Quebec
N.Y. Islanders at St. Louis
Edmonton at Pittsburgh
Detroit at Washington
Winnipeg at Los Angeles
Vancouver at Calgary

WEDNESDAY, FEBRUARY 25
Boston at Hartford
Montreal at Chicago
N.Y. Rangers at Toronto
Edmonton at New Jersey

THURSDAY, FEBRUARY 26
Quebec at Boston

St. Louis at Buffalo
Pittsburgh at N.Y. Islanders
Philadelphia at Calgary
Vancouver at Detroit
Winnipeg at Los Angeles

FRIDAY, FEBRUARY 27
Edmonton at Washington

SATURDAY, FEBRUARY 28
*Buffalo at Boston
Quebec at Hartford
New Jersey at Montreal
St. Louis at N.Y. Islanders
*N.Y. Rangers at Detroit
Chicago at Pittsburgh
Vancouver at Toronto
*Los Angeles at Minnesota
Winnipeg at Calgary

SUNDAY, MARCH 1
*New Jersey at Hartford
Vancouver at Buffalo
*N.Y. Rangers at Washington
Philadelphia at Minnesota
St. Louis at Pittsburgh
Los Angeles at Chicago
Calgary at Winnipeg

MONDAY, MARCH 2
Detroit at Boston

TUESDAY, MARCH 3
Boston at N.Y. Islanders
Detroit at Hartford
Buffalo at Philadelphia
Montreal at Calgary
Pittsburgh at Quebec
New Jersey at Washington
St. Louis at Toronto
Minnesota at Los Angeles

WEDNESDAY, MARCH 4
N.Y. Islanders at N.Y. Rangers
Winnipeg at Chicago
Edmonton at Vancouver

THURSDAY, MARCH 5
Boston at Hartford
New Jersey at Buffalo
Washington at Philadelphia
Pittsburgh at Toronto
Minnesota at Detroit
Winnipeg at St. Louis
Los Angeles at Calgary

FRIDAY, MARCH 6
Montreal at Vancouver
Los Angeles at Edmonton

SATURDAY, MARCH 7
*Washington at Boston
Philadelphia at Hartford
Buffalo at Quebec
Montreal at Edmonton
N.Y. Islanders at Toronto
Chicago at New Jersey
Pittsburgh at Minnesota
Detroit at St. Louis

SUNDAY, MARCH 8
Quebec at Buffalo
N.Y. Islanders at Chicago
Calgary at N.Y. Rangers
*New Jersey at Philadelphia
Pittsburgh at Winnipeg
*Vancouver at Los Angeles

MONDAY, MARCH 9
Montreal at Minnesota
Toronto at St. Louis

TUESDAY, MARCH 10
Hartford at Quebec
N.Y. Islanders at Pittsburgh

Calgary at Washington
Detroit at Vancouver

WEDNESDAY, MARCH 11
Boston at N.Y. Rangers
Calgary at Hartford
Buffalo at Los Angeles
Montreal at Winnipeg
Philadelphia at New Jersey
Toronto at Minnesota
Detroit at Edmonton
St. Louis at Chicago

THURSDAY, MARCH 12
St. Louis at Boston
Quebec at Pittsburgh
N.Y. Rangers at Philadelphia

FRIDAY, MARCH 13
Hartford at Winnipeg
Buffalo at Vancouver
N.Y. Islanders at New Jersey
Toronto at Washington

SATURDAY, MARCH 14
*Chicago at Boston
Buffalo at Edmonton
Philadelhia at Montreal
Quebec at Los Angeles
New Jersey at N.Y. Islanders
N.Y. Rangers at Pittsburgh
Washington at St. Louis
Calgary at Toronto
*Detroit at Minnesota

SUNDAY, MARCH 15
Hartford at Edmonton
Philadelphia at N.Y. Rangers
*Detroit at Winnipeg
*Minnesota at Chicago

MONDAY, MARCH 16
N.Y. Islanders at Montreal

TUESDAY, MARCH 17
Boston at Detroit
Buffalo at Calgary
Quebec at Vancouver
N.Y. Rangers at Philadelphia
New Jersey at Edmonton
Los Angeles at Washington
Chicago at Minnesota

WEDNESDAY, MARCH 18
Hartford at N.Y. Rangers
New Jersey at Winnipeg
St. Louis at Pittsburgh
Chicago at Toronto

THURSDAY, MARCH 19
Minnesota at Boston
N.Y. Islanders at Detroit

Los Angeles at Philadelphia
Edmonton at Calgary

FRIDAY, MARCH 20
Montreal at Buffalo
Toronto at Quebec
Pittsburgh at Washington
Winnipeg at Vancouver
Calgary at Edmonton

SATURDAY, MARCH 21
*Los Angeles at Boston
Minnesota at Hartford
Toronto at Montreal
Philadelphia at Quebec
N.Y. Rangers at N.Y. Islanders
New Jersey at St. Louis
Chicago at Detroit

SUNDAY, MARCH 22
*Boston at Washington
*Los Angeles at Hartford
Detroit at Buffalo
Chicago at N.Y. Rangers
Pittsburgh at Philadelphia
*Vancouver at Winnipeg

MONDAY, MARCH 23
Edmonton at New Jersey
St. Louis at Minnesota

TUESDAY, MARCH 24
Toronto at Buffalo
Montreal at Quebec
Washington at N.Y. Islanders
Philadelphia at Pittsburgh

WEDNESDAY, MARCH 25
Edmonton at Hartford
New Jersey at N.Y. Rangers
Minnesota at Toronto
Los Angeles at Detroit
St. Louis at Chicago
Calgary at Winnipeg

THURSDAY, MARCH 26
Edmonton at Boston
Los Angeles at Buffalo
Quebec at Philadelphia
Vancouver at N.Y. Islanders
Winnipeg at Calgary

FRIDAY, MARCH 27
N.Y. Islanders at Washington
St. Louis at N.Y. Rangers
Minnesota at New Jersey

SATURDAY, MARCH 28
*Vancouver at Boston
Pittsburgh at Hartford
Buffalo at Montreal
Chicago at Quebec

*Detroit at Philadelphia
Edmonton at Toronto
Calgary at Los Angeles

SUNDAY, MARCH 29
Boston at Chicago
*Vancouver at Hartford
Edmonton at Buffalo
Montreal at Pittsburgh
*St. Louis at New Jersey
*Minnesota at Washington
Toronto at Winnipeg

MONTREAL, MARCH 30
N.Y. Rangers at Minnesota
Calgary at Los Angeles

TUESDAY, MARCH 31
Boston at Quebec
N.Y. Islanders at St. Louis
Pittsburgh at New Jersey
Toronto at Washington
Winnipeg at Edmonton

WEDNESDAY, APRIL 1
Hartford at Montreal
Washington at N.Y. Rangers
Philadelphia at Detroit
Minnesota at Chicago
Vancouver at Los Angeles

THURSDAY, APRIL 2
Buffalo at St. Louis
Quebec at N.Y. Islanders
New Jersey at Pittsburgh
Calgary at Edmonton

FRIDAY, APRIL 3
Winnipeg at Vancouver

SATURDAY, APRIL 4
Boston at Montreal
N.Y. Rangers at Hartford
Buffalo at N.Y. Islanders
New Jersey at Quebec
Philadelphia at Washington
Detroit at Pittsburgh
Chicago at Toronto
Minnesota at St. Louis
Edmonton at Los Angeles

SUNDAY, APRIL 5
Quebec at Boston
Hartford at Buffalo
Montreal at N.Y. Rangers
N.Y. Islanders at Philadelphia
Washington at New Jersey
*Toronto at Chicago
St. Louis at Detroit
Winnipeg at Calgary
Los Angeles at Vancouver

NOTES

NOTES

NOTES